D0959861

Fourth Edition

MEDICAL RECORDS

AND THE LAW

William H. Roach, Jr., MS, JD, Chicago
Robert G. Hoban, JD, Chicago
Bernadette M. Broccolo, JD, Chicago
Andrew B. Roth, JD, New York
Timothy P. Blanchard, MHA, JD, Los Angeles

Partners of McDermott Will & Emery LLP

American Health Information
Management Association®

JONES AND BARTLETT PUBLISHERS
Sudbury, Massachusetts
BOSTON   TORONTO   LONDON   SINGAPORE

World Headquarters

Jones and Bartlett Publishers	Jones and Bartlett Publishers	Jones and Bartlett Publishers
40 Tall Pine Drive	Canada	International
Sudbury, MA 01776	6339 Ormindale Way	Barb House, Barb Mews
978-443-5000	Mississauga, Ontario L5V 1J2	London W6 7PA
info@jbpub.com	CANADA	UK
www.jbpub.com		

Jones and Bartlett's books and products are available through most bookstores and online booksellers. To contact Jones and Bartlett Publishers directly, call 800-832-0034, fax 978-443-8000, or visit our website, www.jbpub.com.

Substantial discounts on bulk quantities of Joes and Bartlett's publications are available to corporations, professional associations, and other qualified organizations. For details and specific discount information, contact the special sales department at Jones and Bartlett via the above contact information or send an email to specialsales@jbpub.com.

Copyright © 2006 by Jones and Bartlett Publishers, Inc.
ISBN-13: 978-0-7637-3445-9
ISBN-10: 0-7637-3445-4

Library of Congress Cataloging-in-Publication Data

Medical records and the law / William H. Roach Jr. . . . [et al.]. — 4th ed.
    p. ; cm.
    Rev. ed. of: Medical records and the law / William H. Roach Jr. and
the Aspen Health Law and Compliance Center. 3rd ed. 1998.
    Includes bibliographical references and index.
    ISBN 0-7637-3445-4
    1. Medical records—Law and legislation—United States.   I. Roach,
William H. Medical records and the law.
    [DNLM: 1. Medical Records—legislation & jurisprudence—United States
    2. Confidentiality—legislation & jurisprudence—United States.
    3. Disclosure—legislation & jurisprudence—United States.   WX 33
AA1 M3856 2006]
    KF3827.R4R63 2006
    344.7304'1—dc22   2005035744
    6048

Production Credits
Publisher: Michael Brown
Production Director: Amy Rose
Associate Editor: Kylah McNeill
Associate Marketing Manager: Marissa Hederson
Production Assistant: Alison Meier
Manufacturing Buyer: Therese Connell
Cover Design: Kristin E. Ohlin
Composition: Pageworks
Printing and Binding: Malloy, Inc.
Cover Printing: Malloy, Inc.

Printed in the United States of America
10 09 08 07 06   10 9 8 7 6 5 4 3 2 1

Contents

Preface

The nature and use of health information has changed dramatically since the first edition of this book was published in 1985. Patient information that once traveled at the pace of paper in U.S. mail now moves at light speed. With the evolution in how we create, store, retrieve, use, transmit, and protect health information has come new and comprehensive regulation in the form of the Health Insurance Portability and Accountability Act and its voluminous privacy, security, identifier, and code set, and transactions regulations. Patients have emerged in this new regulatory scheme with expanded rights to control their health information. Healthcare providers and governments at all levels have an increased focus on accountability for the quality of health care and the reduction of errors, and rapid access to electronic health records has become an essential and fundamental part of successful quality improvement efforts. The ability to create for every patient a community health record in electronic form, maintained in a health data network—and easily accessible to patients, their healthcare providers, ancillary support providers, and other authorized individuals—is now viewed as providing greater protection for patients, data for important medical and public health research, and enhanced cost savings for all. As the creation of health information in electronic form becomes the norm, health information professionals must increasingly collaborate with information technology professionals to provide secure environments for health information storage and safe methodologies for data transmission. The pace of change will continue to increase as the healthcare industry endeavors to keep up with technological advances. The law, ever conservative, will attempt to accommodate these changes, without restricting innovation and creativity, while balancing the interests of patients in maintaining confidentiality of information, the interests of providers in furthering medical science and treatment, and the interests of governments in making cost-effective health care available to their citizens.

This fourth edition of *Medical Records and the Law* is once again written primarily for students in HIM programs as a comprehensive and accessible text and as a reliable reference source for those professionals in the health information field as well as our colleagues in the legal profession. It addresses the substantial changes brought about by HIPAA and the growth of electronic health records systems and electronic data networks, while retaining and updating the discussion of state laws affecting the use and disclosure of health information. The book also discusses the highly complex interplay of federal and state health information privacy laws. In addition to the considerable new material concerning HIPAA and its regulations, this edition addresses the challenging area of how patient information may be used in connection with medical research involving human subjects.

Health information professionals and their attorneys will face new challenges both in interpreting the laws governing health information and in using the law to find creative and practical solutions to problems that will inevitably arise. We hope you find *Medical Records and the Law* a useful tool in building the right solutions.

Acknowledgments

As with most other large projects at McDermott Will & Emery LLP, producing this edition was a team effort by a group of attorneys and staff. The project was directed by Bill Roach, who was a coauthor of the previous editions and who took advantage of McDermott Will & Emery's routine practice of fielding teams of individuals from multiple offices around the country. We all are indebted to Leatrice Berman Sandler and Nili Yolin, colleagues in our Chicago and New York offices; and to Margaret H. Campbell, now at Ropes & Gray, and Steven D. Morgan, now at Wiley, Fielding & Felding LLP; for their hard work and support. To James Kim, a student at Loyola University Chicago School of Law; Megan Rooney, a student at Northwestern University School of Law; Shantal Alonso, a student at the University of Chicago Law School; and Lisa Kaegi and Sucheta Misra, both students at the University of Michigan Law School— all of whom participated as summer associates in our firm's Chicago office 2005 summer program—we offer our sincere thanks for their excellent work. We could not have produced this edition without the help of Jerry Trenholm, director of library services at our firm; Valerie Krasnoff, a graduate of the University of Michigan Law School and a reference librarian in our Chicago office law library; Brian Troyan, Megan Smith, Mike McMillan, and John Duval, all reference librarians in our Chicago office law library; and June Stafford, a library research specialist in our Washington office law library; and the considerable efforts of our inestimable assistants, Anna Herrera and Betty Sorensen. Michael Brown, Kylah McNeill, and Alison Meier at Jones and Bartlett Publishers had the patience of Job throughout the project and provided the encouragement needed to keep busy attorneys more or less on schedule, for which we are truly grateful.

Bill Roach
Bob Hoban
Bernadette Broccolo
Andy Roth
Tim Blanchard

About the Authors

William H. Roach, Jr., is a partner in the Chicago office of McDermott Will & Emery LLP based in the firm's Chicago office. Mr. Roach's experience includes the formation of regional and national hospital systems; mergers, acquisitions, affiliations, and dispositions of healthcare facilities and systems; joint sponsorship of faith-based healthcare facilities and systems; corporate reorganizations; hospital/physician integration arrangements; health industry joint ventures; creation and implementation of corporate compliance plans; focused compliance reviews; tax-exempt organizations; and medical staff organization, credentialing, and contracts. He has served as in-house general counsel of two large academic medical centers, and he has also represented institutions of higher education in matters relating to governance, student records, joint ventures, and faculty organization. Mr. Roach is a member of the editorial advisory boards of numerous professional journals, including *Briefings on HIPAA* and *Medical Records Briefing*, and a contributing editor of the *Hospital Law Manual*. Mr. Roach is recognized for his experience in the law governing the use of healthcare information and regularly advises healthcare providers, ancillary service providers, and manufacturers concerning HIPAA compliance matters. He received his J.D. from Vanderbilt University Law School, his M.S. from the University of Pittsburgh, and his A.B. from Columbia University.

Robert G. Hoban is counsel in the Chicago office of McDermott Will & Emery LLP. He was previously general counsel to a major suburban Chicago healthcare system, where he also served as its chief planning officer. Since 1975, Mr. Hoban has served as borrower's counsel for more than $1.5 billion of tax-exempt bond financing transactions for hospitals throughout the country, and has served as counsel in connection with hospital restructurings and mergers, revision of corporate and medical staff bylaws, and negotiations of unified medical staff bylaws. He has assisted clients in the development of hospital-physician joint ventures, structuring hospital risk management programs, establishment of physician practice management entities, and other aspects of corporate hospital organization. Mr. Hoban has established ambulatory surgery centers and has acted as a consultant to physicians with regard to practice mergers. He also has experience with the formation of HMOs, PHOs, MSOs, and IPAs; and the construction, financing, and leasing of medical office buildings and imaging centers. Mr. Hoban has also presented seminars on medical staff credentialing, the liability aspects of risk management programs, discharge planning, release of medical records, and the legal concerns of palliative medicine. He received his J.D. from Northwestern University School of Law and his B.A. from Yale University.

Bernadette M. Broccolo is a partner in the Chicago office of McDermott Will & Emery LLP and has been advising health industry organizations for 25 years on legal and regulatory compliance matters, information technology acquisition, and health information privacy. Her general health practice includes federal taxation of exempt organizations, corporate governance and restructurings, hospital-physician relationships, and clinical research compliance counseling. Ms. Broccolo's health information technology practice includes drafting and negotiating agreements for the development and acquisition of healthcare information and telecommunication systems. She also advises health clients on the complex legal considerations involved in the electronic exchange, and other uses and disclosures, of health information, including the requirements imposed by HIPAA and other privacy and confidentiality laws. She is currently serving on the HIPAA Task Force appointed by the governor of the state of Illinois to focus on HIPAA preemption and other state law implications of HIPAA compliance. Ms. Broccolo currently serves as a member of the Governing Council of the American Bar Association's Health Law Section, and is the immediate past chair of the Health Law Section's Tax & Accounting Interest Group. She received her J.D. from the Notre Dame Law School, and her B.S. from Boston College.

Andrew B. Roth is the partner-in-charge of the New York health law practice of McDermott Will & Emery, LLP. Mr. Roth represents health industry clients on transactional and regulatory matters, including healthcare networks, integrated delivery systems, hospitals, managed care companies, physicians, and others. His practice extends to many medical/legal areas, including mergers and acquisitions, fraud and abuse, corporate compliance, and long-term healthcare facility representation. Mr. Roth also has a national practice involving accreditation of graduate medical education programs in academic medical centers and teaching hospitals and the Accreditation Council for Graduate Medical Education (ACGME), and accreditation of medical schools by the Liaison Committee on Medical Education (LCME). He regularly counsels institutions and teaching programs as to compliance with ACGME and Residency Review Committee (RRC) requirements, and medical schools as to compliance with LCME requirements. He works with clients on their periodic reviews and represents them when necessary to rebut adverse evaluations, including handling ACGME or LCME administrative hearings. Mr. Roth has been a frequent contributor to a variety of health industry and other journals. He received his J.D. from Hofstra University School of Law, and his B.A. cum laude from the State University of New York at Stony Brook.

Timothy P. Blanchard is a partner in the Los Angeles office of McDermott Will & Emery LLP. His practice focuses on healthcare regulatory issues, including Medicare and Medicaid billing and payment, fraud and abuse audits and investigations, healthcare compliance programs, HIPAA, medical necessity and utilization review, and certification and licensing. He has written leading articles regarding Medicare medical necessity policy, including "'Medical Necessity' Determinations—A Continuing Healthcare Policy Problem," 37 Journal of Health Law 598 (2004). Mr. Blanchard is a member of the board of directors of the American Health Lawyers Association (AHLA), and chair of the Program Committee for the AHLA Annual Institute on Medicare and Medicaid Payment Issues. He is also a fellow of the Healthcare Financial Management Association (HFMA) and a member of HFMA's Editorial Review Board. Mr. Blanchard has been recognized as a leading healthcare lawyer in Chambers USA America's Leading Business Lawyers. Mr. Blanchard received his J.D. cum laude from St. Louis University School of Law and his M.H.A. from St. Louis University, both in 1986, and his B.S. with honors from Oklahoma State University in 1982.

CHAPTER 1

Introduction to the American Legal System

Chapter Objectives

- Distinguish between public and private law, civil and criminal law, and tort and contract actions.
- Discuss how the federal constitution delineates governmental authority.
- Identify the two specific procedural protections that the due process clause generally requires and when they are required.
- Discuss the concept of equal protection.
- Give examples of the rights encompassed by the constitutional right to privacy.
- Explain what happens when local, state, and federal law overlap.
- Give examples of administrative agencies, describing their source of authority and how they regulate the public.
- Discuss how courts make law, defining the principles of stare decisis and res judicata.
- Name the three branches of government and outline the responsibilities of each.
- Distinguish among trial courts, appeals courts, and supreme courts.
- Explain the relationship between state and federal courts.

Introduction

The law affects many of the judgments that health record administrators, health professionals, and technical staff members must make each day. Their decisions may have significant potential legal consequences.

However, it is impractical, if not impossible, to obtain professional legal advice before making every decision. Accordingly, health information administrators and technicians—and, indeed, all healthcare providers who collect patient-related data—must develop a general understanding of health information law so they will be able to exercise judgment consistent with applicable law and identify problems that require expert legal counsel.

This chapter sets forth general information about the law, with a particular emphasis on the mechanics of the American legal system and the roles of the various branches of government in creating, administering, and enforcing the law of the federal and state governments.

The Nature of Law

According to most definitions, law is, in essence, a system of principles and processes by which people who live in a society create stability and deal with their disputes and problems, seeking to solve or settle them without resort to force. Law governs the relationships among private individuals, organizations, and government. Through law, society establishes standards of behavior and the means to enforce those standards. Law that deals with the relationships between private parties is called private law; public law deals with the relationships between private parties and government. As society has become more complex, the scope of public law has broadened, and the regulation of private persons and institutions has become more pervasive.

Private law is concerned with the recognition and enforcement of the rights and duties of private individuals and organizations. Legal actions between private parties are of two types: tort and contract. In a tort action, one party asserts that wrongful conduct on the part of the other party has caused harm, and the injured party seeks compensation for the harm suffered. In a contract action, one party asserts that, in failing to fulfill an obligation, the other party has breached a contract, and the injured party seeks either compensation or performance of the obligations as a remedy.

An important part of public law is criminal law, which proscribes conduct considered injurious to the public order and provides for punishment of those found to have engaged in such conduct. Public law consists also of an enormous variety of regulations designed to advance societal objectives by requiring private individuals and organizations to follow specified courses of action in connection with their activities. Although there are criminal penalties for those who do not abide by the regulations, the primary purpose of public law is to secure compliance with, and attain the goals of, the law—not to punish offenders.

The formulation of public policy concerning health care has thrust hospitals and other healthcare providers into the arena of legislative debate about containment of healthcare costs, quality of care, medical device safety, research involving human subjects, confidentiality of patient information, e-commerce, labor relations, employment policies, facility safety, and other important issues. The object of public law at both the federal and state level is to deal with societal problems of a broad nature. Law serves as a guide to conduct. Most disputes or controversies that are covered by legal principles or rules are resolved without resort to the courts. Thus, each party's awareness of the law and of the relative likelihood of success in court affects its willingness to modify its original position and reach a compromise acceptable to both sides.

Sources of Law

The four primary sources of law in the American legal system are federal and state constitutions, federal and state statutes, the decisions and rules of administrative agencies, and the decisions of the courts.

The Constitution

The U.S. Constitution is the supreme law of the United States. It establishes the general organization of the federal government, grants certain powers to the federal government, and places certain limits on what the federal and state governments may do.

The Constitution establishes and grants certain powers to the three branches of the federal government—legislative, executive, and judicial. The Constitution also is a grant of power from the states to the federal government. The federal government has only the powers granted to it by the Constitution. These powers are both express and implied. The express powers include, for example, the power to collect taxes, declare war, and regulate interstate commerce. The Constitution also grants the federal government broad implied powers to enact laws "necessary and proper" for exercising its other powers. When the federal government establishes law, within the scope of its powers, that law is supreme. All conflicting state and local laws are invalid. The Constitution also places certain limits on what the federal and state governments may do. The most famous limits on federal power are the first 10 amendments to the Constitution—the Bill of Rights. The basic rights protected by the Bill of Rights include the right to free speech; free exercise of religion; freedom from unreasonable searches and seizures; trial by jury; and the right not to be deprived of life, liberty, or property without due process of law. State powers are limited by the 14th Amendment as follows: ". . . nor shall any state deprive any person of life, liberty or property, without due process of law; nor deny to any person within its jurisdiction the equal protection of the laws." These clauses of the 14th Amendment frequently are referred to as the due process clause and the equal protection clause. As another constitutional limitation on both state and federal governmental power, courts have also recognized an individual right to privacy. This right frequently affects hospitals and healthcare professionals.

Due Process of Law

The due process clause imposes restrictions and duties only on state action, not on private action. Actions by state and local governmental agencies, including public hospitals, are considered to be state actions and must comply with due process requirements. Actions by private individuals at the behest of the state also can be subject to the due process requirements. In the past, private hospitals were considered to be engaged in state action when they were regulated or partly funded by governmental agencies. Today, it is rare for private hospitals to be considered engaged in state action on that basis.

The due process clause applies to state actions that deprive a person of "life, liberty, or property." In that context, a position or a particular status can be considered property. For example, a physician's appointment to the medical staff of a public hospital and a hospital's institutional licensure by the state are considered property rights. Thus, in the first example, the public hospital must provide due process to the medical staff applicant, while in the second, the state and local governmental agencies must provide due process to the hospital applying for licensure.

The process that is due varies somewhat depending on the situation. Due process consists primarily of two elements: the rules being applied must be reasonable and not vague or arbitrary, and fair procedures must be followed in enforcing the rules. In general, two fundamental procedural protections must be offered: notice of the proposed action, and an opportunity to present evidence as to why the disputed action should not be taken. The phrase "due process" in the 14th Amendment, which applies to the states, also has been interpreted by the Supreme Court of the United States to include nearly all of the rights in the Bill of Rights. Thus, state governments may not infringe on those rights.

Equal Protection of the Laws

The equal protection clause also restricts state action. The concept of equal protection is intended to ensure that similarly situated persons are treated in like fashion. As a result, the equal protection clause is concerned with the legitimacy of the classification used to distinguish persons for various legal purposes. The determination of whether a particular difference between persons can justify a particular difference in rules or procedures can be difficult. In general, courts require that the government agency justify the difference with a rational reason. The major exceptions to this standard are the strict scrutiny that courts apply to distinctions based on particular "suspect classifications," such as race or ethnic origin, and the intermediate scrutiny afforded to classifications based on gender.

Right of Privacy

In *Griswold v. Connecticut*, the United States Supreme Court recognized a constitutional right of privacy.[1] In *Whalen v. Roe,* while upholding a New York law to collect individual patient prescription information in triplicate from pharmacies, the Court nonetheless validated that the duty to avoid unwarranted disclosure of personal information has its roots in the Constitution and the right to privacy.[2] Privacy in this context involves two types of interest: an individual interest in avoiding disclosure of personal matters, and an interest in protecting one's independence in making certain important decisions. The Court subsequently has ruled that the constitutional right to privacy is qualified

---

[1] *Griswold v. Connecticut*, 381 U.S. 479 (1965).
[2] *Whalen v. Roe*, 429 U.S. 589 (1977).

and is not fundamental or absolute, as it exists relative to a specific context.[3] The Court has ruled, however, that the right of privacy limits governmental authority to regulate contraception; abortion; other decisions affecting reproduction; private sexual behavior; marriage; family autonomy; and the right to choose, withhold, or withdraw medical treatment.[4] Thus, in the area of health information, the unauthorized disclosure of confidential patient information can give rise to a claim for invasion of privacy based on the federal constitutional right of privacy, the common law, or, more recently, statutory law. (For a more detailed discussion of invasion of privacy claims for the improper disclosure of medical records, see Chapter 11.)

State Constitutions

Each state also has its own constitution. A state constitution establishes the organization of the relevant state government, grants certain powers to that government, and places certain limits on what that government may do.

Statutes

Another major source of law is statutory law, which is the law enacted by a legislature. Legislative bodies include the United States Congress, state legislatures, and local legislative entities, such as city councils and county boards of supervisors. Congress has only the powers delegated to it by the Constitution, but those powers have been interpreted broadly. State legislatures have all powers not denied them by the United States Constitution, by federal laws enacted under the authority of the federal government, or by their state constitutions. Local

---

[3] *Whalen v. Roe*, 429 U.S. 589 (1977) (upholding the right to keep personal information private unless there is harmless and compelling state interest to access individual health information, in this case copies of individual prescriptions filled for patients for the purposes of overseeing prescription use in New York State); *Planned Parenthood v. Casey*, 505 U.S. 833 (1992) (addressing the limits of privacy and autonomy with respect to abortion); *Washington v. Glucksberg*, 521 U.S. 702 (1997); and *Vacco v. Quill*, 521 U.S. 793 (1997) (addressing the limits of privacy and autonomy with respect to assisted suicide).

[4] For several of the above propositions in order, see, e.g., *Griswold v. Connecticut*, 381 U.S. 479 (1965); *Roe v. Wade*, 410 U.S. 113 (1973); *Stenberg v. Carhart*, 120 S. Ct. 2597 (2000); *Lawrence v. Texas*, 539 U.S. 558 (2003); *Cruzan v. Director, Missouri Department of Health*, 497 U.S. 261 (1990).

legislative bodies have only those powers granted by the state. Through statutes or constitutional amendments, some states have granted local governments broad powers authorizing home rule.

When federal and state law conflict, valid federal law supersedes. In certain cases, federal law may preempt an entire area of law, so that state law is superseded even if it is not in direct conflict. In some law, such as bankruptcy law, Congress explicitly preempts dual state regulation. In other areas of the law, the courts find that preemption is implied from the aim and pervasiveness of the federal statutory scheme, the need for uniformity, and the likelihood that state regulation would obstruct the full goals of the federal law. In the area of healthcare law, one of the most frequently applied preemption provisions can be found in the Employee Retirement Income Security Act of 1974 (ERISA). Designed to achieve uniformity in the regulation of healthcare benefits, ERISA's preemption provisions determine whether state law claims will be heard in state or federal court and what damages are available.

When state law and local government rules conflict, valid state law supersedes. In some cases, state law may preempt an entire area of law, so that local law is superseded even if it is not in direct conflict. For example, in *Robin v. Incorporated Village of Hempstead*, the court ruled that New York had preempted the regulation of abortions.[5] Therefore, additional regulation by local authorities was prohibited.

In 1996, Congress passed the Health Insurance Portability and Accountability Act (HIPAA), which created a comprehensive federal scheme for the protection of individually identifiable health information.[6] Until the passage of HIPAA, medical records law was governed largely by state legislation and regulation. Now HIPAA governs the use and disclosure of most health information. The act contains a complex formula for determining whether HIPAA will preempt a state law relating to health information confidentiality. Thus, provisions relating to healthcare information can be found in federal and state healthcare information confidentiality statutes, healthcare provider licensure laws, communicable diseases legislation, child and elder abuse legislation, peer review legislation, and in statutes governing the dying process.

---

[5] *Robin v. Incorporated Village of Hempstead*, 285 N.E. 2d 285 (N.Y. 1972).
[6] 42 U.S.C. § 1320d et seq.

Decisions and Rules of Administrative Agencies

The decisions and rules of administrative agencies are other sources of law. Legislatures have delegated to numerous administrative agencies the responsibility and power to implement various laws. The delegated powers include the quasi-legislative power to adopt regulations and the quasi-judicial power to decide how the statutes and regulations apply to individual situations. The legislative branch has delegated this authority because it does not have the time or expertise to address the complex issues involved in many areas that it believes need to be regulated.

Administrative agencies that have been invested with these powers include the Department of Health and Human Services (DHHS), the Food and Drug Administration (FDA), the National Labor Relations Board (NLRB), and the Internal Revenue Service (IRS). DHHS promulgates regulations governing a broad spectrum of activities related to health care. In 2000 and 2003, DHHS issued detailed regulations pursuant to HIPAA governing the privacy[7] and security[8] of all health information used by healthcare providers, healthcare clearinghouses, and health plans. The FDA promulgates regulations and applies them to individual determinations involving the manufacture, marketing, and advertising of foods, drugs, cosmetics, and medical devices. The NLRB decides how national labor law applies to individual disputes. The IRS promulgates and applies regulations to individual disputes concerning federal taxation.

Many administrative agencies, such as the NLRB, seek to achieve some consistency in their decisions by following the position they adopted in previous cases involving similar matters. That is similar to the way the courts develop the common law, discussed later in this chapter. When dealing with these agencies, it is important to review the body of law that has evolved from their previous decisions.

Administrative rules and regulations are valid only to the extent that they are within the scope of the authority granted by legislation to the agency that has issued them. The Constitution also limits delegation by the legislative branch. The legislature must retain ultimate responsibility and authority by specifying what regulations the administrative

---

7 65 Fed. Reg. 82462 (Dec. 28, 2000) (codified at 45 C.F.R. Parts 160 and 164).
8 68 Fed. Reg. 8334 (Feb. 20, 2003) (codified at 45 C.F.R. Parts 160, 162, and 164).

body may make. In the past, courts often declared delegations to be unconstitutional unless there was considerable specificity. Today, the courts interpret the Constitution as permitting much broader delegation, but the general area of law to be regulated still must be specified.

Congress and many state legislatures have passed administrative procedure acts. These specify the procedures that administrative agencies must follow in promulgating rules or reaching decisions in contested cases, unless an overriding law specifies different procedures. Generally, these laws provide that most proposed rules be published to allow individuals an opportunity to comment before the rules are finalized. Many federal agencies must publish both proposed and final rules in the *Federal Register*. Many states have comparable publications of the proposed and final rules of state agencies. Those involved with hospitals should monitor proposed and final rules through these publications, other publications, or their professional or hospital associations. Administrative agencies often rely on this comment process to learn from the public and from the affected industries of the potential implications of agency proposals.

Court Decisions

The body of judicial decisions is the fourth source of law. In the process of deciding individual cases, the courts interpret statutes and regulations, determine whether specific statutes and regulations are permitted by the relevant state or federal constitution, and create the "common law" when deciding cases not controlled by statutes, regulations, or a constitution.

Disagreements over the application of statutes or regulations to specific situations arise frequently. In some situations, the legislature has granted an administrative agency the initial authority—or discretion—to decide how a law shall be applied. That agency's decision usually can be appealed to the courts. However, courts generally defer to the decisions of administrative agencies in discretionary matters, and limit their review to whether the delegation to the agency was constitutional and whether the agency acted within its authority, followed proper procedures, had a substantial basis for its decision, and acted without arbitrariness or discrimination.

Whether or not an administrative agency is involved, the court still may have to interpret a statute or regulation or decide which of two or more conflicting statutes or regulations apply. Courts have developed several rules for statutory interpretation. In addition, in some states, a statute specifies rules of interpretation. These rules or statutes are designed to help determine the intent of the legislature in passing the law.

The courts also determine whether specific statutes or regulations violate the Constitution. All legislation and regulations must be consistent with the Constitution. The case of *Marbury v. Madison* established the power of the courts to declare legislation invalid when it is unconstitutional.[9]

Many of the legal principles and rules applied by the courts in the United States are the product of the common law developed in England and, subsequently, in the United States. The term "common law" is applied to the body of principles that evolves from court decisions resolving controversies. Common law is continually being adapted and expanded. During the colonial period, English common law applied uniformly. After the American Revolution, each state provided for the adoption of part or all of the then existing English common law. All subsequent common law in the United States has been developed on a state basis, so common law may differ from state to state.

Statutory law has been enacted to restate many legal rules and principles that initially were established by the courts as part of the common law. However, many issues, especially those pertaining to disputes in private law, still are decided according to common law. Common law in a state may be changed by enactment of legislation modifying it or by later court decisions that establish new and different common law.

In deciding specific controversies, courts for the most part adhere to the doctrine of stare decisis, which frequently is described as following precedent. By referring to similar cases decided previously and applying the same rules and principles, a court arrives at the same ruling in the current case as in the preceding one. However, slight differences in the situations presented may provide a basis for recognizing distinctions between precedent and the current case. Even when such differences are absent, a court may conclude that a particular common law rule no longer is in accord with the needs of society, and thus the court may depart from precedent.

One clear example of this departure from precedent in the law affecting hospitals was the reconsideration and elimination in nearly every state of the principle of charitable immunity, which had provided

---

[9]   *Marbury v. Madison*, 5 U.S. (1 Cranch) 137 (1803).

nonprofit hospitals with virtual freedom from liability for harm to patients resulting from wrongful conduct. In state after state over a 30-year period, courts found justification to overrule precedents that had provided immunity, and, thereby, to allow suits against nonprofit hospitals.

Another doctrine that courts follow to avoid duplicative litigation and conflicting decisions is res judicata, which means a thing or matter settled by judgment. When a legal controversy has been decided by a court and no more appeals are available, those involved in the suit may not take the same matters to court again. This is different from stare decisis in that res judicata applies only to the parties involved in the prior suit and the issues decided in that suit. The application of the doctrine of res judicata can be complicated by disagreements over whether specific matters actually were decided in the prior case.

Governmental Organization and Function

This section focuses on the structure of the three branches of government—the legislative, executive, and judicial branches—and the manner in which their functions interrelate. In a simplified summary of the functions of the three branches, the legislature makes the laws, the executive branch enforces the laws, and the judiciary interprets the laws. The three branches of government exist under a vital concept in the constitutional framework of the United States government and of the various state governments: the separation of powers. Essentially, separation of powers means that no one of the three branches of government is clearly dominant over the other two; however, in the exercise of its functions, each branch may affect and limit the activities, functions, and powers of the others.

The concept of separation of powers, which may be referred to as a system of checks and balances, is illustrated by the involvement of the three branches in the federal legislative process. Specifically, when a bill to create a statute is enacted by Congress, representing the legislative branch, and signed by the president, representing the executive branch, the bill becomes law. If the president should veto the bill, a two-thirds vote of each house of Congress can override the veto. Thus, by the president's veto, the executive branch can temporarily prevent a bill from becoming law. If later sessions of Congress do not act favorably on the bill, it will not become law at all. In addition, the president can prevent a bill from becoming law by not taking any action on the bill while Congress is in session. (This inaction by the president is referred to as a "pocket veto.") Finally, a bill that has become law may ultimately be declared invalid by the United States Supreme Court, representing the judicial branch of government, if the Court decides that the law violates the federal Constitution.

Another example of the relationship among the branches of government involves the selection of federal court judges. Individuals nominated by the president for appointment to the federal judiciary, including the Supreme Court, must be approved by the United States Senate. Thus, over time, both the executive and legislative branches can affect the composition of the judicial branch of government.

In addition, while a Supreme Court decision may be final with regard to the specific controversy before the Court, Congress and the president may generate revised legislation to replace a law previously held unconstitutional. The processes for amending the Constitution, while complex and often time consuming, also can serve as a method for offsetting or overriding a Supreme Court decision.

Each of the three branches of government has a different primary function. The primary function of the legislative branch is to enact laws. This process may involve creating new legislation or amending or repealing existing legislation. It is the legislature's responsibility to determine the nature and extent of the need for new laws and for changes in existing laws. By means of a committee system, legislative proposals are assigned or referred for study to committees with specific areas of concern or interest. The committees conduct investigations and hold hearings, at which interested persons may present their views, in order to assist the committee members in their consideration of the bills. Some bills eventually reach the full legislative body, where, after consideration and debate, they may be either approved or rejected. The Congress, as well as every state legislature except Nebraska's, consists of two houses. (Nebraska has only one house.) Both houses must pass identical versions of a legislative proposal before it can be presented to the chief executive.

The primary function of the executive branch is to enforce and administer the law. However, the chief executive—either the governor of a state or the president of the United States—has a role in the creation of law through the power either to approve or to veto a legislative proposal. If the chief executive accepts the bill through the constitutionally established process, the bill becomes a statute, a part of the enacted law. If the chief executive vetoes the bill, it can become law only if the legislative process for overriding the veto is successful.

The executive branch of government is organized into departments. The departments have responsibilities for different areas of public affairs, and each enforces the law within its assigned area of responsibility. Much of the federal law affecting or pertaining to hospitals and other healthcare providers is administered by the Department of Health and Human Services (DHHS). Most states have separate departments with responsibility over health and welfare matters, and those departments administer and enforce most laws pertaining to hospitals and other healthcare providers. Other departments and government agencies also affect the affairs of hospitals and other healthcare providers, however. On the federal level, for example, laws relating to wages and hours of employment are enforced by the Department of Labor. The federal Department of Justice is also a key player in enforcing healthcare fraud and prohibitions against abuse.

The judicial branch of government is responsible for adjudicating and resolving disputes in accordance with the law. Many types of disputes involving hospitals go before the courts. For example, suits against hospitals by patients seeking compensation for harm allegedly suffered as the result of wrongful conduct by hospital personnel are decided by the courts. Hospitals resort to the courts to challenge exercises of authority by government agencies and departments, to have legislation concerning hospitals declared invalid, to collect unpaid hospital bills, and to enforce contracts.

Although many disputes and controversies are resolved without resorting to the courts, in many situations there is no way to end a controversy without submitting to the adjudicatory process of the courts. A dispute taken before a court is decided in accordance with the applicable law; this application of the law is the essence of the judicial process.

Organization of the Court System

To understand the judicial branch of government and the effect of court decisions as precedents, it is necessary to understand the structure of the court system. There are more than 50 court systems in the United States, including the federal court system, each state's court system, the District of Columbia court system, and those of Puerto Rico and other U.S. territories. These courts do not all reach the same decisions on specific issues. Frequently, a majority approach and several minority approaches exist on each issue. Thus, careful review is necessary to determine which court's decisions apply to an individual hospital and, if no decisions are specifically applicable, to predict which approach the relevant courts are likely to adopt.

The federal court system and many state court systems have three levels of courts—trial courts, intermediate courts of appeal, and a supreme court. Some states have no intermediate courts of appeal.

State Court System

The trial courts in some states are divided into special courts that deal with specific issues, such as family courts, juvenile courts, probate courts, and limited courts that deal only with lesser crimes, such as misdemeanors, or with civil cases involving limited amounts of money. Each state has trial courts of general jurisdiction that may decide all disputes not assigned to other courts, or disputes barred from the courts by valid federal or state law.

At the trial court level, the applicable law is determined, and the evidence is assessed to determine the facts. The applicable law then is applied to those facts. It is the judge's role to determine what the law is. If there is a jury, the judge instructs the jury as to the law, and the jury determines the facts and applies the law. If there is no jury, the judge not only determines what the law is, but also determines the facts and applies the law. In either case, the determination of the facts must be based on the evidence properly admitted during the trial, so the facts as heard by the decision maker may not necessarily be what actually happened.

In some cases, everyone agrees on the facts, and the only issues presented to the court concern what the law is. In other cases, everyone agrees what the law is, but there is disagreement over the facts. To determine the facts for purposes of deciding the case, the credibility of any witnesses and the weight to be given to other evidence must be determined. Many cases involve both questions of law and questions of fact. The judge has significant control over the trial even when a jury is involved. If the judge finds that insufficient evidence has been presented to establish a factual issue for the jury to resolve, the judge can dismiss the case or, in civil cases, direct the jury to decide the case in a specific way. In civil cases, even after the jury has decided, the judge can rule in favor of the other side.

Most state court systems have an intermediate appellate court. Usually, this court decides only appeals from trial court decisions. In some states, there are a few issues that can be taken directly to the intermediate appellate court. When an appellate court decides an appeal, it does not accept additional evidence. It uses the evidence presented in the record from the trial court. Appellate courts almost always accept the factual determinations of the jury or judge in the trial court because the trial court saw the witnesses and therefore can judge their credibility more accurately. Usually, the appellate court bases its decision on whether proper procedures were followed in the trial court and whether the trial court properly interpreted the law. However, an appellate court occasionally will find that a jury verdict is so clearly contrary to the evidence that the appellate court will either reverse the decision or order a new trial.

Each state has a single court at the highest level, usually called the supreme court. In some states, the name is different. For example, in New York, the highest court is the Court of Appeals, while trial courts in New York are called supreme courts. The highest level court in each state decides appeals from the intermediate appellate courts or, in states without such courts, from trial courts. The highest level court frequently has other duties, including adopting rules of procedure for the state court system and determining who may practice law in the state, which includes disciplining lawyers for improper conduct.

Federal Court System

The federal court system has a structure similar to that of state court systems. The federal trial courts are the United States district courts and special purpose courts, such as the U.S. Court of Federal Claims, which hears certain claims against the United States. Federal trial courts are fundamentally different from state trial courts because the federal courts have limited jurisdiction. A federal suit must involve either a question of federal law or a dispute between citizens of different states in which the dispute involves an amount of at least $75,000. Federal questions include cases involving possible violations of federal law or of rights under the United States Constitution. When a federal trial court decides a controversy between citizens of different states, the court is acting under what is called its diversity jurisdiction, using federal court procedures but applying the law of the applicable state.

Sometimes federal trial courts will decline to decide state law questions until they have been ruled on by a state court. That is called abstention. It is designed to leave states' issues for state courts and to minimize the federal courts' workload. Federal courts generally will not abstain when there also are important federal questions not affected by the state law question. Some states have procedures by which the federal courts can ask a state court directly to decide a particular question of state law when it is important to the decision of a case before the federal court.

Appeals from the federal trial courts go to a U.S. court of appeals. The United States is divided into 12 areas, called circuits. The circuits are numbered 1 through 11, plus the District of Columbia circuit court, which is called the Court of Appeals for the Federal Circuit.

The nation's highest court is the Supreme Court of the United States, which decides appeals from the U.S. courts of appeals. Decisions of the highest state courts also may be appealed to the U.S. Supreme Court if they involve federal laws or the U.S. Constitution. When the courts of appeals or the highest state courts decline to review a lower court decision, the decision sometimes can be appealed directly to the Supreme Court.

The U.S. Supreme Court has the authority to decline to review most cases. With only a few exceptions, a request for review is made by filing a petition for a writ of certiorari. If the Supreme Court grants certiorari, the record for the lower court decision is transmitted to the Court for review. In most cases, the Supreme Court denies the writ of certiorari. Such a denial does not indicate approval of the lower court decision; it merely means that the Court has declined to review the decision.

Stare Decisis

The preceding description illustrates the complexity of the court systems in the United States. When a court is confronted with an issue, it is bound by the doctrine of stare decisis to follow the precedents of higher courts in the same court system that have jurisdiction over the geographic area in which the court is located. Each appellate court, including the highest court, generally is bound also to follow the precedents of its own decisions, unless it decides to overrule the precedent due to changing conditions.

Thus, decisions from equal or lower courts or from courts in other court systems do not have to be followed. One exception occurs when a federal court decides a controversy between citizens of different states and must follow the relevant state law as determined by the highest court of the relevant state. Another exception is when a state court decides a controversy involving a federal law or constitutional questions and must follow the decisions of the United States Supreme Court. Another situation that may force a court to alter its prior position is a change in the applicable statutes or regulations by the legislature or an administrative agency.

When a court is confronted with a question that is not answered by applicable statutes or regulations and the question has not been addressed by its court system, the court usually will examine the judicial solutions reached in the other systems to decide the new issue. When a court decides to reexamine its position on an issue that it has previously addressed, it often will examine the judicial decisions of the other systems to decide whether to overrule its position. A clear trend in decisions across the country can form a basis for a reasonable legal assessment of how to act even when the courts in a particular area have not decided the issue. However, a court is not bound by decisions in other systems, and it may reach a different conclusion.

Thus, there can be a majority approach to a certain issue that many state court systems follow, and several minority approaches that other states follow. State courts show more consistency on some issues than on others. For example, nearly all state courts have completely eliminated charitable immunity. However, while nearly all states require informed consent to medical procedures, many states determine the information that must be provided to patients by reference to what a reasonable patient would need to know under the circumstances, while several states make the determination by reference to what other physicians would disclose in like circumstances. A few states have not yet decided what reference to use.

Differences in applicable statutes and regulations between states may force courts in different states to reach different conclusions on certain questions. For example, numerous states have enacted legislation that protects from discovery the records of hospital and medical staff review committees, although the extent of protection varies.[10]

---

[10] Discovery is the formal process in court proceedings by which parties disclose information that is relevant to the parties' underlying legal dispute.

Some statutes provide that such records generally are subject to subpoena, discovery, or disclosure;[11] other laws state specifically that such committee records, proceedings, and reports are not discoverable, or the statutes describe such material as confidential or privileged. There also are common exceptions to the nondiscovery statutes, allowing physicians to discover records of staff privilege committees when contesting the termination, suspension, or limitation of their staff privileges. As a result of these variations, courts throughout the country have construed nondiscovery statutes with varying results.

In summary, although it is important to be aware of trends in court decisions across the country, legal advice should be sought before taking actions based on decisions from court systems that have no jurisdiction over the geographic area in which the healthcare provider is located.

---

[11] Generally, a subpoena is a written court order requiring the attendance of the person named in the subpoena at a specified time and place for the purpose of being questioned under oath concerning a particular matter that is the subject of an investigation, proceeding, or lawsuit. In addition, a specific type of subpoena, a subpoena duces tecum, requires that an individual produce specified documents or pieces of evidence.

CHAPTER 2

Medical Records and Managed Care

Chapter Objectives

- Define utilization management and utilization review organization.
- Explain the role of patient information with respect to the utilization management process.
- Compare and contrast the following: HMO, PPO, IPA, GPWW, consolidated medical group, PHO, MSO, foundation model IDS, physician ownership model IDS, PBM, and disease management organization.
- Identify the characteristics of the managed care industry that have changed the nature of patient records.
- Describe the changes in medical records standards made in response to the growth of managed care—whether instituted by legislatures, accreditation organizations, or health information managers.
- Describe the information protected by the HIPAA Privacy Rule and explain how privacy rules affect health plans.

Introduction

Although the medical record originally developed as a business record of individual healthcare providers (primarily hospitals and physicians), it is now a document that supplies health information critical to continuity of care, is subjected to substantial state and federal regulation, and is "owned" as much, if not more, by the patient as by the provider.

Several forces contributed to this transition, including increased emphasis on the importance of documentation in medical training; medical records standards incorporated in accreditation and certification requirements, and the development of formal utilization controls for healthcare services, culminating in the managed care revolution of the late 1900s.

Utilization Review

One factor in the increase in the scope and quality of medical records was a requirement that was beginning to be imposed by payers around mid-century—namely, that providers document the need for, and provision of, services in exchange for payment. The beginning of the Medicare and Medicaid program operations in 1966 was a watershed year for formal utilization review because the program operations required most hospitals and nursing facilities that wished to participate to maintain utilization review programs in order to obtain and maintain certification.[1] In 1972, Congress added an additional layer of review, by professional standards review organizations (later known as peer review organizations and quality improvement organizations),[2] and imposed a specific obligation upon providers to support their provision of services by evidence of medical necessity and quality "in such form and fashion and at such time as may reasonably be required by a reviewing peer review organization in the exercise of its duties and responsibilities."[3] The federal peer review program extended not only to institutions, but also to physicians and other practitioners.[4]

Managed Care

The impetus for the development of utilization review was burgeoning healthcare costs. A related effort by Congress to address quality and

---

[1] See, e.g., 42 C.F.R. § 482.30, requiring most hospitals seeking to participate in the Medicare program to have in effect a utilization review plan that provides for review of services furnished by the institution and by members of the medical staff to patients entitled to benefits under the Medicare and Medicaid programs.

[2] 42 U.S.C. § 1320c-3.

[3] 42 U.S.C. § 1320c-5.

[4] 42 U.S.C. § 1320c-5.

cost of health care is found in the Health Maintenance Organization Act of 1973, which provided for the development and operation of health maintenance organizations (HMOs), primarily in an effort to ensure appropriate coordination and quality of care, but ultimately to contain rising healthcare costs as well.[5] This legislation laid the groundwork for the managed care revolution.

The concept of "managed care" quickly came to include within its umbrella not only HMOs, but also preferred provider organizations (PPOs), "point of service" plans (POSs), and other entities involved in the coordination and delivery of health care. In 1977, indemnity plans accounted for 96 percent of all job based health plan enrollment; by 1998, indemnity plans held only 14 percent of the market; HMOs held 27 percent; POS plans, 24 percent; and PPO plans, 35 percent.[6]

A fundamental tenet of managed care is that coordination of care will produce higher quality, lower cost outcomes. The pioneering HMO model had sought to furnish most, if not all, covered services required by enrollees "in-house" through physicians employed by, and facilities owned and operated by, the HMO. This approach naturally suggested a comprehensive central medical records database. Other forms of managed care organizations had to obtain information concerning enrollees from a broad range of providers and suppliers in order to coordinate care, and compiling and maintaining a centralized database would prove to be more difficult. To understand the medical records issues that arise in the managed care environment, this chapter discusses below the broad range of managed care entities that operate today.

Managed Care Organizations and Related Entities

The term managed care organization (MCO) is now widely used to encompass various forms of healthcare coordination in the United States.

Health Maintenance Organizations

HMOs are organized healthcare systems that are responsible for both financing and arranging for the delivery of a broad range of

---

[5] See *Pegram v. Herdrich*, 530 U.S. 211, 233 (2000).
[6] J. R. Gabel, "Job-Based Health Insurance, 1977–1998: The Accidental System Under Scrutiny," *Health Affairs* (November/December 1999): 67.

comprehensive health services to a defined population. Some HMOs can be viewed as a combination of healthcare insurer and healthcare delivery system. Whereas traditional healthcare insurance companies are responsible for reimbursing covered individuals for the cost of their health care, HMOs are responsible for arranging for the provision of healthcare services to their covered members through affiliated providers who are reimbursed under various methods. There are different models of HMOs, including staff, group practice, network, IPA, and direct contract, depending on the nature of the relationship between the HMO and its participating physicians. Some HMOs provide a point of service (POS) option, which allows enrollees to use nonaffiliated providers for an additional fee. The HMO models below generally reflect an HMO's relationship with its physicians. The degree of control is described graphically on the following continuum:

Level of HMO Control

Point of Service	IPA	Network	Group Practice	Staff Model
•	•	•	•	•

Less Control   Greater Control

Preferred Provider Organizations

Preferred provider organizations (PPOs) are entities through which employer health benefit plans and health insurance carriers contract to purchase healthcare services for covered beneficiaries from a selected group of participating providers. Typically, providers participating in PPOs agree to abide by utilization management and other procedures implemented by the PPO, and agree to accept the PPO's reimbursement structure and payment levels. In return, PPOs often limit the size of their participating provider panels and provide incentives for their covered individuals to use participating providers instead of other providers. In contrast to individuals with traditional HMO coverage, individuals with PPO coverage are permitted to use non-PPO providers, although higher levels of coinsurance or deductibles routinely apply to services provided by the nonparticipating providers.

Independent Practice Associations

An independent practice association (IPA) is a legal entity, the members of which are independent physicians who contract with the IPA for the sole purpose of having the IPA contract with one or more HMOs. IPAs commonly negotiate with HMOs for a capitation rate that covers all physician services. The IPA in turn reimburses the member physicians, although not necessarily by using capitation. The IPA and its member physicians are generally at risk for at least some portion of medical costs. Therefore, if the capitation payment is lower than the required reimbursement to the physicians, the member physicians must accept lower income. Originally, an IPA was an umbrella organization for physicians in all specialties to participate in managed care. IPAs that represent only a single specialty have also emerged, however.

Group Practice Without Walls

Another type of physician group is the group practice without walls (GPWW), representing a more significant step toward integration of physician services. The formation of a GPWW does not require the participation of a hospital, and, in fact, is often formed as a vehicle for physicians to organize without being dependent on a hospital for services or support.

The GPWW comprises private practice physicians who agree to aggregate their practices into a single legal entity, but the physicians continue to practice medicine in their independent locations. The physicians may appear to their patients to be independent, but from the view of a contracting entity (usually an MCO), they are a single group. The GPWW is owned and governed by member physicians.

Consolidated Medical Group

The terms "consolidated medical group" and "medical group practice" refer to a traditional structure in which physicians have combined their resources into a true medical group practice. Unlike the GPWW, in which the physicians combine certain assets and risks but remain in their own offices and continue to practice medicine as they always have, the true medical group is consolidated into a few sites, and functions in a group setting with a good deal of interaction among members of the group and common goals and objectives for group success.

Physician/Hospital Organizations

A physician/hospital organization (PHO) is usually a separate business entity, such as a for profit corporation, that allows a hospital and its physicians to negotiate with third party payers. In its simplest and most common version, the participating physicians and the hospital develop model contract terms and reimbursement levels, and use those terms to negotiate with MCOs. Governance of the PHO is typically shared between hospital managers and physicians.

A PHO represents a first step toward greater integration between a hospital and its medical staff. This type of organization has the advantage of being able to negotiate contracts on behalf of a large group of physicians allied with a hospital. Another advantage of a PHO is its ability to track and use data to manage the delivery system, at least from the standpoints of utilization management and quality assessment.

Management Services Organizations

A management services organization (MSO) represents the evolution of the PHO into an entity that not only provides a vehicle for negotiating with MCOs, but also provides additional services to support physicians' practices. The physicians, however, usually remain independent practitioners. MSOs are based around one or more hospitals with the capacity to provide the administrative support that forms the basis for the organization.

In its simplest form, the MSO operates as a service bureau, providing basic practice support services to member physicians, such as billing, collection, administrative support, and electronic data interchanges (such as electronic billing). The physician remains an independent practitioner under no legal obligation to use the services of the MSO on an exclusive basis.

Foundation Model Integrated Delivery System

A foundation model integrated delivery system (IDS) is one in which a tax-exempt organization, frequently a hospital, creates a not for profit foundation that purchases and operates physicians' practices. Depending on applicable state law, the foundation may be licensed to practice medicine or may be exempt from licensure requirements, and it may employ physicians directly or use hospital funds to purchase the practices directly. The foundation as a subsidiary of a tax-exempt organization usually combines with other affiliated entities to operate an integrated healthcare system. In another model of IDS, the foundation is an entity that exists on its own and contracts for services with medical groups and a hospital. The foundation owns and manages the practices, but the physicians become members of a medical group that in turn has an exclusive contract for services with the foundation. The foundation itself is governed by a board that is not dominated by either the hospital or the physicians and includes lay members.

Physician Ownership Model Integrated Delivery System

The physician ownership model refers to a vertically integrated system in which the physicians hold a significant portion of ownership interest in the healthcare entities that compose the system. In some cases, the physicians own the entire system; in other cases, the physicians own more than 50 percent but less than 100 percent.

Other Managed Care Organizations

Utilization Review Organizations

Utilization management is an essential element of managed care that allows coordination among providers, monitoring of quality, identification of superior or cost efficient providers as well as of inappropriate use of services or facilities, and making medical necessity determinations. Utilization review relies heavily on patient related information. The regulation of utilization review organizations by state legislatures and accreditation associations, including restrictions on the type of medical records information that may be gathered and the uses to which it may be put, has increased significantly over the past decade because of the growing importance of these organizations in managed health care.

Pharmacy Benefits Managers

Pharmacy benefits managers (PBMs) provide managed care services to HMOs, self funded employer group health plans, and government programs. PBMs may be at financial risk for managing the prescription drug utilization of a defined pool of enrollees, or they may simply contract as third party administrators. PBMs negotiate rebates and price concessions from manufacturers or pharmacies. Generally, PBMs combine a variety of managed care techniques to the delivery and financing of prescription drug benefits. These mechanisms include multitiered drug formularies that require varying levels of financial participation by enrollees, such as higher copayments for brand name pharmaceuticals and lower copayments for generics. In addition, PBMs use prospective, concurrent, and retrospective utilization review in order to ensure appropriate usage. Also, PBMs frequently integrate horizontally and own mail order pharmacies, which reduce dispensing fees.

The Impact of Managed Care on Health Information Management

As the number and complexity of organizations and enterprises involved in the delivery of healthcare services increase, the law of health information management has been forced to develop. Medical records professionals, who traditionally have performed highly quantitative and departmentally focused tasks, must now adopt a systems approach to health information management in a managed care environment. Traditional medical records management activities—such as forms control, record content analysis and control, record tracking, release of information monitoring, record storage, and record destruction—are now performed within large and diverse healthcare enterprises, requiring that decision making and problem solving address the system as a whole. The range of personnel, facilities, and equipment that frequently are connected and supported by an information management system also dictates a more global approach to the subject of medical records and the law.

Traditional legal issues affecting the collection, maintenance, and access to medical records information have evolved with today's healthcare systems, and this information increasingly is being collected and stored electronically. These two trends, increased computer automation and dispersed access to the information, have had, and will continue to have, a profound effect on the legal issues surrounding health information management.

The traditional approach to studying the legal issues associated with medical records has focused on the hospital's role in creating and maintaining these documents, and much of the early legislation addressing medical records management focuses on hospitals' responsibilities for ensuring that the information gathered is accurate and complete, and that its confidentiality is protected. Medical records case law also frequently deals with hospitals as primary players in the delivery of healthcare services, often involving claims for improper disclosure of information or access to peer review records.

Today, because managed care is the dominant form of health insurance coverage in the United States, the hospital's prominence as the keeper of the medical record is reduced. A patient may consult many healthcare providers—including primary care physicians, specialists, hospitals, laboratories, surgical centers, and rehabilitation centers—and each of them will participate in creating a record for that patient. Records containing healthcare information are held by numerous individuals and entities in different locations, many of which are part of a network of providers established by a managed care plan. The information gathered by these providers needs to be shared for clinical purposes in the interest of optimal care of individual patients. In addition, managed care plans themselves rely heavily on the data gathered in patient records, and the plans accumulate enormous amounts of this kind of information for cost assessment and utilization review purposes. Employers also become part of this data integration, and frequently collect and store patient related information as part of the process of providing healthcare benefits to their employees and documenting workers' compensation claims.

The penetration of managed care into the healthcare delivery system has also been an impetus for the computerization of patient information as data networking becomes necessary to link providers, payers, employers, and consumers both regionally and nationally. Many healthcare reform proposals include recommendations for information system networks that may achieve managed care goals of cutting costs while safeguarding the quality of patient care. The establishment of this type of data exchange ability, however, has raised significant concerns about protecting the privacy of patient information as the control of any individual provider over the release of the information decreases. Healthcare reform proposals also factor into their recommendations the growing difficulty of determining who owns and assumes ultimate responsibility for protecting against unauthorized access to medical records in electronic format.

HIPAA and State Privacy Rules

The passage of the Health Insurance Portability and Accountability Act (HIPAA) and the implementation of the Privacy Rule in 2002 dramatically changed the way entities use and disclose health information.[7] The Privacy Rule governs the use and disclosure of "protected health information" (PHI), a term that generally includes any health information (including payment related information) that is linked to an identifier (such as a subscriber identification number) that could reasonably be used to identify the individual. Most health plans, healthcare providers, and healthcare clearinghouses are "covered entities" subject to the Privacy Rule. (For a detailed discussion of the Privacy Rule, see Chapter 6.)

Although the Privacy Rule does not govern the issue of health information ownership, the rule requires covered entities to respect individuals' rights with respect to PHI about themselves, including the right to access and amend the PHI under certain circumstances. Notwithstanding this focus on individual privacy rights, the current state of the law with respect to the issue of ownership of medical records is generally that the healthcare provider owns the records, which may be released or accessed only in accordance with the law. Some states have begun to respond to the ambiguities that arise in today's managed care setting, where individual providers are in fact employees of larger healthcare organizations. Florida law, for example, provides that "records owner" refers to "any health care practitioner who generates a medical record after making a physical or mental examination of, or administering treatment or dispensing legend drugs to, any person; any health care practitioner to whom records are transferred by a previous record owner; or any health care practitioner's employer, including but not limited to group practices and staff model HMOs, provided the employment contract or agreement between the employer and the health care practitioner designates the employer as the records owner."[8] The Florida statute goes on to list certain practitioners and entities that are not authorized to acquire or own medical records, but are authorized to maintain such documents under their respective licensing statutes (for example, pharmacies and pharmacists,

---

7 See 45 C.F.R. §§ 160 and 164.
8 See Fla. Stat. § 456.057(a).

nursing home administrators, clinical laboratory personnel). Record owners as defined in the Florida statute bear the responsibility of maintaining a register of all disclosures of medical records information to third parties.

In addition, with legislation in the majority of states imposing on physicians and other licensed healthcare providers the duty to guard against unauthorized disclosures, state legislatures have had to respond to changes affecting the way health care is delivered and recorded. In a minority of states, legislatures have adopted more generic statutes governing healthcare information. Many states (for example, Tennessee) now impose confidentiality requirements on HMOs,[9] and numerous other states impose similar obligations on utilization review organizations, insurance institutions, agents, and insurance support organizations.[10]

Recognized exceptions to patient privacy in mandatory reporting laws relating to child abuse, infectious diseases, or dangers to third parties generally impose a duty to report certain conditions or events; this duty is imposed on the healthcare provider who is closest to the patient in the treatment relationship. These statutes have been in effect for many years, and many did not contemplate the computerized distribution of patient information that is occurring in today's managed care environment. Increasingly, however, managed care plans are acquiring medical records information that can generate the same duty to disclose information as that imposed on primary healthcare providers such as the physician or the hospital. Nonprovider entities—such as IPAs, utilization review organizations, third party administrators, or employer sponsored health plans—that lawfully access patient care information may be considered "healthcare providers" for the purposes of mandatory reporting obligations, even though they do not directly deliver healthcare services to patients. In Maryland, for example, the definition of "healthcare provider" under the state Medical Records Act includes HMOs and the agents, employees, officers, and directors of a healthcare professional or healthcare facility.[11] Because many managed care plans would fall within the statutory definition of "health maintenance organization," the agents of these plans who work in claims processing, utilization review, or cost or utilization assessments have duties

---

9 See Tenn. Code Ann. § 56-32-225.
10 See, e.g., N.Y. Ins. Law § 4905.
11 Md. Code Ann., Health-Gen. II, §§ 4-301 through 4-305.

to disclose patient information under specific circumstances and are protected from liability for good faith disclosure actions.[12]

Changes in Medical Records Standards

State regulations and associations that accredit healthcare organizations have also responded to the growing number of entities that collect patient data by elaborating information management standards that apply to the types of healthcare organizations that have emerged in the managed care environment. For example, the National Committee for Quality Assurance (NCQA) accredits managed care organizations, and has elaborated specific medical records standards that apply to this type of organization.[13] In addition, the Joint Commission on Accreditation of Healthcare Organizations accredits many types of healthcare entities—including hospitals, healthcare networks, and preferred provider organizations (PPOs)—and has standards that govern the type of patient related data they collect. For example, the Joint Commission accreditation standards for healthcare networks govern information management, and require that a record of health information contain sufficient information to facilitate continuity of care among the components of the network.[14] The Joint Commission's PPO *Accreditation Manual* also addresses information management, requiring PPOs to determine appropriate levels of security and confidentiality of data and information while at the same time ensuring that they have adequate capability to integrate and interpret data from various sources.[15] Increasingly, the standards governing medical records and health information must consider the roles of a variety of actors and organizations with respect to a multitude of evolving standards addressing the definition, permitted use, ownership, content, access, reporting, and retention of medical records and health information.

---

[12] See E. J. Krill, "Required Disclosure of Medical Record Information—Applications to Managed Care," in Monograph 3, *Health Care Facility Records, Confidentialing, Computerization, and Security* (American Bar Association Forum on Health Law, July 1995), 11–26.

[13] National Committee for Quality Assurance, *1997 Standards for Accreditation of Managed Care Organizations*, Standards MR 1 through MR 4. See also National Committee for Quality Assurance, *1997 Standards for the Certification of Physician Organizations*, Standards MR 1 through MR 4.

[14] Joint Commission, *1998–2000 Comprehensive Accreditation Manual for Health Care Networks*, Standard IM 6.3.

[15] Joint Commission, *1997 Accreditation Manual for Preferred Provider Organizations*, Standards IM 1 through IM 4.

CHAPTER 3

Medical Records Requirements

Chapter Objectives

- Identify the governmental and private entities that establish medical records requirements.
- List the types of information contained in a patient record.
- Explain why it is important for a record to be complete and accurate.
- Give examples of the information that state law may require in a medical record.
- Discuss the role of CMS with regard to medical records content and retention.
- Describe how private associations address medical records content and retention, giving examples of the information that associations require.
- List the sources of law governing medical records retention, providing examples of state law requirements.
- Define statute of limitations and discuss how a statute of limitations affects record retention practices.
- Explain how medical research and storage space impact medical records retention.
- Give examples of court cases illustrating the importance of medical records retention.
- Recommend considerations for medical records destruction policy.

Records That Must Be Kept

Healthcare providers must maintain a record for each of their patients. This requirement is imposed by state licensure laws and regulations, accreditation standards, professional association guidelines, and conditions of participation in federal reimbursement programs. Judicial opinions have reinforced the requirement that healthcare providers develop and implement proper record keeping procedures, by imposing liability for the failure to maintain a proper record. Policies concerning medical records, therefore, should address the relevant standards of the healthcare organization or provider concerned, and clearly set forth criteria relating to the types of information to be included in each record, the length of time each record must be kept, and the proper methods for final destruction of records.

A patient's medical record consists of four types of data: (1) personal, (2) financial, (3) social, and (4) medical. Personal information usually is obtained upon admission or first visit to the provider, and will include name, birth date, sex, marital status, next of kin, occupation, identification of personal physicians, and other items needed for specific patient identification. Financial data include the names of the patient's employer and health insurance company; types of insurance and insurance policy numbers; Medicare and Medicaid numbers, if any; and other information that will enable the healthcare provider to bill for its services. Social data may include the patient's race and ethnic background, family relationships, community activities, and lifestyle. Social data may also include any court orders or other directions concerning the patient, and other information related to the patient's position in society that may indicate a need for special confidentiality protection.

Medical data form the patient's clinical record, a continuously maintained history of the treatment provided by the healthcare provider. These data include the patient's chief complaint, medical and family histories, results of physical examinations, planned course of treatment, physicians' diagnosis and therapeutic orders, evidence of informed consent, clinical observations, progress notes, consultation reports, nursing notes, reports and results of all procedures and tests—including pathology and clinical laboratory tests and examinations, operative record, radiology and nuclear medicine examinations and treatment, and anesthesia records—and other reports generated during the patient's treatment.[1] Medical data also may include information obtained from outside sources, such as diagnostic tests performed at another facility or laboratory.

---

[1] See *Franklin Square Hospital v. Laubach*, 556 A. 2d 682 (Md. 1989) (holding that fetal-monitor tracings are part of the medical record).

The medical record may be handwritten, typed, or electronic. Regardless of its form, the medical record should be a complete, accurate, and current account of the history, condition, and treatment of the patient and the results of the patient's previous visits with the physician or the hospitalization or outpatient treatment. Use of an electronic health record (EHR) can expand the information network concerning a patient, enhancing completeness and accuracy, as well as enabling immediate availability of the record to authorized personnel. However, EHRs present special concerns, which are addressed in Chapter 13.

The importance of a complete and accurate medical record to the quality of care rendered to a patient is obvious. The medical record is used not only to document chronologically the care rendered to the patient, but also to plan and evaluate treatment and to enhance communication among the patient's physician and other treating healthcare professionals. In addition, medical records must be complete and accurate because of the heavy reliance on this information for scientific research, utilization management, peer review purposes, and appropriate billing for the care given.

Medical records are important legal documents for both the healthcare provider and the patient. An important legal function of medical records is to provide essential evidence in professional negligence actions brought by patients against the healthcare providers who treated them. Because these actions often are litigated two to five years after a patient received the treatment in question, the medical record frequently is the only detailed record of what actually occurred. Some of the healthcare providers who participated in the patient's treatment may not be available to testify or may not remember important details of the treatment. A properly created medical record enables an individual provider or facility to reconstruct the patient's course of treatment and to show whether the care provided was acceptable under the circumstances.[2]

The Legal Health Record

The legal health record is "the documentation of healthcare services provided to an individual during any aspect of healthcare delivery in

---

[2] See, e.g., *Foley v. Flushing Hospital & Medical Center*, 359 N.Y.S. 2d 113 (1974), where an infant plaintiff's medical records provided evidence sufficient to prevent dismissal of a malpractice suit.

any type of healthcare organization."[3] Each healthcare organization must define what is its legal health record. No single definition will fit all organizations.

The American Health Information Management Association (AHIMA) has developed useful guidelines for establishing the components of a legal health record. Considerations include the ease of access to various components of patient care information, medical staff and legal counsel guidance, community standard of care, statutory and regulatory requirements, accreditation standards, and the requirements of third party payers. The roles of the legal health records are to

- Support the decisions made in a patient's care
- Support the revenue sought from payers of health care
- Document the patient's illness or injury, response to treatment, and caregiver decisions

Whether the healthcare organization creates paper records, a combination of paper and electronic records, or a full electronic health record, it must meet all the requirements imposed on it for maintaining records of its services.[4]

The challenge for each healthcare organization is to determine what documents, images, data elements, audio files, and video files constitute its legal health record. AHIMA suggests three steps in making this determination:

- Determine what legal requirements for health records apply to the organization
- Determine whether health records are created in the ordinary course of the organization's business
- Create a matrix or other document that defines each element in what the organization considers its legal health record[5]

As the technology supporting electronic health records advances, new legal issues will arise in connection with defining the legal health

---

[3] American Health Information Management Association, "Update: Guidelines for Defining the Legal Health Record for Disclosure Purposes," *Journal of AHIMA* (September 2005): 64A.
[4] Ibid.
[5] Ibid.

record. Issues concerning whether pop-ups, alerts, and reminders, as well as data from multiple electronic systems and source systems, will have to be addressed. Whether to incorporate into the records various information stored in audio files (for example, recorded patient telephone conversations, physician dictations) and video files (for example, videos of office visits, procedures, and telemedicine consultations) will require careful consideration. As patients create their own personal health records as part of integrated, community-wide health data networks, an organization must determine whether and to what extent these personal health records should be incorporated into its legal health record. In addition to discussing these issues, AHIMA also has developed a detailed list of data and documents to be considered part of the legal health record, as well as information that should not be included.[6]

Content Requirements

The requirements that healthcare providers create and maintain medical records for the patients they treat are found in state and federal statutes and regulations, municipal codes, and accreditation standards. In some state statutes, a general definition of "medical records" provides guidance on what the records should contain. In Colorado, for example, legislation defines "medical record" as "the written or graphic documentation, sound recording, or computer record of services pertaining to medical and health care which are performed at the direction of a physician or other licensed healthcare provider on behalf of a patient by physicians, dentists, nurses, technicians, emergency medical technicians, prehospital providers, or other healthcare personnel," including "such diagnostic documentation as X-rays, electrocardiograms, electroencephalograms, and other test results."[7] The Nevada statute defines healthcare records as "any reports, notes, orders, photographs, X-rays, or other recorded data or information whether maintained in written, electronic or other form which is received or produced by a provider of health care, or any person employed by him, and contains information relating to the medical history, examination diagnosis or treatment of

---

6 Ibid.
7 See Colo. Rev. Stat. § 18-4-412(2)(a) (2004).

the patient."[8] In a few states, hospital licensing statutes set forth the minimum record requirements. The Florida statute is illustrative:

Each hospital . . . shall require the use of a system of problem oriented medical records for its patients, which system shall include the following elements: basic client data collection; a listing of the patient's problems; the initial plan with diagnostic and therapeutic orders as appropriate for each problem identified; and progress notes, including a discharge summary.[9]

The Tennessee statute simply refers to standards prescribed by the hospital licensing board.[10]

For the vast majority of states, however, the regulatory agencies for hospitals, as well as for other healthcare providers, have jurisdiction to establish detailed requirements on medical record content. These rules and regulations have the effect of law.

The regulations issued by these agencies cover a variety of healthcare providers and types of medical information. California regulations on record content requirements for acute care hospitals distinguish between inpatient and outpatient medical records, as well as between records generated by other facilities, including intermediate care facilities, home health agencies, and adult day care centers.[11] Oregon regulations provide general requirements for the contents of medical records, and add specific requirements for surgical, obstetric, emergency department, outpatient, and clinic records.[12]

The Illinois hospital licensing regulation illustrates the detailed record content requirements found in many states:

An adequate, accurate, timely, and complete medical record shall be maintained for each patient. Minimum requirements for medical record content are as follows:

(A) patient identification and admission information;

(B) history of patient as to chief complaints, present illness and pertinent past history, family history, and social history;

---

[8] Nev. Rev. Stat. § 629.021.
[9] Fla. Stat. § 395.3015 (2003).
[10] Tenn. Code Ann. § 68-11-303.
[11] Cal. Code Regs. tit. 22, §§ 70749, 70527, 73423, and 73439.
[12] Or. Admin. R. 333-505.0050.

(C) physical examination report;

(D) provisional diagnosis;

(E) diagnostic and therapeutic reports on laboratory test results, X-ray findings, any surgical procedure performed, any pathological examination, any consultation, and any other diagnostic or therapeutic procedure performed;

(F) orders and progress notes made by the attending physician and when applicable by other members of the medical staff and allied health personnel;

(G) observation notes and vital sign charting made by nursing personnel; and

(H) conclusions as to the primary and any associated diagnosis, brief clinical resume, disposition at discharge to include instructions and/or medications and any autopsy findings on a hospital death.[13]

A few states, however, have regulations that specify only broad areas of information required in a medical record.[14] The Hawaii regulations provide that the "medical records shall clearly and accurately document a patient's identity, the diagnosis of the patient's illness, treatment, orders by medical staff, observations, and conclusion concerning the patient."[15] As the minimum state standard for medical records, other states simply adopt the accreditation requirements of the Joint Commission on Accreditation of Healthcare Organizations (Joint Commission)[16] or the Medicare Conditions of Participation for Hospitals requirements.[17]

Healthcare providers seeking to participate in federal reimbursement programs must satisfy federal regulations governing conditions of participation in those programs, which also impose record maintenance requirements. Regulations issued by the Department of Health and Human Services, Centers for Medicare & Medicaid Services (CMS) require specific categories of healthcare providers to maintain

---

[13] Ill. Admin. Code tit. 77, § 250.1510(b)(2).
[14] See, e.g., Regs. Conn. State Agencies § 19-13-D3(d).
[15] Haw. Admin. R. § 11-93-21(c).
[16] See, e.g., R.I. Code R. 14-090-007 § 25.7; Rules and Regulations for the Licensure of Hospitals in Virginia, 12 Va. Admin. Code § 5-410-370.
[17] See, e.g., 105 Code Mass. Regs. 130.200 (2004).

a clinical record for every patient who receives care and services, requiring in general that these records be maintained in accordance with professional standards, promptly completed, and properly filed and retained.[18]

In addition, the CMS regulations on the Conditions of Participation for some types of healthcare providers also impose specific content requirements. Conditions of Participation for Hospitals, for example, provide that all records must contain the following information as appropriate:

1. evidence of a physician examination, including a health history, performed no more than seven days prior to admission or within 48 hours after admission;
2. admitting diagnosis;
3. results of all consultative evaluations of the patient and appropriate findings by clinical and other staff involved in the care of the patient;
4. documentation of complications, hospital acquired infections, and unfavorable reactions to drugs and anesthesia;
5. properly executed informed consent forms for procedures and treatments specified by the medical staff, or by federal or state law if applicable, to require written patient consent;
6. all practitioners' orders, nursing notes, reports of a treatment, medication records, radiology and laboratory reports, vital signs, and other information necessary to monitor the patient's condition;
7. discharge summary with outcome of hospitalization, disposition of case, and provisions for follow-up care; and
8. final diagnosis with completion of medical records within 30 days following discharge.[19]

Associations that accredit various healthcare organizations frequently impose maintenance standards for clinical records. For example, the Joint Commission's information management standards for

---

[18] See, e.g., 42 C.F.R. § 482.24 (hospitals), 42 C.F.R. § 418.74 (hospices), and 42 C.F.R. § 484.48 (home-health agencies). The CMS Conditions of Participation for Health-Maintenance Organizations require the organization to maintain a medical record-keeping system that accumulates pertinent information relating to Medicare enrollees, and require that this information be made available to appropriate professionals. See 42 C.F.R. § 417.418.

[19] 42 C.F.R. § 482.24(c)(2).

hospitals require that the health information record contain sufficient information to identify the patient; justify the diagnosis, treatment, or services; provide written documentation of the chronology and results of treatment; and facilitate continuity of care among the components of the healthcare system.[20] The Joint Commission's intent statement for this standard delineates the content of the health record—including patient identification; diagnoses; plan of care; medical history; appropriate physical examinations; immunization and screening status; documentation and results of treatments, procedures, and tests; referrals or transfers to other practitioners; and evidence of known advance directives. The Joint Commission's standards for hospitals have a general content requirement similar to the one imposed on healthcare networks. In addition, the standards require that medical records thoroughly document operative or other procedures and the use of anesthesia,[21] and include specific information when a patient is treated in the hospital emergency department.[22]

As the healthcare industry increasingly relies on patient health information for a variety of purposes, what a patient health record *should* contain, irrespective of what it must contain to comply with law, will likely change. AHIMA has published guidelines for determining what the records created by a particular provider would appropriately contain.[23] These guidelines consider the records from four perspectives—legal health record, patient identifiable source data, administrative data, and derived data—and provide procedures for assessing how to define content in each category. This useful development tool enables providers to accommodate the need for different content as the uses of patient records change over time.

Whether or not specific statutory or regulatory guidelines apply, hospitals and other healthcare organizations or providers should adopt formal written policies concerning the content of medical records. The policy may be a detailed list of data required, or may reference other guidelines, such as state statutes, regulations, or pertinent accreditation

[20] Joint Commission on Accreditation of Healthcare Organizations, *2004 Comprehensive Accreditation Manual for Health Care Networks*, Standards IM 6.10 and 6.20.

[21] Ibid., Standard IM 6.30.

[22] Ibid., Standards IM 6.10(18) and 6.40.

[23] American Health Information Management Association, *Practice Brief: Definition of the Health Record for Legal Purposes* (2001), available at http://library.ahima.org/xpedio/groups/public/documents/ahima/-pub_bok1_009223.html.

standards. Generally, detailed policies require closer periodic review to be kept current, while broad policies remain applicable as circumstance and practice change. The policies should balance the need for providing enough specificity to guide medical records clinical practitioners and the organization's staff against the desire to avoid continual policy revisions.

To maintain the currency of their medical records policies, healthcare providers should keep abreast of state, federal, and accreditation association requirements relating to health information. State and national health information associations often publish changes in the applicable law and accreditation standards. All healthcare institutions should develop reliable ways of monitoring new laws and regulations, and ways of communicating any changes to health information professionals and clinical personnel responsible for making entries in records, and to the individuals responsible for making policy recommendations concerning medical records content. This is particularly important for institutions that have implemented EHRs, because the laws governing electronic records of all types are evolving quickly along with the increasing pace of technological development supporting information storage and transmission.

In particular, these individuals should understand the various functions of the medical record and their interrelationships, as well as how those functions are affected by the nature of the specific institution and by current legislative, regulatory, and licensing requirements. Creating an effective record content policy requires the involvement of a variety of disciplines within an organization, and the involvement of providers who deliver care from networks or facilities outside the organization. Policy makers must be willing to find ways to make practical adjustments to medical records content. In doing so, they should strike a balance among the administrative, financial, and other demands placed upon the medical record and the record's basic patient care function.

Record Retention Requirements

In determining how long to retain medical records, a healthcare facility should consider applicable federal or state laws and regulations, and sound administrative policy and medical practice. The nature of the facility and the resources available to maintain documents or information in electronic form for an extended period of time also will influence the facility's retention policy. Achieving a practical and workable medical records retention policy becomes more difficult in an era of cost containment and reduced financial resources.

Institutions and practitioners subject to the requirements of the Health Insurance Portability and Accountability Act (HIPAA)[24] must also retain documentation related to their medical records, as required by the HIPAA regulations, for a period of six years from the date of its creation or the date on which it was last in effect, whichever is later. This documentation may be in written or electronic form.[25]

Numerous factors need to be considered in establishing a retention policy. First and foremost, the policy must respect the applicable statutory and regulatory requirements. Other factors to be considered in defining a retention policy are statutes of limitations and potential future litigation; requirements of the provider's professional liability insurer; the need for records information in medical research and teaching; storage capabilities; cost of microfilming, computerization, and other long term storage methods; and recommendations of provider-specific healthcare associations. The minimum standard for compliance with respect to retention is that which is enunciated in the applicable statutes and regulations. A healthcare provider may establish a retention period longer than the one dictated by statutory or regulatory requirements, however, where other considerations make it prudent to do so.

Statutory and Regulatory Concerns

Medicare Conditions of Participation require hospitals to retain the original record or a legally reproduced form for a period of at least five years.[26] State statutes and regulations also impose specific retention requirements on medical records.[27] In most jurisdictions, record retention requirements, like content requirements, appear in regulations issued by the state licensing agency. Many jurisdictions also have special retention provisions for certain portions of a patient's record (such as X-rays, graphic data, and discharge summaries), special procedures

---

[24] 42 U.S.C. §§ 1320d et seq.
[25] 45 C.F.R. § 164.530(j).
[26] 42 C.F.R. § 482.24.
[27] See, e.g., Alaska Stat. § 18.20.085(a) (2004); Ind. Code Ann. § 16-39-7-1(b) (2004); Miss. Code Ann. § 41-9-69; Tenn. Code Ann. § 68-11-305.

for records of patients who are minors, and other provisions for records pertaining to deceased persons.

A few states impose extended retention requirements. In Connecticut, for example, a hospital must preserve patient records for a minimum of 25 years.[28] New Jersey requires a discharge summary to be kept for each patient for 20 years, with the summary including a recapitulation of the significant findings and events that occurred during hospitalization.[29] The original medical record must be kept for at least 10 years.

Most of the remaining states establish a shorter minimum time for preserving the entire patient record. About half of them require at least a 10-year preservation period, while the rest prescribe some number less than 10. Arizona requires patient medical records to be readily retrievable for at least 7 years, and many other states prescribe a minimum of 5 or 7 years.[30]

In some cases, licensing regulations identify no particular number of years to maintain patient records. Instead, the rules refer to other sources of law to define the minimum requirements of record retention, such as the state statute of limitations for malpractice claims as the minimum retention period,[31] the Conditions of Participation for federal reimbursement programs,[32] or guidelines set by the American Hospital Association.[33]

A few states provide that records may be kept for a minimum number of years plus an additional period determined by the hospital. This additional time could serve the hospital's needs for "clinical, educational, statistical, or administrative purposes,"[34] or could extend for as long as the record has "research, legal, or medical value."[35] Of course, hospitals and other healthcare facilities in any state may retain records beyond the period prescribed by statute or regulation if clinical, legal, or patient care policies indicate such a need. At least one state's regula-

---

[28] Regs. Conn. State Agencies § 19-13-D3(d)(6) (2004).
[29] N.J. Rev. Stat. § 26:8-5.
[30] Ariz. Admin. Code R9-10-228A.10.b. States that have five-year retention periods include Kentucky and Oklahoma. States that have seven-year retention periods include Pennsylvania and Indiana.
[31] See, e.g., Iowa Admin. Code r. 641-51.6(1).
[32] See Mich. Admin. Code r. 325.1021(4).
[33] See, e.g., Ill. Admin. Code tit. 77, § 250.1510(d).
[34] Mo. Code Regs. Ann. tit. 19, § 30-20.021(3)(D)(15).
[35] N.D. Admin. Code § 33-07-01.1-20(1)(b)(3).

tions specify that nothing in the law should be construed to prohibit retention beyond the period prescribed.[36]

In addition to the general retention requirements described above, Medicare Conditions of Participation and several states have special statutory or regulatory provisions governing how long a hospital should maintain specific portions of a patient's record, such as X-rays, scans, and clinical laboratory reports.[37] Healthcare facilities also must comply with retention laws on vital statistics, including records of births and deaths.[38]

Many states prescribe special retention requirements for records of patients who were minors at the time of treatment, usually requiring that these records be kept. These requirements usually indicate that hospitals must keep records until the patient reaches majority plus some additional time, or until the expiration of the general retention requirement, whichever is longer. The prescribed extension ranges from 1 to 10 years beyond the age of majority.

A few states also address the issue of the records of deceased patients. These regulations allow the facility to destroy records of a deceased patient before the expiration of the general retention requirement. In Oklahoma, for instance, the general retention period for hospital medical records, other than for newborns or minor patients, is five years after the patient was last seen, or at least three years beyond the patient's death.[39]

Statutes of Limitations

Another key factor in establishing a record retention policy is the statute of limitations, which is a period of time established by statute, measured in years, within which a party may bring a lawsuit. The time periods vary with the cause of action (for example, contract, tort, or real estate).

Except in the case of minors' records, retaining the record for the statute of limitations period would not impose a burden because

---

[36] Mont. Admin. R. 37.106.402(5).
[37] See, e.g., 42 C.F.R. § 482.26(d)(2); Alaska Stat. § 18.20.085; Cal. Code Regs. tit. 22, § 70751(c); Idaho Code § 39-1394(1).
[38] See, e.g., Rules and Regulations for the Licensure of Hospitals in Virginia, 12 Va. Admin. Code § 5-410-370(H).
[39] Okla. Hospital Standards § 310: 667-19-14(a).

limitation periods generally are shorter than the period the record would be retained for medical reasons. If the statute of limitations were used as a guide, the medical record of a minor would be kept until the patient reaches the age of majority plus the period of the statute. For example, in a state where the age of majority is 21, and the statute of limitations for torts (which are actions for personal injury, such as a lawsuit based on allegedly negligent medical care) is two years, the retention period for a newborn's record would be 23 years; in states in which the age of majority is 18, and the statute of limitations for torts is two years, the retention period for a newborn's record would be 20 years. Although the possibility of an infant's waiting until majority to bring suit is slight, it can happen.[40] Although most suits by minors are brought soon after the accident causing the injury, a healthcare provider is protected best if it retains records until the minor reaches majority and for an additional time equal to the applicable state statute of limitations on tort actions.

Many states extend the period of the statute of limitations for persons who are disabled and not able to handle their own affairs.[41] Thus, if the provider is aware of a patient's prior disability, the provider ought to place the patient's medical record in the "never destroy" category in order to be able to defend itself if a lawsuit were ever to be filed.

Medical Research and Storage Space Considerations

If a hospital or other medical facility engages in extensive medical research, especially retrospective investigations that require detailed medical records data, the institution may wish to establish a long retention period. Moreover, if the medical research conducted in the hospital involves experimental or innovative patient care procedures, the facility is well advised to retain its medical records for at least 75 years. (For a more detailed discussion of the use of health information in research with human subjects, see Chapter 14.)

Another major consideration for a hospital in establishing a retention policy is its capability to store a large number of records. This has been a serious issue for healthcare institutions with paper medical records. Available space, expansion rates, the endurance of the paper

---

[40] See, e.g., *Bettigole v. Deiner,* 124 A. 2d 265 (Md. Ct. App. 1956).
[41] See, e.g., 735 Ill. Comp. Stat. §§ 5/13-211 and 212.

and folders used, the cost of microfilming, and storage safety requirements all affect the institution's ability to retain records. The traditional space saving technology for paper record storage has been microfilming and, more recently, optical disk storage. But microfilming can raise other administrative problems. For example, members of the medical staff might object to the restrictions on the availability of particular records for purposes of research and review, generating additional costs for reading and printing equipment. Some states implicitly or explicitly authorize the microfilming of records.[42]

Where state law and regulations do not specifically authorize microfilming, healthcare facilities nonetheless may microfilm their medical records and destroy the original records in accordance with law or regulations governing record destruction.

As institutions have implemented EHRs, many have begun to scan old paper records into digital media for storage on computer disks or other storage devices. Before deciding on this method of record keeping, however, they should consult applicable laws governing licensure, accreditation, federal Conditions of Participation, and all rules of evidence on the admissibility of copies of business records and patient records at trial. If they are institutions subject to the requirements of HIPAA and the HIPAA regulations governing health information security (Security Rule), they must be prepared to provide the security safeguards required by the Security Rule for electronic protected health information (ePHI).[43] These institutions must also maintain the computer hardware and software capable of reproducing the EHRs from storage media as the institutions continually upgrade their EHR systems. (For a detailed discussion of EHRs and the Security Rule, see Chapter 13.)

A healthcare facility may scan or microfilm its records itself, provided the facility has the proper staff and equipment, or it may send its records to an outside contract service. If a contract service is selected, it should be bound by a written agreement that specifies, among other things, the method of record transfer, the method of reproduction, the quality and cost of the service, the time within which the service will be performed, safeguards against breach of confidentiality, indemnification for loss resulting from the contractor's improper release of

---

[42] See, e.g., Idaho Code § 39-1394(1)(a); La. Rev. Stat. Ann. § 40:2144(E) and(F); Mass. Ann. Laws ch. 111, § 70 (2004); N.J. Rev. Stat. § 26:8-5.

[43] 45 C.F.R. §§ 164.302 to 164.318.

information or loss of records, and procedures for destroying the original records. If the healthcare facility is a HIPAA covered entity, the contractor will be a HIPAA business associate, and the agreement between the facility and the contractor must comply with the business associate agreement requirements of the HIPAA privacy regulations (Privacy Rule). (For a more detailed discussion of the Privacy Rule and its business associate requirements, see Chapter 6.)

Association and Accreditation Agency Guidelines

AHIMA has adopted a policy that recommends retaining patient health information for the following minimum time periods:[44]

Patient health records (adults)	10 years after most recent encounter
Patient health records (minors)	Age of majority plus statute of limitations
Diagnostic images	5 years
Disease index	10 years
Fetal heart monitor records	10 years after infant reaches majority
Master patient index	Permanently
Operative index	10 years
Physician index	10 years
Register of births	Permanently
Register of deaths	Permanently
Register of surgical procedures	Permanently

Most accrediting bodies require healthcare organizations to have policies that address retention of health information in hard copy or in electronic form. Few accrediting agencies prescribe specific retention periods, but instead refer to applicable law and regulation. For example, the Joint Commission on Accreditation of Healthcare Organizations (JCAHO) places the responsibility on hospitals to determine the

---

[44] American Health Information Management Association, *Practice Brief: Retention of Health Information (Updated)* (June 2002), available at http://library.ahima.org/xpedio/groups/public/documents/ahima/-pub_bok1_01245.html.

retention period for medical records information, as determined by law and regulation and the uses of the information for patient care for legal, research, and educational purposes. The Community Health Accreditation Program, however, states that the records of occupationally exposed patients must be retained for 30 years.[45]

Developing a Record Retention Policy

In the final analysis, no blanket record retention rule for all types of healthcare providers can be devised. The length of time medical records should be retained after they no longer are needed for medical and administrative purposes should be determined by the physician or the facility's management with the advice of qualified legal counsel, taking into account all relevant factors, including the feasibility and cost of converting paper records to a storage medium, the availability and cost of storage space, the cost of maintaining retrieval devices, and the possible future need for such records, as well as the legal considerations related to lawsuits. In most professional negligence actions against a healthcare facility or provider, the defendant must show that the care provided was consistent with accepted medical practice at the time and was reasonable under the circumstances. Medical records are essential to the defense of such actions. Although, in the absence of some special relationship or contractual duty between the parties, courts generally reject the existence of a responsibility by one party to preserve evidence or records for another party's potential suit,[46] several courts have recognized a hospital's duty to maintain patient records as a matter of statute or regulation.[47]

Specifically, in cases where the plaintiff had insufficient evidence to pursue a professional liability action against a hospital because the hospital was unable to produce the patient's record, courts have found the facility liable for this independent act of negligence or have ruled that the plaintiff states a cause of action in negligence.

---

[45] For a summary of accrediting-agency rules concerning retention of health information, see American Health Information Management Association, *Practice Brief: Retention of Health Information (Updated)* (June 2002), 2, available at http://library.ahima.org/xpedio/groups/public/documents/ahima/pub_bok1_012545.html.

[46] See *Panich v. Iron Wood Products Corporation*, 445 N.W. 2d 795 (Mich. Ct. App. 1989); *Koplin v. Rosel Well Perforators, Inc.*, 734 P. 2d 1177 (D. Kan. 1987).

[47] See, e.g., *Fox v. Cohen*, 406 N.E. 2d 178 (Ill. Ct. App. 1980).

In one case, a Florida court ruled that a hospital may be sued for its failure to make and maintain patient medical records because state law imposes a duty to make, maintain, and furnish such records to a patient or personal representative upon request.[48] A woman whose husband died during the administration of anesthesia before surgery sued the hospital for negligence. She could not present expert testimony necessary to establish medical malpractice, however, because the anesthesiology records of her husband's treatment could not be located. The appeals court found that a hospital's duty to make and maintain medical records is imposed by state administrative regulations, and that state law further requires that copies of records be provided to patients at their request. The woman was entitled to sue the hospital for negligently breaching these duties, the court concluded, because the hospital otherwise "stands to benefit that the prospect of successful litigation against it has disappeared along with the crucial evidence."

A patient may not be entitled to sue a hospital for its failure to comply with record retention legislation, however, unless the individual also proves damages and a causal connection with the injuries sustained. In one case, a court dismissed a negligence action against a hospital for failing to preserve all the X-rays taken of a patient.[49] A medical malpractice review panel had rejected a malpractice complaint after considering only the X-rays still available. The court stated that the patient had failed to show any damages resulting from the alleged negligence of the hospital, and dismissed the suit.

Destruction of the Record

Upon expiration of the medical records retention period, or after the record has been copied onto microfilm or scanned into a computer, the original record usually may be destroyed. In some states, the method of medical records destruction is controlled by statute and regulation. The Tennessee statute states:

Upon retirement of the record as provided in [this section], the record or any part thereof retired shall be destroyed by burning,

---

[48] See *Bondu v. Gurvich*, 473 So. 2d 1307 (Fla. Dist. Ct. App. 3d Dist. 1984). See also *Thomas v. U.S.*, 660 F. Supp. 216 (D.D.C. 1987).

[49] See *Hryniak v. Nathan Littauer Hospital Association*, 446 N.Y.S. 2d 558 (App. Div. 1982).

shredding, or other effective method in keeping with the confidential nature of its contents. Destruction of such records must be made in the ordinary course of business and no record shall be destroyed on an individual basis.[50]

Other states require that an abstract of any pertinent data in the medical record be created before destroying the record.[51] Healthcare facilities that deliver their medical records to a commercial enterprise for destruction should do so pursuant to a written agreement that sets forth safeguards similar to those discussed for microfilming or scanning agreements, including the method of destruction, safeguards against breach of confidentiality, indemnification provisions, and certification that the records have been destroyed properly. If the facility is a HIPAA covered entity, the contractor engaged to destroy records will be a business associate, and the agreement between the facility and the contractor must comply with the business associate agreement requirements of the Privacy and Security Rules.

Similarly, healthcare providers that destroy their own records also must establish procedures to protect the confidentiality of record information and ensure that records are destroyed completely. The employee responsible for record destruction should certify that the records have been destroyed properly. Whether the records are destroyed commercially or by the facility itself, certificates of destruction should be retained permanently as evidence of disposal.

The appropriate method of destroying health information will depend upon the medium in which it is created. For example, AHIMA recommends that microfilm be pulverized and recycled; that magnetic computerized data, including magnetic tapes, be degaussed; and that write-once/read-many laser disks be pulverized.[52]

Healthcare providers who are subject to HIPAA must also implement policies and procedures that govern the disposal of ePHI or the hardware and electronic media on which the information is stored.[53] The policies and procedures must incorporate safeguards to prevent the

---

[50] Tenn. Code Ann. § 68-11-305(c). See also Idaho Code § 39-1394(1)(d).
[51] Miss. Code Ann. § 41-9-75.
[52] American Health Information Management Association, *Practice Brief: Destruction of Patient Health Information (Updated)* (November 2002), 1, available at http://library. ahima.org/xpedio/groups/public/documents/ahima/ pub_bok1_016468.html.
[53] 45 C.F.R. § 164.310(d).

loss of privacy and security of ePHI. As the types of storage media change with technological advancements, destruction methods will also change, and health information professionals should keep current with best practices in this area.

Even if a facility is not subject to HIPAA, its medical records policies should include provisions governing destruction of records, and these provisions should be applied uniformly. Failure to apply such a policy uniformly or a violation of policy can lead to a damaging inference by a jury in a negligence suit that if the records were available, they would show that the patient had not received adequate care.

Health information that is involved in any continuing investigation, lawsuit, audit, or peer review proceedings should not be destroyed without the advice of qualified legal counsel. Destruction of records relevant to litigation can expose individual information professionals and their employers to serious liability. In addition, healthcare organizations that destroy such information are also subject to a "media sanction"—that is, potentially severely negative coverage in local news media. Therefore, most healthcare providers establish policies for placing these records in secure locations if in paper form, or in secure computer environments, where they can be protected from inadvertent destruction and can be easily retrieved.

CHAPTER 4

Medical Records Entries

Chapter Objectives

- Illustrate how legibility and accuracy are important to the quality of medical records.

- Give examples of how entry errors and poor legibility can create difficulties for a healthcare provider in defending against a claim of poor medical care.

- Explain how inaccurate or incomplete entries can affect claims review and the payment for services.

- Discuss the standards that govern the completeness, accuracy, and legibility of medical records.

- Define what timeliness means with respect to medical records entries, and the consequences of failing to comply with this standard.

- Distinguish between authorship and countersignatures of medical records entries.

- Explain why authentication is a key element of medical records security, and what standards apply to how and when records are authenticated.

- Define auto-authentication and recommend safeguards for auto-authentication systems.

- Discuss how verbal orders affect the quality of medical records entries, and what specific policies should be in place to govern how these orders are received and recorded.

- List the types of errors that occur in medical records entries, and give proper procedures for correcting or altering a medical record.

Introduction

The quality of a patient record depends largely on the individuals making record entries. All healthcare practitioners and others who enter information into patient records must understand the importance of creating complete and accurate records, as well as the legal and medical implications of failing to do so. Because a medical record enables healthcare professionals to plan and evaluate a patient's treatment and ensures continuity of care among multiple providers, the quality of care a patient receives depends directly on the accuracy and legibility of the information the medical record contains. As the use of electronic health records (EHRs) increases, practitioners must master computer applications to assure correct entry of patient care information. The increased emphasis on fraud and abuse prevention in the healthcare industry has further highlighted the importance of proper medical records documentation. The best evidence a healthcare provider can offer against allegations of false claims and billing is the data contained in the patient records that are under scrutiny. In addition, a healthcare facility that fails to comply with medical records standards found in federal and state law risks loss of licensure, accreditation, and eligibility to participate in federal healthcare programs. Finally, healthcare providers run the risk of increased exposure in the event of a medical malpractice suit if the entries they make to medical records do not accurately describe the patient's condition or the treatment provided.

A healthcare organization or provider should strive to ensure that the original entries made to medical records are timely and complete.[1] Corrections to records, although perfectly permissible, can create serious problems, especially for a healthcare provider involved in negligence litigation. Even if the correction improves the accuracy of the record, a correction can generate difficulties if it is improperly made, deteriorates legibility, or cannot be authenticated. In addition, any alterations made simply to improve the defense of a lawsuit or to defraud third-party payers can have serious adverse consequences for a health-

---

[1] For a discussion of ways to improve the quality of documentation in patient medical records, see American Health Information Management Association (AHIMA), *Practice Brief: Best Practices in Medical Record Documentation and Completion* (1999), available at http://library.ahima.org/xpedio/groups/public/documents/ahima/pub_bok1_000043 .html.

care provider, including the imposition of criminal sanctions. For all these reasons, therefore, a healthcare provider's medical records policy should address the timeliness and manner for both creating and updating patient records.

Legible and Complete Medical Records Entries

The medical record often is the single most important document available to healthcare providers or organizations in the defense of a negligence action. Ordinarily, the record is admissible as evidence of what occurred in the care of the patient. (For a discussion of the admissibility of medical records, see Chapter 10.) Without a legible and complete medical record, a healthcare provider may be unable to successfully defend against allegations of improper care. In addition, some courts will allow the jury to resolve in favor of the patient any ambiguities in the patient's record.

Whether the medical record is in paper or electronic medium, entries to it should be made in clear and concise language that can be understood by all the healthcare professionals who treat the patient. An ambiguous or illegible record often is worse than no record, because it documents a failure to communicate clearly, and therefore has an adverse effect on the quality of care.[2] This is particularly important in a managed care delivery system, such as a health maintenance organization (HMO)—where the patient may not have a long-term relationship with one primary physician, and where services are provided by different providers who, in order to fully understand a patient's medical history, rely heavily on the information a medical record contains.

Maintaining a complete record is important not only to comply with licensing and accreditation requirements (for a more detailed discussion relating to these requirements, see Chapter 3), but also to enable a healthcare provider to establish that a patient received adequate care. If a hospital or other healthcare provider can demonstrate by testimony that, in accordance with its policy and procedures, the provider regularly keeps complete and accurate records, the absence of certain notations

---

[2] See AHIMA, *Practice Brief: Ensuring Legibility of Patient Records* (May 2003), available at http://library.ahima.org/xpedio/groups/public/documents/ahima/pub_bok1_018443.html.

may be used to defend against a claim of negligence. In *Smith v. Rogers Memorial Hospital*, the medical records of a hospital patient did not indicate that the patient had complained of certain symptoms.[3] In this case, however, testimony that the hospital's records were generally reliable was important evidence in rebutting the patient's claim that she had complained of the symptoms and had not received proper care.

Similarly, in *Hurlock v. Park Lane Medical Center*, a physician ordered that the patient be turned in bed every two hours, but the medical record did not indicate each time the patient had been turned.[4] The patient argued that the absence of notes was evidence that the nurses negligently had failed to follow the physician's order, causing the patient to develop serious bedsores and necessitating amputation of her leg. Expert testimony established that, although proper nursing practice required notations to be placed in the patient's record, nurses sometimes get very busy and fail to document each action taken for patients—such as the plaintiff—who require special attention. In such cases, accepted nursing practice places patient care in priority over proper documentation. Without any direct evidence that the hospital nurses had failed to turn the patient as directed, equally plausible inferences about the patient's care arose from the medical record, the court ruled, and dismissed the suit.

Conversely, courts have allowed an inference of negligence where hospital records fail to include certain data, or where they fail to comport with adequate medical record keeping in general. In a California case in defense of a malpractice suit, an appeals court ruled that a physician's inability to produce his original records relating to a patient's treatment created an inference of the physician's consciousness of guilt.[5] In another case, a federal appeals court held that a jury was entitled to find, or at least to infer, negligence from an incomplete medical record where the plaintiff developed eye problems associated with an excessive use of oxygen at birth.[6] Given the absence of documentation about the amount of oxygen actually ordered or adminis-

---

[3] *Smith v. Rogers Memorial Hospital*, 382 A. 2d 1025, 1027 (D.C. Ct. App. 1978), *cert. denied*, 439 U.S. 847 (1978).

[4] *Hurlock v. Park Lane Medical Center*, 709 S.W. 2d 872 (Mo. Ct. App. 1985).

[5] *Thor v. Boska*, 113 Cal. Rptr. 296 (Cal. App. 2d Dist. 1974); see also *Bihun v. AT&T Information Systems, Inc.*, 16 Cal. Rptr. 2d 787 (1993).

[6] *Valdon Martinez v. Hospital Presbiteriano de la Comunidad, Inc.*, 806 F. 2d 1128 (1st Cir. P.R. 1986); *Gillis v. United States*, 722 F. Supp. 713, 717 (M.D. Fla. 1989).

tered, the court accepted testimony from the child's father regarding oxygen administration he remembered observing at the hospital. Based on this evidence, the court upheld the jury's finding of negligence.

Other courts, however, have dismissed claims against healthcare facilities that kept incomplete medical records, ruling that a facility cannot be liable for a patient's injuries where the inadequacy of the records does not proximately cause the patient's harm. One case involved a patient under the constant, direct care of an emergency room physician who did not request information about the individual's vital signs before making a diagnosis. The court ruled that the hospital's failure to take and record the patient's vital signs did not proximately cause an exacerbation of the patient's injuries stemming from the physician's misdiagnosis.[7]

Although some courts have allowed juries to infer negligence by healthcare providers based on reasonable conclusions drawn from incomplete patient records, other courts have gone further, allowing juries to presume negligence when records contain significant omissions. A presumption of negligence affects the evidentiary burden of a defendant healthcare provider to a much greater extent than does a mere inference of negligence. In general, a malpractice plaintiff must show each act of negligence with a preponderance of the evidence. If a plaintiff fails to meet this burden, the court will dismiss the suit, even if the facility presents no evidence in its defense. A presumption of negligence shifts the responsibility to the healthcare provider to prove that it acted properly. This shift in the burden of proof makes defending against a malpractice suit more difficult, especially when medical records documenting the treatment provided are incomplete.[8]

Standardized entries for EHRs can create problems when used improperly. Standardized entries are statements that describe a particular, usually routine, patient care procedure. Clinicians may select a standardized entry from a menu in the EHR software program and insert the entry into a patient's medical record. Use of these entries can save time, but if a practitioner selects the wrong entry or does not confirm that all of the language of the entry is appropriate for the patient, an inaccurate or incomplete medical record may result.

---

7 *Yaney v. McCray Memorial Hospital,* 496 N.E. 2d 135 (Ind. Ct. App. 1986).
8 For an interesting discussion on the role medical records play in determining the outcome of a medical-malpractice suit, see L. Stevens, "Let the Record Show . . . ," *American Medical News* (May 26, 1997): 11.

In addition to ensuring the delivery and evidence of adequate patient care, medical records information facilitates payment for services and claims review. The failure to insert proper notations of care on a patient's chart, therefore, may lead not only to a finding of provider negligence with respect to the patient's medical care, but also to difficulties in recovering the financial cost of the care that was provided. This was illustrated in an Arkansas appeals court ruling on the accuracy of a computerized bill containing charges for services and medication that were not reflected in the patient's chart.[9] Because the evidence revealed the strong possibility that the bill contained charges for medication not given, services not rendered, procedures not performed, and supplies not delivered, the court ruled that the bill was insufficient to sustain the hospital's claim for the cost of the patient's medical care.

The importance of complete, accurate, and legible medical records documentation has been highlighted recently in conjunction with healthcare fraud and abuse prevention and the development of corporate compliance programs in many healthcare facilities. Federal and state legislation impose a complex and expanding array of restrictions on the way healthcare providers conduct business and structure relationships among themselves, generally known as fraud and abuse provisions. At the federal level, these provisions are found primarily in the Medicare/Medicaid statute and Stark legislation,[10] and are enforced under the auspices of these statutes, the civil False Claims Act,[11] and a number of other federal laws applicable to fraudulent activities.

The reach of federal legislation governing healthcare fraud and abuse expanded substantially with the enactment of the Health Insurance Portability and Accountability Act (HIPAA).[12] The statute creates a new offense of "health care fraud," defined as "knowingly and willfully executing or attempting to execute, a scheme or artifice to defraud any health care benefit program or to obtain, by means of false or fraudulent pretenses, representations or promises, any of the money owned by or under the custody or control of any health care benefit program." Other federal offenses relating to healthcare fraud created under the new statute include theft or embezzlement, false statements, and obstruction of criminal investigations.

---

[9]   *Tracor/MBA v. Baptist Medical Center,* 780 S.W. 2d 26 (Ark. Ct. App. 1989).
[10] 42 U.S.C. § 1395nn.
[11] 31 U.S.C. §§ 3729 to 3733.
[12] 42 U.S.C. §§ 1320d et seq.

Allegations relating to false claims and fraudulent billing practices are the object of the vast majority of government enforcement initiatives. These practices involve claims for payment under any federal healthcare program in which the item or service provided to the patient is misrepresented or claims for services or supplies substantially exceed what the patient actually needed. To investigate fraud and abuse violations, the Office of Inspector General (OIG) of the U.S. Department of Health and Human Services (DHHS) has broad authority to access the medical records relating to the services that were allegedly misrepresented or falsified in the claims for payment. The information contained in medical records must be complete and accurate, therefore, to allow a healthcare provider to defend against the potentially devastating sanctions that can arise in these instances. (For a more detailed discussion of the OIG's investigative authority, see "Fraud and Abuse Investigations" in Chapter 8).

Statutes, accreditation standards, and professional associations frequently impose standards relating to the legibility, accuracy, and completeness of medical records. Federal Conditions of Participation in Medicare, for example, require that all entries to hospital records be legible and complete.[13] Conditions of Participation for other types of healthcare providers contain similar standards.[14] State law imposes similar requirements on medical records entries, frequently found in the licensing regulations for specific types of facilities,[15] or in regulations governing the medical records created by a broader category of healthcare providers.[16] Accreditation standards frequently impose a variation of the completeness and legibility standard found in state laws. Joint Commission on Accreditation of Healthcare Organizations (Joint Commission) standards of accreditation for hospitals, for example, require that data be collected in a timely, economic, and efficient manner using the degree of accuracy and completeness necessary for the data's required use.[17] Joint Commission standards for managed care plans, integrated delivery networks, and provider-sponsored networks require that member health records be periodically reviewed for completeness,

---

[13] 42 C.F.R. § 482.24(c)(1).

[14] See, e.g., 42 C.F.R. § 416.47(b), which requires ambulatory surgical services to maintain for each patient a medical record that is accurate, legible, and promptly completed.

[15] See, e.g., N.J. Admin. Code tit. 8, § 43G-15.2(b) and Code Me. R. 10-144-112 § 12.E.

[16] See, e.g., Or. Admin. R. 333-505-0050.

[17] Joint Commission on Accreditation of Healthcare Organizations, *2005 Comprehensive Accreditation Manual for Hospitals*, Standard IM.3.10.

accuracy, and timeliness of the information they contain.[18] Principles of medical records documentation developed by a number of professional associations also recommend that a medical record be legible and complete.[19]

To avoid liability and ensure compliance with the numerous laws and standards that govern their operations, therefore, healthcare facilities must be certain that all staff members clearly document the care provided to patients. In sensitive cases when careful observations are essential, all staff members should record with particular precision their contacts with patients. A healthcare provider should never compromise its standards of medical records documentation in the interest of efficiency or cost containment.

Timely Medical Records Entries

Medical records not only must be accurate, but also must be completed in a timely manner. Entries to the record should be made when the treatment they describe is given or when the observations to be documented are made. Specific legal requirements that entries be made within a certain time following a patient's discharge also exist. Regulations on participation in federal reimbursement programs, for example, require that hospital records be complete within 30 days following the patient's discharge.[20] State licensing regulations for healthcare facilities also frequently contain specific time frames for completing records.[21] Joint Commission standards of accreditation for a variety of healthcare organizations also impose timeliness as a standard for gathering medical records data.[22]

---

[18] Joint Commission, *2003–2004 Comprehensive Accreditation Manual for Health Care Networks*, Standard IM.3.2.1.

[19] See AHIMA, Principles of Medical Record Documentation, developed jointly by representatives of AHIMA, the American Hospital Association, the American Managed Care and Review Association, the American Medical Association, the American Medical Peer Review Association, the Blue Cross and Blue Shield Association, and the Health Insurance Association of America.

[20] 42 C.F.R. § 482.24(c)(2)(viii).

[21] See, e.g., Kan. Admin. Regs. 28-34-9a(f); Code Me. R. 10-144-112 §12.E.7 (requiring records of patients discharged to be completed within 15 days after release).

[22] See, e.g., Joint Commission, *2003–2004 Comprehensive Accreditation Manual for Health Care Networks*, Standard IM.2.1; *2004 Comprehensive Accreditation Manual for Hospitals*, Standard IM.6.10, 4.10, 5.10; and *2004–2005 Comprehensive Accreditation Manual for Home Care*, Standard IM.3.

A healthcare facility's bylaws or policies should require medical staff members to complete patient records within the specified time, and should provide an automatic suspension of clinical privileges for those who fail to comply. Usually, the medical records department or health information manager has the responsibility for making sure that records are completed within a specific time. Therefore, this department or manager should establish procedures for notifying attending physicians when records are incomplete.

Some healthcare institutions create incentives to encourage medical staff members to complete medical records in a timely manner. If these incentives have more than incidental economic value, however, institutions may run afoul of state and federal anti-fraud and abuse laws that prohibit giving anything of value in exchange for referrals of Medicare or Medicaid beneficiaries. Because the institutions and their medical staffs are legally required to complete records as specified by law, giving staff members something of real value can be viewed as paying for the referral of their patients. Therefore, hospitals should not establish incentive programs without the advice of qualified legal counsel.

The timeliness of medical records entries is important for many of the same reasons as the standards relating to legibility and completeness. Late entries to medical records mean that the records are in fact incomplete for a period of time, and, like other deficiencies, this can have disastrous consequences in defending against a professional negligence action. In addition, entries that are not contemporaneous with the service provided are less likely to be accurate, and therefore will have less credibility than those made during or immediately after the treatment. If an entry is made after a lawsuit has been threatened or filed, late entries may appear to have been made for the self-serving purposes of establishing a defense rather than for documenting the actual treatment rendered.

Authorship and Countersignatures

As the number and type of people making entries in patient medical records increase, especially in a managed care environment, it becomes increasingly important for healthcare facilities to have policies addressing who may make entries in a record. The purpose of these policies should be to safeguard the quality of patient care and reduce liability exposure.

State law typically does not impose restrictions on the type of professionals who may write entries in the chart. Who may do so is generally a matter of policy within a healthcare facility. Medical records entries are typically authored by the clinical provider who delivers the service to the patient, and, as a rule, any person providing care to a patient should be permitted to document that care in the individual's medical record, regardless of the caregiver's position within the facility.

It is the responsibility of a healthcare facility, therefore, to establish policies that require each practitioner to function within the scope of his or her practice as authorized by state licensing or state certification statutes, or, in the absence of such statutes, as defined by his or her professional competence.[23] Facilities should also define the level of record documentation expected of practitioners working in the institution based on the practitioner's licensure, certification, and professional competence. To the extent that a facility permits physician's assistants, nurse midwives and other advanced practice nurses, podiatrists, dentists, clinical psychologists, and other nonphysician practitioners to provide treatment, it should require them to document their treatment in accordance with the facility's policy.

The entries of certain individuals do, however, require a physician's countersignature. The purpose of countersignatures is to require a professional to review—and, if appropriate, indicate approval of—action taken by another practitioner. Usually, the person countersigning a record entry is more experienced or has received a higher level of training than the person who made the original entry. In any case, the person required to countersign should be the individual who has the authority to evaluate the entry. Countersignatures should be viewed as a means for carrying out delegated responsibility, rather than as additional paperwork.

In most hospitals, for example, licensed house staff members may make entries in patient charts, but attending physicians are required to countersign some or all such entries.[24] In addition, when undergraduate medical students and unlicensed resident physicians make record entries that show the application of medical judgment, medical

---

[23] See Joint Commission, *2005 Comprehensive Accreditation Manual for Hospitals*, Standard IM.6.10-6.60, which requires that the hospital have a complete and accurate medical record reflecting patient assessment and treatment by authorized individuals. See also Joint Commission, *2004–2005 Comprehensive Accreditation Manual for Home Care*, Standard IM.6.10.1, to the same effect.

[24] See, e.g., Code Me. R. 10-144-112 XII.F.3; Miss. Code § 12-000-040, § 1709.4.

diagnosis, prescription of treatment, or any other act defined by applicable state law to be the practice of medicine, these entries should be countersigned by a licensed physician, who may be an attending or a resident physician. In most states, it is a violation of the medical licensure act for anyone to practice medicine without a license unless the individual is practicing under the direct, proximate supervision of a physician licensed to practice in that state. Therefore, without evidence of such supervision, the student or unlicensed resident might be held to have violated state law. The rules governing a physician's countersignature of medical records entries made by other authorized personnel should be set forth in the hospital's medical staff rules and regulations.

Similarly, the entries of undergraduate nursing students should be countersigned by a licensed professional nurse, if such entries document the practice of professional nursing as defined by the state's nursing licensure act. Without evidence of proper supervision, a nursing student practicing professional nursing could be held in violation of the state's nursing licensure act unless the act specifically authorizes nursing students to practice nursing in the course of their studies toward a registered nursing degree.[25] The nursing licensure acts of some states also authorize graduate nurses who have applied for a license to practice professional nursing for a limited time without a license.[26] Graduate, unlicensed nurses in those states may make entries in medical records without countersignature by a licensed nurse. In states that have no specific allowances for practice by such graduates, however, their entries should be countersigned.

In many hospitals, social workers participate in the care of patients and request that they be allowed to make entries in their patients' charts. Generally, there is no prohibition against such entries as long as the information placed in the record is relevant to the patient's treatment. Entries by social service staff members should be limited to relevant factual observations or to data and judgments that such staff members are competent to make. Highly subjective remarks, if essential to the record, must be worded carefully and must be clearly relevant to the patient's care. Social workers should be discouraged from keeping records of their observations and judgments other than those included in the medical record.

---

[25] See, e.g., 225 Ill. Comp. Stat. Ann. 65/5-15.
[26] Ibid.

Authentication of Records

The requirement that the physician or other medical practitioner sign the record or a portion of the record exists in order to ensure authenticity. Data and person/entity authentication are key elements in system reliability and security. Generally, authentication means the corroboration that a person is who he or she claims to be, or, in the context of medical records, that an entry in a patient's record was actually entered (or ordered) by the person authenticating the record.[27] Traditionally, authentication was made by handwritten signature. However, numerous regulatory and accrediting organizations also contemplate authentication by a rubber stamp or computer key. Each method of authentication must be considered in light of the HIPAA regulations governing security of health information (Security Rule), which governs the confidentiality, integrity, and availability of electronic protected health information (ePHI).[28] (For a detailed discussion of the Security Rule, see Chapter 13.)

The HIPAA Security Rule provides two standards to ensure the authenticity of patient records: the Integrity Standard,[29] and the Person or Entity Authentication Standard.[30] First, the Integrity Standard requires covered entities to implement policies and procedures to protect ePHI from improper alteration or destruction. The term "integrity" means that data or information have not been altered or destroyed in an unauthorized manner.[31] To comply with this standard, a covered entity must address whether it should implement electronic mechanisms, such as digital signatures or check-sum technology,[32] to corroborate that ePHI has not been altered or destroyed in any unauthorized manner.[33] Second, the Person or Entity Authentication Standard requires covered entities to implement procedures to verify that a person or entity seeking access to ePHI is who he or she claims to be.[34]

Unlike many state laws and accreditation organization standards (which are discussed later), the Security Rule does not require use of a

---

27   45 C.F.R. § 164.304.
28   See 45 C.F.R., subpt. C.
29   45 C.F.R. § 164.312(c)(1).
30   45 C.F.R. § 164.312(d).
31   45 C.F.R. § 164.304.
32   68 Fed. Reg. 8356 (Feb. 20, 2003).
33   45 C.F.R. § 164.312(c)(2).
34   45 C.F.R. § 164.312(d).

particular technology or method for authentication. Rather, it gives covered entities the discretion to select those security measures that reasonably and appropriately satisfy the requirements of the rule. In deciding which security measures to use, a covered entity must take into account the following factors:

- The size, complexity, and capabilities of the covered entity
- The covered entity's technical infrastructure, hardware, and software security capabilities
- The cost of the security measures
- The probability and criticality of potential risks to ePHI[35]

The HIPAA Security Rule is but one source of authority governing authentication. The Joint Commission accreditation standards for hospitals, for example, require that medical records be authenticated when necessary.[36] At a minimum, entries of histories and physical examinations, operative procedures, consultations, and discharge summaries must be authenticated, but the healthcare facility's policy may designate other types of entries that require authentication in accordance with state law and regulations or the facility's medical staff bylaws.

Examples of authentication systems that would meet this accreditation standard include:

- Computer entries that allow for an online review of the document and entry of a computer code to signify approval
- A procedure in which transcripts are mailed to the author, who reviews the entry and signs and returns a postcard indicating that the records have been reviewed and attesting to their accuracy
- A system that allows for review and approval with a single signature of a list of specific unsigned entries in a record, where the list is permanently retained in the record[37]

Medicare Conditions of Participation require that all entries to a patient's record be authenticated and dated promptly by the person

---

[35] 45 C.F.R. § 164.306(b).
[36] Joint Commission, *2005 Comprehensive Accreditation Manual for Hospitals,* Standard IM.6.10.
[37] Ibid. Standard, Intents, and Examples for Patient-Specific Data and Information, Example of Evidence of Implementation for IM.6.10–6.60.

responsible for ordering, providing, or evaluating the service furnished.[38] The author of each entry must be identified and must authenticate the entry. Under those regulations, authentication may include signatures, written initials, or computer entry.

States also permit authentication by rubber stamp or computer key, in addition to the traditional handwritten signature. All of the states that permit this type of authentication impose controls to safeguard against abuse. The controls ensure that only properly authorized individuals have access to, and use of, the authenticating devices. For example, in California, the State Department of Health Services has regulations providing the following:

> Medical records shall be completed promptly and authenticated or signed by a physician, dentist or podiatrist within two weeks following the patient's discharge. Medical records may be authenticated by a signature stamp or computer key, in lieu of a physician's signature, only when that physician has placed a signed statement in the hospital administrative offices to the effect that he is the only person who:
>
> (1)   has possession of the stamp or key
>
> (2)   will use the stamp or key[39]

Similarly, Arkansas permits physicians to use rubber-stamp signatures if the method is approved in writing by the hospital administrator and the medical records committee, and requires that the stamp be locked in the medical records department when the physician is not using it.[40] Indiana requires that all physicians' orders for medication and treatment be in writing or acceptable computerized form, and be signed by hand or acceptable computerized form in accordance with hospital and medical staff policies. All verbal orders must be authenticated by the physician and documented in the medical record within 48 hours.[41] The Centers for Medicare & Medicaid Services (CMS), the agency within the DHHS principally responsible for the administration of the Medicare and Medicaid programs, warns that the use of alternative

---

[38] 42 C.F.R. § 482.24(c)(1).
[39] Cal. Code Regs. tit. 22, § 70751(g).
[40] Ark. Code 14(B)(8).
[41] Ind. Admin. Code tit. 410, r. 15-1-5(b)(3)(N) and 15-1-5(b)(3)(O).

signature methods, such as signature stamps, creates a risk of misuse or abuse:

> For example, a rubber stamped signature is much less secure than other modes of signature identification. The individual whose name is on the alternate signature method bears the responsibility for the authenticity of the information being attested to. Physicians should check with their attorneys and malpractice insurers in regard to the use of alternative signature methods.[42]

Some states, however, do not specifically address the substitution of rubber stamps or computer keys for the physician's handwritten signature, or else they impose authentication requirements that appear to preclude the use of stamps or computer codes. For example, in Arizona, the person responsible for each entry "shall be identified by initials or signature and, if a rubber stamp or electronic signature code is used to authenticate an order, the person whose signature the stamp or code represents is accountable for its use."[43] In Kansas, each clinical entry must be signed or initialed by the attending physician, who must be identified properly in the record.[44] New Jersey requires that all entries be written in ink, dated, and either signed by the recording person or authenticated through the use of an EHR system.[45]

Because applicable law in these states may be ambiguous or conflicting, hospitals and practitioners seeking to use alternatives to handwritten signatures should consult with qualified legal counsel. Although some courts may be willing to accept an expansive definition of the terms "writing" and "signature," no general rule exists that authentication of medical records may be accomplished by any method other than a written signature. If state law requires a handwritten signature for authentication, the institution must provide for such authentication, even if it maintains its records in computers. In such states, technology that captures digitally an individual's handwritten signature should satisfy the legal requirement and permit the signature to become part of an

---

[42] Memorandum dated July 8, 2004, to State Survey Agency directors from the director, Survey and Certification Group, Centers for Medicare and Medicaid Services, U.S. Department of Health and Human Services.
[43] Ariz. Admin. Code R9-10-228.
[44] Kan. Admin. Regs. 28-34-9a(f).
[45] N.J. Admin. Code tit. 8, § 43G-15.2(b).

EHR. The only other alternative for the institution or state hospital association is to embark on the often long and difficult task of obtaining an amendment of the applicable restrictive state law.

Auto-Authentication

The introduction of computer technology to health information management has provided opportunities to improve the speed and accuracy of the authentication process. Computerizing medical records, however, has introduced a new risk that the technology will replace rather than supplement the role of practitioners and hospital personnel in this process of verifying the accuracy and completeness of medical records. In particular, these concerns have arisen with respect to the process of auto-authentication, in which a physician authenticates a report by computer code before the report is transcribed. Physicians enter an electronic signature, and agree to review and correct transcripts of EHR within a certain time frame. If no corrections are made by the deadline, the record is deemed complete. Although both federal and state authorities allow electronic signatures to replace handwritten ones, they also require that authentication, regardless of the format, attest to the accuracy of the record.[46] To the degree that an auto-authentication system does not allow a physician to make this verification, many regulatory agencies have adopted the position that the authentication requirement is not fulfilled.

Auto-authentication systems frequently contain safeguards that protect some of the essential functions of the authentication process, however. For example, some facilities require physicians to sign an attestation that they will review all records and, unless they request corrections, the medical records department may enter the physician's signature. These attestations may include a provision in which the physician agrees not to dispute the accuracy of any record based on the absence of the physician's signature on any document. Such an agreement provides no supporting evidence that a physician actually reviewed the record, however, and therefore does not resolve concerns regarding the accuracy of the record's contents.

---

[46] See M. Kadzielski and M. Reynolds, "Legal Review: Auto-authentication of Medical Records Raises Verification Concerns," *Topics in Health Information Management* 14 (1): 77–82 (1993).

Other facilities allow physicians to authenticate unsigned progress notes in a medical record by signing a statement on a cover page that they are authenticating all progress reports for a particular hospital stay. A separate authentication is required for other types of reports in the file, including operative reports, physical reports, discharge summaries, and so on. Because progress reports are authenticated by the physician when they are created, these reports are more likely to be accurate and complete.

Under another system of auto-authentication of dictated and transcribed reports, a physician receives a copy of all transcribed reports and a periodic list of unsigned and dictated reports. The physician then indicates next to each report on the list whether he or she wants to sign it or authorize auto-authentication of the report. The level of accountability increases in this type of system because the physician receives a copy of each report and individually selects each report for either signature or auto-authentication.

The Joint Commission states that signatures do not have to be dated if they occur in real time of the entry, and that countersignatures entered into paper records for authentication purposes should be dated when required by state or federal law and by the policies of the institution.[47] A facility should have a system to determine whether the author of an entry acknowledges the entry after it has been transcribed, and a quality control system should monitor the process.

The CMS Medicare Conditions of Participation require authentication of each entry in a medical record and allow authentication by computer.[48] However, CMS has indicated that any failure to obtain a physician's signature with respect to the record in its final form constitutes a deficiency in the authentication requirement.[49]

In addition to exposing healthcare facilities to loss or denial of accreditation, possible sanctions by administrative agencies, and exclusion from the Medicare/Medicaid program, the use of auto-authentication can generate difficulties in offering evidence in litigation, particularly professional liability suits. The outcome of such litigation frequently depends on establishing what actually took place in the course of the plaintiff's

---

[47] See Joint Commission, *2005 Comprehensive Accreditation Manual for Hospitals,* Examples of Evidence of Implementation for IM.6.10.
[48] 42 C.F.R. § 482.24(c)(1)(ii).
[49] "Vladeck Warns Auto-authentication Will Violate Medicare Conditions," *BNA Health Law Reporter* (Oct. 21, 1993): 1423.

treatment. A physician's signature on the medical record gives evidence that the practitioner actually reviewed the record and acknowledged that it represented a complete and accurate record of the patient's course of treatment. Although a signature does not prove conclusively that the physician reviewed the record, it is stronger evidence of such verification than a signature on a separate form authorizing authentication of the record.

Although the introduction of computer technology has enabled hospitals to introduce new methods for facilitating a physician's role in the authentication process, healthcare institutions should not lose sight of their responsibility in creating accurate and complete medical records. Any computer system that does not require physicians to review reports after they have been transcribed is likely to fall short of both federal and state authentication standards, as well as to create serious liability risks for the facility implementing such a system. (For a more detailed discussion of EHRs, see Chapter 13.)

Verbal Orders

In the course of providing patient care, healthcare practitioners often deliver orders verbally. Because of the effect that this practice may have on the quality of patient care, it is important for healthcare facilities to establish standards governing how these orders are received and recorded. Healthcare facilities should require physicians to deliver their orders in writing or by computer entry, except in situations in which verbal orders are unavoidable. Written and computer entry orders are preferable to verbal ones because written and computer entry orders create fewer chances for error.

Hospital licensing regulations in most states require all physician orders to be written in the patient's medical record and authenticated.[50] Indiana requires that (a) all verbal orders be repeated and verified, (b) that the repetition and verification be documented in the patient's medical record, (c) that the record be signed by the professional who took the order, and (d) that if no repetition and verification occurred, the ordering physician must then authenticate and date the verbal order within 48 hours.[51] Other state licensure laws extend the time pe-

---

[50] See, e.g., S.C. Code Ann. Regs. r. 61-16 § 601.6.
[51] Ind. Admin. Code tit. 410, r. 15-1.5-5(b)(3)(O).

riod for signing verbal orders to "as soon as is practical."[52] Joint Commission standards of accreditation for hospitals state more generally that verbal orders from authorized individuals must be accepted and transcribed by qualified personnel as defined in the facility's rules and bylaws.[53] Regardless of licensing laws or accreditation standards, healthcare facilities should require that physicians are responsible for writing their orders in the medical record unless they are not present when the order must be given, and the facilities should also require all verbal orders to be transcribed within a specified time. Policies should also be predicated on the concept that only personnel who are qualified to understand physicians' orders should be authorized to receive and transcribe verbal orders.

Corrections and Alterations

Some medical records entry errors are inevitable. Generally, two kinds of errors occur: (1) minor errors in transcription, spelling, and so on, and (2) more significant errors involving test results, physician orders, inadvertently omitted information, and similar substantive entries.

While most states have no specific statutory or regulatory rules concerning altering medical records, some state regulations specify how corrections should be handled. For example, in Arkansas, errors in medical records must be corrected by drawing a single line through the incorrect entry, labeling the entry as an error, and initialing and dating it.[54] In Massachusetts, healthcare facilities may not erase mistakes, use ink eradicators, or remove pages from the record.[55]

In the absence of such regulations, however, healthcare facilities should enunciate clear rules governing corrections. If the correction is a significant one, a senior person designated in the facility's policy should review the correction to determine whether it complies with the institution's guidelines for record amendments. Obvious minor errors, such as spelling, do not require intervention by senior personnel. As a general

[52] See, e.g., Neb. Admin. Code 9-006.07A2-.07A3.
[53] See Joint Commission, *2005 Comprehensive Accreditation Manual for Hospitals*, Standard IM.6.5.
[54] Ark. Code 14(A)(6). See also N.J. Admin. Code tit. 8, § 8:43G-15.2(l) (corrections shall be made by drawing a single line through the error and initialing and dating the correction).
[55] 105 Code Mass. Regs. 150.013(B).

rule, the person who made the incorrect record entry should correct the entry. If that is not possible, healthcare practitioners should make only those changes that are within their scope of practice as defined by state licensing and state certification laws. A registered nurse, for example, should not amend a physician's medication order unless directed to do so by the physician.

The person correcting a charting error in a paper record should use a single line to cross out the incorrect entry, then enter the correction, initial the correction, and enter the time and date the correction was made. In an EHR, the method for correcting a error is dictated by the application software, which in any event should document the original entry and the time and by whom it was made, and the corrected entry and the time and by whom the correction was made. Mistakes in the record should not be erased, obliterated, or deleted, because erasures, obliterations, and deletions could arouse suspicions in the minds of jurors as to the contents of the original entry. A single line drawn through incorrect entries—or, in an EHR, the ability to retrieve the original and the corrected entries—leaves no doubt as to the original information being corrected. Where a correction requires more space than is available near the original entry, the person correcting the record should enter a reference to an addendum to the record, and then enter the lengthy correction in the addendum. The application software of an EHR program should clearly indicate that a particular entry has been corrected.

Any appropriate amendments made at the patient's request should be included in an addendum to the record. The HIPAA Privacy Rule gives patients the specific right to amend their health information, and gives healthcare providers the right under certain circumstances to deny the requested amendment. Healthcare providers must follow the amendment procedures set forth in the Privacy Rule.[56] (For a more detailed discussion of the patient's right to request amendments, see Chapter 6.) Although a patient may wish to submit an amendment to his or her medical record, a healthcare provider is not required to accept the amendment if the provider determines that the health information involved was not created by the provider, is not part of the patient's medical record and was not used to make decisions about the patient, would not be available under HIPAA for the patient's inspection, or is

---

[56] See, generally, 45 C.F.R. § 164.526.

accurate and complete.[57] If the provider denies the requested amendment, the provider must provide the patient with the basis for its denial, along with other information concerning the patient's rights with respect to the requested amendment.[58] If the provider accepts the amendment, it should follow its normal record amendment policies with respect to how it implements the amendment. A physician who considers the amendment inappropriate should discuss the matter with the patient.

A few states have regulations that address changes or amendments to medical records at the request of parties. In Maryland, legislation requires healthcare providers to establish a procedure by which an interested person may request an addition or correction to a medical record.[59] If the facility does not make the requested change, it must permit the individual to insert a statement of disagreement in the record. The facility must also provide either a notice of the change or a statement of disagreement, and provide this notice or statement to every person to whom it previously disclosed inaccurate, incomplete, or disputed information within the preceding six months.[60] New York law also allows a qualified person to challenge the accuracy of information in a medical record. In the event that a facility refuses to amend a record in accordance with the person's request, the facility must allow the individual to write a statement challenging the accuracy of the record, and must include the statement as part of the permanent record.[61] HIPAA will not likely preempt these state laws if they provide additional protection for the patient (that is, give the patient greater rights of access to, or control over, their health information). To the extent that HIPAA gives patients greater protection with respect to their health information, however, HIPAA will likely preempt these state laws. (See Chapter 6 for discussion of the preemption provisions of HIPAA.)

In the event of a threatened or actual suit by a patient against a healthcare provider or facility, no changes should be made in the patient's medical record without first consulting defense counsel. Attempts to alter medical records entries to favor the providers are always

---

[57] 45 C.F.R. § 164.526(a)(2); see also 45 C.F.R. § 164.526(d).
[58] Ibid.
[59] Md. Code Ann., Health-Gen. § 4-304(b)(1).
[60] Md. Code Ann., Health-Gen. §§ 4-304(b)(5)(1) and § 4-304(b)(6)(ii).
[61] 10 N.Y. Comp. Codes R. & Regs. § 405.10(a)(7).

inappropriate and usually do not help their defense, particularly if the patient has obtained a copy of the record before the changes were made.

If the patient can show that the record was altered without justification, the credibility of the entire record may be undermined. In a Connecticut case, for example, nurses rewrote an entire section in the medical record of a patient who was injured while hospitalized. The court held in the patient's subsequent negligence action against the hospital that:

> [i]n addition to all the other evidence in the case, the significance of the revised hospital record should not be overlooked. Although the defendant understandably attempts to minimize what was done by characterizing the action as merely one of ordering expanded notes and by attributing it to poor judgment, the trier [of fact] was not required to be so charitable. An allowable inference from the bungled attempt to cover up the staff inadequacies . . . was that *the revision indicated a consciousness of negligence.* The court so charged and the jury could so find. [Emphasis added.][62]

If a healthcare facility or provider that is involved in a negligence suit discovers that an original record entry is inaccurate or incomplete, the facility or provider should request that clarifications or additions to the record be placed in a properly signed and dated addendum to the record. In addition, deliberately altering a medical record or writing an incorrect record may subject a healthcare provider to statutory sanctions. In some states, a practitioner who makes a false entry on a medical record is subject to license revocation for unprofessional conduct.[63] In addition, as is discussed above, altering or falsifying a chart for purposes of wrongfully obtaining Medicare or state healthcare funds is a crime under federal law, and subjects the violator to a substantial fine or imprisonment.[64]

---

[62] *Pisel v. Stamford Hospital,* 430 A. 2d 1 (Conn. 1980).
[63] See, e.g., Ky. Rev. Stat. Ann. § 311.595(10).
[64] 42 U.S.C. § 1320a-7b(a).

CHAPTER 5

Document Consent to Treatment

Chapter Objectives

- Distinguish between express and implied consent
- Identify the information that must be disclosed for informed consent
- Briefly distinguish informed consent and the authorization required by the HIPAA Privacy Rule
- Explain what a patient must show to prove causation in a consent case
- Describe the emergency exception to the informed consent requirement
- Define the therapeutic privilege and waiver of consent
- Outline how informed consent applies to criminal suspects and prisoners
- Identify who can give consent
- Discuss the effect of refusal of consent
- Discuss the application of informed consent to minors
- Distinguish between emancipated minors and mature minors
- Compare the responsibility for obtaining consent among physicians and other healthcare providers, facilities, and organizations
- Outline the requirements for informed consent documentation and explain that documentation of HIPAA authorizations relating to the use and disclosure of health information may be combined with informed consent documentation

(continues)

- Distinguish between the different types of consent forms and their uses
- Discuss how and when consent may be withdrawn
- Briefly explain the HIPAA preemption rule

Introduction

Healthcare providers must obtain proper authorization before performing diagnostic or therapeutic procedures on patients.[1] Consent may be express or implied, and may be obtained from the patient or the patient's authorized representative, if the patient is incapacitated. In most instances, the law requires that the patient be given sufficient information concerning the nature and risks of the recommended and alternative treatments so that the consent is an informed consent. Generally, if the patient decides not to consent, the examination or procedure cannot be performed. In some circumstances, however, the law overrides the patient's decision and provides authorization for involuntary treatment, such as in emergencies and for compulsory treatment for certain conditions, such as mental illness, so long as required procedures are followed.

The primary responsibility for obtaining informed consent for treatment falls on physicians and other healthcare practitioners, rather than on a healthcare institution, facility, or organization, such as a hospital, group practice, clinic, health maintenance organization (HMO), or hospice. The law in this area has developed primarily in the hospital context, with courts and statutes generally establishing that hospitals are not liable for failing to obtain a particular patient's informed consent. There are several important exceptions to the general rule, however. Hospitals and other healthcare institutions and facilities may be liable for failure to obtain consent from a patient if the unconsented to procedure is performed by a hospital employee rather than by an independent contractor. As a practical matter, hospitals frequently assist nonemployee members of its medical staff by obtaining written confir-

---

[1] At least one state court has held that the informed consent requirement applies only to surgical procedures, however: *Morgan v. MacPhail*, 704 A. 2d 617 (Pa. 1997) (informed consent not required for injection of steroids).

mation of the patient's consent. However, once a hospital or other corporate healthcare entity assumes this responsibility, it must consistently comply with its own policies and practices or face increased potential for liability. In addition, a corporate healthcare entity is legally responsible for the adequacy of its organizational consent requirements, policies, and procedures.

Beyond liability to patients, federal, state, and private accreditation requirements mandate that informed consent be obtained and documented. For example, the Medicare Conditions of Participation for Hospitals require properly executed consent forms as part of the medical record.[2] The Joint Commission on Accreditation of Healthcare Organizations (Joint Commission) requires accredited hospitals—as well as home care organizations, ambulatory care organizations, and mental health services that are part of accredited networks—to obtain informed consent.[3] Federal and state laws may create a liability risk by prescribing consent procedures in special situations, such as in connection with a clinical study.[4] State laws may also require written consent documentation on a more general basis, as part of regulatory schemes such as health facility or HMO licensure laws and patients' rights statutes. Thus, healthcare administrators, medical records administrators, and individual healthcare providers must be familiar with the legal principles on patient consent and the proper documentation of consent.

In addition to these requirements for informed consent, the Health Insurance Portability and Accountability Act (HIPAA),[5] and its implementing privacy regulations (Privacy Rule) require certain covered entities to obtain legal permission to use and disclose an individual's protected health information (PHI) unless an exception applies.[6] HIPAA and its implementing regulations created a whole new set of legal obligations applicable to health plans, healthcare insurers, healthcare clearinghouses, and those who receive data from such entities. (For a detailed discussion of HIPAA and the Privacy Rule, see Chapter 6.)

---

[2]   42 C.F.R. § 482.24(c)(2)(v).
[3]   Joint Commission on Accreditation of Healthcare Organizations, *2004 Comprehensive Accreditation Manual for Hospitals*, Standard RI. 2.40.
[4]   See, e.g., 45 C.F.R. § 46. See Chapter 14 for a more detailed discussion of the laws relating to medical research records.
[5]   42 U.S.C. §§ 1320d et seq.
[6]   45 C.F.R. pts. 160 and 164, published in the Federal Register at Standards for Privacy of Individually Identifiable Health Information, 67 Fed. Reg. 53181-53273 (Aug. 14, 2002).

The consent requirement, the decision making roles of patients and their representatives, the exceptions to the consent requirement, and the function of the medical record in the patient consent process are discussed in this chapter. The chapter concludes with a discussion of the HIPAA requirements relating to authorization to use or disclose an individual's PHI, distinguishing the HIPAA authorization requirements from the informed consent requirements. The chapter also contains an explanation of the extent to which the HIPAA Privacy Rule preempts state statutes relating to the privacy of medical records information.

Legal Theories of Consent

The common law long has recognized the right to be free from harmful or offensive touching. The intentional harmful or offensive touching of another person without authorization is called battery. The earliest medical consent lawsuits arose in England in the 18th century. In those early cases, when surgery was done without consent, the court found the surgeon liable for battery. Modern courts also have found physicians liable for battery if the physicians do not obtain their patients' consent.

Courts apply a different legal theory, however, when the patient consents to the procedure but does not have sufficient information to make an informed decision. Today, nearly all courts have adopted the position that failure to disclose the necessary information so the patient can make an informed decision regarding a procedure's risks and benefits does not constitute a battery, but rather, constitutes negligence under the informed consent doctrine. Moreover, many courts also require that a healthcare provider provide a patient with information regarding the provider's own financial and other interests in a given course of treatment.[7]

Express and Implied Consent

Consent may be either express or implied. Express consent is consent given by direct words, either orally or in writing. For some procedures,

---

[7] See *Moore v. Regents of the University of California*, 793 P. 2d 479 (Cal. 1990) (holding that a patient stated a valid claim for lack of informed consent when the physician failed to disclose an economic interest in the research).

particularly those involving reproduction and testing for sexually transmitted diseases, state laws require express written consent. The Medicare Conditions of Participation for Hospitals, include specific requirements for the content of a hospital consent form. Otherwise, either oral or written consent can be legally sufficient authorization where express consent is necessary. However, because it often is difficult to prove oral consent if a dispute arises, providers should almost always seek written consent.

Implied consent is consent inferred from the patient's conduct and consent presumed in certain emergencies. When a patient voluntarily submits to a procedure with apparent knowledge of the nature of the procedure, the courts usually will find implied consent. For example, in a famous early consent case, the court found that a woman had given her implied consent to being vaccinated by extending her arm and accepting the vaccination without objection.[8] In a 1983 case, a court held that a patient who revoked his express written consent to a surgical procedure, but who then silently acquiesced to preoperative medication and submitted to surgery, had given implied consent.[9]

When Is Consent Implied?

Consent is implied in almost all medical emergencies, unless the healthcare provider has reason to believe that consent would be refused—for example, if the patient previously had refused treatment. This emergency exception to the consent requirement applies when there is an immediate threat to life or health *and* the patient is incapacitated and cannot give consent. In an early Iowa case, the court found implied consent to the removal of a patient's mangled limb that had been run over in a train accident.[10] The court accepted the physician's determination that the amputation was necessary to save the patient's life. However, courts have disagreed on whether pain alone is enough justification to find implied consent, although an early New York decision held pain to be a significant factor in establishing a finding of implied consent.[11] Some states have enacted laws that formalize the emergency exception. In California, informed

---

[8] *O'Brien V. Cunard S.S. Co.*, 28 N.E. 266 (Mass. 1891).
[9] *Busalacchi v. Vogel*, 429 So. 2d 217 (La. Ct. App. 1983).
[10] *Jackovach v. Yocom*, 237 N.W. 444 (Iowa 1931).
[11] *Sullivan v. Montgomery*, 279 N.Y.S. 575 (N.Y. City Ct. 1935).

consent for even experimental treatments is not necessary if the patient is in a life threatening situation and unable to give informed consent, and if certain other conditions are met.[12]

Some courts have found implied consent to extensions or modifications of surgical procedures beyond the scope specifically authorized when unexpected conditions arise, and when the extension or modification is necessary to preserve the patient's life. Many surgical consent forms attempt to minimize disagreements regarding the scope of authorization by including explicit authorization of extensions or modifications to preserve the patient's life or health.

Some courts have addressed whether a patient has given implied authorization for the substitution of one practitioner for another. Generally, unless an emergency or other special circumstance occurs, a patient's consent constitutes authorization only for a particular practitioner to perform a particular procedure; deviation from that authorization may invalidate the consent. If the patient refuses to consent to treatment by a certain caregiver, then that caregiver is prohibited from engaging in treatment. Likewise, if the primary physician chooses an assistant to whom the patient objects, that assistant is precluded from participating in the procedure.[13] For example, one court allowed a patient who specifically requested that no male healthcare provider view or touch her unclothed body during childbirth to pursue a battery claim against a male nurse who attended delivery.[14] The patient's physician had assured her that the male nurse would not see her unclothed.

Informed Consent

The term "informed consent" refers to the process in which a patient is apprised of a procedure's risks and benefits, and freely consents to undergo the proposed treatment. Simply requiring the patient to sign a form does not satisfy informed consent requirements, because the form itself serves merely as evidence of the informed consent process. On the other hand, it is important to document consent or the lack of consent.

---

[12] Cal. Health & Safety Code § 24177.5.

[13] See, e.g., *Kenner v. Northern Illinois Medical Center*, 517 N.E. 2d 1137 (Ill. Ct. App. 1987); *Johnson v. McMurray*, 461 So. 2d 775 (Ala. 1984).

[14] *Cohen v. Smith*, 648 N.E. 2d 329 (Ill. Ct. App. 1995); *Chadwick v. Al-Basha*, 692 N.E. 2d 390, 393 (Ill. Ct. App. 1998).

Although not legally conclusive, a well written, properly executed consent form is strong evidence that informed consent was given. Generally, a legally effective consent form must

- be signed voluntarily;
- describe the procedure for which the consent was given;
- show that the consenting person understood the nature of the procedure, the risks involved, and the probable consequences.

The courts have developed two standards for determining the adequacy of the information the physician has given the patient during the informed consent process: (1) the reasonable physician standard, and (2) the reasonable patient standard. In states using the first standard, physicians have a duty to provide the information that a reasonable medical practitioner would offer under the same or similar circumstances.[15]

The second and more modern standard has been adopted by an increasing number of states. Under the reasonable patient standard, the extent of the physician's duty to provide information is determined by the information needs of the patient, rather than by professional practice. Information that is material to the patient's decision must be disclosed. Some states have adopted this standard through legislation. In Pennsylvania, for example, state law requires physicians to inform a patient of the nature of the proposed treatment, the risks associated with the treatment, and the alternatives that a reasonable patient would consider material to the decision whether to undergo treatment.[16] The recently revised Medicare Conditions of Participation also appear to have adopted the reasonable patient standard.[17]

What Information Must Be Disclosed?

Generally, a physician or other healthcare provider must disclose the following categories of information to a patient:

- diagnosis
- nature and purpose of the proposed treatment

---

[15] See, e.g., *Natanson v. Kline*, 350 P. 2d 1093 (Kan. 1960).
[16] 40 Pa. Consol. Stat. § 1301.811-A.
[17] 42 C.F.R. § 482(c)(2)(v).

- risks and consequences of the proposed treatment
- probability that the proposed treatment will be successful
- feasible treatment alternatives
- the identity of the person who will be performing the procedure
- alternatives and prognosis if the proposed treatment is not given

Although this is the generally accepted list of items that should be discussed, a healthcare provider should include all information that the provider knows or reasonably should know would be material to the patient's decision making process.

Most of the cases concerning informed consent involve allegations that the provider failed to reveal sufficient information as to the risks and consequences of the procedure. However, not all risks must be disclosed. For example, risks that are very remote and improbable generally can be omitted, because a person in the patient's position would not likely find them material to the consent decision.[18] Similarly, some risks with a very high probability could be considered to be so commonly known that the physician is not required to mention them. If the provider can document that the patient had knowledge of risks and consequences from other sources, such as from a prior course of treatment or from discussions with another healthcare provider, the patient's consent may be considered informed. Court cases examining what information must be conveyed to patients are highly dependent on the circumstances. Examples follow:

- In an Arizona case, a patient told a physician that preserving his ability to work was crucial in determining a course of treatment.[19] The court ruled that the physician should have informed the patient of the risks that could affect his ability to work.
- A physician treating a minor patient for a concussion should have informed the patient's parents that a computed axial tomography (CAT) scan would reveal bleeding in the brain, even if there was only a 1 to 3 percent chance that the patient suffered that condition.[20]
- A physician may not have fulfilled his duty to fully disclose the risks of breast reduction surgery when he warned a patient that scarring

---

[18] See, e.g., *Lemke v. United States*, 557 F. Supp. 1205 (D.N.D. 1983).
[19] *Hales v. Pittman*, 576 P. 2d 493 (Ariz. 1978).
[20] *Martin v. Richards*, 531 N.W. 2d 70 (Wis. 1995).

could occur, but responded to the patient's questions by telling her that she should not worry and would be happy with the results.[21]

- A physician who did not disclose that his own lack of experience increased the risk that serious impairment could result from aneurysm surgery might be liable, because information that should be revealed to patients is not limited to complications intrinsic to the procedure.[22]

- A physician who recommended and performed laser surgery as a treatment for a viral wart on the cervix failed to obtain informed consent because he failed to advise the patient of the treatment option of doing nothing.[23]

Patients also have sued when their refusal to consent to treatment was not sufficiently informed. In California, the courts have extended the informed consent doctrine to require informed refusal. In the California case that established this concept, the court ruled that a physician could be liable for a patient's death from cancer of the cervix, based on the physician's failure to inform the patient of the risks of not consenting to a recommended Pap smear.[24] The Pap smear probably would have led to discovery of the patient's cancer in time to begin treatment that would have extended her life. The California informed consent rule also requires the primary physician to disclose the risks of not consulting a specialist.[25]

Proving Causation

Often the most difficult element for the patient to prove in an informed consent case is causation. The patient must show a link between the inadequate informed consent and the injury by proving that he or she would not have consented if the risk that occurred had been disclosed. The courts have developed two standards for this proof. Some jurisdictions apply an objective standard, determining what a reasonable person in the patient's position would have decided if informed of the risk.[26] Other courts apply a subjective standard, determining whether the

---

21 *Korman v. Mallin*, 858 P. 2d 1145 (Alaska 1993).
22 *Johnson ex rel. Adler v. Kokemoor*, 545 N.W. 2d 495 (Wis. 1996).
23 *Wecker v. Amend*, 918 P. 2d 658 (Kan. Ct. App. 1996).
24 *Truman v. Thomas*, 611 P. 2d 902 (Cal. 1980).
25 *Moore v. Preventive Medicine Medical Group, Inc.*, 223 Cal. Rptr. 859 (Ct. App. 1986).
26 *Canterbury v. Spence*, 464 F. 2d 772 (D.C. Cir.), *cert. denied*, 409 U.S. 1064 (1972).

patient involved in the lawsuit would have refused to consent to the procedure if informed of the risk.[27] Either of these standards provides substantial protection for the conscientious healthcare provider who discloses the major risks, and whose patient suffers from a more remote risk. For example, in a Massachusetts case, a court held that a physician was not liable for failure to obtain informed consent where the risk he failed to disclose was remote.[28] The physician did not advise a pregnant patient whose membranes had ruptured that waiting for labor to proceed naturally posed a risk of streptococcus pneumonia for the infant, who died five days after birth. The court ruled in favor of the physician, ruling that because the risk of infection was negligible, disclosure would not have been material to the patient's decision to allow labor to proceed naturally.

Medical Experimentation and Research

Innovative treatments trigger special consent requirements, beyond properly informing the patient of risks and benefits. Federal, state, and local laws on human experimentation and the protection of human research subjects impose strict requirements for obtaining patient consent.[29] These laws contain specific safeguards for research subjects and guidelines for informed consent, establishing detailed standards for documentation and record retention. The requirements vary depending on the legal status of the experimental treatment, agreements between the healthcare provider or research sponsor and government authorities, and healthcare facility policies and procedures. Thus, medical records requirements should be carefully examined whenever a patient undergoes an experimental treatment or takes part in a clinical study.

Exceptions to the Informed Consent Requirement

The courts have recognized four situations in which consent is required, but informed consent (that is, adequate disclosure) is not necessarily required: emergencies, the therapeutic privilege, patient waiver, and treatment of criminal suspects or patients in custody.

---

[27] *Feeley v. Baer*, 679 N.E. 2d 180 (R.I. 1972).
[28] *Wilkinson v. Vesey*, 295 A. 2d 676 (Mass. 1997).
[29] 45 C.F.R. § 109(b) and 46 C.F.R. § 116.

Emergencies

In some circumstances, the patient is competent and able to consent to treatment, but the healthcare provider does not have time to provide full disclosure of all possible treatment alternatives before initiating care. This situation does not meet the strict parameters of the emergency doctrine, discussed earlier, in which the patient is incapacitated and consent is presumed. For example, in a New Mexico case, a patient suffered from a snakebite that required immediate treatment.[30] The court recognized that even when there is time to secure consent, certain emergency situations may allow only an abbreviated disclosure of information as to the required treatment. Hospitals (the setting where such emergencies are most likely to be presented) should insist that staff engage in consultation with patients as time and circumstances permit. Findings supporting the existence of an emergency should be noted on the patient's record, with particular emphasis on the nature, immediacy, and magnitude of the threat. The initialing of such notations by consultant physicians is advisable. At the least, the physicians' names should be recorded.

Therapeutic Privilege

Many courts recognize an exception to the informed consent doctrine, called therapeutic privilege, that permits a physician to withhold information when disclosure of information poses a significant threat of detriment to the patient. Courts have carefully limited the therapeutic privilege by making it applicable only when the physician fears that the information might lead the patient to forgo needed therapy. Instead, physicians should rely on this privilege only when they can document that a patient's anxiety is significantly above the norm. In a federal appeals case, the court ruled that when the therapeutic privilege applies, the risk information must have been disclosed to a relative who would not have been paralyzed by anxiety.[31]

Statutes and regulations may also set the parameters of the therapeutic privilege.[32] In California skilled nursing facilities, for example,

---

[30] *Crouch v. Most*, 432 P. 2d 250 (N.M. 1967).

[31] *Lester v. Aetna Casualty & Surety Company*, 240 F. 2d 676 (5th Cir.), *cert. denied*, 354 U.S. 923 (1957); but see *Nishi v. Hartwell*, 473 P. 2d 116 (Haw. 1970) (duty to make full disclosure arises from the physician patient relationship and is owed only to the patient).

[32] See, e.g., Del. Code Ann. tit. 18, § 6852(b)(3).

a physician may choose not to inform a patient of the risks of treatment if objective facts documented in the patient's record demonstrate that the disclosure would so seriously upset the patient that the patient would not have been able to rationally weigh the risks of refusing the recommended treatment. In such a case, unless inappropriate, the physician must obtain informed consent from the patient's representative.[33]

Patient Waiver

Some cases have indicated that a patient can waive the right to be informed before giving consent.[34] However, state laws and regulations may also narrowly define the circumstances in which waiver is appropriate, such as requiring the patient to initiate the waiver, requiring the substituted consent of a representative, or allowing waiver only where risks are minimal. New York law, for example, states that it is a defense to a suit for failure to obtain informed consent if the patient assured the medical practitioner that he or she would undergo the treatment regardless of the risk, or told the practitioner that he or she did not want to be informed.[35] A physician should not suggest a waiver, but instead should encourage reluctant patients to be informed. If the patient persists, the waiver should be documented in the patient's medical records and carefully witnessed. The documentation should describe the patient's waiver and the physician's effort to properly inform the patient.

Treatment of Criminal Suspects and Prisoners

In some instances, healthcare providers are asked by law enforcement officers to perform procedures on unconsenting patients. A healthcare provider might be asked to conduct a medical examination that will result in the discovery of criminal evidence (such as a test for alcohol or drugs in a suspect's blood), or to treat a prisoner against his or her wishes for venereal disease, drug addiction, or mental illness. In some states, healthcare providers are protected by state laws that grant them immunity when acting on the request of a police officer.[36] State laws

---

[33] Cal. Code Regs. tit. 22, § 72528.
[34] See, e.g., *Putensen v. Clay Adams, Inc.*, 12 Cal. App. 3d 1062 (Ct. App. 1970).
[35] N.Y. Pub. Health Law § 2085-d.
[36] See, e.g., N.Y. Veh. & Traf. Law § 1194.

may specifically address what procedures may be performed in the absence of prisoner consent.

For example, Florida law authorizes the treatment of prisoners for venereal disease;[37] Maryland law allows prisoners to be enrolled in drug treatment programs;[38] Tennessee law authorizes complete physical examinations of prisoners, including blood tests;[39] and the Iowa code implies consent (which may be withdrawn) by drivers to be tested for blood alcohol.[40]

Several cases have addressed the appropriateness of procedures ordered by police officers or courts, such as pumping of a suspect's stomach to recover drugs.[41] However, those cases involve the constitutional rights of the patient, not the liability of the healthcare provider. Healthcare providers who are requested to perform examinations or administer treatment to a prisoner without consent should consider whether a state law, regulation, or court order authorizes the medical intervention. The provider should not rely on the police officer's assurance that the procedure is permitted by law, and should document in the medical record the source of the authority to treat.

Distinguishing Informed Consent and HIPAA Authorization

The HIPAA Privacy Rule[42] establishes the conditions under which protected health information (PHI) may be used or disclosed, and the means by which individuals will be informed of such uses and disclosures.[43] Except where otherwise permitted or required, a covered entity may not use or disclose an individual's PHI without that individual's authorization.[44] A covered entity must document and retain any signed authorization and ensure that the authorization contains the required core elements.[45] Generally, an authorization focuses

---

[37] Fla. Stat. Ann. § 384.32.
[38] Md. Code Ann. § 9-603.
[39] Tenn. Code Ann. § 41-4-138.
[40] Iowa Code Ann. § 321J.6.
[41] *Rochin v. California*, 342 U.S. 165 (1952).
[42] 45 C.F.R. pts. 160 and 164.
[43] 45 C.F.R. §§ 164.506, 164.508, and 164.510. See Chapter 6 for a fuller discussion of the HIPAA Privacy Rule.
[44] 45 C.F.R. § 164.508.
[45] 45 C.F.R. §§ 164.508(b)(6) and 164.508(c).

on privacy risks—stating how, why, and to whom the PHI will be used and/or disclosed, and providing a description of how the confidentiality of records will be protected, among other things.[46] An informed consent, on the other hand, provides individuals with a description of the relevant treatment or procedure and of its anticipated risks and/or benefits. (For a detailed discussion of the authorization required by the Privacy Rule, see Chapter 6.)

Who Can Give Consent

The person who makes the consent decision must be legally and actually competent to make the decision, and must be informed of the risks and benefits involved, unless one of the exceptions applies. Competent adults and some mature or emancipated minors make decisions regarding their own care. Someone else must make the decisions for incompetent adults and other minors.

Competent Adults

The age of majority is established by the legislature of each state. In most states, legal majority is now 18 years of age. In some states, a person can be considered an adult before the statutory age of majority by taking certain actions, such as getting married or serving in the armed forces.

An adult is competent if (1) a court has not declared the person incompetent, and (2) the person generally is capable of understanding the consequences of alternatives, weighing the alternatives by the degree to which they promote his or her desires, and choosing and acting accordingly. There is a strong legal presumption of competence. For example, in one case, a court found a woman competent to refuse the amputation of her gangrenous leg even though her train of thought sometimes wandered, her conception of time was distorted, and she was confused on some matters.[47] The fact that her decision was medically irrational and would lead to her death did not demonstrate incompetence. The court believed that she understood the alternatives and the consequences of her decision.

---

[46] Ibid.
[47] *Lane v. Candura*, 376 N.E. 2d 1232 (Mass. App. Ct. 1978).

Competence is not necessarily determined by psychiatrists. A practical assessment of competence should be made by the healthcare provider who obtains the consent or accepts the refusal. When it is difficult to assess competence, consultation with a specialist should be considered. If the provider suspects an underlying condition that affects brain function, the consultant should be a psychiatrist or other appropriate specialist. These assessments should be documented in the medical record.

Refusal of Consent

Competent adults have the right and capacity not only to consent to medical treatment, but also to refuse such treatment. A treatment refusal must be honored regardless of the basis on which it is grounded.

Some patients refuse treatment on religious grounds. The religious beliefs of Jehovah's Witnesses, for example, prohibit them from receiving blood transfusions. The majority of courts have ruled that such patients have the right to refuse blood transfusions even if such refusal will lead to their death.[48] Terminally ill competent adult patients constitute another category of those who may refuse consent to treatment. Documentation of their wishes in the medical record is addressed in detail in Chapter 8.

In these sensitive situations, hospitals and physicians should seek the advice of qualified legal counsel if the patient's refusal is a serious threat to health, as long as the delay involved in seeking that guidance would not further endanger the patient's life. Healthcare providers should exercise extreme caution when administering treatment to an unconsenting patient in the absence of a court order or other clear authority.

Incompetent Adults

If a patient is not competent to give informed consent or informed refusal, the patient's guardian—or, if no guardian exists, the representative of the incompetent adult patient—makes consent decisions on the patient's behalf. Representatives of patients have a narrower range of permissible choices regarding that person than they would have

---

[48] See, e.g., *In re Melideo*, 390 N.Y.S. 2d 523 (1976); *In re Brown*, 478 So. 2d 1033 (Miss. 1985).

concerning their own care. In addition, the known wishes of the patient should be considered in reaching decisions about treatment.

When a court rules that a person is incompetent, the court designates an individual to be the incompetent person's guardian. The guardian has the legal authority to make most of the decisions regarding the incompetent person's care.

Because some patients who actually are incompetent never have been determined to be incompetent by a court, they may have no legal guardian unless they had executed a document that empowered someone to be the surrogate decision maker. When decisions must be made concerning their care, it is common practice to seek a decision from the next of kin or others who have assumed supervision of the patient. In many states, statutes[49] or court decisions[50] support that practice. Most states allow residents to execute a standard form, known as a healthcare power of attorney, for the purpose of designating someone who can make medical decisions for the person when he or she is unconscious or otherwise unable to give informed consent. Persons who take advantage of these laws know that when difficult decisions must be made, there will be little time wasted trying to have a court appoint a guardian.

If the incompetence is temporary, the medical procedure should be postponed until the patient is competent and capable of making the decision, unless the postponement presents a substantial risk to the patient's life or health; in this case, consent will be implied from the emergency.

Certain procedures, such as sterilization and organ donation, require special consideration. Traditionally, neither the courts nor a guardian can authorize involuntary sterilization of incompetent minors or adults without specific statutory authority.[51] Healthcare providers should not perform sterilization procedures on incompetents without appropriate legislative authority, case law authority, or a court order.

As for organ transplants involving incompetents as donors, the courts generally examine the situation to establish whether the procedure is in the best interest of the incompetent person. In some cases, courts have concluded that operations, such as kidney transplants, are

---

[49]   See, e.g., Miss. Code Ann. §§ 41 through 41-3.
[50]   See, e.g., *Farber v. Olkon*, 254 P. 2d 520 (Cal. 1953).
[51]   See, e.g., *Hudson v. Hudson*, 373 So. 2d 310 (Ala. 1979).

not in the patient's best interest.[52] Other courts, however, have been willing to find indirect benefit to the incompetent sufficient to support consent to the procedure. Some courts have upheld the right of a guardian to authorize kidney donations because of the close relationship between the donor and the proposed recipient, the emotional injury to the donor if the recipient were to die, and the reasonable motivations of the patient and the patient's parent or guardian.[53]

Minors

Parental or guardian consent should be obtained before treatment is given to a minor unless (1) the patient requires emergency treatment, (2) a statute grants the minor the right to consent, or (3) a court or other legal authority orders treatment.

Emergency Care

As with adults, consent for treatment of a minor is implied in medical emergencies when an immediate threat to the patient's life or health exists. Most states have statutes addressing this issue.[54] If the healthcare provider believes that the patient's parents would refuse consent to emergency treatment, and if time permits, the provider should seek court authorization for treatment or notify the appropriate government agency responsible for seeking court authorization. If the patient requires immediate treatment, the provider in most cases should treat the minor, even if the parents object. Healthcare administrators should establish policies for responding to these situations.

Emancipated Minors

Emancipated minors may consent to their own medical care. In most states, minors are considered emancipated when they are married or otherwise no longer subject to parental control or regulation and are not supported by their parents. The specific factors necessary to establish

---

[52] See, e.g., *In re Guardianship of Pescinski*, 226 N.W. 2d 180 (Wis. 1975); *Curran v. Bosze*, 566 N.E. 2d 1319 (Ill. 1991).

[53] See, e.g., *Strunk v. Strunk*, 445 S.W. 2d 145 (Ky. 1969); *Hart v. Brown*, 289 A. 2d 386 (Conn. Super. Ct. 1972).

[54] See, e.g., 410 Ill. Comp. Stat. § 210/3(a).

emancipation usually are established by statute and vary from state to state. Some states require that the parent and child agree on the emancipation, so that a minor cannot become emancipated in those states simply by running away from home. In some states, emancipation is established by the courts, and no statutory definition of emancipation exists. Because the doctrine of emancipation is unsettled in many states, healthcare providers should try to obtain the consent of a parent in addition to that of the minor, or consider the existence of another basis upon which to treat a minor without parental or guardian consent (such as an emergency). A well written policy established with the advice of qualified legal counsel will help guide practitioners confronted with this issue.

Mature Minors

Mature minors may consent to some medical care under common law and constitutional principles and under the statutes of some states. Many states have statutes that authorize older minors to consent to any medical treatment. In other states, the age limits and scope of treatments to which a minor may consent vary. Many states have special laws concerning minors' consent to treatment for venereal or other communicable diseases and substance abuse without regard to age.

Most courts reject chronological age as the sole factor in determining maturity, and tend to balance a number of factors.[55] In one case, the Supreme Court of Illinois ruled that a mature minor has the right to refuse life sustaining medical treatment if state interests in preserving life, protecting third party interests, preventing suicide, and maintaining the ethical integrity of the medical profession do not outweigh this right.[56] In this case, a 17-year-old patient needed blood transfusions to treat leukemia, but both she and her mother refused consent on religious grounds. The court held that the mature minor had the right to refuse medical treatment.

Consent requirements for minors seeking abortions are regulated largely by state law. The law varies from state to state, and currently is in a condition of flux. State statutes usually provide that a minor can avoid the necessity of parental consent by proving to a court that he or

---

[55] See, e.g., *Cardwell v. Bechtol*, 724 S.W. 2d 739 (Tenn. 1987).
[56] *In re E.G.*, 549 N.E. 2d 322 (Ill. 1989).

she is a mature minor capable of making such a decision on his or her own.

Generally, when treating a minor, a healthcare provider should urge the minor to involve his or her parents in making consent decisions. When a mature minor refuses to permit parental involvement, the healthcare provider can give the necessary care without substantial risk based on the minor's consent alone, unless there is likelihood of harm to the minor or others that can be avoided only through parental involvement. When the likelihood of such harm arises, parents usually should be involved, unless state law forbids notifying them.

Parental or Guardian Consent

Either parent can give legally effective consent for treatment of a minor child, except when the parents are legally separated or divorced. When the parents are legally separated or divorced, usually the consent of only the custodial parent must be obtained unless there is an agreement between the parents that both must consent to treatment. This often is specified in state statutes. The provider should rely upon the parent or parents to provide information concerning who has authority to consent to the minor's care. If a provider knows or suspects that one parent objects, the provider should use caution and seek the advice of its legal counsel.

Responsibility for Obtaining Consent

It is the treating physician's responsibility to provide the necessary information to the patient concerning the patient's condition and proposed treatment, and to obtain informed consent before proceeding with diagnostic and therapeutic procedures. Other independent practitioners who order procedures have a similar responsibility concerning those procedures. Historically, the hospital, facility, or other healthcare setting where care is rendered generally was not liable for the failure of the physician or other independent practitioner to obtain informed consent unless the practitioner is an employee or otherwise acting on behalf of the corporate entity.[57] Some states have codified this principle

---

[57] See, e.g., *Fiorentino v. Wenger*, 227 N.E. 2d 296 (N.Y. 1967).

in their statutes. For example, Ohio law states: "No hospital, home health agency, or provider of a hospice care program shall be held liable for a physician's failure to obtain an informed consent from his patient prior to a surgical or medical procedure or course of procedures, unless the physician is an employee of the hospital, home health agency, ambulatory surgical center or provider of a hospice care program."[58]

The courts have ruled overwhelmingly that hospitals do not have an affirmative obligation to monitor the content of disclosures given by nonemployed healthcare practitioners to patients being treated within the hospital's facilities to ensure that consent is informed.[59] This reasoning also applies to other types of healthcare facilities and organizations. However, there are circumstances that may lead to consent related liability for these entities:

- The physician that failed to obtain informed consent is an employee of the facility. Liability of an employee may be "imputed" or attributed to the employer based on the reasoning that employers are responsible for supervising their employees.
- The facility knew, or should have known, that a physician did not comply with informed consent requirements but failed to intervene. In this case, a court may hold that the facility negligently breached its own duty to provide quality care to the patient.
- The facility's procedures for requiring, documenting, or verifying consent did not comply with the standards of the medical community, or the facility did not comply with its own policies, procedures, or usual practices with regard to a particular patient. As in the previous example, under these circumstances, the facility may be liable for breaching its direct duty to protect patients.

Another issue that may arise is the question of which provider has the duty to disclose when there is more than one provider involved in rendering care. Courts have held that if a primary treating physician

---

[58] Ohio Rev. Code Ann. § 2317.54.
[59] See, e.g., *Petriello v. Kalman*, 576 A. 2d 474 (Conn. 1990); *Pauscher v. Iowa Methodist Medical Center*, 408 N.W. 2d 355 (Iowa 1987); *Kershaw v. Reichert*, 445 N.W. 2d 16 (N.D. 1989). But see *Magana v. Elie*, 439 N.E. 2d 1319 (Ill. Ct. App. 1982), in which an Illinois appeals court ruled that a hospital may have a duty to its patients to ensure that independent medical staff physicians inform them of the risks of, and alternatives to, surgery.

remains active in the patient's treatment, that physician must obtain informed consent.[60] Responsibility for disclosure also may depend on whether the primary treating physician has asked for a consultation with another physician or whether the patient has been referred to a second physician. To avoid confusion, healthcare administrators should make certain that medical staff bylaws or policies clearly allocate the responsibility of obtaining informed consent.

The role of nonphysician healthcare practitioners (such as nurses and physician's assistants) in the consent process varies among care settings. A typical approach to delineating the role of nonphysician employees in hospitals is to limit their role to (1) screening for completion of a consent form to ascertain that the hospital has documented the patient's consent in accordance with established hospital policy, and (2) informing the responsible physician when the patient has concerns or questions about the consent form, seems to be confused about the proposed treatment, or has withdrawn or retracted consent. If the physician does not respond appropriately, hospital employees should notify medical staff and hospital officials so they may determine whether intervention is necessary. (For a more detailed discussion of seeking and documenting responsible intervention, see Chapter 8.)

Other healthcare entities permit nonphysician providers to obtain the required signature of the patient on the consent form once the physician has informed the patient of proposed procedures and has obtained the patient's verbal authority to proceed with treatment. In some practices or facilities, nonphysicians may provide some or all of the information necessary for the patient to give an informed consent. Although these approaches can provide the patient with the information he or she needs for an informed consent, involving nonphysicians in the consent process could negatively affect the physician-patient relationship by reducing the opportunity for adequate communication. Involving nonphysicians also could shift the liability for inadequacies of consent from the (typically independent) physician to the nonphysician's employer. To avoid those adverse consequences, some healthcare entities prohibit nonphysicians from obtaining consent. State law should be considered closely when developing a policy on who may participate in the consent process, because statutes and court decisions

---

[60] See, e.g., *Jones v. Philadelphia College of Osteopathic Medicine*, 813 F. Supp. 1125 (E.D. Pa. 1993); *Ritter v. Delaney*, 790 S.W. 2d 29 (Tex. App. 1990); *Jacobs v. Painter*, 530 A. 2d 231 (Me. 1987).

often outline who is or may be responsible for obtaining informed consent. In Maine, for example, regulations specifically permit certified registered nurse anesthetists to verify consent.[61]

Documentation

Consent is not merely a form, despite common belief to the contrary. The patient and everyone involved with providing health care should understand that obtaining the patient's consent means obtaining the patient's authorization for diagnosis and treatment. Once the patient has authorized the proposed care, it is important to document that authorization in the patient's medical record. Many commentators agree that the best way to document informed consent is to obtain the signature of the patient or the patient's representative on an appropriate form. Other experts recommend that the physician write a detailed note in the medical record reflecting the discussion of consent with the patient or the patient's representative. This approach is recommended out of concern that courts will view a consent form as all the information given to the patient, and not believe the physician's testimony that additional information was provided. Some forms used today, however, may be more detailed than a practitioner's note in the medical record. A combination of a signed consent form and a notation in the patient's medical record is another method for documenting consent.

A typical consent policy outlines the circumstances under which a signed consent form is required. The types of procedures that may trigger a signed consent requirement include the following:

- major or minor invasive surgery
- procedures that involve more than a slight risk of harm
- forms of radiological therapy
- electroconvulsive therapy
- experimental procedures
- HIV tests
- sterilization
- abortion

---

[61] Code Me. R. § 02-380-008-1(3)(c)(2).

- organ donation
- other procedures for which consent forms are required by statute or regulation

In developing or applying a policy on the use of consent forms, healthcare managers should be aware that the actual process of providing information to the person giving consent and of determining the person's ability to make a decision is more important than the consent form. The form is only evidence of the consent process and is not a substitute for the consent process. A senior manager or medical staff officer should be responsible for determining that actual consent exists even when a consent form has been lost or inadvertently not signed before treatment, or when other circumstances make it difficult to obtain the necessary signature. In all cases, the information on a consent form must be consistent with the information given the patient by the physician. If the physician wishes to provide information different from that on the standard consent form, the physician should revise the form before the patient signs it.

Types of Consent Forms

Once the decision has been made to use a consent form rather than making a detailed note in the medical record, the type of form must be selected. There are two basic approaches to consent forms: the short consent form (also called a general or battery consent form) and the long consent form (also called a detailed or special consent form). These approaches to consent documentation are described below.

A third approach is not advisable, but should be noted. In the past, many hospitals asked patients being admitted for care to sign a consent form authorizing any procedure their physician wished to perform. These forms are known as blanket consents or admission consents. Courts have ruled that blanket consent forms are not evidence of consent to major procedures because the procedure is not specified on the form. Because admission consent forms may serve as valid evidence of consent to minor procedures and noninvasive treatments with insignificant risk of harm, some attorneys recommend their continued use. However, most believe that these admission forms provide no more protection than the implied consent that is inferred from admission and submission to minor procedures.

Short Consent Forms

The short consent form provides space for the name and description of the specific procedure, and states that (1) the person signing has been told about the medical condition, consequences, risks, and alternative treatments; and (2) all the person's questions have been answered to his or her satisfaction. The short form does not list the particular risks and benefits that were described to the patient. This type of consent form usually will defeat a claim of battery if the proper person signs the form and if the procedures described in the form are the ones performed on the patient. Following the procedures for the use of the form also provides support for the healthcare provider's position that the person who signed was informed adequately. However, it is possible that the person who signed the short consent form could convince a court that he or she did not give informed consent, because he or she did not receive information as to consequences, risks, and alternatives to the treatment. When the short form is used, testimony of the healthcare providers who participated in the informed consent process, rather than the form itself, will serve as the most important evidence of informed consent. For this reason, practitioners who use the short form are well advised to make detailed notes in the patient's medical record regarding the risks and benefits that were discussed in the informed consent process.

Long Consent Forms

Some healthcare organizations use forms that include a detailed description of the patient's medical condition, proposed procedure, consequences, risks, and alternatives to treatment. These detailed forms may be mandated by statute, such as in the case of federally funded sterilizations and research involving human subjects. When a long form is used, it is much more difficult for the patient to prove that the information in the form was not disclosed, because the form bears the patient's signature. The healthcare provider may handwrite the risks, benefits, alternatives, and other pertinent information on the long form, or else the form may be preprinted. A preprinted detailed form for a particular procedure should be updated to reflect changes in the risks, benefits, and alternatives to the procedure so that the form does not become obsolete. Because the preprinted long form contains a full description of risks and benefits, there is a danger that healthcare providers may come to rely on the form as an inadequate substitute for the consent process, rather than explaining the information carefully to each patient and ascertaining that the patient understands. Consent policies and procedures, as well as staff education, should be used to guard against this possibility.

Challenges to Consent Forms

As stated earlier, although consent forms are strong evidence of informed consent, they are not conclusive. The person challenging the adequacy of the consent process will have an opportunity to convince the court that informed consent was not actually obtained. For example, the person who signed the form may prove that he or she was not competent as a result of the effects of medication. Thus, it is important that the explanation of a procedure's risks, benefits, and alternatives be given, and that the signature be obtained at a time when the consenting party is capable of understanding the decision being made. Consent forms may be challenged on the basis that the wording was too technical or that the form was written in a language the patient could not understand. Although persons are presumed to have read and understood documents they have signed, courts will not apply this presumption in the face of such challenges.

As a result, it is important that forms are understood by the person signing them. If the person has difficulty understanding English, someone—preferably a healthcare organization employee capable of understanding the technical information, or an agency that specializes in translating medical information—should translate the form. It is advisable to have consent forms in the primary languages used by a substantial portion of the patients served by the healthcare organization or practice. However, it is usually sufficient to have the form translated orally and to have the translator certify that the form and discussion of the procedure have been translated orally for the person signing the form. If a patient refuses to sign a consent form, but is willing to give oral consent after receiving an adequate explanation of the procedures, the fact of oral consent and the reason for the patient's refusal to sign should be documented on the consent form, along with the witnessed signature of the person obtaining the verbal consent.

A consent form also may be challenged on the grounds that the signature was not voluntary. Because in order to prove that the signature was coerced, the person signing would have to prove that there had been some threat or undue inducement, it is difficult to prove coercion.

However, if a physician misrepresents the probability of death or injury involved in refusing to undergo the proposed procedure, the patient or the patient's representative might be successful in showing coercion, and thereby invalidate the patient's prior consent.

Withdrawal of Consent

Unless specified by statute, there is no absolute limit on the period of validity of a consent or the documentation of that consent by a signature on a consent form. If the patient's condition or the available treatments change significantly, the earlier consent no longer is valid, and a new consent should be obtained.

Whenever a patient refuses to consent to, or withdraws consent for, treatment, the patient's physician should be notified, and written acknowledgment of the refusal or withdrawal should be obtained from the patient after the physician has discussed with the patient the implications of the refusal or withdrawal. These steps generally will protect the healthcare provider and organization from liability. If the patient refuses to sign a form releasing the healthcare organization and provider from responsibility for the consequences of refusal or withdrawal of consent, these facts should be documented thoroughly in the medical record.

Because a claim that consent was withdrawn becomes more credible as time passes, it may be advisable to periodically obtain informed consent for patients with ongoing treatment. For example, some hospitals obtain a new consent each time the patient is admitted. The consent may be obtained in a physician's office before the admission, provided that the time between the consent and the admission is not too long. Some policies require consent forms to be signed no more than 30 days before the procedure; others require new consents periodically, especially in outpatient treatment settings. Carefully prepared policy should establish guidelines governing the validity and expiration of patient consent.

Impact of State Statutes

When developing forms, healthcare administrators must consider state statutes. In some states, statutes provide that if the consent form contains certain information and is signed by the appropriate person, it creates a presumption of informed consent. For example, in Iowa, a written consent is presumed to be an informed consent if it describes the nature and purpose of the procedure consented to—including specific risks listed in the statute, such as death, brain damage, and quadriplegia—as well as an acknowledgment that the patient's questions have been answered satisfactorily.[62] Such statutes indicate how the courts will treat forms containing only the information specified in the statute. Although it is not a violation of these statutes to use a form that contains different language from that outlined in the statute, healthcare organizations should be sure that a decision to use forms that do not meet the statutory requirements is based on careful consideration of the risks. In any case, organizations should not adopt such forms without the advice of their legal counsel.

Impact of the Medicare Conditions of Participation

In spite of the case law holding hospitals generally not to be liable for a physician's failure to obtain consent, the Medicare Conditions of Participation[63] and the hospital accreditation standards of the Joint Commission[64] both obligate a hospital to have policies that require physicians to obtain informed consent to procedures. Further, both specify what must be set forth on the consent form. The Medicare Conditions of Participation require the following:

- Patient name or name of legal guardian
- Name of the hospital
- Listing of the procedures
- Name of primary practitioner
- Names of others who will have a significant role in the procedure and a listing of significant surgical tasks
- Risks of the procedure
- Alternatives to the procedure
- Signature of the patient or legal guardian
- Signature of a "professional person" who witnessed the patient's signature
- Name and signature of the person who explained what the procedure was and its risks

---

[62] Iowa Code Ann. § 147.137.
[63] 42 C.F.R. § 482.24(c)(2)(v).
[64] Joint Commission, *2004 Comprehensive Accreditation Manual for Hospitals*, Standard RI.240.

Finally, the very concept of what is "informed consent" is addressed:

- Situations where the patient consents to a procedure and information was withheld from the patient, where, if the patient had been informed of that information, the patient may not have consented to the procedure or made the same decisions, would not be considered informed consent

In light of the requirements of the Medicare Conditions of Participation, all hospitals should examine their informed consent policies and modify them to comply with the requirements. Hospitals should also do their own audit of compliance, just as a federal surveyor would.

HIPAA Preemption

Finally, in evaluating the impact of state statutes that arguably govern the privacy of healthcare information, healthcare managers must consider the HIPAA Preemption Rule.[65] Under the general HIPAA preemption rule, HIPAA regulations preempt any contrary provision of state law unless the state law falls in one of the specifically enumerated exceptions to the general rule.[66] In particular, state laws will not be preempted where they relate to the privacy of individually identifiable information and are more stringent than the HIPAA requirements in regard to protecting the privacy of individually identifiable health information or granting individuals access to their medical records.[67] In addition, state laws relating to reporting of disease, injury, child abuse, birth or death; or relating to public health surveillance, investigation, or intervention; or relating to the auditing, licensure, or certification of health plans, facilities, or individual healthcare providers are not preempted.[68] Finally, a state may submit to the Secretary of Department of Health and Human Services a request to except a provision of state law from preemption on certain specified grounds.[69] Certain states, such as California, have published detailed analyses of the preemptive

---

[65] 45 C.F.R. § 160.201 et seq. discuss HIPAA preemption of state law.
[66] 45 C.F.R. § 160.203.
[67] 45 C.F.R. §§ 160.203(b) and 160.202.
[68] 45 C.F.R. §§ 160.203(c) and (d).
[69] 45 C.F.R. § 160.204.

effect of the HIPAA regulations on various state statutes.[70] However, HIPAA preemption analysis is complex, and generally one should seek legal counsel in determining the extent to which a given state's laws are preempted by the new HIPAA Privacy Rule. (For a more detailed discussion of HIPAA preemption, see Chapter 6.)

---

[70] See, e.g., the California Office of HIPAA Implementation (CalOHI) Web site at http://www.ohi.ca.gov/state/calohi/ohiHome.jsp.

Access to Health Information

Chapter Objectives

- Describe the types of health information protected by confidentiality laws
- Explain the general rule regarding ownership of medical records information
- Describe the key provisions of the HIPAA Privacy Rule, to whom they apply, and how they affect access to health information
- Summarize other federal confidentiality laws that may affect health information
- Describe what is meant by the exercise of professional judgment
- Give examples of state laws that protect the confidentiality of medical records information
- Summarize the rights of patients and third parties to access medical records information, including sensitive information such as alcohol and drug abuse patient records and psychiatric records
- Explain the law governing access to protected health information by individual patients and their personal representatives
- Describe the authority allowing healthcare providers to charge record duplication fees
- Summarize the additional rights provided to individuals in federal health information protection laws
- Summarize the laws or accreditation standards governing the use of medical records in utilization review and quality assurance activities
- Describe the rights and obligations of business associates
- Summarize the additional rights provided to individuals in federal health information protection laws

Introduction

This chapter discusses medical records confidentiality requirements and the general legal principles governing access to patient healthcare information. Healthcare organizations and providers must be aware of the various federal and state laws governing the confidentiality of medical records information. The Health Insurance Portability and Accountability Act[1] and the regulations issued under HIPAA governing the privacy of health information (Privacy Rule)[2] and the security of such information (Security Rule)[3] set a federal "floor," or minimum standard, governing uses and disclosures of most health information used by health plans, healthcare clearinghouses, and certain healthcare providers and entities that use health information in performing services on their behalf. State statutes and regulations that are not preempted by HIPAA also govern uses and disclosures of health information. When state law and the Privacy Rule conflict, the preemption provisions of the Privacy Rule determine whether state law or the Privacy Rule controls.

A variety of access issues can arise in a healthcare setting, including access to medical records by or on behalf of the patient, access to the medical records of minors, and staff access to medical records information. Patient records containing unusually sensitive health information, such as psychiatric and drug or alcohol abuse records, may have stricter confidentiality and release requirements. Healthcare organizations should also be aware of the law regarding disclosures for medical research. (See Chapter 14 for a discussion of the use of health information in research involving human subjects.) To comply with all of these laws, each healthcare organization must devise an effective record security procedure that protects and preserves both the physical medical record and the patient's general interest in confidentiality. Utilization review laws and standards issued by voluntary accreditation organizations may also govern how healthcare organizations and providers may grant access to medical records information. Healthcare organizations and providers should consult the law in their jurisdictions to understand fully their obligation to keep patient information confidential and the circumstances in which medical records information may be used or disclosed.

---

[1]   42 U.S.C. §§ 1320d et seq.
[2]   45 C.F.R. §§ 160 and 164.
[3]   45 C.F.R. §§ 164.302 et seq.

Healthcare organizations and practitioners may be held liable for improperly disclosing patient information. In addition to facing statutory penalties, healthcare facilities, organizations, and providers may be liable under common law theories, including defamation, invasion of privacy, and breach of physician-patient privilege. (Liability for improper uses and disclosures is discussed in Chapter 11.)

In addition to the right of patients to access their health information, HIPAA creates other rights in individuals with respect to their medical records. These include a right to notice of a healthcare entity's privacy practices, a right to receive an accounting of certain uses and disclosures of their information, a right to request restrictions on uses and disclosures, a right to receive communications about their information in a confidential manner, and a right to request amendments to their health information.

Types of Health Information

Not all health information is protected from unauthorized access. The Privacy Rule addresses the uses and disclosures of information that is, or can be, identified with a particular individual. Information that is so general that no individual can be associated with it is not subject to HIPAA privacy protection or to the protection of most state laws. The Privacy Rule describes in considerable detail the information that is subject to its protection, and also provides certain limited ways in which healthcare providers and others may alter health information in order to use it without a patient's permission. Most state medical records laws generally have extended privacy protection to information that identifies an individual, but these laws have not defined protected information with as much detail.

Protected Health Information

The Privacy and Security Rules apply to individually identifiable health information. The rules define "health information" quite broadly as information that is created or received in any form or medium by a healthcare provider, health plan, public health authority, employer, life insurer, school or university, or healthcare clearinghouse, and that "relates to the past, present, or future physical or mental health or condition of an individual, the provision of health care to an individual, or the past, present, or future payment for health services provided to an individual."[4] "Individually identifiable health information" is health information that can be identified with an individual or reasonably could be used to identify an individual.[5] "Protected health information" (PHI) is defined in the rules as individually identifiable health information that is transmitted by electronic media, maintained in electronic form, or transmitted in any other form or medium.[6] PHI does not include education records covered by the Family Educational Rights and Privacy Act,[7] certain records described in that act that have substantial privacy protection,[8] or employment records held by an employer.[9]

De-Identification of Health Information

Health information that does not identify an individual or cannot be used to identify an individual is not subject to HIPAA privacy protection. The Privacy Rule permits covered entities to use and disclose "de-identified information" for their own purposes or for use by another entity.[10] Therefore, if a covered entity can de-identify PHI for a particular use or disclosure, it can lawfully avoid the privacy protection requirements of the Privacy Rule because de-identified information is not PHI.[11] For example, a covered entity does not need a business associate agreement with an organization to which it discloses only de-identified information. (See the discussion of business associates in this chapter.) "De-identified information" is information that does not identify the individual and that the covered entity has no reasonable basis to believe can be used to identify the individual.[12] A covered entity demonstrates that the information has been de-identified by using a statistical determination of a small risk of identification or by meeting the safe harbor requirements provided in the Privacy Rule.

---

[4]   45 C.F.R. § 164.103.
[5]   Ibid.
[6]   45 C.F.R. § 164.501.
[7]   20 U.S.C. § 1232g.
[8]   See 20 U.S.C. § 1232g(a)(4)(B)(iv).
[9]   45 C.F.R. § 164.103.
[10] 45 C.F.R. § 164.502(d)(1).
[11] 45 C.F.R. § 164.502(d)(2).
[12] 45 C.F.R. § 164.514(a).

The statistical analysis to determine that information has been properly de-identified must meet several requirements. The person conducting the analysis must be an expert in statistics—that is, a person with appropriate knowledge of and experience with generally accepted statistical and scientific principles and methods for rendering information not identifiable with individuals.[13] Using such principles and methods, the expert must determine that the risk is very small that the information could be used, alone or in combination with other reasonably available information, by an anticipated recipient to identify an individual.[14] The expert must document the methods and results of the analysis that justifies his or her conclusions.[15]

Covered entities meet the de-identification safe harbor if they have removed an enumerated list of identifiers and have *no actual knowledge* that the remaining information could be used to identify an individual.[16] The list of identifiers includes 18 data elements that contain information from which someone might determine an individual's identity.[17] Although it may create a clear safe harbor, removing these identifiers from health information may also render the resulting de-identified information useless for many activities.

If any organization or individuals other than the covered entity or its workforce participate in the de-identification process, the covered

---

[13] 45 C.F.R. § 164.514(b)(1).
[14] 45 C.F.R. § 164.514(b)(1)(i).
[15] 45 C.F.R. § 164.514(b)(1)(ii).
[16] 45 C.F.R. § 164.514(b)(2)(ii).
[17] They are names; all geographic subdivisions smaller than a State, including street address, city, county, precinct, zip code, and their equivalent geocodes, except for the initial three digits of a zip code if, according to the current publicly available data from the Bureau of the Census, the geographic unit formed by combining all zip codes with the same three initial digits contains more than 20,000 people; the initial three digits of a zip code for all such geographic units containing 20,000 or fewer people is changed to 000; all elements of dates (except year) for dates directly related to an individual, including birth date, admission date, discharge date, date of death; and all ages over 89 and all elements of dates (including year) indicative of such age, except that such ages and elements may be aggregated into a single category of age 90 or older; telephone numbers; facsimile numbers; electronic mail addresses; social security numbers; medical record numbers; health plan beneficiary numbers; account numbers; certificate/license numbers; vehicle identifiers and serial numbers, including license plate numbers; device identifiers and serial numbers; web Universal Resource Locators (URLs); Internet Protocol (IP) address numbers; biometric identifiers, including finger and voice prints; full face photographic images and any comparable images; and any other unique identifying number, characteristic, or code. 45 C.F.R. § 164.514(b)(2)(i).

entity must follow the patient authorization and business associate agreement requirements of the Privacy Rule. The business associate agreement should, among other things, do the following:

- Articulate clearly and in detail the criteria and procedures the business associate will use to mask, scrub, aggregate or otherwise remove the HIPAA identifiers
- Describe in detail the intended form and content of the information once de-identified
- Require the business associate to take certain steps to assure that the personnel who will be handling the PHI as part of the de-identification process are aware of the strict privacy and confidentiality obligations applicable to their access to, and use of, the data on the covered entity's behalf
- Permit the covered entity periodically to inspect the records of the business associate relating to such scrubbing and masking in order to verify compliance with de-identification criteria and procedures

If the entity's workforce will de-identify the information, the entity should have detailed internal documentation of the criteria and procedures its personnel must use for masking, scrubbing, aggregating, or otherwise removing the HIPAA identifiers.

The disclosure of a code or other means to enable coded or otherwise de-identified information to be re-identified with an individual, however, constitutes disclosure of PHI. Any information that has been re-identified will be considered PHI and may be used or disclosed only in accordance with the Privacy Rule.[18]

The Privacy Rule does not apply to use and disclosure of de-identified information. Therefore, the covered entity would not need to have a business associate agreement or other written agreement with a third party to allow the third party to use and redisclose the de-identified information. Nonetheless, a written agreement documenting the fact that the third party is being given access to, and the right to use, only de-identified data can be a useful compliance strategy. The agreement should include, among other provisions:

- A detailed description of the de-identified form and content of the data being exchanged

---

[18] 45 C.F.R. § 164.502(d)(2)(i) and (ii).

- An express statement that the third party will not have access to any keys or codes that can be used to identify the individuals whose data have been de-identified
- A provision allowing the covered entity to inspect the data being used by the third party to confirm that the third party is accessing and using only the de-identified data

Limited Data Set

When the Privacy Rule was first published, healthcare and medical research organizations expressed concerns about the limited usefulness of de-identified information. The Department of Health and Human Services (DHHS) responded in 2002 with modifications to the Privacy Rule by creating a "limited data set," which a covered entity may use or disclose to third parties without the individual's authorization.[19] A limited data set is PHI from which certain, but not all, identifiers of the individual or of his or her relatives, employers, or household members have been removed.[20] Information in a limited data set does not meet the safe harbor for de-identified information because fewer identifiers are removed to create a limited data set than are removed to create de-identified information.

Covered entities may use PHI to create a limited data set only for research, public health, and healthcare operations (see the discussion of healthcare operations in this chapter), and may disclose PHI to a business associate to create a limited data set.[21] Therefore, a limited data set cannot be used for payment, marketing, or certain fund-raising activities, among other things.

Covered entities may not use or disclose a limited data set without entering into a "data use agreement" with the recipient of the limited data set.[22] A data use agreement is similar to a business associate agreement, and must contain virtually all of the same contract provisions,

---

[19] 45 C.F.R. § 164.514(e)(1).
[20] The identifiers are names; post addresses (other than town and city, state, and ZIP code); telephone numbers; facsimile numbers; e-mail addresses; social security numbers; medical records numbers; health plan beneficiary numbers; account numbers; certificate/license numbers; vehicle identity, serial and license numbers; device identifiers and serial numbers; web Universal Resource Locators (URLs); Internet Protocol address numbers; biometric identifiers (e.g., finger prints); and full-face photographic or comparable images. 45 C.F.R. § 164.514(e)(2).
[21] 45 C.F.R. § 164.514(e)(3).
[22] 45 C.F.R. § 164.514(e)(4)(i).

except those relating to the exercise of certain individual rights under the Privacy Rule. (See the discussion of business associate agreements in this chapter.) The data use agreement must do the following:

- Establish the permitted uses and disclosures of the limited data set by the third party (the agreement may not permit the recipient to use or further disclose the information except in accordance with the Privacy Rule)
- Establish who may use or receive the limited data set
- Require the third party to agree not to re-identify the information or contact the individual
- Contain adequate assurances that the third party will use appropriate safeguards to prevent use or disclosure of the data except in accordance with the agreement
- Require the third party to report to the covered entity any use or disclosure of the data not permitted by the data use agreement, if the third party becomes aware of such use or disclosure
- Require the third party to ensure that any of its agents or subcontractors to whom it discloses the data agree to the same restrictions and conditions that apply to the third party under the data use agreement[23]

A covered entity is not liable for a breach of the data use agreement by the third party unless the covered entity knows of a pattern of activity of the recipient that constitutes a violation of the agreement, and the covered entity does not take action to cure the breach or terminate the agreement. If such cure or termination efforts are made but are unsuccessful, the covered entity must discontinue disclosure of the PHI and report the breach to the Secretary of DHHS.[24]

Uses and disclosure of a limited data set must also comply with the minimum necessary standard of the Privacy Rule (which is discussed later in this chapter). Covered entities do not have to account for uses and disclosures of a limited data set under the Privacy Rule's accounting requirements.[25]

---

[23] 45 C.F.R. § 164.514(e)(4)(ii)(C).
[24] 45 C.F.R. § 164.514(e)(4)(iii).
[25] 45 C.F.R. § 164.528(a)(1)(viii).

Designated Record Set

The Privacy Rule defines an individual's "designated record set" as any item, collection, or grouping of information maintained by or for a covered entity to make decisions about the individual.[26] (See the discussion of covered entities in this chapter.) For purposes of this definition, the term "record" means any item, collection, or grouping of information that includes PHI and is maintained, collected, used, or disseminated by or for a covered entity.[27] These records include the medical and billing records a covered healthcare provider maintains, and the enrollment, payment, claims adjudication, and case- or medical-management records a health plan maintains. Health information that is identifiable with the individual but is not used to make decisions about the individual is not a designated record set. Thus, oral health information obtained from a patient but not recorded in his or her medical record would not be designated a record set, nor would information collected for peer review purposes.[28]

The designated record set is significant for the Privacy Rule because the record set determines the information to which the patient has a right of access under the rule. (See the discussion of an individual's rights under HIPAA later in this chapter.)[29]

Ownership of the Medical Record

As a general rule, a healthcare facility or provider owns a patient's medical record subject to the patient's interest in the information the record contains. In many states, the basic rule of record ownership is established by statute.[30] Many state statutes provide that medical records are the property of the organization or provider that maintains or possesses the records. For example, the South Carolina statute states that the

---

[26] 45 C.F.R. § 164.501.
[27] Ibid.
[28] See 65 Fed. Reg. 82605-82606 (Dec. 28, 2000).
[29] For a good summary of the definition of the designated record set and recommendations concerning the information it should contain, see American Health Information Management Association (AHIMA), *Practice Brief: Defining the Designated Record Set* (2003), available at http://library.ahima.org/xpedio/groups/public/documents/ahima/pub_bok1_017122.html.
[30] See, e.g., Tenn. Code Ann. § 68-11-304(a)(1); Miss. Code Ann. § 41-9-65.

"[p]hysician is the owner of medical records in his possession that were made in treating a patient and of records transferred to him concerning prior treatment of the patient."[31]

Many states with specific rules on medical records ownership include these provisions in their state hospital licensing regulations. A typical regulation provides that medical records are the property of the hospital and shall not be removed from its premises except to respond to legal process.[32]

Although the healthcare organization owns the physical medical record, many states have traditionally given the patient an interest in the information contained in the record.[33] The Privacy Rule codifies as federal law an individual's right to assert an interest over the PHI included in that record, including the right to access and seek amendments to the PHI.[34] Thus, the patient has an ownership interest in the information contained in the medical record. Although state laws concerning a patient's access remain enforceable if they provide the patient greater access to his or her information, the Privacy Rule will preempt any state law that gives an individual less access to the information or fewer rights with respect to the information than does the Privacy Rule. (See the discussion of HIPAA preemption of state law in this chapter.)

Courts have recognized that a patient has the right to access health information, such as a copy of medical records or an interpretation of an X-ray, even though the patient might not have a right to possess the original medical records or an X-ray negative.[35] In the absence of statutory or regulatory authority, a few courts have held that a medical record is hospital property in which the patient has a limited property interest. Moreover, this interest has been extended to a health insurer's access to hospital records for the purpose of settling an insurance claim on behalf of the patient where the patient had authorized disclosure.[36]

---

[31] S.C. Code Ann. § 44-115-20; see also Va. Code Ann. § 32.1-127.1:03.

[32] See, e.g., 902 Ky. Admin. Regs. 20:016(11)(c); Or. Admin. R. 333-505-050(12); 28 Pa. Code § 115.28; Tenn. Code Ann. § 68-11-304(a)(1).

[33] See, e.g., La. Rev. Stat. Ann. § 40:1299.96; N.H. Rev. Stat. Ann. § 332-I:1.

[34] 45 C.F.R. § 164.526(a).

[35] See *Cannell v. Medical & Surgical Clinic*, 315 N.E. 2d 278 (Ill. Ct. App. 1974), explained by *Clay v. Little Company of Mary Hospital*, 660 N.E. 2d 123 (Ill. Ct. App. 1995); *McGarry v. J. A. Mercier Company*, 262 N.W. 296 (Mich. 1935).

[36] *Bishop Clarkson Memorial Hospital v. Reserve Life Insurance Company*, 370 F. 2d 1006, 1011 (8th Cir. 1965).

The court recognized that the "records maintained by [the hospital] pertaining to care and treatment of patients and to expenses incurred by patients . . . [were] the property of the hospital." However, the court granted access to the insurer because the patient in this case had authorized disclosure.[37] The Privacy Rule's protection of health information confidentiality does not change the state rules governing the ownership of the physical record.

Although a patient may have a statutory interest in information contained in the medical record, there is no independent constitutional right to such information. In a New York case, a former mental patient writing a book about her experiences was denied access to her medical records by her treating hospitals.[38] At trial, the patient argued that the hospitals had violated her federal constitutional rights. The district court ruled that the hospitals' withholding of information did not violate any of the patient's rights, including her right to information as a corollary to her right of free speech, her right of privacy, her freedom from unreasonable searches and seizures of property, or deprivation of her property without due process of law. In affirming the district court opinion, the court of appeals refused to recognize that psychiatric patients have a constitutionally protected property interest in the direct and unrestricted access to their records. Although the Privacy Rule now grants individuals the right to access PHI about themselves, even mental health records (but not psychotherapy notes), this right is a statutory right elaborated in federal regulations and is not a constitutional right.

A health maintenance organization (HMO), managed care organization (MCO), or other third party administrator (TPA) owns the medical records it maintains, even if the health plan sponsor is a self insured employer. An employer might try to obtain access to confidential patient information held by a TPA by claiming ownership of the medical records. However, even if the TPA is an agent of the employer, not all material used by the TPA belongs to the employer. The relationship between most TPAs and employers is that of independent contractor. In that case, ownership interests are established by state law. No law in

---

[37] *Pyramid Life Insurance Company v. Masonic Hospital Association of Payne County*, 191 F. Supp. 51 (W.D. Okla. 1961). See also *Wallace v. University Hospitals*, 164 N.E. 2d 917, 918 (Ohio C.P. 1959), *modified and aff'd*, 170 N.E. 2d 261 (Ohio Ct. App. 1960).

[38] *Gotkin v. Miller*, 379 F. Supp. 859 (E.D.N.Y. 1974), *aff'd*, 514 F. 2d 125 (2d Cir. 1975). In many jurisdictions, the rules governing access to the medical records of mental health patients are more restrictive than those for other types of medical treatment.

any state provides that information obtained or maintained while providing healthcare services to the beneficiaries of a self insured employer is the property of the employer. Just as courts have determined that providers, not the patients who engage them, own the medical records, a court likely would find that a TPA owns its own records. Accordingly, patient information can be released only in accordance with federal and state confidentiality laws.[39] (See the discussion of access to medical records information by employers later in this chapter.)

When questions of medical records ownership arise, the attorney for the healthcare organization or provider should be aware that, although the institution owns the medical records, patients generally have a right to review the information in those records. Patients' access to their health information is governed primarily by the Privacy Rule, by other federal law governing health information, and by state law. Taking into account all the applicable law and working closely with their health law attorneys, healthcare organizations should develop policies and procedures that direct how individuals may access the records the organizations maintain.

Summary of Confidentiality Requirements

The obligation of healthcare organizations and providers to keep medical records confidential is governed by a patchwork of federal and state law. Generally, the Privacy Rule sets a federal floor or minimum standard governing the use, disclosure, maintenance, and transmission of PHI by covered entities. States also may regulate these uses and disclosures, and may impose obligations that are considerably more restrictive than those set forth in the Privacy Rule. Most states have statutory requirements protecting the confidentiality of medical records information, although these statutory protections often vary between states and within a state, depending on who holds the information.

Federal Law

Most health information is protected by federal law. Sources of federal protection of medical records information include the Constitution,

---

[39] *Humana Medical Plan, Inc. v. Fischman*, Nos. 98-3651, 99-0311, 1999 WL 1243873 (Fla. Dist. Ct. App., Dec. 22, 1999); G. Bogossian, "MCO's Protection of Confidential Information" (paper presented at National Health Lawyers Association Health Law Update and Annual Meeting, June 5–7, 1996).

HIPAA and the HIPAA regulations, the Privacy Act, the Freedom of Information Act, and the Medicare Act.

Constitution

The constitutional right to privacy provides very limited protection for patient health information. The Supreme Court noted that in some situations the duty to avoid disclosing confidential medical records information has its roots in the Constitution. Yet an absolute privacy interest in confidential medical records information does not exist.[40] Constitutional claims are further limited by the requirement that any violation of the right to privacy must be caused by a government or a governmental agency.

HIPAA: The Health Insurance Portability and Accountability Act

HIPAA, together with the HIPAA regulations, is the first comprehensive federal scheme for protecting health information.[41] HIPAA comprises the following five titles, each of which regulates a different aspect of health care:

- Title I: Health Care Access, Portability, and Renewability
- Title II: Preventing Fraud and Abuse, and Administrative Simplification
- Title III: Tax Related Provisions
- Title IV: Application and Enforcement of Group Health Plan Requirements
- Title V: Revenue Offsets

The privacy, security, and transaction standards of HIPAA are the regulations promulgated under Subtitle F of Title II, known as the act's "Administrative Simplification" provisions. The Administrative Simplification provisions are anything but simple, however.

Congress articulated three purposes for the regulations promulgated under the HIPAA Administrative Simplification provisions:

---

[40] *Whalen v. Roe*, 429 U.S. 589 (1977).
[41] 42 U.S.C. §§ 1320d et seq. See also *U.S. Department of Justice v. Reporters Commission for Freedom of the Press*, 489 U.S. 749 (1989); *Tucson Women's Clinic v. Eden*, 379 F. 3d 531 (9th Cir. 2004).

- To protect and enhance the rights of consumers by providing them access to their health information and controlling the inappropriate use of that information
- To improve the quality of care "by restoring trust in the system" among consumers, providers, and others involved in the delivery of care
- To improve the efficiency and effectiveness of healthcare delivery by creating a national framework for health privacy protection[42]

The general directive of HIPAA's Administrative Simplification requirements is to streamline the health system by standardizing electronic healthcare transactions to reduce costs.[43] However, Congress recognized that by enhancing the electronic transmission of confidential health information, it would facilitate the widespread disclosure of private information. Therefore, the Administrative Simplification requirements also establish privacy and security standards that must be met in order to protect the information that now flows so easily through electronic health data networks (HDNs).

The key components of the HIPAA Administrative Simplification provisions are:

- Standards for electronic transmission of claims, payment, and other administrative transactions using health information. The regulations establishing these standards were issued in final form on August 17, 2001.[44]
- National standard healthcare provider identifier. Final regulations were published on January 23, 2004.[45]
- National standard employer identifier. The final regulations establishing these identifiers were issued on May 31, 2002.[46]
- Security and electronic signature standards. Final regulations were published on February 20, 2003.[47]
- Standards for privacy of individually identifiable information. The final regulations establishing the privacy standards were published

---

[42] 65 Fed. Reg. 82462, 82463 (Dec. 28, 2000).
[43] 42 U.S.C. § 1320d-1(b).
[44] 65 Fed. Reg. 50311 (Aug. 1, 2000).
[45] 69 Fed. Reg. 3434 (Jan. 23, 2004).
[46] 67 Fed. Reg. 38009 (May 31, 2002).
[47] 68 Fed. Reg. 8334 (Feb. 20, 2003).

on December 28, 2000; became effective on April 14, 2001; and were modified on August 14, 2002.[48]

- National health plan identifiers. No rules have yet been promulgated (in proposed form or otherwise) for this component of the Administrative Simplification provisions.
- Enforcement. Interim final regulations establishing Privacy Rule enforcement procedures were issued on April 17, 2003.[49] DHHS characterized these regulations as the "first installment" of the enforcement rule. More comprehensive enforcement regulations were proposed on April 18, 2005.[50] These regulations are known as the Enforcement Rule.
- Claims attachments. No rules have yet been promulgated (in proposed form or otherwise) for this component of the Administrative Simplification provisions.
- National individual identifiers. No rules have yet been promulgated (in proposed form or otherwise) for this component of the Administrative Simplification provisions.

The privacy, security and transactions, and code set regulations issued under HIPAA by DHHS are known as the Privacy Rule,[51] the Security Rule,[52] and the TCS Rule, respectively.[53] The Privacy Rule governs the use and disclosure of PHI, and addresses how healthcare providers, clearinghouses, and health plans handle health information in the conduct of their affairs. The Security Rule establishes standards for the protection of the physical security of electronic PHI (ePHI), and, together with the Privacy Rule, provides for the comprehensive protection of PHI. The TCS Rule establishes federal standards for the computer codes that may be used in routine business transactions concerning the billing and payment for healthcare services. HIPAA is an extensive statute that also governs a variety of other activities that are not within the scope of this text.

The Privacy and Security Rules apply to PHI used or disclosed by "covered entities." The rules define covered entities as healthcare

---

[48] 65 Fed. Reg. 82462 (Dec. 28, 2000); 67 Fed. Reg. 53182 (Aug. 14, 2002).
[49] 68 Fed. Reg. 18895 (Apr. 17, 2003).
[50] 70 Fed. Reg. 20224 (Apr. 18, 2005).
[51] 45 C.F.R. §§ 160 and 164.
[52] 45 C.F.R. §§ 164.302 through 164.318.
[53] 45 C.F.R. §§ 162.100 through 162.1802.

providers, clearinghouses, and health plans that conduct the financial and administrative transactions described in the TCS Rule.[54] (See the discussion of covered entities later in this chapter.) "Health care provider" is defined as a provider of medical and health services (as defined by the Social Security Act[55]) and any other person or organization who furnishes, bills, or is paid for health care in the normal course of business.[56]

The Privacy Rule applies to virtually any access to PHI for any reason by any personnel of a covered entity. "Use" is defined as "the sharing, employment, application, utilization, examination, or analysis" of information identifiable with an individual.[57] "Disclosure" is defined as "the release, transfer, provision of access to, or divulging in any other manner of information."[58]

The Privacy and Security Rules also indirectly apply to noncovered entities (such as reimbursement consultants, accounting firms, and information system vendors) that use the covered entity's PHI in the course of performing "business associate" functions on behalf of the covered entity. To allow a business associate to use or disclose its PHI, a covered entity must contractually obligate the business associate to comply with certain provisions of the Privacy and Security Rules, such as protecting the confidentiality of PHI it obtains from or through the covered entity.[59] Thus, the scope of the rules is quite broad. (See the more detailed discussion of business associates later in this chapter.)

Generally, the Privacy Rule follows traditional state law governing disclosure of health information. Healthcare organization managers will find many of the Privacy Rule requirements similar to familiar state confidentiality laws. However, the Privacy Rule also imposes new, more burdensome requirements on healthcare providers and, together with the Security Rule and the TCS Rule, creates a substantial compliance challenge for the healthcare industry.

---

[54] 45 C.F.R. § 160.102.
[55] 42 U.S.C. §§ 1395x(s) and 1395x(u).
[56] 45 C.F.R. § 160.103.
[57] 45 C.F.R. § 164.501.
[58] 45 C.F.R. § 164.501.
[59] For a list of the elements that must be included in a business associate agreement, see 45 C.F.R. § 164.504(e); see also 67 Fed. Reg. 53264 (Aug. 14, 2002) for sample provisions for a business associate agreement. Prior to creating or using a business associate agreement, covered entities should consult with qualified legal counsel.

The general rule under HIPAA is that the use or disclosure of PHI requires the patient's permission, unless the use or disclosure falls within an exception established by the Privacy Rule or by state law that HIPAA does not preempt (typically, a state law providing more stringent protections for PHI or greater access for the patient to his or her PHI). Covered entities are required to safeguard PHI by limiting uses and disclosures of PHI to those permitted by HIPAA or applicable state law.

The HIPAA Security Rule complements the Privacy Rule, but is more limited in scope than the Privacy Rule. The Security Rule applies only to ePHI in any way it may be stored or transmitted.[60] The Security Rule also applies to ePHI regardless of whether it is transmitted in a standard transaction governed by the TCS Rule. (For a more detailed discussion of the TCS Rule, see Chapter 13.) The Privacy Rule addresses the uses and disclosures of PHI, and the Security Rule establishes standards for the physical protection of information while it is being stored or transmitted. The Privacy Rule also contains a security requirement for PHI maintained in any form.[61] Therefore, although this requirement is stated in general terms, covered healthcare providers would be wise, to the extent practicable, to extend to all PHI the same security protections they must provide under the Security Rule. Together, the Privacy and Security Rules provide a comprehensive scheme for protecting individually identifiable health information used by covered entities.

The Security Rule makes no distinction between internal and external communications of ePHI or between transmissions using electronic media and physical movement of information from one location to another in any removable or transportable electronic storage medium. The rule covers transactions over the Internet, extranet, leased lines, dial-up lines, and private networks. The Security Rule also applies to ePHI used by a covered entity's workforce who work at home. Paper and voice transmissions are not subject to the Security Rule, however.[62]

The Security Rule establishes standards for the physical protection of ePHI both as it is transmitted and as it is stored, and sets forth the following four basic security requirements for covered entities:

---

[60] 45 C.F.R. § 164.306.
[61] 45 C.F.R. § 164.520(c).
[62] 68 Fed. Reg. 8337 (Feb. 20, 2003).

- Ensure the confidentiality, integrity, and availability of all ePHI that the covered entity creates, receives, maintains, or transmits
- Protect against any reasonably anticipated threats or hazards to the security or integrity of such information
- Protect against any reasonably anticipated uses or disclosures of such information that are not otherwise permitted or required by the Privacy Rule
- Ensure compliance with the Security Rule by its workforce

The Security Rule sets forth what DHHS expects covered entities to do to protect the security and integrity of ePHI, but generally leaves to the covered entities how best to do it. The Security Rule provides standards that covered entities must meet, and implementation specifications that describe both mandatory and discretionary actions for achieving the rule's security standards. (See the more detailed discussion of the Security Rule in Chapter 13.)

Constitutional challenges to the Privacy Rule have thus far been unsuccessful. In an action for declaratory relief from HIPAA and the Privacy Rule filed by medical associations and physicians, the court ruled that HIPAA is not an impermissible delegation of legislative authority, the Privacy Rule is not beyond the scope of the congressional grant of authority, and HIPAA and the Privacy Rule are not impermissibly vague.[63]

Privacy Act

The Privacy Act of 1974,[64] designed to give private citizens some control over information collected by the federal government, restricts the type of information that a federal agency lawfully may collect concerning an individual citizen or legal alien, and limits the uses of such information. Under the Privacy Act, an agency may maintain only information that is relevant and necessary to its authorized purpose.[65] An agency may not disclose any information about a private individual through any means of communication to any person or other agency

---

[63] *South Carolina Medical Association v. Thompson*, No. 02-2001 (4th Cir., Apr. 25, 2003); see also *Association of American Physicians & Surgeons, Inc. v. Department of Health & Human Services*, No. H-01-2963 (S.D. Tex., June 17, 2002).
[64] 5 U.S.C. § 552a.
[65] 5 U.S.C. § 552a(e)(1).

except as authorized in writing by the person or under certain conditions described in the act.[66]

The Privacy Act also requires each federal agency to allow individuals to gain access to their records or any information pertaining to them and copy any or all of the information.[67] Individuals also may make requests to amend or modify their records, and the agency must either make the changes or provide an explanation for declining to do so.[68] In certain cases, the head of the agency must review the decision to deny a requested change.[69]

The Privacy Act allows an agency to disclose information about an individual without that person's consent only in certain circumstances. Disclosures may be made: to officers and employees of the agency who need the information to perform their duties; under the Freedom of Information Act; for certain statistical and law enforcement purposes; to Congress, the Comptroller General, or the National Archives and Records Administration; pursuant to a valid court order; or where a person shows compelling circumstances affecting the health or safety of the individual to whom the information relates.[70]

The Privacy Act provides civil remedies for individuals aggrieved by an agency's failure to comply with the law.[71] An injured individual may bring suit against the agency in federal court, may possibly enjoin the agency from continuing its action and, may possibly recover reasonable attorney fees and court costs. The act provides for criminal fines against an officer or employee of an agency for certain willful violations of the statute.[72]

It is important to emphasize that the Privacy Act applies only to federal agencies and to government contractors. Hospitals and other healthcare facilities operated by the federal government, therefore, are bound by the act's requirements with respect to the disclosure of the medical records of their patients. In addition, medical records maintained in a records system operated under a contract with a federal government agency are subject to the Privacy Act.[73] MCOs that provide

---

[66] 5 U.S.C. § 552a(b).
[67] 5 U.S.C. § 552a(d)(1).
[68] 5 U.S.C. § 552a(d)(2).
[69] 5 U.S.C. § 552a(d)(3).
[70] 5 U.S.C. § 552a(b)(8).
[71] 5 U.S.C. § 552a(g)(1).
[72] 5 U.S.C. § 552a(i)(1); *Bavido v. Apfel*, 215 F. 3d 743 (7th Cir. 2000).
[73] 5 U.S.C. § 552a(m)(1).

health insurance to government employees and MCOs with Medicare contracts are also covered by the act.[74] Private or state owned hospitals and MCOs that do not contract with the federal government generally are not subject to civil or criminal liability under the act for their unlawful disclosure of patient information or for any unlawful disclosure by a federal agency to which the hospital properly reports. The fact that a hospital or other healthcare facility receives federal funding or is subject to federal regulation does not automatically subject it to the act.[75]

The Privacy Act is subject to the terms of the HIPAA Privacy and Security Rules. Thus, if a federal agency or contractor is a covered entity under HIPAA, it must also comply with the HIPAA Rules.[76] If a particular use or disclosure is permitted by the Privacy Rule but is prohibited by the Privacy Act, the agency or contractor may not make the use or disclosure. If the disclosure is permitted by the Privacy Act but prohibited by the Privacy Rule, the agency or contractor must exercise its discretion to comply with the Privacy Rule and not disclose the information.

USA Patriot Act

Although the passage in 2001 of the USA Patriot Act ("Patriot Act"), a direct result of the September 11, 2001, attack on the World Trade Center in New York City, did not per se amend the privacy protections of HIPAA or the Privacy Act of 1974, the Patriot Act's Section 215 gives law enforcement agencies additional powers to obtain personal medical and health information for national security and foreign security purposes. Section 215 amended Sections 501 through 503 of the Foreign Intelligence Surveillance Act of 1978 to enable law enforcement officers to obtain business records from third parties.[77] The term "business records" includes medical records held by healthcare providers. Accordingly, the director of the Federal Bureau of Investigation is empowered to request a court order to obtain "tangible things" for an investigation to protect against international terrorism or clandestine activities. Although this provision offers the ostensible protection that

---

[74] 42 C.F.R. § 417.486(c).
[75] *Adelman v. Discover Card Services*, 915 F. Supp. 1163 (D. Utah 1996); *DeHarder Investment Corporation v. Indiana Housing Finance Authority*, 90 F. Supp. 606 (S.D. Ind. 1995); *St. Michael's Convalescent Hospital v. California*, 643 F. 2d 1369 (9th Cir. 1981).
[76] 65 Fed. Reg. 82482 (Dec. 28, 2000).
[77] 50 U.S.C. § 1861 et seq.

such investigations of a person in the United States cannot be based solely on activities protected by the First Amendment, and that business records can be obtained only with a court order seeking information consistent with an investigation of international terrorism or clandestine intelligence activities, the Patriot Act reduced the "showing" required to obtain such an order from the traditional criminal law standard of "probable cause" to a lesser standard requiring only certification that an authorized investigation is under way. Such a court order and corresponding subpoena for business records will not disclose that they have been issued for foreign intelligence purposes, and third parties, in this case healthcare providers, are expressly prohibited from disclosing such requests for medical information to their patients. Therefore, although the Patriot Act did not specifically alter privacy and confidentiality protections embedded in existing law, as a practical matter, institutional and personal expectations concerning privacy have been affected.[78]

Freedom of Information Act

The Freedom of Information Act (FOIA), enacted in 1966, provides public access to information on the operations and decisions of federal administrative agencies.[79] A hospital does not become a federal agency by receiving federal funds, so FOIA applies to few hospitals outside of the hospital systems run by the Department of Veterans Affairs and the Department of Defense. The law provides that specific categories of information are available to the public unless one of the nine specific exceptions to the general rule of disclosure applies. Medical records may be exempt from FOIA under specific circumstances.

FOIA requires each federal agency to make certain information available for public inspection and copying, including final opinions, concurring and dissenting opinions, and orders made in the adjudication of cases;[80] statements of policy and interpretations adopted by the

---

[78] USA Patriot Act, Pub. L. No. 107-56, § 215, 115 Stat. 276, 287–288 (2001); Charles Doyle, "The USA Patriot Act: A Legal Analysis," CRS Report RL31377 (Congressional Research, 2002); American Civil Liberties Union (ACLU), *Section 215 FAQ* (October 24, 2002), available at http://www.aclu.org/Privacy/Privacy.cfm?ID+11054&c=130; ACLU, *FAQ on Government Access to Medical Records* (May 30, 2003), available at http://www.aclu.org/news/NEWPRINT.dmf?ID+12747&c=27, last visited July 5, 2005.
[79] 5 U.S.C. § 552.
[80] 5 U.S.C. § 552(a)(2)(A).

agency and not published in the *Federal Register*;[81] and administrative staff manuals and instructions that affect a member of the public.[82] Each agency must make the information available unless the materials are published promptly and copies offered for sale.[83]

All other records, except those specifically excluded under FOIA, must be made available promptly to any person upon request if he or she reasonably describes such records and complies with the agency's published rules covering the time, place, and fee for inspecting and copying.[84] Each agency also is required to maintain and make available a current index for public inspection and copying. The index must provide identifying information as to matters covered by FOIA.[85] However, when it makes available an opinion, statement of policy, interpretation, or staff manual or instruction, an agency may delete identifying details in order to prevent a clearly unwarranted invasion of an individual's personal privacy. In each case, justification for the deletion must be explained fully in writing.[86]

Nine specific exceptions to the general FOIA disclosure are provided.[87] One of these, known as "Exception Six," covers personnel and medical files and similar files, the disclosure of which would constitute a clearly unwarranted invasion of personal privacy.[88]

To qualify for protection from FOIA disclosure, medical records information must satisfy the three elements described in Exception Six:

- The information must be contained in a personnel, medical, or similar file
- Disclosure of the information must constitute an invasion of privacy
- The invasion clearly is unwarranted[89]

---

[81] 5 U.S.C. § 552(a)(2)(B).
[82] 5 U.S.C. § 552(a)(2)(C).
[83] 5 U.S.C. § 552(a)(2).
[84] 5 U.S.C. § 552(a)(3).
[85] 5 U.S.C. § 552(a)(2).
[86] Ibid.
[87] 5 U.S.C. § 552(b).
[88] 5 U.S.C. § 552(b)(6).
[89] *Sims v. CIA*, 642 F. 2d 562 (D.C. Cir. 1980), *rev'd and aff'd on other grounds*, 471 U.S. 159 (1985); see also *Citizens for Environmental Quality Inc. v. U.S. Department of Agriculture*, 602 F. Supp. 534, 537 (D.D.C. 1984), characterizing where the court's analysis under Exception Six as a two-step inquiry to determine: first, whether information sought is contained in personnel, medical, or similar files; and second, whether release would constitute a clearly unwarranted invasion of personal privacy.

An agency seeking to withhold information has the burden of showing that the requested material satisfies each and every element of Exception Six.[90]

In determining whether the information sought falls within this exception, the relevant consideration is whether the privacy interests associated with the information are similar to interests that generally arise from personnel or medical information, and not whether the data are recorded in a manner similar to a personnel or medical file.[91] A file is considered similar to personnel and medical files if it contains intimate details of an individual's life, family relations, personal health, religious and philosophical beliefs, and other matters that, if revealed, would prove personally embarrassing to a person of normal sensibilities. Whether file materials are similar turns on whether the facts that would be revealed would infringe on some privacy interest as highly personal or as intimate in nature as that at stake in personnel and medical records.

Once a court determines that requested information is the type of material covered by Exception Six, it must address whether disclosure of such information would constitute an invasion of privacy. Several courts have emphasized that Exception Six was intended to prevent public disclosure of intimate details about an individual's life, such as marital status, legitimacy of children, identity of fathers of children, medical conditions, welfare payments, alcohol consumption, family fights, and reputation.[92] On the other hand, information connected with commercial matters, business judgments, or professional relationships is not covered by the exception.[93]

If a court concludes that the release of information would constitute an invasion of personal privacy as contemplated by Exception Six, it must balance the personal interest in preventing disclosure against the public interest in obtaining access to the information.[94] In this regard, courts have interpreted the language "clearly unwarranted invasion of personal privacy" as an expression of a congressional policy that favors

---

[90] *Sims v. CIA,* 562, 566.

[91] *Harbolt v. Department of State,* 616 F. 2d 772, 774 (5th Cir. 1980), *cert. denied,* 449 U.S. 856 (1980).

[92] *Sims v. CIA,* 562, 574, quoting *Rural Housing Alliance v. U.S. Department of Agriculture,* 498 F. 2d 73, 77 (D.C. Cir. 1974).

[93] *Sims v. CIA,* 562, 574, citing *Board of Trade of Chicago v. Commodity Futures Trading Commission,* 627 F. 2d 392, 399–400 (D.C. Cir. 1980).

[94] *Sims v. CIA,* 562, 573.

disclosure, and as an instruction to tilt the balance in favor of disclosure.[95] An agency seeking to prevent the release of information under Exception Six therefore must make a detailed and factual showing of the likely consequences of disclosure in individual cases.[96] The possibility of embarrassing an agency or speculation about the identity of an individual that would result from disclosure will not outweigh the public interest.[97]

An agency is required to provide reasonably segregable nonexempt portions of an otherwise exempt record to any person requesting such record.[98] Federal agencies that maintain medical records or have legitimately obtained medical records are required, both by the Privacy Act and by this exception to FOIA, to withhold disclosure of such records unless a court, in balancing individual and public interests in the information, orders disclosure or unless such records are requested by Congress.

Although original medical records maintained by a federal agency are exempt from disclosure under Exception Six, disclosure under FOIA may be required of any information taken from these records in connection with government funded medical research and incorporated into research reports to a sponsoring agency. Determining whether the data belong to the researchers or to the agency is crucial in resolving a request for access under these circumstances because only the agency is subject to FOIA.

The U.S. Supreme Court has ruled that "written data generated, owned, and possessed by a private controlled organization receiving federal study grants are not 'agency records' within the meaning of the [Freedom of Information] Act when copies of those data have not been obtained by a federal agency subject to the FOIA.[99] Federal participation in the generation of the data by means of a grant from the Department of Health, Education, and Welfare (DHEW) does not make the private organization a federal 'agency' within the terms of the

---

[95] *Sims v. CIA*, 562, 575; *Citizens for Environmental Quality Inc. v. U.S. Department of Agriculture*, 534, 538.

[96] *Sims v. CIA*, 562, 575.

[97] *Sims v. CIA*, 562, 573 n. 139; *Citizens for Environmental Quality Inc. v. U.S. Department of Agriculture*, 534, 538.

[98] 5 U.S.C. § 552(b).

[99] *Forsham v. Harris*, 445 U.S. 169 (1980); see also *U.S. Department of Justice v. Tax Analysts*, 492 U.S. 136 (1989); *Missouri ex rel. Garstang v. U.S. Department of the Interior*, 299 F. 3d 745 (8th Cir. 2002).

Act."[100] The Court held that the grantee's data would become agency records if it could be shown that the agency directly controlled the day-to-day activities of the grantee.[101]

Healthcare organizations and hospitals receiving federal funds for medical research can minimize the risk of disclosure of research data under FOIA, therefore, by limiting the agency's supervision of studies conducted by staff. The healthcare organization or hospital also should obtain the agency's acknowledgment that the data are confidential and will not be disclosed except as required by law.

The Privacy Rule imposes additional requirements upon federal agencies that are subject to the rule, that operate Privacy Act systems of records, and that must comply with FOIA. The Privacy Rule permits uses or disclosures that are required by law if the uses or disclosures meet the relevant requirements of the law. Although disclosures under FOIA fall within this provision, an agency must analyze each request for health information on a case-by-case basis, and determine whether, in complying with FOIA, the agency may apply an exception or exclusion and remove PHI from the requested information.[102] If presented with a request for PHI, the agency should first determine whether FOIA requires disclosure of the information or if a FOIA exemption or exclusion applies. In most cases, Exception Six will apply to the disclosure of PHI. The agency should then determine whether the requested information applies to a deceased person. Under the Privacy Act, privacy rights are extinguished upon death of the individual, but under FOIA, it is appropriate for an agency to consider the privacy interests of the decedent's family under Exception Six. Thus, it is possible in most cases for a federal agency to comply with both the terms of FOIA and the Privacy Rule requirements that protect the confidentiality of PHI.

Medicare Conditions of Participation

The Medicare Conditions of Participation require institutions participating in the Medicare and Medicaid programs to keep medical records confidential. The Conditions of Participation apply to a number of institutions participating in federal healthcare programs,

---

[100] *Forsham v. Harris,* 169, 171.
[101] *Forsham v. Harris,* 169, 180.
[102] 65 Fed. Reg. 82482 (Dec. 28, 2000).

including hospitals, MCOs, long term care facilities, home health agencies, substance abuse agencies, and hospices.[103]

Federal Substance Abuse Confidentiality Requirements

The Drug Abuse Prevention, Treatment, and Rehabilitation Act of 1972 and related amendments and the Comprehensive Alcohol Abuse and Alcoholism Prevention, Treatment, and Rehabilitation Act of 1970 and amendments,[104] all amending the Public Health Service Act, and the related federal regulations[105] establish a comprehensive regulatory scheme for the protection of substance abuse patient health information. (See the discussion of substance abuse records later in this chapter.) The federal substance abuse confidentiality law applies to most alcohol and drug abuse treatment, and prohibits the disclosure of information concerning such treatment except as specifically authorized. Although providers of substance abuse treatment will likely be subject to both the federal substance abuse confidentiality regulations and the HIPAA Privacy Rule, conflicts between the rules will not exist in most cases. The Privacy Rule permits, but does not require, PHI to be disclosed in certain circumstances that are not permitted under the Public Health Service Act. Because the Privacy Rule provisions are permissive, it is possible for a covered entity subject to the Public Health Service Act to comply with the act's more restrictive protections for substance abuse treatment information and not permit disclosure of the information. A provider subject to the Privacy Rule, therefore, would not violate its provisions by not disclosing the information. The reverse is also true. The disclosures that the Public Health Service Act permits but does not require can be made without violating either that act or the Privacy Rule. Finally, a healthcare provider should be able to provide the notices that must be given to the patient under the Public Health Service Act and the Privacy Rule without creating a conflict between these two regulatory schemes.

Other Federal Confidentiality Laws

In promulgating the HIPAA Privacy and Security Rules, DHHS took the position that covered entities could comply with the rules and with

---

[103] See, e.g., Conditions of Participation for Hospitals, 42 C.F.R. § 482.24(b)(3).

104 42 U.S.C. §§ 4541 et seq.; 21 U.S.C. § 1101.

[105] 42 C.F.R. §§ 2.1 through 2.67.

other federal laws that created protections for, or required disclosures of, PHI.[106] When apparent conflicts exist, DHHS believes that covered entities should attempt to comply with both laws. For example, the Privacy Rule permits, but does not require, certain uses and disclosures of PHI. If another federal law prohibits such a use or disclosure, a covered entity would simply exercise its discretion whether or not to engage in that use or permit that disclosure. In doing so, it would violate neither the Privacy Rule, which does not require it to make that use or disclosure, nor the other federal law, which prohibits the use or disclosure. Nevertheless, covered entities should exercise caution in how they use, disclose, maintain, and transmit PHI that is subject to both the Privacy and Security Rules and to other federal laws. They should determine what other federal laws apply to their operations, whether conflicts between those laws and the Privacy or Security Rules exist, and, if so, whether these conflicts are irreconcilable.[107] This is a process that will require the assistance of their health law counsel, particularly if conflicts between federal laws appear irreconcilable.

State Law

To date, the Privacy and Security Rules are the broadest source of authority governing uses and disclosures of PHI. These rules set a federal floor or minimum standard governing how covered entities use, disclose, maintain, and transmit PHI. States also regulate health information privacy, and their laws generally survive federal preemption unless they are directly contrary to the Privacy or Security Rule, or stand as an obstacle to the rules' implementation.[108] A healthcare provider or organization should not rely upon a state law until it has determined that the law has not been preempted by HIPAA. (See the discussion of preemption later in this chapter.)

---

[106] See 65 Fed. Reg. 82481 through 82487.

[107] Other federal laws to consider include the Americans with Disabilities Act, 42 U.S.C. §§ 12101 et seq.; appropriation laws; the Children's Online Privacy Protection Act, 15 U.S.C. §§ 6.501 et seq.; the Developmental Disabilities Assistance and Bill of Rights Act, 42 U.S.C. §§ 15001 et seq.; the Fair Credit Reporting Act, 15 U.S.C. §§ 16.01 et seq.; the Fair Debt Collection Practices Act, 15 U.S.C. §§ 16.01 et seq.; the Family and Medical Leave Act, 29 U.S.C. §§ 2601 et seq.; the Controlled Substances Act, 21 U.S.C. §§ 801 et seq.; Medicare, 42 U.S.C. §§ 1301 et seq. and 1395 et seq.; Medicaid, 42 U.S.C. §§ 1396 et seq.; the Indian Self-Determination and Education Assistance Act, 25 U.S.C. §§ 450 et seq.; and federal common law.

[108] See 45 C.F.R. §§ 160.201 through 205 regarding preemption of state law.

This text does not address whether each state law it references has been preempted, nor does it attempt the enormous task of determining what state laws have been preempted. The discussion of state laws in these chapters is intended to give the reader an understanding of the types of laws that states have enacted with respect to the use and disclosure of health information. Because the Privacy Rule adopted many of the rules traditionally imposed by state law, many state laws have not been preempted by HIPAA, and therefore are still relevant for any covered healthcare organization. Entities subject to the Privacy and Security Rules must identify their own state laws that create requirements concerning health information *in addition to those imposed by the rules.* Those state laws, together with the Privacy and Security Rules and any other applicable federal laws (such as those governing drug and alcohol abuse), constitute the body of law governing their use of an individual's health information.

State Medical Records Statutes and Regulations

Statutory provisions concerning health information often are scattered throughout a state's code. For example, confidentiality requirements can be found in a state's medical records act, hospital licensing act, medical practice act, HMO act, or statutes dealing with human immunodeficiency virus (HIV). Often these statutes protect only certain information—such as hospital medical records or physician's records. Some states might not impose confidentiality requirements on all entities that hold patient information. A state might require a physician to keep a patient's medical record confidential, but not impose a similar requirement on an insurer even though the insurer has the same information. The difficulties for healthcare organizations operating in multiple states in dealing with the patchwork quilt of state laws have been reduced to a considerable extent because of the minimum requirements established by HIPAA. Until states conform their medical records laws to HIPAA, however, healthcare organizations must still cope with state laws that may provide greater protections for an individual's health information and are therefore still enforceable. Consequently, despite HIPAA, protection of health information can vary from state to state, leading to situations in which information is given greater protection in one state than in another. The lack of uniform standards and the variation in the law among the states will continue to cause difficulty where interstate healthcare transactions, telemedicine, and ERISA health plans are common.[109]

Most states have traditionally required physicians and other licensed healthcare providers to keep their medical records confidential.[110] The confidentiality provisions of the Privacy and Security Rules have established these requirements as federal law applicable to all states. Some states have adopted confidentiality rules that are more protective of health information than those provided by the Privacy Rule. For example, in its patient records privacy law, Virginia defines "record" to include any communication made by a patient to a provider and any other information acquired in confidence by a provider in the course of treatment.[111] Some states prohibit redisclosure by the individual or entity receiving the patient information without a new patient authorization.[112] Because these provisions extend protection to more information than is subject to the protection of the Privacy and Security Rules, healthcare organizations and providers should continue to comply with them.

As with physicians, most states require healthcare institutions to keep their medical records confidential. Many states locate these requirements in a licensing and regulation act. For example, Florida's hospital and licensing act provides that patient records are confidential, and explains that the records may not be released without the patient's consent except under a narrow set of circumstances.[113] The Illinois Nursing Home Care Act provides that a resident's records are confidential.[114] Illinois law governing long term care facilities states that all information contained in a resident's record is confidential,

[109] For a survey of law in this area, see L. Gostin, Z. Lazzarini, and K. Flaherty, *Legislative Survey of State Confidentiality Laws, with Special Emphasis on HIV and Immunization, Final Report* (presented to the U.S. Centers for Disease Control and Prevention, the Council of State and Territorial Epidemiologists, and the Task Force for Child Survival and Development—Carter Presidential Center, Georgetown University Law Center, July 1996).

[110] See, e.g., Cal. Civ. Code § 56.05(e) (where the confidentiality requirement extends to medical doctors, doctors of osteopathy, chiropractors, and anyone else licensed or certified under the state's Business and Professions Code); Cal. Civ. Code § 56.10; Md. Code Ann., Health-Gen. § 4-302.

[111] Va. Code § 32.1-127.1:03(B).

[112] See, e.g., Md. Code Ann., Health-Gen. § 4-302(d).

[113] Fla. Stat. Ann. § 395.3025(4).

[114] 210 Ill. Comp. Stat. § 45/2-206.

and the facility must obtain written consent of the resident or a guardian prior to releasing the records.[115] Regarding the general rule requiring patient authorization for use or disclosure, the Privacy Rule adopted many of the exceptions that have traditionally been found in state laws.[116] Thus, many state laws that allow uses or disclosures of PHI without patient authorization are not contrary to the Privacy Rule, and therefore remain enforceable.

Insurers and MCOs increasingly require patient information before making utilization review or reimbursement decisions. Some states have enacted statutory provisions requiring HMOs or other insurers to keep patient information confidential. For example, a statute in Colorado concerning HMOs provides that any data or information pertaining to the diagnosis, treatment, or health of any enrollee is confidential and may be disclosed only under very limited circumstances or upon the consent of the individual.[117]

Few states have enacted legislation protecting the confidentiality of patient information held by the patient's employer. One state that has passed legislation protecting this information is California, where the law provides that employers who receive medical information are required to develop procedures to ensure the confidentiality of this information. The California statute also states that the healthcare information may be used only for administering and maintaining employee benefit plans.[118] Employers that are not healthcare providers, health plans, or healthcare clearinghouses are not subject to the confidentiality requirements of the Privacy Rule, but must comply with such state privacy laws. (Access to employee health information by an employer is discussed more fully later in this chapter.)

Some states have enacted patients' rights legislation that covers the confidentiality of medical information. For example, New Jersey's Patient Bill of Rights Act specifies that all patients admitted to a hospital licensed in the state are entitled to privacy and confidentiality of all records.[119] Illinois has a patients' rights statute that protects a variety of health information. The Illinois Patient Rights Act directs physicians, healthcare providers, health services corporations, and insurance

---

[115] Ill. Admin. Code tit. 77, § 390.1630.
[116] See, generally, 45 C.F.R. § 164.512.
[117] Colo. Rev. Stat. § 10-16-423.
[118] Cal. Civ. Code § 56.20.
[119] N.J. Stat. Ann. § 26:2H-12.8(g).

companies not to disclose the nature or details of services provided to patients. The act has several exceptions to this directive, however. Disclosure may be made to the patient; to the party making treatment decisions if the patient is not capable of making them; to parties directly involved with providing treatment or processing payment for that treatment; to parties responsible for peer review, utilization review, and quality assurance; and to those parties where disclosure is authorized or required under the law.[120]

Some states have adopted comprehensive health information statutes. The states of Montana and Washington have adopted the Uniform Health Care Information Act (UHCIA).[121] The UHCIA forbids a healthcare provider, an individual who assists a healthcare provider in the delivery of health care, or an agent or employee of a healthcare provider from disclosing healthcare information without the patient's written authorization. However, the UHCIA has some exceptions to this general rule, allowing disclosure in several situations—including to an individual providing health care to the patient, to an individual needing this information for quality assurance or peer review purposes, and to immediate family members of the patient or to any other individual known to have a close personal relationship with the patient—if the disclosure is made in accordance with good medical or professional practice and the patient has not instructed the provider otherwise. Many of the provisions of the UHCIA are consistent with the Privacy Rule, and thus remain enforceable.

State Open Records Laws

Many states have freedom of information laws granting public access to records maintained by state agencies.[122] In some states, the statute is called the public records law or the open records law. Like the federal Freedom of Information Act (FOIA), these laws typically contain exceptions for records, including medical records, where disclosure would constitute an unwarranted invasion of personal privacy.[123] A few states

---

[120] 410 Ill. Comp. Stat. § 50/3.

[121] Mont. Code Ann. §§ 50-16-501 through 50-16-553; Wash. Rev. Code §§ 70.02.005 through 70.02.904.

[122] See, e.g., Ala. Code § 36-12-40; Fla. Stat. Ann. § 119.01; Md. Code Ann., State Gov't., § 10-611.

[123] See, e.g., 5 Ill. Comp. Stat. § 140/7.

exempt all public hospital medical records from the public records law[124] or include them in a list of public records available only upon court order and in other limited circumstances.[125] Most case law arising under the state acts deals with determining whether a private interest in confidentiality outweighs the public interest in disclosure.

In *Child Protection Group v. Cline*,[126] for example, a West Virginia court outlined five factors for determining whether release of personal information under the state freedom of information act would constitute an "unreasonable" invasion of privacy: (1) whether disclosure would result in a substantial invasion of privacy, and, if so, how serious the potential consequences would be; (2) whether the extent or value of the public interest and the purpose or object of individuals seeking the information justify disclosure; (3) whether the information was available from other sources; (4) whether the information was given with an expectation of confidentiality; and (5) whether it is possible to mold relief to limit the invasion of privacy.[127] After examining these issues, the court in this case authorized release of a bus driver's psychiatric records to parents of schoolchildren after the driver acted in a manner raising serious questions about his ability to operate the bus safely.

Whether specific documents are the kind covered by an exception to a state public records law sometimes is unclear. In *Head v. Colloton*, for instance, a state hospital objected to an attempt to access its bone marrow transplant registry under the Iowa Public Records Act, arguing that the registry was protected from disclosure under the statutory exemption to the act for "hospital and medical records of the condition, diagnosis, care, or treatment of a patient or former patient, including outpatient."[128] Although the court decided that only hospital records relating to patient care and treatment are exempt from disclosure under the law, it concluded that the bone marrow records related to a patient and therefore were not accessible.

The New Hampshire Supreme Court, in *Hawkins v. New Hampshire Department of Health and Human Services*, determined that patient

---

[124] See, e.g., La. Rev. Stat. Ann. § 44:7; Miss. Code Ann. § 41-9-68.
[125] See, e.g., Iowa Code Ann. § 22.7.
[126] *Manns v. City of Charleston Police Department*, 550 S.E. 2d 598 (W. Va. 2001); *Child Protection Group v. Cline*, 350 S.E.2d 541 (W. Va. 1986).
[127] *Child Protection Group v. Cline*, 350 S.E. 2d 541 (W. Va. 1986). See also *Bodelson v. City of Littleton*, No. 00CA1945, 2001 WL 1204536 (Colo. Ct. App., Oct. 11, 2001).
[128] *Head v. Colloton*, 331 N.W. 2d 870 (Iowa 1983); see also *Poole v. Hawkeye Area County Action Program, Inc.*, 666 N.W. 2d 560 (Iowa 2003).

Medicaid claims information stored within the state agency's computer system constituted a public record under the state's right to know law, and that the agency was required to disclose the requested information.[129] The court also noted that the cost of producing the information is not a factor in determining whether it constitutes a public record. The Supreme Court of Georgia has held, however, that information not compiled, prepared, received, or maintained in the course of a state agency's operations is not a public record under the Georgia Open Records Act, and the agency is not required under Georgia law to create new records according to criteria conceived by a citizen making a request for information under the act.[130]

The Privacy Rule imposes additional requirements upon state agencies that are subject to the rule and that must comply with state open records acts. The Privacy Rule permits uses or disclosures that are required by law if the uses or disclosures meet the relevant requirements of the law. A state agency must analyze each request for health information on a case-by-case basis, and determine whether, in complying with state law, it may apply an exception or exclusion and remove PHI from the requested information.[131] If presented with a request for PHI, the agency should first determine whether the state law requires disclosure of the information or if an exemption or exclusion applies. In many states, an exception for health information will apply. Thus, it may be possible for a state agency to comply with both the terms of the applicable state law and the requirements of the Privacy Rule protecting the confidentiality of PHI.

Relationship of HIPAA to State Laws: HIPAA Preemption of State Laws

The regulations promulgated under HIPAA for the protection of PHI preempt contrary state laws, with certain exceptions.[132] (See the discussion of preemption as a judicial doctrine in Chapter 1.) This means that for some conflicting state law, the federal law controls over the

---

[129] No. 2000-012, 2001 WL 1661846 (N.H., Dec. 31, 2001).
[130] *Schulten, Ward & Turner, LLP v. Fulton-DeKalb Hospital Authority*, No S00A0772 (Ga., Sept. 11, 2000).
[131] See discussion at 65 Fed. Reg. 82482 (Dec. 28, 2000) concerning a federal agency's response to a FOIA request for PHI.
[132] 42 U.S.C. § 1320d-7(a)-(c); 45 C.F.R. § 160.203.

state law. The definition of "state law" in the HIPAA preemption provision is broad, and includes a constitution, statute, regulation, rule, common law, or any other state authority having the effect of law.[133] County, municipal, or other local laws having the force and effect of state law, as well as evidentiary privileges recognized as state law, all fall within the definition.[134]

Although HIPAA creates national standards for protecting the privacy of health information, it permits states to enact laws that grant individuals greater rights with respect to their health information or provide greater protections for that information. The HIPAA Preemption Rule applies only with respect to entities covered by HIPAA. Therefore, laws that would be preempted by HIPAA because they apply to covered entities will not be preempted when they apply to entities that are not subject to HIPAA. For example, a municipal fire department that provides emergency health services but does not bill for those services is not a covered entity under HIPAA, and thus is not required to comply with the Privacy Rule. Nonetheless, such a department obtains individually identifiable health information as part of its operations and will be subject to applicable state laws that protect the confidentiality of health information. A hospital in the same state to which the fire department takes its emergent patients will likely be a HIPAA covered entity that must comply with the Privacy Rule. Thus, the state laws that may apply to the fire department in this example will not apply to the hospital because the state statutes are contrary to the Privacy Rule and provide less protection than the rule does for the patients' health information.

As this example demonstrates, the enactment of HIPAA and the adoption of the Privacy and Security Rules have *not* created uniform law protecting the confidentiality of health information throughout the United States, but instead have resulted in a substantially more complex legal environment for many healthcare organizations and providers. Over time, states may amend their laws to be more consistent with HIPAA. Until then, covered entities must determine what state laws still apply to their operations. Determining whether a state law is preempted can be challenging, and must be undertaken for each provision of state law applicable to the use, disclosure, maintenance,

---

[133] 45 C.F.R. § 160.202; 65 Fed. Reg. 82581 (Dec. 28, 2000).
[134] 65 Fed. Reg. 82581 (Dec. 28, 2000).

and transmission of PHI. While various health industry trade associations and law firms have produced preemption analyses for certain states, new legislation in those states makes it difficult to rely upon preemption analyses that are more than a few months old. These analyses provide a good starting point, but covered entities should consult with legal counsel experienced in HIPAA preemption analysis to determine whether a particular state law governing health information remains enforceable.

The HIPAA preemption analysis requires several steps. First, a covered entity must determine whether a state law (as defined above) is contrary to the Privacy Rule. A state law is contrary to the Privacy Rule if a covered entity cannot comply with both laws or if the state law is an obstacle to accomplishing the purposes of HIPAA's privacy protections.[135]

If the state law is contrary to requirements of the Privacy Rule, covered entities must then determine whether an exception to the HIPAA general preemption rule applies. The preemption rule applies to all state laws contrary to the Privacy Rule, except laws that

- the Secretary of DHHS determines are necessary for certain purposes specified in the regulations (for example, to prevent fraud and abuse) or have as their principal purpose the regulation of controlled substances;
- relate to certain public health activities (for example, reporting of child abuse, disease, injury, birth defects);
- require health plans to provide access to information for management or financial audits, program monitoring, or licensure certification of facilities or individuals; or
- relate to health information privacy and are more stringent than the HIPAA Privacy Rule.[136]

If the state law is contrary to the Privacy Rule and does not meet the first three of these exceptions, the covered entity must determine whether the state law is "more stringent" than the Privacy Rule.

To qualify for this exception, the state law must meet two tests: the relationship test and the more stringent test. The state law will meet

---

[135] 45 C.F.R. § 160.202.
[136] 45 C.F.R. § 160.203(a)-(d).

the relationship test if it is related to health information that is identified with an individual. A state law that governs health information that cannot be related to an individual (for example, it meets the requirements of de-identified information under the Privacy Rule) will not fall within this exception. The state law must also have the specific purpose of protecting health information or must affect such information in a clear, direct, and substantial way.[137]
The state law must also meet the more stringent test. Specifically, a state law is more stringent if it achieves at least one of the following:

- Gives the individual greater rights to access or amend his or her health information or requires the delivery of more information to the individual about the use or disclosure of his or her health information or his or her rights with respect to that information
- Provides greater restrictions on the use of health information by, or disclosure of such information to, a third party
- Imposes greater requirements for the individual's authorization for use or disclosure of health information or reduces the coercive effect of the circumstances surrounding the authorization
- Creates a higher standard for record keeping or accounting for disclosures of health information
- Otherwise provides greater privacy protection for the individual[138]

Once it has completed this rather complicated analysis, a covered entity should be able to determine whether to comply with the applicable provisions of the Privacy Rule or the state law. Changes in the state law will require a fresh preemption review. Some states have begun to tailor their health information privacy laws to HIPAA.[139] This should reduce the complexity of preemption determinations.[140]
The Privacy Rule also provides a mechanism by which anyone, including a state, may request that DHHS except a provision of state law

---

[137] 45 C.F.R. § 160.202.
[138] Ibid. For early interpretations of this provision, see *United States ex rel. Pogue v. Diabetes Treatment Centers of America*, No. 99-3298 (D.D.C., May 17, 2004); *Law v. Zuckerman*, No. CBD-01-1429, 2004 WL 438327 (D. Md., Feb. 27, 2004); and *United States ex rel. Stewart v. The Louisiana Clinic*, No. 99-1767, 2002 WL 31819130 (E.D. La., Dec. 11, 2002).
[139] See, e.g., Tex. Health & Safety Code Ann. §§ 181.100 et seq.
[140] For another, more detailed approach to preemption analysis, see Workshop for Electronic Data Interchange, *Preemption White Paper: Final Version—April 2003*, 15.

from preemption by HIPAA. The determinations the Secretary of DHHS makes with respect to such requests will be published in the *Federal Register* and will be effective until the state law or the federal standard is materially changed so as to eliminate the rationale for the exception, or until the Secretary revokes the exception based on a determination that the grounds supporting the exception no longer exist.[141]

International Privacy Standards

The privacy laws of other countries may be applicable to an organization's use or disclosure of health information. Healthcare providers and others doing business in other countries will be subject to the privacy standards imposed on the health information identifiable with the citizens of those countries. For example the European Union has adopted the European Union Directive concerning the use and movement of individually identifiable information (EU Directive), which requires EU states to enact laws consistent with the EU Directive.[142] These laws govern the uses and disclosures of personal information, including health information, of EU citizens. They protect and regulate data, and thus apply to any person or organization that obtains the data. In addition, they determine whether personal information of an EU citizen may be transferred into the United States or other countries. Unfortunately, even with the enactment of HIPAA, the EU has not recognized the United States as a country possessing adequate protection for the privacy of personal information, and would prohibit the movement of such information to this country but for the EU's approval of the Safe Harbor Privacy Principles issued by the U.S. Department of Commerce in 2003. So long as an organization publicly discloses its commitment to meet the requirements of this safe harbor and is subject to the jurisdiction of the appropriate federal government enforcement agencies, it may receive personal information from the EU concerning EU citizens.[143] This is important for academic medical centers and

---

[141] 45 C.F.R. §§ 160.204 and 205.

[142] Directive 95/46/EC, *Official Journal of the European Communities (O.J.)*, L. 281 (Nov. 23, 1995).

[143] For a more expansive analysis of EU privacy law, see A. Wetherfield, "Protecting Personal Information—Over There: A Look at Privacy in the European Union," *Business Law Today* 51 (November/December 2004); S. Bernstein, R. Weisser, A. Bauer, and R. Massey, "Transfer of Clinical Research Data from the European Union to the United States," *BNA Medical Research Law & Policy* (Apr. 7, 2004).

other organizations that participate in research protocols involving citizens of EU countries. (For a more detailed discussion of applicable international law, see Chapter 14.)

What the EU Directive illustrates is the complexity of the laws of foreign jurisdictions and the need for any healthcare provider or other organization that collects, uses, or transmits the information of foreign citizens to understand the requirements of these laws.

Accreditation Organizations

Hospitals, MCOs, and healthcare organizations that seek accreditation from private authorities are required to meet standards concerning medical records confidentiality. The Joint Commission on Accreditation of Healthcare Organizations—which accredits various entities including hospitals, home health agencies, and MCOs—has standards regarding the management of information. For example, entities accredited under the Joint Commission's healthcare network standards are required to develop a process to protect the confidentiality of medical records information.[144] The National Committee for Quality Assurance (NCQA), which accredits managed care entities, also has standards concerning medical records confidentiality. For example, accredited MCOs must have complete policies and procedures for ensuring member confidentiality, in particular health information.[145]

Accreditation standards are not law. They are the measures by which accrediting organizations determine whether to grant an accreditation to an organization. Although an accreditation may have significant consequences for the organization in terms of reputation, and although governmental agencies may delegate to accrediting bodies certain survey tasks, an accrediting organization does not have the power to impose legal sanctions. The ultimate sanction for not meeting accreditation standards is loss of accreditation. Most healthcare organization accreditation standards that concern the confidentiality of health information require the development of systems and policies to protect patient privacy. Few of these standards require greater protections for health information than those imposed by the Privacy and

---

[144] Joint Commission on Accreditation of Healthcare Organizations, *1996–1997 Comprehensive Accreditation Manual for Health Care Networks*, Standard IM 2.

[145] National Committee for Quality Assurance, *Standards for the Certification of Managed Care Organizations*, Standard RRA (2004/2005).

Security Rules. Therefore, an organization may meet accreditation standards and still not be in compliance with the rules.

HIPAA Covered Entities

The HIPAA Privacy and Security Rules apply to PHI used or disclosed by covered entities. Covered entities are healthcare providers, healthcare clearinghouses, and health plans that conduct the financial and administrative transactions described in the TCS Rule.[146] If an individual provider or an organization does not fit within the definitions of a healthcare provider, clearinghouse, or health plan, the rules do not apply to its use or disclosure of PHI. Thus, the rules will not regulate employers, life insurance companies, or public agencies that deliver Social Security or welfare benefits. Other federal and state privacy laws may apply to these entities, however.

Healthcare Providers

The rules define a healthcare provider as a provider of services (as defined in Section 1861(u) of the Social Security Act[147]), a provider of medical or health services (as defined in Section 1861(s) of the act[148]), and any other person or organization who furnishes, bills, or is paid for health care in the normal course of business.[149] Health care is defined comprehensively as care, services, or supplies related to the health of an individual, and includes, but is not limited to, each of the following:

* Preventive, diagnostic, therapeutic, rehabilitative, maintenance, or palliative care; and counseling, service, assessment, or procedure; with respect to the physical or mental condition or functional status of an individual, or that affects the structure or function of the body

---

[146] 45 C.F.R. § 160.102.
[147] 42 U.S.C. § 1395x(u).
[148] 42 U.S.C. § 1395x(s).
[149] 45 C.F.R. § 160.103. These services include physician services and the services and supplies provided as part of a physician's services to outpatients, hospital outpatient services, hospital outpatient diagnostic services, outpatient physical therapy services, rural health clinic services, home dialysis supplies and equipment, certified nurse-midwife services, psychologist services, durable medical equipment, and necessary ambulance services.

- Sale or dispensing of a drug, device, equipment, or other item in accordance with a prescription[150]

Thus, the rules intend to capture a broad spectrum of providers and are not limited just to physicians and hospitals. Titles and labels used by health professionals do not determine whether they fall within the HIPAA definition of healthcare provider; their activities are the determining factor. Anyone who provides health care can qualify, including nutritionists, online pharmacies, social workers, and public health nurses.[151] Moreover, direct contact with the patient is not a prerequisite, so clinical laboratories, manufacturers, and healthcare suppliers who are considered providers by Medicare, and other entities that provide health care to a patient indirectly through others, may be healthcare providers under the rules.[152]

The other requirement of the definition is that the entity conduct standard HIPAA transactions as defined by the TCS Rule. If the physician is employed by a hospital, and the hospital bills for the physician's services, the physician does not conduct standard transactions and would not be a covered healthcare provider. If the physician bills for his or her own healthcare services, the physician will become a covered healthcare provider. Likewise, a physician who conducts medical research and does not perform standard transactions with respect to those research activities is not a covered healthcare provider, even if the researcher provides health care as part of the research. The rules do not apply to a researcher in his or her role as a researcher. If the researcher also provides health care and conducts standard transactions with respect to that care, the rules will apply to the researcher with respect to those provider activities, as opposed to research activities.[153] (For a more detailed discussion of the use of health information in research, see Chapter 14.)

Healthcare Clearinghouses

The rules also apply to healthcare clearinghouses. A healthcare clearinghouse is defined as a public or private entity—including a billing

---

[150] 45 C.F.R. § 160.103.
[151] 65 Fed. Reg. 82573 through 82574 (Dec. 28, 2000); 63 Fed. Reg. 25320 (May 7, 1998).
[152] 65 Fed. Reg. 82574 (Dec. 28, 2000).
[153] 65 Fed. Reg. 82575 (Dec. 28, 2000).

service, repricing company, community health management information system or community health information system, and "value added" networks and switches—that perform either of the following functions:

- Processes or facilitates the processing of health information received from another entity in a nonstandard format or containing nonstandard data content into standard data elements or a standard transaction
- Receives a standard transaction from another entity and processes or facilitates the processing of health information into nonstandard format or nonstandard data content for the receiving entity[154]

Clearinghouses translate information from one form into another form and play a major role in helping covered entities comply with the TCS Rule. Organizations may conduct other activities, such as a billing service, on behalf of one or more healthcare providers, but they will not be covered clearinghouses unless they meet the specific criteria of the definition.[155] Most clearinghouses will qualify as business associates of covered entities, and therefore must comply with the provisions of the rules applicable to business associates.

Health Plans

The rules also apply to organizations that function as group health plans or health insurance issuers, which provide for, or pay the cost of, medical care, as defined in Section 2791(a)(2) of the Public Health Service Act.[156] The definition includes the following:

1. A group health plan, which is defined as an employee welfare benefit plan as defined by the Employee Retirement Income Security Act (ERISA),[157] including insured and self insured plans, to the extent that the plan provides medical care and has 50 or more participants or is administered by an entity other than the employer that established the plan[158]

---

[154] 45 C.F.R. § 160.103.
[155] 65 Fed. Reg. 82573 (Dec. 28, 2000).
[156] 42 U.S.C. § 300gg-91(a)(2) & (b)(2); 45 C.F.R. § 160.103.
[157] 29 U.S.C. § 1002(1).
[158] 45 C.F.R. § 160.103.

2. A health insurance issuer, which is defined as an insurance company, service, or organization that is a licensed insurer subject to state insurance regulation[159]

3. An HMO, which is defined as a federally qualified HMO or state recognized or regulated HMO[160]

4. Part A or Part B of the Medicare program under Title XVIII of the Social Security Act[161]

5. The Medicaid program under Title XIX of the Social Security Act[162]

6. An issuer of a Medicare supplemental policy, as defined in Section 1882(g)(1) of the act[163]

7. An issuer of a long term care policy, excluding a nursing home fixed indemnity policy

8. An employee welfare benefit plan or any other arrangement that is established or maintained for the purpose of offering or providing health benefits to the employees of two or more employers

9. The healthcare program for active military personnel under Title 10 of the U.S. Code

10. The veterans' healthcare program under 38 U.S.C. Chapter 17

11. The Civilian Health and Medical Program of the Uniformed Services (CHAMPUS), as defined in 10 U.S.C. § 1072(4)

12. The Indian Health Service program under the Indian Health Care Improvement Act[164]

13. The Federal Employees Health Benefits Program[165]

14. An approved state child health plan under Title XXI of the Social Security Act, providing benefits for child health assistance that meet the requirements of Section 2103 of the act[166]

15. The Medicare Advantage program under Parts C and D of Title XVIII of the act[167]

---

[159] Ibid.
[160] Ibid.
[161] 42 U.S.C. §§ 1301 et seq., and §§ 1395 et seq. The government agency that administers a government program that qualifies as a health plan is the covered entity. Thus, the Centers for Medicare & Medicaid Services (CMS) is the covered entity. 65 Fed. Reg. 82578 (Dec. 28, 2000).
[162] 42 U.S.C. §§ 1396 et seq.
[163] 42 U.S.C. § 1395ss(g)(1).
[164] 25 U.S.C. §§ 1601 et seq.
[165] 5 U.S.C. §§ 8901 et seq.
[166] 42 U.S.C. §§ 1397aa et seq.
[167] 42 U.S.C. §§ 1395w-21 et seq.

16. A high risk pool that is a mechanism established under state law to provide health insurance coverage or comparable coverage to eligible individuals

17. Any other individual or group plan, or combination of individual or group plans, that provides, or pays for the cost of, medical care, as defined in Section 2791(a)(2) of the Public Health Service Act

The definition excludes, however, any policy, plan, or program to the extent that it provides, or pays for the cost of, excepted benefits that are listed in Section 2791(c)(1) of the Public Health Service Act,[168] such as disability, liability, and accident insurance programs.[169] A government funded program, other than those listed in the definition of health plan, whose principal purpose is other than providing, or paying the cost of, health care, or whose principal activity is the direct provision of health care to persons or the making of grants to fund such care, is also excluded.[170] Therefore, programs such as the Food Stamp Program would not be health plans under the rules.

Exercise of Professional Judgment

Like many comprehensive regulatory schemes, the Privacy Rule gives clear, precise direction for some situations, provides no direction at all for others, and creates ambiguity for yet others. In numerous situations discussed in this text, the Privacy Rule requires covered entities to exercise their judgment as to whether the circumstances required by the rule for a use or disclosure of PHI without patient authorization actually exist.[171] In exercising their judgment, covered entities are expected to adhere to the same standards of performance they otherwise would be expected to meet in carrying out their activities. A physician, therefore, would be expected to exercise the same judgment as that of a reasonable, competent physician faced with the same circumstances. If a dispute arises as to whether the physician met this standard in the exercise of his or her judgment, the question ultimately would be decided in a court of law.

---

[168] 42 U.S.C. § 300gg-91(c)(1).
[169] 45 C.F.R. § 160.103.
[170] Ibid.
[171] See, e.g., 45 C.F.R. § 510(a)(3)(i)(B), 45 C.F.R. § 512(c)(1)(iii)(A), 45 C.F.R. § 512(f)(3)(ii)(C).

Minimum Necessary Rule

Even when a use or disclosure of PHI is permitted, covered entities must determine how much information to use or disclose. The Privacy Rule establishes a general standard governing the amount of PHI that covered entities may use or disclose: they must limit the use or disclosure to the minimum amount of information necessary to accomplish the intended purpose of the use or disclosure.[172] This is known as the "minimum necessary rule." This rule also applies when a covered entity requests PHI from another covered entity. The minimum necessary rule does not apply, however, to any of the following uses and disclosures:

- for treatment purposes
- to the individual who is the subject of the PHI
- made pursuant to the individual's valid authorization
- needed by the Secretary of DHHS for ensuring compliance with HIPAA
- required by other law
- required for compliance with other provisions of the Privacy Rule[173]

The Privacy Rule applies the minimum necessary rule differently to routine or recurring requests for PHI and to nonroutine requests. Covered entities must adopt policies or standard protocols that describe what is the minimum necessary PHI for each particular type of routine request. For example, the protocol for responding to a subpoena duces tecum might provide that the minimum PHI necessary is the information specified in the subpoena, provided the subpoena meets the requirements for legal process set out in the Privacy Rule. These policies must specify the amount of PHI that should be disclosed to each category of employee who requires the use or disclosure of PHI. Routine requests do not require specific, individual determinations of what is the minimum necessary disclosure. They simply require that the disclosures be made in accordance with established policies.[174] To respond appropriately to nonroutine requests, covered entities must develop and apply criteria for determining what in each instance is the minimum

---

[172] 45 C.F.R. § 164.502(b)(1).
[173] 45 C.F.R. § 164.502(b)(2).
[174] 45 C.F.R. § 164.514(d)(3).

necessary information to provide. This will require covered entities to review against established criteria each such request individually as it is made.[175] However, DHHS does not expect covered entities to restructure, upgrade, or redesign their existing facilities and computer systems to meet the minimum necessary rule.[176]

The minimum necessary rule is a reasonableness standard, which gives covered entities flexibility to address their unique circumstances and make their own judgments as to what PHI is reasonably necessary for the purpose of the use or disclosure. Covered entities are not required to limit uses or disclosures of PHI to those that are absolutely needed to achieve the stated purpose. DHHS expects covered entities to approach disclosures of PHI consistent with the best practices and guidelines used by healthcare providers to limit the unnecessary disclosure of health information. The Privacy Rule is not intended to override professional judgment and standards with respect to preventing inappropriate access to such information.[177]

In some cases, covered entities may rely upon the determinations of others as to what PHI is minimally necessary for a particular use or disclosure. The Privacy Rule permits, but does not require, such reliance when the request for PHI is made by any of the following:

- a public official for disclosures permitted by the rule
- another covered entity
- a person who provides professional services for the entity as a member of its workforce or as a business associate (see the discussion of business associates later in this chapter)
- a researcher with appropriate documentation from an institutional review board or privacy board (see the discussion concerning research in Chapter 14)[178]

When requests are made by a public official or a professional, the covered entity may rely upon the representations they make that the

---

[175] 45 C.F.R. § 164.514(d)(3)(ii).
[176] U.S. Department of Health and Human Services, *Standards for Privacy of Individually Identifiable Health Information* (Dec. 3, 2002), 27, available at http://www.hhs.gov/ocr/hipaa/.
[177] U.S. Department of Health and Human Services, *First Guidance on New Patient Privacy Protections* (July 6, 2001), 17, available at http://www.hhs.gov/ocr/hipaa.
[178] 45 C.F.R. § 164.514(d)(3)(iii).

requested information is the minimum necessary for the stated purpose.[179] The Privacy Rule does not require a covered entity to rely on any of the individuals described above. A covered entity has the discretion to make its own determination as to whether the PHI requested is the minimum necessary for the stated purpose.[180] If a covered entity and any of these requesters disagree as to what information is minimally necessary, the parties should negotiate to resolve the issue.[181]

The minimum necessary rule prohibits the release of a patient's entire medical record, unless the release is specifically justified on a case-by-case basis as the minimum amount of PHI necessary for the intended purpose,[182] the disclosure is one described in the covered entity's policies as requiring the entire record to be disclosed, or the disclosure is not subject to the minimum necessary rule.[183] A covered entity may disclose the entire medical record, even if it contains information provided by another or previous healthcare provider.[184] Covered healthcare providers are frequently requested by plaintiffs' attorneys in professional liability lawsuits to release the plaintiff's entire medical record. This type of disclosure will fall under the exceptions to the minimum necessary rule for disclosures to the patient, disclosures pursuant to a valid authorization, and disclosures required by law (if made in accordance with a valid subpoena duces tecum).

The minimum necessary rule also applies to the business associates of a covered entity. (See the discussion of business associates later in this chapter.) By contract, a business associate may not use or further disclose PHI in a manner that would violate the Privacy Rule if done by the covered entity. The agreement between the covered entity and its business associate, therefore, must require the business associate to comply with the minimum necessary requirements imposed upon the covered entity. Given this requirement, a covered entity may reasonably rely upon the requests for information of another covered entity's business associate as the minimum necessary.[185]

---

[179] 65 Fed. Reg. 82545 (Dec. 20, 2000).
[180] Department of Health and Human Services, *First Guidance*, 16.
[181] Department of Health and Human Services, *Standards for Privacy*, 28.
[182] 45 C.F.R. § 164.514(e)(5).
[183] Department of Health and Human Services, *First Guidance*, 19.
[184] Department of Health and Human Services, *Standards for Privacy*, 27.
[185] 45 C.F.R. § 164.504(3)(2)(i); Department of Health and Human Services, *Standards for Privacy*, 27.

The minimum necessary rule is difficult to implement. It requires the exercise of judgment and the close coordination of a covered entity's policies and procedures with the activities of its workforce. Until DHHS provides more specific guidance or the courts provide more precise interpretations of the rule, covered entities should consult with qualified legal counsel in developing practical medical records policies, and should make a good faith effort to apply the rule in a rational way. As has always been the case, erring on the side of protecting the patient's confidentiality is the safest approach when the Privacy Rule defies reasonable interpretation.

Hybrid Entities, Affiliated Covered Entities, and Organized Healthcare Arrangements

The Privacy and Security Rules create hybrid entities, affiliated covered entities (ACEs), and organized healthcare arrangements (OHCAs) to accommodate organizations that carry out functions that are covered by the rules, and noncovered functions and organizations that wish to be treated as one covered entity for purposes of complying with the rules. These provisions of the rules recognize the increasing complexity of the healthcare delivery system and the need for many organizations to coordinate their information privacy and security practices.[186]

Hybrid Entities

The rules define a hybrid entity as a single organization that meets all of the following criteria:

- It is a covered entity
- Its business activities include both functions covered by the rules and noncovered functions
- It designates its components that will be subject to the rules[187]

Thus, a complex organization may have several covered components, which the rules refer to as "health care components." A function will be a healthcare component if it would fit the definition of "covered

---

[186] See 65 Fed. Reg. 82637 through 82640 (Dec. 28, 2000).
[187] 45 C.F.R. § 164.103.

entity" if it were a separate legal entity (for example, it is a healthcare provider that transmits health information in electronic form in connection with a transaction that is subject to HIPAA). For example, a university that would not ordinarily be a covered entity for HIPAA purposes but that provides to students healthcare services which are not otherwise exempted from HIPAA could be a hybrid entity. The university would be a covered healthcare provider. Its activities include both covered services (for example, student health services) and noncovered services (for example, teaching history). If the university designates its student health service as a covered healthcare component, the university will be a hybrid entity. The university might also provide other healthcare activities that would be subject to the rules. For example, it might operate a course in speech therapy that involves a speech clinic, or it might operate a health plan.

The larger organization, the university in the previous example, would be responsible for ensuring that its covered components comply with the rules.[188] This means that the healthcare components must fulfill all the requirements the rules impose on any covered entity concerning the use, maintenance, storage, disclosure, and transmission of PHI. The greater organization must comply with all of the implementation standards of the rules, including creating appropriate policies and procedures, notice of privacy practices, and patient rights with respect to its PHI. It must treat the noncovered components of the hybrid entity as though they were separate and distinct legal entities, and must make certain that its healthcare components do not disclose PHI to noncovered components of the organization in a manner that would violate the rules.[189] The healthcare component must also protect from unauthorized access or use by the noncovered components any ePHI that it creates or receives.[190] The rules do not specify the safeguards required to protect covered components. Each hybrid organization is responsible for developing its own safeguards that enable it to comply with the regulations.

Covered components are free to disclose PHI to noncovered components in ways that are permitted by the regulations. For example, a university's healthcare component may disclose PHI to the university's office of general counsel because the provision of legal services is part of

---

[188] 45 C.F.R. § 164.105(a)(2)(iii).
[189] 45 C.F.R. § 164.105(a)(2)(ii)(A).
[190] 45 C.F.R. § 164.105(a)(2)(ii)(D).

healthcare operations, and covered entities may use or disclose PHI for such operations.[191]

In hybrid entities in which employees have duties in both a healthcare component and a noncovered component, special care must be taken to prevent the improper use or disclosure of PHI. In the healthcare component of their work, these employees may create or receive PHI. In their work for a noncovered component, the employees may not use or disclose this PHI in a manner that would violate the Privacy or Security Rule.[192] The organization's policies and procedures should establish firewalls between its covered and noncovered components, and should give clear directions to its workforce concerning the privacy and security requirements for its covered healthcare components.

The rules do not permit a healthcare component to contain noncovered components unless those components perform functions covered by HIPAA or conduct activities that would make them a business associate of a covered healthcare component (assuming the two were separate legal entities).[193] The objective of these requirements is to keep the distinction between covered and noncovered components clear, and thus facilitate the covered healthcare components' compliance with the rules.

Affiliated Covered Entities

Unlike a hybrid entity, ACEs are separate organizations that are under common ownership or control.[194] "Common ownership" exists if an entity possesses an ownership interest of 5 percent or more in another entity.[195] "Common control" exists if an entity has the power, directly or indirectly, to exercise significant influence or to direct the actions of another entity.[196] Thus, two hospitals organized under the same parent organization would be under common control if the parent has the power to influence the two hospitals' activities (for example, by having the power to elect the hospitals' directors). Likewise, two separate home health companies, 50 percent of whose stock is owned by an-

---

[191] 65 Fed. Reg. 82638 (Dec. 28, 2000).
[192] 45 C.F.R. § 164.105(a)(2)(ii)(E).
[193] 45 C.F.R. § 164.105(a)(2)(iii)(C)(2).
[194] 45 C.F.R. § 164.105(b)(1).
[195] 45 C.F.R. § 164.103.
[196] Ibid.

other company, are under common ownership. Unrelated organizations may not become ACEs, because DHHS believes that their information practices will be too dissimilar.[197]

Organizations become "affiliated" when they designate themselves a single entity for purposes of complying with the rules. For example, several hospitals under common control might designate themselves as an ACE. A healthcare component of a hybrid entity also may affiliate with another covered entity.[198] ACEs commonly establish joint privacy and security policies, procedures, and forms,[199] and must use a single notice of privacy practices.[200] (See the discussion of the notice of privacy practices later in this chapter.) In considering whether to form an ACE, organizations that operate in more than one state should evaluate whether it will be practical for them to use a single form of notice. Because they are treated as one covered entity, ACEs may also share PHI without having to enter into business associate agreements. (See the discussion of business associates later in this chapter.) The rules are not clear as to whether, as one covered entity, ACEs must present one response to individuals seeking to exercise their various HIPAA rights, or whether each covered entity in the affiliated group must relate to those individuals. If the ACE chooses to coordinate its response with respect to individual HIPAA rights, it should make this clear in its notice of privacy practices.

However, each covered entity in an affiliated group retains responsibility for its compliance with the rules.[201] If a covered entity performs multiple covered functions (for example, those of a healthcare provider and those of a health plan), it must comply with all the rules applicable to each function.[202] If an individual relates to the covered entity for only one of its covered functions, the entity may use or disclose the individual's PHI only in connection with that function.[203] Thus, if organizations in the ACE operate different covered functions, they will be able to share an individual's PHI only if the individual has a relationship with each function.

---

[197] 65 Fed. Reg. 82637 (Dec. 28, 2000).
[198] 45 C.F.R. § 164.105(b)(2)(i)(A).
[199] See, generally, 65 Fed. Reg. 82637 through 82640 (Dec. 20, 2000).
[200] 65 Fed. Reg. 82552 (Dec. 20, 2000).
[201] 65 Fed. Reg. 82503 (Dec. 20, 2000).
[202] 45 C.F.R. § 164.504(g)(1).
[203] 45 C.F.R. § 164.504(g)(2).

Organizations that intend to affiliate must exercise caution to prevent their affiliation from creating vicarious liability for each other's wrongful acts under applicable state law. They should state in their affiliation agreement and their joint notice of privacy practices that they are affiliating only for purposes of sharing PHI and coordinating their information policies and procedures. They should also consult with qualified legal counsel in developing their affiliation.

Documentation of Designations

Organizations designate themselves as hybrid entities or affiliated covered entities simply by creating a written or electronic record that they have done so. An organization that wishes to be recognized as a hybrid entity must designate which of its components are healthcare components. Separate organizations that wish to be recognized as affiliated under the rules must designate themselves as such, and must retain the record of that designation for six years from the date it is created or the date it was last in effect, whichever is later.[204]

Organized Healthcare Arrangement

The rules also describe arrangements in which participants need to share PHI about their patients in order to manage and benefit their common enterprise. The participants are separate covered entities that are clinically or operationally integrated. The key ingredient is that patients have an expectation that they will receive services from an integrated and jointly managed arrangement.

The rules provide for five types of OHCAs. The most common type is the clinically integrated care setting in which patients receive health care from more than one provider.[205] A hospital and its medical staff working together in the hospital setting to provide health care to their patients is an example of this integrated OHCA. Here, the need exists for care providers—physicians, nurses, technicians, and others—to share health information required in order to provide quality treatment to patients. The OHCA provisions were added to the final Privacy Rule to enable participants in these arrangements to continue legitimate information sharing.[206]

---

[204] 45 C.F.R. § 164.105(c) and § 164.530(j).
[205] 45 C.F.R. § 160.103.
[206] 65 Fed. Reg. 82494 (Dec. 28, 2000).

The second type of OHCA is an organized system of health care in which more than one covered entity participates, and in which the participating covered entities participate in certain joint activities and hold themselves out to the public as participating in a joint arrangement.[207] These activities must include at least one of the following:

- Utilization review, in which healthcare decisions by participating covered entities are reviewed by other participating covered entities or by a third party on their behalf
- Quality assessment and improvement activities, in which treatment provided by participating covered entities is assessed by other participating covered entities or by a third party on their behalf
- Payment activities, if the financial risk for delivering health care is shared by participating covered entities through the joint arrangement, and if PHI created or received by a covered entity is reviewed by other participating covered entities or by a third party on their behalf for the purpose of administering the sharing of financial risk[208]

A good example of this type of OHCA is an independent practice association formed by a large group of physicians who share common financial risk through withhold pools or other devices designed to create incentives for efficient operations. The physicians need not be under common ownership, but they must conduct one of the practice management activities listed above. The rules recognize that covered entities in these arrangements must share PHI in order to conduct their operations.[209]

The remaining three types of OHCAs involve group health plans and include the following types of plans:

- A group health plan and either health insurance company or HMO, but only with respect to PHI created or received by the health insurance company or HMO where the PHI relates to individuals who are or have been participants or beneficiaries in the plan
- A group health plan and one or more other group health plans, each of which is maintained by the same plan sponsor

---

[207] 45 C.F.R. § 164.103.
[208] Ibid.
[209] 65 Fed. Reg. 82494 (Dec. 28, 2000).

- Group health plans maintained by the same sponsor and health insurance companies or HMOs, but only with respect to PHI created or received by those health insurance companies or HMOs where the PHI relates to individuals who are or have been participants or beneficiaries in any of the group health plans

These definitions recognize that group health plans must often coordinate with insurance companies and HMOs to serve plan participants. Employers often provide health insurance benefits through more than one group health plan, all of which may need to coordinate their activities for plan participants.[210]

The rules treat an OHCA as operating one healthcare enterprise, and permit the covered entities in the OHCA to share PHI for treatment, payment, and healthcare operations of the OHCA.[211] For example, a hospital may disclose PHI to physicians with staff privileges at the hospital as part of hospital's training of medical students.[212] Covered entities participating in an OHCA may also share PHI for treatment, payment, and healthcare operations if they have or had a relationship with the individuals whose PHI is disclosed and if the disclosure is for a quality related operations activity.[213] The rules are silent, however, as to whether covered entities in an OHCA are subject to the same multiple covered functions limitation that applies to an affiliated covered entity.

OHCAs may also use a joint notice of privacy practices, may deliver one notice for all the services provided by the covered entities in the OHCA, and may collect from a patient one acknowledgment of receipt of the notice.[214] The entities participating in the OHCA must agree to abide by the terms of the notice with respect to PHI created or received in connection with OHCA activities, and the notice must meet the content and other requirements of the rules for the notice. The content of a joint OHCA notice, however, may be changed to describe the participating entities in the OHCA, the OHCA's activities,

---

[210] 65 Fed. Reg. 82494 through 82495 (Dec. 28, 2000).
[211] 45 C.F.R. § 164.506(c)(5).
[212] Department of Health and Human Services, *Standards for Privacy*, 57.
[213] 45 C.F.R. § 164.506(c)(4). The quality-related activities must be those described in the first two paragraphs of the definition of "health care operations" at 45 C.F.R. § 164.501, and include quality assessment and improvement, outcomes evaluation, competence review, and training activities.
[214] 45 C.F.R. § 164.520(d).

and the delivery sites to which the joint notice applies. Although the rules require no formal declaration by covered entities participating in an OHCA that they are an OHCA, the entities should include this information in their joint notice of privacy practices. Doing so will give clear notice to patients that they are receiving care from an integrated system.

Each covered entity in an OHCA is responsible for responding to individuals exercising their HIPAA rights, except the right to receive a notice of privacy practices. Participating covered entities may not, therefore, respond collectively to an individual's request to review his or her PHI, or to amend that PHI, or to take the other actions permitted by HIPAA.

A business associate relationship is not created by the mere participation in an OHCA,[215] and the rules do not require participating entities to create business associate agreements for the activities they conduct jointly.[216] The minimum necessary requirements of the rules apply to disclosures of PHI among participating covered entities in an OHCA.[217] (See the discussions of business associates and the minimum necessary rule in this chapter.)

Under state law, the formation of an OHCA may create exposure for participating covered entities to joint and several liability for wrongful acts of another participating entity. Therefore, entities should seek the advice of qualified legal counsel, use care in negotiating their OHCA contracts, and evaluate the insurance and indemnification implications of an OHCA. They should also consider stating in the OHCA's joint notice of privacy practices that they formed the OHCA only for the purpose of sharing PHI in accordance with the rules.

Uses and Disclosures of Medical Records Information

The medical record is a confidential document, and access to it generally should be limited to the patient or his or her authorized representative, the attending physician, and other staff members possessing legitimate interests in the record relating to the patient's care. Usually a

---

[215] 45 C.F.R. § 160.103.
[216] Department of Health and Human Services, *Standards for Privacy,* 43.
[217] 45 C.F.R. § 164.502(b).

parent must authorize disclosure of a minor's medical record. However, in some situations, the minor may be able to authorize disclosure of medical records information. Certain types of health information— such as psychiatric records, records of alcohol and drug abuse treatment, and genetic testing information are particularly sensitive. In addition to the protections afforded by the Privacy and Security Rules, special state laws may govern access to these medical records, usually imposing stricter requirements for confidentiality. Both federal and state laws permit access to medical records under specific circumstances without patient authorization. Health information professionals involved with the release of medical information must understand all of these rules and exceptions.

Access by or on Behalf of the Patient

Individuals have a right to access their own PHI that is held by a covered entity, subject to limited exceptions. This right is codified both in the Privacy Rule[218] and in virtually every state's laws.[219] The Privacy Rule grants individuals the right of access to inspect and obtain a copy of PHI about the individual, so long as the PHI is maintained in the designated record set.[220] (See the discussion of a designated record set earlier in this chapter.) This right does not extend to psychotherapy notes; to information compiled in reasonable anticipation of, or for use in, a civil, criminal, or administrative action or proceeding; or to PHI maintained by certain covered entities.[221]

The covered entity may require individuals to make requests for access in writing, provided that it informs individuals of such a requirement.[222] The covered entity must act on a request for access no later than 30 days after receipt of the request.[223] This means that the covered entity must notify the individual whether it will grant or deny the access requested, and such notice must comply with the Privacy Rule.[224] The 30-day deadline may be extended under certain circumstances,

---

[218] 45 C.F.R. §§ 164.502(a)(2) and 164.524.
[219] See, e.g., S.C. Code Ann. § 44-115-30; Conn. Gen. Stat. § 20-7c(b); Cal. Health & Safety Code § 123110; Ga. Code Ann. §§ 31-33-2 and 31-33-3.
[220] 45 C.F.R. § 164.524(a)(1).
[221] 45 C.F.R. § 164.524(a)(1)(i) through (iv).
[222] 45 C.F.R. § 164.524(b)(1).
[223] 45 C.F.R. § 164.524(b)(2).
[224] For denial notices, see 45 C.F.R. § 164.524(d).

such as when the PHI requested is not maintained or accessible by the covered entity on site.[225]

If the covered entity grants the individual's request to access PHI, the entity must provide the requested access (including inspection or obtaining a copy, or both) in designated record sets.[226] This includes arranging with the individual for a convenient time and place to inspect or obtain a copy of the PHI, or mailing the copy of the PHI if the individual so requests.[227] The covered entity may discuss the scope, format, and other aspects of the request for access with the individual as necessary to facilitate the timely provision of access.[228] If the same PHI that is the subject of a request for access is maintained in more than one designated record set or at more than one location, the covered entity is required to produce the PHI only once in response to the request.[229] The covered entity must provide the individual with access to the PHI in the form or format requested by the individual, if it is readily producible in such form or format; or, if not, in a readable hard copy form or such other form or format as agreed to by the covered entity and the individual.[230] In lieu of providing access to the PHI, the covered entity may provide a summary or explanation of the PHI, provided that the individual agrees in advance to receive an explanation and to pay any applicable fees for producing it.[231]

Most state laws expressly allow a patient or authorized representative to examine and copy the patient's medical records.[232] To the extent that these state laws do not conflict with the Privacy Rule or to the extent that they provide greater protections for the individual, the state laws will apply. (See discussion of state law preemption by HIPAA earlier in this chapter.) Under state laws, the person seeking access typically must make a written request and pay reasonable clerical costs before the records become available.[233] The healthcare organization or provider usually is responsible only for making the records available at

---

[225] See 45 C.F.R. § 164.524(b)(2).
[226] 45 C.F.R. § 164.524(c)(1).
[227] 45 C.F.R. § 164.524(c)(3).
[228] Ibid.
[229] 45 C.F.R. § 164.524(c)(1).
[230] 45 C.F.R. § 164.524(c)(2)(i).
[231] 45 C.F.R. § 164.524(c)(2)(ii).
[232] See, e.g., Md. Code Ann., Ins., § 4-403; Wis. Stat. Ann. § 146.82.
[233] See, e.g., N.H. Rev. Stat. Ann. § 332-I:1; Mont. Code Ann. §§ 50-16-526 and 50-16-541.

reasonable times and places. For example, in California, facilities must provide for patient inspection of records within five working days of the request, and must provide copies within 15 working days and upon payment of fees.[234] Georgia also requires hospitals to provide records access to patients upon receipt of a written request,[235] but allows the institutions to require payment of the copying and mailing costs before releasing the records.[236]

Depending upon the state, a patient may be able to review his or her medical records while he or she is still in the hospital. Many statutes allow patients to review their records upon request during the course of hospitalization.[237] Other statutes grant patients an unrestricted right of access to their medical records only after discharge from the hospital.[238] Florida, for example, has a law that a licensed facility, upon receiving a written request after discharge of the patient, must furnish a patient or patient representative a true and correct copy of the record.[239] The Privacy Rule right of access is available to hospitalized patients as well as to patients who have been discharged from the hospital.

In addition to meeting its legal obligations, a hospital may have some practical reasons for allowing a patient to examine the records during hospitalization. Hospitals should consider whether refusal to permit such an inspection will create unnecessary problems for the institution and its staff. An inpatient who is denied access to a chart may become hostile and more difficult to treat. Moreover, the patient may be more likely to file a claim against the hospital if treatment ends in a poor result.

Therefore, unless the attending physician has a reasonable basis for believing that disclosure of the medical record will harm the patient, the hospital should allow the individual to review the record. In some instances, a record review coordinated by the patient's attending physician will enhance the patient's understanding of actions taken by the physician, thereby promoting better hospital patient relations and decreasing the likelihood of any claims being filed against the facility. It

---

[234] Cal. Health & Safety Code § 123110.
[235] Ga. Code Ann. §§ 31-33-2 and 31-33-3.
[236] *Cotton v. Med-Cor Health Information Solutions, Inc.*, 472 S.E. 2d 92 (Ga. Ct. App. 1996), *cert. denied*, No. S96C1434 (Ga., Oct. 4, 1996) (unpublished); Ga. Code Ann. § 31-33-3.
[237] See, e.g., Minn. Stat. § 144.335(2).
[238] See, e.g., 735 Ill. Comp. Stat. Ann. § 5/8-2001.
[239] Fla. Stat. Ann. § 395.3025(1).

may also result in greater compliance by the patient with agreed upon treatment plans. If inpatients are allowed to examine their records, however, the hospital should employ its customary record security procedures. (Record security is discussed in Chapter 13.)

Under certain circumstances, a covered entity may wish to deny an individual's request to access his or her PHI. The Privacy Rule permits a covered entity to deny an individual access without providing the individual an opportunity to have the denial reviewed by an independent licensed healthcare provider in the following five instances:

- An individual may be denied access without review if the PHI is excepted from the right of access because it is not being maintained in a designated record set (see the discussion of designated record set earlier in this chapter)[240]
- A covered entity that is a correctional institution (or a covered healthcare provider acting under the direction of the correctional institution) may deny, in whole or in part, an inmate's request to obtain a copy of PHI, if obtaining such copy would jeopardize the health, safety, security, custody, or rehabilitation of the individual or of other inmates, or the safety of any officer, employee, or other person at the correctional institution or responsible for the transporting of the inmate[241]
- An individual's access to PHI created or obtained by a covered healthcare provider in the course of research that includes treatment may be temporarily suspended for as long as the research is in progress, provided that certain conditions are satisfied (see the discussion of the use of health information in research in Chapter 14)[242]
- An individual's access to PHI that is contained in records that are subject to the Privacy Act (see the discussion on the Privacy Act earlier in this chapter) may be denied without review, if the denial of access under the Privacy Act would meet the requirements of that law[243]
- An individual's access may be denied without review if the PHI was obtained from someone other than a healthcare provider under a

---

[240] 45 C.F.R. § 164.524(a)(2)(i).
[241] 45 C.F.R. § 164.524(a)(2)(ii).
[242] 45 C.F.R. § 164.524(a)(2)(iii).
[243] 45 C.F.R. § 164.524(a)(2)(iv).

promise of confidentiality, and the access requested would be reasonably likely to reveal the source of the information[244]

A covered entity may deny an individual access to his or her PHI in other circumstances, but unlike the situations described above, the individual has the right to have such a denial reviewed by a licensed healthcare professional. This independent reviewer is designated by the covered entity to act as a reviewing official, and does not participate in the original decision to deny access.[245] The following three denial situations are subject to independent review:

- A licensed healthcare professional has determined that the access requested is reasonably likely to endanger the life or physical safety of the individual or another person[246]
- The PHI makes reference to another person (unless such other person is a healthcare provider), and a licensed healthcare professional has determined that the access requested is reasonably likely to cause substantial harm to such other person[247]
- The request for access is made by the individual's personal representative, and a licensed healthcare professional has determined that the provision of access to such personal representative is reasonably likely to cause substantial harm to the individual or another person[248]

Regardless of whether a denial is subject to review, the covered entity must, to the extent possible, give the individual access to any other PHI requested after excluding the denied PHI.[249]

Many state statutes allow the healthcare organization or provider to refuse to grant the patient's request for disclosure where the individual seeks access to psychiatric information, where release of psychiatric information would be detrimental to the patient's mental health,[250] or where release of any medical information would adversely affect the

---

[244] 45 C.F.R. § 164.524(a)(2)(v).
[245] 45 C.F.R. § 164.524(a)(4).
[246] 45 C.F.R. § 164.524(a)(3)(i).
[247] 45 C.F.R. § 164.524(a)(3)(ii).
[248] 45 C.F.R. § 164.524(a)(3)(iii).
[249] 45 C.F.R. § 164.524(d)(1).
[250] See, e.g., Cal. Health & Safety Code § 123115(b); Colo. Rev. Stat. § 25-1-801; Okla. Stat. Ann. tit. 76, § 19.

general health of the person.[251] To the extent that these state laws do not conflict with the Privacy Rule or to the extent that they provide greater protections for the individual, the state laws will apply. (See the discussion of state law preemption by HIPAA earlier in this chapter.) In some instances, the psychiatric patient can obtain at least a summary of the records following termination of the treatment program.[252] In New York, the provider may deny access to a patient's records where the requested information can reasonably be expected to cause substantial and identifiable harm to the subject or to others, and where that harm outweighs the right to access.[253] In most states where a patient lawfully can be denied access to records, however, the healthcare organization may be required to deliver copies of the record to the patient's representative or attorney.[254]

Several state statutes contain special provisions concerning a patient's access to particular portions of the record, such as X-rays,[255] others have separate rules governing access by a minor patient,[256] and still others allow a provider to prepare a summary of the record for inspection and copying rather than permit the patient access to the entire record.[257]

Some of the state laws restricting individuals' access to their health information will not survive HIPAA preemption with respect to the operations of covered entities, because they conflict with the rights the Privacy Rule grants to individuals to gain access to their PHI. However, as discussed above, the Privacy Rule recognizes circumstances in which an individual's access to his or her information is inappropriate. State laws that contain the same, or less severe, restrictions on individual access are still enforceable.

Some statutes and regulations providing patient access to their records prescribe a time limit for a response. For example, New York requires the provider to respond to a request to review records within

---

[251] See, e.g., Haw. Rev. Stat. § 622-57; Me. Rev. Stat. Ann. tit. 22, § 1711; Minn. Stat. § 144.335(2)(c).

[252] See, e.g., Colo. Rev. Stat. § 25-1-801(1)(a).

[253] N.Y. Pub. Health Law § 18(3)(a).

[254] See, e.g., Haw. Rev. Stat. § 622-57; Me. Rev. Stat. Ann. tit. 22, § 1711; Minn. Stat. § 144.335(2)(c) (provider may withhold information from patient and may supply the information to appropriate third party).

[255] See, e.g., Cal. Health & Safety Code §§ 123110(c) through (e).

[256] See, e.g., Cal. Health & Safety Code § 123115; N.Y. Pub. Health Law § 18(2)(c).

[257] See, e.g., Cal. Health & Safety Code § 123130; Minn. Stat. § 144.335(2)(b).

10 days after receiving the request.[258] California law requires the hospital to provide for inspection of records within 5 working days after receiving a request, and to provide copies of the record within 15 days.[259] Minnesota law states that a provider must furnish copies of a medical record to a patient "promptly" after receiving the request.[260] State law that allows covered entities to respond to an individual's request for access to his or her PHI after the 30-day response time established by the Privacy Rule will likely be found to have been preempted by HIPAA, and the 30-day requirement will apply. State laws that require covered entities to respond in less than 30 days will likely not be preempted by HIPAA. Because the laws in each state vary with respect to the time allowed for a response, every healthcare organization and provider must check requirements in its own area. Where the state laws are silent on the matter, a healthcare organization or provider who is subject to HIPAA should comply with the patient access requirements of the Privacy Rule.

In the absence of statute or regulation, courts in some jurisdictions have recognized a common law duty to allow a patient limited access to records.[261] In *Cannell v. Medical & Surgical Clinic*, for instance, the court found that the fiduciary qualities of the physician patient relationship require the provider to disclose medical data to the patient or agent upon request, and that the patient need not engage in legal proceedings to attain higher status in order to receive such information.[262] Other courts have held that, although a hospital may have a common law duty to disclose all or part of a patient's record, there is no obligation to do so free of charge.[263] However, because the Privacy Rule and the vast majority of states now by statute or regulation recognize a patient's right of access, courts are less likely to become involved in enunciating legal precedent on this issue.

---

[258] N.Y. Pub. Health Law § 18(2)(a).

[259] Cal. Health & Safety Code § 123110(b).

[260] Minn. Stat. § 144.335(2)(b).

[261] See, e.g., *Hutchins v. Texas Rehabilitation Commission*, 544 S.W. 2d 802 (Tex. App. 1976); *In re Weiss*, 147 N.Y.S. 2d 455 (Sup. Ct. 1955).

[262] 315 N.E. 2d 278 (Ill. Ct. App. 1974); see also *Clay v. Little Company of Mary Hospital*, 660 N.E. 2d 123 (Ill. Ct. App. 1995); *Emmett v. Eastern Dispensary & Casualty Hospital*, 396 F. 2d 931 (D.C. Cir. 1967); *Parkson v. Central DuPage Hospital*, 435 N.E. 2d 140 (Ill. Ct. App. 1982).

[263] However, because the vast majority of states now grant statutory recognition to a patient's right of access, courts are less likely to become involved in enunciating legal precedent on this issue.

As covered entities under the Privacy Rule, health plans must permit the enrollee/subscriber access to PHI. In addition to the Privacy Rule, the NAIC Privacy Protection Model Act requires MCOs that are insurers to give enrollees access to information about themselves, as well as the chance to correct or object to the accuracy of the information.[264] Under ERISA, plan participants and their authorized representatives have the right to review documents used to support claim denials.[265] These documents include medical records used to justify the denial.[266] Finally, an MCO that is an ERISA plan fiduciary may have to provide plan participants access to healthcare information held by the MCO. The reasoning discussed above concerning the fiduciary qualities of the physician patient relationship can also be applied to the MCO participant relationship.[267]

Access, Uses, and Disclosures with the Patient's Authorization

The general rule is that one may not disclose an individual's health information except as permitted or required by law or with the individual's valid authorization. The Privacy Rule and the statutes or regulations of many states follow this rule, and require that, when uses or disclosures of health information are made pursuant to an authorization, the use or disclosure must be consistent with the authorization.[268] The Privacy Rule also describes circumstances in which a covered entity must give the patient an opportunity to agree or to object to a particular use or disclosure of his or her PHI,[269] and the rule describes situations in which no authorization is required at all.[270]

Privacy Rule Requirements for Authorizations

The Privacy Rule specifies the minimum information that the written authorization must contain, and permits covered entities to place addi-

---

[264] National Association of Insurance Commissioners, Insurance Information and Privacy Protection Model Act, Model #670-1, § 8.

[265] 29 C.F.R. § 2560.503-1(g).

[266] *Harless v. Research Institute of America*, 1 F. Supp. 2d 235 (2d Cir. 1998); *Groves v. Modified Retirement Plan*, 803 F. 2d 109 (3d Cir. 1986).

[267] Bogossian, "MCO's Protection."

[268] 45 C.F.R. § 164.508(a).

[269] See, generally, 45 C.F.R. § 164.510.

[270] See, generally, 45 C.F.R. § 164.512.

tional elements in their authorizations. The following are the minimum required elements of an authorization,[271] all of which must be in plain language:[272]

- A specific description of the information to be used or disclosed
- The identification of the person or persons, or the class of persons, authorized to make the requested use or disclosure
- The identification of the person or persons, or the class of persons, to whom the covered entity may make the use or disclosure
- A description of the purposes for the requested use or disclosure[273]
- A statement of the individual's right to revoke the authorization in writing[274]
- A statement concerning the ability or inability of the covered entity to condition treatment, payment, enrollment, or eligibility for benefits on whether the individual signs the authorization
- A statement notifying the individual of the potential that PHI disclosed pursuant to the authorization may be redisclosed by the recipient of the PHI, and thus would no longer be protected by the Privacy Rule
- An expiration date or an expiration event that relates to the individual or the requested use or disclosure[275]
- The signature of the individual, or the signature of the individual's representative and a description of the representative's authority, and the date signed

The Privacy Rule establishes special rules for compound authorizations and conditional authorizations. A conditional authorization is one that a covered entity requires before it will provide treatment,

---

[271] See 45 C.F.R. § 164.508.

[272] 45 C.F.R. § 164.508(c)(3).

[273] "At the request of the individual" is sufficient if the individual does not disclose the purpose. 45 C.F.R. § 164.508(c)(1)(iv).

[274] If the covered entity has included in its notice of privacy practices required by the Privacy Rule a description of any exceptions to the individual's right to revoke the authorization and the ways in which he or she may effect a revocation, the authorization must also contain a reference to the entity's notice. If the information is not in the notice, it must be included in the authorization. 45 C.F.R. § 164.508(c)(2)(i).

[275] The Privacy Rule permits researchers to use "end of the research study," "none," or similar language if the authorization is for the use or disclosure of PHI for research, including for the creation or maintenance of a research database or repository. 45 C.F.R. § 164.508(c)(1)(v).

payment, enrollment in a health plan, or eligibility for benefits.[276] A compound authorization is one that is combined with one or more other authorizations or permissions. The rule prohibits combining an authorization for the use or disclosure of PHI with any other consent or authorization, except for (1) an authorization for the use or disclosure of PHI for a research study, which may be combined with any other type of written permission; and (2) an unconditional authorization for a use or disclosure of psychotherapy notes, which may also be combined with any other type of written permission.[277] The rule also prohibits a covered entity from using a conditional authorization, unless one of three exceptions applies:

- A covered healthcare provider may condition research related treatment on the receipt of an authorization for the use or disclosure of PHI for such research
- Prior to an individual's enrollment in a health plan, the plan may condition enrollment or eligibility for benefits on the provision of an authorization if the plan meets the requirements set forth in the rule
- A covered entity may condition treatment on receipt of an authorization if the treatment is provided solely for the purpose of creating PHI for disclosure to a third party[278]

The Privacy Rule declares an authorization to be defective if its expiration date or event has passed or occurred, if it was improperly prepared, if the covered entity knows it was revoked, if it is a prohibited compound or conditional authorization, or if it contains any material information that is false.[279]

State Law Requirements for Authorizations

Some states have enacted statutes or adopted regulations that specify the elements that must be contained in an authorization for the use or disclosure of medical records. Maryland, for example, requires the patient's authorization to be written, dated, and signed by the patient or his or her authorized representative, and to:

---

[276] 45 C.F.R. § 164.508(b)(4).
[277] 45 C.F.R. § 164.508(b)(3).
[278] 45 C.F.R. § 164.508(b)(4).
[279] 45 C.F.R. § 164.508(b)(2).

- state the name of the healthcare provider;
- identify to whom the information is to be disclosed;
- state how long the authorization is valid (up to a year, except in cases involving criminal justice referrals and nursing home residents); and
- apply only to a record created by the provider, unless the authorization states in writing that a record received from another provider will be disclosed and that the other provider has not prohibited the disclosure.[280]

Maine has a similar but more detailed statute that tracks more closely the requirements of the Privacy Rule.[281] Texas requires an authorization that meets the requirements of the Privacy Rule to accompany any claim filed against a physician or healthcare provider for medical malpractice.[282]

State laws that require more information in an authorization than is required by the Privacy Rule should not be preempted by HIPAA, because they give the individual greater rights with respect to the protection of their PHI. With respect to healthcare providers, practitioners, and other organizations that are subject to the Privacy Rule, state laws that require fewer elements than those specified in the rule will likely be preempted. With the help of qualified legal counsel, covered healthcare organizations should carefully analyze the authorization requirements of their state laws against those of the Privacy Rule to determine what they must include in authorizations for use or disclosure of PHI.

Before a healthcare organization provides third party access with the patient's authorization, the organization may take reasonable precautions to verify the authority of the person seeking the information. Some state statutes specifically authorize hospitals to take these measures.[283] Courts also have recognized a hospital's right to verify the validity of a patient's authorization. In one case, a state appeals court held that a hospital records clerk properly refused to release certain files on the basis of a signed authorization form containing alterations that were unacceptable under hospital records policy.[284] On the other hand, a hospital will

---

[280] Md. Code Ann. § 4-303.
[281] Me. Rev. State tit. 22, § 1711C.3; see also Tex. Health & Safety Code § 241.152; Wash. Rev. Code § 70.20.030; Cal. Civ. Code § 56.11.
[282] Tex. Civ. Prac. & Rem. Code § 74.052.
[283] See, e.g., Cal. Health & Safety Code § 123110(d).
[284] *Thurman v. Crawford*, 652 S.W. 2d 240, 242 (Mo. Ct. App. 1983).

be liable under state law[285] and the Privacy Rule[286] for unreasonably restricting access to medical records, because such action would be tantamount to a refusal to release the records.

Determining who is the patient's representative for purposes of accessing records also can generate difficulties. The Privacy Rule provides that state or other applicable law governs the issue of who qualifies as an adult's or emancipated minor's personal representative.[287] If, under applicable law, a person has authority to act on behalf of an individual who is an adult or an emancipated minor in making decisions related to health care, a covered entity must treat such person as a personal representative with respect to PHI relevant to such personal representation.[288] As the following case illustrates, however, determining who qualifies under state law may be challenging. In *Emmett v. Eastern Dispensary & Casualty Hospital*, the son of a deceased patient requested to see his father's medical record in order to bring a wrongful death action against the hospital.[289] However, the hospital refused to release the records because the son was not the father's administrator, and therefore not the father's legal representative. The court ruled that, although the decedent's proper legal representative is the only person authorized to bring a suit for wrongful death, the purpose of such a suit is to benefit the spouse and next of kin. Therefore, the court concluded, the hospital's duty of disclosure to the patient extended to the patient's son, his only surviving relative and next of kin.

Notwithstanding state law, however, the Privacy Rule permits covered entities to elect not to recognize the authority of a person to act as the patient's representative if the covered entity has a reasonable belief that the patient has been, or may be, subjected to domestic violence, abuse, or neglect by that person, or if treating that person as the patient's representative could endanger the patient. In such a case, the covered entity, in the exercise of its professional judgment, may decide that recognizing that person as the representative would not

---

[285] *Thurman v. Crawford. Emmett v. Eastern Dispensary & Casualty Hospital.* Minn. Stat. § 144.335(1)(a); Cal. Health & Safety Code § 123110(a); see also N.Y. Pub. Health Law § 17 (release of medical records) and N.Y. Pub. Health Law § 18 (access to patient information).

[286] 45 C.F.R. § 160.506.

[287] 45 C.F.R. § 164.502(g)(2); see also 65 Fed. Reg. 82633 (Dec. 28, 2000).

[288] 45 C.F.R. § 164.502(g)(2).

[289] *Emmett v. Eastern Dispensary & Casualty Hospital.*

be in the patient's best interest.[290] In exercising its professional judgment in this situation, covered entities must act as a prudent organization or individual provider would under the same or similar circumstances.

Revocation of Authorizations

The Privacy Rule permits an individual at any time to revoke an authorization that he or she has given in accordance with the rule, provided the revocation is written. The requirement that the revocation be in writing can be misleading however. For a revocation to be effective with respect to a covered entity, the entity must have knowledge of the revocation. If a covered entity has knowledge of a revocation, it must, "to the greatest extent practical," cease using or disclosing the PHI described in the authorization. But the covered entity's knowledge of a revocation need not come directly from a written document. For example, an individual might give a government agency an authorization for the agency to obtain PHI from healthcare providers who have treated the individual. If the individual later revokes that authorization in writing, but neither the individual nor the government agency informs the individual's healthcare providers, the providers would not have knowledge of the revocation, and thus would not be required to comply with it. If the individual telephoned one of the providers and advised him or her of the revocation, however, that provider would have knowledge of the revocation given in writing to the agency, and thus would have to comply with the revocation.

The practical course for a covered entity to follow, therefore, is to make a reasonable inquiry into any notice of revocation of any authorization upon which the entity wishes to rely for the use or disclosure of PHI. Knowledge becomes a burden, and a covered entity that learns in any manner of a possible revocation would be well advised to make a reasonable effort to determine whether the patient issued a valid revocation, and, if so, to honor it.

The revocation provisions of the Privacy Rule have one exception for healthcare settings: an authorization is irrevocable to the extent that a covered entity has taken action in reliance upon it. Thus, a covered entity is not required to retrieve PHI that had been disclosed before the

---

[290] 45 C.F.R. § 164.502(g)(5).

valid authorization was revoked, and its use of PHI in accordance with that authorization before the revocation does not become invalid when the patient revokes the authorization.

States have also adopted statutes governing how an individual may revoke an authorization. For example, Maine permits an individual to revoke his or her authorization at any time—either in a signed writing; an electronic communication bearing the individual's unique identifier and the date; or orally, in which case the provider must record receipt of the oral revocation and the date. In addition, the revocation must be retained in the individual's healthcare information.[291] Maryland requires a revocation to be written, and makes the revocation effective when the provider receives it.[292] Both states make clear that actions taken by a provider in reliance on an authorization the patient revoked are not affected by the revocation. These laws will apply to healthcare organizations and practitioners who are not subject to the Privacy Rule, and will apply to HIPAA covered entities to the extent that the laws have not been preempted by the rule.

Access by Family and Friends

Healthcare providers are frequently asked for health information by the family and friends of their patients. Under the general rule of protecting health information confidentiality, providers would not be able to release the information without patient authorization. The Privacy Rule contains an exception to the general rule, however, and permits, under certain circumstances, covered entities to disclose a patient's PHI to his or her relative, friend, or designated representative (for example, spouse, roommate, boyfriend, colleague, neighbor). However, the PHI must be directly relevant to the recipient's involvement in the patient's health care or payment for health care.[293]

This includes using PHI to find the patient's relative, friend, or representative, and to notify the person of the patient's location, general condition, or death.[294] For example, a hospital might use the patient's

---

[291] Me. Rev. Stat. tit. 22, § 1711-C.5; see also Wash. Rev. Code § 70.20.040; Cal. Civ. Code § 56.15.
[292] Md. Code Ann. § 4-303(d).
[293] 45 C.F.R. § 164.510(b)(1).
[294] 45 C.F.R. § 164.510(b)(1)(ii).

medical records information to notify his family that he had been admitted from the emergency room following a heart attack.

The covered entity may make these disclosures, however, only if the patient agrees to them or, if the patient is able to express his or her wishes, is given an opportunity to object to the disclosures and does not object. If the patient is unable to give permission, and the provider exercises professional judgment to determine from the circumstances that the patient does not object, the provider may disclose information.[295] For example, if a roommate brings a confused and ill patient to the emergency room, the hospital could reasonably infer that the patient would not object to the release of his or her general condition to the roommate. In any case in which the patient is not present or is unable to express his or her wishes, the covered entity may release to the relative, friend, or representative only information that is directly relevant to that person's involvement in the patient's care.[296] For example, releasing past medical history not pertinent to the patient's current illness would be prohibited.

When the Privacy Rule was proposed, many expressed concern that the regulations ignored common practice and would prevent a relative from collecting prescriptions from a pharmacy on the patient's behalf. In fact, the final regulations state that a covered entity may exercise its judgment to permit such practices,[297] and DHHS clarified that it did not intend to prohibit a person from picking up prescriptions, X-rays, or medical equipment on the patient's behalf.[298]

The regulations also permit a covered entity to disclose PHI to government or private disaster relief organizations (for example, the American Red Cross) to enable them to carry out their disaster relief activities.[299] For example, a disaster relief organization might need the information to notify family of a patient's condition or to assist the family in obtaining necessary medical care. The provider is expected to exercise its professional judgment in determining that such disclosures are in the patient's best interest. (See the discussion concerning the exercise of professional judgment in this chapter.)

---

[295] 45 C.F.R. § 164.510(b)(2).
[296] 45 C.F.R. § 164.510(b)(3).
[297] 45 C.F.R. § 164.510(b)(3).
[298] Department of Health and Human Services, *First Guidance*, 10.
[299] 45 C.F.R. § 160.510(b)(4).

Facility Directories

The Privacy Rule permits healthcare providers to use PHI to create directories of patients in their facilities. But the provider must inform the patient of its policies concerning directory information, and must give the patient the opportunity to opt out of the directory or to restrict the amount of his or her information in the directory. This notice and opt out or restriction may be oral or written.[300]

Unless the patient objects, the directory may include the patient's name, location in the facility, general condition (for example, good, fair, stable, critical, and so on), and religious affiliation.[301] The provider may disclose all the directory information to clergy, and all the information except religious affiliation to anyone who asks for the patient by name.[302] Providers may disclose religious affiliation only to clergy,[303] and may release directory information to a member of the clergy, even if the clergyman does not request the patient's information by name.[304] However, the Privacy Rule does not require a covered entity to inquire concerning a patient's religious affiliation, and does not require an individual to supply that information; the Rule does not even require a covered provider to maintain a registry.[305] For example, some providers maintain strict restrictions on the use of directory information for celebrity patients or others in whom news media would likely be interested. (See the discussion of celebrity patient records in Chapter 8.)

If the patient is incapacitated or is being treated in an emergency, and thus is unable to express his or her wishes concerning directory information, the provider may release directory information if the provider exercises its professional judgment to determine that the release is in the patient's best interest. If the patient has objected in the past to release of directory information, the provider should not disclose the information until the patient has had a chance to reconsider. When the patient is awake and aware, the provider must give him or her an opportunity to opt out of the directory or restrict the information in the directory.[306] A patient may express his or her objection orally or in writing.[307]

---

[300] 45 C.F.R. § 164.510(a).
[301] 45 C.F.R. § 164.510(a)(1)(i).
[302] 45 C.F.R. § 164.510(a)(1)(ii)(B).
[303] 45 C.F.R. § 164.510(a)(1)(ii)(A).
[304] 65 Fed. Reg. 82522 (Dec. 20, 2000).
[305] Ibid.
[306] 45 C.F.R. § 164.510(a)(2) and (3).
[307] 65 Fed. Reg. 82522 (Dec. 20, 2000).

Records of Minors

Emancipated Minors

The Privacy Rule treats adults and emancipated minors alike, and gives to emancipated minors the same authority over their PHI that adults have.[308] Whether a minor is emancipated will be determined by applicable state law. (See Chapter 5 for a discussion of what constitutes emancipation.)

Unemancipated Minors

Generally, a healthcare organization or provider may disclose the medical record of an unemancipated minor patient only with authorization from one of the parents of that individual. Parents typically are allowed access to such records on behalf of an unemancipated minor patient, and the Privacy Rule generally upholds this position.[309] If a guardian has been appointed to act in the child's behalf, only the guardian may access the patient's records and authorize release of information to others.

With respect to the use or disclosure of an unemancipated minor's PHI, the Privacy Rule requires covered entities to recognize the authority of a person who, under applicable state law, is qualified as the personal representative of that minor in making decisions related to health care.[310] In most cases, the person will be the minor's parent and will be able to exercise the minor's rights with respect to PHI. To this general rule, the Privacy Rule contains three exceptions:

- State or other law does not require the consent of a parent or other person before the minor can obtain a particular healthcare service and the minor consents to the service. For example, a state law may authorize an adolescent to obtain drug abuse treatment without parental consent and the adolescent alone consents to the treatment.
- A court determines, or other law authorizes, someone other than the parent to make treatment decisions for a minor. For example, a court will sometimes grant to someone other than the parent the authority to make healthcare decisions for a minor. In some cases, the court will reserve that authority to itself.

---

[308] 45 C.F.R. § 160.103. See 65 Fed. Reg. 82634 (Dec. 28, 2000).
[309] See 45 C.F.R. § 164.502(g)(3).
[310] 45 C.F.R. § 164.502(g)(3)(i).

- A parent or guardian agrees to a confidential relationship between the minor and a healthcare provider with respect to a healthcare service. For example, a physician might ask the parent of an adolescent whether the physician may talk with the child confidentially about a health problem, and the parent agrees. [311]

Clearly, the drafters of the Privacy Rule struggled with whether the rule should permit disclosure of PHI concerning sensitive healthcare services to minors. In addition to the complex rules described above, the Privacy Rule contains a provision that permits a covered entity to disclose an unemancipated minor's PHI to his or her parent or guardian if such disclosure is permitted by state or other law, if the parent or guardian qualifies under the Privacy Rule as the minor's representative, or if state or other law permits access to the PHI. If state or other law prohibits disclosing the minor's PHI to a parent or guardian, however, a covered entity may choose to disclose or to deny disclosure of the PHI to the parent or guardian. The decision of whether to disclose the minor's PHI in these circumstances must be made by a licensed healthcare professional in the exercise of professional judgment.[312]

The interplay of the Privacy Rule and applicable state law is important here. In many instances, it will be difficult to weave state law and the Privacy Rule into a coherent rule without a careful preemption analysis of the state law.

A number of state statutes governing access to medical records include specific directions about disclosing the records of a minor. For example, Minnesota defines the term "patient" to include a parent or guardian of a minor, and then directs each hospital to provide copies of the record to the "patient" upon request.[313] The California statute has separate provisions dealing with access to a minor's records and disclosure of such records to third parties.[314] The provision on access provides that any adult patient, any minor patient authorized by law to consent

---

[311] 45 C.F.R § 164.502(g)(3)(i)(A) through (C). See also Department of Health and Human Services, *Standards for Privacy*, 32, for a good explanation of the Privacy Rule's complex provisions concerning a minor's PHI.

[312] 45 C.F.R. § 164.502(g)(ii).

[313] Minn. Stat. § 144.335(1)(a).

[314] Cal. Health & Safety Code § 123110(a); see also N.Y. Pub. Health Law § 17 (release of medical records) and N.Y. Pub. Health Law § 18 (access to patient information).

to treatment, and any patient representative shall be entitled to inspect patient records upon written notice and payment of reasonable fees. However, a minor patient shall be entitled to inspect only records pertaining to health care of the type for which the minor may lawfully consent.

Notwithstanding the general right of access granted to a minor's representative under California law, a representative may not access the minor's records if the minor has a right of inspection under the general rule of patient access by virtue of his or her authority to consent to the type of medical treatment described in the record.[315] In addition, a healthcare provider may deny access to a minor's representative if the healthcare provider determines that access would have a detrimental effect on the provider's professional relationship with the minor.[316] The California statute defines "representative" as a parent or guardian of a minor who is a patient or former patient.[317]

A minor patient may authorize release of medical information to third parties if the information was obtained during the course of providing healthcare services to which the minor lawfully could consent under other provisions of the law.[318] In all other cases, the minor's legal representative must consent.[319]

The New York law on access to a minor's record is similar to California's; however, New York allows the provider to deny access where release of information would have a detrimental effect on an infant's relationship with parents or guardian.[320] Further, a minor patient's records involving abortion or venereal disease never can be released to the parent or guardian.[321] In all other cases, the parent or guardian can authorize release to third parties.

---

[315] Cal. Health & Safety Code § 123115(a)(2).
[316] Ibid. See *In re Daniel C.H.*, 269 Cal. Rptr. 624 (Ct. App. 1990), in which the court applied this provision to deny a parent access to a minor child's psychotherapy records. The parent contended that he was entitled to access the child's confidential communications because, as a parent, he has the right to receive information concerning the medical condition of his child. The court ruled, however, that access would cause substantial harm to the child, who might refuse to be open with the therapist out of fear of disclosure to the parent.
[317] Cal. Health & Safety Code §§ 123105(c) through (e).
[318] Cal. Civ. Code § 56.11(c)(1).
[319] Cal. Civ. Code § 56.11(c)(2).
[320] N.Y. Pub. Health Law § 18(2)(c) and § 17.
[321] N.Y. Pub. Health Law § 17.

The statutes of many states simply are not clear on the question of parental or guardian access to a minor's records. Most statutes permit access with the consent of the patient,[322] or with the consent of the patient or his authorized representative.[323] In those states, healthcare organizations and providers should follow the general rule and obtain the authorization of the minor's parent before disclosing the patient's records to third parties. However, when the minor has the authority under state law to consent to medical treatment, the minor must give his or her consent to disclose this information, even to the minor's parents or legal guardians.

In this regard, healthcare organizations and providers must carefully examine the statute for the definitions of terms such as "patient" and "representative," because not all states define those terms in the same way. Moreover, the same state may provide one definition under the provisions on direct access, and another definition for disclosure to third parties.

Most importantly, a healthcare organization or provider treating or planning to treat a young person must double check the legal age for giving consent to the particular treatment involved. Although a "minor" in most states is a person under 18 years of age,[324] many jurisdictions create exceptions for certain types of medical treatment. For example, in California, a 12-year-old may consent to mental health treatment if the child presents a serious danger to self or others, or has been the victim of alleged incest or child abuse;[325] and an emancipated minor of any age lawfully can consent to any hospital, medical, or surgical care.[326] In Illinois, a 17-year-old can consent to a blood donation.[327]

Given the complexity of the Privacy Rule provisions governing use and disclosure of unemancipated minors' PHI, covered healthcare providers are well advised to develop effective policies and procedures to guide their employees and professional staffs concerning the health information of these minors.

---

[322] See, e.g., Colo. Rev. Stat. § 25-1-801(1)(a); Fla. Stat. Ann. § 395.3025(1); Haw. Rev. Stat. § 622-57.
[323] See, e.g., Me. Rev. Stat. Ann. tit. 22, § 1711; Tenn. Code Ann. § 68-11-304(a)(1).
[324] See, e.g., Cal. Fam. Code § 6500.
[325] Cal. Fam. Code § 6924(b).
[326] Cal. Fam. Code §§ 7002 and 7050.
[327] 210 Ill. Comp. Stat. Ann. § 15/1.

Access for Treatment, Payment, or Healthcare Operations

Access to PHI by the staff of a covered entity is controlled largely by the Privacy Rule, which permits an entity's use and disclosure of PHI for its own treatment, payment, or healthcare operations.[328] A covered entity may also disclose PHI for the treatment activities of a healthcare provider,[329] and for the payment activities of a healthcare provider or another covered entity.[330] Thus, the rule permits any staff of a healthcare provider to gain access to the patient's medical record without the patient's authorization, for the purpose of providing health care to the patient. The rule defines "treatment" broadly as

> the provision, coordination, or management of health care and related services by one or more health care providers, including the coordination or management of health care by a health care provider with a third party; consultation between health care providers relating to a patient; or the referral of a patient for health care from one health care provider to another.[331]

DHHS intended for the Privacy Rule to facilitate the normal exchange of health information by healthcare practitioners, and wished to avoid placing barriers that would impair an individual's access to health care or impede caregivers' ability to provide treatment effectively.[332] Thus, a hospital may use an individual's PHI to provide treatment to the individual and to consult with other healthcare providers about the individual's treatment. One physician may send a copy of a patient's medical records to a specialist physician with whom a consultation is necessary for the patient's treatment. Also, a physician may, without the patient's authorization, disclose PHI to a pharmacist as part of a prescription for a patient, because the disclosure is for treatment purposes.[333] When a healthcare provider discloses PHI for purposes of

---

[328] 45 C.F.R. § 164.506(c)(1).
[329] 45 C.F.R. § 164.506(c)(2).
[330] 45 C.F.R. § 164.506(c)(3).
[331] 45 C.F.R. § 164.501.
[332] See 65 Fed. Reg. 82626 (Dec. 28, 2000); Department of Health and Human Services, *Standards for Privacy*, 56.
[333] See, generally, Department of Health and Human Services, *Standards for Privacy*, 56.

treating a patient, a recipient may be a provider who is not covered by the Privacy Rule.[334] DHHS also relies upon various codes of professional ethics to ensure that exchanges of PHI between healthcare providers respect the patient's confidentiality.

The business and professional staffs of a covered entity may also use and disclose PHI for the entity's own payment activities. The Privacy Rule defines "payment" to include virtually all functions needed to bill for and obtain payment for services rendered by health plans and healthcare providers, and to determine eligibility or coverage by a health plan.[335] Payment includes billing, claims management, collection activities, reinsurance payments, utilization review activities, disclosures to consumer reporting agencies of certain elements of PHI, and related healthcare data processing. Thus, a healthcare provider may disclose a patient's PHI as part of a claim to a health insurance plan for payment for treatment services provided to the patient, or may communicate with the spouse of a patient for the purpose of obtaining payment. Members of a covered entity who must use or disclose PHI for these activities must restrict their use or disclosure to these legitimate purposes.

A covered entity may also use PHI for its own healthcare operations. The Privacy Rule defines "health care operations" very broadly to include the management and operational activities of an organization or practice—such as quality improvement activities; assessing the competence or qualifications of healthcare professionals; training programs; accreditation, certification, licensing, and credentialing activities; underwriting, premium rating, and other activities relating to the creation, renewal, or replacement of health insurance or health benefits; provision of professional services, such legal, auditing, business consulting, and planning; business management and general administrative activities; and the resolution of internal grievances. The sale or transfer to, or the merger of, all or parts of one covered entity with another covered entity or with an organization that will become a covered entity at the conclusion of the transaction is also considered to be healthcare operations. But note that when a covered entity makes reports to consumer credit reporting agencies, the information it may disclose is limited to the name and address of the provider or health plan making the report, and to the following data about the individual:

[334] Ibid.
[335] 45 C.F.R. § 164.501.

name and address, date of birth, Social Security number, payment history, and account number.[336] The covered entity may make these reports itself or through a third party functioning as a business associate. (See the discussion of business associates later in this chapter.)[337]

The Privacy Rule also permits a covered entity to make limited disclosures of PHI to others for their healthcare payment operations. The applicable provisions of the rule are complicated, but they are designed to permit the types of interactions among healthcare providers and payers that have become accepted practice over the years and that are necessary for the efficient operation of the healthcare industry. Under the rule, a covered entity may disclose PHI to another covered entity or to any healthcare provider (whether or not it is covered by the Privacy Rule) for the payment activities of the recipient.[338] Thus, a physician may give a patient's health plan coverage information to a laboratory that needs the information to bill for services the laboratory provided to the physician with respect to the patient. Likewise, a hospital may give a patient's payment information to an ambulance company that transported the patient to the hospital so that the company is able to bill for its treatment services.[339]

The Privacy Rule is more restrictive with respect to a covered entity's disclosures to other covered entities for their healthcare operations. Such disclosures are permitted only if each of the disclosing and recipient entities has or had a relationship with the patient, if the patient's PHI pertains to that relationship, and if the disclosure is for a quality related healthcare operations activity (such as a quality improvement program) or for the purpose of fraud and abuse detection or compliance.[340] For example, the Privacy Rule would permit a hospital's disclosure of a patient's PHI to the quality assurance department of a nursing home to which the hospital transferred the patient. Also, if two covered entities participate in an OHCA, one entity may disclose PHI to another for any joint healthcare operations conducted by the OHCA.[341] Thus, where a hospital and its independent medical staff have formed an OHCA, the hospital may disclose patients' PHI to a

---

[336] Ibid.
[337] Ibid.
[338] 45 C.F.R. § 164.506(c)(3).
[339] Department of Health and Human Services, *Standards for Privacy*, 56.
[340] 45 C.F.R. § 164.506(c)(4).
[341] 45 C.F.R. § 164.506(c)(5).

physician staff member who participates in the hospital's training of medical students. The hospital and the physician are covered entities participating in an OHCA, and medical education is a joint healthcare operation. (See the discussion of OHCAs earlier in this chapter.)

State law and standards promulgated by accreditation agencies such as the Joint Commission permit disclosure of confidential patient information under certain conditions. Several state statutes permit the release, without patient authorization, of confidential patient information to qualified personnel for the purpose of conducting audits, program evaluations, official surveys, education, and quality control activities.[342] In addition, the Joint Commission states says that clinical and administrative data can be aggregated and analyzed to support decisions, track overtime trends, make comparisons within the organization and among organizations, and improve performance.[343] These activities would be permissible under the Privacy Rule.

Some state statutes provide that hospital or healthcare organization staff members can have access to patient records. In most states, hospital licensing regulations permit access to patient records by "authorized" personnel or persons granted access by hospital policy for purposes related to the patient's care.[344] The hospital then is made responsible for ensuring that only authorized persons review the records.[345] Some states, such as Rhode Island, permit qualified personnel and healthcare providers within the system to have access to medical records for the purpose of coordinating care.[346] State law may also permit release of patient information for administrative reasons, such as for billing purposes.[347] Finally, the confidentiality statutes in many states expressly permit access to patient records by healthcare providers and others for purposes of providing diagnosis or treatment and during medical emergencies.[348]

---

[342] See, e.g., R.I. Gen. Laws § 5-37.3-4(b)(3); Cal. Civ. Code § 56.10.

[343] Joint Commission, *1997 Hospital Accreditation Manual*, Standard IM.8 through IM 8.1.12; Joint Commission, 1997 Accreditation Manual for Preferred Provider Organizations, Standard IM.4 through IM 4.3.

[344] See, e.g., Cal. Civ. Code § 56.10(c)(1); Fla. Stat. Ann. § 395.3025(4)(a); Wis. Stat. Ann. § 146.82(2).

[345] See, e.g., 902 Ky. Admin. Regs. 20:016(11)(C)(1); Mo. Code Regs. Ann. tit. 19, § 30-20.0213(D)(7).

[346] R.I. Gen. Laws § 5-37.3-4(b)(5).

[347] See, e.g., Wis. Stat. Ann. §§ 146.82(2) and (3).

[348] See, e.g., Cal. Civ. Code § 56.10(c)(1); Fla. Stat. Ann. § 395.3025(4)(a); R.I. Gen Laws § 5-37.3-4(b)(1).

State laws such as these, which permit healthcare practitioners to use and disclose PHI for the patient's treatment, are generally consistent with the Privacy Rule. But, as with all state laws that affect health information, healthcare providers must use caution in applying state laws for which a preemption analysis has not been conducted. (See the discussion of HIPAA preemption of state laws earlier in this chapter.)

Access to certain patients' records is expressly governed by some state and federal laws. For example, there are special federal statutes and regulations on access to certain alcohol or drug abuse treatment records (discussed later in this chapter). These provide for the general confidentiality of drug and alcohol patients' records, with an exception for disclosure to persons in connection with their duties to provide diagnosis, treatment, or referral for treatment of abuse.[349] There also is a statutory exception to confidentiality for release of patient records information during a bona fide medical emergency.[350]

Some states also address alcohol and drug abuse patient records. These laws typically provide an exception to the general ban on disclosure of such records for the exchange of information relating to the patient's treatment among qualified personnel involved in the treatment.[351] Other states incorporate the federal alcohol and drug abuse regulations directly into their own laws.[352]

Some states have special laws on staff access to records of mental health patients[353] and AIDS patients.[354] Not all staff members have access to those types of records. Again, the laws vary from state to state, and healthcare organizations should consult the particular rules applicable to them.

Accreditation organizations such as the Joint Commission and the NCQA require healthcare and physician organizations to be especially careful about maintaining the confidentiality of sensitive information.[355] In its Management of Information Standards, the Joint

---

[349] 42 C.F.R. § 2.12(c)(3).

[350] 42 U.S.C. § 290dd-2(b)(2)(A); 38 U.S.C. § 7332(b)(2)(A).

[351] See, e.g., Wis. Stat. Ann. § 51.30(4).

[352] See, e.g., Md. Code Ann., Health-Gen., § 8-601(c).

[353] Wash. Rev. Code Ann. § 71.05.390.

[354] See, e.g., Haw. Rev. Stat. § 325-101.

[355] See Joint Commission, *1997 Hospital Accreditation Manual,* Intent of Standard IM.2 through IM.2.3; Joint Commission, *1997 Accreditation Manual for Preferred Provider Organizations,* Intent of Standard IM.2; Joint Commission, *1996–1997 Comprehensive Accreditation Manual for Health Care Networks,* Standard IM.2 through IM.2.3.

Commission recognizes that some data are more sensitive and require a higher level of confidentiality.[356]

Healthcare organizations must carefully develop policies and procedures for staff members to follow to obtain access to PHI. The Privacy Rule requires covered entities to develop and implement policies that are designed to comply with the provisions of the rule. (See discussion of HIPAA administrative requirements later in this chapter.) The organization should next decide who has access to what information. Healthcare organizations should consider allowing access on a need-to-know basis. Access may differ depending upon the staff member's job title, responsibilities, and function. For example, physicians do not need to access information on all patients; their access should be limited to the patients that they are treating. Certain parts of the medical record may be very sensitive and require extra protection of the patient's privacy. A healthcare organization might choose to store sensitive portions of the medical record, such as psychiatric records, in a separate location.[357] (See also the discussion of information security in Chapter 13.)

Access by Employers

Recognizing that employers have responsibilities under state and federal laws that require them to use or disclose PHI (for example, reports related to safety in the workplace), the Privacy Rule permits certain disclosures of information to an employer about one of its employees. However, the person making the disclosures must be a healthcare provider, such as a plant physician, who is engaged by an employer to provide care to its employees. The disclosures can be only for the following purposes, and the provider must notify the patient that his or her PHI will be disclosed to the employer for these purposes.

* To conduct medical surveillance of the workplace or to determine whether an individual has a work related illness or injury (the information disclosed must be limited to findings concerning at least one of these purposes, however)

---

[356] Joint Commission, *1995 Management of Information Standards*, 40–41. The Management of Information Standards, which currently are being phased in, are directed to hospitals and healthcare networks.

[357] Ibid., 40–45.

- To fulfill the employer's obligations under state or federal occupational health, mine safety, or similar laws[358]

The Privacy Rule codifies a legal fiction that employers are distinct from the group health plans that they offer to employees. A group health plan, or an HMO or insurer with respect to that group health plan, generally may not permit access to employee PHI by the plan sponsor (that is, the employer) unless permitted by the Privacy Rule.[359] Notwithstanding this general prohibition, and recognizing a plan sponsor's legitimate need for nonclinical PHI about its employees in limited situations, the Privacy Rule permits plan sponsors to access PHI about employees for specified purposes. For example, a plan sponsor may need to access PHI for plan administration purposes,[360] or for obtaining premium bids from HMOs or insurers for providing insurance coverage under the group health plan.[361] Group health plans may not disclose PHI to the plan sponsor for the purpose of employment related actions or decisions, such as terminating employees with high cost sicknesses.[362] Given the acute sensitivity surrounding this issue, and the need in some cases to amend plan documents prior to disclosure, a records administrator should consult legal counsel prior to granting an employer access to employee PHI.

Mental Health Records

Recognizing the sensitivity of health information concerning mental health treatment, the Privacy Rule and many state laws provide special rules for the use or disclosure of mental health treatment information. The Privacy Rule differentiates between psychotherapy notes and other health information generated in connection with mental health treatments. It establishes additional protections for psychotherapy notes, but treats other mental health treatment information as PHI

---

[358] 45 C.F.R. § 164.512(b)(1)(v).
[359] See generally, 45 C.F.R. § 164.504(f).
[360] The term "plan administration" means administration functions performed by the plan sponsor of a group health plan on behalf of the group health plan, and excludes functions performed by the plan sponsor in connection with any other benefit or benefit plan of the plan sponsor. 45 C.F.R. § 164.504(a).
[361] 45 C.F.R. § 164.504(f)(1)(ii)(A).
[362] 45 C.F.R. § 164.504(f)(3)(iv).

that is subject to the rule's general protections of confidentiality and to the exceptions that permit uses and disclosures for certain purposes.

"Psychotherapy notes" are a mental health professional's notes concerning his or her counseling session with an individual or group. These notes are kept separate from the medical record. The definition excludes prescription records and summaries of diagnosis, functional status, treatment plans, symptoms, prognosis, and progress, all typically found in the patient's medical records.[363] The Privacy Rule requires a covered entity to obtain the authorization of the patient for the use or disclosure of psychotherapy notes, unless the use or disclosure falls into one of the following exceptions:[364]

- The use of the notes by their originator for treatment purposes
- A covered entity's use or disclosure for its own training of mental health personnel under supervision or to defend itself against a legal proceeding brought by the patient
- Pursuant to a request by the Secretary of DHHS for compliance purposes
- When required by law
- Health oversight activities with respect to the originator of the notes
- When required by a coroner or medical examiner
- When necessary to protect the health or safety of a person or the public

Although the Privacy Rule permits individuals to obtain access to their PHI, it provides an exception for psychotherapy notes. A covered entity, including the physician who created them, is not required to disclose the notes to the patient.[365] In addition, covered entities may choose not to disclose mental health records to an individual if they determine that granting access may cause the patient or another person serious harm. This rule applies in three situations:[366]

- When a licensed healthcare professional determines that access is reasonably likely to endanger the life or physical safety of the patient or another person

---

[363] 45 C.F.R. § 164.501.
[364] 45 C.F.R. § 164.508(a)(2).
[365] 45 C.F.R. § 164.524(a)(1)(i).
[366] 45 C.F.R. § 164.524(a)(3).

- When the PHI contains a reference to another person (other than another healthcare provider), and the covered entity determines that access is reasonably likely to cause substantial harm to the other person
- When the access is requested by the patient's personal representative, and a licensed healthcare professional determines that access is reasonably likely to cause substantial harm to the patient or another person

The determinations required for the application of these exceptions to the general access rule must be made in the exercise of professional judgment. (See the discussion of the application of professional judgment earlier in this chapter.) These limited circumstances in which an individual may be denied access to mental health records were intentionally designed into the Privacy Rule as a reflection of DHHS's belief that more was to be gained by giving an individual greater access to his or her PHI than was permitted in many state laws.[367]

In some states, the rules on access to the medical records of mental health patients differ from those applicable to medical records generally. In past years, mental health patients were denied access to their medical records even where non-mental health patients in the same jurisdiction had such a right. It was widely believed that authorizing psychiatric patients to review their records would be injurious to their health. The Privacy Rule has preempted these laws to the extent that they prevent an individual from gaining access to his or her mental health treatment information, other than psychotherapy notes. To the extent that state laws give additional protection or greater access to mental health records, HIPAA will not preempt, and healthcare providers should follow the more stringent state laws.

For example, in New Jersey, the statute governing psychiatric patients makes confidential all records that directly or indirectly identify an individual who is receiving or has received mental health services, except if the person or legal guardian consents.[368] Such a provision, granting the patient a statutory right to records confidentiality, can be construed to create a corresponding implied right of access for the patient. A federal trial court has ruled that this provision allows patients

---

[367] See 65 Fed. Reg. 82733 (Dec. 20, 2000).
[368] N.J. Stat. Ann. § 30:4-24.3.

confined in mental institutions to obtain access to all of their records maintained by the state, even if their guardians do not consent to disclosure, unless the state can challenge the patients' capacity to give informed consent.[369]

State legislation in some jurisdictions allows mental health patients to petition a court to seal the records of treatment. Under New York legislation, for example, patients must demonstrate by competent medical evidence that they are not currently suffering from mental illness, that they have not received inpatient services for treatment of mental illness for a period of three years, and that the interests of both the petitioners and society would be served best by sealing the records.[370] One court has ruled that society has an interest in sealing mental health records to remove the barriers that would prevent a former psychiatric patient from participating fully in society without fear of stigma or discrimination.[371] In the absence of a statutory right to expunge mental health records, some courts have authorized such action for records that result from an illegal commitment or illegal involuntary examination proceeding involving falsehood or perjury.[372]

Under the Privacy Rule and most state laws, a person authorized by a competent patient may obtain access to that patient's records, including those relating to mental health treatment but excluding psychotherapy notes. If a patient is incompetent, the duly authorized legal guardian may access the records in the same manner as a competent patient.[373] However, the healthcare organization or provider should request to see the appropriate authorization before permitting access by a person who claims to be acting on behalf of an incompetent patient. Under state law, a guardian who has been appointed for a specific purpose does not necessarily have the authority to review an incompetent patient's records.[374] The Privacy Rule defers to state laws for the determination of the qualifications of a person to act as a personal representative for purposes of granting authority to use or disclose PHI.

Similarly, where an incompetent patient has a guardian assigned by a court to act in the person's best interests, the healthcare organization

---

[369] *Bonnie S. v. Altman*, 683 F. Supp. 100 (D.N.J. 1988).

[370] N.Y. Mental Hyg. Law § 33.14(a)(1) and (b).

[371] *Smith v. Butler Hospital*, 544 N.Y.S. 2d 711 (Sup. Ct. 1989).

[372] *Johnston v. State*, 466 So. 2d 413 (Fla. Dist. Ct. App. 1985), citing *Wolfe v. Beal*, 384 A. 2d 1187 (Pa. 1978).

[373] 45 C.F.R. § 164.502(g)(2). See also *Gaertner v. State*, 187 N.W. 2d 429 (Mich. 1971).

[374] See, e.g., *In re Patarino*, 142 N.Y.S. 2d 891 (Ct. Cl. 1955).

or provider should be careful not to release the records to other persons associated with the patient. In one case, for example,[375] the mother of an involuntarily committed minor requested access to records pertaining to her daughter's treatment, but the child's court appointed guardian objected. The mother alleged, but could not prove, that decisions made by the hospital were not in the best interests of her daughter. The court denied the mother's request, emphasizing that one purpose of appointing a guardian is to protect the minor from parental efforts to terminate treatment for reasons unrelated to the best interests of the child.[376] (See also the discussion of access to the records of minors earlier in this chapter.)

Alcohol and Drug Abuse Patient Records

Provisions in the Public Health Service Act address access to the records of drug or alcohol abuse patients.[377] Under these provisions, records of the "identity, diagnosis, prognosis, or treatment" of any patient maintained in connection with the performance of any educational, training, treatment, rehabilitative, or research program concerning drug or alcohol abuse may not be disclosed except for certain purposes and under certain circumstances.[378] Any person or program that releases information in violation of the act is subject to criminal fines.[379]

The Secretary of DHHS has promulgated regulations on access to records of alcohol and drug abuse patients covered by the act.[380] The

---

[375] *In re J.C.G.*, 366 A. 2d 733 (N.J. Hudson County Ct. 1976).

[376] Cases involving a guardian purportedly acting on behalf of a mental-health patient should be distinguished, however, from those involving an "interested person" who may have independent rights under state law to participate in mental-health proceedings affecting a patient. See, e.g., *In re Wollan*, 390 N.W. 2d 839 (Minn. Ct. App. 1986), where the court granted records access to the sister of a mentally ill and dangerous patient as an "interested person" entitled to notification of any change in the patient's status and the right to request review of the change of status under Minnesota law. See also *In re New York News, Inc.*, 503 N.Y.S. 2d 714 (1986), where the court granted a newspaper access to sealed mental-health records as a party "properly interested" in such records under applicable New York law.

[377] Originally enacted as the Drug Abuse Prevention, Treatment, and Rehabilitation Act. See, generally 21 U.S.C. §§ 1101 through 1800 and the Comprehensive Alcohol Abuse and Alcoholism Prevention, Treatment, and Rehabilitation Act, 42 U.S.C. §§ 4541 through 4594.

[378] 42 U.S.C. § 290dd-2(a).

[379] 42 U.S.C. § 290dd-2(f).

[380] The regulations are codified at 42 C.F.R. §§ 2.1 through 2.67.

regulations, like the statutes, generally prohibit disclosure of certain types of information about an alcohol or drug abuse patient except as specifically authorized.[381]

Virtually every alcohol and/or drug abuse treatment center is subject to the act and the DHHS regulations. Under the regulations, any facility operating a "program" that is "federally assisted" falls within the scope of the act.[382] "Federal assistance" is defined broadly to include any program that receives a state or municipal grant if the state or local government in turn has received any unrestricted grants or funds from the federal government.[383] If contributions to a program are deductible under federal income tax law, the program is regarded as a recipient of federal financial assistance. Few programs are totally privately funded, receive no tax deductions for contributions, and/or are neither licensed nor regulated by the federal government. Accordingly, almost every drug or alcohol abuse program is governed by the act.[384]

"Program" refers to an individual, partnership, corporation, governmental agency, or other legal entity that holds itself out, in whole or part, as providing—and does provide—alcohol or drug abuse diagnosis, treatment, or referral for treatment. For a general medical care facility or any part of it to qualify as a "program," the facility must have an identified unit that provides such services, or medical personnel whose primary function is to provide such services and who are identified as providers of such services.[385] The terms "diagnosis," "treatment," "alcohol abuse," and "drug abuse" are defined specifically in the regulations.[386]

The provisions for the release of information apply only if an individual is a "patient" under the act. The regulations define "patient" as

---

[381] 42 C.F.R. §§ 2.12(a) and 2.13(a).

[382] 42 C.F.R. § 2.12(a)(1)(ii).

[383] However, if a state receives federal money earmarked for certain purposes not including an alcohol- or drug-abuse treatment program, a facility receiving state funds is not subject to the federal laws governing alcohol- and drug-abuse patient records. See *Listion v. Shelby County*, No. 93007-3 R.D. (Tenn. Ct. App., Oct. 23, 1987) (unpublished).

[384] Whenever a person or program seeks to invoke the protection of the federal statute and regulations in order to assure the confidentiality of patient records, that person or program bears the burden of demonstrating the applicability of the federal laws. See *Samaritan Health Services v. City of Glendale*, 714 P. 2d 887 (Ariz. Ct. App. 1986), where the facility claiming protection under 42 U.S.C. § 290ee-3 failed to show that it operated a program subject to the law; see also *State v. Gullekson*, 383 N.W. 2d 338 (Minn. Ct. App. 1986).

[385] 42 C.F.R. § 2.11.

[386] Ibid.

any individual who has requested or received a diagnosis or treatment for alcohol or drug abuse at a federally assisted program.[387] A hospital emergency room does not qualify as a "program" for purposes of the act unless its primary function is to provide "drug and alcohol abuse services or it holds itself out to the public as providing these services."[388]

An alcohol or drug abuse treatment program under the act may not disclose any information, recorded or not, that would identify a patient as an alcohol or drug abuser—either directly, by reference to other publicly available information, or through verification by another person.[389] This blanket prohibition clearly covers a broad range of information about a patient, including nonwritten information and indirect indications of a patient's identity.[390]

Healthcare organizations subject to the act must be wary of implicit disclosure of confidential information. If a general care hospital or other healthcare organization fails to disclose information about a drug or alcohol abuse patient when it routinely discloses such information about other patients, the facility could be liable for implicitly admitting that the patient was being treated for drug or alcohol abuse. Hospitals and healthcare organizations, therefore, should delete such patients from their directories unless the individuals consent to having their presence acknowledged. Although that practice will protect the patients' identities as required by the alcohol and drug abuse regulations, it can create other problems. For example, hospitals that maintain patient directories at their switchboards and information desks may encounter difficulties. In identifying drug or alcohol abuse patients, healthcare organizations must devise methods that do not allow its personnel to release information inadvertently.

The medical records of alcohol and drug abuse patients may be disclosed with their consent under certain circumstances. The regulations provide a list of elements required for lawful consent, along with a sample consent form.[391] These regulations were amended in 1987 to allow

---

[387] Ibid.

[388] 42 C.F.R. § 2.12(e); see also *Center for Legal Advocacy v. Earnest,* 320 F. 3d 1107 (10th Cir., Feb. 25, 2003).

[389] 42 C.F.R. § 2.12(a)(1)(i).

[390] But see *State v. Brown,* 376 N.W. 2d 451 (Minn. Ct. App. 1985), where the court held that personal observations made to police officers by a counselor at a drug-treatment center relating to a patient's parole for drug-related offenses were not "records" under the regulations, even if reduced to writing by the counselor.

[391] 42 C.F.R. §§ 2.31(a) and (b).

greater flexibility for the wording of the consent.[392] In general, the consent must be in writing, signed by the patient or authorized signatory, and must describe the kind of information to be disclosed and the purpose for disclosure. The person releasing the medical records must notify the recipient of the fact that the recipient in turn is bound by the regulations and prohibited from further disclosure.[393] A facility releasing information in accordance with this provision should document its notice to the recipient in writing; a routine form letter sent to each recipient of alcohol and drug abuse patient records would facilitate meeting this requirement.

Under the regulations, minors may consent to the release of their drug and alcohol abuse records if, under state law, they may consent to the treatment.[394] The regulations do not address directly the circumstances under which a minor may consent to such treatment, but instead, expressly defer to state law on the issue. Consequently, a minor's ability to consent to the release of treatment records covered by the act will vary from state to state. Where state law mandates parental consent to alcohol and drug abuse treatment for a minor, the regulations require parental consent to any disclosure of information relating to such treatment.[395] Federal regulations also specifically authorize disclosure to parents or guardians of facts relevant to reducing a substantial threat to a minor's life or physical well being where the individual lacks capacity to make a rational decision about whether to release the records.[396] The regulations also contain a special provision on release of information by incompetent patients.[397]

Disclosure without consent is permitted under limited circumstances. For example, disclosure to medical personnel may be made in a medical emergency posing an immediate threat to health.[398] A program proceeding under this provision must enter all of the following information directly into the patient's record:

---

[392] See *M.A.K. v. Rush-Presbyterian–St. Luke's Medical Center*, No. 90527, 2001 WL 1632294 (Dec. 20, 2001).
[393] 42 C.F.R. § 2.32.
[394] 42 C.F.R. § 2.14(b).
[395] 42 C.F.R. § 2.14(c); 42 C.F.R. § 2.14(c).
[396] 42 C.F.R. § 2.14(d); 42 C.F.R. § 2.14(d).
[397] 42 C.F.R. § 2.15.
[398] 42 C.F.R. § 2.51(a).

- the name of the medical personnel to whom disclosure was made and their affiliation with any healthcare facility
- the name of the individual making the disclosure
- the date and time of the disclosure
- the nature of the emergency[399]

Another important exception to the general ban on disclosure without the patient's consent applies to communications between persons who need the information to perform duties arising out of diagnosis, treatment, or referral for treatment of alcohol or drug abuse. However, such exchanges of information are permitted only if they occur within a program or between a program and an entity that has direct administrative control over the program.[400] The ban on disclosure does not apply to communications between a program and a "qualified service organization,"[401] defined as including companies providing data processing, bill collecting, lab work, legal work, and other services to the program.[402] On the other hand, the ban on disclosure is expressly extended to third party payers; to entities with direct administrative control over programs receiving information from the program related to diagnosis, treatment, or referral; and to persons receiving information from a covered program with the patient's consent as provided under the regulations.[403] This provision could apply to MCOs that, for example, receive protected information related to payment of benefits even though the MCO does not maintain actual treatment records.

Disclosure without consent may be made for audit and evaluation[404] or for research purposes.[405] The regulations provide for additional measures in these situations to protect patient information and identification. The regulations allow certain disclosures of information to the Food and Drug Administration (FDA) in situations where a tainted drug may threaten the health of an individual under the FDA's

---

[399] 42 C.F.R. § 2.51(c).
[400] 42 C.F.R. § 2.12(c)(3).
[401] 42 C.F.R. § 2.12(c)(4).
[402] 42 C.F.R. § 2.11.
[403] 42 C.F.R. § 2.12(d)(2).
[404] 42 C.F.R. § 2.53.
[405] 42 C.F.R. § 2.52.

jurisdiction.[406] Other exceptions are made for disclosures to law enforcement officials relating to a patient's commission of, or threat to commit, a crime on program premises or against program personnel,[407] and for reporting suspected child abuse or neglect under state law.[408]

Disclosure without consent also may be made in response to a court order.[409] A person with a legally recognized interest in disclosure of records covered by the federal provisions may apply for a court order to use the records for noncriminal purposes.[410] In general, the act provides that an order for disclosure may be issued only for good cause.[411] For "good cause" to exist, the evidence must demonstrate that the information is not available through other means or would not be effective, and that the public interest and need for disclosure outweigh the potential injury to the patient, the physician patient relationship, and the treatment services.[412]

If the records are to be used in a criminal investigation or prosecution of a patient, different criteria govern their release. These criteria relate to the seriousness of the underlying crime; the value of information in the records to the investigation or prosecution; the unavailability or ineffectiveness of other ways to obtain the information; the public interest and need for disclosure versus the potential injury to the patient, physician patient relationship, and the ability of the program to provide services to others; and the availability of independent counsel for the person holding the records.[413]

Many of the programs subject to the federal laws on alcohol and drug abuse patient records also are governed by the Privacy Rule and state law, including state rules on confidentiality and state mandatory reporting laws. The operation of these sets of rules may create conflicts for the program.

The federal alcohol and drug abuse regulations provide that the statutes authorizing them do not preempt state law.[414] They instruct that if disclosure permitted by the federal regulations is prohibited

---

[406] 42 C.F.R. § 2.51(b).
[407] 42 C.F.R. § 2.12(c)(5).
[408] 42 C.F.R. § 2.12(c)(6).
[409] See, e.g., 45 C.F.R. § 164.512(e).
[410] 42 C.F.R. § 2.64; see also *Center for Legal Advocacy v. Earnest.*
[411] 42 U.S.C. § 290dd-2(b)(2)(C); see also 42 C.F.R. § 2.64.
[412] 42 C.F.R. § 2.64(d).
[413] 42 C.F.R. § 2.65(d).
[414] 42 C.F.R. § 2.20.

under state law, federal law should not be interpreted to authorize a violation of the state law. On the other hand, the regulations provide that state law may not authorize or compel any disclosure prohibited by the federal regulations. In other words, if the federal law permits disclosure prohibited by state law, the disclosure is not to be made; and if federal law prohibits disclosure, disclosure should not be made, regardless of the state law governing the issue. Nevertheless, a program subject to both sets of rules must be careful to release only the particular information required by state law. Any release of information beyond that required by state law constitutes a breach of the federal substance abuse regulations.

Several states have enacted their own provisions for access and disclosure of alcohol and drug abuse patient records.[415] These statutes typically impose a general ban on disclosure of records by covered programs except as provided in the law. Exceptions to confidentiality generally are created for disclosures relating to financial and compliance audits and program evaluations, between qualified personnel involved in the patient's treatment, and to qualified persons responding to a medical emergency. Alcohol and drug abuse treatment programs in each state must be aware of the particular state laws applicable to them in addition to the federal laws governing their patient records, and must determine whether the Privacy Rule preempts relevant state laws.

Treatment programs that also qualify as covered entities under the Privacy Rule also will be subject to the privacy requirements of the rule. This means that the programs must determine whether a particular use or disclosure of alcohol and drug abuse patient records is permitted by both the substance abuse regulations and the Privacy Rule. DHHS has taken the position that the Privacy Rule does not conflict with the Public Health Service Act or the substance abuse regulations.[416] The Privacy Rule is for the most part a set of permissive regulations that permit, but do not require, disclosure of PHI. Where other laws, such as the substance abuse regulations, are more restrictive, it is possible for an organization that is subject to both laws to comply with the more restrictive (that is, more protective) law without violating either law. For example, the substance abuse regulations permit disclosure of patient

---

[415] See, e.g., Md. Code Ann., Health-Gen., § 8-601(c); Wis. Stat. Ann. § 51.30(4).
[416] 65 Fed. Reg. 82482 (Dec. 28, 2000).

records information with a consent form that includes a prohibition against further disclosure by the recipient of the information. The Privacy Rule includes no such requirement for patient authorizations. Programs subject to both laws should comply with the more restrictive substance abuse regulations. However, the Privacy Rule treats medical records numbers as PHI, and generally prohibits their disclosure without authorization. The substance abuse regulations permit disclosure of record numbers under limited circumstances. Programs that are covered entities should follow the more restrictive Privacy Rule with respect to record numbers. Given the complexity of these laws, DHHS has published guidance for alcohol and drug abuse treatment programs that are also covered entities as to how to comply with both regulatory schemes.[417]

Genetic Information

The Human Genome Project (HGP) has raised many legal issues. The goal of the HGP is to map the location of genes in the human genome. Researchers have already successfully identified the genes responsible for diseases such as Huntington's disease, amyotrophic lateral sclerosis (Lou Gehrig's disease), and cystic fibrosis. The HGP is also identifying genes associated with diseases caused by environmental and social influences as well as by hereditary factors, such as breast and colon cancer, diabetes, and hypertension.

Breaching the confidentiality of genetic information can make an individual vulnerable to discrimination by insurance companies or employers. In addition, the offspring of these individuals can be susceptible to the same form of discrimination because they, too, might have inherited genes making it more likely that they will develop a particular disease. Recognizing the sensitivity of genetic information, the U.S. Court of Appeals for the Ninth Circuit has stated that genetic information is entitled to the highest expectation of privacy.[418]

The Privacy Rule also extends confidentiality protection to genetic information. It treats all biometric identifiers as unique to the individual, and requires them to be stripped from health information in order

---

[417] U.S. Department of Health and Human Services, *The Confidentiality of Alcohol and Drug Abuse Patient Records Regulation and the HIPAA Privacy Rule: Implications for Alcohol and Substance Abuse Programs* (June 2004).

[418] *Bloodsaw v. Lawrence Berkeley Laboratory*, 135 F. 3d 1260 (9th Cir., Feb. 3, 1998).

to remove the information from the rule's protection.[419] (See the discussion of de-identified health information earlier in this chapter.) In addition, when law enforcement officials request PHI for the purpose of locating individuals, the rule permits covered entities to disclose only certain limited elements of information. One of the elements that covered entities are not allowed to disclose in response to such a request is an individual's DNA or DNA analysis.[420] Otherwise, the Privacy Rule treats genetic information as part of PHI, and thus subject to all of the protections the rule affords.

In response to concerns about genetic privacy, many states have passed legislation regulating access to genetic information. For example, Texas law prohibits certain group health benefit plans from disclosing or redisclosing genetic information without the patient's express written consent.[421] Illinois has a similar restriction: the Genetic Information Privacy Act requires a patient's written consent to release the fact that he or she has undergone genetic testing or to release the results of such tests.[422] Georgia's statute provides that genetic test information is confidential and privileged. In addition, an insurer that possesses genetic information may not release the information to any third party without the written consent of the individual tested.[423] In Missouri, genetic test information cannot be released before fully informing the individual of the scope of information that will be released, as well as the risks, benefits, and purposes of disclosure and the identity of those to whom the information will be released.[424] Colorado's genetic privacy law applies to health insurers, HMOs, nonprofit hospitals, and medical surgical and health services corporations.[425] Under the statute, information derived from genetic testing is confidential and privileged. It may not be released for purposes other than diagnosis, treatment, and therapy without the written consent of the patient. Any entity that receives genetic test information may not use or keep the information for any nontherapeutic purpose, or for a purpose connected with the provision of coverage for health, group disability, or long term care insurance.[426]

---

[419] 45 C.F.R. § 164.514(e)(2)(xv).
[420] 45 C.F.R. § 164.512(f)(2)(ii).
[421] Tex. Ins. Code § 546.001 et seq.
[422] 410 Ill. Comp. Stat. §§ 513/15 and 513/30.
[423] Ga. Code Ann. § 33-54-3; see also La. Rev. Stat. Ann. § 40:1299.6.
[424] Mo. Rev. Stat. § 191.317.
[425] Colo. Rev. Stat. § 10-3-1104.7.
[426] See also Md. Code Ann., Ins., § 27-909.

In some states, an individual's interest in protecting the confidentiality of genetic information may be outweighed by the state's interest in protecting others. For example, in *Johnson v. Superior Court*, the California Court of Appeal found that the state's interest in protecting the health of a child outweighed a sperm donor's health information privacy.[427] In this case, the facts indicated that the sperm donor's family may have had a history of serious kidney disease. The parents of the child conceived with the donor's sperm moved to compel the donor to produce health information that might reveal the donor's medical and family history.

Record Duplication and Fees

Although healthcare organizations and providers have a duty to permit patients and their representatives to inspect and copy their medical records, healthcare organizations and providers are not obligated to do so at their cost. The authority to charge duplication fees and the amounts of those fees are governed by the Privacy Rule and by state statutory or case law.

The Privacy Rule allows covered entities to impose a reasonable, cost based fee for duplication. This fee may include only the cost of copying, including the cost of supplies and labor of copying; postage (if applicable); and preparing an explanation or summary of the PHI (if applicable).[428] If hard copies are made, the fee could include the cost of paper. If electronic copies are made to a computer disk, the fee could include the cost of the computer disk.[429] The Privacy Rule prohibits covered entities from charging any fees for retrieving or handling the information or for processing the request.[430]

State law also governs duplication fees charged to individuals. Although some of the statutory or regulatory provisions on fees enunciate a "reasonable" standard to determine the amount, many other states have stipulated specific maximum amounts that may be charged for these services. For example, in Louisiana, a provider may require pay-

---

[427] 80 Cal. App. 4th 1050 (Ct. App. 2000).
[428] 45 C.F.R. § 164.524(c)(4).
[429] 65 Fed. Reg. 82557 (Dec. 28, 2000).
[430] Ibid.

ment of a reasonable copying charge before releasing a patient's medical record. The amount may not exceed $1.00 per page for the first 25 pages, $0.50 for pages 26 through 500, and $0.25 per page thereafter. Hospitals may charge a maximum handling charge of $10.00, other healthcare providers may charge a maximum handling charge of $5.00, and all providers may charge actual postage.[431]

The fees that a state establishes for copying and postage are presumed reasonable by the Privacy Rule, but the rule declares to be unreasonable any state established fees for reimbursement for the cost of retrieving or handling PHI, and therefore preempts those state laws.[432] Over time, states will likely conform their duplication fee provisions to the Privacy Rule. Until then, covered entities must assess whether fees set forth in state statutes are permissible under the Privacy Rule. (See the discussion of HIPAA preemption of state law earlier in this chapter.)

In the absence of a state statute, courts have applied a reasonableness standard to a hospital's right to charge fees for accessing a medical record. For example, a court in Mississippi held that a hospital that was obligated to disclose record information to the patient could charge a fee for reproducing that information.[433] In an Illinois case, a court held that the hospital properly refused to reproduce and release voluminous patient records when it received only a form request and offer to pay for "reasonable access."[434] The court ruled that the hospital properly could allow the person making the request to review the full record and indicate what parts he was willing to pay to have copied.

Whether the authority to charge an access fee derives from legislation or from case law, the price a provider charges for reproducing any portion of a patient's medical record should be based on the actual or reasonable cost to duplicate and deliver the portions requested. A healthcare organization should not make a profit from a patient's request for copies of his or her records, and the preamble commentary to the Privacy Rule would support this position—it specifically states that the fee should not impede the ability of individuals to copy their

---

[431] La. Rev. Stat. Ann. § 40:1299.96(A)(2)(b).
[432] 65 Fed. Reg. 82557 (Dec. 28, 2000).
[433] *Young v. Madison General Hospital*, 337 So. 2d 931 (Miss. 1976).
[434] *Rabens v. Jackson Park Hospital Foundation*, 351 N.E. 2d 276 (Ill. Ct. App. 1976).

records.[435] Again, the numerous pronouncements by state courts concerning the fees that a provider may charge for reproducing health information are now subject to the Privacy Rule preemption requirements. To the extent that a state court gives greater protection to the confidentiality of health information or provides greater rights to the individuals with respect to their PHI, the court's decision will prevail. But if a court has decided that duplication fees may include, for example, the cost of retrieving a medical record, the court's decision will be preempted by the Privacy Rule.

In responding to patient requests for photocopying records, a healthcare organization may contract with a third party to perform the work. Whenever the healthcare organization makes such an arrangement, it must ensure confidentiality of the records in its contract with the party providing the copying services. Under the Privacy Rule, these contractors are "business associates" of the covered entity, and the contractual arrangements between the covered entity and its business associates must comply with the business associate provisions of the rule. (See the discussion of business associates later in this chapter.) In an Illinois case, an appeals court ruled that hospitals that send patient medical records to photocopy shops to be reproduced when patients ask for copies of their records are not violating state law regarding confidentiality.[436] Under Illinois law, a hospital can use independent contractors, agents, or employees in providing patients access to their records, the court held. Finally, the court refused to find that ministerial duties, such as photocopying, breach a patient's right to confidentiality, as long as the photocopying is done in a reasonable manner.

Alternatively, patients might choose to rent a portable photocopy machine and copy the records themselves. Under the Privacy Rule, patients choosing that option will not be required to reimburse the healthcare organization for retrieving the file, but may be required to reimburse for time spent by a healthcare organization employee super-

---

[435] The inclusion of a fee for copying is not intended to impede the ability of individuals to copy their records. Rather, it is intended to reduce the burden on covered entities. If the cost is excessively high, some individuals will not be able to obtain a copy. See 65 Fed. Reg. at 82557 and 82735 (Dec. 28, 2000).

[436] *Clay v. Little Company of Mary Hospital.* The relevant part of Illinois law provides as follows: "Examination of records. Every . . . hospital shall . . . permit the patient, his or her physician or authorized attorney to examine the hospital records . . . kept in connection with the treatment of such patient, and permit copies of such records to be made by him or her or his or her physician or authorized attorney. . . ." 735 Ill. Comp. Stat. § 5/8-2001.

vising the copying. A patient does not have the right to unsupervised off premises inspection and copying of records under the Privacy Rule[437] or under state law.[438] (See the discussion of an individual's right to access his or her PHI earlier in this chapter.)

QIO Record Keeping

The Tax Equity and Fiscal Responsibility Act of 1982[439] created the current statutory framework for quality improvement organizations (QIOs) by repealing the earlier Professional Standards Review Organization (PSRO) program and the Peer Review Organization (PRO) program.[440]

The Social Security Act uses the term "utilization and quality control peer review organizations" to describe those entities, now called QIOs, which contract with CMS for the performance of the function prescribed in Title XI of the Social Security Act. CMS regulations provide an extensive regulatory framework for CMS's quality initiative governing the provision of Medicare and Medicaid services, which begins with a focus on hospital and nursing homes, but also broadly applies to grant programs in health, HMOs, Medicaid, and Medicare.[441] Under the current statute, "utilization and quality control peer review organization," means an entity composed of a substantial number of licensed doctors of medicine and osteopathy in the area representative of practicing physicians, or an entity with a sufficient number of such physicians available under arrangement to assure adequate peer review of services provided by the various specialties and subspecialties.[442]

At least one member of the QIO's governing body must be an individual representing consumers.[443] A QIO must be able to perform the required review functions efficiently and effectively, and must measure

---

[437] 45 C.F.R. § 164.524(a).

[438] *Paterna v. Zandieb*, 515 N.Y.S. 2d 54 (App. Div. 1987).

[439] 42 U.S.C. §§ 1320c through 1320c-12.

[440] 67 Fed. Reg. 36539 (May 24, 2000).

[441] 42 C.F.R. § 400.200 (general definitions) and pts. 475, 476, and 480, subpt. B (focusing on acquisition, protection, and disclosure of QIO information).

[442] 42 U.S.C. §§ 1320c-1(1)(A) & (B).

[443] 42 U.S.C. § 1320c-1(3).

the pattern of quality of care provided in the area against objective criteria that define acceptable and adequate practice.[444]

QIOs are charged with a number of functions. Most importantly, they must review some or all of the professional activities conducted by physicians and providers who receive federal reimbursement under Medicare. In conducting these reviews, QIOs must determine: (1) whether services and items were reasonable and medically necessary, (2) whether the quality of services met professionally recognized standards, and (3) whether inpatient services could have been provided more economically on an outpatient basis or in an inpatient healthcare facility of a different type.[445] The statute also requires QIOs to conduct certain other reviews, including readmissions occurring within 31 days of discharge[446] and some or all ambulatory surgical procedures.[447]

In carrying out its functions, a QIO must collect and maintain records of relevant information, and permit access to such records and use of the collected information as required by the Secretary of DHHS, subject to the statutory provisions prohibiting disclosure of certain QIO information.[448] Under the QIO regulations,[449] CMS or any person, organization, or agency authorized by DHHS or federal statute to monitor a QIO will have access to, and may obtain copies of, medical records of Medicare patients maintained by institutions or healthcare practitioners.[450] The statute and regulations address access and disclosure of medical records and QIO information in other contexts considered below.

QIO Access to Individual Patient Records

The act grants QIOs broad authority to access patient records and other information. First, it provides that each QIO shall examine the pertinent records of any practitioner or provider of healthcare services subject to its review,[451] and may require the institution or practitioner

---

[444] 42 U.S.C. § 1320c-1(2).
[445] 42 U.S.C. §§ 1320c-3(a)(1)(A) through (C).
[446] 42 U.S.C. § 1320c-3(a)(13).
[447] 42 U.S.C. § 1320c-3(d).
[448] 42 U.S.C. § 1320c-3(a)(9)(A).
[449] 42 C.F.R. §§ 475.1 through 476.100 and 480.001 through 480.143.
[450] 42 C.F.R. §§ 476.88; 480.103.
[451] 42 U.S.C. § 1320c-3(a)(7)(C).

to provide copies of records or information to the QIO.[452] Second, a QIO is authorized to access and require copies of Medicare records or information held by intermediaries or carriers if the QIO determines that such material is necessary to carry out its review functions.[453] Third, a QIO has the right to all information collected by institutions or other entities for QIO purposes.[454] The regulations add that a QIO may have access to records of non-Medicare patients in accordance with its quality review responsibilities under the act if authorized by the institution, practitioner, or patients in accordance with state law.[455] The Privacy Rule permits covered entities to disclose PHI to health oversight agencies such as QIOs.[456] Clearly, QIOs have authority to review and copy confidential patient medical records and related information collected by physicians, facilities, intermediaries, and carriers.

Third Party Access to Information Collected by a QIO

The statute provides that, in general, any data or information acquired by a QIO in the exercise of its duties and functions shall be held in confidence and not disclosed except as specifically authorized under the law.[457] A QIO may disclose information to the extent necessary to carry out the purposes of the statute.[458] It also may release information for purposes specifically authorized by statute, including to assist with investigations into cases and/or patterns of fraud or abuse; with matters where a risk to the public health is presented; with issues involving state licensing, certification, or accreditation; and with health planning.[459] A QIO may disclose information as authorized by the Secretary of

---

[452] 42 C.F.R. § 476.78 (b)(2).
[453] 42 C.F.R. §§ 476.80; 480.103.
[454] 42 C.F.R. §§ 476.88; 480.113.
[455] 42 C.F.R. § 480.111.
[456] See 45 C.F.R. § 164.512(d). A health oversight agency means an agency or authority of the United States, a state, a territory, a political subdivision of a state or territory, or an Indian tribe, or a person or entity acting under a grant of authority from or contract with such public agency, including the employees or agents of such public agency or its contractors or persons or entities to whom it has granted authority, that is authorized by law to oversee the health care system (whether public or private) or government programs in which health information is necessary to determine eligibility or compliance, or to enforce civil rights laws for which health information is relevant. 45 C.F.R. § 164.501.
[457] 42 U.S.C. § 1320c-9(a).
[458] 42 U.S.C. § 1320c-9(a)(1).
[459] 42 U.S.C. §§ 1320c-9(a)(3) and 1320-9(b).

DHHS to assure adequate protection of the rights and interests of patients, practitioners, or providers of health care.[460]

QIOs are required to provide reasonable physical security measures to prevent unauthorized access to the information and to ensure the integrity of the data.[461] The QIO must instruct its officers and employees, as well as employees of healthcare institutions participating in its activities, of their responsibility to maintain confidentiality. No individual participating in the QIO review process on a regular basis shall have authorized access to confidential QIO information unless that person has been properly trained and has signed a statement indicating an awareness of the legal penalties for unauthorized disclosure.[462] QIO information may be stored in a shared health data system unless such storage would prevent the QIO from complying with the regulations.[463] QIO information may not be disclosed by the shared health data system unless the source of the information consents or the QIO requests disclosure as permitted by the regulations.[464]

The regulatory provisions governing disclosure of QIO information distinguish "confidential" from "nonconfidential." "Confidential information" is defined as any of the following:

- Information that explicitly or implicitly identifies an individual patient, practitioner, or reviewer
- Sanction reports and recommendations
- Quality review studies that identify patients, practitioners, or institutions[465]

The phrase "implicitly identifies" is defined to mean "data so unique or numbers so small that identification of an individual patient, practitioner, or reviewer would be obvious."[466] Nonconfidential information is not defined by the regulations, but the term presumably refers to information falling outside the definition of "confidential information."

A QIO is required to disclose nonconfidential information to any person upon request. Such information may relate to the norms, crite-

---

[460] 42 U.S.C. § 1320c-9(a)(2).
[461] 42 C.F.R. § 480.115(a).
[462] 42 C.F.R. § 480.115(d).
[463] 42 C.F.R. §§ 480.143(a) and (b).
[464] 42 C.F.R. § 480.143(c).
[465] 42 C.F.R. § 480.101(b).
[466] Ibid.

ria, and standards used for initial screening of cases and other review activities; routine reports submitted by the QIO to CMS to the extent they do not contain confidential information; and quality review studies from which the identification of patients, practitioners, and institutions has been deleted.[467] A QIO also must disclose to state or federal health planning agencies all aggregate statistical information that does not implicitly or explicitly identify individual patients, practitioners, or reviewers.[468] In addition to these mandatory disclosures, a QIO may disclose any of the above nonconfidential information to any person, agency, or organization on its own initiative.[469]

The regulations generally require a QIO that intends to disclose nonconfidential information to give 30-day advance notice to any institution identified in the material and to provide a copy to the institution. The institution may submit written comments to the QIO that must be included with the information disclosed or forwarded separately.[470] Where the QIO plans to disclose "confidential information," it also must give advance notice. If the request for information comes from a patient or patient representative, the QIO must provide the notice to the practitioner who treated the patient.[471] On the other hand, if the request comes from an investigative or licensing agency, the QIO must: (1) notify the practitioner or institution, (2) provide the practitioner or institution with a copy of the requested information, and (3) include comments submitted by the practitioner or institution in the disclosure to the agency.[472]

There are three exceptions to the general requirement that a QIO give advance notice to a practitioner or institution before confidential information is disclosed:

- If a QIO determines that the requested information is necessary to protect against an imminent danger to individuals or the public health, notice of the disclosure may be sent to the practitioner or institution at the same time the disclosure is made, rather than 30 days in advance[473]

---

[467] 42 C.F.R. § 480.120(a).
[468] 42 C.F.R. § 480.120(b).
[469] 42 C.F.R. § 480.121.
[470] 42 C.F.R. § 480.105(a).
[471] 42 C.F.R. § 480.105(b)(1).
[472] 42 C.F.R. § 480.106(b)(2).
[473] 42 C.F.R. § 480.106(a).

- If the disclosure is made during a fraud and abuse investigation conducted by the Office of Inspector General (OIG) or the Government Accountability Office (GAO), no notice is required[474]
- If the disclosure is made during a fraud and abuse investigation conducted by any other state or federal agency, no notice is required if the agency specifies in writing that the information is related to a potentially prosecutable criminal offense[475]

All disclosures of confidential information by a QIO must be accompanied by a written statement informing the recipient that the information may not be further disclosed except as provided by the regulations.[476]

QIO records that identify patients are not subject to subpoena or discovery in a civil action, including an administrative, judicial, or arbitration proceeding.[477] However, this last restriction does not apply to DHHS, OIG, or GAO, or to administrative subpoenas issued during the course of DHHS program audits and investigations, or during administrative hearings held under the Social Security Act.[478]

There is no access or disclosure of QIO information beyond that described in the statute and regulations.[479] That provision is designed to avoid the litigation experienced under the former PSRO law where attempts to characterize PSROs as federal agencies under FOIA led to conflicting court decisions.[480]

Patient Access to QIO Information

Generally, a QIO must disclose patient identifying information in its possession to that individual or his or her representative upon written request, provided that all other patient and practitioner identifiers have been removed.[481] First, however, the QIO must discuss the appropriateness of disclosure with the patient's attending practitioner. If the

---

[474] 42 C.F.R. § 480.106(b)(1).
[475] 42 C.F.R. § 480.106(b)(2).
[476] 42 C.F.R. § 480.104(a)(2).
[477] 42 C.F.R. § 480.138(a)(3).
[478] 42 C.F.R. § 480.138(b)(1).
[479] 42 C.F.R. § 480.138(b)(2).
[480] See, e.g., *Public Citizen Health Research Group v. Department of Health, Education & Welfare*, 668 F. 2d 537 (D.C. Cir. 1981).
[481] 42 C.F.R. § 480.132(a)(1).

practitioner states that the released information could harm the patient, the QIO must disclose the material to the patient's representative rather than directly to the patient.[482] If the patient is mentally, physically, or legally unable to designate a representative, the QIO must disclose the information to a person responsible for the patient as determined by the QIO in accordance with the regulations.[483] The QIO must disclose patient information directly to the patient unless knowledge could be harmful.[484]

Utilization Review and Quality Assurance

In addition to their uses in medical research, patients' records play a critical role in each healthcare organization's effort to improve the quality of healthcare services and to increase the efficiency with which the services are provided. Patients' records are a primary source of data for such utilization review and other quality assurance activities. Healthcare providers and health law practitioners must be aware of the statutes, regulations, and judicial opinions in their jurisdictions that affect the ability to use medical records for these purposes.

Two types of review processes occur in hospitals. The first type is the federal QIO system, part of the Medicare program governed by federal statute and regulation,[485] which is discussed more fully above. The second type of review is hospital utilization review and quality assurance. These two review programs are conducted by hospital staff members and consist of in-house monitoring of both the quality and cost of providing services. The basic requirements for these review programs are set forth in the standards of accreditation adopted by the Joint Commission and in various state laws.

Quality assurance and utilization review programs also are an important aspect of managed health care. State laws usually condition issuance of an HMO or MCO certificate of authority on the submission and approval of a quality assurance program. Statutes and regulations mandating quality assurance activities vary in terms of level of detail.[486]

---

[482] 42 C.F.R. §§ 480.132(a)(2) and (c)(2).
[483] 42 C.F.R. § 480.132(c)(3).
[484] 42 C.F.R. § 480.132(c)(1).
[485] See, generally, 42 C.F.R. §§ 480.101 through 480.143.
[486] See, e.g., Idaho Code § 41-3905(6)(a); Md. Code Ann., Health-Gen., §§ 19-705.1(d), (e), and (f).

State laws also vary widely on utilization review. Many laws, however, indicate that the HMO must have procedures for developing, compiling, evaluating, and reporting statistics relating to the cost of its operations, the pattern of utilization of its services, and the availability and accessibility of its services.[487]

Accreditation organizations have standards related to quality assurance and utilization review. The Joint Commission standards applicable to hospitals, PPOs, and healthcare networks are categorized under "Leadership" and "Improving Organizational Performance."[488] The standards concentrate on the monitoring, evaluation, and comparison of various data in order to identify and correct problems. In its Standards for the Certification of Physician Organizations, the NCQA has developed standards for quality management and improvement as well as for utilization management.[489] Like the Joint Commission standards, the NCQA standards stress collecting and analyzing data in order to monitor service and improve performance.

Although utilization management and quality assurance rely on many data sources, the most valuable sources clearly are patients' medical records. Many states have enacted laws protecting the confidentiality of medical records used in utilization management and quality assurance functions. For example, some states require entities applying for a utilization review organization (URO) license to submit information about the URO's policies for protecting the confidentiality of medical records.[490] In addition, many state laws require UROs to protect the confidentiality of medical information.[491] An Illinois statute provides that all information used in the course of internal quality control or in other ways designed to improve patient care is strictly confidential. However, a claim of confidentiality may not be used to deny a physician access to any information used to make a decision in any

---

[487] See, e.g., Ga. Code Ann. § 33-21-3(b)(3).

[488] Joint Commission, *1997 Hospital Accreditation Standards*, Standards LD.1 through LD4.5 and PI.1 through PI.5.1; Joint Commission, *1997 Accreditation Manual for Preferred Provider Organizations*, Standards LD.1 through LD.5.1 and PI.1 through PI.4.1; Joint Commission, *1996–97 Comprehensive Accreditation Manual for Health Care Networks*, Standards LD.1 through LD.6 and PI.1 through PI.5.1.

[489] National Committee, *Standards for the Certification of Physician Organizations*, QI Standards 1 through 14, UM Standards 1 through CR (Credentialing Standards 1-12 and RR (Members Rights) Standards 1-4 (2004).

[490] See, e.g., Md. Code Ann. § 15-10B-05; R.I. Gen. Laws § 23-17.12-4.

[491] See, e.g., La. Rev. Stat. Ann. § 22:3075; Ala. Code § 27-3A-5(a)(7); Minn. Stat. § 62M.08.

HMO proceeding concerning the physician's services or the physician's staff privileges.[492]

Many states have enacted statutes authorizing disclosure of patient records to staff quality control, peer review, and medical review committees. Some of these statutes provide that a healthcare practitioner may release confidential patient information to a peer review committee.[493] On the other hand, the Nebraska law states that a provider is obligated to give a review committee information it requests.[494] Other statutes indicate that physicians or other healthcare practitioners who provide information to a review committee are immune from liability if their actions were taken in good faith.[495] Each type of statute permits review committees access to confidential patient information as is relevant and necessary to carry out their functions.

Some states without statutes specifically granting record access to quality control committees may have case law that permits disclosures. In a Missouri appeals court case, for example, a staff physician sought to prevent the disclosure of his patients' records to a hospital committee that was investigating his qualifications and competency.[496] Missouri had a physician patient privilege statute that decreed that a physician was incompetent to testify as to any information received during a professional consultation with a patient. The physician argued that the privilege should prevent the use of patient records in a competency determination because that would constitute a type of testimony at what basically was a hearing. The court reviewed the privilege's history and noted that no state ever had treated the privilege as an absolute prohibition against a physician's disclosure. After balancing the parties' opposing interests, the court concluded that the privilege was inapplicable because "[t]he public's interest in the disclosure of the information to the internal staff of the hospital and in assuring proper medical and hospital care outweigh[ed] the patient's interest in concealment."[497]

If a third party asks to review records for utilization management and quality assurance purposes, the healthcare organization will need

---

[492] 735 Ill. Comp. Stat. § 5/8-2101.
[493] See, e.g., Alaska Stat. § 18.23.010(b); Cal. Civ. Code § 56.10(c)(4).
[494] Neb. Rev. Stat. § 71-2047.
[495] See, e.g., Conn. Gen. Stat. Ann. § 19a-17b; Del. Code Ann. tit. 24, § 1768; Fla. Stat. Ann. § 766.101(3)(a).
[496] *Klinge v. Lutheran Medical Center*, 518 S.W. 2d 157, 161 (Mo. Ct. App. 1975).
[497] Ibid.

to evaluate each request individually to determine if the patient has given permission for the release of his or her health information. The healthcare organization will need to review a copy of the agreement that the patient signed when he or she enrolled in the health plan to determine if that agreement authorizes representatives of the plan to access medical records. If the patient has not provided such an authorization, his or her medical records should not be released before obtaining the patient's written authorization.

State quality assurance and utilization management laws vary from state to state. Healthcare administrators and health law practitioners therefore should consult the statutes, regulations, and case law in their jurisdictions before authorizing the use of patients' medical records for quality assurance and utilization review.

Business Associates

The HIPAA Privacy and Security Rules apply to both covered entities and their business associates. The relationship between a covered entity and its business associate is an important one, and is governed by specific provisions of the rules. These provisions recognize that covered entities must engage a variety of vendors to provide services needed to enable the entities to conduct business, and that many of those vendors must use PHI in order to provide their services. To provide additional confidentiality protection for PHI, the rules impose on covered entities a number of contracting requirements that indirectly extend the coverage of HIPAA beyond just "covered entities" to their business associates. These requirements apply to a broad spectrum of business relationships and transactions between covered entities and the organizations from whom they obtain products and services.

Qualifying as a Business Associate

A business associate relationship arises when the right to use or disclose PHI belongs to the covered entity, and another person is using or disclosing that information to perform a function on behalf of, or to provide services to, the covered entity. In general, a covered entity may disclose PHI to a business associate and may allow a business associate to create or receive PHI, or maintain or transmit ePHI, on its behalf, if the covered entity obtains satisfactory assurances, through a written agreement, that the business associate will appropriately safeguard the information.[498]

Persons who on behalf of a covered entity perform any of the following functions that involve the use or disclosure of individually identifiable health information will be business associates. This is not an exclusive list, so performing other similar services for a covered entity in connection with an activity related to health care or health information would likely create a business associate relationship.

- Claims processing or administration
- Data analysis, processing, or administration
- Utilization review
- Quality assurance
- Billing
- Benefit management
- Practice management
- Repricing[499]

Thus, an independent medical transcriptionist that provides transcription services to a physician, an independent billing company providing services to a home health agency, and a third party administrator that assists a health plan with claims processing are all business associates. One covered entity may be a business associate of another covered entity. For example, if one healthcare provider provides services, such as compliance training for employees, to another healthcare provider, a business associate relationship will arise, and the two providers must enter into a business associate agreement. If one covered entity is permitted under the rules to disclose PHI to another covered entity, that disclosure may be made directly to a business associate who is acting on behalf of the recipient covered entity.[500]

Persons who use or disclose PHI to perform any one of the following categories of services for covered entities are also considered business associates:

- Legal
- Actuarial

---

[498] 45 C.F.R. §§ 160.103 and 164.314(a).
[499] 45 C.F.R. § 160.103.
[500] Department of Health and Human Services, *Standards for Privacy*, 47.

- Accounting
- Consulting
- Data aggregation
- Management
- Administration
- Accreditation
- Financial[501]

This is an exclusive list. The Privacy Rule includes no other professional services. Thus, an accrediting organization of a hospital, a law firm providing professional liability defense services to a hospital, a hospital providing data aggregation services for other hospitals, and a physician's accounting firm would all qualify as business associates.

A business associate agreement is not required for disclosures of PHI or transmissions of ePHI by a covered entity to a provider concerning treatment of an individual or by a group health plan to the plan sponsor.[502] Therefore, a hospital is not required to execute a business associate agreement with a specialist to whom it refers a patient and transmits the patient's health information. Likewise, a hospital laboratory is not required to execute such an agreement with a reference laboratory to which it discloses PHI for treatment purposes. This broad exception eliminates the need for a business associate agreement between a hospital and a member of its medical staff for disclosures for treatment purposes.

The business associate requirements also do not apply to the disclosure of PHI or transmissions of ePHI by a group health plan, health insurer, or HMO to the plan sponsor (if separate rules for plans are satisfied), or to disclosures of PHI or transmissions of ePHI by a health plan that is a government program providing public benefits, if an individual's eligibility or enrollment is determined by another entity, the activity is authorized by law, and other requirements are met.[503] The regulations and corresponding commentary also carve out certain other relationships from business associate status:

1. *Members of a covered entity's workforce.*[504] "Workforce" is defined as employees, volunteers, trainees, and others whose work is under

---

[501] 45 C.F.R. § 160.103.
[502] 45 C.F.R. §§ 164.308(b)(2) and 164.502(e)(1)(ii).
[503] Ibid.
[504] 45 C.F.R. § 160.103.

the direct control of the covered entity, regardless of whether they are paid.[505] The "direct control" requirement would exclude most independent contractors, because tax and other rules generally require the covered entity to not assert any direct control over a contractor in order to avoid treating that contractor as an employee. Some ambiguity exists as to whether a health organization's directors (for example, those on board committees that would review PHI regularly as part of peer review or other activities) are part of its workforce, because directors are not under the "direct control" of the organization. They also do not fit clearly into the definition of business associate. Until DHHS provides further guidance on this point, a healthcare organization should treat its directors who have more than incidental access to PHI as members of its workforce, and should include them in required HIPAA training.

2. *Covered entities performing business associate type functions as part of an OHCA.*[506] The HIPAA regulations define an OHCA to include a clinically integrated care setting in which individuals typically receive health care from more than one healthcare provider; an organized system of health care in which more than one covered entity participates, and in which the participating covered entities hold themselves out to the public as participating in a joint arrangement, and participate in joint activities that include certain utilization review, quality assessment or payment activities; and certain arrangements between group health plans and insurers or HMOs.[507] (See the discussion of OHCAs earlier in this chapter.)

3. *Entities that are merely conduits for information* (for example, the U.S. Postal Service or the electronic equivalent, financial institutions that process consumer payments for health care), assuming that the covered entity complies with HIPAA's minimum necessary disclosure rule.[508]

4. *Entities that do not use PHI but may have incidental exposure to PHI.* A hospital's janitorial services, a law firm that does not routinely view a provider's PHI, or an electrician doing construction work for a physician's office are examples.[509]

---

[505] Ibid.
[506] Department of Health and Human Services, *Standards for Privacy,* 48.
[507] 45 C.F.R. § 160.103.
[508] 65 Fed. Reg. 82476 (Dec. 20, 2000).
[509] Department of Health and Human Services, *Standards for Privacy,* 42. See also 45 C.F.R. § 164.502(a)(1).

5. *Researchers for research purposes.* PHI is normally disclosed to re-searchers in accordance with a patient authorization or in a limited data set. Researchers are not business associates because they do not conduct activities regulated by HIPAA, such as healthcare operations, and do not provide one of the services described above.[510] (See the discussion of uses and disclosures of health information for research in Chapter 14.)

Generally, a healthcare provider is not a business associate of a payer. Thus, a hospital that submits a claim to a health plan is not a business associate of the plan, because in this case both covered entities are acting on their own behalf. If the hospital provides a service on behalf of the plan, such as case management, it would become the plan's business associate.[511] The selling or providing of computer software to a covered entity does not create a business associate relationship if the vendor does not have access to the covered entity's PHI. If it does have access to PHI in order to provide the software, the covered entity should enter into a business associate agreement with the vendor.[512]

In addition, if a law requires a business associate to perform a function on behalf of, or provide a service to, a covered entity, the covered entity need not comply with the business associate contracting requirements if doing so violates the requirements of that other law. In this case, the covered entity must make a good faith effort to obtain the business associate's assurances of compliance with HIPAA. If that effort is unsuccessful, the covered entity must document the reasons it could not obtain the assurances.

In general, a covered entity may disclose PHI to a business associate and may allow a business associate to create or receive PHI on its behalf, if the covered entity obtains satisfactory assurances, through a written agreement, that the business associate will appropriately safeguard the information.[513] The regulations set forth several required elements of business associate agreements. These elements establish restrictions on the use, disclosure, maintenance, and transmission of the PHI (including ePHI) by the business associate, and these restrictions are designed to achieve compliance with HIPAA. Business associates

---

[510] Department of Health and Human Services, *Standards for Privacy,* 43.
[511] Ibid., 52–53.
[512] 45 C.F.R. §§ 164.314(a)(2)(ii)(B) and 164.504(e)(3)(i)(B).
[513] 45 C.F.R. §§ 164.308(b)(1) and 164.502(e)(1).

may not avoid the business associate contracting requirements by self certifying or being certified by a third party as compliant with the Privacy and Security Rules.[514]

Requirements for Business Associate Agreements

HIPAA requires that covered entities have a written agreement with each vendor who is a business associate, and that the agreement do all of the following:

1. Set forth permitted uses and disclosures of PHI that the business associate may make
2. Require a business associate to:
    *   Not use or disclose the PHI, except as permitted by the contract or required by law
    *   Have appropriate administrative, physical, and technical safeguards in place to prevent misuse and inappropriate disclosure of PHI
    *   Report to the covered entity any attempted or successful unauthorized access, use, disclosure, modification, or destruction of PHI
    *   Require the same safeguard and disclosure conditions or restrictions on its agents and subcontractors
    *   Make PHI available to individuals for access and copying (if it is maintained in the designated record set)
    *   Make PHI available so that amendments to PHI can be made, as needed, and update the PHI to include any such amendments (if it is maintained in the designated record set)
    *   Make available to the covered entity any information needed to provide patients with an accounting of disclosures of their PHI
    *   Make practices, books, and records available to DHHS
    *   Return or destroy all PHI on termination of the contract—or, if that is not possible, limit disclosures of PHI beyond the termination of the contract
3. Allow the covered entity to terminate the contract if the business associate commits a serious violation of the contract, including the confidentiality, privacy, and security provisions of the agreement[515]

---

[514] Department of Health and Human Services, *Standards for Privacy*, 46.
[515] 45 C.F.R. §§ 164.314(a)(2) & 164.504(e)(2).

In addition, DHHS has provided model contract language that it believes will help covered entities implement the business associate agreement requirements.[516] Covered entities are not required to use the model language, and DHHS makes clear that the model language alone does not constitute a binding contract.

The regulations contain contract requirements that give patients the right to access and request amendments to the records containing their PHI. However, DHHS's model language confirms that a business associate agreement does not need to contain the business associate's commitment to accommodate patients' requests for access to, or amendments of, their PHI if the business associate does not hold the PHI in a designated record set. The regulations define designated record set for healthcare providers as an individual's medical and billing records that a covered entity maintains, including any records the covered entity uses to make decisions about the individual.[517] PHI maintained outside of these records, therefore, would not be subject to the access and amendment provisions of the business associate agreement. (See the discussion of designated record sets earlier in this chapter.)

Non-HIPAA Required Provisions for Business Associate Agreements

In addition to the HIPAA required business associate agreement provisions, covered entities should consider other provisions designed to address the appropriate allocation between the parties of the potential risks associated with a HIPAA violation. The principal risks for the covered entity include the imposition of civil monetary penalties under HIPAA, as well as exposure to other liability—such as damages in a lawsuit brought by an individual whose PHI has been inappropriately used or disclosed under state law theories (for example, violation of state privacy statutes, common law privacy rights, or negligence standards). The principal risks for the business associate include breach of contract remedies that are specified in the agreement or available under applicable law, and potential exposure to the criminal sanctions under HIPAA. (See the discussion of penalties for HIPAA violations in Chapter 11.)

---

[516] http://www.hhs.gov/ocr/hipaa/contractprov.html.
[517] 45 C.F.R. § 164.501.

The following additional business associate agreement provisions should be considered in allocating these risks between the business associate and the covered entity when the business associate will have the right to access and/or use PHI of the covered entity or its affiliates for purposes of performing services for, or a function on behalf of, the covered entity. This is not an exclusive list, and covered entities should tailor their business associate agreements to fit the circumstances of their size, complexity, and operations. They should consult with experienced qualified legal counsel in preparing and negotiating these agreements.

Indemnification and insurance. The covered entity should seek indemnification (for itself and its affiliates) by the business associate against any claim, cost, or damage arising from a breach by the business associate of its obligations in connection with security, privacy, or confidentiality of PHI. The terms of the general indemnification provision in the agreement can be modified to include such rights. Ideally, the indemnification obligation should also be supported by a commitment to insure that obligation so that the business associate will be financially able to fulfill the indemnification obligations.

Exclusion from limitation of liability. Generally, limitation of liability clauses include both a cap on direct damage liability and a disclaimer against any consequential, indirect, special, or punitive damages (that is, damages other than direct damages). Damages resulting from a third party's breach of PHI use, privacy, security, or confidentiality obligations are likely to be considered consequential, special, or indirect damages. Therefore, the covered entity should consider whether such damages should be expressly excluded from liability limitations and disclaimers.

Minimum necessary representations. As discussed earlier in this chapter, the Privacy Rule provides that, if reasonable under the circumstances, a covered entity may rely on a requested disclosure of PHI as the minimum necessary for the stated purpose if the information is requested by another covered entity or if the information is requested by a professional who is a business associate of the covered entity for purposes of providing professional services to the covered entity, provided that the professional represents that the information requested is the minimum necessary for the stated purposes.[518] Therefore, the covered entity should request the business associate to make appropriate minimum necessary representations in the agreement.

---

[518] 45 C.F.R. § 164.514(d)(3)(iii).

Right to cure. The business associate standard of the Privacy Rule states that a covered entity is not in compliance with that standard if the covered entity knew of a pattern of activity or practice of the business associate that constituted a material breach or violation of the business associate's obligations, unless the covered entity took reasonable steps to cure the breach or end the violation, as applicable.[519] Therefore, the covered entity should expressly preserve the right to cure a breach by the business associate. The covered entity should have the right to terminate the agreement and seek related remedies, however, even if it is able to cure the breach.

Burden of proof for injunctive relief. In the event of the business associate's unauthorized use or disclosure of PHI, the covered entity must be able to act in order to prevent further unauthorized use or disclosure. Thus, the agreement should include an express acknowledgment and stipulation by the business associate as to the burden of proof a covered entity would need to meet in order to obtain an injunction in such a situation. This acknowledgment and stipulation would include a statement that any such breach would result in irreparable harm to the covered entity, and that the covered entity has the right to seek an injunction and other legal and equitable rights and remedies available under the law.

Data ownership. The agreement should contain an express, unequivocal statement that, as between the business associate and the covered entity, the covered entity is the owner of the PHI.

Controlling responses to subpoenas. Unless the business associate is another covered entity, the business associate may not be sufficiently knowledgable about the legal, business, and strategic considerations involved in disclosing PHI in response to a subpoena. In many, if not all, cases, the covered entity should therefore require the business associate to notify the covered entity of, and to allow the covered entity to control a response to, a subpoena or any other discovery request or judicial or administrative order mandating that the business associate disclose PHI that the covered entity has made available to the business associate.

Security policies and procedures. Unless the business associate agreement includes detailed provisions relating to the Security Rule, the agreement should also include a general statement that the business associate will comply with the covered entity's security policies and procedures.

---

[519] 45 C.F.R. § 164.504(e)(1)(ii).

Liability for Acts or Omissions of Business Associates

Only a covered entity serving as a business associate may be directly liable for a violation of HIPAA arising from its acts and omissions as a business associate. In contrast, the actions of a business associate that is not itself a covered entity will be attributed to the covered entity on whose behalf it is acting or providing services, but only if that covered entity knows of the wrongful activity of the business associate and fails to take action to address it. A covered entity is responsible for the HIPAA noncompliance of its business associate if the covered entity knew of a pattern of activity or practice of the business associate that constituted a material breach of the HIPAA required provisions of the agreement, unless the covered entity took reasonable steps to cure the breach or terminated the agreement with its business associate.[520] The regulations do not define "knowledge," but the preamble to the Privacy Rule states that knowledge may arise from "substantial and credible evidence."[521] Thus, the rule reduces the extent to which a covered entity must monitor the activities of its business partners, but requires the entity to take reasonable corrective action if it learns of a problem.

The extent to which a covered entity must inquire concerning a business associate's ability to comply with a business associate agreement will depend upon the covered entity's analysis of the risks involved in the relationship. The following controls have been suggested as prudent due diligence by a covered entity:[522]

- The data criticality analysis, required by the Security Rule, which examines whether the PHI includes particularly valuable or sensitive information[523]
- A background check to identify any risk factors
- An independent assessment of the business associate's security and privacy protections for PHI
- Confirmation of entity status and availability for service of legal process
- Determination of the jurisdiction whose laws will apply and the

---

[520] 45 C.F.R. § 164.314(a)(1)(ii); 45 C.F.R. § 164.504(e)(1)(ii).
[521] 65 Fed. Reg. 82505 (Dec. 28, 2000).
[522] J. R. Christiansen, *An Integrated Standard of Care for Healthcare Information Security: Risk Management, HIPAA and Beyond* (American Health Lawyers Association, 2005), 169.
[523] 45 C.F.R. §306(b)(2)(iv).

appropriate venue for any legal action to enforce the business associate agreement[524]

- Contractual provisions describing the business associate's obligations in detail and a right to audit its contractual compliance
- Establishing an incident response plan for dealing with privacy and security breaches
- A prohibition against subcontracting without the covered entity's prior approval

However, the business associate may be directly exposed to liability for the criminal penalties under HIPAA for the violations resulting from its breach of the HIPAA required provisions of the business associate agreement.

Additional Patient Rights Under HIPAA

The HIPAA Privacy Rule creates significant rights for patients to help them understand and control how their health information is used and disclosed. Most state laws, although protecting the confidentiality of health information, have not provided the additional rights now afforded individuals by the Privacy Rule. Comments from the health industry concerning the proposed Privacy Rule criticized these new rights as creating a substantial, unnecessary, and expensive burden on healthcare providers, but DHHS remained firm in its belief that HIPAA requires the additional protections the rights provide.[525] The final Privacy Rule establishes the following principal rights for individuals.

Right to Notice of How a Covered Entity Will Use and Disclose PHI

The Privacy Rule has introduced the concept of notice to the protection of health information, and requires a covered entity to inform individuals of the policies and procedures it has adopted to protect the privacy of PHI, and to inform them of their rights with respect to their

---

[524] This control will be especially important for offshore outsourcing arrangements.
[525] See, generally, 65 Fed. Reg. 82720 through 82744 (Dec. 28, 2000).

PHI. Covered entities must give individuals notice of these privacy practices and rights generally at the beginning of their relationship, so that the individuals will be able to decide whether to continue in the relationship, and, if so, to exercise their rights to protect their privacy. The purpose of the notice provisions is to focus individuals on privacy issues and to prompt them to have discussions with their healthcare providers and health plans concerning privacy matters.[526]

The rule requires certain covered entities to give an individual notice of (a) the uses and disclosures the covered entities may make of his or her PHI, (b) the individual's rights with respect to the privacy of the PHI, and (c) the covered entities' duties concerning the PHI. Because the notice relates to the specific privacy practices of a particular covered entity, each affected covered entity must develop its own notice and provide it to each person from whom it obtains PHI. All covered entities except the following must give a HIPAA notice:

- A group health plan that creates or receives no PHI other than summary health information or enrollment or disenrollment information, and that provides benefits only through contracts with insurance companies or HMOs[527]
- Healthcare clearinghouses that create or receive PHI only as a business associate of another covered entity[528]
- A correctional institution that has a covered healthcare provider component[529]

A business associate of a covered entity is not required to give a notice of privacy practices, but is required to adhere to the privacy practices of the covered entity.[530]

Who Must Receive Notice and Give Acknowledgment

A covered healthcare provider with a direct treatment relationship with a patient must provide notice to the patient and obtain the patient's

---

[526] Department of Health and Human Services, *Standards for Privacy*, 103.
[527] 45 C.F.R. § 164.520(a)(2).
[528] 45 C.F.R. § 164.500(b)(1).
[529] 45 C.F.R. § 164.520(a)(3).
[530] Department of Health and Human Services, *Standards for Privacy*, 108.

written acknowledgment that he or she has received the notice.[531] If the individual is an adult, the covered entity should deliver the notice to the individual. If the individual is an unemancipated minor with a personal representative (usually a parent), the notice should be delivered to the personal representative. If the patient is an adult who is legally incompetent and who has a personal representative, the personal representative should receive the notice. Emancipated or unemancipated minors who are legally authorized to consent to health care are treated as adults and should receive the notice.[532]

Except in emergency situations, only a covered healthcare provider that has a direct treatment relationship with an individual must (a) make a good faith effort to obtain a written acknowledgment of receipt of the notice, and (b) document its good faith efforts. If the provider is unable to obtain an acknowledgment, it must document the reasons why the acknowledgment was not obtained. This requirement applies to both paper and electronic notices.[533]

Patients react differently to the often complex notices they receive from providers. Some may simply refuse to sign the provider's acknowledgment form. If this occurs, the provider's personnel should simply document the occurrence and include the reason given, if any, why the individual refused. If a patient who receives his or her notice by mail neglects to return the acknowledgment form, the provider should place a copy of the acknowledgment form in the record with an indication that it was mailed, so that the record will show that the individual failed to return the form. A covered provider is not in violation of the Privacy Rule if the patient chooses not to return the requested acknowledgment.[534] This is a commonsense standard; providers should make a reasonable effort to obtain an acknowledgment and create a clear record of the facts describing any inability to obtain one.

Content of the Notice

The notice must be written in plain language that the average person can understand.[535] To protect individuals who have limited proficiency in English, the Civil Rights Act requires any recipient of federal funds

---

[531] 45 C.F.R. § 164.520(c)(2).
[532] Department of Health and Human Services, *Standards for Privacy*, 111.
[533] 45 C.F.R. § 164.520(c)(2)(ii).
[534] Department of Health and Human Services, *Standards for Privacy*, 109.
[535] 45 C.F.R. § 164.520(b)(1).

to take information it gives the general public and to make that information available in the languages commonly used by individuals in the entity's service area.[536] Most likely, the covered entities most affected by this requirement will be healthcare providers. These providers should evaluate their service area demographics and prepare HIPAA notices that will communicate effectively with their patients.

The privacy regulations specify in detail what the notice must contain, but do not specify the form or format of the notice. The government has provided no form notice. The notice must contain all of the essential components described in the regulations and may include other provisions.[537] It also must include any information required by state and federal laws not preempted by the Privacy Rule.

Every notice must contain a prominently displayed header: "THIS NOTICE DESCRIBES HOW MEDICAL INFORMATION ABOUT YOU MAY BE USED AND DISCLOSED AND HOW YOU CAN GET ACCESS TO THIS INFORMATION. PLEASE REVIEW IT CAREFULLY."[538] In addition, the notice must contain all of the following information:

- A description, with at least one example, of the types of uses and disclosures the covered entity may make for each of their treatment, payment, and healthcare operations
- A description of each of the other purposes for which the covered entity is permitted or required to use or disclose PHI without the individual's authorization (see the discussion of such uses and disclosures of medical record information earlier in this chapter)
- A statement that other uses or disclosures will be made only with the individual's written authorization, which he or she may revoke to the extent permitted by the Privacy Rule
- A description of any additional limitations on the use or disclosure of PHI that may be imposed by state or other law
- An effective date, which may not be sooner than the date the notice is published
- The name or title and telephone number of the person or office to contact at the covered entity for further information[539]

---

[536] See Ex. Ord. No. 13166, 65 Fed. Reg. 50121 (Aug. 11, 2000).
[537] 45 C.F.R. § 164.520(b)(1).
[538] 45 C.F.R. § 164.520(b)(1)(i).
[539] 45 C.F.R. § 164.520(b)(1).

If the covered entity engages in the following uses of PHI, its notice must contain:

- A statement that the covered entity may contact the individual to provide appointment reminders or information concerning treatment alternatives or other health related benefits or services of possible interest to the individual
- A statement that the covered entity may contact the individual to raise funds for the covered entity
- If the covered entity is a group health plan or an insurance company or HMO supporting a group health plan, a statement that PHI may be disclosed to the plan's sponsor[540]

The notice must disclose the following information concerning the individual's rights with respect to PHI, and a brief statement as to how the individual may exercise these rights:

- The right to receive the notice electronically
- The right to complain to the covered entity and to the Secretary of DHHS if the individual believes his or her privacy rights have been violated, a description of how to file a complaint with the covered entity, a statement that the covered entity may not retaliate for a complaint to request restrictions on certain uses and disclosures of PHI, and a statement of the covered entity's right to reject such request
- The right to receive confidential communications of PHI
- The right to inspect and copy PHI
- The right to amend PHI
- The right to receive an accounting of certain disclosures of PHI
- The right to receive a paper copy of the HIPAA notice upon request, even if the individual has agreed to receive notice electronically[541]

Although not specifically required by the regulations, a covered entity may wish to consider including certain other rights and protections afforded to individuals under the regulations, including the right to opt

---

[540] 45 C.F.R. § 164.520(b)(1)(iii).
[541] 45 C.F.R. § 164.520(b)(1)(iv) and (vi).

out of certain uses and disclosures and the right to provide prior written authorization of certain uses and disclosures. The notice must also state that the covered entity:

- Is required by law to maintain the privacy of PHI and to provide the individual with the notice of privacy practices
- Is required to comply with the terms of the notice currently in effect
- Reserves the right to revise its notice with respect to all the PHI it maintains and to specify how it will provide individuals with a revised notice[542]

The Privacy Rule permits covered entities to include optional additional provisions. If a covered entity chooses to further limit the uses and disclosures the rule otherwise permits it to make, the entity may describe those limitations in its notice. However, the rule prohibits it from including a limitation affecting its right to use or disclose PHI as required by law or to avert a serious threat to health or safety.[543]

The Privacy Rule also permits a covered entity to provide a "layered notice" to the individual. A layered notice is a two part notice consisting of a brief summary of the individual's rights and other information and the more detailed HIPAA notice described above. Some covered entities may wish to use the layered notice as a more reader friendly communication with the individual. Layered notices are acceptable as long as the communication contains all the notice elements required by the Privacy Rule.[544]

Changes to the Notice

Covered healthcare providers with a direct treatment relationship with an individual must make a revised notice available to patients who request it and to patients who have a first service delivery after the effective date of the revisions.[545] If a covered provider has a physical delivery site, the provider also must have the revised notice available at the site for individuals to take with them, and must post the revised notice in a clear and prominent location where it is reasonable for individuals to be

---

[542] 45 C.F.R. § 164.520(b)(1)(v).
[543] 45 C.F.R. § 164.520(b)(2).
[544] Department of Health and Human Services, *Standards for Privacy*, 108.
[545] 45 C.F.R. § 164.520(b)(2)(iv).

able to read it. The covered entity need not send a copy of the revised notice to individuals who received a prior version of its notice, unless one of them requests a copy of the revised version.[546] A covered entity that revises its notice is not required to obtain an additional acknowledgment of receipt of the notice from individuals who received a prior version. An acknowledgment must be obtained only at the first service delivery.[547] An affected health plan must inform individuals then covered by the plan of a material revision to its notice within 60 days of the revision.[548]

Time and Manner of Giving Notice

When and how to give notice depends in part on whether the covered entity is a healthcare provider with a direct treatment relationship with the individual or whether it is a group health plan.

Health plans that are required to give the notice must do so at time of enrollment to new enrollees and within 60 days of a material revision to the plan. At least every three years, health plans must also notify persons covered by the plans that the notice is available and how to obtain a copy of it. Notice to the named or primary insured person is considered to be notice to that person and all dependents. If the health plan has more than one notice, it must give the person making the request the notice that is applicable to him or her.[549] Health plans are not required to obtain an acknowledgment of receipt of notice.[550]

In a non-emergency treatment situation, covered health providers with a direct treatment relationship with an individual must provide the notice no later than the date of delivery of the first service to that individual.[551] The first service is usually the first face-to-face encounter in the provider's office or other service location. However, first service could be by telephone or e-mail, and the Privacy Rule is designed to be flexible enough to accommodate these types of encounters.[552] For example, if the first service is by telephone, the provider should send the notice and request for acknowledgment to the patient by mail or e-mail

---

[546] Department of Health and Human Services, *Standards for Privacy*, 112.
[547] Ibid., 108.
[548] 45 C.F.R. § 164.520(c)(1)(i)(C).
[549] 45 C.F.R. § 164.520(c)(1).
[550] Department of Health and Human Services, *Standards for Privacy*, 109.
[551] 45 C.F.R. § 164.520(c)(2)(i)(A).
[552] Department of Health and Human Services, *Standards for Privacy*, 109.

on the same day if possible.[553] If the initial telephone contact is merely for the purpose of obtaining pretreatment information or for scheduling the appointment, the notice requirements do not apply. In that situation, the provider should provide notice at the time the patient appears for the treatment appointment.[554] In emergency situations, the provider must provide the notice to the individual as soon as reasonably practicable after the emergency treatment has been provided.[555]

If the provider maintains a physical service delivery site, the provider must have copies of the notice available for individuals seeking services to take with them, and must post the notice in a clear and prominent location for such individuals.[556] The rule requires that the entire notice be posted, but does not prescribe the manner or format of posting, so providers have discretion to design their postings in a manner most suitable to their treatment setting.[557] Posting the notice is not a substitute for providing the notice to each patient.[558]

Healthcare providers with an indirect treatment relationship are *not* required to provide the notice, but they must provide the notice upon request.[559] These providers typically deliver health care to individuals based on the orders of another healthcare provider, and provide services or products, or report the diagnosis or results, directly to another healthcare provider, who furnishes these products or services to the individual. For example, a radiologist and, in some cases, a clinical laboratory are providers with an indirect treatment relationship.

Requirements for Electronic Notice

A covered entity that maintains a Web site that provides information about the covered entity's customer services or benefits must prominently post its notice on the Web site and make the notice available electronically through the Web site.[560] The notice must be provided automatically in response to the patient's first requests for service.[561] A

---

[553] Ibid.
[554] Ibid., 112.
[555] 45 C.F.R. § 164.520(c)(2)(i)(B).
[556] 45 C.F.R. § 164.520(c)(2)(iii).
[557] Department of Health and Human Services, *Standards for Privacy*, 111.
[558] Ibid., 112.
[559] 65 Fed. Reg. 82723 (Dec. 28, 2000).
[560] 45 C.F.R. § 164.520(c)(3)(i).
[561] 45 C.F.R. § 164.520(c)(3)(iii).

covered entity may provide its notice to an individual by e-mail, if the individual agrees to electronic notice and if such agreement has not been withdrawn. The electronic notice must be timely made in accordance with all other aspects of the notice procedure for the applicable covered entity. In addition, if the covered entity knows that the e-mail transmission has failed, it must provide a paper copy of the notice to the individual.[562] An individual who receives the notice in electronic form retains the right to obtain a paper copy of the notice from a covered entity upon request.

Joint Notices

Separate covered entities participating in an OHCA may each use a separate notice or may issue a joint notice if:

- The joint notice otherwise satisfies all the other essential elements of the notice
- They agree to abide by the terms of the notice with respect to the PHI created or received by them as part of their participation in the OHCA
- The joint notice identifies with reasonable specificity the entities, service delivery sites, or classes of service delivery sites to which the joint notice applies
- The joint notice states that the covered entities participating in the OHCA will share PHI with one another as necessary to carry out the treatment, payment, and healthcare operations relating to the OHCA[563]

(See the discussion of OHCAs earlier in this chapter.) If any one participating covered entity in an OHCA provides the joint notice to an individual, it will satisfy the notice requirement for all participating covered entities.[564] Thus, if a hospital and its medical staff function as an OHCA, and the hospital provides the notice when the patient is first seen at the hospital, the notice distribution requirement of the

---

[562] 45 C.F.R. § 164.520(c)(3)(ii).
[563] 45 C.F.R. § 164.520(d).
[564] 45 C.F.R. § 164.520(d)(3).

rule will have been met. If the OHCA uses a joint notice, only a participating provider with a direct treatment relationship must attempt to obtain the individual's acknowledgment of receipt of the joint notice.

Legally separate covered entities may designate themselves (including any healthcare component of such covered entity) an ACE if all of the covered entities designated are under common ownership or control. An ACE is required to produce and distribute only one notice. Therefore, if one of the covered entities included as part of the single ACE provides notice to a patient, all of the participating entities will have met the rule's notice requirements.[565] (See the discussion of ACEs earlier in this chapter.)

Right to Have Access to, Inspect, and Copy PHI

A covered entity must permit an individual to request access to the PHI in his or her designated record set. The covered entity may deny the request under certain circumstances, but must provide a procedure for reviewing certain denials. Individuals also have the right to obtain a copy of their PHI, but may be required to pay for reasonable duplication costs. The patient's right of access under the Privacy Rule is discussed in greater detail in the section of this chapter titled "Access by or on Behalf of the Patient."

Right to Request Restrictions on the Uses and Disclosures of PHI for Treatment, Payment, and Healthcare Operations

The Privacy Rule gives an individual the right to request that a covered entity restrict the use or disclosure of his or her PHI in connection with treatment, payment, or healthcare operations; for the purposes of notifying family and friends of the individual's health status; and for their involvement in the individual's health care.[566] Covered entities, especially covered healthcare providers, should discuss the requested restrictions with the individual and explain any risks that might arise from the restrictions.[567] Covered entities are not required to agree to a

---

[565] 45 C.F.R. § 164.105(b)(1).
[566] 45 C.F.R. § 164.522(a)(1)(i).
[567] 65 Fed. Reg. 82553 (Dec. 28, 2000).

restriction unless they are required to do so under state law. If they do agree, however, they must document the restriction and, unless an exception applies, abide by it until it is terminated.[568] Formal documentation is not required; a simple note in the patient's medical record would be sufficient.[569] Many covered entities will likely prefer to develop a standard form by which an individual may request a restriction, and place the completed form in the individual's medical record. The documentation also may be in an electronic medium. Covered entities must maintain their documentation at least six years from date it was created or the date it was last in effect, whichever is later.[570]

If a covered entity agrees to a restriction, the entity must abide by the restriction, except in the following circumstances. If the use or disclosure is made to the individual to whom the PHI relates or is required to treat the individual in an emergency,[571] the covered entity is not subject to the restriction, but it must request any recipient of the PHI not to redisclose it.[572] The patient's restriction also does not apply to PHI used in facility directories in accordance with the Privacy Rule, or to uses and disclosures that may be made without the patient's authorization and for which the patient is not given an opportunity to object, and those needed by the Secretary of DHHS to investigate the covered entity's compliance with HIPAA.[573]

Covered healthcare providers should exercise their judgment with respect to patient requests for additional restrictions, particularly if the patient needs additional privacy protection. This will likely be the case for celebrity patients and for patients suffering from an illness or procedures knowledge of which could adversely affect the patient's relationship with family and friends (for example, sexually transmitted disease, AIDS treatment, abortion). (See discussion of use and disclosures of health information concerning these special circumstances in Chapter 8.) If a covered entity has accepted an individual's requested restriction, the restriction will also apply to that covered entity's business associates, with two exceptions: the use of PHI that the business

---

[568] 45 C.F.R. §§ 164.522(a)(1)(iii) through (v).
[569] 65 Fed. Reg. 82553 (Dec. 28, 2000).
[570] 45 C.F.R. § 164.530(j).
[571] 45 C.F.R. § 164.522(a)(1)(iii).
[572] 45 C.F.R. § 164.522(a)(1)(iv).
[573] 45 C.F.R. § 164.522(a)(1)(v).

associate needs to manage its business, and for data aggregation.[574] A covered entity therefore must inform its business associates of any restrictions it has accepted on use and disclosure of PHI that is disclosed to the business associates.

If a covered entity has agreed to the patient's additional restriction, the entity may terminate its agreement if the patient provides a written agreement or request to terminate the restriction, if the patient provides an oral agreement and the covered entity documents it, or if the entity notifies the patient that it is terminating the agreement. If the covered entity terminates its agreement, the termination applies only to PHI created or received after the covered entity has informed the patient of the termination. The restriction to which the covered entity agreed will continue to apply to PHI created or received before the restriction terminated.[575]

The individual may terminate the restriction at any time.[576] Covered entities should obtain the individual's termination in writing or document the individual's oral termination and maintain the records in the same manner as the original restriction.

DHHS expects that covered entities, especially covered providers, will discuss any requested restrictions with the individual and explain any risks that might arise from the restriction. DHHS was particularly concerned that a restriction on use or disclosure could compromise the ability of providers to render necessary health care to the individual in the future.[577] The Privacy Rule addresses this concern in part by permitting a covered entity to use or disclose PHI, or to disclose PHI to a healthcare provider, in violation of an agreed upon restriction if the individual requires emergency treatment. If PHI is disclosed for emergency treatment, the disclosing entity must request the recipient provider not to further disclose or use the PHI.[578] The commentary to the Privacy Rule makes clear that the rule does not address the question of whether a covered entity will be liable for an individual's future injury resulting from the entity's agreement to his or her request for a

---

[574] U5 Fed. Reg. 82728 (Dec. 28, 2000).
[575] 45 C.F.R. § 164.522(a)(2).
[576] 45 C.F.R. § 164.522(a)(2)(i).
[577] 65 Fed. Reg. 83553 (Dec. 28, 2000).
[578] 45 C.F.R. § 164.522(a)(1)(iii).

restricted disclosure of health information. Such questions of liability will be decided by state law.[579]

Right to Request to Receive Confidential Communications

The Privacy Rule also entitles individuals to request that covered healthcare providers communicate PHI by alternative means or at alternative locations.[580] An individual may prefer, for example, that his or her family (or an abusive spouse) not be aware of a particular illness or treatment, and therefore the individual may request a hospital or physician to send health information to a place of employment rather than to the home. An individual may also request that communications be in a sealed envelope rather than on a postcard. Likewise, a health plan must accommodate such requests if the individual clearly states that the disclosure of information from the health plan in the normal course of business could endanger the individual.[581] For example, a person may not wish to disclose an explanation of health plan benefits to individuals in his or her household who may become abusive.

Covered entities are not expected to accommodate unreasonable requests for alternative means of, or locations for, communications. The reasonableness of a request must be determined solely on the basis of the administrative difficulty of complying with it. A covered healthcare provider or health plan may not refuse a request simply because the individual's reason seems unfounded.[582] In addition, a healthcare provider may not require the individual to provide an explanation for the request.[583] A covered entity, however, may require an individual to make the request in writing, including a statement for a health plan that disclosure could endanger the individual, and may refuse the request if the individual does not provide sufficient information concerning how payment will be handled or does not specify the means of communication desired or the address of an alternative delivery site.[584]

---

[579] 65 Fed. Reg. 82727 (Dec. 28, 2000).
[580] 45 C.F.R. § 164.522(b)(1).
[581] 45 C.F.R. § 164.522(b)(2).
[582] 65 Fed. Reg. 82553 (Dec. 28, 2000).
[583] 45 C.F.R. § 164.522(b)(2)(iii).
[584] 45 C.F.R. § 164.522(b)(2)(ii).

Right to Request Restrictions on the Uses and Disclosures for Which an Authorization Is Not Required

The Privacy Rule gives individuals the right to object to, or request restrictions on, the use or disclosure of PHI to family or friends involved in their care, or to public health or other organizations authorized to participate in disaster relief activities.[585] These uses and disclosures are discussed in greater detail in the section of this chapter titled "Access by Family and Friends."

Right to Request an Amendment to PHI

The Privacy Rule permits individuals under certain circumstances to request a covered entity to amend their PHI. The purpose of this rule is to ensure that individuals' health information is accurate and complete and that inaccurate information will not be used to their detriment.[586] This is not an unqualified right to alter a medical record, however, and covered entities may accept or reject a request for amendment.[587] The intent of the Privacy Rule is not to create a perfect record or to permit substantive reviews to the medical decisions documented in the record. The goal is to establish a standard of reasonable accuracy and completeness.[588]

Nature of the Right to Amend

An individual's right to request an amendment applies only to health information maintained in a designated record set.[589] (See the discussion of designated record sets earlier in this chapter.) Therefore, if a hospital receives a request for an amendment, but the information that is the subject of the request is not part of the hospital medical record and does not use the information as a basis for making decisions concerning the patient, the Privacy Rule would not apply, and the hospital would have no HIPAA obligation to accept or respond to the request.

---

[585] 45 C.F.R. § 164.510.
[586] 65 Fed. Reg. 82736 (Dec. 28, 2000).
[587] 65 Fed. Reg. 82737 (Dec. 28, 2000).
[588] 65 Fed. Reg. 82558 (Dec. 28, 2000).
[589] 45 C.F.R. § 164.526(a)(1).

If a state law creates a right in an individual to amend his or her health information, however, and that law is not preempted by HIPAA, the hospital would be required to comply with the state law.

If a covered entity notifies them in advance of its requirements, the entity may require individuals to submit their requests for amendment in writing and to state the reasons for the amendments.[590] If it has met these conditions, a covered entity will not be required to act on a requested amendment that does not satisfy its required procedures.[591] A covered entity must document the titles of persons or offices it designates to receive requests for amendments, and maintain this information in writing (which includes electronic storage) for at least six years.[592]

The individual or the individual's personal representative may request an amendment to the individual's PHI. A personal representative is someone who has the authority under applicable law to act on behalf of the individual.[593]

If a covered entity receives notice from another covered entity that the designated record set it holds has been amended, the receiving entity must amend the record accordingly.[594] The Privacy Rule does not require a covered entity to amend its designated record set if it receives notice of an amendment from someone other than the individual or his or her personal representative or from another covered entity, but any healthcare provider should consider, and possibly address in its health information policies and procedures, how the provider will respond if it receives credible information that one of its patient's records has been amended.

Accepting an Amendment

Most covered entities will accept any requested amendment that corrects an error in the record or otherwise improves the record. If it accepts any part of the amendment, a covered entity should make the accepted amendment by identifying the records affected by the amendment and appending or providing a link to the amendment. The

---

[590] 45 C.F.R. § 164.526(b)(1).
[591] 65 Fed. Reg. 82558 (Dec. 28, 2000).
[592] 45 C.F.R. § 164.526(f).
[593] See 45 C.F.R. § 164.502(g).
[594] 45 C.F.R. § 164.526(e).

amendment may be an actual change in the record or may be the addition of a document or a link in an electronic record that contains the additional information requested. To implement the amendment, covered entities should follow their established record amendment policies. For example, many hospitals require that any alteration of a medical record include the identity of the person making the change and the date on which it is made. (See Chapter 4 for a discussion of alterations to the medical record.)

The covered entity also must take each of the following actions:

- Notify the individual that it has accepted his or her request (this notice need not include an explanation of why the amendment was accepted or any physician's signature)
- Ask the individual to identify any persons who have received PHI about the individual and who should receive the amendment
- Obtain the individual's agreement to disclose the amendment to those persons

The covered entity must then provide the amendment to the persons identified by the individual and persons the covered entity knows have, and may rely upon, the individual's PHI (for example, the covered entity's business associates and other covered entities who treated the individual).[595]

A covered entity must act on a request for amendment, either to accept or deny it, within 60 days of receiving a request. If it accepts a request, the covered entity must make the amendment and issue the notifications described above within those 60 days. If it rejects any part of the request, the entity must give the individual the written denial described below within that time. The regulations allow a covered entity one additional 30-day extension in which to act if it notifies the individual within the first 60 days of the reason for the delay and the date it expects to respond.[596]

Denying an Amendment

A covered entity may deny a requested amendment if it determines that the PHI involved meets any one of the following qualifications:

---

[595] 45 C.F.R. § 164.526(c)(3).
[596] 45 C.F.R. § 164.526(a)(2).

- Was not created by the covered entity[597]
- Is not part of a designated record set
- Would not be available under the Privacy Rule for an individual's inspection (see the discussion of an individual's access to PHI elsewhere in this chapter)
- Is accurate and complete[598]

Its denial must be given to the individual in writing in plain language, and must include all of the following:

- The basis for the denial
- Notice of the individual's right to submit a written statement disagreeing with the denial, and instructions on how to submit it
- If no statement of disagreement is submitted, notice of the individual's right to ask that his or her original request and the covered entity's denial be included with any future disclosure of the PHI
- A description of how the individual may complain to the covered entity or to the Secretary of DHHS, including the contact information for the covered entity's privacy officer, contact person, or office[599]

The covered entity may set a reasonable limit on the length of a statement of disagreement. If the individual submits a statement of disagreement, the covered entity may, but is not required to, prepare a rebuttal statement. If it chooses to create a rebuttal, the covered entity must send a copy to the individual.[600]

Future Disclosures of Amended Records

The covered entity must attach, physically or electronically, the request for amendment, its denial, any statement of disagreement, and any rebuttal statement to the designated record set that was the subject of the

---

[597] A covered entity may not use this rationale if the individual gives it a reasonable basis to believe that the creator of the PHI is no longer available to make the amendment (e.g., has gone out of business). 45 C.F.R. § 164.526(a)(2)(i).

[598] A covered entity may, but is not required to, amend the PHI even if it believes the PHI is accurate and complete. 65 Fed. Reg. 82738 (Dec. 28, 2000).

[599] 45 C.F.R. § 164.526(d)(1).

[600] 45 C.F.R. § 164.526(d)(2) and (3).

initial request.[601] Any future disclosure of that record must include these materials or, if the covered entity prefers, an accurate summary of them.[602]

The Privacy Rule acknowledges that a covered entity may not be able to include these materials in disclosures made in the form of a HIPAA standard transaction because the standard computer code sets may not contain the free text fields necessary to accommodate additional materials. If this is the case, the covered entity may disclose these materials to the recipient in a separate electronic transmittal.[603] This is an exception to the HIPAA TCS Rule that requires PHI to be transmitted in standard transactions using HIPAA standard code sets.

Right to Receive an Accounting of Disclosures of PHI

The Privacy Rule gives an individual the right to request a list of a covered entity's disclosures of his or her PHI.[604] The purpose of the accounting requirement is to inform individuals as to the disclosures and recipients of their PHI, to enable them to exercise their other rights under the rule, to enable them to monitor how covered entities are complying with the rule, and to permit them to address any privacy concerns they may have with a covered entity.[605] The requirement reflects the conclusion of the 1977 report of the Privacy Protection Study Commission that individuals should receive an accounting of disclosures of their health information.[606] The rule's accounting provisions are a substantial additional requirement for covered entities, a requirement that is not found in most state health information privacy laws. Although many health information systems in large providers and health plans are now electronic, the administrative burden for covered entities is substantial.

The Privacy Rule is specific as to what a covered entity must include in an accounting and how it must respond to an individual's request for the accounting. The accounting must include disclosures made by the

---

[601] 45 C.F.R. § 164.526(d)(4).
[602] 45 C.F.R. § 164.526(d)(4)(i) and (ii).
[603] 45 C.F.R. § 164.526(d)(4)(iii).
[604] 45 C.F.R. § 164.528(a)(1).
[605] 65 Fed. Reg. 82739 (Dec. 28, 2000).
[606] Privacy Protection Study Commission, *Personal Privacy in an Information Society* (Privacy Protection Study Commission, July 1977), 306–307.

covered entity and its business associates during the six years prior to the date of the requested accounting or for such shorter period as the individual may prescribe.[607] (See discussion of business associates earlier in this chapter.) The accounting must include all of the following information for each disclosure:

- The date of the disclosure
- The name and address of the person who received the PHI
- A brief description of the PHI disclosed
- A brief description of the purpose of the disclosure, unless the disclosure was made in response to a DHHS investigation or for a purpose that the rule permits without an individual's authorization, in which case the accounting need provide only a copy of the request for that disclosure[608]

If a covered entity makes multiple disclosures to the same person or organization pursuant for a single purpose permitted by the Privacy Rule, the entity may provide a summary accounting of those disclosures rather than an accounting for each disclosure.[609] Individuals are entitled to one accounting free of charge from a covered entity in any 12-month period, but must pay a reasonable, cost based fee for any additional accountings they request during that time. If the covered entity imposes such a fee, it must notify the individuals of the fee in advance and give them an opportunity to withdraw their additional requests.[610] A covered entity must respond to a request for an accounting within 60 days of its receipt—unless it is unable to do so, in which case the entity is permitted one 30-day extension if it notifies the requesting individual of the delay and the reason for it.[611]

The accounting must include all disclosures the covered entity made, except for disclosures:

- To carry out treatment, payment and healthcare operations. DHHS decided that requiring an accounting for these disclosures would be unduly burdensome on covered entities.[612] Thus, an accounting

---

[607] 45 C.F.R. § 164.528(a)(1) and (3).
[608] 45 C.F.R. § 164.528(b)(2).
[609] 65 Fed. Reg. 82743 (Dec. 28, 2000).
[610] 45 C.F.R. § 164.528(c)(2).
[611] 45 C.F.R. § 164.528(c)(1).
[612] 65 Fed. Reg. 82740 (Dec. 28, 2000).

need not include disclosures to a person involved in the patient's healthcare treatment. Most of the disclosures a covered healthcare provider makes fall into this exclusion. (See the discussion of treatment, payment, and healthcare operations earlier in this chapter.)

- To the individual. An individual will be aware of these disclosures and will not need an accounting of them.
- Incident to a use or disclosure otherwise permitted or required by the Privacy Rule. The rule permits or requires various disclosures of PHI. A covered entity need not account for disclosures of PHI that are merely incidental to those disclosures, so long as it has met the rule's other requirements (for example, minimum necessary disclosures).
- Pursuant to an authorization properly completed by the individual. Again, if the individual authorized the disclosure, it is presumed that he or she is already aware of it.
- For the covered entity's directory or to family and others involved in the individual's care or for other notifications permitted by the regulations (for example, notifying a family member of the patient's condition).
- For lawful national security or intelligence purposes.
- To correctional institutions or law enforcement officials for the purposes specified in the Privacy Rule (for example, for the care of inmates, safety of officers, law enforcement in the institutions).
- As part of a limited data set. Information disclosed in a limited data set contains too few personal identifiers to require an accounting.
- That occurred prior to the HIPAA compliance date for the covered entity (that is, April 14, 2003, for most covered entities).[613]

The amount of PHI disclosed does not affect whether the disclosure must be in the accounting. Even if a covered entity discloses only a small amount of PHI, the accounting must include the disclosure unless it falls into one of these exceptions. The fact that informing individuals of reports to public health agencies might cause people to avoid treatment so that their diseases would not be reported is not a reason to exclude those disclosures from an accounting.[614]

An accounting must include *disclosures* and not uses. The accounting primarily informs individuals to whom their PHI has been disclosed,

---

[613] 45 C.F.R. § 164.528(a)(1).
[614] 65 Fed. Reg. 82740 (Dec. 28, 2000).

not how it is being used. The downstream disclosures made by other recipients of the PHI need not be included in the covered entity's accounting. Thus, if a hospital discloses information to a physician's office for purposes of healthcare treatment, and the physician discloses that PHI to another person, the hospital should not include the physician's disclosure in the hospital's accounting.[615]

The Privacy Rule creates a limited exception for disclosures a covered entity has made to a health oversight agency or to law enforcement officials. Informing the patient of these disclosures may compromise a lawful investigation. If an agency or law enforcement official requests a covered entity to temporarily suspend an individual's right to an accounting because an accounting may impede the agency's activities, the covered entity must do so. The request may be oral, in which case the covered entity must document the request and the identity of the agency or official making it. If the request is oral, an individual's right may be suspended for no more than 30 days. If the agency or official submits a written request to the covered entity for a suspension, the suspension may continue for the time specified in the written request.[616]

A covered entity must maintain certain documentation relating to accountings for a period of six years from the date the information is created. The entity must maintain all of the information needed to comply with the accounting requirement of the rule, a copy of the accountings provided to individuals, and the titles of the persons or offices at the covered entity who are responsible for receiving and responding to accounting requests.[617]

Right to Report Violations of the Regulations to the Secretary of DHHS

The Privacy Rule and the Enforcement Rule give individuals two methods for filing complaints if they believe a covered entity has failed to comply with the Privacy Rule. They may complain directly to the covered entity, or they may report the violation to the Secretary of DHHS.

Each covered entity must establish in its HIPAA policies a process by which individuals may make complaints concerning the entity's pri-

---

[615] 65 Fed. Reg. 82742 (Dec. 28, 2000).
[616] 45 C.F.R. § 164.528(a)(2).
[617] 45 C.F.R. § 164.528(d).

vacy policies and procedures, the entity's compliance with those policies and procedures, and the entity's compliance with the requirements of the Privacy Rule.[618] The covered entity must retain documentation of all complaints in written or electronic form for a period of six years from the date the documentation is created or the date it was last in effect, whichever is later.[619] Most covered entities would prefer that an individual register a complaint with them rather than with a government enforcement agency. Thus, it would be advantageous to have a complaint procedure that patients can easily understand and follow.

If a person believes that a covered entity is not complying with the compliance principles of the Enforcement Rule or with the requirements of the Privacy Rule, he or she may file a complaint with the Secretary of DHHS.[620] The complaint must be written but may be filed electronically. It must also name the covered entity, describe the nature of its violation, and provide other information the Secretary may prescribe.[621] Complaints must be filed within 180 days of when the person knew, or should have known, of the violation, but the Secretary may waive this time limit if there is good cause to do so.[622] Instructions for filing complaints electronically or in writing are available on the CMS Web site.[623]

The right to file a complaint extends also to members of a covered entity's workforce, who may disclose PHI as part of a whistle blower report of improper conduct by the covered entity, although the Privacy Rule does not prescribe the precise manner in which the report is to be made.[624]

Verifying Identity and Representations

Healthcare organizations and practitioners must use care in verifying that individuals requesting patient health information are who they say

---

[618] 45 C.F.R. § 164.530(d).
[619] 45 C.F.R. § 164.530(j).
[620] 45 C.F.R. § 160.306(a).
[621] The specific information to be included is set forth on the DHHS Web site at http://answers.hhs.gov/cgi-bin/hhs.cfg/php/enduser/std_alp.php.
[622] 45 C.F.R. § 164.530(b).
[623] http://www.cms.hhs.gov/hipaa/hipaa2/default.asp.
[624] 45 C.F.R. § 164.502(j)(1).

they are. State laws provide little guidance as to what actions constitute adequate verification, but the Privacy Rule prescribes specific steps to verify identity.

Under the Privacy Rule, a covered entity is required as a general rule to verify the identity of anyone requesting PHI, unless the covered entity already knows the requester's identity and the requester's authority to have access to the PHI.[625] Thus, a physician who knows his or her patient is not required to verify the patient's identity or authority to access the patient's PHI. Verification is not required for disclosures of PHI to facility directories or to family members and others involved in the patient's care. (See the discussion of these disclosures earlier in this chapter.)

Before a covered entity may disclose PHI in certain circumstances, the Privacy Rule requires the person requesting PHI to make representations or provide documentation. For example, a law enforcement official seeking PHI in connection with a law enforcement activity must represent, among other things, that the PHI is needed to determine whether a crime has been committed. In these instances, the covered entity must obtain the representation or documentation and may rely upon it if, on its face, the representation or documentation meets the requirements of the Rule and if that reliance is reasonable.[626] As a general rule, therefore, covered entities should not rely on any representation or documentation that is in some way suspicious. If any doubt exists, it is better to err on the side of protecting the confidentiality of health information, even if that means seeking the intervention of a senior manager of or legal counsel for the covered entity.

When public officials or their agents request PHI, special rules apply. The Privacy Rule permits covered entities to rely upon any of the following to verify identity:

- A badge or other official credentials presented personally
- A request presented on appropriate government letterhead
- If the disclosure is to an agent of a public official, a written statement on appropriate government stationery that the requester is acting under the government's authority, or a contract or other documentation substantiating the requester's status[627]

---

[625] 45 C.F.R. § 164.514(h)(1)(i).
[626] 45 C.F.R. § 164.514(h)(2).
[627] 45 C.F.R. § 164.514(h)(2)(ii).

The covered entity may rely on any of the following to verify the public official or agent's authority to obtain PHI:

- A written or oral statement of the legal authority under which the request is made
- Any subpoena, warrant, order, or other legal process issued by a grand jury, court, or administrative tribunal[628]

In situations in which the Privacy Rule gives individuals an opportunity to object to the disclosure of their PHI, a covered entity will fulfill the verification requirements of the rule if it exercises its professional judgment. (See the discussion of the exercise of professional judgment earlier in this chapter.) If the covered entity is disclosing PHI to prevent a serious threat to health or safety, the entity will fulfill its verification requirements if it acts in good faith.[629]

The Privacy Rule gives the Secretary of DHHS the authority to investigate the alleged violation and, if a violation has occurred, to attempt to correct the problem through informal efforts. If the Secretary and the covered entity cannot resolve the matter through these means, the Secretary may issue written findings of noncompliance, which may then subject the covered entity to legal sanctions under HIPAA.[630] (See the discussion of HIPAA sanctions in Chapter 11.)

If a covered entity becomes aware of a violation, because a person has filed a complaint with it or with the Secretary or from any other source, the entity must take action to the extent possible to mitigate the harmful effects of the violation.[631] The requirement to mitigate applies to violations by the covered entity or its business associates. To protect the individual's right to complain of violations, the Privacy Rule prohibits a healthcare provider from requiring a patient to waive his or her right to file a complaint as a condition for the provision of healthcare treatment, payment, enrollment in a health plan, or eligibility for plan benefits.[632] In addition, a covered entity may not retaliate against or intimidate any person for exercising his or her rights under the Privacy Rule or for testifying in an enforcement hearing.[633]

---

[628] 45 C.F.R. § 164.514(h)(2)(iii).
[629] 45 C.F.R. § 164.514(h)(2)(iv).
[630] 45 C.F.R. § 160.312(a).
[631] 45 C.F.R. § 164.530(f).
[632] 45 C.F.R. § 164.530(h).
[633] 45 C.F.R. § 164.530(g).

HIPAA Administrative Requirements

The Privacy and Security Rules impose on most covered entities administrative requirements that are necessary to implement the privacy and security protections prescribed in the rules. These include regulations that govern record keeping, privacy, and security personnel; training; mitigation of damages; and the like. These requirements apply to all covered entities except group health plans that provide benefits solely through a contract with a health insurer. Imposing the administrative requirements on these plans would create an unreasonable burden given the limited PHI they maintain. These plans are subject to the Privacy Rule's prohibition against intimidation or retaliation. (See the related discussion earlier in this chapter.)[634]

Policies and Procedures

The Privacy Rule requires each covered entity to establish such written policies and procedures as are necessary, given its size and the nature of its operations, to enable it to comply with the requirements of the rule.[635] The purpose of this requirement is to ensure that important decisions concerning individuals' privacy rights are made thoroughly and not in an ad hoc manner and to facilitate workforce HIPAA training.[636] The Privacy Rule does not specify the content of these policies and procedures, but leaves to each covered entity the discretion to design its policies and procedures to fit its unique structural and operational characteristics. Most large healthcare providers have had policies and procedures governing their medical records operations, but their HIPAA privacy policies and procedures will likely be much more extensive and must be coordinated with their notice of privacy practices. (See the discussion of notice earlier in this chapter.)

Documentation

In addition to privacy and security policies and procedures, the Privacy and Security Rules require covered entities to document many of their actions and to retain various documentation in connection with the

---

[634] 65 Fed. Reg. 82564 (Dec. 28, 2000).
[635] 45 C.F.R. § 164.530(i).
[636] 65 Fed. Reg. 82749 (Dec. 28, 2000).

use, disclosure, and protection of PHI. This documentation must be retained for a period of six years from the later of the date on which the documentation was created and the date on which it was last in effect. Documentation must be written, but may be written in electronic form.[637]

Personnel

A covered entity must designate and document a privacy official[638] and a security official,[639] who are responsible for developing the entity's required policies and procedures. These individuals may be the contact persons to whom complaints of violations are directed or who provide additional information about the privacy practices described in the entity's privacy notice. (See the discussion of privacy notices earlier in this chapter.) If the entity prefers not to name its privacy and security officials as the contacts, it may designate an office to receive complaints.[640] The designated privacy official and security official may be, but are not required to be, the same person.

Training

Training should be a major component of any covered entity's HIPAA compliance program. The Privacy and Security Rules require a covered entity to provide training for its workforce, but do not specify how a covered entity must organize its training program. The training must be appropriate and sufficient for members of the workforce to carry out their functions in the covered entity.[641] The rules define "workforce" as employees, volunteers, and others who work under the direct control of the covered entity.[642] Thus, most independent contractors would not be part of the workforce because the entity would not have direct control over their work.

All current members of a covered entity's workforce should now be trained concerning compliance with the Privacy and Security Rules,

---

[637] 45 C.F.R. §§ 164.316(b) and § 164.530(j).
[638] 45 C.F.R. § 164.530(a)(1).
[639] 45 C.F.R. § 164.308(a)(2).
[640] 45 C.F.R. § 164.530(a).
[641] 45 C.F.R. § 164.308(a)(5)(i); 45 C.F.R. § 164.530(b)(1).
[642] 45 C.F.R. § 160.103.

and new members of the workforce must receive training within a reasonable period after they begin work. If the covered entity revises its HIPAA policies and procedures such that members of the workforce are materially affected, those individuals must receive additional training for those changes.[643] Periodic recertification of workforce members who have been trained is unnecessary.[644] Covered entities must document that they have provided the required HIPAA training and must maintain their records for the prescribed period.[645] Many covered entities have created or acquired Web based HIPAA training materials that enable workforce members to train individually, to confirm through testing their understanding of the rules, and to automatically document each completed session of required training. Other, often smaller covered entities conduct in-person training sessions that are appropriate for their size and operations.

Sanctions Imposed on Workforce

Covered entities must establish sanctions to be imposed on their workforce members who violate the provisions of the Privacy Rule or the policies and procedures that the covered entities establish in accordance with the rule.[646] Imposition of sanctions is not required, however, in connection with disclosures of PHI by whistle blowers in accordance with the rule or as a means of retaliating against a workforce member who has filed a complaint with the Secretary of DHHS, has testified or assisted in an investigatory hearing, or has opposed in good faith an act that is unlawful under the rule.[647] As a general matter, covered entities may not intimidate or retaliate against members of its workforce for these actions, or against individuals for exercising their Privacy Rule rights. Covered entities may not compel individuals to waive their rights to file complaints with the Secretary concerning Privacy Rule violations.[648] In this context, the term "individuals" includes individual persons, organizations, or groups, such as oversight agencies and advocacy groups.[649] It should be noted that whistle blower protection does

---

[643] 45 C.F.R. § 164.530(b)(2).
[644] 65 Fed. Reg. 82745 (Dec. 28, 2000).
[645] 45 C.F.R. § 164.530(b)(2)(ii).
[646] 45 C.F.R. § 164.530(e)(1).
[647] 45 C.F.R. § 164.530(e)(2).
[648] 45 C.F.R. § 164.530(g) and (h).
[649] 65 Fed. Reg. 82748 (Dec. 28, 2000).

not extend to disclosures by members of the workforce to friends or news media.[650]

Duty to Mitigate

If a covered entity becomes aware of a use or disclosure of PHI in violation of the Privacy Rule by a member of its workforce or by a business associate or contractor, the entity must take reasonable steps to mitigate the harmful effects of the violation.[651] The covered entity's duty arises only if it has actual knowledge of harm and if it is practicable to reduce the harm. For example, if a covered entity learns that it inadvertently disclosed PHI without authorization in a domestic abuse situation, the entity must promptly notify the patient and the appropriate authorities and alert them to the potential danger.[652]

Safeguards

The Privacy Rule contains a general requirement that covered entities have appropriate administrative, technical, and physical safeguards to protect PHI from any use or disclosure that would violate the rule.[653] The Security Rule, which was published after the Privacy Rule, sets forth much more detailed requirements for the security of PHI.[654]

---

[650] 65 Fed. Reg. 82748 (Dec. 28, 2000).
[651] 45 C.F.R. § 164.530(f).
[652] 65 Fed. Reg. 82748 (Dec. 28, 2000).
[653] 45 C.F.R. § 164.530(c)(1).
[654] See 45 C.F.R. § 164.302 et seq.

CHAPTER 7

Reporting and Disclosure Requirements

Chapter Objectives

- Give examples of mandatory reporting laws
- Explain how the Privacy Rule affects a provider's obligations under mandatory disclosure laws
- Discuss the persons or facilities subject to the reporting requirement under mandatory disclosure laws
- Give examples of information that must be included in a child abuse report and an adult abuse report
- Summarize the requirements of communicable disease reporting laws
- Discuss whether mandatory reporting laws apply to managed care organizations

---

Introduction

Many state laws and some federal laws require or permit the disclosure of confidential medical records information without the patient's consent. Certain disclosures, such as child abuse reports, are mandatory; others are permissive. Some laws require hospitals and other facilities to make reports; other laws place the responsibility for making reports on the individual healthcare professional. Certain laws may also permit or require managed care organizations (MCOs) to disclose confidential medical records information.

Disclosure of medical records information under statutory or regulatory requirements does not subject a healthcare organization or practitioner to civil liability, even if the disclosure is made against the patient's express wishes. Healthcare organizations and providers must be aware of the special disclosure rules applicable in their jurisdictions because the rules often vary among states. In addition, health information professionals must understand who is responsible under applicable laws, as well as the organization's policies for filing a report and when reports should be made.

The major development in recent years in the law governing mandatory disclosure of medical records information was the publication in late 2000 of final privacy regulations (Privacy Rule) under the Health Insurance Portability and Accountability Act (HIPAA).[1] This comprehensive federal statutory scheme preempts conflicting state law, unless the state law creates more stringent protection for health information. (See the discussion of the Privacy Rule in Chapter 6.) Although the Privacy Rule permits the disclosure of protected health information (PHI) in accordance with a state law requirement, the disclosure must be made in the manner prescribed by the rule. As a general rule, if the state mandatory reporting statute specifies a different method of reporting, one must comply with HIPAA and the Privacy Rule. The preemption provisions of the Privacy Rule are complex, and organizations and practitioners covered by HIPAA should seek the advice of qualified legal counsel in determining whether a given state law or HIPAA controls. (See the discussions of preemption in Chapters 1 and 6). In this chapter, we discuss a number of state laws to illustrate the positions the states have taken on mandatory reporting. An exhaustive preemption analysis of these laws, however, is beyond the scope of this book.

Disclosures Required by Law

The Privacy Rule is a permissive regulation—that is, it generally does not require covered entities to disclose PHI, but rather, permits them to do so under certain circumstances. (See the definition of covered entity in Chapter 6.) The primary exception to this principle is the obligation created by the rule for covered entities to disclose PHI to an individual at that person's request.

---

[1] 42 U.S.C. §§ 1320d et seq.

The Privacy Rule permits covered entities to disclose PHI when such disclosures are required by law.[2] The Privacy Rule defines "required by law" to mean a mandate contained in a law that compels an entity to use or disclose PHI and that is enforceable in a court of law.[3] This term includes, but is not limited to, the following:

- Court orders and court ordered subpoenas
- Subpoenas or summons issued by a court, grand jury, a governmental or tribal inspector general, or an administrative body authorized to require the production of information
- A civil or an authorized investigative demand
- Medicare Conditions of Participation with respect to healthcare providers participating in the program
- Statutes or regulations that require the production of information, including statutes or regulations that require such information if payment is sought under a government program providing public benefits[4]

A covered entity may use or disclose PHI to the extent that such use or disclosure is required by law and the use or disclosure complies with, and is limited to, the relevant requirements of such law.[5] The Privacy Rule contains provisions permitting disclosures in accordance with state laws requiring the reporting of victims of abuse, neglect, or domestic violence; the release of information in judicial or administrative proceedings; or disclosures for law enforcement purposes.[6] Thus, covered entities may comply with most applicable state laws requiring disclosure of PHI.

Child Abuse and Neglect

Laws in most jurisdictions require hospitals and healthcare practitioners to report cases of actual or suspected child abuse. The Privacy Rule permits a covered entity to disclose PHI to a public health authority or other appropriate government authority authorized by law to receive

---

2 45 C.F.R. § 164.512(a).
3 45 C.F.R. § 164.103.
4 Ibid.
5 45 C.F.R. § 164.512(a)(i).
6 45 C.F.R. § 164.512(a)(2) referring to §§ 164.512(c), (e), and (f).

reports of child abuse or neglect.[7] The exact list of persons and facilities subject to the reporting requirement varies among the states, and persons working in various healthcare institutions should be familiar with their state's particular child abuse law. It is important for healthcare organizations and practitioners to understand who in their facility must report child abuse, when reports are due, and what information must be presented in a report. Although most statutes provide civil liability protection for persons required to report, similar protections are not afforded to voluntary reports or release of extra information not required or permitted by law. In addition, the Privacy Rule permits the disclosure of only the minimum amount of PHI that is necessary to achieve the purpose of the disclosure. (See the discussion of the minimum necessary rule in Chapter 6.)

To comply with child abuse reporting requirements, healthcare organizations must first determine whether a patient is a "child" under the relevant statute. A "child" for abuse reporting purposes is not necessarily synonymous with "minor" under state law. Definitions of these terms vary in different state laws. In Massachusetts, for example, child abuse reports must be filed for all persons under 18 years of age who satisfy other criteria for reporting.[8] In New York, an "abused child" may be older than 18 in some cases.[9]

Some states have broad mandatory requirements that all "persons" with certain knowledge of child abuse make a report.[10] This type of statute imposes obligations on all personnel, not only on practitioners who treat victims of child abuse. Most statutes require reporting by healthcare practitioners and others who know, or have "reason" to suspect or believe, that a child they know or observe in their official or professional capacity is abused or neglected.[11]

Other states impose mandatory reporting obligations on specific categories of people, including designated healthcare professionals. Practitioners and other healthcare workers subject to mandatory re-

---

[7]   45 C.F.R. § 164.512(b)(1)(ii).
[8]   Mass. Gen. Laws ch. 119, § 51A.
[9]   N.Y. Soc. Serv. Law § 412.
[10] See, e.g., 23 Pa. Consol. Stat. § 631; N.J. Stat. Ann. § 9:6-8.10; Tenn. Code Ann. § 37-1-403(a).
[11] See, e.g., Fla. Stat. Ann. § 39.201(1)(a); Md. Code Ann., Fam. Law, § 5-704; N.Y. Soc. Serv. Law § 413.

porting may be listed directly in the child abuse reporting provisions,[12] or may be cross referenced to the state healthcare professional licensing statute. Most child abuse reporting requirements are mandatory for health practitioners; at least one state, Mississippi, has a permissive child abuse reporting law.[13]

In some states, the list creates a fixed group of professionals subject to reporting.[14] In other states, the list is merely illustrative, stating that all individuals who provide healthcare services, including those listed, must report.[15] In a few states, persons involved with hospital admissions have an explicit duty to report, along with practitioners.[16]

Only certain conditions diagnosed in children are reportable, and the child abuse statute in each state includes definitions of conditions that trigger the duty to report. Some statutes define an "abused and neglected" child as a single term.[17] Others distinguish "abuse" from "neglect."[18] Still others provide definitions of other related terms such as "sexual abuse."[19] Some states refer to abuse by the child's parent or other person responsible for the child's welfare.[20] A few statutes mandate a global imperative: if any person believes that a minor is or has been a victim of abuse that is not accidental in nature, the abuse must be reported.[21]

The definitions in every state generally include both physical and mental harm or threats of harm caused by the acts or omissions of certain persons. Sexual abuse, unusual punishment, or unexplained physical injuries constitute signs of abuse under most laws.[22] Impairment of the child's ability to perform or function and other signs of emotional or psychological distress indicate potential abuse in many states.[23]

---

[12] See, e.g., Haw. Rev. Stat. § 350-1.1(a); Md. Code Ann., Fam. Law, § 5-704(a); N.Y. Soc. Serv. Law § 413.

[13] Miss. Code Ann. § 93-21-25.

[14] See, e.g., N.Y. Soc. Serv. Law § 413.

[15] See, e.g., Fla. Stat. Ann. §§ 39.201(1)(a) and (b); Haw. Rev. Stat. § 350-1.1(a).

[16] See, e.g., Fla. Stat. Ann. § 39.201(1)(b)(1).

[17] See, e.g., Haw. Rev. Stat. § 350-1.

[18] See, e.g., Fla. Stat. Ann. §§ 39.01(2) and (45); La. Rev. Stat. Ann. §§ 603(1) and (14); D.C. Code Ann. §§ 4-1340.01(2) and (3); see also New York law, which defines "abused child" and "maltreated child" separately. N.Y. Soc. Serv. Law §§ 412(1) and (2).

[19] See, e.g., Cal. Penal Code § 11165.1.

[20] See, e.g., Fla. Stat. Ann. § 39.01(1); Haw. Rev. Stat. § 350-1; La. Rev. Stat. Ann. § 603.

[21] See, e.g., Ariz. Rev. Stat. Ann. § 13-3620(A).

[22] See, e.g., Fla. Stat. Ann. § 39.01; Haw. Rev. Stat. § 350-1.

[23] See, e.g., Haw. Rev. Stat. § 350-1.

Exploitation and abandonment are typical elements of child abuse, along with failure to provide adequate supervision, food, clothing, shelter, or health care.[24] Most statutes require specific information to be included in a child abuse report. Typically, the name of the person making the report, the name and address of the child, the extent of the child's injuries, and the child's current whereabouts must be disclosed, along with other pertinent information relating to the cause of abuse and the identity of the individual or individuals responsible.[25] Massachusetts requires the child's age and sex to be disclosed in addition to the child's parents' names and addresses.[26] In New York, persons making the reports must reveal their identities and any actions they have taken, including photographs or X-rays and removal or keeping of the child.[27]

Persons who comply with the reporting provisions generally are immune under the statute from any resulting civil or criminal liability.[28] Several courts have extended civil immunity to reports made in good faith but based on a negligent diagnosis.[29] California legislation that grants immunity to healthcare providers when they make mandated reports of child abuse also protects providers from liability when they make reports that are not required but merely are authorized under the law.[30] On the other hand, persons who fail to make required reports or who knowingly make false reports may be criminally liable.[31]

Most child abuse statutes stipulate that both the report and the identity of the individual who makes it are confidential.[32] Moreover, in most states, disclosures authorized by such laws do not violate the physician-patient privilege that otherwise would prevent the use of confidential medical information at trial or in other legal proceedings. (For a more extensive discussion of how physician-patient privilege operates in conjunction with child abuse reporting laws, see Chapter 10.)

---

[24] See, e.g., Fla. Stat. Ann. § 39.01; Haw. Rev. Stat. § 350-1.
[25] See, e.g., N.Y. Soc. Serv. Law § 415; Tenn. Code Ann. § 37-1-403(c); Wash. Rev. Code Ann. § 26.44.040.
[26] Mass. Ann. Laws ch. 119, § 51A.
[27] N.Y. Soc. Serv. Law § 415.
[28] See, e.g., Fla. Stat. Ann. § 39.203; Haw. Rev. Stat. § 350-3.
[29] See, e.g., *Maples v. Siddiqui*, 450 N.W. 2d 529 (Iowa 1990).
[30] See *Ferraro v. Chadwick*, 270 Cal. Rptr. 379 (Ct. App. 1990); *rev. denied*, No. 501657 (Cal., Aug. 15, 1990) (unpublished).
[31] See, e.g., Haw. Rev. Stat. § 350-1.2; Mass. Ann. Laws ch. 119, § 51A.
[32] See, e.g., Fla. Stat. Ann. § 39.203; Haw. Rev. Stat. § 350-1.4; Tenn. Code Ann. § 37-1-612.

Abuse of Adults and Injuries to Disabled Persons

Many states have enacted reporting requirements for cases of known or suspected abuse of senior citizens, institutionalized persons, nursing home residents, and persons suffering from physical or mental impairments.[33] Like the child abuse statutes discussed above, the laws on abuse of adults typically define terms such as "abuse" and "neglect," and require various health practitioners to report instances where they have a reasonable basis for believing that such abuse or neglect has occurred. The statutes usually list the kinds of information to be included in a report, such as the identity of the person reporting, the name and address of the victim, the time and place of the incident of abuse, the name of the suspected wrongdoer, and other information concerning the victim's statements and persons with knowledge of the incident. A practitioner usually may make an initial incident report by telephone, then follow up with a written report within a certain time period.

Most jurisdictions have general reporting requirements. Some states also require reports based on particular diagnoses of institutionalized or disabled adults. For example, Maryland mandates general reports of abuse suffered by developmentally disabled[34] or mentally impaired persons.[35]

The Minnesota Vulnerable Adult Act defines the terms "vulnerable adult," "abuse," and "neglect," and requires certain individuals to report known abuse or neglect where the professional has reasonable cause to believe that maltreatment is occurring or has occurred, or who has knowledge that a vulnerable adult has sustained an unexplained physical injury.[36] The Minnesota act extends immunity for reports made in good faith under the law, and imposes criminal liability on individuals who are required by law to report and who intentionally fail to report. The act also imposes liability for damages on those who negligently fail to report.[37]

The Privacy Rule establishes more stringent requirements for abuse cases other than child abuse. The Privacy Rule provision concerning child abuse permits covered entities to disclose PHI in accordance with

---

[33] See, e.g., Cal. Welf. & Inst. Code §§ 15600 through 15657.3; Fla. Stat. Ann. §§ 415.101 through 415.113; Iowa Code §§ 235B.1 through 235B.20.
[34] Md. Code Ann., Health-Gen. § 7-1005.
[35] Md. Code Ann., Health-Gen. § 10-705.
[36] Minn. Stat. Ann. § 626.557.
[37] Minn. Stat. Ann. §§ 626.557(5) and (7).

state law, and generally defers to state law for the specific information to be provided to the public health or other governmental agency.[38] The rule permits covered entities to disclose PHI about an individual that the covered entity reasonably believes to be a victim of abuse, neglect, or domestic violence. The PHI may be disclosed to a government authority that is authorized by law to receive such reports, if any one of the following requirements is met:

- The disclosure is required by law and complies with, and is limited to, the relevant requirements of such law
- The disclosure is permitted but not required by law, and either of two conditions are met: (a) the covered entity, exercising its professional judgment, believes the disclosure is necessary to prevent serious harm to the individual or to others; or (b) the individual is incapacitated and unable to authorize the disclosure, and the covered entity receives a representation from the law enforcement officer or other public official authorized to receive the abuse report that the information will not be used against the victim and that an immediate enforcement effort that relies upon the information disclosed would be materially and adversely affected by delaying the disclosure
- The individual agrees to the disclosure[39]

Thus, a challenging situation for the healthcare practitioner or other covered entity is one involving a state statute that does not *require* an abuse report but permits one. In that situation, the covered entity must meet the additional requirements described above before it may disclose PHI pursuant to the state law. (See the discussion of the exercise of professional judgment in Chapter 6.)

A covered entity making a disclosure under this provision may be under an obligation to inform the patient promptly that a report has been or will be made, except in two circumstances. If the covered entity, exercising its professional judgment, believes that informing the individual would place the individual at risk of serious harm, the entity has no obligation to inform. Likewise, if the covered entity would be informing a personal representative, such as a family member, and the en-

---

[38]   See 45 C.F.R. § 164.512(b).
[39]   45 C.F.R. § 164.512(c).

tity reasonably believes that the personal representative is responsible for the victim's injury and that informing this person would not be in the best interests of the victim, the covered entity has no duty to inform.[40]

Controlled Drug Prescriptions and Abuse

Some states require physicians and others to identify patients obtaining prescriptions for certain controlled drugs, and to prepare and maintain records open to inspection or to report patient names to the appropriate state or federal agency.[41]

Other states require physicians to report diagnoses of drug abuse. New Jersey requires healthcare practitioners to report the names of drug dependent persons within 24 hours after determining that the person uses a controlled dangerous substance for purposes other than treatment of sickness or injury as prescribed and administered under the law.[42] Such a report is confidential, however, and not admissible in a criminal proceeding.[43]

In most circumstances, a covered entity would be able to comply with these state laws under the Privacy Rule's provisions permitting disclosures required by law,[44] disclosures for public health activities,[45] or those for law enforcement purposes.[46]

Occupational Diseases

A few states require physicians to report diseases or abnormal health conditions caused by, or related to, conditions in the workplace.[47] The reports typically are made to the state's department of public health, and usually include the name, address, occupation, and illness of the patient, and the name and address of the patient's employer. The reports are confidential except for statistical purposes and in extreme

---

[40] 45 C.F.R. § 164.512(c)(2).
[41] See, e.g., Mass. Ann. Laws ch. 94C, § 24; N.Y. Pub. Health Law § 3333.
[42] N.J. Stat. Ann. § 24:21-39; but see *Commonwealth v. Donoghue*, 358 N.E. 2d 465 (Mass. App. Ct. 1976), where a Massachusetts state court struck down its drug abuse reporting statute as unconstitutionally vague because practitioners could not define the term "chronic use," which triggered such reports under the existing version of the law.
[43] N.J. Stat. Ann. § 24:21-39.
[44] 45 C.F.R. § 164.512(a).
[45] 45 C.F.R. § 164.512(b).
[46] 45 C.F.R. § 164.512(f).
[47] See, e.g., Tex. Health & Safety Code Ann. § 84.004.

medical emergencies.[48] The purpose of these statutes is to enable public health officials to investigate occupational diseases and to recommend methods for eliminating or preventing them.

The Privacy Rule does not apply to employers, unless they are also covered entities as defined by the rule. However, if an employer provides health care in the workplace through a plant physician, nurse, or other practitioner, or operates a workplace clinic and those practitioners and facilities meet the definition of covered entity, they will be subject to the Privacy Rule and must comply with the rule's disclosure requirements.

The Privacy Rule provisions concerning the release of an employee's PHI by an employer permit such disclosures if the employee authorizes the disclosure or if all of the following four conditions are met:

- The covered entity is a healthcare provider employed by the employer or engaged by the employer to conduct medical surveillance of the workplace or to evaluate whether the employee has a work related illness or injury
- The disclosed PHI consists of findings concerning a work related illness or injury or surveillance of the workplace
- The employer needs such findings in order to comply with federal law (for example, the Occupational Safety and Health Act) or similar state law requiring the employer to record such workplace related illness, injury, or surveillance
- The covered entity notifies the employee in writing that such PHI has been disclosed to the employer[49]

These provisions were included in the Privacy Rule to ensure that employers are able to obtain the information that they need to comply with relevant federal and state law designed to promote healthier and safer workplaces.[50]

Abortion

Several states require hospitals and practitioners to report abortions they perform, along with a variety of information about the patient

---

[48] Tex. Health & Safety Code Ann. § 84.006.
[49] 45 C.F.R. § 164.512(b)(1)(v).
[50] 65 Fed. Reg. 82670 (Dec. 28, 2000).

(such as year of birth, race, marital status, and state and county of residence), the procedure, and any resulting complications, although the names of the patient and provider may not be disclosed.[51] Some states impose independent reporting requirements on physicians who diagnose a woman as having complications from an abortion, including the name and location of the facility, if known.[52] A few states require reports only for abortions performed on minors.[53] At least one court has upheld the requirement that physicians disclose the names and addresses of women receiving abortions as rationally related to a compelling state interest in maternal health and not an infringement upon the physician-patient relationship, the right to an abortion, or any personal right of privacy.[54]

The Privacy Rule permits these reports under the provisions governing disclosures required by law[55] and disclosures for public health activities.[56]

Birth Defects and Other Conditions in Children

Many states require or permit health practitioners and others to report diagnoses of various birth defects and children's conditions to the state department of health.[57] Reportable conditions include congenital and acquired malformations and disabilities,[58] sudden infant death syndrome (SIDS),[59] sentinel birth defects,[60] Reye's syndrome,[61] diseases of the eyes of infants,[62] and abnormal spinal curvature.[63] These reports are permitted under the Privacy Rule provisions governing disclosures required by law[64] and disclosures for public health activities.[65]

---

[51] See, e.g., Fla. Stat. Ann. § 390.0112; Tex. Health & Safety Code Ann. § 245.011.
[52] See, e.g., 720 Ill. Comp. Stat. Ann. 510/10.1.
[53] See, e.g., Ala. Code § 26-21-8(c).
[54] See, e.g., *Schulman v. New York City Health and Hospital Corporation*, 342 N.E. 2d 501 (1975).
[55] 45 C.F.R. § 164.512(a).
[56] 45 C.F.R. § 164.512(b).
[57] See, e.g., N.J. Rev. Stat. § 26:8-40.21; Wis. Stat. Ann. § 253.12.
[58] See, e.g., Ala. Code § 21-3-8; Fla. Stat. Ann. § 383.14.
[59] See, e.g., Cal. Health & Safety Code § 102865.
[60] See, e.g., Md. Code Ann., Health-Gen., § 18-206.
[61] See, e.g., Mass. Ann. Laws ch. 111, § 110B.
[62] See, e.g., Mass. Ann. Laws ch. 111, § 110.
[63] See, e.g., Tex. Health & Safety Code Ann. § 37.003.
[64] 45 C.F.R. § 164.512(a).
[65] 45 C.F.R. § 164.512(b).

Cancer and Other Registries

Many states require that information from the medical records of patients suffering from cancer or other diseases be disclosed to central state or regional registries.[66] These registries usually contain demographic, diagnostic, and treatment information about patients who suffer from the same or similar diseases, and are designed to provide raw data for studies concerning the incidence of a disease in the population; long-term prognosis of the disease; type, duration, and frequency of treatment rendered to patients with the disease; and other indicators of the healthcare industry's ability to manage the disease. Usually operated by statewide, tax-exempt organizations funded by federal grants, the registries rely to a large extent on the cooperation of individual hospital registries, and obtain patient information directly from participating hospitals pursuant to agreements between the hospitals and the registry.

If these reports are required as part of a public health authority's collection of disease information, they would be permitted under the Privacy Rule provision governing disclosures for public health activities.[67] If the reports are made to a private agency, such as a private academic medical center or a not for profit organization, for the purpose of medical or scientific research, the provisions of the Privacy Rule governing disclosures for research purposes would control. (See a discussion of those provisions in Chapter 14.)

Death or Injury from Use of a Medical Device

The federal Safe Medical Devices Act requires hospitals to report any death resulting from the use of a medical device to the U.S. Department of Health and Human Services (DHHS) within 10 days of discovery.[68] The hospital must identify in the report the device's manufacturer, if known, and must notify the manufacturer when a device caused or contributed to a patient's serious illness or injury. If the hospital cannot determine the manufacturer, the report of the illness or injury must be sent to the U.S. Food and Drug Administration (FDA).[69]

---

[66] See, e.g., Cal. Health & Safety Code § 103885; Fla. Stat. Ann. § 385.202; Haw. Rev. Stat. § 324-21.
[67] 45 C.F.R. § 164.512(b).
[68] 21 U.S.C. § 360(i).
[69] 21 C.F.R. § 803.30(a)(2).

The Joint Commission on Accreditation of Healthcare Organizations (Joint Commission) also requires compliance with the Safe Medical Devices Act as one of its accreditation standards.[70]

The Privacy Rule provides that a covered entity may disclose PHI to a person subject to the jurisdiction of the FDA with respect to an FDA regulated product or activity for which that person has responsibility, for the purposes related to the quality, safety, or effectiveness of the product or activity.[71] This provision would permit a covered entity to:

- Collect or report adverse events, product defects, or problems (including problems with the use or labeling of a product) or biological product deviations
- Track FDA regulated products
- Enable recalls, repairs or replacement, or lookback (including locating and notifying individuals who have received products that have been recalled, withdrawn, or are the subject of the lookback)
- Conduct post-marketing surveillance[72]

The terms used in this section of the Privacy Rule have both their commonly understood meanings and any specialized definitions created by the Food, Drug, and Cosmetic Act.[73] Therefore, covered entities should be familiar with the interplay of HIPAA and that act with respect to disclosures to the FDA.

Communicable Diseases

Communicable disease reporting laws require hospitals and practitioners to inform public health authorities of cases of infectious, venereal, or sexually transmitted diseases. These are among the oldest compulsory reporting statutes in many states. The statutes or regulations usually list the particular diseases that must be reported, and direct practitioners to give local public health officials the patient's name, age, sex, address, and identifying information, as well as the

---

[70] Joint Commission on Accreditation of Healthcare Organizations, *2005 Comprehensive Accreditation Manual for Hospitals*, Standard EC.6.10.7.

[71] 45 C.F.R. § 164.512(b)(1)(iii).

[72] Ibid.

[73] 21 U.S.C. § 321 et seq.; see also 65 Fed. Reg. 82525 (Dec. 28, 2000).

details of the illness.[74] State health agencies may have authority to request patient records for purposes of healthcare cost containment, professional regulation, and the conduct of professional disciplinary hearings; establishing a trauma registry and regulatory system; and conducting epidemiological investigations.[75] Such disclosure should include only the information required by the statute.

The majority of states have enacted special laws governing reports of acquired immunodeficiency syndrome (AIDS) and human immunodeficiency virus (HIV) cases. Many of the statutes require both AIDS and HIV to be reported; the information required in these reports varies from state to state. Providers should know what information should be released in their jurisdictions. (For a detailed discussion of access and disclosure issues involving AIDS and HIV patients' records, see Chapter 9.)

A few states have laws authorizing hospitals to disclose confidential information when emergency medical personnel come into contact with a patient suffering from a reportable condition.[76] The procedures for notifying the emergency personnel vary among the states, and hospitals should know the proper routine before releasing any information. Some states allow the hospital to directly notify the person at risk; others require the hospital to notify authorities at the state board of health, who then contact the emergency personnel. In either case, the hospital usually is precluded from revealing the name of the afflicted patient.

The Privacy Rule permits covered entities to disclose PHI for public health activities,[77] and to a person who may have been exposed to a communicable disease or may otherwise be at risk of contracting or spreading a disease or condition, if the covered entity or public health authority is authorized by law to notify such person as a necessary adjunct to a public health intervention or investigation.[78]

Covered entities may also make reports concerning communicable disease under the Privacy Rule provision that authorizes disclosures made to avert a serious threat to health or safety. Such disclosures must

---

[74] See, e.g., Ala. Code §§ 22-11A-1 through 22-11A-73; Fla. Stat. Ann. §§ 384.21 through 384.34; Haw. Rev. Stat. §§ 325-2 & 325-3.
[75] See, e.g., Fla. Stat. Ann. § 395.3025.
[76] See, e.g., Cal. Health & Safety Code § 1797.188; Fla. Stat. Ann. § 395.1025; 5310 C.F.R. §§ 35.11 and 35.12; 5410 C.F.R. § 35.33.
[77] 45 C.F.R. § 164.512(b).
[78] 45 C.F.R. § 164.512(b)(1)(iv).

be consistent with other applicable federal law, state law, and standards of ethical conduct. The threat of harm must be serious and imminent, and the disclosure must be to someone reasonably able to prevent or reduce the threat. This includes the person or persons who are the targets of the threat.[79]

Misadministration of Radioactive Materials

Federal regulations require hospitals or practitioners using radioactive materials in the practice of nuclear medicine to obtain a federal license,[80] and to report to the Nuclear Regulatory Commission any event in which the administration of radioactive material (a) results in a dose above a significant increment from that which has been prescribed, (b) is to the wrong person, or (c) is delivered by the wrong mode of treatment or route of administration.[81] These reports are permitted under the Privacy Rule provisions governing disclosures required by law.[82]

Death

All deaths must be reported so that authorities are informed in the event the deceased was the victim of a crime and so that accurate statistical records can be kept. Death certificates usually are signed by the physician pronouncing the death. Any suspicious or unusual deaths must be reviewed by state authorities to rule out criminal activity. Unnatural deaths usually are referred to the medical examiner for review. The medical examiner usually reviews cases involving suicides, deaths caused by criminal neglect, any type of violent death, or any type of death under suspicious or unusual circumstances. The medical examiner may conduct an investigation or perform an autopsy to determine the cause of death.[83]

The Privacy Rule permits covered entities to report deaths of individuals as part of public health activities.[84] Covered entities may also

---

[79] 45 C.F.R. § 164.512(j)(i).
[80] 10 C.F.R. §§ 35.11 and 35.12.
[81] 10 C.F.R. § 35.33.
[82] 45 C.F.R. § 164.512(a).
[83] See, e.g., Cal. Health & Safety Code §§ 102850 through 102870; N.J. Stat. Ann. 52:17B-88.
[84] 45 C.F.R. § 164.512(b)(1)(i).

disclose the decedent's PHI to a law enforcement official for the purpose of alerting law enforcement of the death of the individual, if the covered entity has a suspicion that such death may have resulted from criminal conduct.[85]

Gunshot and Knife Wounds

Most states require the reporting of certain types of wounds that ordinarily result from some type of criminal activity. Gunshot and knife wounds are always included. A state may, however, require the reporting of any wound apparently inflicted by a sharp instrument or that may have resulted from a criminal act. For example, New York requires the reporting of any wound inflicted by a sharp instrument that may result in the death of the victim.[86] Iowa requires reporting of wounds that appear to have resulted from criminal acts.[87]

State laws that require reporting may provide criminal prosecution or civil or administrative sanctions against the professional who fails to report the appropriate incident. Failure to report may be the basis of professional disciplinary action against the professional as well. On the other hand, a professional making such a report required by law is usually given immunity from any type of civil liability for making the report.

The Privacy Rule permits covered healthcare providers providing emergency health care in response to a medical emergency, other than such emergency on the provider's premises, to disclose PHI to a law enforcement official if such disclosure appears necessary to alert law enforcement to any of the following:

- The commission and nature of a crime
- The location of such crime or of the victim of the crime
- The identity, description, and location of the perpetrator of the crime[88]

If the provider believes that the medical emergency resulted from abuse, neglect, or domestic violence, however, the provider must dis-

---

[85] 45 C.F.R. § 164.512(f)(4).
[86] N.Y. Penal Law § 265.25.
[87] Iowa Code Ann. § 147.111.
[88] 45 C.F.R. § 164.512(f)(6)(i).

close PHI in accordance with the Privacy Rule provisions governing reports of such injuries.[89]

Other Health Related Reporting Requirements

Hospitals and practitioners in the various states may be required or permitted to report other instances of health related conditions and injuries to the appropriate state department of public health. Examples of miscellaneous reporting laws include instances of veterans' exposure to Agent Orange or other causative agents,[90] diagnosis of brain injuries in patients,[91] burn injuries and wounds in cases of suspected arson,[92] cases of cerebral palsy,[93] identities of women who took diethylstilbestrol (DES) during pregnancy,[94] environmentally related illnesses and injury,[95] and lead poisoning.[96]

Wisconsin requires reports by coroners and medical examiners concerning the results of mandatory blood tests performed on victims of snowmobile[97] and boating[98] accidents. That state allows a physician to report a patient's name and other information to the state department of transportation without the patient's consent when the physician believes that the patient's physical or mental condition affects his or her ability to reasonably control a motor vehicle.[99]

Some states provide reimbursement for certain health services provided to qualified persons. Facilities wishing to participate in these programs typically are subject to reporting requirements as to the care provided. Programs may involve primary healthcare services,[100] maternal and infant care,[101] or other services funded by the state.

---

[89] 45 C.F.R. § 164.512(f)(6)(ii); see also 45 C.F.R. § 164.512(c).
[90] Iowa Code Ann. §§ 36.1 through 36.10; Tex. Health & Safety Code Ann. §§ 83.001 through 83.010.
[91] 59 Iowa Code § 135.22.
[92] La. Rev. Stat. Ann. § 14:403.4.
[93] Mass. Ann. Laws ch. 111, § 111A.
[94] N.J. Stat. Ann. § 26:2-116.
[95] Haw. Rev. Stat. § 321-314.
[96] Cal. Health & Safety Code §§ 124125 through 124160.
[97] Wis. Stat. Ann. §§ 350.15 and 350.155.
[98] Wis. Stat. Ann. § 30.67.
[99] Wis. Stat. Ann. § 146.82(3)(a).
[100] See, e.g., Tex. Health & Safety Code Ann. §§ 31.001 through 31.017.
[101] See, e.g., Tex. Health & Safety Code Ann. §§ 32.001 through 32.021.

The Privacy Rule generally would permit these miscellaneous disclosures under the provisions governing disclosures required by law,[102] and those for public health activities.[103]

Required Disclosure by Managed Care Organizations

Although the duty of hospitals and healthcare providers to report child abuse and other medical conditions is fairly well established, an MCO's duty to disclose this same information is not quite as clear. MCOs possess a large amount of patient and medical records information that they use for utilization review, quality assurance, or other evaluation processes. The same laws that require healthcare providers or hospitals to disclose confidential patient information may also permit or require MCOs to disclose this information. Although many of the statutes were written with healthcare providers or hospitals in mind, some of the statutes, particularly concerning mandatory reporting of abuse, are broad enough to include MCOs.

In some states, nonprovider entities are subject to mandatory reporting requirements even though they do not directly deliver healthcare services to patients. In Maryland, for example, the definition of "health care provider" under the state's Medical Records Act includes HMOs and the agents, employees, officers, and directors of a healthcare professional or a healthcare facility.[104] Maryland requires a healthcare provider to disclose medical records information for the purposes of investigating suspected abuse or neglect of a child or an adult.[105] Accordingly, MCOs that lawfully come into contact with patient information through, for example, claims processing or utilization review tasks have a duty to disclose patient information under certain circumstances and are protected from liability for good faith actions.[106] Similarly, Hawaii requires "[e]mployees or officers of any public or private agency or institution, or other individual, providing social, medical, hospital, or mental health services . . ." to report suspected child

---

[102] 45 C.F.R. § 164.512(a).
[103] 45 C.F.R. § 164.512(b).
[104] Md. Code Ann., Health-Gen., § 4-301(a).
[105] Md. Code Ann., Health-Gen., § 4-306.
[106] Md. Code Ann., Health-Gen., § 4-308. See Edward J. Krill, "Required Disclosure of Medical Record Information—Applications to Managed Care," in Monograph 3, *Health Care Facility Records: Confidentiality, Computerization, and Security* (American Bar Association Forum on Health Law, July 1995), 11–25.

abuse.[107] Depending upon the structure of the MCO, employees or officers of the MCO may be required to make a report.

In many states, statutory language may be broad enough to encompass MCOs. Many reporting statutes require or allow "any" person to report suspected abuse or neglect. For example, Arizona law provides that any person other than one required to report may report suspected child abuse and will received immunity for making such a report.[108] Other states, such as Florida, require "any" person who has reasonable cause to suspect that a child is abused or neglected to make a report.[109] Statutes requiring or allowing "any" person to report suspected abuse can allow or require MCO employees to make such a report.

MCOs should carefully examine the laws in the states in which they operate to determine whether the statutes in these states are written broadly enough to require or allow disclosure of otherwise confidential patient information. Research may reveal that MCOs and their employees have a duty to disclose patient information. Although some states may permit but not require MCOs to disclose medical records information under certain circumstances, MCOs should determine whether they would be immune from liability for disclosing this information before developing a workplace policy concerning this issue.

The Privacy Rule will not apply to an MCO's use or disclosure of health information unless the MCO is a covered entity as defined by the rule. However, an MCO may be subject to the rule if the MCO functions as a business associate of a covered entity and has agreed by contract to abide by the provisions of the rule. If the MCO is subject to the Privacy Rule, the MCO must also determine whether the particular state laws governing its use or disclosure of PHI have been preempted by HIPAA, and then design its privacy policies and procedures accordingly. (For a discussion of HIPAA's preemption provisions, see Chapter 6.)

Health Oversight

Hospitals and healthcare practitioners in some states may be required to disclose health information to government agencies that are charged

---

[107] Haw. Rev. Stat. § 350-1.1.
[108] Ariz. Rev. Stat. § 13-3620.
[109] Fla. Stat. Ann. § 415.504; see also Md. Code Ann., Fam. Law, § 5-705.

with overseeing health care in those states. These include state insurance commissions, state health professional licensure and professional disciplinary boards, and state Medicaid fraud control units, each of which often is authorized by statute to conduct investigations and to obtain information in the furtherance of their regulatory duties.[110]

The Privacy Rule defines a "health oversight agency" as a government or Indian tribal agency or authority or its agent that is authorized by law to oversee the healthcare system (whether public or private) or government programs in which health information is necessary to determine eligibility or compliance, or to enforce civil rights laws for which health information is relevant.[111] The rule permits a covered entity to disclose PHI to health oversight agencies for their oversight of the healthcare system, government benefit programs, entities subject to government regulation, and entities subject to civil rights laws if those oversight activities are authorized by law and if health information is relevant to those activities.[112] These disclosures are limited to the information that health oversight agencies are authorized by law to receive. The Privacy Rule creates no new rights in the agencies to obtain health information or to conduct investigations, however.[113]

The Privacy Rule also attempts to provide guidance concerning when a covered entity may disclose PHI under the health oversight agency provisions, and when it should disclose under the law enforcement provisions. If the individual is the subject of an agency investigation, and the investigation does not arise from alleged healthcare fraud, a covered entity should follow the rules governing disclosures to law enforcement officials.[114] (See the discussion of disclosures to law enforcement officials in Chapter 8.) Notwithstanding this distinction, however, covered entities may also disclose PHI to a health oversight agency that, in conjunction with another governmental agency, is conducting a joint investigation that is not related to health.[115]

---

[110] Fla. Stat. Ann 395.3025.
[111] 45 C.F.R. § 164.501.
[112] 45 C.F.R. § 164.512(d).
[113] 65 Fed. Reg. 82528 (Dec. 28, 2000).
[114] 45 C.F.R. § 164.512(d)(2).
[115] 45 C.F.R. § 164.512(d)(3).

CHAPTER 8

Documentation and Disclosure: Special Areas of Concern

Chapter Objectives

- Discuss state statutes, accreditation standards, and the Emergency Medical Treatment and Active Labor Act (EMTALA) requirements pertaining to the content of emergency department records

- Discuss documentation and disclosure concerns associated with celebrities, hostile patients, possible child and adult abuse victims, and adoption records

- Outline documentation requirements and related obligations placed on healthcare providers by the Patient Self-Determination Act (PSDA)

- Distinguish among advance directives, living wills, and durable powers of attorney for health care, and discuss statutory requirements for documentation

- Explain how do-not-resuscitate (DNR) orders impact healthcare providers' decisions on patient treatment

- Recommend documentation steps to protect healthcare providers from liability triggered by disagreements among professional staff

- List purposes for which managed care organizations (MCOs) may legitimately request access to patient healthcare information, and recommend procedures for ensuring authorized disclosure

- Discuss the scope of law enforcement agencies' authority to obtain access to medical records

- Discuss the use of search warrants to obtain medical records, and give examples of court-approved warrantless searches of healthcare facilities

(continues)

- Outline the differences between a subpoena and a court order, and recommend procedures for healthcare records professionals to follow in responding to subpoenas
- Discuss the increasing trend of fraud and abuse investigations and appropriate response strategies for healthcare providers
- Outline statutory/regulatory requirements and recommended procedures related to the disposition of medical records upon change of ownership or closure

Introduction

This chapter discusses a number of special problems involving documentation and disclosure of medical records that arise frequently in healthcare settings. Some of these problems are derived simply from the fact that healthcare organizations provide medical services for special categories of patients on a daily basis, and special documentation issues arise in dealing with these patients. These categories include patients in need of emergency care, celebrity patients, hostile patients, victims of child abuse, patients who refuse treatment, dying patients, and recently deceased persons (that is, dead bodies that require authorization for autopsy). Finally, special attention to documentation is also required in situations that involve none of these patient categories. For example, careful documentation is particularly important where patient care has generated disagreements among professional staff as to the appropriate treatment or medication. As will be discussed in the first part of this chapter, individuals making medical records entries relating to any of these areas must be extraordinarily precise and objective in their notations.

Healthcare professionals, and particularly health information professionals, regularly encounter special disclosure issues. These issues are commonly triggered by certain requests for medical records made by individuals other than the patient. Such requests include managed care organizations' requesting an enrollee's record information for purposes of utilization review or quality improvement, adoptees or adoptive parents requesting health-related information about biological parents, state and federal investigators seeking relevant information in the course of law enforcement activities, and attorneys or agency officials requesting information that may bolster their positions in a pending legal or enforcement action. Some of the disclosure problems arising in these situations are discussed in the second part of this chapter, with a particular emphasis on the potentially competing interests that come into play in deciding whether disclosure is appropriate. Other special problems involving access, however, are discussed in Chapters 6 and 7. In all of these situations, the healthcare organization is best prepared if it has developed, with the assistance of qualified health law counsel, a workable and appropriate policy to provide its personnel and medical records practitioners with a consistent protocol.

The chapter concludes with a discussion of two additional areas of concern for healthcare records professionals in today's rapidly changing healthcare environment: medical records containing test results as reported from outside diagnostic and laboratory facilities, and record maintenance and retention when a healthcare facility is either undergoing a change of ownership or permanently closing its doors. As more and more facilities contract with independent laboratories for particular services, and form alliances or other healthcare delivery networks to achieve more cost-effective and higher quality patient care, medical records practitioners must be aware of the health information management issues arising from these developments.

Special Documentation Concerns

Emergency Department Records

Various state and federal regulations and laws discussed throughout this book govern medical records, including emergency department records.[1] Some state laws and regulations specify the information to be recorded; other states specify which broad areas of information concerning the patient's treatment must be included, or simply declare that the medical record shall be "adequate," "accurate," or "complete." State hospital licensure rules and regulations also may provide requirements and standards for the general maintenance, handling, signing, filing,

---

[1] Medicare Conditions of Participation formerly specifically addressed emergency service or emergency department records, but now no longer separately address emergency department records. See 42 C.F.R. § 482.24.

and retention of medical records. (For a more detailed discussion of these laws, regulations, and standards, see Chapter 3.)

In addition, some states specifically regulate the contents of emergency department records. Alaska requires that the emergency services record contain patient identification, the time and means of transportation to the facility, current condition, diagnosis, record of treatment provided, condition on discharge or transfer, and disposition, including instructions given for follow-up care.[2] Arkansas specifies content requirements for emergency department records, and mandates that they must be completed immediately or within 24 hours of the patient's visit.[3] Maine and Oklahoma establish detailed standards for what constitutes a complete emergency room medical record.[4] Meanwhile, Maine specifies the requisite content of emergency department records, and also requires that all such records contain documentation of notification of appropriate authorities in suspected medicolegal cases.[5] In Oklahoma, regulations require that an emergency medical record contain documentation if a patient leaves against medical advice.[6]

The Joint Commission on Accreditation of Healthcare Organizations (Joint Commission) also has established standards for emergency care records. The standards for accreditation of hospitals provide that, in addition to the information required for all medical records,[7] emergency care records should contain:

- The time and means of arrival
- The patient's leaving against medical advice
- Conclusions at the termination of treatment, including final disposition, patient's condition at the time of discharge, and any instructions for follow-up care[8]

---

2   Ala. Admin. Code tit. 7, § 12.870(f). See also Wis. Admin. Code § 124.24(2)(d) (emergency department record must contain patient identification; history of disease or injury; physical findings; lab or X-ray reports, if any; diagnosis; record of treatment; disposition of case; authentication; and other appropriate notations, such as patient's arrival time, time of treatments, and time of patient discharge or transfer).
3   Ark. Reg. 007 05 Carr 003 § 15b.
4   Code Me. R. 10-144-112, ch. XIX.M.2(a-j); Okla. Admin. Code § 310:667-19-11.
5   Code Me. R. 10-144-112, ch. XIX.M.2(k).
6   Okla. Admin. Code § 310:667-19-11(a)(12).
7   Joint Commission on Accreditation of Healthcare Organizations, *2005 Accreditation Manual for Hospitals*, Standard IM. 6.10.
8   Ibid., Standard IM. 6.10.18.

The Joint Commission also states that a copy of an emergency care record should be available to the practitioner or medical organization responsible for follow-up care.[9] Finally, in accordance with the Emergency Medical Treatment and Active Labor Act (EMTALA),[10] discussed next, the Joint Commission requires that a hospital's decision to refer, transfer, or discharge a patient to a different level of care or another health professional or setting be based on the patient's needs and the organization's capability to provide the care needed.[11]

The importance of establishing complete and accurate emergency care records increased significantly with the enactment of federal legislation designed to prevent the transfer of hospital patients for economic reasons. In 1985, Congress enacted EMTALA as part of the Consolidated Omnibus Budget Reconciliation Act of 1986 (COBRA).[12] As an amendment to the Medicare statute, COBRA's emergency care requirements apply to every hospital that participates in the Medicare program and that has an emergency room. COBRA, sometimes called the federal "antidumping" law, was enacted largely out of legislative concern that hospital emergency departments were turning away or transferring patients who could not pay for treatment but needed emergency medical care.

Because COBRA has detailed requirements, and because violations may lead to serious administrative consequences as well as liability (discussed below), hospital administrators should review their emergency department procedures for compliance with this important federal law. Under COBRA, any hospital with an emergency department must provide an appropriate medical screening examination (MSE) to any individual who comes to the department and requests treatment for a medical condition. A hospital must use ancillary services routinely available to the emergency department when providing medical screening. A hospital cannot delay an MSE, further medical examination, or treatment to inquire about the individual's method of payment or insurance status.[13]

Although COBRA was enacted to prevent disparate treatment of patients without insurance, it also prohibits disparate emergency

[9] Ibid.
[10] 42 U.S.C. § 1395dd.
[11] Joint Commission, *2005 Comprehensive Accreditation Manual for Hospitals*, Standard PC.15.20.
[12] 42 U.S.C. § 1395dd.
[13] 42 U.S.C. § 1395dd(a) and (h).

department treatment of patients enrolled in managed care plans. For example, a hospital would violate COBRA by sending a patient to an HMO for a full examination after a partial MSE at the hospital, because the hospital is not providing the HMO patient with the same MSE provided to other patients.[14]

Although the emergency care provisions of COBRA contain no specific requirements for documentation of an MSE, a hospital should carefully document this type of patient care in order to defend against charges that it violated the law. Accordingly, the emergency department should create and retain a record of each MSE it conducts. If the MSE indicates that the individual does not have an emergency condition, the hospital will have satisfied its obligations under the law. For evidence purposes, however, emergency department records should demonstrate that the MSE was conducted and that such a conclusion was reached.

Proper documentation is particularly important if the individual refuses to consent to the MSE or refuses to undergo recommended treatment. The hospital is required to obtain, or attempt to obtain, the individual's written informed consent to refuse treatment.[15] Similarly, if a hospital offers to transfer the individual and informs the person of the risks and benefits of the transfer, but the individual refuses to consent, the hospital will have fulfilled its obligations under the law.[16] A hospital must take all reasonable steps to obtain written informed consent when an individual has refused an examination, treatment, or transfer.[17]

Documentation on the stabilization of a patient's condition or on a transfer must be accurate and complete in order to demonstrate that the hospital complied with its duties under COBRA. The documentation should indicate the status of the individual's condition and the treatment provided to achieve stabilization. In the event of a transfer, the record also should include a statement by medical personnel that, within reasonable medical probability, no material deterioration of the patient's emergency medical condition will result from the transfer or

---

[14] Healthcare administrators should note that courts generally have ruled that managed care organizations, including HMOs, cannot be held responsible for COBRA violations. See, e.g., *Dearmas v. Av-Med., Inc.,* 814 F. Supp. 1103 (S.D. Fla. 1993) (physicians and HMOs are not subject to liability for failing to satisfy COBRA requirements).

[15] 42 U.S.C. § 1385dd(b)(2).

[16] 42 U.S.C. § 1395dd(b)(3).

[17] 42 U.S.C. §§ 1395dd(b)(2) and (3).

will occur during the transfer process.[18] In addition, COBRA requires that specific records accompany the patient to the receiving facility. At the time of the transfer, the transferring hospital must send a copy of all available medical records related to the emergency conditions— including observations of signs or symptoms, preliminary diagnosis, treatment provided, results of any tests, the informed consent to transfer or the physician's certification, and the name and address of any on-call physician who has refused or failed to appear within a reasonable time to provide necessary stabilizing treatment.[19] Healthcare managers also should know that states have become increasingly involved in the problems of patient transfer, and thus, in some jurisdictions, appropriate documentation and the implementation of hospital policies regarding patient transfers is necessary to prove compliance with state antidumping laws.[20]

If the person conducting the MSE (for example, a physician or other "qualified" individual) determines that the patient has an emergency medical condition or is in active labor, the hospital must stabilize the patient before discharge.[21] The hospital may transfer a patient who has not been stabilized only upon the signed certification of a physician that the benefits of the transfer outweigh the risks. If a physician is not physically present in the emergency department at the time of transfer, a "qualified medical person" may sign a certification after consultation with a physician, but the physician must subsequently countersign the certification.[22]

At least two federal appeals courts interpreting COBRA have examined whether a physician actually evaluated the risks and benefits of transfer. COBRA certification must be a true assessment, not merely a

---

[18] 42 C.F.R. § 489.24(b).

[19] 42 C.F.R. § 489.24(d)(2)(ii). COBRA also requires that hospitals with emergency departments adopt a policy to ensure that records of all patient transfers are maintained for at least five years.

[20] See, e.g., Tex. Health & Safety Code Ann. § 241.027 (hospital licensing statute requiring hospitals to adopt procedures to ensure that patient transfers are accomplished through hospital policies that result in medically appropriate transfers; the statute specifies the policies' content, including the steps physicians must take in making patient transfer determinations and in documenting transfers).

[21] See, e.g., 42 C.F.R. § 489.24(a) through (b). The qualifications for who may perform an MSE are not outlined in federal regulations; rather, the relevant regulations require only that hospital bylaws or rules identify which individuals are qualified to perform screening examinations.

[22] 42 C.F.R. § 489.24(d).

signature, according to one of the earliest cases to arise under the law. The Fifth Circuit ruled that a physician's failure to weigh the medical risks and benefits before transferring a severely hypertensive woman in active labor violated the law. Although the physician had signed the "Physician's Certificate Authorizing Transfer," the court concluded that he had not engaged in a meaningful weighing of the risks and benefits.[23] The Ninth Circuit, on the other hand, has ruled that a hospital did not violate COBRA by failing to enumerate the risks and benefits of a patient's transfer on a form, if the hospital could show that a physician actually considered the medical risks and benefits. In refusing to impose COBRA liability, the court concluded that even though the hospital technically violated a record-keeping provision, the purpose of the statute was satisfied in light of evidence demonstrating that the physician deliberated over the risks and benefits before signing the transfer certification form.[24]

COBRA's enforcement provisions impose a civil monetary penalty of up to $50,000 for each violation against hospitals that negligently violate the law, or up to $25,000 against those with fewer than 100 beds. Hospitals that fail to substantially meet the COBRA requirements are subject to suspension or termination of their Medicare provider agreements.[25] Although many hospitals have been fined, only a few have had their Medicare provider agreements terminated. Civil suits are another potential consequence of COBRA violations. An individual who suffers personal harm as a direct result of a hospital's violation of the law can sue the hospital for personal injury damages and equitable relief.[26]

Given the significant enforcement action in this area and the potential costs of legal violations, hospital managers should work with hospital legal counsel in reviewing institutional policy and procedures to ensure full compliance with all applicable federal and state statutes and regulations pertaining to emergency department records and record-keeping requirements.

---

[23] *Burditt v. U.S. Department of Health & Human Services*, 934 F. 2d 1362, 1372 (5th Cir. 1991).

[24] *Vargas ex rel. Gallardo v. Del Puerto Hospital*, 98 F. 3d 1202 (9th Cir. 1996). More recently, the Ninth Circuit affirmed this interpretation in an unpublished opinion. See *Kilcop v. Adventist Health, Inc.*, 2000 U.S. App. LEXIS 18733 (9th Cir. 2000), *1, *5.

[25] 42 U.S.C. § 1395dd(d)(1); 42 C.F.R. § 489.53.

[26] 42 U.S.C. § 1395dd(d)(2). Courts have consistently ruled that physicians cannot be found liable under COBRA. However, hospital administrators should know that state

Celebrity Patients

When patients subject to close scrutiny by news media are hospitalized for conditions that might be embarrassing for them, special care often must be taken to protect records confidentiality. Although news media take an interest in patients who may have become newsworthy temporarily, they often use more aggressive tactics in obtaining information concerning celebrities. As a result, some hospitals have established special procedures for handling celebrity patient records. The procedures typically allow the patient to control the amount and type of information released unless otherwise required by law. This approach is consistent with the HIPAA Privacy Rule, which gives the patient the opportunity to object even to listing his or her name in the institution's directory, and the right to request restrictions on the use or disclosure of his or her health information.[27]

As an extra precaution against unauthorized disclosure, some hospitals omit the patient's name from the record or use a code name that corresponds to a master code maintained by the medical records director and hospital chief executive officer.[28] Also, the celebrity patient has the right to request an alias name; upon receiving such a request, the hospital should assign the alias name upon admission of the patient, use that name throughout the patient's visit, and then make necessary corrections to the records after discharge. The hospital also may adopt a policy reserving its right to issue an alias to a patient if it considers this action to be in the best interest of the patient and the medical facility admitting the patient. Although assigning an alias may give added protection to the patient, it may conflict with state statutes and

laws may provide for individual liability for COBRA violations, and that hospitals found liable may be able to recover from individuals who actually committed the violations. See *McDougal v. Lafourche Hospital Services District No. 3,* No. 92-2006, 1993 U.S. Dist. LEXIS 7381 (E.D. La., May 25, 1993) (unpublished) (allowing hospital to recover damages from staff physician); but see *Griffith v. Mt. Carmel Medical Center,* 842 F. Supp. 1359, 1365 (D. Kan. 1994) (holding that a jury award cannot be apportioned between hospital and physician in COBRA suits, and noting that an action for indemnity is more appropriate).

[27] 45 C.F.R. §§ 164.510(a)(2) and (3).

[28] Some healthcare institutions prefer using an alphanumeric code in place of the patient's real name, rather than assign a generic name (e.g., "John Doe"). One code format, for example, is a combination of the patient's initials and business office account number.

regulations. Thus, the use of aliases should be employed only with the advice of qualified legal counsel.

Policies and procedures should be established to quickly assess the need for patient anonymity at admission and assign an alias if necessary. For example, the hospital should have policies that specify exactly which senior managers are empowered to authorize patient anonymity, and which departments should be notified to ensure greater protection of that anonymity (for example, security, public relations, and/or administration). Some hospitals place celebrity patients' medical records in a special secure file accessible only to the medical records director and other designated persons. This approach may not provide the same degree of protection as the former method, but it is not likely to violate state law record content requirements. A spokesperson, preferably an individual experienced in healthcare public relations, should be designated to address any inquiries received from the media or any other authorities.[29] The hospital also should establish procedures to ensure that any information approved for release is consistent and accurate, and that any information regarding the patient's condition or presence in the facility is released only upon the patient's authorization. (For a more extensive discussion of media access to medical records, see "Invasion of Privacy," covered in Chapter 11.)

Health information professionals developing special procedures for handling the records of patients who request anonymity should consider a number of possible steps for preventing unauthorized disclosure, including:

- Replacing the patient's name with an assigned code or alias on all bed boards, bulletin boards, and patient room signs
- Restricting computer access to those users who need to know the patient's identity to perform their jobs, and employing mechanisms that will alert a security officer when a system user attempts to access information beyond his or her security clearance
- In facilities with paper record systems, designating one individual

---

[29] Healthcare administrators should consider advising designated spokespersons to follow established guidelines when releasing information about patients. See, e.g., Society for Healthcare Strategy and Market Development, American Hospital Association, *Updated Guidelines for Releasing Information on the Condition of Patients* (Chicago, 2003), available at http://www.ihaonline.org/hipaa/Guidelines%20FINAL.pdf.

to be responsible for controlling access to the restricted medical record
- Providing employees, medical staff members, students, and volunteers with specific training about their responsibility to protect the confidentiality of medical records information, and requiring them to sign a nondisclosure agreement
- Allowing access to the patient's record after the patient has been discharged only to those employees with a valid need to know (for example, those involved in the record completion process)

Health information professionals and risk managers should establish a system for performing periodic audits to ensure that policies in this area are being followed and are still effective.

Hostile Patients

Hostile patients present problems for everyone in a healthcare facility. Whether the hostility arises from the patient's condition, general nature, or the treatment received at the institution, the hostile individual often is more inclined to take legal action if a problem in treatment actually occurs. Moreover, hostile patients may be less inclined to remember all the facts of a treatment situation or to view them in a light favorable to the healthcare facility, and therefore physicians and other healthcare personnel should take greater care in documenting hostile patients' treatment.

No special rules of law apply to hostile patients' records, but healthcare practitioners should take a commonsense approach to documentation in such records. All relevant staff members should be trained to recognize the hostile patient, and should know that prudent handling of that patient's medical care must include the creation of a detailed medical record that leaves little ambiguity about the care that has been provided. Obviously, such staff members also should avoid making derogatory remarks about a hostile patient in the medical record. Remarks of this nature contribute nothing to the ability of other practitioners to care for the patient, and instead generate the risk that these comments will be used by the litigious hostile patient as further proof of the practitioners' bad faith. A medical record should contain remarks concerning the patient's hostility only if such conduct is clinically relevant, and, in those cases, notations should be limited to concise descriptions in clinical terms.

Recording Indicators of Child or Elder Abuse or Domestic Violence

When the physician assesses a child or an adult covered by the state's laws governing domestic violence or the treatment of senior citizens, disabled adults, institutionalized adults, or nursing home residents to determine whether reasonable cause exists to believe the patient is abused, neglected, or the victim of domestic violence, careful notations must be made in the medical record. Specifically, a detailed and objective documentation and description of all pertinent physical findings should be noted clearly in the record. In addition, any tests performed or photographs taken to document the suspected abuse or injury should be noted carefully. This information will be the basis upon which a determination of abuse is made, and thus attention to detail in recording the information is very important. The record should include a history of the injury, including details reported by the parent, guardian, or other person of how the injury allegedly happened, date and time of the injury, sequence of events, names of witnesses, interval between the injury and the time that medical attention was sought, and identities of the interviewers. If the parents, guardians, or other caregiver and patient are interviewed separately, the date, time, and place of each session should be documented. (For a more detailed discussion of disclosure and reporting issues in relation to records indicating abuse, see "Special Disclosure Concerns" later in this chapter.)

Patients Refusing Treatment and/or Near Death

The medical record plays a critical role in right-to-die situations. Whether it is the patient who makes the decision to withdraw or not accept life-sustaining medical treatment, or whether it is someone designated to act on the patient's behalf, the medical record will be the primary, if not sole, source documenting the appropriateness of the decision. In either case, the patient's medical record should clearly set forth all relevant information concerning his or her treatment decision and plan before the physician gives a directive to withdraw or forgo life-sustaining treatment for a patient. The following sections discuss some of the laws, regulations, and standards containing medical records requirements pertinent to end-of-life decision making.

Background

It is well established that competent adults have the right to refuse treatment unless state interests outweigh that right. Courts have long recognized that a patient's right to make decisions concerning medical care necessarily includes the right to decline medical care.[30]

A patient's ability to personally exercise the right to determine medical treatment does not exist if the individual is incompetent. Some patients who never have expressed their wishes regarding treatment become irreversibly incompetent and unable to communicate. Others never have had an opportunity to express their wishes because of youth or mental retardation. With increasing frequency, courts are confronting these issues, and many have concluded that because competent adults have the right to refuse treatment, there must be a means for the same right to be exercised on behalf of incompetent patients.

The United States Supreme Court addressed this issue in the well-publicized *Cruzan* case.[31] In that case, the parents of a young woman in a persistent vegetative state since her injury in an automobile accident in 1983 requested court authorization to remove the gastrostomy tube through which their daughter received life-sustaining nutrition and hydration. The Court recognized that a competent person has the right to refuse medical treatment, but that an incompetent patient is unable to exercise such a right. The Court stated that "a State may apply a clear and convincing evidence standard in proceedings where a guardian seeks to discontinue nutrition and hydration of a person diagnosed to be in a persistent vegetative state," and that the Constitution gives "a competent person a constitutionally protected right to refuse lifesaving hydration and nutrition."[32] A state has the authority to set standards governing how this right may be exercised on behalf of an incompetent patient, and how to ensure that the decision respects as much as possible the wishes expressed by the patient while competent, the Court ruled.

---

[30] See, e.g., *White v. Chicago & North Western Railway Company*, 124 N.W. 309 (Iowa 1910); *State v. McAfee*, 385 S.E. 2d 651 (Ga. 1989); *McKay v. Bergstedt*, 801 P. 2d 617 (Nev. 1990).

[31] *Cruzan v. Director, Missouri Department of Health*, 497 U.S. 261 (1990). See also *Vacco v. Quill*, 521 U.S. 793, 797–805 (1997).

[32] *Cruzan v. Director.*

In another, highly publicized case, the courts upheld a spouse's decision to end the patient's life support. Theresa Marie Schindler Schiavo suffered cardiac arrest and fell into a comatose state in 1990 at the age of 27.[33] Florida law provided that a decision made by such a proxy to refuse life-prolonging procedures must be supported by "clear and convincing evidence."[34] Ms. Schiavo's husband, Michael Schiavo, petitioned the court to remove the feeding tube from his wife and was opposed by Ms. Schiavo's parents, the Schindlers. First, the district court found that physicians' testimony and examination of Ms. Schiavo was sufficient to categorize Ms. Schiavo as being in a "Persistent Vegetative State" (PVS), as defined by Florida law.[35] Second, the district court held that the "clear and convincing evidence" standard was met by statements made by Ms. Schiavo concerning her desire not to be supported by artificial means, and the court therefore entered an order authorizing the discontinuance of artificial feeding and hydration.[36] The Florida appellate court affirmed the district court's opinion and refused to order the reinsertion of the feeding tube in 2001, resulting in the first of several removals and subsequent reinsertions of Ms. Schiavo's feeding tube (removed and reinserted in 2001, removed and reinserted in 2003, and removed again in 2005).[37] Subsequently, Mr. Schiavo and the Schindlers went through several years and many layers of litigation that resulted in reinsertion and re-removal of the feeding tube until intervention by the Florida Legislature, which authorized the governor to order a one-time stay, specifically for Ms. Schiavo's case, to prevent withholding of nutrition and hydration. This action was later found to be unconstitutional. This resulted in subsequent congressional intervention and appeals to the federal court system. By denying the plaintiffs' motions for temporary restraining orders to prevent withholding of hydration and nutrition,[38] the federal district and appellate court decisions effectively resulted in an affirmation of the

---

[33] *In re Schiavo*, 780 So. 2d 176, 177 (Fla. Dist. Ct. App. 2001).

[34] Ibid.

[35] Fla. Stat. § 706 requires the patient's attending or treating physician and at least one other consulting physician to separately examine the patient and come to the same conclusion and document this in the medical record.

[36] *In re Schiavo*, 176, 177.

[37] *In re Schiavo*, 176, 179–180; see Obsidian Wings: Terry Schiavo, available at http://obsidianwings.blogs.com/obsidian_wings/2005/03/terri_schiavo.html, for a narrative description of the events leading up to Ms. Schiavo's eventual death.

[38] See, e.g., *Schiavo v. Schiavo*, 403 F. 3d 1289 (11th Cir. 2005).

general principle of patient autonomy as established by the New Jersey Supreme Court in *In re Quinlan*,[39] where the constitutional right to privacy was held to include a right to refuse medical treatment, and by the U.S. Supreme Court in *Cruzan*. Finally, the county medical examiner determined upon autopsy that "no treatment could have remotely improved [Ms. Schiavo's] condition.[40]

Both the federal and state legislatures have responded to the need to formalize the decision-making process for competent and incompetent patients who are faced with life-sustaining treatment decisions. As discussed next, legislation at the federal level imposes duties on healthcare providers to inform patients of their right to accept or refuse medical treatment, and every state has some type of statute that regulates patients' right to specify, in advance of incompetency, what medical measures should be used to sustain their lives. Moreover, the JCAHO requires all healthcare organizations to have policies and procedures regarding decisions to forgo or withdraw life-sustaining procedures.

Patient Self-Determination Act

Legislation requiring that all federally funded facilities inform patients of their rights under state law to accept or refuse medical treatment was enacted as part of the Omnibus Budget Reconciliation Act of 1990, more commonly referred to as the Patient Self-Determination Act (PSDA).[41] Since December 1, 1991, when the PSDA took effect, healthcare providers and institutions that receive Medicare or Medicaid funding have been required to inform patients of their legal right to accept or refuse medical or surgical treatment, and the right to formulate advance directives.[42] "Advance directive" is defined as a written instruction, such as a living will or durable power of attorney for health care, recognized under state law and relating to the provision of medical care when the individual is incapacitated.[43] Covered providers include, but are not limited to, hospitals, clinics, rehabilitation facilities,

---

[39] *In re Quinlan*, 355 A. 2d 647 (N.J. 1976).
[40] "Schiavo Autopsy Says Brain, Withered, Was Untreatable," *New York Times* (June 16, 2005).
[41] See Omnibus Budget Reconciliation Act of 1990, Pub. L. No. 101-508, 104 Stat. 1388, codified at 42 U.S.C. § 1395cc(f).
[42] 42 U.S.C. § 1305(b)(1)(a)(1)(A)(i).
[43] 42 U.S.C. § 1395cc(f)(3).

long-term care facilities, home health care agencies, hospice programs, and HMOs. Under the PSDA, each state must prepare a written description of its law on advance directives, and distribute this information to hospital patients, residents in a skilled nursing facility, HMO enrollees, or recipients of home health care and hospice program services.[44]

In accordance with the law, healthcare facilities must develop written policies requiring that patients receive legal information on the exercise of their rights as well as information about the facility policy itself.[45] Written information distributed by the healthcare provider must have two components: a summary of individual rights under state law, and the provider's written policy as to implementation of those rights.[46] The appropriate state agency should furnish the state law summary to facilitate uniformity among institutions. The provider itself is required to draft a written policy regarding patients' legal rights, and to provide a copy of it to patients at the time of admission.[47] The PSDA requires only that a patient's medical record indicate whether or not the individual has an advance directive, and does not specifically require that a copy of the directive be obtained and made part of the medical record. State law, however, may otherwise impose this duty on attending physicians or hospitals. In general, healthcare organizations would be well advised to require that the advance directive be made a part of the medical record, with provisions for confirming its continued validity upon any readmission or renewal of services.

Joint Commission standards require that healthcare organizations comply with the PSDA and that their policies and procedures describe the means by which patients' rights under the PSDA are protected and exercised.[48] A patient's rights as defined in these standards include the opportunity to create advance directives, the access to information necessary to make informed decisions about medical treatment, and the right to participate in discussions of the ethical issues that may arise during the individual's care. According to the intent of the Joint Com-

---

[44] 42 U.S.C. § 1395cc(f)(2).
[45] 42 U.S.C. § 1395cc(f)(1).
[46] Ibid.
[47] Ibid.
[48] See Joint Commission, *2005 Comprehensive Accreditation Manual for Hospitals*, Standard RI.2.70; Joint Commission, *2003–2004 Comprehensive Accreditation Manual for Health Care Networks*, Standards RI.3, RI.3.1, RI.3.2, and RI.3.3.

mission standard on advance directives, documentation of whether or not a patient has signed an advance directive should be placed into the record.[49] Moreover, patients must have the opportunity to review and revise advance directives, and hospitals upon request should help or refer patients for assistance in formulating advance directives.[50]

Living Will Legislation

The most widely available instrument for recording future healthcare related decisions is the living will. Most states have enacted legislation recognizing a competent adult's right to prepare a document that provides direction as to medical care if the adult becomes incapacitated or otherwise unable to make decisions personally. Many states' living will laws encompass "natural death acts" or statutory provisions allowing a living will to be specifically applied if the patient is suffering from a terminal condition or is irreversibly unconscious.[51]

Living will legislation covers a variety of topics, including procedures for executing such a document, physician certification of terminal illness or irreversible coma, immunity from civil and criminal liability for providers who implement the decisions, and the right to transfer a patient to another facility if a provider cannot follow the directive for reasons of conscience. As a general rule, the more precise and exact the living will's directions are, the more likely it is that healthcare providers will comply with the will.

Although some state laws used to contain statutorily dictated wording for written directives, the trend has been away from mandating the contents of living wills and toward requiring that they contain "substantially" or "essentially" the same information as the statutory model. North Carolina law states that the statutory form "is specifically determined to meet the [legislative] requirements," implying that other forms would be acceptable if they met the same requirements.[52] West

---

[49] Joint Commission, *2005 Comprehensive Accreditation Manual for Hospitals*, Standard RI.2.80.4.

[50] Ibid.

[51] The terminology varies from state to state. See, e.g., Cal. Health & Safety Code § 7180 ("irreversible cessation of circulatory and respiratory functions" or "irreversible cessation of all functions of the entire brain, including the brain stem"); Ark. Code Ann. § 20-17-201(6) ("permanently unconscious"); N.C. Gen. Stat. § 90-321(a)(4) ("persistent vegetative state"); W. Va. Code § 16-30-3(g).

[52] N.C. Gen. Stat. § 90-321(d).

Virginia law states that a directive "may but need not be in the form specified in the statute and may include other specific directions."[53] Arkansas provides that, in the absence of knowledge to the contrary, a healthcare provider may presume that a declaration complies with the law and is valid.[54]

State legislation also specifies the formality with which the directive must be executed. All of the acts require witnesses, and some of the acts disqualify certain people from being witnesses—such as relatives, those who will inherit the patient's estate, those who have claims against the patient's estate, the attending physician, and employees of the physician or hospital.[55] Normally, the witnesses' qualifications are not of concern to the hospital or physician because a directive usually includes a certification by the witness that they are not disqualified.

State laws also specify the means to revoke a directive. Written revocations generally must meet minimal requirements: they must be signed, dated, and communicated to the attending physician. In most states, any verbal revocation is effective upon communication to the attending physician.[56] If a copy of the directive is in the medical record, and the healthcare organization receives notice of revocation, a note should be entered on the directive stating that the patient has revoked it.[57] If the original directive is in the record, usually a patient cannot revoke it by physical destruction.

State law also defines the effect of a directive. Most state statutes specify that any physician may decline to follow the directive, but then must make an effort to transfer the patient to a physician who will follow it.[58] Some states provide that a directive shall not apply while the patient is pregnant.[59]

State legislation generally makes it a crime to interfere with the proper use of directive forms.[60] Unauthorized cancellation or conceal-

---

[53] W. Va. Code § 16-30-4(g).
[54] Ark. Code Ann. § 20-17-211.
[55] See, e.g., W. Va. Code § 16-30-4(b); Kan. Stat. Ann. § 65-28,103(a).
[56] See, e.g., W. Va. Code § 16-30-18(3); N.C. Gen. Stat. § 90-321(e); Tex. Health & Safety Code Ann. § 166.042.
[57] See, e.g., W. Va. Code § 16-30-18(a).
[58] See, e.g., Tex. Health & Safety Code Ann. § 166.045(c); W. Va. Code § 16-30-12; Or. Rev. Stat. § 127.625(2)(c) (physician must notify healthcare representative, who must make a reasonable effort to transfer the patient).
[59] See, e.g., Kan. Stat. Ann. § 65-28,103(a); Tex. Health & Safety Code Ann. § 166.049.
[60] See, e.g., Tex. Health & Safety Code Ann. § 166.097.

ment of a directive in order to interfere with a patient's wish not to be treated may constitute a criminal misdemeanor or grounds for professional disciplinary action. State law also usually makes it a felony to engage in falsification or forgery of a directive or to withhold knowledge of revocation in order to cause actions contrary to the patient's wishes when those actions hasten death.[61]

Durable Power of Attorney

A power of attorney is a written document that authorizes an individual, as an agent, to perform certain acts on behalf of, and according to the written directives of, another—the person executing the document—from whom the agent obtains authority. The agent is called the attorney-in-fact, and the person executing the document is called the principal. Most states have adopted the Uniform Durable Power of Attorney Act, which provides that the subsequent disability or incompetence of the principal does not affect the attorney-in-fact's authority.[62] For the power of attorney to have any legal effect, however, the principal must be mentally competent when executing the instrument. The requirements governing witnesses and notarization of the instrument typically vary with state law. Because of the lack of uniformity in state laws, it is possible that a power of attorney valid in one state may not be enforceable in other jurisdictions. Healthcare providers should always seek legal counsel to determine the validity of an out-of-state power of attorney, and healthcare organizations should specifically require such consultation in relevant policies.

Such legislation is general in nature, however, and is not tailored to healthcare decision making. For this reason, most states have enacted legislation authorizing durable powers of attorney specifically for healthcare decisions.[63] Under these statutes, the state authorizes the appointment of an individual who is specifically empowered to make personal healthcare-related decisions for another person in the event the latter becomes incapacitated. Many state statutes provide model forms that include specific choices for the conditions under which life-sustaining treatment may be withdrawn.

---

[61] Tex. Health & Safety Code Ann. § 166.048.
[62] See Uniform Probate Code, Sec. 20201, 8 U.L.A. 74 (1983).
[63] See, e.g., 755 Ill. Comp. Stat. Ann. §§ 45/4-1 through 45/4-12; Ariz. Rev. Stat. §§ 36-3221 through 36-3224; Cal. Prob. Code §§ 4600 through 4805; D.C. Code §§ 21-2205 through 21-2210.

The exact wording of durable powers of attorney for health care varies from state to state and, like that of living wills, is dictated largely by models contained in the statutes. In general, these documents grant agents full power and authority to make healthcare decisions for principals to the same extent that principals themselves would if they were competent. In exercising this authority, the agent must, to the extent possible, make decisions that are consistent with the principal's desires using the substituted judgment doctrine,[64] or that are based on what the agent believes to be the principal's best interests.[65] The power of attorney can enumerate specifically the principal's desires as to different types of life-sustaining measures, admission or discharge from facilities, pain relief medication, and anatomical gifts. It also should allow the agent to gain access to the principal's medical records to be able to make informed decisions.

Of paramount importance is the actual determination of the principal's disability or incompetence. The durable power of attorney should state who will determine the principal's incompetence, and should set the standards to be used in making that determination. It is best for one or more physicians, named in the document or chosen according to a procedure established in the document, to determine incompetence.[66] Disability and incompetence should be defined in the durable power of attorney, and should be mutually acceptable to the principal and physicians involved. Copies of the durable power of attorney should be given to the attorney-in-fact, the principal's physician, and close family members. As an additional safeguard, the document also should be included in the patient's medical record.

A competent principal can revoke the durable power of attorney at any time. The instrument also may be terminated if it contains an expiration clause. An expiration clause allows the principal periodically to reconsider the directives in the writing.

---

[64] Substituted judgment means that the decisions of the surrogate should be based on what the patient would have decided if he or she had been able to do so at the time; in most states, it is the legal standard that applies in the absence of an explicit statement of desires in an advance directive. See, e.g., Idaho Code § 39-4505; D.C. Code § 21-2006(c); Cal. Prob. Code § 4604.

[65] The American Bar Association Commission on Legal Problems of the Elderly has adopted a model Health Care Powers of Attorney containing this broad grant of authority. See also D.C. Code § 21-2006(c)(2).

[66] The ABA model suggests that incapacity should be determined by the agent and the attending physician.

As with living will legislation, state statutes governing durable power of attorney for health care usually impose criminal penalties for failing to conform with the healthcare agency provided for under the statutes. Falsification or forgery of a healthcare agency with the intent to cause withholding or withdrawal of life-sustaining or death-delaying procedures contrary to the principal's intent, which thereby hastens the death of the patient, may be subject to felony charges.[67]

Healthcare providers view the durable power of attorney for health care as a more flexible instrument than a living will. The scope of a living will generally is limited to situations where the patient is either terminally ill or permanently unconscious. The power of attorney, on the other hand, can apply to a wider range of situations in which the patient is unable to communicate a choice regarding a healthcare decision. In addition, the power of attorney allows the agent to make any decision regarding an incapacitated patient's health care and is not limited to specific life-sustaining measures.

Do-Not-Resuscitate Orders

The term "cardiopulmonary resuscitation" (CPR) describes a procedure developed over the past two decades to reestablish breathing and heartbeat after cardiac or respiratory arrest. The most basic form of CPR, which is being taught to the public, involves recognizing the indications for intervention, opening an airway, initiating mouth-to-mouth breathing, and compressing the chest externally to establish artificial circulation. In hospitals, and in some emergency transport vehicles, CPR also can include the administration of oxygen under pressure to the lungs, the use of intravenous medications, the injection of stimulants into the heart through catheters or long needles, electric shocks to the heart, insertion of a pacemaker, and open-heart massage. Some of these procedures are highly intrusive and even violent in nature.

To ensure that CPR is not initiated where the patient's advance directive prohibits it, common practice is to write "Do not resuscitate" (DNR) or "No CPR" on the orders for the patient's treatment. The order is directed to on-call staff members who, because of the urgency of cardiac arrest, are unable to consult with the patient or primary care physician as to the desired course of treatment. Many institutions call

---

[67] See, e.g., 755 Ill. Comp. Stat. Ann. § 45/4-9.

the CPR team by announcing "Code Blue," so the order might read "No Code Blue." DNR orders provide an exception to the universal standing order to provide CPR. For prehospital and emergency department care, consent for CPR is implied unless a valid, written advance directive states otherwise. With respect to emergency care, the presumption at law is that the patient would choose to be resuscitated were he or she able to express such an opinion. Moreover, the American Medical Association (AMA) Council on Ethical and Judicial Affairs has stated that "[e]fforts should be made to resuscitate patients who suffer cardiac or respiratory arrest except when circumstances indicate that administration of cardiopulmonary resuscitation (CPR) would be inappropriate or not in accord with the desires or best interest of the patient."[68]

Joint Commission standards require that healthcare organizations establish policies and procedures regarding the decision to withhold resuscitative services.[69] Moreover, state statutes in this area typically require that the physician who is primarily responsible for the patient's care is the only person who may write DNR orders and inscribe them in the patient's medical record.[70] An appropriate consent form or refusal of treatment form should also be signed by the patient, the patient's family, or the patient's surrogate or proxy; a physician must obtain the informed consent of a competent patient or of an incompetent patient's family or other representative before entering a DNR order. Typically, hospital policies require daily review of DNR orders to determine if they remain consistent with the patient's condition and the desires of the patient or patient's representative.

If a patient is incompetent, a healthcare provider should proceed with caution before placing a DNR order in the medical record or failing to respond in the event of cardiopulmonary arrest, unless a written advance directive such as a living will clearly indicates the patient's choice. In one leading case, a court ruled against a physician who, after concluding that a patient was incompetent, issued a no-code order in

---

[68] American Medical Association, *Code of Medical Ethics*, E-2.22.
[69] Joint Commission, *2005 Accreditation Manual for Hospitals*, Standards RI.2.80, PC.9.30; Joint Commission, *2003–2004 Accreditation Manual for Health Care Networks*, Standard RI.3.2.
[70] See, e.g., Alaska Stat. § 18.12.010(b); Ga. Code Ann. § 31-39-4; Md. Code Ann., Health-Gen., § 5-.602(f)(2).

response to a relative's request.[71] Although a nurse gave evidence that the patient was able to communicate coherently up to a few minutes before his death, the physician relied on the patient's sister, who requested the DNR order. No efforts were made to resuscitate the patient when he stopped breathing. The court held that the patient should have been consulted before the physician gave the DNR order. In addition, the court noted that a year prior to the incident, the patient had suffered from the same type of illness and recovered. Thus, there was a good possibility that the patient would have survived if there had been concerted resuscitation efforts.

Moreover, a physician must explain the nature of the treatment to be withheld from an incompetent patient before obtaining consent from the patient's family or other representative. The representative of an incompetent patient should be informed concerning the nature of the treatment to be denied. It is worth noting, however, that a physician typically is not required to obtain court approval before entering a DNR order.[72] If a patient is a ward of the state, however, the physician may need to obtain court approval before entering a DNR order.[73]

Although some states have enacted statutes that prohibit the use of DNR orders outside the hospital setting, at least 35 other states have advance directive legislation that either specifically permits emergency medical personnel to honor certain out-of-hospital DNR orders or leaves open the opportunity for the state's medical community to develop standards in this area.[74] In many of these states, statutes, regulations, or medical society standards provide that, if certain conditions are met by physician and patient, DNRs in these situations will be recognized and honored by emergency medical services (EMS) personnel responding to calls for patients suffering cardiopulmonary arrest. In Wisconsin, for example, a recently enacted statute allows certain indi-

---

[71] *Payne v. Marion General Hospital,* 549 N.E. 2d 1043 (Ind. Ct. App. 1990).

[72] See, e.g., *In re Quinlan, cert. denied, Gavger v. New Jersey,* 429 U.S. 922 (1976); *In re Dinnerstein,* 380 N.E. 2d 134 (Mass. App. Ct. 1978). See also *Severns v. Wilmington Medical Center, Inc.,* 421 A. 2d 1334 (Del. 1980) (authorizing DNR order, but failing to state whether court authorization always is required); *In re Jobes,* 529 A. 2d 434, 449 (N.J. 1988) ("judicial review of such decisions is not necessary or appropriate").

[73] See *Custody of a Minor (No. 1),* 434 N.E. 2d 601, 608 (Mass. 1982) (holding that "[a]bsent a loving family with whom physicians may consult regarding the entry of a 'no code' order, this issue is best resolved by requiring a judicial determination").

[74] In some states, such standards are considered to be medical protocols appropriately promulgated by the medical community, rather than enacted by the state legislature.

viduals to request a DNR bracelet from his or her physician. If the bracelet is found on the patient's wrist (and the bracelet is not defaced in any way), emergency healthcare personnel will not undertake CPR measures.[75] The statute also provides that no physician, EMS worker, or other healthcare professional may be held criminally or civilly liable, or otherwise disciplined, if they withhold or withdraw resuscitation from a patient with a DNR order. In New Jersey, recently released guidelines for out-of-hospital DNR orders provide that such orders will be considered valid only if the DNR form is completed, signed and dated by both the patient and his or her physician, and displayed prominently in the patient's home or presented to medical personnel who respond to an emergency call, or if the patient is wearing an appropriately recognized DNR bracelet.[76]

Deceased Patients and Autopsy Authorizations

The Privacy Rule permits covered healthcare providers to disclose PHI without authorization to a coroner or medical examiner for the purpose of identifying a deceased person, determining a cause of death, or other purposes authorized by law.[77] If they suspect that a person has died as a result of criminal conduct, covered healthcare providers may also disclose PHI of the deceased person to a law enforcement official for the purpose of alerting the official of the death.[78]

Autopsies are the most frequent cause of litigation involving hospitals and dead bodies. Autopsies are performed primarily to determine the cause of a patient's death. This finding can be crucial in detecting crime or ruling out transmittable diseases that may be a threat to the public health. More frequently, the cause of death can determine whether death benefits are payable under insurance policies, workers' compensation laws, and other programs.

Community mores and religious beliefs have long dictated respectful handling of dead bodies. Societal views have evolved now to the point that a substantial portion of the population recognizes the benefit of autopsies. Out of respect for those who continue to find them unacceptable, the law requires appropriate consent before an autopsy can be

---

[75] Wis. Stat. § 154.19. See also Fla. Stat. § 401.45; Fla. Admin. Code Ann. r. 64E-2.031.
[76] Medical Society of New Jersey, *Out of Hospital DNR Order Guidelines* (2003).
[77] 45 C.F.R. § 164.512(g).
[78] 45 C.F.R. § 164.512(f)(4).

performed, except when one is needed to determine the cause of death for public policy purposes. The consent to the autopsy, whether given by the decedent, by family members, or by other persons authorized to do so in the particular state, must be documented in the patient's medical record. A few states require that an autopsy be authorized in writing. Many states include telegrams and recorded telephone permissions as acceptable forms of authorization. Common law does not require that the authorization be documented in a particular way, so evidentiary considerations are the primary basis for deciding the appropriate form of consent. A written authorization or recorded telephone authorization obviously is the easiest to prove.[79]

Recording Disagreements Among Professional Staff

All members of the medical team have a duty to take reasonable actions to safeguard the lives of their patients. Physician's assistants, nurse-practitioners, nurses, and other healthcare professionals often are given the responsibility of monitoring and coordinating patient care. Thus, in the exercise of reasonable professional judgment and to minimize possible liability for negligence, nonphysician medical professionals may be expected to intervene to clarify or object to physicians' orders that they believe are improper. Courts have upheld such interventions.[80] Courts also have recognized that nurses and other nonphysician medical professionals, including pharmacists, have an independent duty to patients, and so can be held liable for failing to question physicians' orders.[81] Accordingly, nurses and other medical professionals must document their efforts to fulfill their duty to object to improper orders, and must document their attempts to obtain responsible intervention to settle a professional disagreement. At the same time, it is important to create a medical record that is so objective and factual that

---

[79] See, e.g., *Lashbrook v. Barnes*, 437 S.W. 2d 502 (Ky. Ct. App. 1969).

[80] See, e.g., *Carlsen v. Javurek*, 526 F. 2d 202 (8th Cir. 1975).

[81] See, e.g., *Gassen v. East Jefferson General Hospital*, 628 So. 2d 256, 259 (La. Ct. App. 1993) (holding that "a pharmacist has a limited duty to inquire or verify from the prescribing physician clear errors or mistakes in the prescription"); *Riff v. Morgan Pharmacy*, 508 A. 2d 1247 (Pa. Super. Ct. 1986) (holding pharmacist liable for failing to warn patient or inform her physician of inadequacies in prescription's instructions); *Norton v. Argonaut Insurance Company*, 144 So. 2d 249 (La. Ct. App. 1962) (holding nurse liable for administering fatal dose to patient as result of not contacting physician about apparently erroneous medication order).

it could not be used as evidence against the physician or the institution in a negligence action.

There are no clear answers to the medical records issues presented in instances of disagreements among physicians and other medical professionals. However, several suggested approaches may be helpful. If hospital policy requires that resolution of disagreements be documented in the medical record, all persons making entries in patients' medical records should be trained as to proper documentation in these situations. Entries in the medical record should be objective, concise, and completely factual rather than judgmental. The more complex the intervention, the more care the nurse or other professional must take in documenting the facts. Statements such as "Dr. Smith is negligent again" or "Dr. Smith's order is incorrect" are unnecessary and inappropriate—and, in the event of any legal action, may be used as evidence against the nurse or other nonphysician healthcare provider, the physician, and the healthcare institution.

There are varying opinions among healthcare professionals concerning whether these kinds of professional discussions and disagreements should be documented in a medical record, and, if so, in what manner. Regardless of the position one takes on the issue, it is clear that a healthcare organization must have a policy covering the question.[82] Otherwise practitioners are left to work out their differences on their own. The latter inevitably leads to inconsistent patient care and record documentation practices, and may result in vindictive or otherwise "dangerous" medical records entries made in the heat of anger.

Special Disclosure Concerns

Use and Disclosures for Marketing Purposes

Healthcare organizations and practitioners may wish to use patient health information for the purpose of marketing their disease-specific goods and services or for the purpose of assisting an external vendor to

---

[82] Disagreements among healthcare professionals have not generated cases on documentation issues, but have resulted in cases involving employment issues. See *Kirk v. Mercy Hospital Tri-County*, 851 S.W. 2d 617 (Mo. Ct. App. 1993), in which the court ruled that discharging a nurse for complaining to other hospital employees about the level of care given by a physician to a hospital patient constituted wrongful discharge.

market its products or services. Using medical records information, providers can determine what goods and services patients might want based on the illnesses for which they were treated, their need for follow-up or recuperative care, and the like. Providers also possess information that is valuable to commercial enterprises that are willing to pay for access to patient data. All providers should consider carefully whether using or disclosing health information for marketing purposes is appropriate.

For all organizations and practitioners subject to the Privacy Rule, special restrictions apply. The Privacy Rule requires covered entities to obtain the patient's authorization for the use or disclosure of PHI for marketing purposes.[83] Therefore, if the proposed communication requires the use of PHI and fits the definition of marketing, a covered entity may not use or disclose the PHI unless it first obtains an authorization that meets requirements of the Privacy Rule, or unless it determines that no authorization is required.

The first step in determining whether the Privacy Rule permits using PHI in a communication without the patient's authorization is to ascertain whether that communication qualifies as "marketing," which is defined in the Privacy Rule as "a communication about a product or service that *encourages the recipient* of the communication to purchase or use the product or service."[84] Thus, if, on its face, the communication encourages the recipient to purchase or use a product or service, the communication is marketing, unless one of the exceptions from the definition applies.

The Privacy Rule recognizes that some forms of communication are common in a healthcare setting, and should not be viewed as marketing, for which a patient authorization is needed. A covered entity is not engaged in marketing, and does not need to obtain an authorization, when it communicates to individuals about any of the following:[85]

- A health-related product or service, or payment for the product or service, provided by the covered entity making the communication (for example, it is not marketing for a physician who has developed a device to treat a particular malady to send an announcement de-

---

[83] 45 C.F.R. § 164.508(a)(3).
[84] 45 C.F.R. § 164.501.
[85] Ibid.; see also 67 Fed. Reg. 53186 (Aug. 14, 2002).

scribing the device to all of his or her patients, whether or not they suffer from that illness)[86]

- Health insurance products that could enhance or substitute for existing plan coverage offered by the covered entity to health plan beneficiaries and members (for example, it is not marketing for a health plan to advise its enrollees about other available health plan coverages)
- Health-related value-added items or services, as long as the items or services are available only to plan enrollees and not to the general public (for example, it is not marketing for a managed care plan to communicate about discounts offered for eyeglasses or health club memberships)
- The individual's treatment (for example, it is not marketing for a physician to refer a patient to a specialist for additional examination, to provide free samples of a prescription drug to a patient, or to send appointment reminders to patients)
- Case management or care coordination for that individual, or directions or recommendations for alternative treatments, therapies, healthcare providers, or settings of care

In addition to these exceptions, the Privacy Rule permits communications without the patient's authorization, even if they constitute marketing, if the communications are made in a face-to-face encounter with the individual or if they involve a promotional gift of nominal value (for example, an inexpensive pen or a refrigerator magnet).[87] Moreover, the definition of marketing does not include communications that merely promote health in a general manner and do not promote a specific product or service. Therefore, promotional materials reminding women to get annual mammograms, and mailings offering information about lowering cholesterol levels, support groups, organ donation, and the like do not require patient authorization.[88]

The Privacy Rule and guidance provided by DHHS are clear with respect to covered entities who are paid by another entity to provide PHI for the other entity's marketing purposes: PHI may not be dis-

---

[86] For additional examples of each exception, see U.S. Department of Health and Human Services (DHHS), *Standards for Privacy of Individually Identifiable Health Information* 72 (Dec. 3, 2002).
[87] 45 C.F.R. §§ 164.508(a)(3)(i)(A) and (B).
[88] DHHS, *Standards for Privacy* 71.

closed for this purpose without the patient's authorization.[89] The rule provides no exceptions to this requirement. In addition, any authorization obtained for uses of PHI for marketing where the covered entity has obtained remuneration, directly or indirectly, must disclose that remuneration will be received.[90] However, for communications that fall outside the definition of marketing, the rule does permit covered entities to obtain remuneration without having to obtain an individual's authorization. For example, a provider that receives payment for sending patients prescription refill reminders is not engaging in marketing.[91]

For covered entities, the use and disclosure of PHI for marketing purposes likely will continue to be a confusing aspect of the Privacy Rule, at least until further guidance from DHHS is forthcoming. In the meantime, all healthcare organizations and practitioners considering this use of patient health information should proceed cautiously.

Use and Disclosures for Fund-Raising

Many not for profit healthcare organizations have substantial development departments charged with generating philanthropic donations in support of the organizations' charitable purposes. In the past, development staff have often used information in medical records to identify patients who might be willing to make substantial gifts or participate in the institutions' volunteer programs.

The Privacy Rule places restrictions on such use of PHI for fund-raising. The rule does not define a covered entity's "fund-raising," but describes the activity as "raising funding for its own benefit."[92] Permissible fund-raising includes appeals for money and sponsorship of events, but does not include royalties or payments for the sale of products of others (except in charitable auctions, rummage sales, and similar events).[93] The only PHI that a covered entity may use or disclose for

---

[89]   45 C.F.R. § 164.501; DHHS, *Standards for Privacy* 66.
[90]   45 C.F.R. § 164.508(a)(3)(ii).
[91]   DHHS, *Standards for Privacy* 67.
[92]   45 C.F.R. § 164.514(f)(1). Not for profit, charitable, and for profit organizations may rely upon the Privacy Rule's provisions governing use of PHI for fund-raising. Although most covered entities that engage in soliciting gifts are charitable organizations, the rule permits taxable entities to use the limited PHI for raise funds.
[93]   65 Fed. Reg. 82718 (Dec. 28, 2000).

fund-raising purposes without the patient's authorization is an individual's demographic information and the dates of health care that was provided to the individual.[94] In the fund-raising context, "demographic information" includes the patient's name, gender, and insurance status, but not information about illness or treatment.[95]

For fund-raising purposes, a covered entity may also disclose this limited PHI to a business associate or to a foundation related to the covered entity.[96] For example, a hospital might engage an outside firm to analyze its medical records to identify possible donors or volunteers. An "institutionally related foundation" is an organization that is a not for profit, charitable organization under Section 501(c)(3) of the Internal Revenue Code (which governs tax-exempt charities), and that has in its articles of incorporation, charter, or other governing documents an explicit link to the covered entity.[97] Most of the foundations that tax-exempt hospitals have created to generate donations and build endowments on behalf of the hospitals would qualify. The Privacy Rule does not limit the number of charitable organizations the foundation may support, so long as the foundation is expressly linked to the covered entity. Thus, a hospital may disclose the limited PHI to a related foundation, if one of the foundation's stated corporate purposes is to raise funds for a hospital group that includes the hospital disclosing the PHI. However, without a patient authorization, a covered entity could not disclose PHI to a community foundation that is not legally related to the covered entity and has only a general purpose of raising funds for medical research or a particular illness.

To use PHI for fund-raising without obtaining a patient's authorization, a covered entity must give the patient notice and an opportunity for the patient to avoid unwanted solicitations. To accomplish this, the covered entity must take all of the following actions:

- Include in its notice of privacy practices a statement that it may contact the individual to raise funds for the covered entity[98]
- Include in its fund-raising materials a description of how the individual may opt out of receiving future solicitations[99]

---

[94]   45 C.F.R. § 164.514(f)(1).
[95]   65 Fed. Reg. 82718 (Dec. 28, 2000).
[96]   45 C.F.R. § 164.514(f)(1).
[97]   65 Fed. Reg. 82546 (Dec. 28, 2000).
[98]   45 C.F.R. § 164.520(b)(1)(iii)(B).
[99]   45 C.F.R. § 164.514(f)(2)(ii).

- For individuals who opt out, make reasonable efforts to protect them from receiving any future fund-raising materials[100]

If a covered entity wishes to use PHI other than the limited PHI described above, it must first obtain the patient's authorization in a form that meets the requirements of the Privacy Rule.

Records Sought by Managed Care Organizations

In today's healthcare environment, healthcare organizations must regularly respond to requests for access to patient healthcare records information from managed care organizations (MCOs). In responding to these requests, healthcare organizations may trigger potential liability risks stemming from the inappropriate generation of, use of, and access to healthcare record information. The HIPAA Privacy Rule specifically permits disclosures of health information for treatment and payment purposes.[101] However, a covered entity, such as a healthcare provider, must make reasonable efforts to limit the protected health information that it uses or discloses to another covered entity, such as an MCO, to the minimum necessary to accomplish the intended purpose of the permitted use or disclosure.[102] (See the discussion of the minimum necessary rule in Chapter 6.) In addition, healthcare organizations must be aware of all relevant state laws relating to medical records and MCOs.[103]

Managed care and the growth of integrated healthcare delivery systems have created greater challenges with respect to protecting unauthorized disclosure and preserving the confidentiality of patient healthcare information. It has become increasingly difficult, for example, to identify all the possible sites where a particular medical record, or a segment of that record, may be located. Where formerly such documentation may have been located at various locations but within only one institution (for example, within a number of hospital departments), now, in addition to these sources, parts of the patient's medical

---

[100] 45 C.F.R. § 164.514(f)(2)(iii).
[101] 45 C.F.R. § 164.502(a)(1).
[102] 45 C.F.R. § 164.502(b)(1).
[103] See 45 C.F.R. at § 160.203 (state laws that are not contrary to the HIPAA Privacy Rule, that are more stringent, or that have been deemed necessary to "ensure the appropriate State regulation of insurance and health plans" are not preempted). Laws relating to medical records and MCOs are more fully discussed in Chapter 2.

records information may be found at numerous other sites, including managed care organizations, utilization management companies, and various member healthcare providers of integrated delivery networks. Each of these entities may be a covered entity or business associate under the Privacy Rule and subject to the rule's privacy requirements.[104]

Although the Privacy Rule has created a new regime that protects the confidentiality of patients' medical records and has increased patients' control over their medical records, it does not preempt many state statutes that carve out exceptions permitting disclosure of patient information without a patient's permission. (For a discussion of HIPAA preemption of state law, see Chapter 6.) Indeed, many state laws exist that permit healthcare providers to review and use patient information for public health reasons[105] or for research purposes.[106] State laws and regulations also contain numerous exceptions, such as mandatory reporting laws, that allow the disclosure of confidential information with or without patient consent. (For a more detailed discussion of exceptions relating to both access and confidentiality, see Chapters 6 and 7.)

Notwithstanding these exceptions, the general principle is that patient records are to be generated and used in a manner that encourages the maintenance of confidentiality, and this principle applies to all healthcare institutions, including MCOs. Federal and state laws discussed throughout this book impose confidentiality and/or disclosure requirements for certain types of medical records, and MCOs are generally subject to these laws. In addition, several other laws obligate MCOs to maintain the confidentiality of healthcare records information. For example, MCOs may fall within the purview of the National Association of Insurance Commissioners Insurance Information and Privacy Protection Model Act, enacted in some form in many states.[107] This model act prohibits insurers from disclosing confidential information about individuals without statutorily prescribed written au-

---

[104] 45 C.F.R. § 160.103.
[105] See, e.g., Mo. Ann. Stat. § 191.656; N.D. Cent. Code § 23-07-05.
[106] See, e.g., Neb. Rev. Stat. § 71-3402; N.M. Stat. Ann. § 14-6-1; 42 C.F.R. § 2(a)(1).
[107] See, e.g., Ariz. Rev. Stat. §§ 20-2101 through 20-2122; Cal. Ins. Code §§ 791.01 through 791.27; Conn. Gen. Stat. §§ 38a-975 through 38a-999a. Pursuant to Ariz. Rev. Stat. § 20-2122, an insurance institution subject to and in compliance with the HIPAA Privacy Rule is deemed to comply with the Arizona Insurance Information & Privacy Protection Act.

thorization of the individual. Accreditation standards[108] and state utilization review statutes,[109] as well as state HMO acts,[110] also typically contain provisions relating to the protection of confidential information and an MCO's obligation to ensure such protection.

Moreover, in managed care settings, contractual obligations often impose a duty to maintain patient information in confidence. Because contracts for managed care services are frequently a controlling source in the uses and format of managed care information, healthcare managers reviewing such contracts (in consultation with legal counsel) should devote special attention to avoiding in provider contracts the inclusion of clauses that are contrary to state or federal requirements regarding confidentiality and access to health information. Qualified legal counsel should be consulted whenever a managed care arrangement or provision within a managed care provider contract gives rise to concerns regarding the negligent or improper granting of access to unauthorized persons, including sharing or disseminating information to MCOs or other non-healthcare-related institutions (for example, employers, utilization management, and insurance companies) without patient permission and for uses other than permitted by state and federal law.

MCOs often have a legitimate purpose for obtaining access to patient healthcare records, such as monitoring discharge planning, case management, or utilization review, or the accreditation or credentialing of a physician who has applied to become a provider. To avoid disputes that may arise between the healthcare facility and the MCO requesting patient healthcare information,[111] health information professionals should develop policies and procedures for dealing with such requests.

One approach is to designate specific individuals to undertake the duties of requesting access to information and responding to such requests. The healthcare facility may want to create a list of authorized users, which should include the names of MCO-designated representatives who will be informed about whom to contact at the facility re-

---

[108] See Joint Commission, *2005–2006 Comprehensive Accreditation Standards for Integrated Delivery Systems Managed Care Organizations*, Standard IM.2.1.10.

[109] See, e.g., Ark. Code Ann. § 20-9-913; Ala. Code § 27-3A-5(a)(7).

[110] See, e.g., Ga. Code Ann. § 33-21-23(a).

[111] For example, the frustrated managed care representative may demand access and threaten to alert the CEO that the healthcare organization has technically breached its contract with the MCO by denying access to such information.

garding access to records, and about the types of information they may access either with or without a patient's permission.[112]

The healthcare facility should also designate its own managed care coordinator or facilitator whose job is to field records access requests from managed care entities. Additionally, the healthcare facility should consider the benefits to be gained by establishing a managed care relations team comprising individuals, such as the coordinator responsible for records requests, who will receive special training in handling potential conflicts with managed care representatives; all members should ultimately know the applicable laws relating to access to confidential patient information and medical staff records.

Other policies that might be developed in this area include:

- Annual review of healthcare records information policy and procedures to make certain that they continue to comply with all applicable federal and state laws
- Education of those responsible for generating and using managed care medical records information, with particular reference to how they should record information so as not to trigger needless denials of claims
- Training of all staff members by risk managers and legal counsel on issues related to the protection of patient healthcare information

To avoid potential liability for negligent granting of access to unauthorized persons or for unauthorized disclosure of information, both healthcare facilities and MCOs should have policies and procedures governing this area.

Records Sought by Parties to Adoption

For the most part, general rules on patient access to medical records do not resolve the competing policy interests that arise when one of the parties to an adoption attempts to access either the original birth records or the medical records of the biological parents. In this area, the issues are more complicated, given that all 50 states have adoption laws that generally cover adoption procedures, the rights of all parties, and the process by which an adoption is accomplished. In almost all in-

---

[112] A similar approach could be taken with respect to access requests involving medical staff files.

stances, court action of one form or another is involved in some aspect of the adoption process, and many state statutes provide that court records on adoption and the adoptee's original birth certificate can be placed under seal and made confidential by court order. Until the 1980s, when new adoption legislation was enacted in many states, most states prohibited access to these adoption records unless a party, generally the adoptee, could demonstrate "good cause" to access the record based on medical or psychological needs. (For a discussion of court decisions in this area, see "'Good Cause' to Obtain Adoption Records Information" in this chapter.)

Although current adoption statutes in many states still have provisions restricting inspection of adoption records except upon court order for good cause shown, most states now require that the adoptive parents receive, at the time of placement for adoption, specific health-related information on the adoptee.[113] Moreover, as discussed later in this section, many states allow individuals who are parties to an adoption (that is, biological parents, adoptive parents, and adoptees) to access certain information via avenues other than court order, including direct requests by adult adoptees who meet specified statutory conditions, mutual consent registries, and confidential intermediary search programs.[114]

In addition to specifically authorizing the direct disclosure of non-identifying health-related information to adult adoptees who request such information,[115] most state adoption statutes now require that certain background physical and mental health information be provided

---

[113] See, e.g., Ala. Code §§ 26-10A-31(a) and (c); Cal. Health & Safety Code § 102705; Colo. Rev. Stat. § 19-1-309.

[114] Note that, even under these newer statutes, parties to adoptions continue to bring constitutional challenges to statutory provisions limiting access to information. See, e.g., *Griffith v. Johnston*, 899 F. 2d 1427 (5th Cir. 1990), *cert. denied*, 498 U.S. 1040 (1991), wherein the court dismissed constitutional challenges to a Texas adoption statute in a case involving adoptive parents who contended that they could not provide necessary care and treatment for their adopted children with special needs because they were denied access to certain background information.

[115] Many of these statutes require that adoptees be 18 years of age or older to obtain such information, although some states impose no age restrictions on the adoptee's right of access. See, e.g., Conn. Gen. Stat. § 45a-746(c) (adult); 750 Ill. Comp. Stat. Ann. § 50/18.4(b) (18 or older); N.D. Cent. Code § 14-15-16 (adult); Or. Rev. Stat. § 109.342(4) (age of majority); Wis. Stat. § 48.432(3)(a)(1) (18 or older). But see Neb. Rev. Stat. § 43-146.02 (no age provision).

to the adoptive parents when the child is placed for adoption.[116] In some states, however, the decision as to whether to disclose information is left to the discretion of the state or private adoption agency.[117] In South Carolina, for example, the release of nonidentifying health information to adoptive parents, biological parents, or adoptees is left to the sole discretion of the chief executive officer of the adoption agency if that individual perceives that the release would serve the best interests of the persons concerned.[118] Some states have chosen to leave the decision to the judiciary, requiring a court order before information can be released.[119]

Although state adoption statutes generally provide for the sealing of original birth certificates, many states now also specify circumstances when the adopted person, or a designated representative for the adopted person, may be allowed access to birth certificate information, as well as other identifying information regarding the biological parents.[120] In addition, many states have amended their adoption statutes to establish mutual consent voluntary registries, which allow biological parents and adopted individuals to register to indicate their willingness to have their identity and whereabouts disclosed to each other under specified circumstances.[121]

Some adoption statutes also provide for obtaining background information by enlisting the services of a "confidential intermediary" who is authorized to contact one or both of the adoptee's biological parents and request information sought by the adoptee.[122]

---

[116] See, e.g., Ala. Code § 26-10A-31(g); Colo. Rev. Stat. § 19-5-207; Conn. Gen. Stat. § 45a-746(b); Ga. Code Ann. § 19-8-23; Haw. Rev. Stat. § 578-14.5(h); 750 Ill. Comp. Stat. Ann. § 50/18.4(a).

[117] See, e.g., Del. Code Ann. tit. 13, § 924 (department of licensed agency may release nonidentifying information to any parties in the adoption).

[118] S.C. Code Ann. § 20-7-1780(D).

[119] See, e.g., D.C. Code Ann. § 16-311; Tenn. Code Ann. § 36-1-138; N.M. Stat. Ann. § 32A-5-40.

[120] See, e.g., Okla. Stat. tit. 10, § 7505-6.6(D) (allowing adult adoptees to obtain, upon request to state registry, an uncertified copy of the original birth certificate, provided certain conditions are met).

[121] See, e.g., 750 Ill. Comp. Stat. Ann. § 50/18.1; Okla. Stat. tit. 10, § 7508-1.2.

[122] See, e.g., Okla. Stat. tit. 10, § 7508-1.3 (state-run confidential intermediary search program); 750 Ill. Comp. Stat. Ann. § 50/18.3a (court-appointed confidential intermediaries may contact adoptee's biological parents either to seek consent to release of identifying information or to ascertain willingness to meet or otherwise communicate information about any physical or mental condition); Colo. Rev. Stat. § 19-5-304 et seq.; N.Y. Dom. Rel. Law § 114(4).

"Good Cause" to Obtain Adoption Records Information

Courts have intervened on numerous occasions to determine whether "good cause" for the release of adoption records exists based on the medical need for such information. A medical necessity generally satisfies the "good cause" requirement of many statutes. In one case involving a female adoptee who was considering having children, a New York appeals court authorized the adoptee's access to any medical reports or nonidentifying related matter in the court records of her adoption, reasoning that "good cause" is demonstrated by concern about genetic or hereditary factors that might impact upon the decision to have children.[123] However, courts also have held that to satisfy the "good cause" requirement, the need to obtain information on hereditary or genetic diseases must be supported with detailed descriptions.[124]

Courts have considered whether "good cause" for the release of adoption records exists based on the psychological need for such information, but generally have been less sympathetic to adoptees' requests for information in these cases than in those involving a request based on medical needs. In one New York case, for example, the adoptee sought both the records of her adoption and the sealed board of health records on her birth.[125] The plaintiff asserted that because she did not know who her biological parents were, she was experiencing psychological problems that impaired her musical skills, she was fearful of entering into an incestuous marriage, and she was unable to establish her religious faith. The court held that the plaintiff had demonstrated only curiosity about the identity of her biological parents, and curiosity would not satisfy the "good cause" requirement.[126]

In recent years, some states have begun to enact legislation specifying what types of information will demonstrate "good cause" for disclosure of, or access to and inspection of, sealed adoption records. For

---

[123] *Chattman v. Bennett*, 393 N.Y.S. 2d 768 (App. Div. 1977).

[124] See, e.g., *Rhodes v. Laurino*, 444 F. Supp. 170 (E.D.N.Y. 1978), *aff'd*, 601 F. 2d 1239 (2d Cir. 1979); *Golan v. Louis Wise Services*, 507 N.E. 2d 275 (N.Y. 1987).

[125] *In re Linda F. M.*, 409 N.Y.S. 2d 638 (Sur. Ct. 1978), *aff'd*, 442 N.Y.S. 2d 963 (App. Div. 1979), *aff'd*, 437 N.Y.S. 2d 283 (App. Div. 1981).

[126] See also *In re Assalone*, 512 A. 2d 1383 (R.I. 1986) (holding that curiosity to discover biological identity is insufficient to establish "good cause" where adoptee's need to know did not arise from any mental or physical ailments); *In re Dixon*, 323 N.W. 2d 549 (Mich. Ct. App. 1982) (holding that denial of access to adoptee claiming "good cause" based on depressive illness was not due to lack of information regarding the adoptee's biological parents).

example, a New York statute provides that certification from a state-licensed physician must cite a serious physical or mental illness to show "good cause" and identify the information required to address such illness.[127]

Responding to Records Requests

Healthcare records personnel usually do not encounter requests from individuals seeking to inspect a medical record where the request is either primarily or incidentally premised on a desire to obtain information about the adoptee's biological parents. Parties to an adoption more often address such requests to either the agency that handled the adoption or the court that entered the adoption order. Requests are also directed to the healthcare institution, however, and healthcare records professionals should recognize that disclosure of such information must be handled carefully to assure protection of patient privacy and compliance with state law. Laws that permit patient access to medical records conflict with adoption laws that require the sealing of court records to protect the privacy of the biological parents. Because of this policy conflict, healthcare organizations responding to a request for information relating to adoption may be presented with dilemmas requiring a difficult weighing of competing interests. To assist in the formulation of an appropriate response to such requests, healthcare records professionals, in consultation with legal counsel, should develop policies and procedures to address disclosure of adoption information.

In developing policies and procedures in this area, health information professionals may be interested in relevant recommendations from the American Health Information Management Association (AHIMA).[128] With respect to disclosure of adoption records information, AHIMA suggests that healthcare records professionals consider the following policies:

- Refer requests for records information from biological parents to the agency that handled the adoption; biological parents of a child

---

[127] N.Y. Dom. Rel. Law § 114(4).

[128] American Health Information Management Association (AHIMA), "Practice Brief: Disclosure of Health Information," *Journal of AHIMA* 67 (9) (1996).

placed for adoption relinquish their right to inspect their child's medical record after the adoption.

- If allowing adoptive parents to inspect the adoptee's medical records for health-related record information, implement a mechanism for ensuring that all identifying information pertaining to the biological parents has been excluded before the medical record is made available to the adoptive parents.
- Refer minor adoptees trying to trace their biological parents to the agency that handled the adoption. Although adult adoptees (that is, age 18 or older) have the right to inspect their medical records (sans information identifying the biological parents), adopted children seeking such information do not have the same right. The healthcare provider should inform the adopted child who is seeking medical history information that such information can be disclosed only in accordance with a court order.[129]

In addition, AHIMA suggests that if the state operates an adoption history program such as a confidential intermediary search program, healthcare records personnel should always encourage requesters, particularly adopted children and biological parents, to contact that program for further assistance.

Records Indicating Child or Elder Abuse

Most states have enacted mandatory reporting laws obligating healthcare personnel who have reason to believe that a child or senior citizen has been abused to report their findings to a designated state agency. These state laws are specifically exempted from preemption by the HIPAA Privacy Rule.[130] These reporting requirements specify the nature and content of the information provided to the state agency. A healthcare organization's staff member who is covered by the statute and who suspects abuse is required by most state laws to notify the person in charge of the institution, who in turn makes the necessary

---

[129] An adopted child's request for such information should be given some consideration only in a situation involving emergent circumstances in relation to continued patient care (and therefore time does not allow for obtaining a court order); even then, the information disclosed should be abstracted from the record, providing only the essential medical information and excluding all identifying information regarding the biological parents.

[130] See 45 C.F.R. § 160.203(c); 45 C.F.R. § 164.512(b)(1)(ii).

report. Also common to many of these statutes is a grant of immunity to persons who make reports in good faith.[131] (For a more detailed discussion of mandatory abuse reporting requirements, see Chapter 7.)

A typical abuse statute authorizes a designated state agency to intervene for the victim's protection and to assist the person committing abuse in finding appropriate counseling or treatment. As the known incidence of abuse has increased with better reporting, the public's interest in abuse prevention has grown. As a result, some laws now declare that any evidence of a child's injuries may be admitted in any legal proceeding arising from the alleged abuse.[132] The public policies supporting child abuse reporting statutes are the protection of children and the reduction of abuse through appropriate counseling.

The reporting requirements of these statutes, however, may conflict with other statutes protecting patient confidentiality. Federal and state statutes addressing disclosure of medical records information in a variety of contexts support the general rule that information in a patient's medical record may not be disclosed without the individual's consent. The evidentiary statutes of many states, for example, establish a privilege that protects statements made in the course of treatment by a physician where a physician-patient relationship exists. This privilege enables a patient (and, in some states, a physician or hospital) to object to any attempt to introduce such statements in a court proceeding.[133] Some states also have enacted statutes that prohibit or restrict disclosure of certain types of patient information in court or elsewhere. The Illinois Mental Health and Developmental Disabilities Confidentiality Act, for example, prohibits the disclosure of information concerning a person undergoing treatment for mental illness or developmental disabilities (as defined by the act), except under certain circumstances.[134] The statute states that all records kept by a therapist or agency in the course of providing mental health or developmental disabilities services to a patient that concern the patient and the service are confidential and may not be disclosed, except as provided in the act.[135]

Courts have long struggled with the conflicting public policies that underlie state mandatory child abuse reporting statutes and state and

---

[131] See, e.g., 325 Ill. Comp. Stat. Ann. § 5/9.
[132] See, e.g., 325 Ill. Comp. Stat. Ann. § 5/10.
[133] See, e.g., 735 Ill. Comp. Stat. Ann. § 5/8-802; N.J. Stat. § 2A:84A-22.2.
[134] 740 Ill. Comp. Stat. Ann. §§ 110/1 through 110/17.
[135] 740 Ill. Comp. Stat. Ann. § 110/3.

federal statutes prohibiting disclosure of certain medical records.[136] A typical dilemma might involve a situation where, in the course of treatment for mental illness or alcoholism, a patient discloses information that suggests or confirms that he or she abused a child. In response to this type of problem, state legislatures have incorporated waivers of the physician-patient privilege into state penal and juvenile codes to accommodate their child abuse statutes, and the courts increasingly favor disclosure in cases involving possible child abuse. However, the extent of disclosure remains ambiguous in many jurisdictions.[137]

The Supreme Court of Minnesota addressed this apparent conflict in a case involving a man charged with three counts of criminal sexual conduct involving his 10-year-old stepdaughter and his 11-year-old niece.[138] State authorities had learned of the abuse from sources other than the defendant's medical records. After his release on bail, while undergoing treatment for depression and alcoholism at a crisis unit, the defendant described his sexual contact with young girls. When state authorities sought to discover his medical records and statements made to the crisis unit, the defendant argued that such information was protected from disclosure under the federal Comprehensive Alcohol Abuse and Alcoholism Prevention, Treatment, and Rehabilitation Act, as well as the state's physician-patient privilege.

The court held that the federal alcoholism treatment act and regulations do not preempt the state's child abuse reporting law. Based on its review of the legislative history of both the state child abuse reporting law and the federal alcoholism treatment statute and regulations, the court concluded that Congress did not intend for state child abuse reporting laws to be preempted by the federal law. The court ruled that the federal alcohol treatment statute's confidentiality of patient records provision does not preclude the use of patient records in child abuse proceedings to the extent required by the state child abuse reporting statute. Emphasizing that the public policy underlying the child abuse reporting statute is to encourage child abusers to seek treatment voluntarily, the court also concluded that the child abuse reporting statute

---

[136] For a discussion of the requirements for a court order for disclosure in child abuse cases, see J. Tomes, *Healthcare Records: A Practical Legal Guide* (Westchester, Ill.: Healthcare Financial Management Association, 1990), 203–218.

[137] See, e.g., Cal. Penal Code § 11171.2(b); N.C. Gen. Stat. § 8-53.1; S.D. Codified Laws § 26-8A-15.

[138] *State v. Andring*, 342 N.W. 2d 128 (Minn. 1984).

abrogates the physician-patient privilege, but only to the extent of permitting the use of information required to be contained in a maltreatment report.[139]

Other courts have held that the statutory waiver of the physician-patient privilege extends to criminal proceedings involving the prosecution of the child abuser. For example, a father who was accused of raping his two children attempted to exclude conversations that he had had with a nurse while seeking treatment for the symptoms of a sexually transmitted disease.[140] During the consultation, the patient had admitted to having had sex with both his son and daughter. The court declared that in accordance with child abuse reporting legislation, the physician-patient privilege did not apply to exclude the conversation from evidence. In adopting the statute, the court concluded, the legislature balanced the need for confidential medical treatment against the need to protect child victims, and opted to provide the broadest possible exceptions to the physician-patient privilege. (For a more detailed discussion of the physician-patient privilege, see Chapter 10.)

Because of the importance of the public policy issues in abuse reporting legislation, courts generally are reluctant to exclude medical records evidence on the basis of physician-patient privilege. Statutory waivers of the privilege, which frequently apply to any proceedings involving abuse, have been interpreted broadly. The cases indicate that states will be permitted to pierce the shield provided by both the federal alcoholism treatment act and state physician-patient privilege, at least to the extent necessary to protect the children involved.

Health Information Sought by Law Enforcement Agencies

As a general rule, healthcare practitioners and organizations should not release medical records or other patient information to law enforcement personnel without the patient's authorization. In the absence of statutory or regulatory authority, a police agency has no authority to

---

[139] *State v. Andring*, 128, 132. Such information includes the identity of the child; the identity of the parent, guardian, or other person responsible for the child's care; the nature and extent of the child's injuries; and the name and address of the reporter.

[140] *State v. Etheridge*, 352 S.E. 2d 673 (N.C. 1987). See also *State v. Bellard*, 533 So. 2d 961 (La. 1988) (holding that waiver of physician-patient privilege in state's child abuse reporting statute applies to criminal proceedings against child abuser).

examine a medical record. Both federal and state law have created exceptions to this general rule, however.

HIPAA Privacy Rule Provisions

Practitioners and organizations that are subject to HIPAA may disclose protected health information (PHI) to law enforcement officials under several specific circumstances. The Privacy Rule defines "law enforcement official" as an officer of any governmental or Indian tribal agency who is empowered by law to investigate a potential violation of law or prosecute a proceeding arising from such violation.[141] A covered entity may disclose limited information in response to a law enforcement official's request made in an effort to identify or locate a suspect, witness, fugitive, or missing person.[142] The information is limited, however, to the individual's name, address, date and place of birth, Social Security number, blood type and Rh factor, type of injury, date and time of treatment, date and time of death (if applicable), and a description of distinguishing physical characteristics.[143] The rule specifically prohibits disclosing any of the individual's

- DNA
- DNA analysis
- Dental records
- Typing, samples, or analysis of body fluids or tissues[144]

Covered entities may also disclose PHI to law enforcement officials pursuant to legal process or otherwise as required by law. If officials present a court order, court-ordered warrant, or a subpoena or summons issued by a court; a grand jury subpoena; or an administrative request, a covered entity may disclose the requested PHI, if all of the following conditions are met:

- The disclosure complies with, and is limited to, the requirements of the legal process

---

[141] 45 C.F.R. § 164.501.
[142] 45 C.F.R. § 164.512(f)(2).
[143] 45 C.F.R. § 164.512(f)(2)(i).
[144] 45 C.F.R. § 164.512(f)(2)(ii).

- The information sought is relevant to a legitimate law enforcement inquiry
- The request is specific and limited in scope to that necessary for the purpose of the request
- De-identified information could not reasonably be used[145]

Law enforcement officials may request PHI concerning an individual who is, or is suspected to be, a victim of a crime. Covered entities may disclose such information if the individual authorizes its disclosure. In cases in which the individual is incapacitated or undergoing emergency care and is unable to give an authorization, a covered entity may disclose the requested PHI if the law enforcement official represents that the information is necessary to a law enforcement activity, that the activity would be adversely affected by delay, that the information will not be used against the individual, and that the disclosure will be in the individual's best interest.[146]

A covered entity may also disclose to a law enforcement official PHI about an individual who has died, if the entity suspects that the death may have resulted from criminal conduct,[147] or if the entity believes that the PHI may be evidence of criminal conduct on its premises.[148] A healthcare provider who is providing emergency health care in response to an emergency that occurred off of the provider's premises may disclose PHI to a law enforcement official if the disclosure appears necessary to alert the official to the commission and location of a crime, the location of a victim of the crime, or the identity of the perpetrator of the crime.[149]

The Privacy Rule is specific in directing that, notwithstanding the rules governing disclosures to law enforcement officials, covered entities must report child and adult abuse and neglect in accordance with the provisions of the rule concerning those disclosures and with applicable state law.[150]

---

[145] 45 C.F.R. § 164.512(f)(1).
[146] 45 C.F.R. § 164.512(f)(3).
[147] 45 C.F.R. § 164.512(f)(4).
[148] 45 C.F.R. § 164.512(f)(5).
[149] 45 C.F.R. § 164.512(f)(6).
[150] See, e.g., 45 C.F.R. § 164.512(f)(6)(ii).

State Law Provisions

Practitioners and organizations that are not covered entities subject to the Privacy Rule must be aware of applicable state law governing disclosures to law enforcement agencies. Under state law, the general rule applies: healthcare practitioners and organizations should not release patient health information to law enforcement personnel without the patient's authorization or a specific statutory or regulatory exception to the rule.

If a law enforcement official provides the facility with a valid court order or subpoena, the healthcare provider or organization, upon the advice of its legal counsel, should provide the information requested. Also, with the advice of their qualified legal counsel, healthcare managers may determine that it would be in the community's best interest to release specific medical records information to law enforcement personnel. In such a situation, the managers may rely on the doctrine of qualified privilege in releasing such information. Under this common law doctrine, a party (the healthcare provider) with a duty or a legitimate interest in conveying the information is permitted to engage in communication to a second party (the law enforcement agency) with a corresponding interest in receiving the particular information. The information transfer must be made in good faith and without malice, and based on reasonable grounds.[151] (For a more detailed discussion of this and other principles of the law of defamation, see Chapter 11.)

The doctrine of qualified privilege, however, protects the healthcare organization only if the law enforcement officer who receives the medical records information acts under the authority of law. Thus, before releasing information, health information professionals should determine that a basis for the request exists and that the officer requesting it is performing official duties. The information released should be limited to what is appropriate for the particular request; in other words, a

---

[151] See *Tarasoff v. Regents of the University of California*, 551 P. 2d 334 (Cal. 1976), where the court held that psychotherapists had an affirmative duty to report a patient to law enforcement agencies because the patient's medical or psychological condition represented a foreseeable risk to third persons. The therapists in this situation should have disclosed information that the patient had threatened to kill the eventual victim because the therapists are protected by the doctrine of qualified privilege. See also *Hicks v. United States*, 357 F. Supp. 434 (D.D.C. 1973), *aff'd*, 511 F. 2d 407 (D.C. Cir. 1975).

patient's entire medical record should not be released unless there are reasonable grounds for doing so.

State law varies widely regarding the release to government agencies of medical records information without patient authorization. Some state statutes allow certain patient records, such as those involving victims of crime or carriers of contagious disease not specifically designated by statute, to be revealed to government officials without the patient's consent in the course of routine police investigations or public health inquiries.[152] Moreover, many states have statutes imposing a duty upon physicians and/or healthcare organizations to report certain kinds of information, such as cases involving gunshot or knife wounds,[153] child abuse (see discussion earlier in this chapter), and disorders affecting a motorist's ability to drive safely.[154] In states having these types of reporting statutes, a patient's consent is not required in order to release the record. In fact, under some statutes, healthcare facilities may be guilty of criminal misdemeanor if they fail to report certain cases. (For a more detailed discussion of such statutory reporting requirements, see Chapter 7.)

Practical Considerations

Requests by law enforcement officials are often difficult to manage because the officials do not present their requests with sufficient information to permit a healthcare provider to make a judgment as to whether it may disclose patient health information, and the officials are impatient or even threatening if the provider does not respond immediately. Police officers have threatened hospital health information professionals with arrest when they refused to release medical records information. The circumstances in which requests are made can be highly charged, and time can be of the essence in apprehending a criminal or protecting a victim.

---

[152] See, e.g., S.C. Code Ann. § 44-22-100(A)(4) (allowing disclosure of medical record information without a patient's consent only in specified circumstances, including when disclosure is necessary in cooperating with law enforcement, health, welfare, and other agencies, or when furthering the welfare of the patient or the patient's family).

[153] See, e.g., N.Y. Penal Law § 265.25. See also Cal. Penal Code § 11160.

[154] See, e.g., 75 Pa. Consol. Stat. § 1518(B). See also Ga. Code Ann. § 40-5-35(b) (physician may report).

Healthcare practitioners and organizations should work with their legal counsel to develop policies, procedures, and training materials that will enable members of their workforce to respond appropriately to law enforcement officials who seek health information. Seeking the intervention of the practitioner's or institution's legal counsel in a dispute with a law enforcement officer or prosecutor can save considerable time and aggravation. In most disputes, the officers simply must be informed that they will be able to obtain the information they seek after they have met the legal requirements for disclosure of health information. This is a task that should be undertaken by legal counsel or a senior manager, not by line health information personnel.

Warrants and Searches

As discussed in the previous section, healthcare organizations have a strong interest in the privacy of their medical records, and as a general rule, they may refuse to release records to law enforcement agencies that do not possess a valid subpoena or other court order for such records. This same rule applies to records sought by government officials, with one exception: government officials may be entitled to search and seize medical records if they first obtain a judicially issued search warrant. Because a search warrant requires the approval of a neutral magistrate and must state specifically the place to be searched, the objects to be seized, and the reason for the search, it effectively precludes general "fishing expeditions" by the government. In recent years, federal and state government officials conducting fraud and abuse investigations have arrived at a healthcare facility's door with a search warrant in hand, and subsequently seized a substantial portion of that facility's patient records and other documents. (For a more detailed discussion of such situations, see "Fraud and Abuse Investigations" later in this chapter.)

The Fourth Amendment to the U.S. Constitution—which protects persons and their houses, papers, and effects from unreasonable searches and seizures—is the source of the search warrant requirement. The amendment is designed "to safeguard the privacy and security of individuals against arbitrary invasions by governmental officials."[155]

---

[155] *Camara v. Municipal Court*, 387 U.S. 523 (1967); *Florida v. Riley*, 488 U.S. 445, 462 (1989); see *New Jersey. v. T.L.O.*, 469 U.S. 325, 335 (1985).

Although the amendment was intended to apply primarily to private residences, its proscription of warrantless searches as presumptively unreasonable applies to commercial premises as well.[156] Generally, therefore, government access to medical records without a search warrant is presumptively unreasonable and violates the Fourth Amendment. Nevertheless, in some instances, courts may determine that government officials are entitled to gain access to medical records even without a search warrant.

Although the search warrant requirement has been associated almost exclusively with criminal investigations, the U.S. Supreme Court has stated specifically that administrative or regulatory searches also come within the Fourth Amendment's scope.[157] Whether a court will impose a warrant requirement on an administrative search, however, depends on whether the search is designed to enforce a general regulatory scheme or is aimed at specific licensed industries. The Supreme Court has imposed a warrant requirement when an administrative search is conducted pursuant to general regulatory legislation that applies to all residences, structures, or employers within a given jurisdiction. For example, the Court has required a warrant in situations involving routine commercial inspections of business premises not open to the public under the Occupational Safety and Health Act of 1970.[158]

The Supreme Court has treated searches of specific licensed industries differently, however, ruling that a warrant may not be required for searches of businesses that either are federally licensed or have a long history of government supervision and pervasive regulation.[159] Lower federal and state courts also have recognized these two basic types of administrative searches (that is, searches pursuant to general regulatory schemes and searches pursuant to specific licensed industries), and have analyzed situations involving government access to healthcare facilities generally and medical records specifically. After making the inquiry into the thoroughness of regulation and determining that the medical facility is not a pervasively regulated business, courts typically have decided whether a warrantless search is reasonable by balancing

---

[156] See *Illinois v. Krull*, 480 U.S. 340, 351 (1987); *Marshall v. Barlow's, Inc.*, 436 U.S. 307 (1978); *New York v. Burger*, 482 U.S. 691, 699 (1987).

[157] See, e.g., *Michigan v. Tyler*, 436 U.S. 499 (1978).

[158] *Marshall v. Barlow's, Inc.* But see *Donovan v. Loue Steer, Inc.*, 464 U.S. 408, 412 (1984).

[159] See, e.g., *United States v. Biswell*, 406 U.S. 311 (1972).

the privacy interests of the institution against the government interest in obtaining the desired information.

Only in certain narrowly defined situations, however, have courts authorized warrantless searches of healthcare facilities. In one case involving a skilled nursing facility, for example, a California appeals court upheld a warrantless inspection of business records.[160] A county health inspector routinely inspected the facility's records, without a search warrant, and discovered that the defendant, a licensee of the facility, had commingled patients' funds with his own. The court rejected the defendant's challenge to the warrantless search on the grounds that the healthcare industry in California had been pervasively regulated and that the state's interest in regulating the industry outweighed the facility's privacy interest. Similarly, a New York court upheld a state statute that authorized thorough warrantless inspections of hospitals, home health agencies, and nursing homes.[161] Because of the overriding interest of the state in protecting nursing home residents, and because of the thorough regulation of nursing homes in New York, the court concluded that such warrantless searches did not violate the Fourth Amendment.

Because hospital patients may be considered a less vulnerable population than nursing home residents, however, the cases described previously are not particularly strong precedents for challenging a warrantless search of medical records at hospitals. Moreover, hospital managers involved in such a challenge may encounter difficulties in attempting to assert that the government has no interest whatsoever in medical records. Instead, hospitals may more effectively rely upon assertions that the government's interest is sufficiently protected by limits established by the warrant-obtaining procedure. Also, because the court's determination regarding the necessity of a warrant may rely on its assessment as to whether the burden of getting the warrant will negate the purpose of making the search, hospitals should consider emphasizing that there are no exigent circumstances that necessitate a warrantless inspection, and that requiring the government to obtain a warrant will not in any way diminish the subsequent inspection of medical records.

Courts also have authorized warrantless searches of pharmacy records. In one case involving the warrantless search of pharmacy

---

[160] *People v. Firstenberg*, 155 Cal. Rptr. 80 (Ct. App. 1979), *cert. denied*, 444 U.S. 1012 (1980).
[161] *Uzzilia v. Commissioner of Health*, 367 N.Y.S. 2d 795 (1975).

records by state health inspectors, the New York court noted that the search was pursuant to statute, and thus upheld the search.[162] Refusing to impose a warrant requirement even though health inspectors had time and opportunity to procure a warrant, the court concluded that pharmacy records in New York are subject to inspection without warning because the pharmacist accepts a state license subject to the right of warrantless inspection, thereby consenting to warrantless searches.

Another category of medical facility for which courts have addressed the validity of warrantless searches comprises healthcare organizations or clinics that perform abortions. A number of federal courts have invalidated statutes allowing warrantless searches of such facilities, typically rejecting the contention that the performance of abortions is a pervasively regulated business.[163] Emphasizing the recognized need for privacy in the physician-patient relationship, such courts have determined that the privacy interest in these cases far outweighs the minimal state interests in sanitary conditions and properly trained personnel.

From the cases discussed above, health information personnel can take away some practical guidance for responding to situations involving a request to review medical records pursuant to a search warrant. The health information professional presented with a search warrant should carefully review the warrant to determine whether it states with requisite particularity the scope of the search and the place to be searched. A court cannot properly issue a warrant based on a government assertion of valid public interest; rather, the government must state specifically why it requires a search of specific medical records. If healthcare managers and other staff members responsible for keeping and maintaining medical records believe that a search warrant is insufficient in this respect, then they may want to consider affirmatively withholding consent to the search. It is important that these individuals understand that consent to an administrative search can be implied easily, and thus an affirmative statement regarding withheld consent may be necessary. However, health information professionals and other

---

[162] *People v. Curco Drugs, Inc.*, 350 N.Y.S. 2d 74 (Crim. Ct. 1973). See also *State v. Welch*, 624 A. 2d 1105 (Vt. 1992).

[163] See, e.g., *Akron Center for Reproductive Health Inc. v. City of Akron*, 479 F. Supp. 1172 (N.D. Ohio 1979), *aff'd in part and rev'd in part on other grounds*, 651 F. 2d 1198 (6th Cir. 1981), 462 U.S. 416 (1983); *Margaret S. v. Edwards*, 488 F. Supp. 181, 215–217 (E.D. La. 1980); *Tucson Women's Clinic v. Eden*, 379 F. 3d 531, 550–551 (9th Cir. 2004).

relevant personnel also should understand the mandatory nature of a valid search warrant, and the necessity of obeying a warrant that states in detail the time and place of the search and the specific records to be searched.

The Privacy Rule authorizes covered entities to disclose PHI for law enforcement purposes in compliance with a court-ordered warrant.[164]

Responding to Subpoenas and Court Orders

Healthcare organizations may be required to release health information pursuant to "legal process," which generally refers to all of the writs that are issued by a court during a legal action or by an attorney in the name of the court but without court review. In general, health information professionals should have a basic knowledge of how to deal with situations involving two types of legal process—the subpoena and the court order.

Subpoenas

Healthcare organizations customarily receive two types of subpoenas: (a) a subpoena *ad testificandum*, which is a written order commanding a person to appear and to give testimony at a trial or other judicial or investigative proceeding; and (b) a subpoena *duces tecum*, which is a written order commanding a person to appear; to give testimony; and to bring all documents, papers, books, and records described in the subpoena. These orders are used to obtain documents during pretrial discovery and to obtain testimony during trial. The form of the subpoena is prescribed by statute in certain states.[165] Generally a valid subpoena provides specifics such as the name of the court; the names of the plaintiff and the defendant; the case docket number; the date, time, and place of the requested appearance; the specific documents sought (for a subpoena *duces tecum*); the name of the attorney who caused the subpoena to be issued; and the signature or stamp of the official authorized to issue the subpoena.

Those authorized to issue subpoenas vary from state to state, but in most states, such persons include judges, clerks of court, justices of the

---

[164] 45 C.F.R. § 164.512(f)(1)(ii)(A).
[165] See, e.g., Kan. Stat. Ann. § 60-245a(c).

peace, and other officials.[166] As officers of the court, attorneys are also empowered to issue subpoenas for the production of records without the prior approval of the court. Many state statutes provide that any competent person not less than 18 years of age may serve subpoenas, but often subpoenas are served in person by local sheriffs (for state courts) or U.S. marshals (for federal courts).[167] The manner of service varies from state to state; in some states, the subpoena may be served by registered or certified mail or delivery to counsel of record, while in others the subpoena must be physically handed to the subpoenaed person by the server. Usually subpoenas must be served within a specified period of time in advance of the required appearance.[168]

Several cases have addressed the legitimacy of disclosing certain medical records in response to a grand jury subpoena. The Supreme Court of Illinois, for example, has ruled that disclosure to a grand jury of the identities of abortion clinic patients does not violate the physician-patient privilege or the patients' constitutional right of privacy.[169] Similarly, a federal circuit court has ruled that a grand jury may gain access to information that psychiatric patients have consented to release from their medical records to insurers for reimbursement purposes, because such consent constitutes a waiver of any physician or psychotherapist privilege that may exist, given the patients' expectation that confidentiality of these

---

[166] In cases brought before federal courts, however, only clerks of the court have the authority to issue subpoenas. See, e.g., Fed. R. Civ. P. 45(a)(3).

[167] See, e.g., Ga. Code Ann. § 24-10-23.

[168] In several states, statutes establish the advance-notice period with specific reference to medical records. In Connecticut, for example, subpoenas for hospital records must be served 24 hours in advance of the time that they are to be produced, unless written notice of the intent to serve the subpoena has been delivered at least 24 hours in advance of the time for production to the person in charge of hospital records. Conn. Gen. Stat. § 4-104; see also N.Y. C.P.L.R. 2306 (subpoena must be served at least three days before records must be produced).

[169] See also *People v. Manos*, 761, N.E. 2d 208, 216 (Ill. Ct. App. 2001) (stating that the case law is clear that revealing patient names alone will not violate privilege); *People v. Florendo*, 447 N.E. 2d (Ill. 1983) (holding that abortion clinic's clients' interests in confidentiality must give way to public's interest in uncovering criminal activity; but see *People v. Doe*, 570 N.E. 2d 733 (Ill. Ct. App. 1991) (holding that identifying information that characterizes a person as a recipient of services, where information sought is not directly related to an immediate or specific law enforcement action, is privileged and confidential); *People v. Smith*, 514 N.E. 2d 211 (Ill. Ct. App. 1987) (quashed subpoena *duces tecum* that sought information identifying abortion clinic's clients). *People v. Florendo*, 282 (holding that abortion clinic's clients' interests in confidentiality must give way to public's interest in uncovering criminal activity); but see *People v. Smith* (quashed subpoena *duces tecum* that sought information identifying abortion clinic's clients).

records might be compromised as a result of the reimbursement process.[170]

Courts also have addressed the issue of the appropriate means for responding to a subpoena for medical records, and have determined that certain responses violate the privacy rights of the person(s) whose medical records are at issue. In one case involving a pharmacy that received a subpoena *duces tecum* to appear in court and produce a customer's five-year prescription drug record, for example, the Supreme Court of Rhode Island held that, by mailing the customer's records directly to the requesting attorney, the pharmacy violated the customer's right to privacy under state law.[171] Although prescription drug information may be subject to disclosure within a legal proceeding, a subpoena alone does not cause the confidential nature of the information to "evaporate," the court cautioned. Rather, privileged healthcare records may be released only in strict compliance with legal process. In this case, the court explained, the pharmacy's unilateral disclosure of the records to the attorney in advance of either court authorization or the customer's consent clearly did not comply with proper judicial process.

Court Orders

Occasionally a state or federal court, or a state commission or other administrative tribunal, orders a healthcare organization to release medical records or other confidential patient information or to produce patient records in court. Written court orders usually are served upon healthcare facilities in a manner similar to that of subpoenas, but also may be issued orally in court to an attorney representing the healthcare

---

[170] See *In re Grand Jury Proceedings*, 220 F. 3d 568, 572 (7th Cir. 2000) (stating that when circumstances suggest that a document might be privileged, it is important that the court consider the totality of circumstances, because documents that appear privileged may have lost that privilege through disclosure or transmittal to a third party); *cf. Doe v. Smith*, No. 98-CV-660, 2000 U.S. Dist. LEXIS 22321, at *10 (E.D.N.Y., Apr. 27, 2000); *In re Pebsworth*, 705 F. 2d 261 (7th Cir. 1983). See also *In re Grand Jury Subpoena*, 710 F. Supp. 999 (D.N.J.), *aff'd without op.*, 879 F. 2d 857 (3d Cir. 1989) (unpublished) (upholding subpoena based on determination that psychotherapist-patient relationship must give way to government's interest in investigating criminal fraud); but see *People v. Helfrich*, 570 N.E. 2d 733 (Ill. Ct. App. 1991) (subpoena quashed in homicide investigation in which government sought all medical record information pertaining to male tenants at treatment center for mentally ill where records were protected by the Illinois Mental Health and Developmental Disabilities Confidentiality Act).

[171] *Washburn v. Rite Aid Corporation*, 695 A. 2d 495 (R.I. 1997).

organization or practitioner. Provided the court order does not violate a statute or regulation, the healthcare organization or practitioner should make every effort to comply with it, although the organization does have the option to contest a court order and present its case to the court before any sanctions for failure to comply are imposed. Failure to comply with a final, valid court order subjects either the person ordered to act or the healthcare organization's corporate officers, if the organization has been ordered to act, to a contempt-of-court citation. Such corporate officers are liable if the institution declines to follow the order, even if a healthcare manager or other staff member is the person who decides not to follow the order.

A court order requiring the disclosure of medical records will not violate the statutory physician-patient privilege if "sufficient steps" are taken to safeguard the identity of the patient involved.[172] Although the state supreme court had ruled previously that a trial court's order requiring physicians to disclose the names, addresses, and means of contacting patients they had treated undermined the purpose and intent of the physician-patient privilege, the question remained as to whether the removal of all information in medical records that tended to identify the patients would render the records discoverable. In this case, the appeals court, noting that the state supreme court had objected only to identification of the patients, ruled that the disclosure of anonymous records is permissible.

HIPAA and State Compliance Requirements

The Privacy Rule speaks specifically to disclosures of PHI by covered entities for judicial and administrative proceedings. The rule permits covered entities to disclose PHI in such proceedings in response to a court order, but only the PHI that has been expressly authorized by the order.[173] The Privacy Rule provision governing subpoenas is more complicated. If a covered entity receives a subpoena, it may disclose the requested PHI if the covered entity receives assurance from the party seeking the PHI that reasonable efforts have been made by that party to ensure that the person for whom information is requested has been

---

[172] *Terre Haute Regional Hospital, Inc. v. Trueblood*, 600 N.E. 2d 1358 (Ind. 1992); *Ziegler v. Superior Court*, 656 P. 2d 1251 (Ariz. Ct. App. 1982).
[173] 45 C.F.R. § 164.512(e)(1)(i).

given notice of the request or to secure qualified protective order.[174] The assurance required by the rule with respect to notice to the affected individual can be satisfied if the covered entity receives a written statement and accompanying documentation showing that all of the following requirements have been met:

- The requesting party has made a good faith attempt to give the individual written notice so as to permit him or her to raise objections to the court or administrative tribunal
- The notice included sufficient information about the proceeding in which the PHI was requested to permit the individual to raise a meaningful objection
- The time by which the individual must raise an objection has passed, and no objection was filed or all objections have been resolved by the court or tribunal

The assurance required by the rule with respect to obtaining a qualified protective order can be satisfied if the covered entity receives a written statement and accompanying documentation showing that the parties to the dispute have agreed to a qualified protective order and have presented it to the court or tribunal, or if the party seeking the PHI has requested a qualified protective order from the court or tribunal.[175] A qualified protective order is an order of a court or tribunal or a stipulation by the parties to the proceeding that prohibits the parties from using the PHI for any purpose other than the proceeding and requires the return to the covered entity or the destruction of the PHI or copies of it at the end of the proceeding.[176] In any event, the Privacy Rule permits a covered entity to disclose PHI in response to lawful process without these assurances if the covered entity itself makes reasonable efforts to give the individual notice of the request or the opportunity to seek a qualified protective order.[177] This notice may be delivered to the individual's attorney, or the subpoena itself may qualify as sufficient notice to the individual if the subpoena contains all the required elements.[178]

---

[174] 45 C.F.R. § 164.512(e)(1)(ii).
[175] 45 C.F.R. §§ 164.512(e)(1)(iii) and (iv).
[176] 45 C.F.R. § 164.512(e)(1)(v).
[177] 45 C.F.R. § 164.512(e)(1)(vi).
[178] www.hhs.gov/ocr/hippa.

When a covered entity must disclose PHI in a judicial or administrative proceeding for its own benefit (for example, when seeking payment for services it has provided), the Privacy Rule offers specific guidance. The DHHS Office for Civil Rights, which is charged with the responsibility for enforcing the rule, has explained that disclosures of this type are permitted under the rule provisions concerning disclosures for healthcare operations.[179] In addition, it can be argued that these disclosures are permitted for purposes of obtaining payment,[180] as required by law,[181] or as part of a government oversight function or investigation.[182]

Healthcare organizations that are not subject to the Privacy Rule should comply with valid legal process properly served upon them in the manner prescribed by applicable state law. In recent years, many states have enacted statutes establishing compliance procedures with specific reference to subpoenas of medical records.[183] In states that have not enacted such statutes, the subpoena of medical records is treated like any other subpoena. Health information professionals should be aware of current developments in their own states in this rapidly changing area of the law. Without reasonable justification, failure to correctly comply with a subpoena is punishable as contempt of court.

The time permitted for compliance with subpoenas of medical records varies from state to state. In some states, for example, statutes require the healthcare organization to comply by the date specified on the subpoena.[184] Other state statutes provide for a specific time period for compliance.[185] Generally the records must be sealed, then enclosed in an envelope, and may be opened only with the court's authorization. Most states expressly permit copies to be submitted in lieu of the original documents. A few states specify that the court may subpoena the originals if the copies are illegible or if their authenticity is in dispute.[186]

In several states, records furnished in compliance with legal process must be accompanied by an affidavit from the healthcare organization's

[179] Ibid.
[180] 45 C.F.R. § 164.506(c)(1).
[181] 45 C.F.R. § 164.512(a).
[182] 45 C.F.R. § 164.512(d).
[183] See, e.g., Conn. Gen. Stat. § 4-104; Ky. Rev. Stat. Ann. § 422.305; N.Y. C.P.L.R. 2306.
[184] See, e.g., N.Y. C.P.L.R. 2306(b).
[185] See, e.g., Va. Code Ann. § 8.01-413(B) (within 15 days of receipt of request).
[186] See, e.g., Ala. Code § 12-21-6; Nev. Rev. Stat. Ann. § 52.355(1).

records custodian to certify the records' genuineness, attesting that any copy of a record is a true copy and that the records were prepared by personnel of the healthcare organization, staff physicians, or persons acting under control of either.[187] In addition, these statutes provide that if the hospital possesses none, or only part, of the records described in the subpoena, the custodian must make certification to this fact in the affidavit. A subpoena may also require the custodian to attend the proceeding for which the records are requested. In most cases, the director of the medical records department is served with a subpoena because he or she is deemed to have custody of the medical records. However, very few states define the term "custodian." Some states do specify that the custodian may be any person who prepares records, such as a physician, nurse, or therapist, or anyone entrusted with the care of the records.[188]

No healthcare organization is expected to respond to requirements that would be considered unreasonable, and, in consultation with legal counsel, health information professionals should develop appropriate responses under such circumstances. The healthcare organization certainly has no obligation to respond if it receives a subpoena after the date upon which it is required by statute to be served, or if the subpoena arrives after the designated response date that appears on the document. The healthcare organization also may claim unreasonableness if the subpoena commands presentation of records so voluminous that they cannot be reproduced by the return date given, or so old that they are not in the organization's possession.

Turning to the healthcare organization's legal counsel is usually the best course of action in any matter that requires dealing with other attorneys who have made unreasonable demands for medical records. If the subpoena was initiated by a plaintiff in an action against the healthcare organization, the organization should consider not complying with the subpoena, and instead demanding that the plaintiff file a motion to produce the records. In so doing, the healthcare organization is provided with the opportunity to argue against disclosure. If the health information manager believes that a subpoena is invalid or improper, the healthcare organization should consider having its attorney file a motion to quash the subpoena.

---

[187] See, e.g., Miss. Code Ann. § 41-9-109; Ark. Code Ann. § 16-46-305; Nev. Rev. Stat. Ann. § 52.325(2); Ala. Code § 12-21-6.
[188] See, e.g., Nev. Rev. Stat. Ann. § 52.260(6)(a).

The person designated to process subpoenas of medical records should respond in accordance with a procedure established by the healthcare organization and approved by its attorney. The procedure should include at least the following steps:

- Examination of the records subject to subpoena to make certain that they are complete, that signatures and initials are legible, and that each page identifies the patient and the patient's identification number
- Examination of the records to determine whether the case forms the basis for a possible negligence action against the healthcare organization, and, if so, notification of the appropriate managers, legal counsel, or risk managers
- Removal of any material that may not properly be obtained in the jurisdiction by subpoena, such as, in some cases, notes referring to psychiatric care, copies of records from other facilities, or correspondence
- Enumeration of each page of the medical record, and marking of the total number of pages on the record jacket or cover sheet of a printed electronic record
- Preparation of a list of the medical records contents to be used as a receipt for the record if the record must be left with the court or an attorney (most medical records departments use a standard form for this purpose and retain a copy of the record provided)
- In responding to legal process, use of a photocopy or electronic copy of the record, whenever possible, rather than the original

With respect to the last step, if the original paper medical records must be sent, a healthcare organization should have an established procedure for such deliveries to the court, including the designation of a person to deliver originals in person. A typical procedure is to prepare a signature document to be signed by the clerk of the court, accepting responsibility for the record's safekeeping and safe return at the culmination of proceedings. Health information professionals should recognize that they lose all control over medical records that are placed in the mail, and that if original records are subsequently lost through the mail or otherwise, this may present a serious problem in the event of a negligence action brought against the healthcare organization. Providing electronic health information eliminates these problems because the original records do not leave the information system in which they are created. From a practical point of view, only a paper or electronic copy of an electronic record can be provided.

Fraud and Abuse Investigations

Aggressive enforcement of healthcare fraud and abuse prohibitions by the Department of Health and Human Services (DHHS) through its Office of Inspector General (OIG) have expanded the likelihood that healthcare facilities will one day confront this type of investigation. It is not uncommon for a healthcare facility to learn that it is the object of an OIG investigation when federal agents arrive at its place of business, brandishing search and seizure warrants and taking possession of a significant portion of the facility's internal documentation, including all active and inactive patient files. It is important for health information professionals to understand the nature and scope of this type of government investigation, given the implications such an investigation can have for medical records integrity and confidentiality.[189]

Every federal agency has an inspector general who is responsible for ferreting out waste, fraud, and abuse in that agency's programs. Although the inspector general's offices in several other agencies are involved in healthcare fraud and abuse investigations, the DHHS OIG is the most significant player in this area because it oversees the largest federal government insurance programs. To exercise its authority, the DHHS OIG has the right to subpoena documents with respect to both civil and criminal investigations.[190] The OIG subpoena represents one of the primary methods used by investigators and prosecutors to obtain information in healthcare fraud and abuse cases. These subpoenas may be used in OIG audits, evaluations, or investigations, and may be served on parties that have no immediate connection with the entity under investigation.[191]

In addition to its subpoena authority, the OIG has "immediate access authority," which derives from its right to impose a permissive exclusion from the Medicare/Medicaid program against an individual or

---

[189] Note that fraud investigations (and search and seizure of patient records) may also be initiated by state government officials who are acting pursuant to state law and have valid search warrants. See, e.g., *Brillantes v. Superior Court of Los Angeles County*, 58 Cal. Rptr. 2d 770 (Ct. App. 1996) (patient records seized as part of a Medi-Cal fraud investigation).
[190] See 5 U.S.C. Appx. § 6(a)(4).
[191] See *United States v. Art-Metal U.S.A.*, 484 F. Supp. 884 (D.N.J. 1980).

entity that fails to give the OIG immediate access to review any documents and data necessary to the performance of its statutory duties.[192] Regulations that implement this authority provide that the government must submit a reasonable request for the documents, signed by the OIG, to the provider.[193] The request must include all of the following:

- A statement of authority for the request
- The entity's or individual's rights
- The definitions of "reasonable request" and "immediate access"
- The penalties that would be imposed for failure to comply

The request also must include information suggesting that the entity or individual has violated statutory or regulatory requirements under specific statutes relating to healthcare fraud.

A provider fails to grant immediate access if it does not produce or make available for inspection and copying all requested records within 24 hours of the request. If the government reasonably believes that the requested documents are at imminent risk of being altered or destroyed, it is not required to give the provider the 24-hour period prior to granting access. In addition, according to the preamble in the regulations, a provider does not have the right to learn about the nature of the allegations from the agents who arrive on-site to conduct an immediate access investigation.

As a condition of their participation in the Medicare and Medicaid programs, all healthcare providers are required to provide to the government the records used in determining appropriate reimbursement, and this requirement encompasses investigations conducted by the OIG within the scope of its fraud and abuse enforcement authority.[194] A Medicare or Medicaid beneficiary essentially waives any state-established physician-patient privilege regarding his or her medical records. If the Medicare or Medicaid program requests the medical records relating to one of its beneficiaries, then those records must be turned over to the program.

---

[192] 42 U.S.C. § 1320a-7(b)(12).
[193] 42 C.F.R. § 1001.1301.
[194] See 42 C.F.R. § 482.24.

It is important that healthcare providers be adequately prepared to respond to an OIG investigation. To protect legitimate business interests, personnel should be trained to respond properly to subpoenas, search warrants, and unannounced visits by government agents. Appropriate strategies include retaining outside counsel, maintaining the integrity of internal documentation, reviewing and negotiating the scope of the subpoena, negotiating the response period to produce the requested documents, collecting that documentation and forwarding it to legal counsel for review, and finally, producing the documents for the OIG.

If the government requests mainly billing and medical records, an index can be created to assist in locating the documents. The index may include the location of paper records by records number and storage location, or computer locaters for electronic records. However, in tracking the particular billing practices that are usually the focus of government scrutiny, it is often helpful to create a database for cataloging the documents produced to the government. This database could include the basic information related to each document, such as the author, the recipient, and a document description. A database is helpful in cataloging documents because each document can be coded as relating to a particular issue and as being responsive to one or more of the subpoena requests. Of course, the scope and efficiency of these cataloging efforts depend in large part on the number of documents that have been produced and the types of documents requested by the OIG.

Oversight for HIPAA Compliance

DHHS Investigations

HIPAA establishes in the DHHS Office for Civil Rights the authority to enforce compliance with the Privacy and Security Rules. The Privacy Rule gives DHHS, as part of its oversight responsibility, the ability to obtain PHI in connection with the enforcement of, or other compliance activities related to, the Privacy and Security Rules.[195] Thus, covered entities are required to disclose PHI if DHHS requests it in connection with an investigation to determine compliance with HIPAA. DHHS may obtain access to the covered entity's facilities, books, records,

---

[195] 45 C.F.R. §§ 164.502(a)(2)(ii) and 160.310.

accounts, and other information, including PHI, during the covered entity's regular business hours, provided the information is relevant to the requirements of the Privacy and Security Rules. If the secretary of DHHS believes that an urgent need for access to information is required (for example, records may be destroyed), he or she may authorize access to the covered entity at any time and without notice.[196] DHHS may have authority to gain access to a covered entity under other federal law. (See, for example, the discussion of fraud and abuse investigations in this chapter.)

The HIPAA regulations governing enforcement and compliance prohibit the secretary of DHHS from disclosing PHI that the agency receives in the course of an investigation concerning the Privacy or Security Rule, unless doing so is necessary for ascertaining or enforcing compliance with the rules or is otherwise required by law.[197]

Disclosures by Whistle-blowers or Crime Victims

If a member of a covered entity's workforce or its business associate believes in good faith that the covered entity has engaged in conduct that is unlawful; violates professional or clinical standards; or endangers patients, workers or the public, he or she may disclose PHI without violating the Privacy Rule.[198] The disclosure must be to one of the following:

- A health oversight agency or public health authority with authority to regulate the conduct in question or the covered entity's operations or to an accrediting organization
- An attorney he or she has retained for the purpose of seeking legal advice concerning the matter[199]

The Privacy Rule prohibits a covered entity from intimidating or retaliating against anyone who exercises his or her rights under the rule, including whistle-blowers.[200] Practitioners and organizations subject to

---

[196] 45 C.F.R. § 160.310(c).
[197] 45 C.F.R. § 160.310(c)(3).
[198] 45 C.F.R. §§ 164.502(j)(1).
[199] 45 C.F.R. §§ 164.502(j)(1)(ii).
[200] 45 C.F.R. §§ 164.530(g).

the rule and those that are not covered entities would be ill-advised to do anything that would impair actions of a whistle-blower acting in good faith. The best defense against whistle-blowers is an effective compliance program that reduces conduct that would provide the basis for a whistle-blower report.

A covered entity also does not violate the Privacy Rule if one of its workforce members is a crime victim and discloses PHI in a report to law enforcement officials. The victim, however, may disclose only the following information pertaining to the suspect criminal:

- Name and address
- Date and place of birth
- Social Security number
- ABO blood type and Rh factor
- Type of injury
- Date and time of treatment
- Date and time of death, if applicable
- A description of distinguishing physical characteristics (for example, height, weight, gender, race)[201]

Use of Outside Test Reports in Hospital Patients' Records

Numerous hospitals permit the use of test reports from outside clinical laboratories and diagnostic centers to satisfy preadmission or preoperative test requirements, and such reports are entered into hospital patients' medical records. Hospital administrators and risk managers should be aware that the hospital's policies regarding the use of outside test reports may trigger special concerns, particularly in two areas: licensure and accreditation and antitrust law.

Licensure and Accreditation

The Joint Commission standards require that hospitals have a system that ensures that pathology and clinical laboratory services and consultation are readily available to meet patients' needs, and that provides for the prompt performance of adequate testing, either on-site

---

[201] 45 C.F.R. §§ 164.502(j)(2).

or in a reference/contract laboratory.[202] Accordingly, while the patient is under the hospital's care, all laboratory testing must be done in the hospital's laboratories or in approved reference laboratories. When outside laboratories are used for testing hospital patients, the Joint Commission requires that the hospital's director of pathology and clinical laboratory services recommend reference laboratory services to the medical staff for acceptance. If the hospital does not have centralized pathology and clinical laboratory services, the medical staff must establish a mechanism to identify acceptable reference and/or contract laboratory services; such laboratories must meet applicable federal standards for clinical laboratories (the Clinical Laboratory Improvement Amendments of 1988, otherwise known as CLIA).[203]

Some state licensing acts also impose controls on the use of outside laboratories for testing of hospital patients. In Illinois, for example, a hospital may use outside laboratories only if three conditions are met: (a) the outside laboratory is either part of a hospital licensed under the Illinois Hospital Licensing Act or approved to provide these services as a laboratory under the Illinois Clinical Laboratory Act; (b) the original report from the outside laboratory is contained in the medical record; and (c) the conditions, procedures, and availability of examinations performed in the outside laboratory are in writing and available in the hospital.[204]

In formulating a policy on outside testing sources, a hospital should assess the risk and likelihood of poor quality performance by outside testing sources as well as the ease of monitoring those sources' compli-

---

[202] See Joint Commission, *2005 Comprehensive Accreditation Manual for Hospitals*, Standards PC.16.10 through 16.60. Note that the accreditation standards in this area apply only to hospitals that perform limited laboratory testing (otherwise referred to as waived testing), or that refer all testing to outside laboratories. Waived testing procedures are specifically defined in the standards as those that meet requirements to be classified as waived tests under CLIA '88, 42 U.S.C. § 493.15 (federal regulation listing waived tests); Joint Commission, *2005 Comprehensive Accreditation Manual for Hospitals*, Standard PC-16 (noting that tests are constantly evaluated for inclusion in the waived-test category, and suggesting reference to the FDA, CDC, and CMS Web sites for the most up-to-date information regarding testing categorization and CLIA requirements). Hospitals that perform moderate- or high-complexity testing are subject to distinct Joint Commission standards for physician office laboratories, specialty, and subspecialty testing and reference laboratories. See, e.g., Joint Commission, *2005–2006 Laboratory Accreditation Standards* and *2005–2006 Laboratory and Point-of-Care Testing Accreditation Standards*.

[203] Joint Commission, 2005 Accreditation Manual for Hospitals, Standards PC.16.10 through 16.60.

[204] Ill. Admin. Code tit. 77, §§ 250.510(b) and (c)(3).

ance with the hospital's quality assurance standards. The policy should require that the original report from the outside facility be placed into the hospital's medical records, that the name of the outside source be placed into the report, and that there be some mechanism for ensuring that the outside source meets all relevant federal regulatory, state licensing, and accreditation requirements.[205]

Under circumstances demonstrating that quality assurance should be of concern, a hospital policy may allow for the exclusion of outside test reports from medical records and for the prohibition on the use of such reports to meet preadmission or preoperative testing requirements—unless the outside source is recommended by the relevant department head; approved by the medical staff; and complies with all relevant laws, regulations, and accreditation standards. However, as discussed in the next section, refusal to accept outside test reports may give rise to antitrust concerns, and thus legal counsel should be consulted when drafting a policy in this area.

Antitrust Issues

Potential antitrust problems arise when a hospital proposes to exclude all outside test reports from its medical records. Such exclusionary conduct can create substantial antitrust risk, particularly if a competitor, such as an outside laboratory or diagnostic testing facility, can demonstrate that it was injured by that conduct and that the hospital had an anticompetitive intent in implementing a restrictive policy regarding outside test reports. A competitor could assert that the hospital unlawfully monopolized, or attempted to monopolize, the relevant market by implementing a blanket prohibition on outside test reports, with the intent to use its existing market power to create barriers to the entry of additional competitors for diagnostic service.[206] By demonstrating that its ability to enter the market was reduced due to the hospital's exclusion of outside test reports, the competitor may sufficiently demon-

---

[205] See, e.g., 42 C.F.R. § 482.27 (requiring hospitals that participate in the Medicare program to ensure that all laboratory services provided to their patients are performed in Medicare-approved facilities).

[206] Such conduct would constitute a violation of Section 2 of the Sherman Act, which prohibits monopolization and attempted monopolization. See 15 U.S.C. § 2.

strate economic harm resulting from the hospital's conduct, and therefore establish a prima facie claim of antitrust violation. A competitor also could assert that the hospital's exclusionary policy constitutes an illegal tying arrangement involving a tie-in between hospital services and diagnostic testing, and that, by this arrangement, the hospital unlawfully foreclosed competition in the market for diagnostic testing by exercising its power in the market for hospital services.[207]

Other, less restrictive alternatives—such as the imposition of strict guidelines for acceptable outside testing—may be appropriate and may help avoid exposure to antitrust liability or the expense of antitrust litigation. Those guidelines should be uniform for all outside facilities whose test reports are included in the medical records. For example, outside laboratories could be required to meet the standards for a particular class of licensed laboratories under applicable state licensing laws, assuming that this requirement also is met by any other laboratories whose results would be included in medical records. Hospitals should seek the advice of qualified antitrust legal counsel in formulating policy with respect to outside laboratory vendors.

Change of Ownership or Closure: Disposition of Records

The rapidly changing healthcare environment has prompted many mergers[208] and acquisitions[209] as healthcare facilities strive to streamline their operations and improve their competitive positions. In this process, healthcare facilities are faced with a change of ownership or, in some cases, closure (for instance, where an unacquired facility is unable

---

[207] Such conduct would violate Section 1 of the Sherman Act, which prohibits any contracts, combinations, or other conspiracies in restraint of trade. See 15 U.S.C. § 1. Courts have established key elements necessary for establishing a tying claim, and if these criteria are met, the tying of two products has been condemned as a per se violation of the Sherman Act.

[208] A merger is a corporate transaction that involves one corporation being absorbed into a second corporation (the "new entity"), which takes on all of the rights and obligations of the first corporation.

[209] There are two types of acquisitions: an asset acquisition and a stock acquisition. An asset acquisition is a corporate transaction that involves one corporation acquiring part or all of the assets of another corporation, and generally the acquiring corporation takes on agreed-upon rights and obligations of the selling corporation. A stock acquisition is a corporate transaction that involves one corporation acquiring part or all of the stock of another corporation, and generally the acquiring corporation assumes only the rights and liabilities of an owner of the stock in the acquired corporation, and does not directly assume any of the acquired corporation's rights or liabilities.

to compete with larger integrated healthcare networks). The management of health information is one of many critical issues to be considered when a healthcare organization undergoes a change of ownership by merger or acquisition or closes its doors and withdraws from the healthcare market. These circumstances should be significant to any health information manager or risk manager because the healthcare organization's obligation to maintain the safety and confidentiality of its patient records continues after a change of ownership or closure.

The Privacy Rule includes in the definition of healthcare operations the sale, transfer, merger, or consolidation of all or a part of a covered entity with another covered entity or with an entity that will become a covered entity.[210] Because the rule permits covered entities to use or disclose PHI for healthcare operations without the patient's authorization, covered entities are able—in the course of mergers, sales, and other changes of ownership involving another covered entity—to disclose the PHI they maintain. Thus, organizations and practitioners covered by the Privacy Rule have considerable flexibility to comply with applicable state law governing disposition of medical records in such transactions.

The procedures for handling patient records in these transactions are set forth in state law and regulations, which vary across the country. Healthcare records professionals also can turn to various guidelines published by national professional organizations.[211] In most cases, however, the better source of information is any applicable state law that covers the disposition of records in the event of change of ownership or closure,[212] and any additional guidance offered by state national hospital and health information management associations.[213] There are

---

[210] 45 C.F.R. § 164.501.

[211] See, e.g., H. Rhodes, "Practice Brief: Managing Health Information in Facility Mergers and Acquisitions," AHIMA (1996), available at http://library.ahima.org/xpedio/groups/public/documents/ahima/pub_bok1_022080.html; P. Wanerus, "Managing Health Information Through a Merger," *Journal of AHIMA* 65 (4): 55 (1994); American Hospital Association Ad Hoc Committee for Hospital Closures, *Guidelines for Managing Hospital Closures* (Chicago: American Hospital Association, 1990); M. D. Brandt, "Practice Brief: Protecting Patient Information After a Facility Closure" (AHIMA, 2003), available at http://library.ahima.org/xpedio/groups/public/documents/ahima/pub_bok1_ 022080.html.

[212] See, e.g., Cal. Code Regs. tit. 22, § 70751(e); Ill. Admin. Code tit. 77, § 250.120(f).

[213] See, e.g., Colorado Health & Hospital Association, *Guidelines for Consent to Care and Release of Health Information* (Colorado Health & Hospital Association, 2004); Iowa Health Information Management Association, *Iowa Guide to Medical Records Laws* (Iowa Health Information Management Association, 2003).

several ways for a healthcare organization to handle the disposition of its records, depending on whether a change of ownership or a closure is involved.

Change of Ownership

Some states have statutory or regulatory guidelines regarding the management of health information in the event of change of ownership (for example, during the process of a merger or acquisition).[214] Most require that the new entity comply with all legal, regulatory, and accreditation requirements regarding the disposition, maintenance, and retention of healthcare records. Statutory and regulatory provisions in this area also may require the new entity to merge the old entity's active records with its records, and prepare a retention schedule that meets the needs of patients and others who legitimately require access to these records. Accordingly, health information professionals and risk managers for facilities involved in a merger and/or acquisition or that are otherwise undergoing a change of ownership should verify with legal counsel that health information arrangements within the merger transaction satisfactorily meet all federal and state law requirements,[215] as well as accreditation standards.[216] In addition, legal counsel should be consulted whenever a merger or acquisition or other network formation gives rise to any liability concerns in relation to protecting the confidentiality of patient healthcare records information.

---

[214] See, e.g., Cal. Code Regs. tit. 22, § 70751(e); Mass. Gen. Laws ch. 111, § 70 (hospitals, institutions for unwed mothers, and clinics); Or. Admin. R. 333-505-0050(17); S.C. Code Regs. 61-16 § 601.7(c); Tex. Admin. Code tit. 25, § 133.21 (hospitals).

[215] Aside from state licensing requirements, for example, many healthcare facilities will need to ensure compliance with the Medicare Conditions of Participation and Interpretive Guidelines, which provide that a medical record must be maintained for each inpatient and outpatient, and that records may be combined into a single unit record or maintained in two different systems as long as an adequate cross-referencing mechanism is in place. See 42 C.F.R. § 482.24; State Operations Manual, Appendix A—Survey Protocol, Regulations & Interpretive Guidelines for Hospitals, § 482.24.

[216] See, e.g., Joint Commission, *2005 Accreditation Manual for Hospitals,* Standards IM.3.10 and 4.10, which require that healthcare organizations use a patient information system to quickly assemble all relevant information from components of a patient's record when a patient is treated. The Joint Commission also requires healthcare facilities to provide written notification of significant change of ownership or control within 30 days of such changes. See, e.g., Joint Commission, *2005 Comprehensive Accreditation Manual for Hospitals.*

In general, when ownership changes and the facility remains open to patients, custody of the records should be transferred to the new governing body, but the files should remain stored at the healthcare organization. In some states, this arrangement is required by law.[217] In California, for example, before the change in ownership occurs, both parties must submit written documentation informing the Department of Health Services that the newly licensed facility will take custody of the prior licensed facility's patient records, or that some other arrangement has been made whereby the records remain available to both parties and to other authorized persons.[218]

After licensure, regulatory, and accreditation requirements have been evaluated, the newly formed healthcare organization must address the many operational issues that are involved with health information management in the context of mergers and acquisitions. In this respect, a critical consideration in any merger or acquisition is integration of the merging entities' information systems. The new healthcare organization will need to inventory existing information systems and technology and then develop plans to consolidate these systems. Although significant savings may be realized through consolidating software licenses and maintenance contracts, careful advance planning and consultations with legal counsel are necessary to ensure compliance with the terms of such licensure agreements.[219]

If the consolidation of information systems results in the discontinuation of one or more existing systems, AHIMA recommends that healthcare records professionals consult with legal counsel to obtain more information about precautions that should be taken under these circumstances, such as:

- Ensuring that all final data, including diagnostic and procedures codes and billing information, have been entered, and that all work, such as transcription of dictated reports, has been completed
- Facilitating ongoing access to old files by saving and reformatting them for compatibility with any new systems and, with any such data transfer, implementing appropriate audit trails
- Assessing the need for retaining and accessing existing databases, especially abstract databases

---

[217] See, e.g., Or. Admin. R. 333-505-0050(17); S.C. Code Regs. 61-16 § 601.7(c).
[218] Cal. Code Regs. tit. 22, § 70751(e).
[219] See Rhodes, "Practice Brief: Managing Health Information."

- Assessing the need for archiving data in their original form or for retaining reports or records in hard copy, microfilm, or other media for future use[220]

AHIMA makes a number of other recommendations in its practice brief on health information management in the context of merger and acquisitions. Some important objectives for healthcare personnel responsible for handling health information needs during a change-of-ownership process, or for facilitating the integration of health information during a postmerger or acquisition transition, include:

- Developing and implementing a records retention policy to meet the needs of patients and other legitimate users, and to ensure compliance with legal, regulatory, and accreditation requirements—this is particularly important with respect to mergers and acquisitions resulting in the closure of health facilities
- Assessing the compatibility and functionality of existing information systems, and formulating a plan that, to the greatest extent possible, allows for the integration of these systems
- Ensuring the maintenance of existing databases in an accessible form if there is any anticipated need for that data in the future
- Employing or contracting with health information management professionals to evaluate the options and implement plans for integrating information systems, as needed[221]

Closure

When a healthcare facility closes or a medical practice dissolves, there is a continuing obligation to maintain the confidentiality of patients' healthcare information and to assure that such information is available if it is needed in the future. Healthcare records professionals should work closely with the state licensing agency when arranging for the preservation of medical records upon closure or change in ownership. Although some states have no specific laws governing the disposition of records under these circumstances, the state licensing agency is likely to provide guidance for handling records in a manner that preserves

---

[220] Ibid.
[221] Ibid.

confidentiality and ensures the availability of the records for access by patients.

In developing procedures for the disposition of patient records upon closure of the healthcare facility, health information professionals must consider a number of statutory and regulatory requirements, including state licensing and record retention laws, as well as Medicare requirements and, if applicable, federal laws governing records of patients undergoing treatment for alcohol and drug abuse. Many states require approval from the state department of health or licensing authority before implementing any plan regarding disposition of records upon closure.[222]

When a healthcare organization closes, the records usually must be transferred to another location. Most state laws do not specify where the records should be kept; however, they require the healthcare organization to notify the licensing agency in writing about the arrangements made for safekeeping of the records.[223] This notification should include the location of the storage facility and the name of the person acting as custodian.[224] In some states, the licensing agency will accept custody of the records after closure. At least one state requires the healthcare organization to index the records and deliver them to the agency for safekeeping.[225] Most states, however, encourage the closing healthcare organization to transfer its records to another healthcare facility in the area.[226] Nebraska requires the closing hospital to transfer records to the licensed facility to which the patient is transferred; otherwise, the closing hospital should dispose of all remaining records by shredding, mutilation, incineration, or other equally effective protective measure.[227] Utah regulations suggest returning the records to the attending physician if that person still is in the community.[228] Where no other facility is located nearby (for example, in remote rural areas) and

---

[222] See, e.g., La. Rev. Stat. 40:2109(E); La. Admin. Code tit. 48I, ch. 93, § 9307.

[223] See, e.g., Cal. Code Regs. tit. 22, § 70751(d); Kan. Admin. Regs. 28-34-9a(d)(2); 902 Ky. Admin. Regs. 20:016(3)(11)(3); N.J. Admin. Code tit. 8, § 43G-15.1(c); N.D. Admin. Code § 33-07-01.1-20(1)(a)(4).

[224] Ibid.

[225] See Tenn. Code Ann. § 68-11-308; Tenn. Dept. of Health Hospital Rule 1200-8-1-.06(f).

[226] See, e.g., Ind. Admin. Code tit. 410, r. 15-1-9(2)(b)(2)I; Miss. Code Ann. § 41-9-79.

[227] Neb. Admin. R. & Regs. tit. 175, ch. 9, § 006.07A5.

[228] Utah Admin. Code 432-100-33(4)(e) (regulation also allows a hospital to store its records at another hospital or approved medical records storage facility).

no physician wants to keep the records, the files might be stored at the closest government office, a reputable commercial storage company, or a law firm.

In general, the closing healthcare organization must notify the licensing agency of its arrangements for record keeping before the closing is completed.[229] In addition, closing healthcare organizations should notify former patients as to how to obtain access to their records should the need arise.[230] In some states, before patients' records are transferred to an archive facility or another healthcare facility, patients must receive reasonable notification—if not by letter, then by publishing a series of notices in the local newspaper.[231]

Contractual provisions regarding the disposition of records come into play when a healthcare facility closes as part of a sale of that facility to another healthcare organization. In this situation, patient records may be considered assets and may be included in the sale of the property.[232] AHIMA recommends that a sales agreement contain a provision allowing the closing facility the right to access or obtain copies of patients' records as needed. Another advisable provision is one that allows the facility the right to reclaim the patient records if the new owner later decides to sell to a third party.[233]

Contractual obligations will also likely arise when a facility closes without a sale. In this case, the facility must make arrangements to have patient records transferred to another healthcare facility or otherwise appropriately stored (for instance, archived with the state government or stored in a reputable commercial storage facility). Prior to transferring the records, a written agreement should be signed by the closing healthcare facility and the facility accepting transfer of the records; because the closing facility remains responsible for ensuring that records are stored safely for the required length of time, the agreement should thoroughly outline the terms and obligations of both facilities.

---

[229] See, e.g., Ill. Admin. Code tit. 77, ch. I, § 250.120(k) (90 days' notice); Utah Admin. Code 432-2-14 (30 days' notice); Cal. Code Regs. tit. 22, § 70751(d) (48 hours' notice).

[230] See, e.g., Colo. Dept. of Health Standards for General Hospitals ch. IV, § 4.2.2; 28 Pa. Code § 115.23.

[231] See, e.g., Wis. Stat. § 146-819(2).

[232] If the facility is sold to an organization other than a healthcare entity, patient records should not be included in the assets available for purchase, and the facility should take steps to transfer patients' records to an archive or to another appropriate healthcare provider. See Brandt, "Practice Brief: Protecting Patient Information."

[233] See Brandt, "Practice Brief: Protecting Patient Information."

AHIMA advises that contractual provisions should be carefully drafted and very specific if a closing healthcare facility must transfer patient records to a storage firm. Among the provisions AHIMA recommends for inclusion in a written contract between the healthcare facility and the storage firm are the following:

- Agreement to keep all information confidential and to disclose patient records information only to authorized representatives of the healthcare facility or upon written authorization from the patient or his or her legal representative
- Prohibition against selling, sharing, discussing, assigning, transferring, or otherwise disclosing confidential information with any other individuals or business entities
- Agreement to protect information against theft, loss, unauthorized destruction, or other unauthorized access
- Return or destruction of information at the end of the agreed-upon retention period
- Assurance that healthcare providers, patients, and other legitimate users will have access to the information as needed[234]

Once the records of a closed healthcare organization have been moved, they must be preserved safely for some time. In Pennsylvania, a special law requires that records be stored at least 5 years after a hospital discontinues its operations. After that time, a hospital wishing to destroy any remaining records may do so after notifying the public and providing opportunity for patients to claim their files.[235] In Tennessee, records may be destroyed 10 years after the hospital closes.[236] Many state laws, however, do not specifically address the duration of the time period for record retention upon closure of a healthcare organization. Health information professionals also must be careful to ensure compliance with any applicable retention requirements under federal law; if the facility participates in the Medicare program, for example, it must retain records in their original or legally reproduced form for at least 5 years to comply with Medicare Conditions of Participation.[237] (For a more detailed discussion of record retention requirements, see Chapter 3.)

---

[234] Ibid.
[235] 28 Pa. Code § 115.23(c).
[236] Tenn. Hospitals Rules & Regs. § 1200-8-1-06(f).
[237] See 42 C.F.R. § 482.24(b)(1).

Health information professionals should be aware of one important consideration to be factored into any determination of how long records must be kept after a facility closes (assuming that no state law specifies the retention period): the state's malpractice statute of limitations for both adults and minors. The retention period should be at least as long as, and preferably longer than, the period of time specified by such statute-of-limitations provisions.[238] Also, according to AHIMA, the healthcare organization should contact its malpractice insurance carrier regarding closure and disposition of records. Wherever the records are stored, the closing healthcare organization and the carrier must be provided with access after closure if a malpractice claim is later filed. (For a more detailed discussion of records retention and its importance for purposes of defending against malpractice claims, see "Developing a Record Retention Policy" in Chapter 3.)

After an established retention period has come to an end, the healthcare facility may consider giving original records directly to patients. AHIMA cautions, however, that original records should never be given out to patients during the required retention period, because the healthcare facility and other legitimate requesters may need access to these records for business reasons.

Finally, special issues related to disposition of records upon closure arise for facilities covered by the Confidentiality of Alcohol and Drug Abuse Patient Records Regulation.[239] If a program covered by these federal regulations is "taken over or acquired" by another program, the acquired program must notify its patients of the change in ownership and obtain written consent to transfer custody of the records to the new owner or to another program designated by the patient; in the absence of such consent, the acquired program must delete all patient identifying information from the records or destroy them.[240] This provision applies regardless of whether the physical site of the program changes

---

[238] AHIMA recommends a retention period longer than the state's malpractice statute of limitations because, in some cases, that statute will not begin to run until the potential plaintiff learns of the causal relationship between an injury and the care received. Moreover, the appropriate retention period for the records of patients who are minors is the period of time up to the patient's reaching the age of majority plus the period of the state's statute of limitations, unless otherwise provided by state law. Brandt, "Practice Brief: Protecting Patient Information."

[239] 42 C.F.R. §§ 2.1 through 2.67.

[240] 42 C.F.R. § 2.19(a).

or remains the same after the ownership change. Patients who refuse consent to transfer their records to the acquiring program or some other facility must withdraw from treatment. The original program then may edit or destroy the records pursuant to the regulations, unless another legal requirement directs the facility to preserve the records for some additional period of time.[241]

Although the obligation to obtain consent from every patient may be burdensome for many facilities, DHHS has determined that the burden is outweighed by the public policy to protect the confidentiality of substance abuse patients' records. When a substance abuse treatment program completely discontinues operations, it must destroy all medical records except those for any patients who consent to having their records transferred to another program, or unless a different law requires the records to be maintained.[242] Records kept pursuant to another legal requirement must be sealed and labeled.[243] According to DHHS, this other legal requirement may be a state law governing the disposition of medical records during a closure or change in ownership, or the applicable statute of limitations for malpractice claims. When the retention period expires, the federal regulations authorize destruction of the records.[244] Although the federal rules do not require the program to notify patients before destroying their records, other federal or state laws may contain such a notification requirement; thus, healthcare records professionals uncertain of the law in this area should obtain legal counsel prior to destroying records for which the retention period has expired.

---

[241] 42 C.F.R. § 2.19(a)(1) and (2).
[242] Ibid.
[243] 42 C.F.R. § 2.19(b)(1).
[244] 42 C.F.R. § 2.19(b)(2).

CHAPTER 9

HIV/AIDS: Mandatory Reporting and Confidentiality

Chapter Objectives

- Outline statutory/regulatory requirements for mandatory reporting of HIV/AIDS cases to state and local health departments
- Describe restrictions contained in provisions of state HIV/AIDS statutes intended to protect the confidentiality of HIV/AIDS information
- Discuss common exceptions specified in state HIV/AIDS statutes prohibiting the disclosure of HIV test results without the test subject's written informed consent
- Explain the limits on disclosure of HIV/AIDS test results of the patient (in circumstances where exceptions apply) and of the healthcare provider.
- Describe statutory provisions allowing disclosure of HIV/AIDS information pursuant to a court order, and give examples of how courts respond to petitions for such orders
- Describe civil and criminal liability provisions of state HIV/AIDS statutes, and compare with common law liability for unauthorized disclosure of HIV/AIDS information
- Recommend steps to protect patient privacy and confidentiality of HIV/AIDS information
- Discuss mandatory reporting and confidentiality of HIV/AIDS records
- Discuss the impact of the HIPAA Privacy Rule and Security Rule

Introduction

One of the more significant problems in medical records management is the treatment of records of patients who have acquired immune deficiency syndrome (AIDS) or are human immunodeficiency virus (HIV)–positive. The complexity and variety of the laws governing these records can interfere with the ability of record managers to cope with the demands of government agencies, researchers, hospital administrators, and the patients themselves. It is important, therefore, for healthcare records managers to understand the laws applicable to such records and to keep abreast of legal developments as they occur.

The issues presented by records containing HIV- and AIDS-related information continue to complicate the operation of health institutions' health information services departments, particularly with respect to special confidentiality and reporting provisions. Most states impose a duty on physicians and/or healthcare facilities to report all cases of "contagious," "infectious," or "sexually transmitted" diseases to the department of health. The Health Insurance Portability and Accountability Act (HIPAA) regulations governing the privacy of health information (Privacy Rule) permit disclosures required by state law.[1] The statutory or regulatory definitions of reportable diseases typically include AIDS, as all states must report AIDS cases to the federal Centers for Disease Control and Prevention (CDC). In addition to these general reporting laws, special reporting laws for AIDS and related conditions are in effect in most states. (For a more detailed discussion of mandatory reporting statutes, see Chapter 7.)

In conjunction with these reporting statutes, many states also have enacted special confidentiality statutes governing the disclosure of AIDS-related information in patients' medical records. These statutes typically prohibit the attending physician and healthcare facility from releasing such information to persons other than the patient and the department of health. Most of these statutes, however, also list several exceptions that permit disclosure of AIDS-related information under specified circumstances to specified individuals or entities—including medical professionals, emergency assistance personnel, spouses, sexual and needle-sharing partners, epidemiologists and researchers, blood banks, medical facilities handling body parts of the deceased, funeral

---

[1]   45 C.F.R. §164.512(b)(1)(i).

directors, correctional facilities, managed care and peer review organizations, employers, schools, and insurance companies (for the purposes of making insurance payments). Courts also can order disclosure of AIDS patients' records in circumstances not addressed directly by legislation. These laws are important because they authorize the release of information in a patient's records without the individual's consent—and, in some cases, despite his or her protests.

The question of when AIDS-related information may be disclosed without consent is a particularly sensitive issue because of the strong interests involved. The patient wants to prevent any disclosure of information because of the personal nature of the disease and the stigma attached to it, and the public interest in fostering medical treatment and encouraging blood and organ donations is perhaps best served by the assurance of donor and patient confidentiality. Healthcare providers need to know the patient's condition in order to protect themselves from the virus while providing proper care to the patient. The government seeks access to AIDS-related information in order to conduct scientific research and monitor the spread of the disease. Finally, third parties, such as spouses, need to know whether their partners are carriers of the deadly virus. This chapter discusses the statutory and regulatory requirements in this area, with a focus on the difficult balancing of conflicting interests that often comes into play in disclosure determinations.

The Privacy and Security Rules provide the same protections for health information concerning HIV and AIDS as they do for other protected health information (PHI). Therefore, the focus on this information must be whether state laws that provide greater protections (and, therefore, are not likely to be preempted by HIPAA) apply, and whether the healthcare provider or other covered entity has complied with them. (For a detailed discussion of the Privacy Rule and HIPAA preemption of state law, see Chapter 6.)

Duty to Report

All states have statutes and/or regulations requiring healthcare providers to report AIDS cases to the state or local department of health, and a majority of states require HIV and/or ARC (AIDS-related complex) reporting as well. The reporting laws and regulations vary widely as to who has the duty to report; some place the duty of reporting on the attending physician and/or the laboratory that performs a test that concludes with a positive result,[2] while others require hospitals, clinics, blood banks and plasma centers, and other entities such as health maintenance organizations (HMOs) to report AIDS and/or HIV cases;[3] some states require reporting from a combination of all these sources.[4] Minnesota has enacted what appears to be the only state statute containing a self-reporting provision that requires healthcare workers diagnosed with HIV to report that information to the commissioner of health no more than 30 days after learning of the diagnosis or 30 days after becoming licensed or registered by the state.[5] The Minnesota law also requires healthcare workers who personally know of another healthcare worker's failure to comply with infection control procedures to report that to the appropriate licensing board or a designated hospital official within 10 days.[6]

Reporting laws governing HIV- and AIDS-related information also vary with respect to what information must be reported. Many states require the patient's name and address to be disclosed in the report, along with age, race, and sex,[7] while a few states prohibit the release of identifying information unless set criteria are met.[8] Some states have statutes that permit the test subject, upon request, to remain unknown—in other words, the patient who consents to testing has the right to anonymous testing.[9] Under these statutes, patients also may be

---

[2] See, e.g., Ark. Code Ann. § 20-15-904 (physician); Fla. Stat. Ann. § 384.25(1) (physician and laboratory); Kan. Stat. Ann. §§ 65-6002(a) and (b) (physician, administrator of medical facility, and laboratory).

[3] See, e.g., 410 Ill. Comp. Stat. Ann. § 310/4(b); Iowa Code §§ 141A.6 (2) through (4).

[4] See, e.g., Colo. Rev. Stat. §§ 25-4-1402(1) and (2); Mich. Stat. Ann. § 333.5114 ("any person or governmental entity"); Wis. Stat. § 252.15(7)(b); Ala. Code § 22-11A-2.

[5] Minn. Stat. § 214.19, sub. 2.

[6] Minn. Stat. § 214.19, sub. 4.

[7] See, e.g., Colo. Rev. Stat. § 25-4-1402(4); Md. Code Ann., Health-Gen., § 18-201(b); Mich. Comp. Laws § 333.5114(1); Wis. Stat. § 252.15(7)(b); N.D. Cent. Code § 23-07-02.1; Or. Admin. R. 333-018-0010.

[8] See, e.g., Or. Admin. R. 333-018-0030(3)(a)(A) through (E) (anonymous reporting unless the HIV-infected person fits into specified categories, including persons who: have donated blood or tissue in the past year, have a criminal record involving sex offenses, are under six years of age, or request assistance in notifying partners). See also 410 Ill. Comp. Stat. Ann. § 310/4 (registry of reported cases of AIDS and ARC to be identified by code rather than number).

[9] See, e.g., Fla. Stat. Ann. § 384.25(7)(a); 410 Ill. Comp. Stat. § 305/6; Me. Rev. Stat. Ann. tit. 5, § 19203-B. See also Ind. Code § 16-41-6-2.5 (applies to prenatal healthcare providers).

permitted to execute an HIV test consent form in a manner that does not reveal their identity; for example, patients may choose to execute the document not by signing their names, but instead by using an alias or a coded number, which the healthcare provider must then use in identifying the test subject, the test sample, and the test results. In states with such anonymous testing programs, reported cases of AIDS and HIV infection from anonymous testing sites usually do not include patient-identifying information.[10]

Mandatory disclosure laws in most states also require the attending physician and/or laboratory to submit a written report on a patient within a specified number of days after a reportable diagnosis has been confirmed.[11] In Maryland, for example, the director of a medical laboratory in which serum samples are tested for HIV must submit a report within 48 hours of an HIV-positive test result, and the report must contain statistical data but no identifying information.[12] Other institutions that obtain or process semen, blood, or tissue must obtain a blood sample from all potential donors in order to test for HIV, and all positive test results must be reported to the department of health.[13]

A growing number of states require the identity of persons with either AIDS or HIV to be reported.[14] Michigan law, for example, requires all persons who obtain a positive HIV result for a test subject to report the name, address, age, race, and sex of the test subject within seven days.[15] Reports must be filed with both state and local health departments, and only licensed clinical laboratories are exempt from those requirements. However, patients who submit to HIV testing in a physician's private practice office or the office of a physician engaged by an HMO may request their doctor not to reveal their name, address, or telephone number.[16]

---

[10] Mich. Comp. Laws § 333.5113(2)(b)(iii); W.Va. Code § 16-3C-2(c).
[11] See, e.g., Fla. Stat. Ann. § 384.25(1) (not to exceed two weeks); Iowa Code § 141A.8(3) (seven days); Kan. Stat. Ann. § 65-6002(a) (one week); Md. Code Ann., Health-Gen., § 18-205(a) (48 hours); Mich. Comp. Laws § 333.5114(1) (seven days). See also Cal. Health & Safety Code § 1603.1 (72 hours; applies to blood banks and plasma centers that have received tainted blood).
[12] Md. Code Ann., Health-Gen., §§ 18-205(a)(1) and (b)(2)(ii)(2).
[13] Md. Code Ann., Health-Gen., § 18-334(b)(2)(i).
[14] See, e.g., Ala. Code E § 22-11A-2; Ark. Code Ann. § 20-15-904(b); Colo. Rev. Stat. § 25-4- 1402(1); Mich. Comp. Laws § 333.5114(1); Wis. Stat. § 252.15(7)(b).
[15] Mich. Comp. Laws § 333.5114(1).
[16] Mich. Comp. Laws § 333.5114(3).

In at least one state, a state supreme court has ruled that a mandatory disclosure statute that requires physicians to report to the state department of health the names and addresses of patients who are HIV-positive or suffer from AIDS is not unconstitutional.[17] An Alabama statute imposing this requirement was challenged by a physician who was willing to report certain statistical data, but refused to provide the names and addresses of patients; the department of health sued to compel the physician's full compliance with the reporting statute. The physician argued that the statute violates the equal protection clause because sellers of confidential HIV-testing kits and out-of-state laboratories that evaluate test results are not required to report the names and addresses of purchasers. In rejecting this argument, the court concluded that out-of-state testing labs and testing kit vendors are not similarly situated to those individuals required to report HIV and AIDS cases. The court therefore ruled that the reporting requirement was constitutional. The labs do not know the identity of the persons who are being tested, and the testing-kit vendors sell kits without knowing whether a particular purchaser is HIV-positive or suffers from AIDS, the court explained. The court thus affirmed a lower court decision ordering the physician to disclose identifying information as required by the statute.

Protecting Confidentiality of HIV-Related Information

The Privacy Rule and the Security Rule

As a general rule, a covered entity may not disclose PHI without the patient's authorization, unless the Privacy Rule specifically permits the disclosure. If the information is created in a blind HIV test, so that the data contain no patient identifiers, the information is not PHI and is not entitled to HIPAA Privacy Rule protection. If the HIV/AIDS information contains patient identifiers, covered entities may disclose it if required to do so by state law (for example, mandatory reporting statutes), in connection with public health agency activities (such as disease prevention), protection of individuals' health or safety (for example, permitted disclosures to individuals who may be exposed to HIV or AIDS), and other purposes described in the rule. (For a more

---

[17] *Middlebrooks v. State Board of Health*, 710 So. 2d 891 (Ala. 1998).

detailed discussion of permitted disclosures under the Privacy Rule, see Chapter 6.) Therefore, if a state law requiring the disclosure of such data is not preempted by HIPAA, a covered entity may disclose the information in accordance with the requirements of the applicable state law.

The challenge for covered entities who receive, maintain, use, or transmit HIV- or AIDS-related information is obtaining accurate HIPAA preemption analyses of relevant state law, and developing policies and procedures that provide required protections for such information. In many states, the preemption analysis will result in applying state laws that provide greater protection for this data.

HIV- or AIDS-related information that qualifies as PHI also requires the security safeguards described in the Security Rule. (For a detailed discussion of these safeguards, see Chapter 13.) Thus, for such data, covered entities must provide safeguards that are appropriate to their size and operations. State law may also require additional security protections for HIV- or AIDS-related information.

State Law

For covered entities in states whose relevant law is not preempted by HIPAA, and for organizations not subject to HIPAA, state law will control the use and disclosure of HIV- or AIDS-related information.

In addition to protecting the confidentiality of medical records in general and of medical records containing information about sexually transmitted diseases, many states have statutes specifically directed at protecting the confidentiality of HIV- or AIDS-related information and records. These confidentiality statutes usually provide that, except in specified circumstances, no person may disclose the identity of an HIV test subject, and test results and an individual's HIV status must be kept confidential and recorded in a manner that does not reveal the test subject's identity.[18]

Many statutes also prohibit the disclosure of test results without the test subject's written informed consent.[19] Some statutes strictly limit the sharing of HIV test results to persons with a statutorily defined

---

[18] Confidentiality provisions in this area typically prohibit disclosure of the identity of a person who has undergone an HIV test regardless of the results of the test.

[19] See, e.g., Fla. Stat. Ann. § 381.004 (3)(a); 77 Ill. Admin. Code. § 697.140 (a)(2); La. Rev. Stat. Ann. § 40:1300.16; R.I. Code R. 14-040-006, §15.1.

"need to know," making distinctions among personnel within a single healthcare facility. Massachusetts prohibits disclosing HIV test results without the patient's written consent, and recognizes no exceptions.[20] Other states provide exceptions that specify when disclosure is permissible without the patient's written consent. New York, for example, prohibits the release of HIV-related information except with consent of the patient, but then specifies more than a dozen exceptions for disclosure without the patient's consent.[21] (For a more detailed discussion of disclosure exceptions, see "Statutory Provisions Regarding Disclosure," next in this chapter.)

The first exception often listed in these confidentiality statutes permits access to test results to the person obviously most interested in such information: the test subject or the subject's legally authorized representative.[22] A second common exception permits disclosure of test results to any person(s) designated in a written authorization or otherwise legally effective release executed by the test subject or the subject's authorized representative.[23] (For a more detailed description, see "Disclosure to Third Parties with Patient Authorization" later in this chapter.) Thus, a healthcare provider who orders an HIV test for a patient may inform the patient or his or her representative of the results without liability.[24] Although these confidentiality statutes create special civil and criminal liability for unauthorized disclosures (for example, where none of the exceptions applies), they are not intended to discourage healthcare practitioners from indicating the results of an HIV test in a patient's file.[25]

In a small office setting, such as a physician's or group practice's office, test results can be maintained in a separate confidential file, with access limited to the patient's physician. In a larger institutional setting,

---

[20] Mass. Gen. Laws ch. 111, § 70F.
[21] N.Y. Pub. Health Law §§ 2782(1)(a) through (o). See also Cal. Health & Safety Code §§ 121015 and 121035 through 121070.
[22] See, e.g., Del. Code Ann. tit. 16, § 1203(a)(1); 410 Ill. Comp. Stat. Ann. § 305/9(a); N.Y. Pub. Health Law 18 § 2782.
[23] See, e.g., Del. Code Ann. tit. 16, § 1203(a)(2); 410 Ill. Comp. Stat. Ann. § 305/9(b); N.Y. Pub. Health Law § 2782(1)(b); Me. Rev. Stat. Ann. tit. 5, § 19203(3).
[24] However, a patient may sue a healthcare provider for negligently advising the patient that he or she has tested HIV-positive. See *Johnson v. United States*, 735 F. Supp. 1 (D.D.C. 1990).
[25] See, e.g., N.Y. Pub. Health Law § 2782(8) ("confidential HIV-related information shall be recorded in the medical record of the protected individual").

however, protecting confidentiality of test results is more problematic. Establishing separate confidential files may not be feasible. Recognition of this problem underlies the provisions in some state HIV confidentiality statutes that permit HIV test results to be recorded in a patient's medical record.[26] Some states elaborate further by providing that, if HIV test results are recorded in patients' medical records, this must be done in a manner that does not permit a person to learn a patient's HIV status by some means other than reading the record. Regulations promulgated under the Illinois AIDS confidentiality statute, for example, require that HIV test results be disclosed to healthcare providers and researchers only in a manner that does not reveal the identity of the subject of the test or with the subject's consent in accordance with the statute.[27] Accordingly, records containing AIDS-related information should not bear distinguishing labels or marking; for instance, the healthcare records manager should avoid placement of such information in a separate, distinctive colored document or file within the patient's medical record.

Statutory Provisions Regarding Disclosure

Disclosures Permitted by the Privacy Rule

The Privacy Rule contains provisions that permit covered entities to disclose HIV- or AIDS-related information under circumstances that are covered in most related state laws. These provisions are discussed below. For example, the Privacy Rule permits a covered entity to disclose PHI, including HIV- or AIDS-related information, to prevent a serious and imminent threat to the health or safety of a person, provided that the disclosure is "consistent with applicable law and standards of ethical conduct."[28] Thus, under this provision, a physician could reasonably take the position that disclosure of a patient's HIV- or AIDS-related information to coworkers or employees who may have contact with the patient is a permitted disclosure to protect the recipients' health and safety, and hospital emergency room staff could disclose HIV- or AIDS-related information to paramedics who treated an AIDS victim.

---

[26] See, e.g., Cal. Health & Safety Code § 120985(a); N.Y. Pub. Health Law § 2782(8).
[27] Ill. Admin. Code § 697.140(b).
[28] 45 C.F.R. § 164.512(j).

The Privacy Rule also permits disclosures of PHI without a patient's authorization for public health activities, to individuals who may have been exposed to a communicable disease, in connection with persons who may be victims of abuse or neglect, in compliance with state law, and for other enumerated purposes. Where state laws require disclosure of HIV- or AIDS-related information for one or more of these purposes, therefore, state law and the Privacy Rule will likely be compatible, and covered entities should comply with state law requirements.

Disclosure to Third Parties with Patient Authorization

Many of the HIV confidentiality laws allow the patient to authorize release of test results to third parties.[29] This provision permits a healthcare practitioner to release confidential information to persons who otherwise are precluded from access to the patient's records. A patient might authorize release to any insurance company, employer, or school. The practitioner should require that such release be in writing and signed by the patient or the patient's representative. A copy of the release should be attached to the patient's records. These laws generally are consistent with the Privacy Rule and, if they require the same or similar authorization from the patient, will not be preempted.

Disclosure to Healthcare Workers

Most confidentiality laws, whether general or AIDS-specific, allow information to be released to medical personnel involved in the patient's care and without the patient's consent.[30] The Privacy Rule specifically permits the disclosure of PHI for the purpose of treating the patient. Under these circumstances, authorizing the disclosure of HIV- and AIDS-related information can serve several purposes. To facilitate proper medical treatment for AIDS victims, many statutes authorize release of AIDS information to the patient's medical provider, who is thereby authorized to place the results of an HIV test directly into the patient's record.[31] Physicians often are authorized to reveal information

---

[29] See, e.g., Del. Code Ann. tit. 16, § 1203(a)(2); 410 Ill. Comp. Stat. Ann. § 305/9(b); N.Y. Pub. Health Law § 2782(1)(b); Me. Rev. Stat. Ann. tit. 5, § 19203(3); Va. Code Ann. § 32.1-36.1(2).

[30] See, e.g., Cal. Civ. Code § 56.10 (c)(1); see also N.C. Gen. Stat. § 130-143(3).

[31] See, e.g., Cal. Health & Safety Code § 120985(a); W.Va. Code § 16-3c-3(a)(5).

directly to other healthcare providers for purpose of treating the patient.[32] In addition, the laws reflect a concern for the safety of medical workers who are at risk for HIV infection during performance of their duties. Several statutes authorize the attending physician to reveal an HIV patient's identity to other healthcare workers who come into contact with body fluids or body parts of the patient, or who work directly with HIV patients.[33]

Some statutes permit disclosure upon finding that the healthcare worker has a "reasonable" or "medical" need to know the information in order to provide proper care. Other laws allow disclosure whenever generally relevant to the patient's treatment. Many of the laws are unclear, however, as to whether the authorized disclosures are permissive or mandatory. This question bears on the ability of a concerned worker to demand that a physician confirm the test results of a patient who the worker suspects is positive for the virus. Many statutes also are unclear as to whose interests must be analyzed for purposes of such disclosure—the worker's or the patient's. For example, a "need to know" for purposes of providing patient care may refer to the worker's need to take precautions to prevent becoming infected while rendering treatment to the patient; on the other hand, the "need to know" might relate to special treatments available only for AIDS patients.

Not every healthcare worker involved with the patient has a legitimate need to know that the person has been tested for HIV; only a limited class of medical practitioners have access to such information under HIV confidentiality statutes. In California, for example, the results of an HIV test may be recorded in the subject's record and otherwise revealed without the patient's consent to providers of care for purposes of "diagnosis, care, or treatment of the patient."[34] Accordingly, the results of an HIV test may be disclosed to a healthcare provider's agent or employee who provides "direct patient care and treatment."[35] Similarly, Maine authorizes disclosure of HIV test results to the healthcare provider designated by the patient, and the patient's

---

[32] See, e.g., Cal. Health & Safety Code § 120985(a); Haw. Rev. Stat. § 325-101(a)(10); Iowa Code § 141.23(1)(d); Me. Rev. Stat. Ann. tit. 5, § 19203(2); Mich. Comp. Laws § 333.5131(5)(a)(iii); W.Va. Code § 16-3c-3(a)(5).

[33] See, e.g., Cal. Health & Safety Code §§ 120985(a) and 121010(b) through (e); Kan. Stat. Ann. § 65-6004(a); 410 Ill. Comp. Stat. Ann. § 305/9(h).

[34] Cal. Health & Safety Code § 120985(a).

[35] Cal. Health & Safety Code § 121010(c).

physician then may make results available only to other providers working directly with that person, and only for the purpose of providing direct patient care.[36] These provisions appear to be permissive, and it is unclear whether a provider of direct care could successfully demand that the physician confirm that a suspected AIDS patient had indeed tested positive for the HIV infection.

In Delaware and Iowa, HIV confidentiality statutes provide that no person may disclose the identity of any subject of an HIV test, or the results thereof, in a manner that permits identification of the test subject—except, among other circumstances, to an authorized agent or employee of a healthcare provider if: (a) that provider is authorized to obtain the test results, (b) the agent or employee provides patient care or handles or processes specimens of body fluids or tissues, and (c) the agent or employee has a medical need to know such information in order to provide health care to the patient.[37] These statutes seem to reflect concern for the patient, rather than for the safety of healthcare workers, because the third prong of the test—the employee's medical need to know—must be tied into the purpose to provide health care to the patient. Thus, the medical aspect of the need to know refers to the patient's medical interests, not the employee's own health concerns.

Illinois has adopted a similar three-part test for disclosing AIDS information to other healthcare providers; however, the third prong of that test requires only that the employees have a need to know the information.[38] Similarly, Missouri allows the release of HIV test results to "health care personnel working directly with the infected individual who have a reasonable need to know the results for the purpose of providing direct patient health care."[39] Again, it is unclear whether the "reasonable need to know" relates to the worker's safety or to the patient's proper care. In either case, the Missouri law is fairly typical in limiting the circle of disclosure to persons directly involved with the patient. New Hampshire's HIV confidentiality statute also is concerned for the patient's treatment; the relevant provision of that statute provides that a physician or other healthcare provider may disclose information pertaining to the identity and test results of the person tested to other physicians and healthcare providers directly involved in that

---

[36] Me. Rev. Stat. Ann. tit. 25, § 19203(2).
[37] Del. Code. Ann. tit. 16, § 1203(a)(3); Iowa Code § 141.23(1)(c).
[38] 410 Ill. Comp. Stat. Ann. § 305/9(c).
[39] Mo. Rev. Stat. § 191.656(2)(b).

person's health care when the disclosure of such information is necessary to protect the health of the person tested.[40]

In contrast, Kentucky and Hawaii have HIV confidentiality statutes that allow for much greater discretion on the part of the physician. Although Kentucky law authorizes the release of medical information only to the physician retained by the person infected with AIDS or another sexually transmitted disease, the statute is silent on the extent to which the physician may release such information to coworkers involved in the patient's care, except in the case of an emergency when information may be released to protect the life or health of the patient.[41] Hawaii allows disclosure of AIDS, ARC, and HIV information by the patient's healthcare provider to another healthcare provider "for the purpose of continued care of [or] treatment of the patient."[42] These broadly written provisions rely upon the judgment of the physician on the question of disclosure, but allow release of the information in an emergency to the extent necessary to protect the life or health of the patient.

Other states' HIV confidentiality statutes demonstrate more concern for persons other than the patient and those that provide direct care for the patient, such as other healthcare professionals. In Texas, the HIV confidentiality statute is permissive, but provides that results of an HIV test may be released to a physician, nurse, or other healthcare personnel who have a "legitimate" need to know the results to provide for their protection and the patient's health and welfare.[43] The New York confidentiality provision authorizes release of confidential HIV-related information only to an agent or employee of a health facility or health provider if three conditions are met: (a) the agent is permitted to access medical records, (b) the facility is authorized to obtain HIV information, and (c) the agent either provides health care to the protected individual or maintains medical records for billing or reimbursement.[44] The statute then provides that a provider or facility is authorized to receive HIV-related information when knowledge of such material is "necessary to provide appropriate care or treatment to the protected individual or a child of the individual."[45]

---

[40] N.H. Rev. Stat. Ann. § 141-F:8(IV).
[41] KY. Rev. Stat. Ann. § 214.420(3)(e).
[42] Haw. Rev. Stat. § 325-101(a)(10).
[43] Tex. Health & Safety Code Ann. § 81.103(b)(5); see also Idaho Code § 39-610.
[44] N.Y. Pub. Health Law § 2782(1)(c).
[45] N.Y. Pub. Health Law § 2782(1)(d).

Like the New York law, Utah's statute in this area provides for disclosure to a healthcare provider, healthcare personnel, and public health personnel with a "legitimate need to have access to the information in order to assist the patient, or to protect the health of others closely associated with the patient."[46] The statute expressly notes that the above language does not create a duty to warn third parties, but is designed to assist providers in treating and containing AIDS, HIV, and other infectious diseases.[47] This provision clearly authorizes disclosure to certain medical personnel working closely with the patient, but also extends to family members, sexual partners, and needle-sharing partners.[48] (For a more detailed discussion of other state statutes addressing this subject, see "Disclosure Without Consent to Spouse or Needle-Sharing Partner" in this chapter.) Many laws also permit disclosure of a patient's identity to facilities that procure, process, distribute, or use blood, other body fluids, body parts, tissues, or organs.[49]

The statutes discussed above govern the release of all HIV-related information. Others focus directly on disclosure of the reports submitted to the department of health. Colorado, as described above, has a mandatory AIDS and HIV reporting law applicable to healthcare workers,[50] which provides that reports containing HIV-related information held by a healthcare provider or facility, physician, clinic, blood bank, or other agency shall be strictly confidential and shall not be released, shared, or made public except as provided.[51] Louisiana has a special law requiring a hospital to notify a nursing home of an HIV patient's condition when the hospital transfers the patient to the home. A

---

[46] Utah Code Ann. § 26-6-27(2)(h); see also Idaho Code § 39-610.

[47] Utah Code Ann. § 26-6-27(2)(h); see also Cal. Health & Safety Code § 121015(c).

[48] Although the state legislation authorizes disclosure to healthcare workers treating the patient, it is possible that courts will impose a duty on patients to reveal whether they have AIDS. See, e.g., *Boulais v. Lustig,* 1992 Cal. LEXIS 65, No. BC038105 (Super. Ct. 1993) (unpublished), in which a surgical technician successfully sued a patient for fraudulently concealing the fact that she had AIDS when filling out forms before undergoing surgery. After the technician was cut with a scalpel while removing sutures, the patient revealed her HIV-positive status. The technician had not been wearing gloves at the time of the exposure, and although the technician consistently tested negative for HIV postexposure, the court awarded her damages for fraud, but refused to award her damages for negligent infliction of emotional distress.

[49] See, e.g., N.Y. Pub. Health Law § 2782(1)(e); Va. Code Ann. § 32.1-36.1(A)(8); Wis. Stat. § 252.15(5)(a)(4).

[50] Colo. Rev. Stat. § 25-4-1402.

[51] Colo. Rev. Stat. § 25-4-1404(1).

similar duty is placed upon a nursing home transferring an HIV patient to a hospital.[52]

Disclosure Without Consent to Emergency Medical Personnel

Many confidentiality statutes allow the release of HIV-related information without the patient's consent to medical technicians who provide emergency care to an HIV-positive patient.[53] The statutes vary, however, in the purpose for such disclosure. Some link disclosure to the health of the patient, others indicate a concern for the safety of the emergency workers, and many others reflect an ambiguous balance between the two concerns.

In some states, for example, confidential HIV-related information may be released to medical personnel in a "medical emergency" to the "extent necessary to protect the health or life of [the patient].[54]" The relevant statutory provision in Hawaii defines "medical emergency" as any disease-related situation that threatens life or limb.[55] Other states authorize disclosure to healthcare providers rendering medical care when knowledge of HIV test results is "necessary" to provide "appropriate emergency care or treatment" to the patient.[56] These laws demonstrate concern for the patient's treatment.

Other state statutes in this area reflect a predominant concern for the safety of rescue workers. For example, Illinois allows release of the identity of the subject of an HIV test to "[a]ny health care provider or employee of a health facility, and any firefighter or any EMT-A or EMT-I, involved in an accidental direct skin or mucous membrane contact with the blood or bodily fluids of an individual which is of a nature that may transmit HIV, as determined by a physician in his medical judgment."[57] Similarly, the Wisconsin HIV confidentiality statute permits the release of HIV-positive test results to persons who, in rendering care to the victim of an emergency or accident, are significantly

---

[52] La. Rev. Stat. Ann. § 40:1099(B)(2); Miss. Code Ann. § 41-23-1(5).
[53] See, e.g., Cal. Health & Safety Code § 121010(e); Colo. Rev. Stat. § 25-4-1404(1)(C); Del. Code Ann. tit. 16, § 1203(a)(4); Fla. Stat. § 384.29(1)(d); Wis. Stat. § 252.15 (5)(11).
[54] See, e.g., Colo. Rev. Stat. § 25-4-1404(1)(c); Fla. Stat. § 384.29(1)(d); Iowa Code § 141.10(1)(c); Kan. Stat. Ann. § 65-6002(c)(4); Ky. Rev. Stat. Ann. § 214.420(3)(e).
[55] Haw. Rev. Stat. § 325-101.
[56] See, e.g., Del. Code Ann. tit. 16, § 1203(a)(4).
[57] 410 Ill. Comp. Stat. Ann. § 305/9(h).

exposed to the victim, provided that a physician certifies in writing that the emergency caregiver has been significantly exposed, and that this certification accompanies any request for disclosure.[58]

A few states impose an affirmative duty on an attending physician or healthcare facility to respond to inquiries by emergency rescuers regarding contact with a patient later diagnosed with a contagious disease or virus including HIV;[59] under such statutes, rescuers entitled to receive such information include paid or volunteer firefighters, emergency medical technicians, rescue squad personnel, and law enforcement officers. Such statutes typically require that the rescue worker be notified within 48 hours after confirmation of the patient's diagnosis, and that the information be communicated to emergency care personnel in a manner that protects the confidentiality of both the patient and rescuer. In Maryland, each medical care facility must develop and disseminate written procedures for exposure notification. A facility or provider acting in good faith under this section is not liable for failure to give notice of exposure where the rescuer does not properly initiate the process as developed.[60] Other statutes in this area are permissive; Washington law, for example, authorizes certain emergency rescuers and other healthcare workers who come into significant contact with the blood and/or other body fluids of another person to request that an HIV test be performed on that person; the requester is then entitled to know the results.[61] California outlines detailed procedures to follow under circumstances where an exposed worker requests an evaluation of the exposure by a physician, including measures to be taken in relaying information regarding HIV status to the exposed worker.[62]

Disclosure Without Consent to Spouse or Needle-Sharing Partner

Many states have confidentiality statutes that provide for notification of an HIV patient's spouse, needle-sharing partner, or other "contact" at

---

[58] Wis. Stat. § 252.15(5)(11).
[59] See, e.g., La. Rev. Stat. Ann. § 18-213(e); Mich. Comp. Laws § 333.20191(5).
[60] Md. Code Ann., Health-Gen., § 18-213(i)(1).
[61] Wash. Rev. Code § 70.24.105(2)(h).
[62] Cal. Health & Safety Code § 121135.

risk for the infection.[63] A small minority of states authorize the release of HIV test results to the spouse of the test subject, but not to other sexual partners.[64] These provisions usually are permissive and do not create a duty on the part of the physician to warn all third parties.[65] Thus, a contact who develops the virus but who was not informed of the risk by the partner's physician cannot bring a lawsuit against the physician under the statute. On the other hand, a physician who reveals the risk to a contact as authorized is not liable to the patient for breach of confidentiality.[66] This exception in South Carolina's disclosure law, for example, simply states that a physician or state agency identifying and notifying a spouse or known contact of a person having HIV infection or AIDS is not liable for damages resulting from the disclosure.[67]

State statutes containing mandatory HIV notification provisions do exist, although they are few in number.[68] Such statutes require the health department or the healthcare provider to notify persons at risk, and typically specify the circumstances when the requirement applies. Oregon, for example, requires healthcare providers to report the names of HIV-infected persons to the health department specifically for purposes of partner notification in two circumstances: (1) when the patient requests assistance in notifying partners; or (2) without the patient's consent, when the patient's partner is not a member of certain population groups who may have a high risk of HIV infection (that is, hemophiliacs, prostitutes, intravenous drug users, homosexuals).[69] Before

---

[63] See, e.g., Cal. Health & Safety Code § 121015 (spouse, sexual partner, or needle-sharing partner); Haw. Rev. Stat. § 325-101(a)(4) (sexual or needle-sharing contact); 410 Ill. Comp. Stat. Ann. §§ 305/9 and 325/5.5(b) (spouse and contacts); Kan. Stat. Ann. § 65-6004(b) (spouse or partner); Mich. Comp. Laws § 333.5131(5)(b) (contacts); N.Y. Pub. Health Law § 2782(4) (contact); W.Va. Code § 16-3C-3(d) (sex and needle-sharing partners and other contacts). One survey estimates that the HIV confidentiality statutes in 39 states contain statutory exceptions allowing disclosures to spouse, needle-sharing partners, or other contacts (e.g., sexual partners).

[64] See, e.g., Tex. Health & Safety Code Ann. § 81.103(b)(7); Va. Code Ann. § 32.1-36.1(A)(11).

[65] See, e.g., Cal. Health & Safety Code § 121015(c); 410 Ill. Comp. Stat. Ann. § 305/9(a); Kan. Stat. Ann. § 65-6004(c); N.Y. Pub. Health Law § 2782 (4)(c); W.Va. Code § 16-3C-3(e).

[66] See, e.g., Cal. Health & Safety Code § 121015(a); 410 Ill. Comp. Stat. Ann. § 305/9(a).

[67] S.C. Code Ann. § 44-29-146; see also W.Va. Code § 16-3C-3(d).

[68] See, e.g., Mich. Comp. Laws § 333.5131(5)(b); Or. Admin. R. 333-018-0030.

[69] Or. Admin. R. 333-018-0030 (3)(a) (D) and (E).

notifying the health department, however, the healthcare provider must have tried unsuccessfully to persuade the patient voluntarily to notify his or her partners.

Under North Carolina's notification scheme, patients are required to notify all past (since the date of infection, if known) and future sexual partners of their infection.[70] If a physician knows the identity of the spouse of an HIV-infected patient, and has not notified the spouse after obtaining the patient's consent, then the physician must report the identity of the spouse to the department of health. In doing so, the physician fulfills the statutory requirement to notify exposed and potentially exposed persons.

Whether mandatory or permissive, these notification laws usually require the physician to protect the identity of the patient when making such disclosures.[71] For example, California provides that a physician or surgeon having the results of a confirmed positive HIV test of a patient under his or her care cannot be held criminally or civilly liable for disclosing to a person reasonably believed to be the spouse, sexual partner, or needle-sharing partner, or to the county health officer, the patient's test result; in disclosing the possibility of exposure to HIV to sexual partners who are not spouses, however, the healthcare provider must not disclose any identifying information about the individual believed to be infected.[72] Further, before any disclosure, the physician must discuss the importance of notification with the patient, attempt to obtain the patient's voluntary consent for notification of any contacts, and, regardless of whether consent is granted, inform the patient of the physician's intent to notify the patient's contacts of their being at risk.[73]

A physician who wishes to notify a contact under one of these laws should discuss such plans in depth with the patient. The physician should remind the patient of the moral obligation to disclose the con-

---

[70] N.C. Admin. Code tit. 10A, r. 41A.0202(1)(e).
[71] According to one estimate, only two states specifically permit disclosure of the name of the HIV-positive patient by the health department. See, e.g., Ohio Rev. Code Ann. § 3701.243 (B)(1) (a) (authorizing disclosure of HIV test results and the identity of person tested to spouse or any sexual partner); Mich. Comp. Laws § 333.5114a (5) (b) (allowing disclosure of identity of person tested, but only if that person consents to such disclosure).
[72] Cal. Health & Safety Code § 121015(a). The provision is permissive, however, and thus imposes no duty on the part of the physician to notify any of these contacts. See, e.g., Cal. Health & Safety Code § 121015(c).
[73] Cal. Health & Safety Code § 121015(b).

dition to third parties at risk. In addition, patients should be aware that some states impose criminal liability on an HIV carrier who knowingly engages in activities likely to spread the virus.[74] The physician should fully document the discussion in the patient's record. If, after this consultation, the patient still refuses to reveal the condition to sexual partners or to others at risk, the physician then may contact the third parties directly; however, the physician should not proceed in a manner that identifies the patient. The physician also should be sensitive to the effect of the notification on a third party that may be completely unaware of the situation. Although HIV notification provisions in most state statutes do not create a duty to warn third parties, other federal or state laws may impose such an obligation.[75]

Moreover, case law, which did not involve patients who participated in high risk behavior, in a few states appears to create a duty to warn for healthcare providers, and there is no statute protecting them from liability for failure to warn. In Vermont, for example, the state supreme court has imposed a "duty to warn" on mental health professionals who know, or should know, that a patient poses a serious risk of danger to an identifiable victim,[76] and this ruling could be extended to other healthcare professionals, particularly with respect to notifying spouses of known HIV-positive patients.[77]

In at least one state, however, a court has held to the contrary on the issue of whether there is a duty to warn the spouse of a hospitalized patient who has tested positive for HIV where no blood transfusion is involved; a District of Columbia appeals court ruled that hospital employees owed no duty to warn the husband of such a patient.[78] The

---

[74] See, e.g., Fla. Stat. Ann. § 384.24.

[75] For example, one federal law might be relevant in this respect. The laboratory Medicare and Medicaid Conditions of Participation require hospitals to take action when they learn that they have received a blood product at increased risk of transmitting HIV. See 42 C.F.R. § 482.27(c). Under these regulations, if a blood bank notifies a hospital that a previous blood donor has tested HIV-positive, the hospital must dispose of the donor's blood or blood products and follow specified procedures to notify patients who received blood or blood products derived from the donor.

[76] *Peck v. Counseling Service*, 499 A. 2d 422 (Vt. 1985). See also *Tarasoff v. Regents of the University of California*, 551 P. 2d 334 (Cal. 1976).

[77] See also *Reisner v. Regents of the University of California*, 37 Cal. Rptr. 2d 518 (Ct. App. 1995) (HIV-infected person who contracted virus from his girlfriend can sue hospital for failing to inform girlfriend that she had received HIV-tainted blood transfusion at hospital).

[78] *N.O.L. v. District of Columbia*, 674 A. 2d 498 (D.C. 1995).

husband, who was separated from his wife when she was hospitalized, but later reunited with her, sued the hospital for emotional distress, arguing that he had suffered psychologically upon learning at least one year after the hospitalization that his wife had tested HIV-positive at that time. The court dismissed the suit, finding that the hospital did not owe the husband any duty to disclose his wife's test results, but rather, that a duty was owed to the wife to not disclose the information to anyone without her written consent.

Other Permissible Disclosures Without Patient Authorization

In addition to the common exceptions described in the previous sections, disclosure of HIV-related information is permitted under many statutes to numerous other parties—including blood banks and organ donors, epidemiologists or other researchers, correctional facilities, schools, HMOs or other healthcare facilities, and insurance companies.[79] Most states allow, rather than require, release of this information; some states, however, mandate that HIV test results be disclosed to school officials, blood donors, correctional officials, and law enforcement authorities who are investigating criminal offenses that may have resulted in HIV transmission.[80] (See "Duty to Report," discussed previously in this chapter.) Some confidentiality statutes also permit release of information to health facility staff committees, accreditation committees, and oversight review organizations.[81] In addition, New York allows disclosure to an authorized agency in connection with foster care or adoption of a child, to insurance companies or their agents to the extent necessary to reimburse healthcare providers for health services, and to the medical directors of correctional facilities.[82] Wisconsin authorizes release to a funeral director or person who performs an autopsy on an HIV patient, to a coroner, and to a sheriff or keeper of a prison.[83]

---

[79] See, e.g., Ohio Rev. Code § 3701.248; Fla. Stat. § 381.004(3)(e).

[80] See, e.g., Cal. Health & Safety Code §§ 121055, 121060, and 121070; N.Y. Pub. Health Law § 2782(1)(l)-(o).

[81] See, e.g., Del. Code Ann. tit. 16, § 1203(a)(7); 410 Ill. Comp. Stat. Ann. § 305/9(f); N.Y. Pub. Health Law § 2782(1)(f); W.Va. Code § 16-3C-3(a)(8).

[82] N.Y. Pub. Health Law §§ 2782(1)(h), (i), and (n). See also Haw. Rev. Stat. § 325-101(a)(6) through (10).

[83] Wis. Stat. §§ 252.15(5)(a)(7), (12), and (13).

Disclosure of Healthcare Provider's Status to Patients

Healthcare facilities also must confront the difficult issue of whether to reveal a healthcare worker's HIV status to patients. In this regard, it is important to distinguish between disclosure before treatment and disclosure after treatment. Guidelines issued by the CDC address both situations; the guidelines recommend that an HIV-positive worker notify prospective patients of the worker's HIV status before the patients undergo exposure-prone invasive procedures, and that disclosure after treatment should be decided on a case-by-case basis.[84] More specifically, the CDC describes the case-by-case approach to decisions as to whether patients should be notified of possible exposure as a determination involving the "assessment of specific risks, confidentiality issues, and available resources." The CDC also recommends that decisions regarding notification and follow-up studies should be made in consultation with state and local public health officials.

Some states also require healthcare workers who perform exposure-prone procedures to notify prospective patients of their seropositive status and to obtain written consent from patients before patients undergo exposure-prone procedures.[85] A New Jersey court has upheld a hospital's requirement that an HIV-positive surgeon disclose his HIV status to prospective patients as part of the informed consent procedure.[86] In Maryland, an appeals court has allowed two patients of a surgeon who died of AIDS to sue his estate based on the claim that he had failed to inform them before surgery that he was infected with HIV.[87] A physician's duty of care must include disclosure that an operating surgeon's HIV-positive status poses a risk, however minimal, of transmission of the AIDS virus during surgery, the court concluded.

With respect to disclosure after exposure, a hospital may make the decision to inform patients that a provider who treated them is HIV-positive. Some states allow notification of an individual who may have been exposed to HIV through contact with an HIV-infected provider, as

---

[84] See, e.g., Centers for Disease Control and Prevention, *Morbidity and Mortality Weekly Report* (July 12, 1991).

[85] See, e.g., Tex. Health & Safety Code Ann. § 85.205(c).

[86] See *Estate of Behringer v. Medical Center at Princeton*, 592 A. 2d 1251 (N.J. Super. Ct. Law Div. 1991).

[87] *Faya v. Almaraz*, 620 A. 2d 327 (Md. 1993).

well as an investigation of the healthcare provider.[88] In states that have HIV confidentiality statutes that forbid such disclosure, however, the hospital would need to obtain court authorization before disclosing such information. In a Pennsylvania case, for example, the high court allowed a hospital to disclose the identity of an AIDS-infected obstetrics-gynecology resident to patients who had been treated by the resident.[89] Two hospitals where the physician had worked requested court permission to disclose the physician's name and medical information to more than 200 patients who had been associated to some degree with the physician in the course of their treatment. Under Pennsylvania law, information derived from HIV testing must remain confidential, but courts may authorize disclosure of such information if there is a compelling need to do so. The court emphasized in this case that the physician was involved in invasive surgical procedures where the risk of sustaining cuts and exposing patients to tainted blood was high. His medical problem became a matter of public concern the moment he picked up a surgical instrument and became involved in surgical procedures, the court declared. After weighing the physician's privacy interests against the interests of public health, the court concluded that the latter should prevail, given the potential risks for transmission of the disease.

Disclosure by Court Order

The Privacy Rule contains specific provisions governing how a covered entity may respond to a court order or subpoena. A covered entity may disclose PHI in a judicial or administrative proceeding in response to a court order, so long as the disclosure is limited to scope of the order.[90] The covered entity may disclose PHI in response to a subpoena or other discovery request, provided that the entity follows the procedures set out in the Privacy Rule.[91] (For a more detailed discussion of disclosures in response to legal process, see Chapter 8.)

---

[88] 410 Ill. Comp. Stat. Ann. §§ 325/5.5(b) and (c). See also *Estate of Doe v. Vanderbilt University, Inc.*, 824 F. Supp. 746 (M.D. Tenn. 1993) (when hospital becomes aware that an HIV-positive worker participated in exposure-prone procedures, it has a duty to decide whether to initiate a "lookback" program, and attempt to inform patients who may have been exposed to HIV).

[89] *In re Milton S. Hershey Medical Center of Pennsylvania State University*, 634 A. 2d 159 (Pa. 1993).

[90] 45 C.F.R. § 164.512(e).

[91] Ibid.

Many state confidentiality statutes include standards by which a court may authorize disclosure of the results of a patient's HIV test. Some statutes allow disclosure under a "lawful court order";[92] others require the person seeking access to show a "compelling need," with no other means of acquiring the information.[93] In determining whether a compelling need exists, the court must balance the petitioner's interest against the patient's privacy interest and the public interest.[94] The public interest will not be served if disclosure deters future testing; fosters discrimination;[95] or discourages donations of blood, organs, or semen.[96] The petitioner may be required to show that other ways of obtaining the information are not available or would not be effective.[97] Many statutes also provide that the patient's true name may not be included in any documents filed with the court—a pseudonym must be substituted. The test subjects must be given notice and opportunity to participate in the proceedings if not already a party. All proceedings are conducted in camera unless the test subject agrees to a hearing in open court, or unless the court determines that a public hearing is necessary to the public interest and proper administration of justice.[98]

Court Orders and Disclosure in Blood Donor Cases

Even in the absence of such statutory directives, courts have struggled to balance the interests involved when one person requests disclosure of medical information relating to another person. Numerous cases in this area have involved claims by patients who contracted AIDS through blood transfusions and who request the facility that provided blood to produce a list of donors' names and addresses. Such cases generally involve malpractice claims against a hospital or blood supplier or both, in which a patient attempts to discover the identity of the donor

---

92 Wis. Stat. § 252.15(5)(a)(9).
93 See, e.g., 35 Pa. Consol. Stat. § 7608 (A); Iowa Code § 141.23(1)(g)(1). See also Haw. Rev. Stat. § 325-101 (a)(11) (court order upon showing of good cause).
94 See, e.g., Del. Code Ann. tit. 16, § 1203(a)(10)(a); W.Va. Code § 16-3C-3(a)(9)(i).
95 See, e.g., Del. Code Ann. tit. 16, § 1203(a)(10)(a).
96 See, e.g., Fla. Stat. Ann. § 381.004 (3)(f)(9)(a); Ky. Rev. Stat. Ann. § 214.181 (5)(c) (9)(a); S.C. Code Ann. § 44-29-136 (A).
97 See, e.g., Del. Code Ann. tit. 16, § 1203(a)(10)(a); Mich. Comp. Laws Ann. § 333.5131(3)(a)(ii).
98 See, e.g., Del. Code Ann. tit. 16, § 1203(a)(10)(d); Haw. Rev. Stat. § 325-101 (a)(11); W.Va. Code § 16-3C-3(a)(9)(iv).

who provided the contaminated blood. The patient frequently alleges that access to the blood donor's identity is necessary in order to establish whether the hospital or supplier used proper screening and testing procedures when they accepted the blood.

Courts are divided on the issue of whether a donor's right to privacy outweighs an individual patient's need to prove negligence on the part of a healthcare provider in a malpractice suit. Some courts that have considered the issue have refused to order blood collection facilities to reveal the identities of donors. The Florida Supreme Court, for example, ruled that the privacy interests of donors and society's interest in maintaining a strong volunteer blood donation program outweigh a patient's need to prove the source of his AIDS contamination in a personal injury suit.[99] The court ruled that the release of the blood donor's records would result in an undue invasion of privacy, and added that discovery should be denied so that donors would not be deterred from donating blood for fear that someone would be able to inquire into their private lives by obtaining their blood records. Similarly, a federal trial court in South Carolina ruled that a patient who sued a blood bank after she acquired HIV from a blood transfusion was not entitled to discover the identity of the donor because the donor's interest in privacy and the public interest in protecting voluntary blood programs outweighed the patient's interest in the case.[100]

However, other courts have held that the patient's interest in discovering the identity of the donor outweighs the donor's privacy rights. The Louisiana Supreme Court allowed a patient who tested HIV-positive after a blood transfusion to discover the identity of a donor who had tested HIV-positive.[101] The court ruled that the patient's interest in discovering the identity of the donor outweighed both the donor's privacy interest and public policy considerations favoring nondisclosure. The court emphasized that the donor already had tested HIV-positive, that the patient sought only to identify the donor of one specific unit of blood, and that the patient needed to identify the donor in order to evaluate the blood center's screening process.[102] One court

---

[99]   *Rasmussen v. South Florida Blood Services*, 500 So. 2d 533 (Fla. 1987).

[100] *Doe v. American Red Cross Services*, 125 F.R.D. 646 (D.S.C. 1989).

[101] *Most v. Tulane Medical Center*, 576 So. 2d 1387 (La. 1991).

[102] See also *Sampson v. American National Red Cross*, 139 F.R.D. 95 (N.D. Tex. 1991); *Tarrant County Hospital District v. Hughes*, 734 S.W. 2d 675 (Tex. App. 1987); *Long v. American Red Cross*, 145 F.R.D. 658 (S.D. Ohio 1993).

has allowed a patient to sue a blood donor identified through information inadvertently provided by the Red Cross.[103] The court held that the patient's right to litigate her claim against the donor substantially outweighed the individual privacy rights and public interest in maintaining a safe and adequate blood supply, especially in light of evidence suggesting donor misconduct.

Some courts have resolved blood donor cases by allowing, but limiting, disclosure, such as by requiring the blood collection agency to reveal the name of the infected donor to the court, which then relays relevant communications between the patient and the donor.[104] One court that adopted this method also directed that communications between the donor and that person's lawyer and the court be maintained with redacted signatures in a sealed envelope marked "Confidential."[105] Another court that permitted discovery of donors' identities ordered the plaintiff not to communicate with the donors or undertake further discovery.[106]

Liability for Unauthorized Disclosure of HIV-Related Information

Healthcare providers' unauthorized disclosure of information relating to a patient's HIV status can lead to liability based on violation of HIV confidentiality or other relevant statutes. Liability provisions of most HIV confidentiality statutes create special civil and criminal liability for persons who make unauthorized disclosures of HIV test results. Civil liability gives the test subject a private cause of action for damages against the person who disclosed the information; criminal liability, on the other hand, allows the state attorney to prosecute the offender and impose fines and/or a jail sentence.

In most states, a person who consciously disregards the statute is subject to harsher penalties than one who is negligent. In California, for example, any person who negligently discloses the results of an HIV test to any third party in a manner that identifies or provides identifying

---

[103] *Coleman v. American Red Cross*, 979 F. 2d 1135 (6th Cir. 1992), complaint dismissed on other grounds, 145 F.R.D. 422 (E.D. Mich. 1993).
[104] *Belle Bonfils Memorial Blood Center v. District Court*, 763 P. 2d 1003 (Colo. 1988). See also *Watson v. Lowcountry Red Cross*, 974 F. 2d 482 (4th Cir. 1992).
[105] *Watson*, 482, 487–488.
[106] *Tarrant*, 684.

characteristics of the person to whom the test results apply is liable to a civil penalty of up to $1,000 (to be paid to the test subject); the civil penalty to be assessed for willful disclosure, however, is up to $5,000 (to be paid to the test subject).[107] In Virginia, any person who willfully or through gross negligence makes any unauthorized disclosure is liable for a civil penalty of up to $5,000 per violation, payable to a special state fund,[108] and the person who is the subject of an unauthorized disclosure may recover actual damages or $100, whichever is greater, plus reasonable attorneys' fees and court costs.[109] Wisconsin provides for actual damages and costs, plus exemplary damages of up to $5,000 for an intentional violation.[110] In addition to receiving damages and attorneys' fees, an aggrieved party in Illinois may request other appropriate relief, including an injunction.[111] Colorado provides for a criminal penalty only, imposing misdemeanor fines not less than $500 or greater than $5,000, and/or imprisonment not less than six months or greater than two years.[112]

Based on common law grounds, healthcare providers may also be sued for unauthorized disclosure of information relating to a patient's HIV status. In one California case in which a healthcare provider disclosed a patient's HIV status to an insurance carrier, a state appeals court allowed the patient to sue the healthcare provider based on the state's constitutional right to privacy.[113] After receiving treatment for injuries sustained at work, a patient told the physician's nurse to be careful because he was HIV-positive, but made it clear that he was disclosing the information solely for the purpose of protecting healthcare professionals. The physician's report mentioning AIDS as a possible source of the patient's symptoms was sent to the insurance company, the insurance carrier, and the Workers' Compensation Appeals Board. The court found that the circumstances surrounding the patient's disclosure clearly demonstrated his anticipation that the information would remain private. Enforcing such reasonable expectations of privacy fosters disclosure of HIV-positive status only when necessary and

---

[107] Cal. Health & Safety Code § 120980.
[108] Va. Code § 32.1-36.1(B).
[109] Va. Code § 32.1-36.1(C).
[110] Wis. Stat. § 242.14(4).
[111] 410 Ill. Comp. Stat. Ann. § 305/13.
[112] Colo. Rev. Stat. § 25-4-1409(2).
[113] *Estate of Urbaniak v. Newton*, 277 Cal. Rptr. 354 (Ct. App. 1991).

protects against misuse of information, the court held, concluding that the disclosure was protected under the constitutional right to privacy. In another case, a New Jersey hospital was found liable for failing to protect the confidentiality of a diagnosis of AIDS in a staff physician who had been treated at the facility.[114] The test results were placed in the physician's medical chart, which was kept at the nurses' station on the floor where the physician was an inpatient. There were no restrictions on access to the record. Within hours of the diagnosis, the physician's condition was widely known within the hospital. The court found the hospital negligent for failing to take reasonable precautions regarding access to the physician's record. (For a more detailed discussion of liability arising from improper disclosure of medical records information, see Chapter 11). Covered entities who use or disclose HIV- or AIDS-related information in violation of the Privacy or Security Rule will be subject to the criminal or civil sanctions prescribed by HIPAA. These include substantial fines and imprisonment. (For a more detailed discussion of these sanctions, see Chapter 11.)

Recommended Policies and Procedures

Healthcare providers frequently encounter situations requiring them to balance their duty to protect third parties from the spread of the disease with their duty to protect the privacy of individuals who are infected with HIV. Individuals tested for HIV and/or treated for AIDS must be assured that information shared with healthcare professionals will remain confidential. Without such assurance, patients may withhold critical information that could affect the quality and outcome of care, safety of healthcare workers, and reliability of the information. In developing policies and procedures to safeguard patient privacy and the confidentiality of information relating to HIV infection, healthcare records managers may want to consider guidelines in this area issued by the American

---

[114] *Estate of Behringer*. See also *Goins v. Mercy Center for Health Care Services*, 667 N.E. 2d 652 (Ill. Ct. App. 1996) (hospital security officer exposed to HIV-positive patient's blood can sue hospital for breach of confidentiality based on hospital's failure to keep secret the officer's HIV testing and results).

Health Information Management Association (AHIMA),[115] which recommends implementation of the following measures:

- Develop screening programs to provide confidential testing of individuals and communication of their test results.
- Implement a system that ensures that specific, written informed consent is obtained from the individual or his or her legal representative prior to voluntary testing, followed by posttest counseling provided by a qualified healthcare professional.
- Maintain health records of patients infected with HIV along with other patients' records in a secure area with restricted access; segregation of records based on HIV status should be avoided, because such a system may call attention to the patient's HIV status.
- Manage HIV-positive healthcare workers according to guidelines outlined by the CDC and state and federal laws. The healthcare worker's privacy must be balanced against the risk of transmission to patients, employees, and others. If questions arise, the facility's legal counsel should be involved in resolving the related questions.
- Unless directed otherwise by the physician, medical coders should code only from diagnoses listed in the medical record, and not from laboratory data or test results when a diagnosis is not clearly stated.

In addition, AHIMA emphasizes that healthcare facilities must implement clear policies and procedures for disclosure of health information related to HIV/AIDS, and for continual monitoring of such procedures to ensure consistent compliance. Depending on state law, the facility may be required to report the name of the person tested or other identifying information to local health authorities; however, within the facility, a patient's serological status should be disclosed only as needed for diagnosis, management, or treatment. Others who may review patient health records for administrative purposes (such as quality improvement, billing, and risk management) must ensure that this information is handled in a confidential manner. Information should be disclosed to other legitimate users only with specific written authoriza-

---

[115] American Health Information Management Association, *Practice Brief: Managing Health Information Relating to Infection with the Human Immunodeficiency virus (HIV)(Updated)*, available at http://library.ahima.org/xpedio/groups/public/documents/ahima/pub_bok1_000048.html.

tion of the patient or his or her legal representative or upon receipt of a valid subpoena.[116] Information disclosed to authorized users should be limited strictly to that required to fulfill the purpose stated on the authorization. Authorizations for release of "any and all information" without specifically mentioning HIV or AIDS should not be honored. Due to the sensitivity of this information, it should not be transmitted via facsimile machine or disclosed over the telephone unless urgently needed for patient care. Redisclosure of information relating to HIV/AIDS should be prohibited, unless otherwise required by state law.

---

[116] Some states require a court order for release, thus protecting the records of HIV/AIDS patients from discovery by subpoena.

CHAPTER 10

Discovery and Admissibility of Medical Records

Chapter Objectives

- Distinguish between discoverability and admissibility
- Define the physician-patient privilege and discuss its effect on discovery and admissibility
- Describe the healthcare provider's role in protecting health information from discovery
- Explain waiver of the physician-patient privilege and give examples of how the privilege may be waived
- Define hearsay
- Define the business record exception and its application to medical records
- List other types of records containing patient information that may be sought in discovery
- Describe the peer review privilege and what types of records it protects from discovery
- Recommend steps to protect peer review records from discovery
- Outline the factors that affect whether incident reports are protected from discovery

Introduction

Medical records often play critical roles in legal actions. For example, medical records information is central to workers' compensation claims, disability insurance claims, personal injury suits, and medical malpractice suits. Consequently, patients and other parties to legal actions typically seek every record that may be relevant to their controversy, including patient medical records, quality assurance and other committee records, hospital incident reports, and other types of documents that may contain information about patients.

Whether records are discoverable by parties to a lawsuit, or are admissible during the course of a trial, may significantly affect the outcome of the claim. At the outset, it is important to distinguish between the discoverability of evidence and the admissibility of evidence.

- Discoverability refers to access to documents or witnesses by parties to a legal proceeding. A document or information is discoverable if it must be produced to the party who requests it.
- Admissibility concerns whether documents, objects, or testimony may be admitted formally into evidence at the trial phase of a litigation. The judge, jury, or other decision maker (such as an arbitrator in an arbitration proceeding) may consider only evidence that has been admitted.

The legal standard for determining whether something is admissible is more stringent than the standard for discoverability. Thus, health information may be discoverable by parties in advance of, or in the early stages of, a legal proceeding, but may not be admissible into evidence during the trial or hearing itself. The judge, administrative hearing officer, or panel will apply the rules of evidence to determine whether a record is discoverable or admissible. Because these rules vary from state to state, it is important for healthcare administrators and health information professionals to refer questions on this subject to their qualified legal counsel. Counsel will interpret applicable rules and help prepare appropriate arguments for or against discoverability or admissibility.

Discoverability of Medical Records

Discovery is pretrial access to either witnesses or documents, allowing parties to a suit to learn (that is, to "discover") facts and possible evidence in the case. The standard for what information and documents must be revealed is broad, allowing parties to obtain most items reasonably calculated to lead to the discovery of admissible evidence. A variety of methods exist for discovering information, including:

- Conducting an oral deposition (a question and answer session) of a party or witness
- Obtaining court permission to examine documents or other objects
- Sending written requests for copies of documents
- Sending written lists of questions, known as interrogatories, to parties and/or other witnesses

Because the confidentiality of medical information needs to be preserved in the absence of some compelling reason justifying its disclosure, courts sometimes require an in camera inspection of patient records during discovery, rather than allowing records to be freely copied and distributed to the parties. In this type of inspection, the judge will personally review the medical records requested, and make a determination as to what information should be revealed.

When health information professionals receive a request to examine or copy patient records, the request may come from a patient, the patient's attorney, or another party to a lawsuit involving the patient. A subpoena or court order to produce documents also may be served on a healthcare provider, facility, or organization, perhaps requiring the medical records custodian to appear in person with the requested records. Federal or state fraud or other investigators may appear without advance notice and demand to examine patient records. Individuals and organizations not subject to the Health Insurance Portability and Accountability Act (HIPAA)[1] must comply with the rules of the jurisdiction in which they are located governing discovery and admissibility of evidence. Entities subject to HIPAA must comply with the HIPAA privacy regulations (Privacy Rule) and any state laws that are not preempted by HIPAA. The Privacy Rule sets forth specific requirements that covered entities must meet when disclosing protected health information (PHI) in response to search warrants, court orders, and other legal processes. (See Chapters 6 and 7 for a more detailed discussion of the Privacy Rule, and see Chapter 8 for a more detailed discussion of disclosures of PHI in judicial proceedings.) Policies and procedures should specify how to respond to each type of request for access to records. These procedures should be clearly written and be consistent with the legal and ethical duties of healthcare providers.

---

[1]   42 U.S.C. §§ 1320d et seq.

Physician-Patient Privilege

Patients or healthcare providers may seek to shield health information from discovery by asserting the physician-patient privilege. Even if a court, hearing officer, or other decision maker rules that a medical record is discoverable, the physician-patient privilege, as noted earlier, may later preclude the record's admissibility into evidence. Nearly every state has a statute that protects communications between a patient and a physician from disclosure in judicial or quasi-judicial proceedings under specified circumstances. In addition, courts in jurisdictions in which no statutory privilege exists have created such a privilege as a matter of common law.[2] The purpose of this privilege is to encourage the patient to disclose to the physician all information necessary for treatment, no matter how personal or sensitive.[3]

Statutory privilege provisions vary from state to state. Four aspects to examine when assessing the privilege conferred under a state law are:

- The categories of healthcare providers covered by the statute
- The scope and extent of the patient's privilege to prevent disclosure by the healthcare provider
- The extent to which the provider may exercise the patient's privilege
- The nature of the proceedings in which the privilege may be raised

In Illinois, for example, the statute provides that no physician, surgeon, psychologist, nurse, mental health worker, therapist, or other healing art practitioner may disclose information acquired while professionally attending a patient, if the information was necessary to serve the patient, except in specified circumstances. These specified circumstances include:

- Homicide trials
- Malpractice actions against the healthcare practitioner
- Actions where the patient's physical or mental condition is an issue, including any action in which the patient seeks damages for personal injury, death, pain and suffering, or mental or emotional injury[4]

---

2   See Wanda Ellen Wakefield, Annotation, *Physician–Patient Privilege as Extending to Patient's Medical or Hospital Records*, 10 A.L.R. 4th 552.
3   Ibid.
4   735 Ill. Comp. Stat. Ann. § 5/8-802.

Virginia's privilege statute protects the information that a licensed practitioner of any branch of the healing arts acquires in treating a patient in a professional capacity if the information is necessary to treat the individual. However, the Virginia law states that the information may be disclosed when the physical or mental condition of a patient is at issue, when a patient unlawfully attempts to procure a narcotic, when necessary for the care of the patient, to protect the practitioner's rights, in connection with the operations of a healthcare facility or health maintenance organization (HMO), or to comply with state or federal law.[5]

In litigation between the patient and others, it is not the healthcare provider's concern or right to assert the privilege or to oppose a records subpoena. However, the court may order the provider to permit examination of medical records without disclosing confidential communications.[6]

When a patient seeks to discover the medical records of other patients who are not parties to the legal action, a healthcare provider may be able to assert the physician-patient privilege on behalf of the nonparty patients.[7] The effectiveness of the provider's assertion depends, of course, on the applicable state statute. Healthcare providers and medical records professionals must proceed carefully, with the advice of counsel, because courts have ruled on the discovery of these records based on a variety of grounds.

- In a Georgia case, the court allowed evidence of orthodontic treatment provided by a dentist to patients other than the plaintiff.[8] The court stated that the evidence was admissible to contradict any possible testimony by the dentist that, in similar cases, similar treatment had not resulted in the same unfortunate results.
- In a Maryland case in which a physician was being sued for malpractice, a second physician was serving as an opposing expert witness. The state's highest court ruled that the defendant could not challenge the opposing expert witness by introducing the expert's

---

[5] Va. Code Ann. § 8.01-399.

[6] See *In re D.M.C.*, 331 N.W. 2d 236 (Minn. 1983); *In re Larchmont Gables, Inc.*, 64 N.Y.S. 2d 623 (Sup. Ct., Westchester Co., 1946).

[7] See Dag E. Ytrebert, Annotation, *Discovery, in Medical Malpractice Action, of Names of Other Patients to Whom Defendant Has Given Treatment Similar to That Allegedly Injuring Plaintiff*, 74 A.L.R. 3d 1055.

[8] *Gunthorpe v. Daniels*, 257 S.E. 2d 199 (Ga. Ct. App. 1979).

patients' records.[9] Although Maryland state law allows a healthcare provider to release the records of any patient if the records will assist in defending a lawsuit, that statute did not apply in this case, because the defendant physician did not wish to disclose his own patients' records.

- A Florida court allowed an obese patient suing for malpractice to obtain the records of other obese patients treated by her obstetrician.[10] Although a state law requires notice to nonparty patients before their records can be disclosed, the patients' names and addresses would have to be divulged to implement that requirement. The court ruled that redacting the identifying information made the notice requirement inapplicable, and ordered the physician to produce the records.

Unless applicable law requires healthcare providers to disclose medical records information of a nonparty patient under the particular circumstances presented, it would be prudent for such providers to assert the confidential communications privilege on behalf of the patient, even though the patient is not a party to the lawsuit. A physician who asserts the privilege improperly, however, and refuses to provide records when required to do so, may be subject to sanctions. Thus, the advice of counsel should be sought whenever a broad request for nonparty patient records is received.

Waiver of the Physician–Patient Privilege

The physician–patient privilege belongs to the patient rather than to the physician. The patient may waive this privilege expressly or impliedly. What constitutes a valid waiver has been the subject of considerable litigation. Many courts have held that an individual who files a lawsuit that places his or her physical or mental health in issue impliedly waives the physician–patient privilege.[11] For example, a patient who seeks compensation for physical injuries or "pain and suffering" generally must allow opposing parties to review medical records infor-

---

[9] *Warner v. Lerner,* 348 Md. 733 (1998).

[10] *Amente v. Newman,* 653 So. 2d 1030 (Fla. 1995).

[11] *Carr v. Schmid,* 105 Misc. 2d 645, 432 N.Y.S. 2d 807 (Sup. Ct., N.Y. Co., 1980); J. R. Kemper, Annotation, *Commencing Action Involving Physical Condition of Plaintiff or Decedent as Waiving Physician–Patient Privilege as to Discovery Proceedings,* 21 A.L.R. 3d 912.

mation pertinent to the evaluation and treatment of those injuries. As mentioned above, state statutes may also specify that the privilege is waived under those circumstances.[12] Even if a patient waives the physician-patient privilege by putting his or her physical or mental condition at issue in a lawsuit, however, the scope of the waiver may be limited. For example, a New York appellate court has held that a patient who alleged medical malpractice during her pregnancy did not waive her privilege as to medical records outside of that pregnancy.[13] A Florida court has ruled that a patient suing for medical malpractice waives the physician-patient privilege only as to information exchanged between the patient and the defendant physician, and not between the patient and subsequent physicians.[14]

A number of courts have ruled that the privilege is not waived unless it is evident that the patient intended to waive it.[15] In one case, for example, a Missouri appellate court ruled that a patient had not waived his privilege by turning his records over to his insurer. The court held that doing so was not an unequivocal demonstration that the patient intended to abandon the privilege.[16] Rather, it was an act consistent with the intention to reveal confidential information only to the extent necessary to obtain treatment and payment. On the other hand, once the privilege is actually waived in one context, a patient may be precluded from asserting it in another context. For example, a Michigan court held that a patient who disclosed his medical records in an action against him (alleging that he injured a young child in a car accident) may not object to discovery of the same records in a later suit against his physicians.[17]

Physician-Patient Privilege vs. the Public Interest

Some courts have held that the physician-patient privilege may give way to an important public interest.[18] For example, when dealing with a child care or custody case, courts are likely to find that the interest of

---

[12] See, e.g., 735 Ill. Comp. Stat. Ann. § 5/8-802.
[13] *Murphy v. LoPresti*, 232 A.D. 2d, 648 N.Y.S. 2d 169 (2d Dep't 1996).
[14] *Acosta v. Richter*, 671 So. 2d 149 (Fla. 1996).
[15] See, e.g., *Schaffer v. Spicer*, 215 N.W. 2d 134 (S.D. 1974).
[16] *State ex rel. Gonzenbach v. Eberwein*, 655 S.W. 2d 794 (Mo. Ct. App. 1983).
[17] *Landelius v. Board of Regents*, 556 N.W. 2d 472 (Mich. 1996).
[18] See, e.g., *People v. Doe*, 107 Misc. 2d 605, 435 N.Y.S. 2d 656 (Sup. Ct., Westchester Co., 1981); Wakefield.

the child outweighs the parents' interest in keeping their medical records confidential.[19] This balance may be struck at the legislative level also. The Illinois confidential communications statute specifically provides that the privilege does not apply in civil or criminal actions arising out of the filing of a report under Illinois's Abused and Neglected Child Reporting Act.[20] In this situation, a court may attempt to partially protect the physician-patient privilege by allowing a private examination of medical records by the court and other parties, rather than admitting entire records into evidence.

Courts have held that the prosecution of a crime is an important public interest.[21] Courts also have generally permitted the broadscale discovery of patient records in the context of fraud investigations. In a New York case, a trial court ruled that a hospital under investigation for Medicare violations was required to turn over the billing and medical records of 96 former patients to a grand jury. Noting that "the privilege was never intended to prevent disclosure of evidence of a crime," the court refused to grant the hospital's request to quash the grand jury's subpoenas.[22] Similarly, a California court ruled that a physician whose records were seized as part of a Medi-Cal fraud investigation was not entitled to a hearing to assess whether the physician-patient privilege protected the records. The court found that allowing a physician accused of fraud to assert the privilege would serve the physician's, rather than the patients', interest.[23] In an Ohio fraud investigation, a court ruled that a physician could not assert the physician-patient privilege as a shield from criminal prosecution. Although the records seized from the physician's office were admissible in that case, the court cautioned that they were required to be redacted by concealing the patients' names.[24]

A federal district court in Maryland found another public interest in the investigation of licensees by the state's medical review board of professional conduct.[25] In this case, a group of patients challenged an ad-

---

[19] See, e.g., *Bieluch v. Bieluch*, 462 A. 2d 1060 (Conn. 1983); *In re Baby X*, 293 N.W. 2d 736 (Mich. Ct. App. 1980); *In re Doe Children*, 402 N.Y.S. 2d 958 (Fam. Ct. 1978); Wakefield.
[20] 735 Ill. Comp. Stat. Ann. § 5/8-802(7).
[21] See, generally, Wakefield.
[22] *People v. Doe*. See also *In re Pebsworth*, 705 F. 2d 261 (7th Cir. 1983).
[23] *Brillantes v. Superior Court of Los Angeles County*, 51 Cal. App. 4th 323 (Ct. App. 1996).
[24] *Ohio v. McGriff*, 669 N.E. 2d 856 (Ohio Ct. App. 1996).
[25] *Patients of Dr. Barbara Solomon v. Board of Physician Quality Assurance*, 85 F. Supp. 2d 545 (D. Md. 1999).

ministrative subpoena issued by the state board to their physician for the physician's medical records. In rejecting the patients' request for a temporary restraining order preventing disclosure of the records to the board, the court held that the state board's mandate to investigate physicians outweighs the patients' rights to privacy. In so ruling, the court stated that "[i]t is beyond doubt that society has a deep interest in ensuring, through its government agencies, that practicing physicians meet moral and professional standards. Investigations are necessary and may involve the subpoenas of medical records . . . allowing individual patients to block Board investigations—as the patients seek to do here—would hinder the Board's ability to protect public health."[26]

HIPAA's Treatment of the Physician–Patient Privilege

The treatment of the physician–patient privilege under HIPAA is in flux at this writing. In part, this is a result of the failure of the Privacy Rule to provide any guidance concerning the issue of whether HIPAA permits the privilege to be waived so as to allow the patient's health information to be admitted into evidence in court. This, in turn, presents the question of whether HIPAA preempts state laws that allow waiver under the circumstance described above. The problem arises primarily in two situations. In one, a party to a litigation seeks to discover and admit the medical records of another person (for example, the records of the decedent in a wrongful death case). In the other, a healthcare provider seeks to disclose the plaintiff's medical records as part of the defense in a professional negligence lawsuit. Several courts have addressed these questions, with mixed results. (For a detailed discussion of the Privacy Rule and HIPAA preemption, see Chapter 6.)

Some courts have held that the Privacy Rule does not preempt state law providing for a waiver of the privilege. They based their holdings on their conclusion that records sought pursuant to a court order or subpoena may be disclosed in accordance with the Privacy Rule's provisions

---

[26] *Patients*, 545, 548. See also *Jane Doe et al. v. Maryland Board of Social Work Examiners*, 862 A. 2d 996 (Md. 2004) (finding that if social work client privilege or privacy rights "were to take precedence over the Board's interest in investigating allegations that one of its licensees was acting in violation of his or her professional obligations, the lack of access to client treatment records could impede a meaningful investigation into that conduct and discovery of a further basis for disciplinary action").

permitting such disclosures, therefore eliminating any conflict between state law and the Privacy Rule that would trigger a preemption.[27] Other courts have concluded that the Privacy Rule does preempt state law, and that the party seeking to disclose or admit the medical records is precluded from doing so without the patient authorization required by the Privacy Rule.[28] These cases demonstrate the difficulties that can arise in analyzing preemption by HIPAA of state laws, and it is likely that court decisions on this issue, because it affects state laws governing physician-patient privilege, will continue to be mixed as courts struggle to interpret and apply the preemption rule to unique state statutes.

It is also likely that valid arguments will be presented against HIPAA preemption and in support of state laws waiving the privilege and permitting the disclosure of PHI in legal proceedings. Parties may rely on several provisions of the Privacy Rule in making these arguments. Disclosures of PHI made in accordance with a court order, subpoena, or other discovery request are consistent with the Privacy Rule's provisions expressly permitting such disclosures.[29] In addition, where a state statute waives the physician-patient privilege, it can be argued that disclosure of the patient's PHI is required by law and may be disclosed in accordance with the Privacy Rule's provision permitting disclosures that are required by law.[30] These arguments are consistent with the position that the Department of Health and Human Services (DHHS) took in its commentary to the Privacy Rule—namely, that that DHHS did not intend to alter the rules of discovery.[31]

Healthcare organizations and practitioners who are confronted with the question of whether the physician-patient privilege has been, or can be, waived in a particular judicial proceeding should seek the advice of qualified legal counsel. This aspect of the Privacy Rule is likely to remain complex and difficult to negotiate until a majority of courts agree on the appropriate interpretation of the HIPAA preemption rules or until DHHS provides specific guidance on the issue.

---

[27] *Hawes v. Golden*, No. 03CA008398, 2004 WL 2244448 (Ohio Ct. App., Sept. 22, 2004); *Smith v. American Home Products Corporation*, 855 A. 2d 608 (N.J. Super. Ct. Law Div. 2003).
[28] *Law v. Zuckerman*, 307 F. Supp. 2d 705 (U.S.D.C. Md. 2004); *Keschecki v. St. Vincent's Medical Center*, 785 N.Y.S. 2d 300 (Sup. Ct. Richmond Co. 2004).
[29] 45 C.F.R. § 164.512(e).
[30] 45 C.F.R. § 164.512(a).
[31] See 65 Fed. Reg. 82554 (Dec. 28, 2000).

Admissibility of Medical Records

As a general matter, medical records are admissible into evidence.[32] All evidence, including medical records information, must be relevant, material, and competent before it can be admitted. Although these three terms often are used as synonyms, they have distinct meanings.

* Evidence is relevant if it tends to prove or disprove a fact at issue in the case
* Evidence is material if it is important to an issue in the case
* Evidence is competent if it is fit and appropriate proof

Thus, a party seeking to admit medical records into evidence must show that the records meet all three tests—unlike in discovery, where a party seeking access to medical records need only argue that the records might be admissible, or might lead to the discovery of admissible evidence.

Medical Records as Hearsay

Hearsay is an out-of-court statement that is introduced into a legal proceeding for the purpose of proving the truth of the facts asserted in that statement. Under traditional rules of evidence, a patient care record is hearsay. Generally, hearsay is not admissible into evidence because the person who actually made the statement is not available to be cross-examined. Consider the example of a nurse who has made an entry regarding the patient's blood pressure. The following problems may result if the record is admitted into evidence as proof of that blood pressure:

* The opposing side cannot ask the nurse about mistakes that the individual may have made in transcribing the record

---

[32] See, generally, James D. Lawlor, Annotation, *Admissibility Under Uniform Business Records as Evidence Act or Similar Statute of Medical Report Made by Consulting Physician to Treating Physician*, 69 A.L.R. 3d 104; Lawlor, Annotation, *Admissibility Under Business Entry Statutes of Hospital Records in Criminal Case*, 69 A.L.R. 3d 22; Lawlor, Annotation, *Admissibility of Hospital Record Relating to Cause or Circumstances of Accident or Incident in Which Patient Sustained Injury*, 44 A.L.R. 2d 553; Donald M. Zupanec, Annotation, *Admissibility Under State Law of Hospital Record Relating to Intoxication or Sobriety of Patient*, 80 A.L.R. 3d 456; Jean F. Rydstrom, Annotation, *Admissibility of Hospital Records Under Federal Business Records Act*, 28 U.S.C. § 1732(a), 9 A.L.R. Fed. 457.

- The jury cannot observe the nurse's demeanor and judge the nurse's veracity
- The jury will be unable to check the records as it would if the records were part of the nurse's testimony in the courtroom

Business Records Exception to the Bar on Hearsay

Although medical records are hearsay, they may be admitted into evidence on other grounds. Many states have enacted the "business records exception" to the bar on hearsay, which allows documents such as medical records to be admitted into evidence without requiring that the person who actually made the entries be available for cross-examination, if the medical records qualify as business records. Business records are typically defined as documents that are made in the regular course of business at the time that, or within a reasonable time after, the recorded event occurred, and under circumstances that reasonably might be assumed to accurately reflect the actual event.[33] Other documents retained by healthcare providers, facilities, and organizations that may qualify as business records include billing records, discharge summaries, and record extracts.[34]

Even if a medical record qualifies as an admissible business record, other standards of admissibility rules may preclude *information in the record* from being entered into evidence. In a patient care record, observations that healthcare providers are trained to make, and that they routinely make in the course of treating patients, will be admissible. In one case, for example, a physician's observation that the patient was intoxicated on arrival at the hospital was held to be admissible.[35] In another, statements regarding the cause of a construction worker's crushed foot were admissible because the information was relevant to diagnosis and treatment.[36] Generally, information in the medical record will be inadmissible if it is not relevant to the patient's diagnosis or treatment. For example:

- A statement in a hospital discharge summary that a patient had fallen from a catwalk around an oil tank was not admissible because

---

[33] See, e.g., Fla. Stat. § 90.803; N.D. Cent. Code § 31-08-01.
[34] *Sandegren v. State*, 397 So. 2d 657 (Fla. 1981).
[35] *Rivers v. Union Carbide Corporation*, 426 F. 2d 633 (3d Cir. 1970).
[36] *Santucci v. Govel Welding, Inc.*, 168 A.D. 2d 845, 564 N.Y.S. 2d 518 (3d Dep't 1990).

the summary was not made at or near the time of the injury, the information was not used to diagnose or treat the patient, and the record did not indicate who gave the physician the information or when it was given[37]

- A statement that an injured bicyclist was not wearing a helmet and accidentally ran into a stationary car was not admissible because the evidence did not indicate who made the statement, and someone other than the bicyclist could have given the information to the hospital staff[38]

- A statement by a truck driver that she slipped on diesel fuel and fell was not admissible because the information was not necessary to the driver's diagnosis or treatment[39]

Other Exceptions to the Bar on Hearsay

Even if a medical record does not qualify as a business record, it may be admissible if it qualifies under another exception to the hearsay rule. Because statements in certain categories are considered to be free of the untrustworthiness and inaccuracy that underlie most out-of-court assertions, they may be admitted into evidence even when the person making the statements is unavailable to testify. (For example, statements made in a moment of surprise are considered trustworthy because the person would have had no time to fabricate a false statement.) Such exceptions include:

- Declarations against interest
- Spontaneous exclamations
- Statements made for medical diagnosis and treatment
- Dying declarations
- Admissions of a party[40]

State statutes also may make medical records admissible under hearsay exceptions for public or official records. This is especially true when state statutes require public hospitals to keep records. The rationale is that the record-keeping requirement ensures that the information

---

[37] *Benson v. Shuler Drilling Company,* 871 S.W. 2d 552 (Ark. 1994).
[38] *Barrera v. Wilson,* 668 A. 2d 871 (D.C. 1995).
[39] *Carton v. Missouri Pacific Railroad Company,* 798 S.W. 2d 674 (Ark. 1990).
[40] See, generally, Fed. R. Evid. 803; Okla. Stat. § 12-2803.

in the record will be reliable. Hospital records also may be admissible under workers' compensation laws. Under Illinois law, for example, medical records, certified as true by a hospital officer and showing medical treatment given to an employee in the hospital, are admissible as evidence of the medical status of the workers' compensation claimant.[41]

Other Healthcare Documentation

Aside from patient records, there are many types of documentation that a healthcare facility, organization, or provider may wish to keep confidential. By the same token, patients and others may seek these documents in the course of a malpractice or other lawsuit. Examples include:

- Credentialing committee minutes, records, and reports
- Joint Commission on Accreditation of Healthcare Organizations and other accreditation surveys and recommendations
- State inspection reports and recommendations
- Mortality committee minutes and records
- Incident reports
- Grand rounds presentations
- Surgical reviews
- Infection control committee minutes and records
- Evaluations of healthcare providers
- Peer review records
- Medical call center protocols
- Care protocols
- Practitioner training materials
- Licensing applications and documents
- Operating room records, such as logs
- Risk management data
- Patient representative/ombudsman records
- Patient complaints
- Profiling data
- Quality improvement documentation
- Utilization review reports

---

[41] 820 Ill. Comp. Stat. Ann. § 305/16.

Generally, these types of records are discoverable unless they are specifically shielded by a state statute. Admissibility, however, may hinge on whether the records fall within an exception to the bar on hearsay. The state statutes that may create a privilege for these categories of records are too various to discuss here. However, two types of documents with a well-established history regarding discovery and admissibility serve as examples: peer review records and incident reports.

Peer Review Records

Healthcare facilities and organizations are required by a variety of governmental, regulatory, and accrediting authorities to establish and maintain programs to monitor and improve the quality of the patient care they provide. What constitutes a "peer review record" will be determined generally by state statutes. Many statutes define the term broadly enough to include the records of almost any quality improvement activity, so long as it is conducted by a committee charged with the responsibility for reviewing the quality of healthcare practitioners in the organization. Documentation relating to broad quality initiatives that do not focus on the performance of individual practitioners, however, may fall outside the statutory definition of "peer review," and may not be afforded protection from discovery.

Quality assurance and peer review programs rely on committees that collect data and generate records on the performance of individual physicians or the treatment of patients. Hospital medical staffs, for example, generally have a medical executive committee, a credentials committee, and various performance evaluation committees to carry out their functions. The value of peer review is well established. In a Connecticut case, the federal district court said that "[t]he overriding importance of these review committees to the medical profession and the public requires that doctors have unfettered freedom to evaluate their peers in an atmosphere of complete confidentiality. No chilling effect can be tolerated if the committees are to function effectively."[42]

The potential value of records generated by such committees to a person suing for negligence is clear, and the demand for access to such records has created a substantial body of law.

The first step in determining whether a peer review record is discoverable or admissible is to examine state statutory and case law.

---

[42] *Morse v. Gerity*, 520 F. Supp. 470 (D. Conn. 1981).

Although there is a great deal of variety between states, similar issues should be considered when analyzing a peer review confidentiality statute:

- Whose communications are protected? Does the statute create a privilege only for peer review committee members, for example, or also for individuals who make reports to the committee? Is the peer review protection limited to physicians, or are other healthcare practitioners included?
- What committees are protected? Some statutes protect the activities of hospital medical staff committees, while others might include other quality assurance, peer review, and utilization review committees individually or generally. The activities of ad hoc committees or individuals, acting outside of bylaws or other established parameters, are not likely to be protected.
- What is the subject of the communication at issue? Generally, statutes require that, to be protected, a committee activity must be motivated by patient care concerns.
- Who is seeking the peer review records? Some statutes specifically allow physicians challenging peer review decisions (on antitrust or defamation grounds, for example) to obtain committee records.
- What communications and information are protected? Some statutes designate as confidential official committee proceedings and reports, but allow independent discovery of information provided to the committee. The identities of committee members and witnesses might also be subject to discovery. State laws might allow discovery of communications volunteered to a committee, but disallow as confidential any information developed at the request of the committee.
- Are there other laws that might create a privilege? With some exceptions, federal laws create a privilege for information provided to qualified quality improvement organizations (QIOs).[43]
- On what authority are the records sought? Some state statutes protect peer review records from subpoena, discovery, or disclosure; other laws simply declare the records confidential or privileged.

The following cases illustrate the high degree of variability in court decisions regarding the discovery of peer review records:

---

[43] 42 U.S.C. § 1320c-9.

- The Pennsylvania peer review privilege does not apply to physician credentialing records created by an independent practitioner model HMO, according to the high court in that state.[44] An independent practice association (IPA) HMO does not come within the definition of healthcare provider in the peer review statute because it is neither a direct provider nor an administrator of a healthcare facility.
- Physician credentialing documents were discoverable in a physician's suit against a hospital for discriminating against him in violation of the Americans with Disabilities Act (ADA), a Louisiana court ruled.[45] Although a state law peer review privilege existed, the court ruled that federal law, which provides no similar privilege, applied.
- The statutory peer review privilege in North Dakota applies only to those committees mandated by the statute, the high court in that state ruled.[46] The court rejected the argument that the activities of all committees performing quality assurance functions are privileged, limiting coverage to committees specifically enumerated in the statute.
- A federal district court in New York held that peer review, quality assurance, and credentialing materials were discoverable in a physician's suit against a hospital for retaliatory harassment, including refusing to recommend renewal of the physician's privileges.[47] The court determined that, although the requested materials were voluminous, they could possibly contain information necessary to prove disparate treatment, which outweighed the protected interest of confidentiality.

Admissibility of Peer Review Records

Even if they are not protected from discovery by state law, peer review and quality assurance committee records may be inadmissible as hearsay. Unlike patient records, committee minutes and reports often do not meet the formal requirements of the business records exception to the hearsay rule. Peer review and quality assurance committees do not generate records at, or reasonably soon after, the time at which the

---

[44] *McClellan v. Health Maintenance Organization,* 686 A. 2d 801 (Pa. 1996).
[45] *Robertson v. Neuromedical Center,* 169 F.R.D. 80 (M.D. La. 1996).
[46] *Trinity Medical Center. v. Holum,* 544 N.W. 2d 148 (N.D. 1996).
[47] *Franzon v. Massena Memorial Hospital,* 189 F.R.D. 220 (N.D.N.Y. 1999).

discussed events occurred. Moreover, committee records usually contain conclusions or opinions that generally are inadmissible.

Another option for a party seeking to admit medical staff committee records into evidence is to obtain the records and allow an expert witness to review them before trial. Under the federal rules of evidence, the expert witness may be able to testify as to the content of the records, by expressing an opinion based, in part, on information "perceived by or made known to the expert at or before the hearing."[48] Further, an expert witness may be able to testify concerning the contents of medical records even though the records are found to have been admitted improperly.[49]

Practical Tips

Because state statutes and court decisions on the protection of peer review and quality assurance activities from discovery vary considerably, participants should carefully review and thoroughly understand the applicable law. Healthcare managers should organize and operate peer review and quality assurance activities in a manner designed to obtain the greatest possible protection available, in consultation with qualified legal counsel. Once policies for committee records are in place, all personnel involved in committee activities should be educated as to the importance of meticulously following those policies. All peer review committee minutes and reports should be prepared carefully, and should demonstrate that the committee performed an objective, considered review. Committee minutes should document actions taken on the matter discussed, and not the details of the actual discussion or personal comments made by committee members. Managers should limit distribution of, and access to, committee minutes and reports to as few individuals and files as possible.

Incident Reports

Incident reports are another type of document likely to be sought during healthcare litigation, but these reports are potentially protected from discovery. A healthcare facility or office generates incident reports

---

[48] Fed. R. Evid. 703. See, e.g., *Wilson v. Clark,* 417 N.E. 2d 1322 (Ill.), *cert. denied*, 102 S. Ct. 140 (1981).
[49] See, e.g., *Wilson v. Clark.*

to document the circumstances surrounding an incident, to alert its insurer or defense counsel to a potential liability situation, and to create data with which to monitor the number and type of incidents occurring in the facility. Incident reports are an essential part of good risk and claims management programs, and, like other records, can be a fertile source of information for parties in litigation.

In many states, incident reports are protected from discovery primarily under the attorney-client privilege and the attorney work product rule. Where legal advice is sought from an attorney, communications between the attorney and the client are privileged and may not be disclosed by the attorney unless the client waives the privilege.[50] Therefore, incident reports that are made for purposes of obtaining legal advice based thereon, or those that are kept confidential and allowed to be accessed only by risk managers and attorneys, may not be discoverable.[51] Because dissemination of incident reports can waive the protection of the attorney-client privilege, it is imperative that the circulation of the reports be strictly limited.

The scope and application of any privilege that may protect incident reports from discovery is highly dependent on state law, the allegations in the lawsuit, the job duties of the individuals developing and reviewing the reports, and the surrounding circumstances. The following decisions illustrate the variability of court rulings and the importance of specific, strictly implemented procedures regarding incident reports:

- An Illinois court ruled that a report written by a coordinator in a hospital's risk management department is not discoverable in a malpractice suit against the hospital.[52] The court observed that the hospital relied on the coordinator's advice and opinions in its decision to settle or litigate matters. The coordinator therefore was entitled to the protection of a privilege when communicating with hospital counsel.
- In a New York case, a federal court ruled that a state confidentiality law did not prevent discovery of hospital incident reports in a civil

---

[50] See Alexander C. Black, Annotation, *What Corporate Communications Are Entitled to Attorney Client Privilege—Modern Cases*, 27 A.L.R. 5th 76.

[51] See *Sierra Vista Hospital v. Superior Court*, 56 Cal. Rptr. 387 (Ct. App. 1967); see also *Scripps Health v. Superior Court of San Diego County*, 109 Cal. App. 4th 529 (2003).

[52] *Mlynarski v. Rush Presbyterian–St. Luke's Medical Center*, 572 N.E. 2d 1025 (Ill. Ct. App. 1991).

rights lawsuit involving the kidnapping of an infant on hospital premises.[53] The parents sued the hospital under federal civil rights laws and sought to discover incident reports prepared about the kidnapping. Although, under state law, incident reports are protected from release in medical malpractice lawsuits, the court ruled that the hospital's interests must give way when violations of constitutional law are involved.

- The Iowa Supreme Court ruled that statements prepared by nurses shortly after an incident and in anticipation of litigation were discoverable because two years had elapsed between the incident and the nurses' depositions, and the nurses were able to recall very little of the event.[54]

- The Texas Court of Appeals held that an incident report completed by an individual in the hospital's security department was discoverable in a premises liability suit against the hospital, even though the hospital maintained a policy pursuant to which "incident reports are prepared immediately following an unusual occurrence to facilitate the peer review investigation process."[55] The appeals court found that it was unclear whether the incident report was necessarily produced for the hospital's peer review committee. Rather, the report appeared to have been prepared as a "routine matter" by the hospital's security department "for purposes of general information gathering." The fact that the peer review committee may have considered the report, the court concluded, did not transform the report into a committee record.[56]

- A New York court permitted discovery of postincident investigation reports.[57] A patient alleging that she was misdiagnosed attempted to discover statements and records relating to an investigation of her case. The court found that the reports were not protected from discovery within a New York statute prohibiting disclosure of records relating to medical review functions. Although peer review investigations are protected by the statute, the hospital could not establish that the incident reports constituted a medical review function.

---

[53] *White v. New York City Health and Hospital Corporation,* 88 Civ. 7536 (S.D.N.Y., Mar. 19, 1990) (unpublished).

[54] *Berg v. Des Moines General Hospital Company,* 456 N.W. 2d 173 (Iowa 1990).

[55] *In re Osteopathic Medical Center,* 16 S.W. 3d 881 (Tex. App. 2000).

[56] Ibid., 886.

[57] *Wiener v. Memorial Hospital for Cancer and Allied Diseases,* 114 Misc. 2d 1013, 453 N.Y.S. 2d 142 (Sup. Ct., N.Y. Co., 1982).

Admissibility of Incident Reports

Because incident reports constitute hearsay, they are inadmissible in evidence unless they fall within one of the exceptions to the hearsay rule. The hearsay exception most frequently cited for the purpose of admitting incident reports into evidence is the business records exception, particularly where the party seeking the reports can show that the reports were made in the routine course of business, at or near the time of the occurrence, and were reported under circumstances that would indicate a high degree of trustworthiness.[58] Although some courts have interpreted "business" narrowly, the trend is toward admitting incident reports that meet the requirements of the business records exception.

Practical Tips

Although it is becoming difficult in some jurisdictions to prevent discovery and admission of incident reports, a healthcare facility, office, or organization that has established incident-reporting procedures should take specific actions to protect its reports. It should:

- treat incident reports as confidential documents, clearly marked as such;
- strictly limit the number of copies made and the distribution of the reports in the institution;
- not place a copy of the report in the patient's medical record or in a file on the patient care unit, although it may retain copies with other quality assurance records;
- limit the content of the report to facts, not conclusions or assignment of blame, and place analyses of the cause of an incident in a separate document;
- address the report and any separate analysis of an incident to the attorney or claims manager by name;
- train personnel to complete incident reports with the same care used in completing a medical record; and
- treat incident reports generally as quality assurance records and subject them to the same stringent policies that are applied to other quality assurance records.

---

[58] See *Fagan v. Newark*, 188 A. 2d 427 (N.J. Super. Ct. App. Div. 1963).

CHAPTER 11

Legal Theories in Improper Disclosure Cases

Chapter Objectives

- Describe how HIPAA affects liability for releasing protected health information
- Describe permitted disclosures under HIPAA and the procedures for enforcing HIPAA
- Describe how state statutes affect liability for releasing medical records information
- List the elements of a defamation claim, and describe when releasing patient information might constitute defamation
- Discuss the privileges against liability for releasing patient information
- Describe the effect of a patient's consent to release information
- Distinguish between a defamation claim and an invasion of privacy claim
- List the types of invasion of privacy claims, and give examples in the health information context
- Discuss the potential liability for publishing patient photographs, releasing patient information to obtain reimbursement, and divulging patient information to the news media
- List the elements of a breach of confidentiality claim, and give examples in the healthcare context

Introduction

Healthcare providers and institutions may face civil and criminal liability for a release of medical records information that has not been authorized by the patient or that has not been made pursuant to statutory, regulatory, or other legal authority. The Health Insurance Portability and Accountability Act (HIPAA)[1] provides for civil liability for enforcement actions initiated by the U.S. Department of Health and Human Services (DHHS), and criminal liability for HIPAA violation enforcement actions initiated by the U.S. Department of Justice. State statutes and regulations may provide for criminal or professional disciplinary sanctions for violating statutory confidentiality requirements, as discussed in examples throughout this book. State laws and regulations may also expressly grant individuals the ability to file civil suits and recover particular damages under specified circumstances. Unlike a criminal proceeding, which is initiated by government officials, a civil lawsuit must be instituted by a private individual, who usually seeks an award of monetary damages. Civil liability also may be grounded in "common law," as established by court decisions.

HIPAA Liability

HIPAA places limitations on the release, transfer, provision of, access to, or divulgence of protected health information (PHI). Under HIPAA, a patient may file a complaint with the DHHS alleging that a covered entity has failed to comply with a provision of HIPAA. Chapter 6 includes a detailed discussion of mandatory and permitted disclosures of PHI under HIPAA, and the elements that the DHHS will look for in measuring a covered entity's compliance with the disclosure requirements.

Violations

The secretary of DHHS is authorized to impose civil monetary penalties (CMPs) of $100 for each violation, up to $25,000 per calendar year for all violations of an identical requirement.[2] The Department of Justice may also impose criminal penalties.[3] If an offense is a criminal violation (enforced by the Department of Justice), a CMP may not also be imposed for that violation. Also, a CMP may not be imposed if the

---

[1]   42 U.S.C. §§ 1320d et seq.
[2]   42 U.S.C. § 1320d-5.
[3]   42 U.S.C. § 51330d-6.

person did not know—and could not have known after exercising reasonable diligence—of the violation, or if the failure to comply was due to reasonable cause and not to willful neglect, and if the violation is corrected during the 30-day period (or such longer period determined by an extension granted by the secretary of DHHS) beginning on the first date the person liable for the penalty knew—or, by exercising reasonable diligence, would have known—that the failure to comply occurred. During the correction period, the secretary may provide such technical assistance as he or she considers appropriate, if the secretary determines that the noncompliance was due to an inability to comply. In addition, a CMP may be reduced to the extent that the payment is excessive relative to the compliance failure. The CMP provisions apply to all HIPAA standards, including those contained in the HIPAA regulations governing the privacy of health information (Privacy Rule) and the security of health information (Security Rule). The procedures for imposition of the CMP are those contained in the Social Security Act relating to violations of the Medicare requirements.[4]

The criminal penalties for violating the Privacy and Security Rules are set forth in the Social Security Act and are enforced by the Department of Justice. The penalties include fines ranging from $50,000 to $250,000 and/or imprisonment ranging from 1 to 10 years, depending upon the severity of the offense. Under HIPAA, it is a criminal offense for any person to knowingly use, or cause to be used, a unique health identifier or to obtain or disclose to another person individually identifiable information. The length of the imprisonment and the amount of the fine vary depending upon whether the offense is a basic offense; whether it is committed under false pretenses; and whether it is committed with intent to sell, transfer, or use individually identifiable health information for commercial advantage, personal gain, or malicious harm. Criminal penalties under HIPAA likely fall within the group of federal laws implicated by the federal sentencing guidelines, and thus may be eligible for abatement.

The position taken initially by DHHS was one of assisting HIPAA covered entities in their compliance with the Privacy and Security Rules. DHHS stated in the preamble to the proposed HIPAA enforcement regulations that the department is "committed to promoting and encouraging voluntary compliance with the HIPAA rules through

---

[4] 42 U.S.C. § 1320a-7a.

education, cooperation and technical assistance." During the two years following the effective date of the Privacy Rule, enforcement activities were primarily complaint driven. How long DHHS will take this rather benign enforcement stance is difficult to predict, but one must keep in mind that the department has not hesitated to enforce vigorously other regulatory schemes that provided substantial revenues to the government through fines and penalties. After a reasonable period of time during which covered entities can be expected to conform their operations to the requirements of the Privacy and Security Rules, healthcare organizations can expect more aggressive enforcement efforts by the DHHS Office for Civil Rights (OCR). Proposed regulations published by OCR suggest that the government will take this more stringent approach to enforcement.[5]

Any person who believes that a covered entity is not complying with a provision of HIPAA may file a written complaint with the secretary of DHHS for the secretary's investigation.[6] The secretary may also conduct compliance reviews to determine whether covered entities are complying with the requirements of HIPAA.[7] In addition, the HIPAA regulations include procedures for addressing and resolving investigations, imposition of penalties, and hearings.[8] There is no private cause of action under HIPAA.[9]

To reduce liability for improper disclosure of PHI, covered entities should disseminate clearly written policies and procedures and take care in training their workforce in appropriate disclosures of PHI. In addition, covered entities will want to maintain communication lines between their compliance departments and members of their workforce to encourage open dialogue regarding appropriate uses and disclosures, and may wish to consider implementing a hotline for reporting potential violations or for requests for clarification.

---

[5] 70 Fed. Reg. 20226-20227 (Apr. 18, 2005).
[6] 45 C.F.R. § 164.306.
[7] 45 C.F.R. § 164.308.
[8] 45 C.F.R. §§ 160.500 through 160.572.
[9] See *University of Colorado Hospital Authority v. Denver Publishing Company*, 340 F. Supp. 2d 1142, 1145 (D. Colo. 2004); *O'Donnell v. Blue Cross Blue Shield of Wyoming*, 173 F. Supp. 2d 1176, 1180 (D. Wyo. 2001); *Brock v. Provident American Insurance Company*, 144 F. Supp. 2d 652, 657 (N.D. Tex. 2001); *Means v. Independent Life and Accident Insurance Company*, 963 F. Supp. 1131, 1135 (M.D. Ala. 1997); *Wright v. Combined Insurance Company of America*, 959 F. Supp. 356, 362–363 (N.D. Miss. 1997).

Other Statutory Bases for Liability

Unless preempted by HIPAA, state statutes may impose both criminal sanctions and civil liability on healthcare providers that disclose medical records information without authorization.[10] A Tennessee law, for example, addresses both types of consequences for breaching confidentiality, making a willful violation of the medical records confidentiality statute a misdemeanor. In addition, hospitals (and their employees, medical and nursing personnel, and officers) in that state may be held liable for civil damages for "willful or reckless or wanton" violations of the confidentiality statute.[11] The Illinois Mental Health and Developmental Disabilities Confidentiality Act more specifically lists the civil remedies available to the patient: "Any person aggrieved by a violation of this Act may sue for damages, an injunction, or other appropriate relief. Reasonable attorney's fees and costs may be awarded to the successful plaintiff in any action under this Act."[12]

In some states, statutes impose specific criminal and/or civil penalties for revealing particular types of medical information, such as a patient's human immunodeficiency virus (HIV) status. For example, in Wisconsin, an individual who negligently discloses a patient's HIV status may be liable for actual damages (which compensate for losses suffered and proved by the patient), as well as $1,000 in punitive, or exemplary, damages (which are intended to punish the violator). An individual who intentionally discloses a patient's HIV status may be liable for up to $5,000 in punitive damages. If the disclosure causes bodily or psychological harm to the patient, the violator may be fined up to $10,000 and sentenced to nine months in jail in a criminal proceeding.[13] Additional examples of statutes prescribing remedies for improper disclosure of particular types of medical information are included throughout this book. The remainder of this chapter discusses civil liability for improper disclosure of medical information. There are no private causes of action for violations of HIPAA. However, a breach

---

[10] State statutes that are contrary to a provision of HIPAA are preempted by HIPAA unless the provision of state law relates to the privacy of individually identifiable health information and is more stringent than a standard, requirement, or implementation specification under HIPAA, 45 C.F.R. §§ 160.203(a) and (b).
[11] Tenn. Code Ann. § 68-11-311.
[12] 740 Ill. Comp. Stat. Ann. § 110/15.
[13] Wis. Stat. § 252.15(8).

of any of these state statutes would most likely also be a breach of HIPAA, such that, in any lawsuit, the plaintiff could add the HIPAA violation as further evidence of bad faith by the healthcare provider.

Theories of Liability

Whether a patient suing to recover monetary damages for release of confidential medical information cites statutory or common law authority to pursue a claim, the patient must state a valid legal theory, or cause of action. The patient must then prove the required "elements" of the cause of action to establish that a compensable injury occurred. Three legal theories pertinent to medical information liability are discussed below: defamation, invasion of privacy, and breach of confidentiality.

Defamation

Defamation is one legal theory under which patients may file civil lawsuits for unauthorized disclosure of medical information. To prevail in a suit for defamation, the patient must prove each of the following:

- a false and defamatory statement about the patient
- "publication" of the statement to a third party
- fault on the part of the publishing person
- either injury caused by the statement, or that the statement falls into a category not requiring proof of injury[14]

A communication is defamatory if it "tends so to harm the reputation of another as to lower him in the estimation of the community or to deter third persons from associating or dealing with him."[15] If the individual bringing the defamation suit is a public official or public figure, that individual must also prove that the speaker knew that the statement was false or acted with reckless disregard of its truth or falsity.[16]

---

[14] Restatement (Second) of Torts § 558.
[15] Restatement (Second) of Torts § 559.
[16] See, e.g., *New York Times Company v. Sullivan*, 376 U.S. 254 (1964); *McKinnon v. Smith*, 275 N.Y.S. 2d 900 (Sup. Ct. 1966), *aff'd*, 300 N.Y.S. 2d 520 (App. Div. 1969).

There are two types of defamation. Traditionally, libel is the written form of defamation; slander, on the other hand, is oral. A libel suit may be pursued without proof of actual damages, although slander suits ordinarily require actual damages, unless the statement falls into a special class of defamatory comments.[17] Thus, even oral disclosure of medical records information by a healthcare provider to an unauthorized person could result in an action for defamation, if the information is false and would adversely affect a person's reputation in the community.

However, a patient's chance of obtaining a recovery against a healthcare provider for defamation for release of medical records information is slight. Medical records entries ordinarily are true. As a general rule, truth of the published statement is an absolute defense to a civil cause of action for libel or slander, irrespective of the publisher's motive. Although the rule has been modified in some states to allow application of the truth defense only where the publisher's motive was good, the traditional rule, even as modified, provides substantial protection for healthcare providers.

Patients who sue healthcare providers for defamation must prove that the defamatory statement was published—that is, that it was revealed to someone other than the patient or a healthcare provider. For example, a state appeals court affirmed a judgment in favor of two physicians when the allegedly libelous statement was contained in a letter that the physicians mailed to the patient.[18] The physicians prepared a letter containing the results of a patient's physical examination, including a statement that the patient had had gonorrhea during his marriage. The statement was not true. When the letter arrived at the patient's home, his wife opened the letter and read it to him over the telephone. The patient and his wife sued the physicians for libel, claiming that the defamatory contents of the letter caused marital discord. The court rejected the patient's suit because the letter was sealed and addressed only to the patient. The letter was not published to the patient's wife, except by the patient, who had asked her to read it to him over the telephone.

---

[17] Restatement (Second) of Torts § 568. An individual suing for slander need not prove that he suffered actual harm if the statement imputes a criminal offense, a loathsome disease, a matter compatible with his profession, or serious sexual misconduct. See also Restatement (Second) of Torts § 570.

[18] *Dowell v. Cleveland Clinic Foundation*, No. 59963 (Ohio Ct. App. 1992) (unpublished).

Privileges Against Defamation

Two privileges may serve as a defense for healthcare providers sued for defamation, even if the patient proves all the elements of a defamation claim. These are absolute privilege and qualified privilege. The absolute privilege protects publications made in legislative, judicial, and administrative proceedings. Thus, statements made in those contexts ordinarily do not serve as the basis for a defamation suit. In a Maryland case, for example, a psychologist's courtroom statements during custody proceedings that a father had sexually abused his child were absolutely privileged, although they were defamatory.[19] There are limits to the scope of absolute privilege, however. One court has stated that a physician who discloses medical records information in connection with a court proceeding may lose the protection of absolute privilege upon disclosing medical information unrelated to the court action.[20]

The second type of privilege—known as conditional, or qualified, privilege—provides protection from defamation liability if the person who publishes the statement reasonably believes that the information affects a sufficiently important interest of the publisher, and the recipient's knowledge of the information serves the lawful protection of that interest.[21] Thus, a court examining whether a statement is protected by qualified privilege will examine the publisher's motive and interest in disclosing the information. The extent of the qualified privilege is uncertain and impossible to reduce to a formula. The disclosure must be justified by the importance of the interest served, and it must be called for by a legal or moral duty, or by generally accepted standards of decent conduct.

For example, a hospital was not liable for defamation for indicating on an insurance claim form that an unmarried 14-year-old was pregnant, because the institution had acted within its qualified privilege.[22] The hospital was required to provide a diagnosis to the insurance company in order to receive compensation for its services. Although the diagnosis of pregnancy was incorrect, the court ruled that the hospital

---

[19] *Rosenberg v. Helsinki*, 616 A. 2d 866 (Md. 1992). See also *O'Barr v. Feist*, 296 So. 2d 152 (Ala. 1974) (letter from physician to probate judge absolutely privileged); *Bond v. Pecaut*, 561 F. Supp. 1037 (N.D. Ill. 1983), *aff'd*, 734 F. 2d 18 (7th Cir. 1984) (letter from psychologist relevant to custody proceedings and within judicial privilege).

[20] *Moses v. McWilliams*, 549 A. 2d 950 (Pa. Super. Ct. 1988).

[21] Restatement (Second) of Torts § 594.

[22] *Edwards v. University of Chicago Hospital*, 484 N.E. 2d 1100 (Ill. Ct. App. 1985).

was shielded from liability by a qualified privilege. Specifically, the hospital had acted in good faith and in pursuit of its valid business interest in obtaining compensation. In addition, the statement was limited in scope to the proper purpose, occasion, manner, and parties, having been disclosed only as required on the standard insurance claim forms. As illustrated by this case, the qualified privilege provides important protection against defamation liability for healthcare providers who release potentially defamatory information to insurers, health plans, utilization reviewers, and others with control over payment for medical services. However, healthcare personnel are cautioned to consider other legal theories and statutes, discussed throughout this chapter and elsewhere in the book, that may create liability.

Courts have also applied the qualified privilege against defamation when the interest of a healthcare provider is not directly affected. Such cases may arise when medical records information is disclosed to employers, insurance companies, litigating parties, news media, or others. For example, an insurance company was sued by one of its insureds after the company had informed an agency subscribed to by other life insurance companies that the insured had a heart condition. The court dismissed the suit, holding that the insurance company's disclosure was shielded by qualified privilege.[23] In a later case based on virtually identical facts, a court found that a qualified privilege to exchange medical information was supported by the insurer's and agency's business interest in the information, as well as by the public's interest in the insurance industry.[24] Another court has held that, in an action predating HIPAA and under that state's privacy statute, a qualified privilege protects parties who disclose medical information where the disclosure is reasonably necessary to protect or further a legitimate business interest.[25]

The qualified privilege may also apply when the release of information serves a public duty, such as protecting the community from highly contagious diseases.[26] For example, in an early case, the Nebraska Supreme Court held a physician not liable for disclosing to the owner

---

[23] *Mayer v. Northern Life Insurance Company,* 119 F. Supp. 536 (N.D. Cal. 1953).
[24] *Senogles v. Security Benefit Life Insurance,* 536 P. 2d 1358 (Kan. 1975); see also *Hauge v. Fidelity Guaranty Life Insurance Company,* No. 91-C-20033 (N.D. Ill. 1992) (unpublished).
[25] *Bratt v. International Business Machines Corporation,* 467 N.E. 2d 126 (Mass. 1984).
[26] Annotation, *Libel and Slander: Privilege of Statements by Physician, Surgeon, or Nurse Concerning Patient,* 73 A.L.R. 2d 325.

of a boardinghouse that a patient living there had a venereal disease.[27] In addition to intimating that the diagnosis was incorrect, the court reasoned that the rules of qualified privilege, under the law of defamation, would govern this case. The physician was held to have had a moral or legal duty to disclose his diagnosis to those persons who might be endangered by this contagious disease. In a more recent decision, a physician who misdiagnosed a patient's pelvic inflammatory disease and told the patient's husband that she had gonorrhea was protected by the qualified privilege.[28] In spite of the holdings in these cases, healthcare providers should be wary of revealing information regarding a patient's contagious status to third parties. Many states now have statutes specifying when and to whom such information may be revealed (see examples in Chapter 9). Further, other legal theories, such as those discussed later in this chapter, may serve as a basis for liability.

A request for information by a totally disinterested party, however, never can create a qualified privilege. For a disclosure to be privileged, the party to whom it is made must have a valid interest in obtaining the information. Whether or not the information was requested or volunteered will help to determine whether the publisher acted in good faith or had a moral duty to communicate. Moreover, it is important to remember that the qualified privilege can be lost if the publisher

- knows the statement is false or recklessly disregards its falsity,
- publishes the statement for an improper purpose,
- excessively publishes the statement, or
- lacks reasonable belief that the publication is necessary to protect the interest.[29]

For example, in one case, a physician's notation in a medical record that the patient's wife may have abused her children was protected by qualified privilege. The patient's wife could proceed with a defamation suit, however, because she produced evidence that the physician abused the privilege by acting with malice.[30] She alleged that there was a heated telephone conversation between the physician and her prior to

---

[27] *Simonsen v. Swenson*, 177 N.W. 831 (Neb. 1920); see also *Shoemaker v. Friedburg*, 183 P. 2d 318 (Cal. Ct. App. 1947).
[28] *Thomas v. Hillson*, 361 S.E. 2d 278 (Ga. Ct. App. 1987).
[29] Restatement (Second) of Torts § 594.
[30] *Strauss v. Thorne*, 490 N.W. 2d 908 (Minn. Ct. App. 1992).

the notation, that the physician said he had made the notation to get back at her, and that the physician refused to remove the notation when he learned that his concerns were not reportable to social services.

Consent as a Defense

Even in the absence of a privilege, a healthcare provider will not be liable for the release of medical information if the patient has consented to or authorized the release. A person who knowingly consents to the release of medical records is barred from bringing a defamation suit when those records subsequently are released. In a Minnesota case, for example, a pilot submitted to a chemical dependency evaluation at the request of his employer.[31] Before the analysis, the pilot had consented to the release of information relating to his evaluation and treatment. The records, which contained the diagnosis of alcoholism, were released to the pilot's employer and the employer's insurance company. The pilot sued the facility where the test was performed and the chemical dependency counselor, alleging that they had defamed him with the diagnosis. Although the pilot admitted that he had signed a release, he contended that he did not consent to the release of the defamatory statements because they did not exist at the time he signed the forms. However, the court found no indication that the pilot did not know the implications of the forms that he signed, and no evidence of fraud or malice on the part of those who had prepared the reports. The court concluded that the pilot could not sue for defamation.

Healthcare providers should take care, however, not to exceed the scope of a patient's consent or authorization to release medical records information. If the disclosure of the record exceeds the scope of the authorization given by the patient or other appropriate person, the disclosure will be unauthorized, and therefore unprotected in the event of a defamation suit.

To avoid defamation cases, healthcare personnel are well advised to take the conservative approach and withhold medical records information unless they find exceptionally good reasons to disclose it. They should establish appropriate reasons for disclosure with the help of their legal counsel, and should set forth those reasons in their health information policies.

---

[31] *Williamson v. Stocker*, No. 4-79-335 slip op. (D. Minn., Dec. 21, 1982) (unpublished); see also *Clark v. Geraci*, 208 N.Y.S. 2d 564 (Sup. Ct. 1960).

Invasion of Privacy

A second legal theory upon which a patient could base a suit for improper release of medical information is invasion of privacy. Because health information is highly personal, improper disclosure of patient information to unauthorized individuals, agencies, or news media may make a hospital liable to the patient for an invasion of privacy. A cause of action for invasion of privacy can be based on state common law, state or federal constitutional law, or state statutory law.[32] The purpose of the right is to protect against mass dissemination of information concerning private, personal matters. A claim for invasion of privacy will be successful only if the challenged publication is not a matter of legitimate public concern and would be highly offensive to a reasonable person.[33] Some courts have held that an oral publication alone cannot constitute an invasion of privacy, although others have allowed recovery, especially where the plaintiff proved actual damages.[34]

The theories of defamation and invasion of privacy are similar in terms of the circumstances that may create liability. However, several factors distinguish the two causes of action:

- Truth of the information published is not a defense to an invasion of privacy suit, although it is a defense in a defamation suit. Thus, an unauthorized disclosure even of accurate medical information could subject a hospital to liability for invasion of a patient's privacy.
- To recover for an invasion of privacy, the plaintiff need not prove special damages, unlike the plaintiff in a defamation action, who often must prove that the disclosure actually harmed him or her.
- The two theories provide redress for different types of injury. A cause of action for invasion of privacy focuses on the harm a disclosure has caused to the plaintiff's feelings. Thus, a plaintiff in an action for invasion of privacy may recover even for the disclosure of favorable information. Defamation, on the other hand, focuses on the injury to the plaintiff's reputation.
- Although an action for invasion of privacy often involves publication, it is not a necessary element for recovery. Thus, discovery of

---

[32]   See *A.L.A. v. West Valley City*, 26 F. 3d 989 (10th Cir. 1994).
[33]   Restatement (Second) of Torts § 652D.
[34]   I. J. Schiffres, Annotation, *Invasion of Right of Privacy by Merely Oral Declarations*, 19 A.L.R. 3d 1318.

private information by a single person can invade an individual's privacy. The law of defamation normally requires publication to a second person.

The common law has established several types of invasion of privacy claims:

* unreasonable intrusion upon the seclusion of another
* appropriation of another's name or likeness
* unreasonable publicity of another's private life
* unreasonable publicity that places another in a false light[35]

Invasion of privacy claims based on state or federal constitutions, as opposed to those rooted in common law, occur less frequently. A patient who brings a claim for improper disclosure of medical information based on the federal or state constitution typically must show that the individual had a "reasonable expectation of privacy" concerning the information that was disclosed.[36] Courts will consider factors such as the content of the disclosure and the circumstances under which the patient provided the information to the healthcare worker.

A patient may also sue a healthcare provider under a state statute creating a right to sue for certain invasions of privacy. For example, the Massachusetts statute states that "[a] person shall have a right against unreasonable, substantial, or serious interference with his privacy."[37]

If a patient consents to or authorizes disclosure of patient information, he or she cannot later successfully claim that the disclosure was an invasion of privacy, if the disclosure was within the scope of the consent.[38] Thus, healthcare providers should obtain a patient's written consent or authorization before releasing medical information. If a patient verbally authorizes a disclosure, but refuses to sign an authorization form, healthcare personnel should note the verbal consent, properly sign and date the note, and insert it into the patient's medical record. If the healthcare personnel are covered entities or are employees

---

[35] Restatement (Second) of Torts § 652A.
[36] See, e.g., *Urbaniak v. Newton*, 226 Cal. App. 3d 1128 (Ct. App. 1991).
[37] Mass. Ann. Laws ch. 214, § 1B.
[38] See, e.g., *Clark*. Patient had authorized physician to disclose incomplete information about his illness; plaintiff therefore could not claim that he had not consented to the disclosure of the underlying cause of the illness—alcoholism.

of a covered entity under the HIPAA privacy regulations (Privacy Rule), the patient's authorization must contain the information specified in the Privacy Rule. (See Chapter 6 for a detailed discussion of HIPAA authorizations.)

Healthcare institutions, organizations, and providers should protect against invasion of privacy claims by developing and implementing policies and procedures that address problematic circumstances. Confidentiality policies should be written clearly, avoiding vague language.[39] The following discussion illustrates some problematic circumstances where clear and widely disseminated policies can reduce invasion of privacy liability risks.

Photographs

The use of photographs in medical care creates a potential for invasion of privacy actions under more than one type of claim. Courts have held healthcare providers liable for the *appropriation of likeness* type of invasion of privacy, primarily where the provider exploited the patient for commercial benefit. However, courts also have imposed liability where a healthcare provider used a patient's name or likeness for a noncommercial benefit under the *intrusion upon seclusion* type of invasion of privacy. This theory can lead to liability even if the photographs were not published. In an early Pennsylvania case, for example, the court prohibited a physician from using photographs of a patient's facial development in connection with medical instruction.[40] The court found that even taking the picture without the patient's express consent was an invasion of privacy; in order to establish liability, it was not necessary to show that the physician had used the photographs improperly or had shown them to others. A court in Maine reached a similar conclusion in a case in which a physician photographed a terminally ill patient shortly before his death.[41] The court rejected the physician's argument that his scientific interest in the photograph justified taking the picture. The court held that unauthorized photography under such circumstances

---

[39] See, e.g., *Group Health Plan, Inc. v. Lopez*, 341 N.W. 2d 294 (Minn. Ct. App. 1983).
[40] *Clayman v. Bernstein*, 38 Pa. D. & C. 543 (1940).
[41] *Estate of Berthiaume v. Pratt*, 365 A. 2d 792 (Me. 1976).

would constitute an invasion of privacy, whether or not the photographs were published.[42]

Publication of photographs also may subject healthcare providers to liability under the type of invasion of privacy known as *unreasonable publicity of private life*. For example, a court ruled that a physician had invaded a patient's privacy by using "before-and-after" photos of her face on television and at a department store presentation to demonstrate the effects of a face-lift.[43] The use of the photographs publicized the fact that the patient had had a face-lift, which she found embarrassing and distressing. The court held that the patient's right to privacy outweighed the public's general interest in plastic surgery, and held the physician liable.[44]

Finally, full face photographic images and other comparable images of patients constitute PHI under the Privacy Rule.[45] Therefore, covered entities may disclose these photographs only pursuant to a valid patient authorization or otherwise as specifically permitted by the Privacy Rule.

Health information policies should establish the circumstances under which a patient may be photographed. Photographs taken in connection with scientific research should be part of a research protocol approved by an appropriate institutional review board or privacy board. (For a detailed discussion of the use of health information in human subject research, see Chapter 14.) All other photographs of patients should be taken in accordance with institutional or organizational policies and procedures. In general, these policies should require approval of such photography by an appropriate healthcare administrator.

---

[42] See also *Bazemore v. Savannah Hospital*, 155 S.E. 194 (Ga. 1930). For a discussion of taking unauthorized photographs as invasion of privacy in this and other contexts, see Phillip E. Hassman, Annotation, *Taking Unauthorized Photographs as Invasion of Privacy*, 86 A.L.R. 3d 374.

[43] *Vassiliades v. Garfinckel's, Brooks Brothers*, 492 A. 2d 580 (D.C. 1985).

[44] When an individual's name or likeness is published in connection with a newsworthy event, the person does not have an action for invasion of privacy. See also *Gilbert v. Medical Economics Company*, 665 F. 2d 305 (10th Cir. 1981) (newsworthiness of physician's psychiatric history precludes liability for disclosure). See discussion under "Disclosure to the News Media" in this chapter.

[45] 45 C.F.R. § 164.514(b)(2).

Invasion of Privacy Within the Healthcare Setting

Courts have found an unwarranted intrusion upon the plaintiff's seclusion or private concerns where the defendant monitored the plaintiff's telephone calls or bedroom, invaded the plaintiff's house, or in other ways intruded in an objectionable manner into the plaintiff's concerns. Monitoring a patient's telephone conversations from the hospital may subject an institution not only to liability for invasion of privacy, but also to liability under federal statutes prohibiting the interception of private communications.[46] Also, in allowing nonmedical personnel to witness medical procedures or to examine a patient without the patient's consent, the invasion of the patient's privacy may lead to litigation.[47] Teaching hospitals, especially, should be certain their patients understand that they will be participating in the education and training of medical, nursing, and other students who may observe or assist in treatment.

Payment-Related Disclosures

It is unlikely that a healthcare institution, organization, individual provider, or other personnel will be held liable for invasion of privacy upon releasing medical records information for the purpose of obtaining reimbursement. Court decisions have established that publication of information to an extent reasonably calculated to serve the legitimate interests of the publisher does not constitute a common law invasion of privacy.[48] This restriction is similar to the qualified privilege in defamation actions. Thus, release or disclosure of information in the medical record to individuals such as insurance company representatives and utilization reviewers for purposes of reimbursement ordinarily would not constitute an invasion of the common law right of privacy.[49] At least one court has extended this type of privilege to pro-

---

[46] *Gerrard v. Blackman*, 401 F. Supp. 1189 (N.D. Ill. 1975).

[47] See *Knight v. Penobscot Bay Medical Center*, 420 A. 2d 915 (Me. 1980). The viewing of plaintiff's delivery of a child by the nurse's husband was found, under the circumstances, not to be an invasion of privacy.

[48] See, generally, *Voneye v. Turner*, 240 S.W. 2d 588 (Ky. Ct. App. 1951); *Patton v. Jacobs*, 78 N.E. 2d 789 (Ind. Ct. App. 1948); *Lewis v. Physicians & Dentists Credit Bureau*, 177 P. 2d 896 (Wash. 1947).

[49] *Pennison v. Provident Life & Accident Insurance Company*, 154 So. 2d 617 (La. Ct. App. 1963) (disclosure to plaintiff's insurance company not an invasion of privacy); *Edwards* (no liability where hospital publishes diagnosis in standard insurance claim form to obtain payment); Joel E. Smith, Annotation, *Exchange Among Insurers of Medical Information Concerning Insured or Applicant for Insurance as Invasion of Privacy*, 98 A.L.R. 3d 561.

vide a shield from liability for even constitutional invasion of privacy.[50] The court held that an employer who reviewed prescription drug benefit records for the purpose of controlling costs did not violate an employee's constitutional right to privacy. The prescription drug records, obtained by the employer's drug benefit vendor, linked employee names with specific medications, revealing that the employee was HIV-positive. The court concluded that the employer's interest in controlling costs outweighed the employee's right to privacy.

In addition, the Privacy Rule specifically permits covered entities to disclose PHI in connection with payment activities without a patient's authorization.[51] Thus, a covered healthcare provider may use or disclose PHI in the course of billing and collecting payment for the services it provided.

Statutory provisions may also protect providers from actions based on payment-related disclosures. In Massachusetts, for example, an exception in the patient bill of rights statute says that confidentiality of records provisions shall not prevent any third-party reimburser from inspecting and copying all records relating to diagnosis, treatment, or other services to determine benefits, as long as the patient's insurance policy permits access to the records.[52]

Disclosure to the News Media

The circumstance most likely to create invasion of privacy questions may be the release of patient information to news entities. (For a related discussion on protecting the confidentiality of celebrity patients, see Chapter 8.) In addition, disclosures to the news media of material that contains PHI are prohibited by the Privacy Rule unless the disclosures are made pursuant to a valid patient authorization or to one of the other provisions of the rule permitting disclosure without an authorization.

A healthcare provider has no legal obligation to disclose medical records information to news media. In some states, statutes limit the dissemination of medical records information to certain entities or individuals that the state has deemed to have a legitimate interest in the information, such as courts, arbitrators, government and private commissions, insurers, employee benefit plans, and medical staffs.[53]

---

[50] *Doe v. SEPTA*, 72 F. 3d 1133 (3d Cir. 1995).
[51] 45 C.F.R. § 164.506(c)(1).
[52] Mass. Ann. Laws ch. 111, § 70E.
[53] See, e.g., Cal. Civ. Code § 56.10.

Before the enactment of HIPAA, healthcare institutions and organizations were permitted to release patient information to the media under certain circumstances, unless prohibited by statute. Announcements of patient admissions, discharges, or births posed no problem, for example, unless a facility specialized in the care of patients with specific diseases that were considered shameful or embarrassing.[54] Since the effective date of the Privacy Rule (April 2003), however, healthcare institutions that are covered entities may not release PHI to news media without the patient's authorization. Covered entities may disclose certain PHI as part of their facility directories so long as they give the patient the opportunity to opt out of a directory.[55] If the patient does not object, the directory may include the patient's name, location in the facility, general condition, and religious affiliation, and the institution may disclose all of the information except religious affiliation to anyone who asks for the patient by name.[56] (For a more detailed discussion of facility directories, see Chapter 6.)

Some health information has always been considered too sensitive to release to news media. A drug or alcohol addiction rehabilitation center, for example, should not release the names of patients. (See the discussion of the disclosure of alcohol and drug abuse patient records in Chapter 6.) Even where releasing general information is permissible, the scope of the information should be considered carefully. To publicize the fact that a particular patient gave birth to a normal healthy baby may not be considered an invasion of privacy, for instance, but to publicize the fact that the baby was conceived through artificial insemination might be actionable.

A healthcare entity that discloses medical records information to the news media may be sued for common law invasion of privacy under two theories: (1) unreasonable publicity of another's private life, or (2) unreasonable publicity that places another in a false light. However, a healthcare provider will not be liable for invasion of privacy if the information disclosed to the news media is newsworthy or a matter of legitimate public interest. If the patient is a public figure, the person's prominence, in itself, makes virtually all of the patient's doings of interest to the public, and therefore not subject to invasion of privacy ac-

---

[54] See *Koudsi v. Hennepin County Medical Center*, 317 N.W. 2d 705 (Minn. 1982).
[55] 45 C.F.R. § 164.510(a).
[56] 45 C.F.R. § 164.510(a)(1)(ii)(B).

tions.[57] Relatively obscure people voluntarily may take certain actions that bring them before the public, or they may be victims of newsworthy occurrences, such as accidents, crimes, and so forth, thus making them of interest to the public.[58] The latitude extended under state law to the publication of the personal matters, names, photographs, and other such information of public figures varies. Under the Privacy Rule, however, such disclosures are prohibited if they contain PHI, unless the patient has provided an authorization or the disclosure is otherwise expressly permitted by the Privacy Rule.

Ordinary citizens who voluntarily adopt a course of action that is newsworthy cannot complain if their names and pictures are published. For example, a patient who filed a $38 million medical malpractice lawsuit in 1991 against a physician was not entitled to sue the physician later for invasion of privacy when the physician informed a newspaper reporter that the patient was HIV-positive.[59] The court held that medical malpractice lawsuits, particularly those for large monetary sums, were a matter of legitimate public interest. By filing such a suit, the patient was precluded from later claiming that his privacy had been invaded by the physician's public comments regarding the suit. The physician revealed the HIV status to explain why the patient had not been diagnosed accurately. Under the Privacy Rule, a physician would not be able to disclose PHI, and certainly not HIV status, to news media without the patient's authorization. If the physician were required to disclose PHI in responsive pleadings in the lawsuit, he or she would have to seek a protective order from the court to prevent the pleadings from becoming public documents. (See the discussion of disclosures of PHI in judicial proceedings in Chapter 8.)

In another case, HIV-positive individuals who revealed their identities in numerous panel discussions, publications, and meetings could not later sue when their names were published in a "living with HIV"

---

[57] See, e.g., *Cason v. Baskin*, 30 So. 2d 635 (Fla. 1947); Jeffrey F. Ghent, Annotation, *Waiver or Loss of Privacy*, 57 A.L.R. 3d 16.

[58] For example, in *Estate of Hemingway v. Random House, Inc.*, 244 N.E. 2d 250 (N.Y. 1968), Ernest Hemingway's widow was unable to recover for invasion of privacy against an author for a memoir describing the widow's personal feelings and relationship with her husband. In *Howell v. New York Post Company*, 612 N.E. 2d 699 (N.Y. 1993), a patient whose photo, showing her walking alongside a public figure on the grounds of a psychiatric facility, was published on the front page of the newspaper could not recover for invasion of privacy.

[59] *Lee v. Calhoun*, 948 F. 2d 1162 (10th Cir. 1991), *cert. denied*, 504 U.S. 973 (1992).

government program guide.[60] By revealing their names in other contexts, they had waived their right to privacy.

An illness or an accident also may be newsworthy.[61] Courts have held that the name and photograph of the victim of a circumstance that itself is newsworthy may be published.[62] However, the court may distinguish between the newsworthiness of the event and the newsworthiness of the identity of the individual involved. One court has ruled that, even when a particular medical condition is of interest to the public, hospitals that reveal the identity of individuals with that condition are subject to invasion of privacy actions.[63] In that case, a married couple who participated in a hospital's in vitro fertilization program sued the hospital for invasion of privacy. The couple attended the hospital's private social function for in vitro participants. Although they refused to be interviewed and avoided a news crew attending the event, the couple appeared on a televised news report. The court ruled that the couple could sue the hospital, reasoning that although in vitro fertilization may be of interest to the general public, individual involvement in such a program is a private matter.

Similarly, a Missouri court held that a magazine could be liable for invasion of privacy when it published the name and picture of a patient in a story titled "Starving Glutton" concerning the patient's hospitalization to treat her constant desire to eat, possibly caused by pancreatic dysfunction.[64] The magazine's employees had obtained the patient's picture by surreptitious means and over her express objections. Holding that the patient was entitled to recover, the court said that "certainly if there is any right of privacy at all, it should include the right to obtain medical treatment at home or in a hospital for an individual per-

---

[60] *Doe v. Marsh*, No. 96-7453 (2d Cir., Oct. 7., 1996) (unpublished).
[61] See, e.g., *The Home News v. New Jersey*, 677 A. 2d 195 (N.J. 1996) (newspaper may receive cause of death information about boy who died under suspicious circumstances).
[62] *Bremmer v. Journal-Tribune Publishing Company*, 76 N.W. 2d 762 (Iowa 1956) (publication of mutilated dead boy's picture); *Kelley v. Post Publishing Company*, 98 N.E. 2d 286 (Mass. 1951) (publication of automobile accident victim's picture); *Jones v. Herald Post Company*, 18 S.W. 2d 972 (Ky. 1929) (publication of picture of murder victim's wife who had struggled with her husband's assailants); *Metter v. Los Angeles Examiner*, 95 P. 2d 491 (Cal. Ct. App. 1939) (publication of picture of one who committed suicide). See also Irwin J. Schiffres, Annotation, *Invasion of Privacy by Use of Plaintiff's Name or Likeness for Nonadvertising Purposes*, 30 A.L.R. 3d 203.
[63] *Y.G. v. Jewish Hospital of St. Louis*, 795 S.W. 2d 488 (Mo. Ct. App. 1990).
[64] *Barber v. Time, Inc.*, 159 S.W. 2d 291 (Mo. 1942).

sonal condition (at least if it is not contagious or dangerous to others) without personal publicity. . . ." The court found that although the patient's ailment was of some interest to the public, her identity was not. Publishing the patient's name and picture, which conveyed no medical information, thus was an invasion of her privacy.[65]

Further, as time passes, the identity of the participant in such an event loses importance, and action for invasion of privacy becomes more likely. However, the publisher need not prove that the event was "currently newsworthy" or published contemporaneously. In determining whether the matter publicized is of legitimate public interest, courts will consider the length of time that has passed between the "event" and publication, along with other factors such as community standards and the importance of the matter published.[66]

Although healthcare providers should be reluctant to release patient information to the news media, release of information of legitimate news value may be appropriate in some cases. In such circumstances, the risk of liability is dependent on the specific nature of the disclosure. The fact that a patient is newsworthy does not require the release of information; it simply may protect the provider who chooses to disclose the information. The patient's condition may not create liability exposure, but disclosing more detailed information or a photograph without the individual's consent should be avoided. A healthcare organization or institution that releases specific information about a patient who participates in a newsworthy event may be protected from an invasion of privacy action. However, the best policy that healthcare administrators can adopt is to refuse to release any information (other than the status of the patient) without the patient's consent.

Breach of Confidentiality

Yet another legal theory under which a patient may sue a healthcare provider who improperly discloses medical records information is breach of confidentiality, also known as breach of physician-patient privilege. The general rule is that a physician who violates the physician-

---

[65] See also *Vassiliades* (plastic surgery patient entitled to expect that photos would not be published, even though plastic surgery is matter of general public interest).

[66] See *Montesano v. Donrey Media Group*, 668 P. 2d 1081 (Nev. 1983), *cert. denied*, 466 U.S. 959 (1984); *Romaine v. Kallinger*, 537 A. 2d 284 (N.J. 1988).

patient privilege is liable to the patient.[67] A patient who successfully sues for breach of the physician-patient privilege is entitled to damages to compensate for harm caused by the disclosure, such as deterioration of a marriage, the loss of a job, or emotional distress.[68]

In some states, the scope, application, and waiver of the privilege are governed by statute.[69] In other states, the privilege was developed in common law, by court decisions. In recognizing the privilege, some courts have relied on a public policy that favors the protection of the confidential relationship between physician and patient. These courts have typically pointed to professional conduct statutes, physician licensing statutes, and medical records confidentiality statutes as evidence of the social importance of the physician-patient privilege.[70]

A Nebraska court has described what a patient must prove to invoke the physician-patient privilege.[71] The patient must show all of the following elements:

- That a physician-patient relationship existed
- That the information was acquired during the relationship
- That the information was necessary for the physician's treatment of the patient in a professional capacity

Which categories of healthcare providers have a duty of confidentiality to their patients has not been definitively established, and varies from state to state. In South Carolina, for example, a court held that a pharmacy patient could sue the pharmacy for defamation, but not for

---

[67] See, e.g., *Crescenzo v. Chane*, 796 A. 2d 283 (N.J. Super. Ct., May 6, 2002); *Stempler v. Speidell*, 495 A. 2d 857 (N.J. 1985); *Anker v. Brodnitz*, 413 N.Y.S. 2d 582 (Sup. Ct. 1979); *Alberts v. Devine*, 479 N.E. 2d 113 (Mass. 1985); *Horne v. Patton*, 287 So. 2d 824 (Ala. 1973). For an overview of which states have recognized this cause of action, see Judy E. Zelin, Annotation, *Physician's Tort Liability for Unauthorized Disclosure of Confidential Information*, 48 A.L.R. 4th 668.

[68] See *MacDonald v. Clinger*, 446 N.Y.S. 2d 801 (App. Div. 1982).

[69] J. R. Kemper, Annotation, *Commencing Action Involving Physical Condition of Plaintiff or Decedent as Waiving Physician-Patient Privilege as to Discovery Proceedings*, 21 A.L.R. 3d 912.

[70] See, e.g., *Bryson v. Tillinghast*, 749 P. 2d 110 (Okla. 1988); *Stempler; Geisberger v. Willuhn*, 390 N.E. 2d 945 (Ill. Ct. App. 1979); *Schaffer v. Spicer*, 215 N.W. 2d 134 (S.D. 1974); *Horne; Hammonds v. Aetna Casualty and Surety Company*, 243 F. Supp. 793 (N.D. Ohio 1965); *Hague v. Williams*, 181 A. 2d 345 (N.J. 1962); *Clark; Berry v. Moench*, 331 P. 2d 814 (Utah 1958).

[71] *Branch v. Wilkinson*, 256 N.W. 2d 307 (Neb. 1977). See also *State v. Randle*, 484 N.W. 2d 220 (Iowa Ct. App. 1992).

breach of confidentiality.[72] A pharmacy employee had falsely told others that the patient was being treated for venereal disease. The court determined that pharmacists have no duty of confidentiality toward their patients. A Rhode Island court ruled that prescription drug information is confidential health information, however.[73] In Indiana, an appeals court rejected a patient's claim that there is a nurse-patient privilege.[74] State statutes may be helpful in identifying the healthcare providers who owe a duty of confidentiality. In Mississippi, for example, all communications made to a physician, osteopath, dentist, hospital, nurse, pharmacist, podiatrist, optometrist, or chiropractor by a patient under his or her charge or by one seeking professional advice are privileged.[75]

The scope of the information protected by the physician-patient privilege also may be a subject of dispute. In some cases, even a physician's list of patients may be protected. The Supreme Court of Nevada, for example, refused to order a plastic surgeon to reveal his patient list, because to do so would have violated the physician-patient privilege.[76] The court ruled that, although disclosure of a patient's name does not always violate the physician-patient privilege, the names are protected if the nature of the treatment is disclosed. To avoid liability for breaching the physician-patient privilege, healthcare providers and facilities providing specialized treatment, such as drug rehabilitation centers, should take care to protect the confidentiality of the identity of their patients. Finally, a Washington court ruled that, pursuant to a Washington statute,[77] a patient may bring a tort action for the damages resulting from an unauthorized disclosure of any patient information related to the health of the patient that was obtained within the physician-patient relationship.[78]

Defenses Against Breach of Confidentiality

As in defamation and invasion of privacy cases, a privilege may serve as a defense to a breach of confidentiality claim against a healthcare

---

[72] *Evans v. Rite Aid Corporation*, 478 S.E. 2d 846 (S.C. 1996).
[73] *Washburn v. Rite Aid Corporation*, 695 A. 2d 495 (R.I. 1997).
[74] *Darnell v. Indiana*, 674 N.E. 2d 19 (Ind. Ct. App. 1996).
[75] Miss. Code Ann. § 13-1-21.
[76] *Hetter v. Sanchez*, 874 P. 2d 762 (Nev. 1994).
[77] Wash. Rev. Code § 7.70.030(1).
[78] *Berger v. Sonneland*, 1 P. 3d 1187 (2001).

provider. For example, a disclosure is typically privileged if failure to divulge medical records information would jeopardize the health or safety of the patient or others.[79] In one case, the Supreme Court of Oklahoma held that a patient could not sue for breach of the physician-patient privilege when a physician revealed medical information to police, leading to the patient's arrest for rape.[80] A patient sought treatment at a hospital for a bite wound on his genitals. A physician who treated the patient later learned that police were looking for a suspected rapist with that injury. The physician told the police about the patient, leading to his arrest. The patient sued the physician for breaching the physician-patient privilege. The court dismissed the suit, holding that the physician-patient privilege was not designed to protect criminals from apprehension. The court also ruled that a public policy exception allows physicians to reveal otherwise confidential medical information when the information will benefit the public.[81]

In several jurisdictions, a patient waives the physician-patient privilege, foreclosing claims for breach of the privilege, by putting information exchanged within the privilege at issue in a lawsuit—for example, a medical malpractice lawsuit.[82] However, courts disagree as to the scope of the waiver. (This issue is discussed in detail in Chapter 10.)

Patient consent to, or authorization for, disclosure is another defense to a breach of confidentiality suit, although the disclosure must be carefully tailored to remain within the scope of the patient's consent or authorization. In an interesting case involving the newspaper publication of a patient's photograph that was taken in a hospital's AIDS clinic waiting room, a New York appeals court ruled that a patient could sue the hospital and a treating physician for breach of privilege because he had consented to the picture only after they had assured him that he would not be recognizable.[83] When the photograph was published, a friend recognized the patient. Although the court ruled that the hospital had not violated the privilege simply by allowing the media to be present in the waiting room of its infectious disease unit, it held that the physician-patient privilege protects the identity of a patient, as well

---

[79] See, e.g., *Horne.*
[80] *Bryson.*
[81] See also *Mull v. String,* 448 So. 2d 952 (Ala. 1984).
[82] See, e.g., *Fedell v. Wierzbieniec,* 485 N.Y.S. 2d 460 (Sup. Ct. 1985). For a discussion of which jurisdictions have adopted this view, see Kemper.
[83] *Anderson v. Strong Memorial Hospital,* 542 N.Y.S. 2d 96 (App. Div. 1989).

as the treatment provided. The court concluded that the hospital and physician had possibly breached the privilege by making such assurances and by not informing the patient that the photographer was with the local media.

The same advice for reducing liability for defamation and invasion of privacy applies to breach of confidentiality. Clearly written and widely disseminated policies and procedures concerning the confidentiality of patient information will decrease the likelihood that confidential information will be released in breach of the physician-patient privilege. Healthcare administrators should implement guidelines that healthcare and health information professionals can understand and follow.

CHAPTER 12

Risk Management and Quality Management

Chapter Objectives

- Introduce the areas of risk management and quality management, and describe the increasing focus in the healthcare industry on reducing medical errors and improving the quality of care

- Compare and contrast risk management and quality management

- Describe the four principal steps in the risk management process

- List some of the data, documents, and records that a risk manager relies on to identify risks

- List the activities that are part of the quality management process

- Discuss the increasing use of health information technology to help reduce medical errors, improve communication, and therefore increase the quality of care and better evaluate various healthcare interventions

- Describe the elements that must be part of an effective compliance program according to the federal sentencing guidelines, and discuss the guidelines for compliance issued by the Office of Inspector General (OIG) of the U.S. Department of Health and Human Services (DHHS)

- Identify laws that a healthcare organization should consider when creating a corporate compliance program

- Discuss the role of medical records as part of the data used in risk management, quality management, compliance activities, and pay for performance initiatives

Introduction

Risk management and quality management programs depend in large measure on medical records and health information professionals for information necessary to identify potential risks. Health information professionals, therefore, can contribute significantly to the success of risk management and quality management programs. To do so, they must have a good working knowledge of risk management principles, risk management and quality management program objectives, and the effect of medical records information on the management of potential risk. Corporate compliance programs also are an important aspect of a healthcare organization's risk management and quality management plans. A compliance program can reduce the risk of criminal prosecution or civil suits, reduce criminal fines, establish a way to communicate legal and organizational requirements to all staff, and monitor compliance with legal and organizational requirements.

This chapter discusses generally the relationship between quality management and risk management; the definition and components of risk management, quality management, and corporate compliance programs; and the use of medical records in these programs.

Increased Scrutiny of Medical Errors and Demand for Improving Quality Care

In 1999, the Institute of Medicine released its landmark report indicating that as many as 100,000 deaths occur each year in the United States because of medical errors and other adverse events that affect patient safety.[1] Since then, concerns about the need to reduce medical errors have yet to dissipate. A major effect of the report has been its ability to encourage improvements in patient safety by key healthcare participants, starting with the federal government.

In 2001, Congress appropriated $50 million for patient safety research. Soon thereafter, Congress named the Agency for Healthcare Research and Quality (AHRQ) as the lead federal agency for patient safety. AHRQ established the Center for Quality Improvement and

---

[1] *To Err Is Human: Building a Safer Health Care System* (Washington, D.C.: National Academy Press, 1999).

Patient Safety, which has become the primary source for developing guidelines and setting standards for furthering patient safety efforts. Some of the areas of risk management that have been, and continue to be, investigated include infection control, clinical incidents, incident reporting policies, fraud, clinical risk management, drug administration, security, the movement of patients, and food hygiene policies.

Nongovernmental organizations such as the Joint Commission on Accreditation of Healthcare Organizations (Joint Commission), the Centers for Medicare & Medicaid Services (CMS), the Centers for Disease Control and Prevention (CDC), the National Patient Safety Foundation, and the Institute for Healthcare Improvement, to name a few, also have undertaken efforts to create guidelines for the performance of in-depth analyses of the underlying causes of medical errors, as well as prospective analyses to create preventive opportunities without actually having to experience the adverse event. These two tasks—risk management and quality management—are widely considered to be the cornerstones for creating an environment geared toward preventing, detecting, and minimizing hazards and the likelihood of medical error.

Relationship Between Risk Management and Quality Management

The purposes of risk management and quality management often are viewed as complementary. The patient-safety aspect of risk management—preventing events most likely to lead to patient injury—is the area of greatest interaction between quality management and risk management. Poor quality care that creates a risk of injury to patients poses financial risks both to healthcare practitioners and to healthcare facilities. Identification and resolution of problems in patient care—the foundations of quality management—ultimately prevent events that may result in patient injury, and consequently reduce the potential risk of malpractice liability to the healthcare provider. Quality management and risk management use similar methodologies to achieve their common aim of ensuring patient safety. Both depend on the establishment of screening criteria, collection and analysis of data pertaining to those criteria, and correction of identified problems through improvements in individual practices and in the system-wide delivery of care throughout an institution.

Nevertheless, quality management and risk management differ in at least one significant respect related to the perspective that each brings to the analysis of data. Quality management generally approaches the identification and analysis of patient care problems and issues from the standpoint of what should occur in, and what goals should be met by, the healthcare organization. Risk management, on the other hand, tends to approach these tasks from the perspective of what should not occur in, and what risks need to be avoided by, that organization. Accordingly, quality management monitors patient care on an ongoing basis, and aims to improve quality of care and prevent adverse outcomes, but risk management focuses on risk identification, protecting the organization's financial and personnel assets, and investigating specific incidents that may have resulted in liability for the organization. Because the sources of data relied on by each of these disciplines are substantially similar, the data may be obtained in a more cost-effective manner if coordinated properly.[2]

In its accreditation manuals, the Joint Commission requires that healthcare organizations demonstrate integration of quality management and risk management functions by showing an appropriate sharing of information between established quality management and risk management committees, and a coordinated approach to resolving identified problems. For example, information obtained through the monitoring and evaluation process conducted in relation to policies and procedures on hospital safety must be shared by quality management and risk management committees, although each committee ultimately reviews such information and conducts further investigation from their different perspectives.

Risk Management

Risk management can be described as a four-step process designed to identify, evaluate, and resolve the actual and possible sources of loss.

1. *Risk identification* is the process of identifying activities that have the potential to expose the organization to the risk of liability or financial loss. Risk management committees and risk managers rely on many data sources to identify risks, including incident reports

---

[2]   See Joint Commission on Accreditation of Healthcare Organizations, *2005 Hospital Accreditation Manual,* Standards PI.1.10, PI.3.10.

and occurrence screening systems, verbal communication, safety and quality management committee reports, and patient complaints. Risk identification is most commonly accomplished retrospectively (based on information on past events or incidents), but is often combined with other approaches, including prospective risk identification (based on an analysis of likely exposures) and concurrent risk identification (based on monitoring of situations and events as they occur).

2. *Risk evaluation* is the process of using analytical skills to determine the potential for risk, and the financial impact that the risk could have on the practitioner or organization. Risk managers attempt to predict the expected loss frequency (how often an identified risk will generate a loss) and loss severity (how much the generated loss will cost), so that the organization may be prepared to address the consequences of loss events and can prioritize necessary risk management efforts. Risk evaluation usually entails analysis of incident reports and claims generated by the healthcare organization, as well as analysis of relevant statistical studies and surveys from industry associations, government agencies, and independent organizations.

3. *Risk handling* is the process of taking steps to respond to the risks that have been identified. Risk managers must analyze available methods for reducing exposure and potential losses and implementing an appropriate course of action. The primary approach utilized for risk handling is *risk control* (preventing losses from occurring in the first place, and reducing the effect of losses that do occur), which can be further classified into several categories, including *risk elimination* (totally avoiding a particular exposure by limiting or completely eliminating an activity, procedure, or particular service) and *risk reduction* (reducing or preventing loss).

4. *Risk monitoring* is the process of continuously monitoring and evaluating the results of risk management initiatives. Risk managers must modify techniques as appropriate, and review risk management processes on an ongoing basis, updating approaches in accordance with changing circumstances or revealed inefficiencies.

To identify risks, a risk manager relies on a wide range of collected data, documents, and records. The following are common information sources used for risk identification purposes:

- Incident and accident reports
- Data on members who utilize greater than average levels of service
- Length of stay data
- Unexpected patient returns for acute care
- Variations from clinical practice guidelines and outcome indicators
- Patient complaints and patient satisfaction surveys
- Accreditation and federal/state inspection reports
- Credentialing, recredentialing, and clinical privileges files
- Audit reports of internal committees or insurance surveyors[3]

The health information management department plays an important role in the risk management function. The department can be responsible for performing the following tasks:

- Supervising data gathering, with documentation of the data produced at all levels
- Training clerical personnel engaged in locating the most useful sources of required information
- Determining the incidence of relevant data requested for the use of committees and individuals
- Screening medical records for compliance with established clinical criteria and designated exceptions or equivalents as established by the medical staff
- Participating in the selection and design of forms used in the medical record and in the determination of the sequence and format of the contents of the medical record
- Suggesting to the professional staff methods of improving the collection and organization of primary source data so as to facilitate retrieval, analysis, tabulation, and display
- Performing continuing informational surveillance of practice indicators or monitors for medical staff review
- Ensuring the provision of a mechanism to protect the privacy of patients and practitioners whose records are involved in quality assessment activities
- Reviewing all requests for access to or copies of medical records by patients and third parties to determine their validity under applicable state law

---

[3] See C. Benda and F. Rozovsky, Liability and Risk Management in Managed Care (Gaithersburg, Md.: Aspen Publishers, 1998), 15:3.

- Reviewing all medical records for which requests or demands for access or copies have been received (for example, from patients and attorneys, or based upon court orders or subpoenas), to determine whether it is apparent from the medical record that the hospital or healthcare organization has potential exposure to liability (department personnel should confer closely with the organization's risk manager and legal counsel in this regard, because the early identification of potential claims can greatly enhance and facilitate the defense of any claim that may be brought against the organization and any of its healthcare practitioners)

Each of these components of a risk management program in the health information management department should be evaluated with respect to the needs of the institution and the available personnel and resources, so that the most effective plans and protocols may be implemented in the hospital or healthcare organization.

Quality Management

The healthcare industry has long recognized the importance of monitoring healthcare services with the goal of improving patient care. In recent years, the terminology and methodology of quality management have changed. Today, continuous quality improvement and total quality management have become predominant terms in the language of healthcare quality management. These terms, and several others, are frequently interchanged, which sometimes can make the vocabulary used to describe new quality management concepts confusing. For the basic overview of quality management contained in this chapter, "quality improvement" and "quality management" are meant to encompass the numerous labels applied to the quality improvement philosophy and process.

The concept of quality management, as applied to a healthcare organization, focuses on all key organizational functions, including governance, management, and support functions, as well as direct patient care. Implementation of quality management efforts involves education at all levels, from top executives to employees paid by the hour, such that the entire organization is following the flow of provided healthcare services from beginning to end, continuously working together to improve quality at every stage of administration and patient care.

Quality management relies on statistical evaluation of data collected during review activities for the overall purpose of improving systems or processes, as opposed to being limited to individual performance. Quality management can include the following activities:

- Review of surgical and other invasive procedures
- Evaluation of drug usage
- Review of medical records
- Review of blood utilization
- Evaluation of pharmacy and therapeutics
- Review of risk management activities
- Review of sentinel events and their restrictions[4]

During the past decade, quality management has started to include outcome research, comparative research, measurement of illness severity, patient satisfaction surveys, and benchmarking. With the advent of managed care, quality management has become more involved in the business needs of health care by compiling data for managed care contracting, report cards, and physician profiling.[5]

Quality management is a multidisciplinary process and can involve many departments, such as the health information management, medical staff, and nursing departments. Some facilities may create multidisciplinary committees to perform quality management activities.[6] Other facilities may have a separate quality management department, or place the responsibility of quality management within the health information management department.

---

[4] A sentinel event is defined by the Joint Commission as "an unexpected occurrence involving death or serious physical or psychological injury, or the risk thereof." It includes those events subject to review under the Joint Commission's Sentinel Event Policy, and may include process variations that do not affect outcomes or results in a particular case, but for which a recurrence carries a significant chance of a serious adverse outcome or result. See Joint Commission, *2005 Hospital Accreditation Manual,* Glossary and Standard PI.2.30.

[5] B. J. Youngberg and D. R. Weber, "Integrating Risk Management, Utilization Management, and Quality Management: Maximizing Benefit Through Integration," in B. J. Youngberg, ed., The Risk Manager's Desk Reference (Gaithersburg, Md.: Aspen Publishers, 1998), 29.

[6] J. A. Meyer, S. Silow-Carroll, T. Kutyla, L. S. Stepnick, and L. S. Rybowski, *Hospital Quality: Ingredients for Success—Overview and Lessons Learned* (Commonwealth Fund, July 2004).

In its various accreditation manuals, the Joint Commission requires accredited healthcare organizations (that is, hospitals, long term care facilities, ambulatory healthcare facilities, healthcare networks, and so on) to improve organizational performance on a continuous and ongoing basis. The Joint Commission defines improvement as activities undertaken by leaders and support staff for the purpose of continuously measuring, assessing, and improving performance of clinical and other processes, and ultimately improving patient health outcomes.[7] Although there are many approaches to improving organization performance, the Joint Commission's standards indicate that all quality management programs should contain the following elements:

- *Plan.* There is a planned, systematic, organization-wide approach to designing, measuring, assessing, and improving performance
- *Design.* New processes that are implemented must be designed well, and must effectively identify and manage sentinel events and reduce patient safety risks
- *Measure.* There must be in place a systematic process to collect data needed to design and assess new processes and identify sentinel events
- *Assess.* There must be a systematic process for assessing collected data to determine whether design specifications for new processes were met
- *Improve.* The hospital or healthcare organization must systematically improve its performance and patient safety, and reduce the risk of sentinel events[8]

The National Committee for Quality Assurance (NCQA), an organization that accredits managed care organizations (MCOs), also focuses on clinical and administrative mechanisms for quality management and improvement, and on the communication process for problem identification, analysis, and follow-up. With respect to quality management, the NCQA requires that the MCO have a well-organized, comprehensive quality management program accountable to its highest organizational levels. The NCQA measures quality management through review of quality management program structure,

---

[7] See, e.g., Joint Commission, *2005 Hospital Accreditation Manual,* Standards PI.1.10 through PI.3.20.
[8] Ibid.

accountability, coordination with management, content, and delegation. The NCQA attempts to answer the following in the course of its
review:

- Does the plan fully examine the quality of care given to its mem-
  bers?
- How well does the plan coordinate all parts of its delivery system?
- What steps does the plan take to make sure members have access to
  care in a reasonable amount of time?
- What improvements in care and service can the plan demonstrate?[9]

During the evaluation process, the NCQA focuses on the tracking of
issues uncovered by the MCO's quality management process, including
whether that process follows problems through to their resolution, and
assesses quality management/quality improvement studies, projects, and
monitoring activities; quality management/quality improvement committees; and governing body reports and meeting minutes.[10]

HIPAA and Risk Management/Quality Management

The Health Insurance Portability and Accountability Act (HIPAA)
and the privacy regulations issued pursuant to it (Privacy Rule) apply
to "covered entities," which include most healthcare providers and certain healthcare organizations and health plans, and create a comprehensive scheme of protection for individually identifiable health
information (protected health information, or PHI).[11] (For a detailed
discussion of the Privacy Rule, see Chapters 6, 7, and 8.) Although
HIPAA restricts the use and disclosure of PHI, the act expressly permits covered entities to use and disclose PHI for their "health care
operations" without the patient's authorization.[12] The definition of
healthcare operations includes:

---

[9] See S. Dasco and C. Dasco, Managed Care Answer Book (Gaithersburg, Md.: Aspen
     Publishers, 1996), 8–14; National Committee for Quality Assurance (NCQA), *Standards
     for Accreditation of Managed Care Organizations: Standards for Quality Management and
     Improvement* (2004).
[10] Ibid.
[11] 42 U.S.C. §§ 1320d et seq.
[12] 45 C.F.R. § 164.502(a)(1)(ii).

- Conducting quality assessment and improvement activities, including outcomes evaluation and development of clinical guidelines
- Population-based activities relating to improving health or reducing healthcare costs
- Protocol development
- Case management and care coordination
- Contacting healthcare providers and patients with information about treatment alternatives
- Reviewing the competence or qualifications of healthcare professionals
- Evaluating practitioner and provider performance
- Conducting healthcare training programs for students, trainees, and practitioners under supervision
- Training nonhealthcare professionals
- Accreditation, certification, licensing, and credentialing activities
- Auditing functions, including fraud and abuse detection and compliance programs
- Resolution of internal grievances[13]

By permitting the activities that are essential to any healthcare quality management program, the Privacy Rule avoids creating barriers to the appropriate use of PHI for quality enhancement.

Healthcare operations for which PHI may be used without patient authorization also include the business management and general administration of the covered entity.[14] Conducting risk management programs, in addition to being related to quality management, is part of a covered entity's overall management functions. Covered entities, therefore, may use and have access to PHI where such information is necessary to the proper conduct of their internal risk management programs.

Most state health information privacy laws are sufficiently broad to permit healthcare providers to use individually identifiable health information for their internal management and operations activities, which, it can reasonably be argued, include quality management and risk management programs. Health information professionals should keep current with legislative developments in their states, however, as more jurisdictions move to increasingly specific privacy protection provisions in their statutes.

---

[13] 45 C.F.R. § 164.501.
[14] Ibid.

Compliance Programs

In response to the proliferation of fraud and abuse legislation and enforcement activities directed at the healthcare industry, many healthcare organizations have developed corporate compliance programs. Compliance programs not only can prevent violations of the law, but also can help to reduce the potential for liability should violations occur. Healthcare providers in all segments of the industry have implemented (and continue to implement) such programs in response to heightened scrutiny and expectations of compliance, and also as part of settlements following healthcare fraud investigations. An effective compliance program can minimize the consequences resulting from a violation of the law, and may, in some cases, convince a prosecutor not to pursue a criminal prosecution. With respect to criminal penalties, the U.S. Sentencing Commission Guidelines, Sentencing for Organizations (Sentencing Guidelines)—which cover every business in the United States, including charitable and not for profit institutions—specifically mandate lesser criminal sanctions for companies that have effective compliance programs in place and that periodically assess the effectiveness of such compliance programs, compared to those which do not.[15] As far as civil sanctions are concerned, the Civil Division of the Department of Justice has a similar philosophy, and often treats defendants more leniently if they have compliance programs in effect.

In designing a compliance program, a healthcare organization should begin with the Sentencing Guidelines' description of the minimum steps that such a program must include. An effective compliance program must include the following:

1. The organization must establish compliance standards and procedures that are reasonably capable of reducing the prospect of criminal or wrongful conduct
2. The organization must assign individuals in high-level personnel positions with the overall responsibility to oversee compliance with the standards and procedures that will be developed after completion of a legal audit

---

[15] U.S. Sentencing Commission Guidelines, Sentencing for Organizations, 56 Fed. Reg. 22,762 (1991), as amended effective Nov. 1, 2004—69 Fed. Reg. 28,994–29,028 (May 19, 2004).

3. In addressing oversight responsibilities, the organization must use due care not to delegate substantial discretionary authority to individuals who the organization knew, or should have known through the exercise of due diligence, had a propensity to engage in illegal activities

4. Once the organization has developed suitable standards and procedures, they must be communicated effectively to all employees and other agents

5. The organization must develop a monitoring and auditing system reasonably designed to detect criminal and other wrongful conduct by its employees and other agents

6. The organization must implement an adequate enforcement and discipline procedure that will ensure consistent enforcement of the compliance standards via an appropriate disciplinary mechanism

7. The organization must take all reasonable steps, including any necessary modifications to its program, to respond to a detected offense and to prevent further similar offenses[16]

In implementing any corporate compliance program, the DHHS Office of Inspector General (OIG), strongly encourages high-level involvement by the healthcare organization's governing body, president and/or chief executive officer, general counsel, and chief financial officer—as well as by other medical, nursing, and administrative personnel—as appropriate, in the development of standards of conduct.[17] The precise actions necessary to implement these steps, however, depend on the size of the organization, the nature of its business, and its history.

For example, the OIG highlights the integral components of a compliance program for hospitals as one that should include, among other things, the following:

- Written standards of conduct that state the organization's goals and ethical requirements of compliance
- An emphasis on exposure to certain risk areas, such as improper billing, false cost reports, patients' freedom of choice, and improper financial arrangements

---

[16] Sentencing Guidelines, at § 8A1.3(k).
[17] U.S. Department of Health and Human Services (DHHS), Office of Inspector General (OIG), Publication of the OIG Compliance Program Guidance for Hospitals, 63 Fed. Reg. 35, n. 8 (Feb. 23, 1998).

- Reinforcement of statutes and regulations addressing claim development and submission
- Guidelines for compliance with medical necessity standards, antikickback and antireferral statutes
- Procedures for proper outpatient coding, admissions and discharges, and supplemental payment considerations (such as improper claims for clinical trials and abuse of diagnosis related group [DRG] outlier payments)[18]
- A mechanism for reviewing whether the organization is properly reporting bad debts to Medicare
- Procedures for providing timely and accurate reporting of Medicare and other federal healthcare program credit balances[19]

Similar components are contained in the OIG guidelines for physicians and small group practices; however, unlike the hospital guidelines, these guidelines do not necessitate the implementation of a full scale compliance program. Instead, the OIG emphasizes a step by step approach to follow in recognition of the unique fiscal and staffing constraints faced by such physician practices.[20]

A healthcare organization's corporate compliance plan should be targeted to the needs of that particular organization. The healthcare organization should determine all areas that could be included in a compliance program by considering whatever federal, state, and/or local statutes, regulations, and ordinances impose criminal or civil sanctions or liability. Although this list is not intended to be exhaustive or complete, the laws that a healthcare organization should consider when creating a corporate compliance program would include the following:

- Antikickback statute and state or local counterparts
- Antitrust laws
- Civil monetary penalties laws
- Emergency Medical Treatment and Active Labor Act (EMTALA)
- Employment-related laws, such as the Americans with Disabilities Act (ADA), the Family and Medical Leave Act (FMLA), and the Fair Labor Standards Act (FLSA)

---

[18] OIG Supplemental Compliance Program Guidance for Hospitals, 70 Fed. Reg. 19, 4859–4862 (Jan. 31, 2005).
[19] OIG, Publication, 8990–8993.
[20] OIG, OIG Compliance Program for Individual and Small Group Physician Practices, 65 Fed. Reg. 194, 59434–59435 (Oct. 5, 2000).

- False Claims Act and state or local counterparts
- Federal fraud statutes, such as mail fraud statute and wire fraud act
- Health Insurance Portability and Accountability Act of 1996 (HIPAA), with specific respect to the Privacy Rule and the Security Rule
- Medical waste management laws
- Medicare and Medicaid Acts
- Patient confidentiality statutes
- Patient Self-Determination Act (PSDA)
- Racketeer Influenced and Corrupt Organizations Act (RICO)
- Safe Medical Devices Act
- Stark law and state or local counterparts
- Tax laws[21]

The health information management department should be integrated with an organization's compliance efforts, because documents are critical to the investigation and enforcement activities of a compliance program. Patient records are an important data source for compliance efforts, particularly for the monitoring and auditing system that must be part of any compliance plan.[22] Healthcare organizations may choose to conduct a preplanning audit addressing financial, accounting, billing, transactional, and quality of care issues. Patient records document the treatment provided by a physician, and can be used to determine whether the organization complied with all applicable laws, standards, and policies and procedures. Patient records are also crucial to the ongoing monitoring that is part of a corporate compliance program. The health information professional's experience in data collection and analysis, physician documentation practices, billing and coding, and data management is essential to compliance efforts.

The health information management department may conduct a medical records audit as part of the institution's compliance program. Some areas that the health information management department may consider for review in this regard include:

- Compliance with the Privacy Rule and Security Rule
- Document retention and destruction policies

---

[21] M. Hanzal, "Understanding the Need for a Corporate Compliance Program," in Youngberg, *Risk Manager's*, 112–113.
[22] *Sentencing Guidelines*, at § 8A1.3(k).

- Medical records documentation that should be available at the time the record is coded, and consideration of whether all physician documentation and test results must be in the medical record
- Procedures that the health information department has in place to ensure that the medical record has adequate documentation and supports the coded diagnoses and procedures
- Education and training of physicians, nurses, coders, and other individuals involved in documentation, coding, and billing[23]

Medical Records in Risk Management, Quality Review, Compliance Activities, and Pay for Performance Initiatives

Patient records form an essential part of the data used in risk management, quality management, and compliance activities. The health information management department and its personnel occupy an important position in ensuring that staff members who have either the authority to make entries in the patient record or the right to examine the record do so in accordance with applicable laws, regulations, and accreditation standards. For Joint Commission–accredited hospitals and healthcare networks, the accreditation standards recognize several purposes for maintaining medical records, which also are important to the proper functioning of a risk management, quality management, or corporate compliance program.

The Joint Commission standards relating to patient-specific data and information recognize several uses for patient or member-specific data. The information may be useful to

- Facilitate patient or member care
- Serve as a financial and legal record
- Aid in clinical research
- Support decision analysis
- Guide performance improvement or document outcomes of care[24]

---

[23] See, L. S. Vincze, "Compliance, Medical Records, and the FBI: Preventing Fraud and Abuse," *Journal of AHIMA* 69(1): 41–42 (1998); S. Prophet and C. Hammen, "Coding Compliance: Practical Strategies for Success," *Journal of AHIMA* 69(1): 52–53 (1998); S. Prophet, "Fraud and Abuse: What You Can Do," *Journal of AHIMA* 69(1): 68–70 (1998).

[24] Joint Commission, *1996 Comprehensive Accreditation Manual for Health Care Networks*, Intent of Standard IM.6; Joint Commission, *2005 Hospital Accreditation Manual*, Intent of Standards IM.6.10 through IM.6.20.

As is evident from the Joint Commission standards, a complete and accurate medical record is necessary to fulfill several important functions: (1) it chronicles the history of a patient's care, and will reveal both the positive and negative aspects, if any, of that patient's dealings with healthcare providers; (2) it will be used, for both risk management and quality management purposes, to evaluate the quality of the care rendered and to identify potential problems with either the system of delivering care or with the providers who deliver it; and (3) it can be used for compliance purposes, either in an audit or to ensure that the organization has complied with all applicable laws and regulations.

Finally, by 2005, there has been a coming together by private payers, employer groups, public interest groups, and the federal government on the concept that higher quality providers, both institutional and professional, should be rewarded for providing higher quality patient care. Measuring patient care for quality requires medical records to be extracted and compiled, and statistics on patient injuries to be analyzed. The standards for the "pay for performance" movement are still evolving, but it is clear that all the issues discussed in this and other chapters concerning access to medical records and other confidential records of providers will affect the final design of these payment programs.

Health information professionals should be an important part of any healthcare organization's risk management, quality management, and corporate compliance programs. Essential to success in these endeavors is the creation of, and access to, reliable information. Health information professionals are often best equipped to provide the knowledge and training needed to implement effective information management strategies.

CHAPTER 13

Electronic Health Records

Chapter Objectives

- Discuss the benefits of electronic health records (EHRs)
- Explain the legal concerns that arise from EHRs
- Identify the sources of law that govern confidentiality of health information, discussing their application to EHRs
- Explain why security is important to an EHR, giving examples of safeguards against unauthorized access, including technological, physical, and user access controls
- Describe the HIPAA security requirements, transactions and code set requirements, and National Provider Identifier requirements
- Describe health data networks and the legal issues they present in connection with the use of EHRs
- Discuss the concerns associated with outside users of EHR information
- Clarify how durability and accuracy requirements apply to EHRs
- Discuss the legal obstacles to admission of EHRs into evidence, and how the obstacles can be overcome
- Discuss the potential security problems of faxed and e-mailed medical information
- Define telemedicine and give examples of current applications, highlighting medical records concerns
- Discuss the Internet as a method of conveying patient-specific information, including risks and safeguards

The Movement to Electronic Health Records

The development and expansion of electronic health records (EHRs) in the past decade have been dramatic. Most institutional healthcare providers and ancillary service providers and many large physician practices have converted to EHRs and electronic financial support systems.[1] In addition, the federal government has recognized that EHRs and related computerized records systems will generate enormous savings for the healthcare industry and society generally. Thus, the government has undertaken numerous initiatives to encourage the adoption of EHRs.[2] It has been shown that fragmented, disorganized, and inaccessible health information adversely affects the quality of health care and patient safety, and that an EHR system can form the basis for dramatically improved quality and safety.[3]

As the health industry moves toward adoption of EHRs, the question arises as to what information an EHR should contain. This will be determined initially by existing state law governing medical records. (See the discussion of medical records content in Chapter 3.) While complying with applicable state law, writers of EHR software must contend with the ability of any electronic record to hold vastly more information than traditional paper records do, and with the need for EHRs to be used in systems that may span several states. A comprehensive consideration of what should constitute a medical record can be found in the practice brief of the American Health Information Management Association (AHIMA), which describes the "legal record" as

---

[1]   American Hospital Association, *Forward Momentum: Hospital Use of Information Technology* (Oct. 2005); "This Time They Really Mean It: Annual Survey Shows Healthcare Organizations Are Committing More Money to IT and Installing [EHRs] Is Now Their Top Priority," *Modern Healthcare* 42 (Feb. 14, 2005).

[2]   See, generally, U.S. Government Accountability Office (GAO), GAO-05-628, *Health Information Technology: HHS Is Taking Steps to Develop a National Strategy* (May 27, 2005), and GAO-04-991R, *HHS's Efforts to Promote Health Information Technology and Legal Barriers to Its Adoption* (Aug. 13, 2004); T. Thompson and D. Brailer, *The Decade of Health Information Technology: Delivering Consumer-Centric and Information-Rich Health Care—Framework for Strategic Action*, U.S. Department of Health and Human Services (July 21, 2004).

[3]   Institute of Medicine, *Key Capabilities of an Electronic Health Record System* (Institute of Medicine, 2003), 2.

the documentation of healthcare services provided to an individual during any aspect of healthcare delivery in any type of healthcare organization. It is consumer- or patient-centric. The legal health record contains individually identifiable data, *stored on any medium*, collected and directly used in documenting health status [emphasis added].[4]

(See the more detailed discussion of the legal health record in Chapter 3.) To demonstrate the impact of EHRs on health information management functions, AHIMA has also prepared a detailed analysis of each function required to maintain a health record as that function would be performed for a paper health record, a hybrid paper-electronic health record, and an EHR.[5] For example, for the function of abstracting data elements, manual retrieval of information from a paper record could be eliminated in an EHR, if the application software automatically captured information for data abstracts. The analysis shows how dramatically information management tasks will change as organizations migrate from paper to electronic record keeping.

The Institute of Medicine has identified the following core functionalities of an EHR:

- Health information and data about patients, including test results, medications, urgent developments, and medical and nursing diagnosis and care
- Results management, allowing for readily accessible results, critical linkages among multiple providers, and improved care coordination
- Order entry/management, permitting provider order entry, improved work flow processes, increased clinician productivity, and reduced undetected errors
- Decision support, so as to enhance clinical performance with computer-assisted diagnosis and disease treatment and management

---

[4] American Health Information Management Association (AHIMA), *Practice Brief: Update: Guidelines for Defining the Legal Health Record for Disclosure Purposes* (Sept. 2005), 64A; *Practice Brief: Core Data Sets for the Physician Practice Electronic Health Record* (Oct. 2003), available at http://library.ahima.org/expdio/groups/public/documents/ahima/pub_ bok1_021607.html.
[5] A. Tegan, et al., "The EHR's Impact on HIM Functions," *Journal of AHIMA* 76 (May 2005).

- Electronic communication and connectivity, facilitating communication among providers and with patients and permitting the development of EHR systems
- Patient support, particularly in the areas of health education, wellness awareness, and self-testing
- Administrative processes, to increase healthcare organizations' efficiency
- Reporting and population health management, enabling more effective monitoring of patient safety and quality of care[6]

Other organizations also continue to develop standards for EHR content and functionality. For example, the eHealth Initiative, with a large and diverse membership of stakeholders in the healthcare industry, has taken up the task of developing standards for the EHR.[7] Other standard-setting organizations will provide further standardization as use of EHRs expands.[8] As the healthcare industry adopts standards for EHRs, a broadly accepted definition will emerge for general use by providers, payors, and other healthcare organizations.

In addition, in recent years, Congress and many states have enacted laws that have supported the development and expanded use of EHRs. The Uniform Electronic Transactions Act (UETA) is a model act that was promulgated by the National Conference of Commissioners of Uniform State Laws in June of 1999 in an effort to make transactions in the electronic marketplace as enforceable as transactions memorialized on paper with manual signatures, without altering any of the substantive rules of law that apply.[9] UETA applies only to voluntary agreements that involve "*electronic records and signatures* relating to a *transaction*, defined as those interactions between people relating to business, commercial and governmental affairs,"[10] and does not apply

---

[6] Institute of Medicine, *Key Capabilities*, 7–11.

[7] See "About e-Health Initiatives," available at http://www.ehealthinitiative.org/about/priorities.mspx.

[8] "E-Health Foundation Launches Prototype for Safe E-Health Information Sharing," *Health Care Daily Report* (June 3, 2005); "Commission Ready to Work on National Health-Records System," *Information Week* (Jan. 11, 2005), available at http://www.informationweek.com/shared/printableArticleSrc.jhtml?articleID=57700565.

[9] Robert A. Wittie and Jane K. Winn, supra note 1, at 2; Uniform Law Commissioners, "Summary: Uniform Electronic Transactions Act," available at http://www.nccusl.org/Update/uniformact_summaries/uniformacts-s-ueta.asp (last visited June 3, 2005).

[10] National Conference of Commissioners of Uniform State Laws, Uniform Electronic Transactions Act § 3 (emphasis added) (hereinafter UETA).

to most transactions subject to the Uniform Commercial Code (UCC).[11] UETA provides that a record or signature may not be denied legal effect or enforceability solely because it is in electronic form, that a contract may not be denied legal effect or enforceability solely because an electronic record was used in its formation, that any law that requires a writing will be satisfied by an electronic record, and that any signature requirement in the law will be met if there is an electronic signature.[12] Although UETA requires an agreement between parties, it does not require an explicit consumer consent in order to disclose information that is required to be made available in writing, as in the case of E-SIGN (which is discussed below). UETA also adopts a technology-neutral standard that provides general standards that can evolve as technology changes.

The Uniform Computer Information Transactions Act (UCITA) is a substantive contract law statute that provides a comprehensive set of rules for licensing computer information, whether computer software or other clearly identified forms of electronic information.[13] The majority of UCITA's regulations act as default rules, meaning that they apply only when the parties have not otherwise agreed, and the regulations can be varied by the parties' agreement through use of an "opt-out" provision of UCITA, in a format similar to that adopted in the UCC.[14] UCITA's scope is limited to "computer information transactions," as defined by the statute, and does not apply to transactions governed by much of the UCC.[15] UCITA applies to, among other things, contracts for the licensing or purchase of software, contracts for software development, and contracts for access to databases through the Internet.[16]

---

[11] UETA § 3.
[12] UETA § 7.
[13] Uniform Law Commissioners, "Summary: UETA."
[14] Ibid.; National Conference of Commissioners of Uniform State Laws, Uniform Computer Information Transactions Act § 104 (hereinafter UCITA).
[15] A computer information transaction is defined as an agreement a primary purpose of which is to require a party to create, modify, transfer, or license computer information or informational rights in computer information; "computer information" is information in electronic form that is obtained from or through the use of a computer or that is in digital or equivalent form capable of being processed by a computer. UCITA §§ 102 and 103.
[16] UCITA § 103. For a description of the exceptions to UCITA and a description of how conflicts in regulation between different laws, such as the Uniform Commercial Code (UCC) and UCITA, are resolved, see UCITA § 103 and Mary Jo Howard Dively, *The New Laws That Will Enable Electronic Contracting: A Survey of the Electronic Contracting Rules in the Uniform Electronic Transactions Act and the Uniform Computer Information Transactions Act*, 38 Duq. L. Rev. 209, 226–227 (2000).

UCITA's electronic contract rules include procedural rules, substantive formation rules, and attribution rules.[17] The procedural rules mirror those in UETA and E-SIGN, generally validating contracts made electronically or using electronic signatures.[18] The formation rules include validation of parties' choices of law[19] and forum,[20] provisions on the manner in which an electronic contract may be formed, rules limiting the enforceability of shrink-wrap and click-wrap contracts,[21] provisions governing access contracts,[22] and provisions limiting the ability of a licensor to exercise electronic self-help.[23] Finally, UCITA also adopts a technology-neutral standard that does not specify implementation of a specific technology.

Several states have adopted a variety of digital signature acts. These statutes are generally modifications based upon the framework of UETA or UCITA. These statutes, following the enactment of E-SIGN, are all subject to the "consistency with E-SIGN" requirement as described above, and are barred from requiring implementation of a single type of technology.

The Electronic Signatures in Global and National Commerce Act (E-SIGN) is federal legislation enacted with two purposes: validating contracts executed using electronic signatures, and protecting consumers by requiring adequate consent to performing transactions electronically.[24] E-SIGN was signed into law June 30, 2000, and became generally effective as of October 1, 2000.[25] E-SIGN is divided into four titles that deal with electronic records and signatures in commerce, transferable records, promotion of international electronic commerce, and the Commission on Online Child Protection.[26] E-SIGN generally provides that a signature, contract, or other record that effects interstate

---

[17] Dively, *New Laws*, 209, 229.
[18] UCITA § 107.
[19] UCITA § 109.
[20] UCITA § 110.
[21] UCITA §§ 201 through 210.
[22] UCITA § 611.
[23] UCITA § 816.
[24] Robert A. Wittie and Jane K. Winn, *Electronic Records and Signatures Under the Federal E-SIGN Legislation and the UETA*, 56 Bus. Law 93 (2000).
[25] Electronic Signatures in Global and National Commerce Act (E-SIGN), Pub. L. No. 106-229, 114 Stat. 464 (2000) (codified at 15 U.S.C. §§ 7001 through 7031). Certain portions of E-SIGN, such as the electronic disclosure and record-keeping provisions, became effective March 1, 2001.
[26] Ibid.

or foreign commerce cannot be denied legal effect, validity, or enforceability solely because it is in electronic form or because an electronic signature or electronic record[27] was used in its formation.[28] In addition, E-SIGN provides that use and acceptance of electronic records and signatures is voluntary for nongovernment agencies, and that E-SIGN does not affect any other underlying law relating to the document that does not require contracts or records to be in nonelectronic form.[29]

E-SIGN imposes record-keeping requirements for electronic records and signatures "in a form that is capable of being retained and accurately reproduced for later reference by all parties or persons who are entitled to retain the contract or other record."[30] However, within the statute, E-SIGN fails to define what parties are "entitled to retain the contract." E-SIGN also imposes a requirement to obtain consumer consents for electronic disclosure of information that is required to be made available in writing to consumers, subject to certain exceptions.[31] E-SIGN also includes a provision that expressly preempts state law, except: (a) state enactments or adoptions of the Uniform Electronic Transactions Act (UETA); (b) where the state law specifies alternative requirements that are consistent with E-SIGN, and the requirements do not require or accord greater legal status to the implementation of a specific technology; and (c) where the state statute was enacted or adopted after enactment of E-SIGN, and the statute makes specific reference to E-SIGN.[32] Therefore, state electronic transactions statutes are required to be "consistent" with E-SIGN and must present a technology-neutral standard.

The Medicare Prescription Drug, Improvement, and Modernization Act of 2003 (MMA) directs the Secretary of the Department of Health and Human Services (DHHS) to develop standards for electronic prescribing of drugs in connection with the prescription drug benefit provided by the MMA.[33] Accordingly, DHHS published proposed

---

[27] E-SIGN defines an "electronic signature" broadly as "an electronic sound, symbol, or process, attached to or logically associated with a contract or other record and executed or adopted by a person with the intent to sign the record"; E-SIGN defines an "electronic record" as "a contract or other record created, generated, sent, communicated, received, or stored by electronic means." 15 U.S.C. § 7006.
[28] 15 U.S.C. § 7001.
[29] Ibid.
[30] Ibid.
[31] Ibid.
[32] 15 U.S.C. § 7002.
[33] Pub. L. No. 108-173.

regulations to provide limited relief from proscriptions against physician self-referrals for referrals in order to promote the adoption of e-prescribing.[34] Using its separate legal authority under the Social Security Act, DHHS also proposed regulations that would create exceptions to the self-referral prohibitions and permit certain nonmonetary remuneration to physicians for the purpose of facilitating the adoption of interoperable EHRs.[35]

Electronic Health Records Systems

The EHR, maintained by healthcare providers, is a critical building block for an EHR system, which can be defined to include the following:

- Longitudinal collection of electronic health information for and about persons
- Immediate electronic access to person- and population-level information by authorized users
- Provision of knowledge and decision support that enhance the quality, safety, and efficiency of patient care
- Support of efficient processes for healthcare delivery[36]

The healthcare system is moving rapidly toward EHRs maintained not just by individual practitioners and institutions, but in a variety of multi-institutional and community-wide networks through which multiple authorized providers of direct and ancillary healthcare services may contribute patient health information to, and retrieve data from, EHRs stored in provider databases or in centralized data warehouses. Acceptance of EHRs and EHR systems will continue to be higher among institutional providers and large physician group practices, but smaller practitioner groups will inevitably adopt EHRs as pressures from government and private payors to use electronic information systems increase.[37]

---

[34] 70 Fed. Reg. 59182 (Oct. 11, 2005).
[35] 70 Fed. Reg. 59015 (Oct. 11, 2005).
[36] Institute of Medicine, *Key Capabilities*, 1.
[37] See Center for Studying Health System Change, *Limited Information Technology for Patient Care in Physician Offices*, Issue Brief No. 29 (Sept. 29, 2004) (showing that 60 percent of physicians in sole or relatively small practices use limited information technology, and more than 50 percent of physicians in large groups and medical school faculties use more extensive information technology).

A growing consensus in government and the healthcare industry has supported the development of community-wide health data sharing among all components of the healthcare delivery system. This effort began in the mid-1980s with the formation of community health information networks (CHINs), which were created to establish centrally located health databases that provided controlled access to authorized users. A variety of legal, financial, and operational obstacles, however, prevented the development of an effective community-wide EHR. In 2004, the Bush administration called for the widespread adoption of an interoperable EHR within 10 years, and established the position of the National Health Information Technology Coordinator, who was charged to develop, maintain, and direct the implementation of a strategic plan to guide the nationwide implementation, in both the private and public sectors, of interoperable health information technology that would reduce medical errors, improve quality, and produce greater value for healthcare expenditures.[38] A strategic plan was developed to achieve that goal.[39] On November 15, 2004, DHHS issued a request for information (RFI) concerning how widespread interoperability of health information technologies and health information exchange could be achieved.[40]

The RFI described the government's vision for a national health information network consisting of regional health information organizations (RHIOs) designed to provide community-wide EHRs accessible to healthcare providers, patients, hospitals, laboratories, and other components of the healthcare delivery system in a particular region. This government effort,[41] together with the contributions of private companies,[42] led to an accelerated exploration of technologies and laws

---

[38] GAO, *HHS's Efforts*, 15.
[39] See Office of the National Coordinator for Health Information Technology, "The Decade of Health Information Technology: Delivering Consumer-Centric and Information-Rich Health Care," available at http://www.hhs.gov/onchit/framework/.
[40] 69 Fed. Reg. 65599 (Nov. 15, 2004).
[41] For a complete description of efforts in support of health information technology, see GAO, *HHS's Efforts*.
[42] See *Modern Healthcare's Daily Dose* (June 1, 2005) (Markle Foundation and Robert Wood Johnson Foundation to provide $1.9 million to connect regional health information networks in California, Indiana, and Massachusetts); *Modern Healthcare* 51 (Apr. 25, 2003) (Horizon Blue Cross Blue Shield of New Jersey and Caremark Rx provide $3 million to subsidize costs for 700 physicians to use electronic prescribing); *Wall Street Journal* online (May 9, 2005) (American Medical Association provides free Internet-based personal health record to physicians); Massachusetts eHealth Collaborative, press release (May 13, 2005) (Blue Cross provides $50 million grant to create HDN in Massachusetts).

needed to create workable information networks and interoperable EHRs.

An interoperable EHR is one that permits the exchange of patient health information among disparate clinicians and other authorized entities in real time and under stringent security, privacy, and other protections. Interoperability is needed to improve quality and efficiency of care, compiling a patient's complete care experience, maintaining a patient's personal health record, providing accessibility to the complete health record, enabling clinicians to make fact-based decisions without error, and permitting the collection of data for biosurveillance and medical research.[43] With interoperable EHRs, individuals may have a personal health record, which is designed to enable them to manage their own health information and to participate as informed consumers in their own health care. This vision of a personal health record sees "an Internet-based set of tools that allows people to access and coordinate their lifelong health information and make appropriate parts of it available to those who need it."[44] The concept of a personal health record fits nicely with the development of RHIOs and other community-based information sharing arrangements or health data networks (HDNs).[45]

The principal legal underpinning for the EHR and EHR systems is the Health Insurance Portability and Accountability Act (HIPAA), which enunciates standards and requirements for the electronic transmission of health information.[46] Moreover, the legal issues associated with the computerization of patient-related data have become increasingly complex as information systems expand beyond the simple electronic capturing of health records within a single healthcare facility. As healthcare providers integrate to provide a relatively seamless continuum of care across a network of participants, the need to integrate information systems has also arisen, generating complex legal issues about the rights and duties of the provider who originates the data, and of the integrated delivery system or network that operates the shared information system.

The use of EHRs, and in particular automated payment systems, also has significant repercussions in the area of healthcare fraud and

---

[43] 69 Fed. Reg. 65599–65600 (Nov. 15, 2004).

[44] Markle Foundation, *Connecting for Health: A Public-Private Collaborative*, Personal Health Working Group, Final Report 3 (July 1, 2003).

[45] For a more detailed discussion of personal health records, see AHIMA, *Health Record Paradigm Shift: Consumer Health Informatics* (2004).

[46] 42 U.S.C. §§ 1320d et seq.

abuse prevention. Violations of healthcare fraud prohibitions are facilitated when a claims payment system is highly automated. Although these systems are designed to accelerate claims processing by catching errors, testing eligibility, matching diagnoses to procedure codes, and returning erroneous claims to the provider, they have also made it possible to identify what combinations of diagnoses, procedures, and charges guarantee payment without any human review. The improved speed and efficiency of automated payment systems also make it possible to augment the volume of these types of claims, and to extend fraudulent activity across multiple patients and payers. Electronic data exchange has also opened the door to new kinds of healthcare fraud, arising from the growing number of computer links to claims information and the addition of electronic funds transfer (EFT) capabilities.

Although the law must race to keep pace with advances in health information technology, much has been accomplished in the past decade to create the legal framework for the EHR, especially with respect to the protection of the privacy of health information and the security of such information used, stored, and transmitted electronically. Nonetheless, a provider who implements an EHR system must still ascertain whether the system will comply with applicable licensure laws and regulations, Medicare requirements, and applicable accreditation requirements. In addition, preserving the confidentiality and integrity, accessibility, accuracy, and durability of medical records in an EHR system presents special problems. EHRs present unique security concerns because of their vulnerability to computer viruses and other sabotage. The early cases of loss of patient confidentiality through computer error or sabotage have resulted in substantial damages to the organizations who failed to provide adequate security.[47] (For a more detailed discussion of liability for unauthorized disclosure of health information, see Chapter 11.) Finally, it is vital that EHR systems be designed, installed, and maintained in a manner that preserves the reliability of records created and stored on such systems so that such records will be admissible as evidence in court and will be credible as evidence.

---

[47] *In re Eli Lilly and Company*, No. C-4047, 2002 FTC LEXIS 22 (May 8, 2002); Federal Trade Commission (FTC), agreement containing consent order: *In re Eli Lilly and Company*, available at http://www.ftc.gov/os/2002/01/lillyagree.pdf; see also "Lilly Privacy Violations Are Settled," *New York Times* (Jan. 19, 2002): C3.

HIPAA Privacy Rule

It is impractical to develop and implement an effective and acceptable EHR without adequate safeguards to protect individual privacy and records stored in electronic media. Studies have shown that the public remains skeptical concerning how well the healthcare industry can protect the confidentiality of health information,[48] and unfortunate examples of loss of privacy are numerous.[49]

With the enactment of HIPAA and the promulgation of the federal HIPAA privacy regulations (Privacy Rule), a comprehensive federal health information privacy protection scheme came into being. Certain provisions of the Privacy Rule present special concerns for the development of EHR systems, such as HDNs, and other shared information arrangements. (To understand fully the discussion in this chapter concerning HDNs, review the detailed discussion of the HIPAA Privacy Rule in Chapter 6 and the discussion of the HIPAA Security Rule later in this chapter.)

Privacy Rule Issues for Interoperable Electronic Health Records

Most users of interoperable EHRs are HIPAA covered entities, and therefore most participants in EHR systems, such as HDNs and other information sharing arrangements, are subject to the Privacy Rule. Their use and disclosure of electronic protected health information (ePHI) is subject to the requirements of HIPAA and the Privacy Rule. Thus, participants in an HDN may not use or disclose ePHI in their HDN without the authorization of the patient, unless the use or disclosure is otherwise expressly permitted by the Privacy Rule. However, if the HDN itself is formed as a separate legal entity (as opposed to operating as a creature of contracts among participating organizations), it will not likely qualify as a covered entity unless it operates as a healthcare clearinghouse, and therefore will not be subject to the Privacy Rule.[50]

---

48 Gallup Organization, *Access Denied: Americans Wary of Information Release* (May 7, 2002).
49 Randall Stross, "Whoops! We Seem to Have Misplaced Your Identity," *New York Times* (May 8, 2005): 5; Associated Press, "FBI Probes Stanford Computer Breach" (May 25, 2005), available at http://www.msnbc.msn.com/id/7983895/; Jeri Clausing, "Report Rings Alarm Bells About Privacy on the Internet," *New York Times* (Feb. 7, 2000): C10; Joseph Menn, "Industry at Odds Over ID Theft Liability," *Los Angeles Times* (Mar. 7, 2005): C1.
50 See 45 C.F.R. § 160.103 for the definition of a clearinghouse.

An HDN may organize itself in a manner that will facilitate the use and disclosure of information among its participants. The Privacy Rule permits legally separate organizations to form themselves into organized healthcare arrangements (OHCAs) to gain additional flexibility in the use and disclosure of ePHI. Participating providers in an HDN may become an OHCA if they are clinically integrated and patients receive care from more than one HDN participant. Organizing an HDN as a data warehouse or community-wide database may help to demonstrate the clinical integration needed to support OHCA status. Otherwise, nonaffiliated HDN participants may become an OHCA if they hold themselves out as a joint arrangement and they engage in joint utilization review or quality assurance or financial risk sharing. Here, the HDN structure might be used to support the analysis of each participant's treatment activities against established norms, and might assist in managing utilization review for all participants. Clearly, however, OHCA status will require participants to do more than just share a common health information network.

If an HDN qualifies as an OHCA, it gains the advantages that OHCA status confers. For example, its participants are not required to enter into business associate agreements for the purpose of disclosing ePHI; except for psychotherapy notes, they would be permitted, without authorization, to disclose ePHI for treatment and for the network's healthcare operations; they may use a joint notice of privacy practices and obtain one patient acknowledgment; and they may designate a single person to serve as a joint privacy officer.

HDN participants might also qualify as affiliated covered entities (ACEs) if they meet either the common ownership or common control test required of affiliated covered entities. This would give them the added advantages of an ACE with respect to exchange of ePHI, joint policies, single notice and acknowledgment, single point for managing HIPAA individual rights, and avoidance of business associate agreements. But, although there are data sharing and management benefits in structuring an HDN as an OHCA or an ACE, each HDN participant also would have to address potential additional liability exposure that it might derive under state law from those arrangements for the actions of the other HDN participants.

If OHCA and ACE status are not available or are undesirable to an HDN's participants, it is likely that they may choose to establish business associate relationships among themselves. Who would be a business associate of whom will depend upon the HDN's structure and role. In an HDN in which each provider maintains its own EHRs and the HDN serves as a pointer to locate a patient's records in whichever providers maintain them, one can argue for or against business associate status. It can be argued that both the HDN and each participant are engaged in the business associate functions of data administration and processing, so each in that model would be a business associate of the others. However, it can also be argued that the HDN merely directs covered entities to each other's health information using a master location registry, and therefore functions as merely an "information conduit" with "incidental contacts" to ePHI, in which case the HDN would not require a business associate agreement with each participating covered entity. As a practical matter, however, the participating covered entities may *want* business associate status for the HDN because it may give them additional control over the HDN's operations and greater protection against improper disclosures of ePHI by the HDN.

But where the HDN provides either separate data warehouses for individual participating providers or one data warehouse for all medical records, the HDN would be providing the data management function for each participant, and therefore should be a business associate of each participant. In these structures, the participants would not likely need to be business associates of each other unless they provide additional business associate services to each other. With respect to the HDN, participating covered entities will have to pay careful attention to required business associate agreement content as they structure their information network.

The Privacy Rule also permits entities governed by the rule to use or disclose protected health information (PHI) for treatment, payment, and healthcare operations. This exception to the rule requiring patient authorization for the use or disclosure of ePHI provides broad latitude to move ePHI within an HDN for treatment purposes, and a variety of operational activities for multiple HDN providers treating the same patient. Depending upon how the HDN is structured and whether its participants are all covered entities, the HDN could perform functions that would fall within the Privacy Rule definition of healthcare operations, including quality assurance, business management, and general administrative activities. In the HDN designed to maintain a community-wide database of health information, the transfer of a provider's health information into the HDN's database may fall under the transfer or consolidation of part of a covered entity with another covered entity, because multiple covered entities would be consolidating their health information in the database. Also, if the HDN creates de-identified information or limited data sets for use by the covered entities in network studies, it would be engaging in healthcare operations.

Another critical issue for interoperable EHRs is how they can be used effectively for research. If created as an integrated record of a patient's health care from multiple providers over time, the EHR will offer researchers longitudinal records for public health and medical research, and the question will be how researchers can obtain lawful access to that information. Using ePHI for research, including maintaining ePHI in a research database indefinitely, requires notice and either patient authorization, an institutional review board (IRB) or privacy board waiver of authorization, or satisfaction of the requirements for one of the limited exemptions from authorization (that is, preparing for research or studying decedents). The HDN's policies and procedures and the EHR's functionality will have to accommodate these requirements as well as the administrative implementation of them among the participants before ePHI in the system can be used effectively for research. In addition, participants, and possibly the HDN itself, will likely be required to comply with other federal law governing research.[51] (For a detailed discussion of the use of PHI in research, see Chapter 14.)

The EHR could be used without patient authorization for studies, such as quality assurance studies, that would constitute healthcare operations. But if those studies amount to a systematic investigation that contributes to generalizable knowledge, they would constitute research for HIPAA purposes, and use of PHI for them would require patient authorization or an IRB or privacy board waiver. So, characterizing research as healthcare operations is risky, and covered entities should do so only with the advice of qualified legal counsel.

The same need to accommodate patient authorization arises in connection with studying longitudinal EHRs for public health purposes, although here covered entities could take advantage of the Privacy Rule authorization exception for disclosures to public health agencies, and the various exceptions for disclosures for certain public health interests (for example, child abuse reporting, prevention of disease, workplace medical surveillance). To qualify for this public health exception, the public health agency must be "legally entitled" to receive information

---

[51] See 45 C.F.R. pt. 46; 21 C.F.R. pts. 11, 50, and 56; Neil F. O'Flaherty and Pamela J. Furman, "FDA Considerations Related to Maintaining Clinical Trial Records in Electronic Form," *Health Lawyers News* (Dec. 2004).

from EHRs maintained in the HDN. One question that may arise, therefore, is whether the public health agency's enabling statute encompasses the study it wants to conduct. The minimum necessary rule will apply unless the disclosure is authorized by the patient or is required by law. If the information sought for either medical or public health research is a limited data set and is used pursuant to a limited data set agreement or is de-identified, the health information involved ceases to be PHI, and the Privacy Rule authorization requirements would not be applicable.

The Privacy Rule gives individuals the right to access their ePHI even if it is located in different designated record sets in different locations. Thus, individuals have access to all the information in their EHR even if the records are maintained in a pointer system HDN in different covered entities. Where PHI is managed in an HDN, a key question that arises is who should be responsible for determining whether one of the exceptions to access applies and for granting individuals' access to their ePHI when access is appropriate. If the data network has no central data repository, and the health information simply remains where it was captured, data access management would likely be the responsibility of each covered entity. Here, the HDN might not have the knowledge necessary to determine whether the individuals are entitled to access to the ePHI or whether some exception to their right of access applies (for example, the health information was created for, or used in, a legal action).

However, if the HDN is structured as a community health records model with a central data depository containing all of an individual's EHR, it might be appropriate to give the HDN greater responsibility, as the business associate of the covered entities, for managing individuals' access, particularly because the EHR that the HDN maintains would consist of the integrated information from multiple participating covered entities. In setting up the HDN, participants will need to decide how individuals will be given access and what the scope of that access will be, and set out in the HDN policies who in the network will be responsible for managing access.

The same kinds of issues arise with respect to the individual's right to request restrictions on disclosures. Participants in a decentralized HDN may simply maintain their current practices with respect to an individual's requests for restrictions. Those in the more centralized community health record model will likely need to agree upon what requests will be granted and what requests will be denied, and whether restrictions will be honored even if HIPAA permits disclosures irrespective of those restrictions. The HDN policies and procedures would need to delineate how the HDN would handle those requests.

With an EHR in an HDN, the possibility increases for many more disclosures of ePHI made at the speed of light, but it is not clear that the burden of accounting for disclosures in compliance with the Privacy Rule will necessarily increase. The HDN participants may take advantage of the HIPAA exceptions to the accounting requirement for disclosures made for healthcare operations or to other participants for treatment purposes, and those disclosures for which an accounting is required would likely be highly automated in an EHR environment. HDN participants would still need to decide who has the responsibility for maintaining the accounting and making it available for individuals who request it.

With respect to HIPAA individual rights, therefore, the challenges in an HDN—that is, beyond the current HIPAA requirements with which any covered entity has to contend now—are likely to be in the allocation of responsibility for managing those rights among the HDN participants and the HDN itself. In the decentralized HDN models, the covered entities themselves are likely to retain control and responsibility; in the centralized models, the HDN will likely have a greater role.

Other Privacy Issues

In designing HDNs that incorporate EHRs, it is important to remember that the Privacy Rule applies only to the healthcare providers, health plans, and clearinghouses—and leaves considerable health information outside of its jurisdiction. This information remains subject to many state laws governing the privacy of health information.

Confidentiality obligations vary from state to state. Many states have general health information confidentiality statutes that apply to specific categories of persons, including healthcare providers, third-party administrators, and employers. Other general confidentiality requirements are imposed on providers in legislation enunciating patients' rights. For the most part, however, confidentiality provisions are found in statutes and regulations that license or otherwise regulate specific categories of providers and their duty to maintain medical records. These requirements apply to the providers maintaining the patient records, and in some instances also apply to those who receive patient information from a regulated provider. Confidentiality requirements also may vary depending on the type of information recorded or the purpose of a particular disclosure of information. (See Chapter 6 for a detailed discussion of state health records confidentiality laws.)

When an EHR is transmitted across state lines, it may not always be clear which state's law applies or which courts will have jurisdiction if a dispute arises over disclosure of an individual's health information. Several factors determine which state has jurisdiction to resolve such a dispute—including where the medical record entries were made, where patient care was delivered, and the location of the medical records. The consolidation of the healthcare industry into national networks of providers located in many different states and the increasing availability of EHR data have highlighted the challenge of identifying applicable confidentiality requirements.

Use of EHRs may also trigger the requirements of confidentiality laws in foreign jurisdictions. (See Chapter 6 for a more detailed discussion of these laws.) For example, the European Union Data Privacy Directive will apply when healthcare organizations collect health information from EU citizens. These organizations and HDNs and other data networks they create may also need to address the privacy requirements of codes of ethics applicable to Internet-based information management systems.[52]

HIPAA Security Rule

The use of an EHR increases the risk of unauthorized disclosure of personal health information, thereby necessitating special safeguards to keep the data confidential. The ease with which personal health information can be collected, stored, and accessed in an EHR system means that, generally, more information is included in a computer-based record than in a paper record. The detailed and sophisticated health information often found in computer-based records—and the trend to-

---

[52] See, e.g., Health Internet Ethics, *Principles for Internet Health Services,* available at http://www.hiethics.org/Principles/indes.esp; Internet Healthcare Coalition, *eHealth Code of Ethics,* available at www.ihealthcoalition.org/ethics/ethics.html; Health On the Net Foundation, *Code of Conduct,* available at http://www.hon.ch/HONcode.

ward use of this data for nonhealth purposes—makes EHRs attractive targets. A single breach of an EHR system's security can lead to disclosure of hundreds—or even thousands—of records and to potentially catastrophic liability for such disclosure, because computers are capable of accessing, copying, and transmitting large numbers of records in an instant.

Automation of the information distribution process and the integration of computer and telecommunication linkages allow widespread access to patient records, not only by the parties involved in providing care, but also by secondary users of the information.[53] Secondary users of patient records information include life, health, and disability insurers; employee health benefit plans and support organizations; educational institutions; both the civil and criminal justice systems; rehabilitation and social welfare programs; credit agencies and banking centers; and others who do not normally participate in HDNs. Accordingly, confidentiality must be maintained and unauthorized access to EHRs prevented, both by inside and outside users of EHR systems and by primary and secondary users of individual health information.

Because the potential for large-scale breaches of data security is much greater in an EHR system, and because a provider bears the greatest risk of liability for unauthorized disclosure, a provider who implements such a system must be sure that the system adequately protects EHR security with respect to both internal and external users of the EHR. Computer system security must therefore balance the need for ready access to patient information by those involved in patient care with the need to protect against unauthorized access and loss of critical health information. This may require a delicate balance between conflicting objectives. On the one hand, a provider may be liable when its records are so highly guarded that health information is not readily available to those treating a patient; on the other hand, the provider can be liable for privacy and security breaches that result from permitting easy access to EHRs by unauthorized personnel or from inadequately safeguarding the EHRs from destruction.

To comply with legal requirements, an EHR system must provide for both system and data security. "Security" can be defined as protecting the integrity, availability, confidentiality, and accountability of

---

[53] U.S. Congress, Office of Technology Assessment (OTA), Protecting Privacy in Computerized Medical Information, OTA-TCT-576 (Washington, D.C.: 1993).

information system resources.[54] Data security exists when data are protected from improper disclosure or unauthorized or unintended alteration. System security implies that a defined system functions in a defined operational environment, serves a defined set of users, contains prescribed data and operational programs, has defined network connections and interactions with other systems, and incorporates safeguards to protect the system against defined threats to the system and its resources and data.[55] Appropriate computer security can generally be achieved through a combination of administrative, physical, and technical measures. It is generally preferable to incorporate the technical safeguards into the system application or program (that is, the EHR system), rather than relying on network infrastructure for security.[56]

The Security Rule, published in the *Federal Register* on February 20, 2003, is one of the major components of the regulations issued pursuant to HIPAA, and is designed to protect the security of ePHI.[57] The rule establishes standards for the physical security of ePHI and, together with the Privacy Rule, provides for the comprehensive protection of PHI. This is the principal body of federal regulations addressing the protections that covered entities using EHRs must create to protect the confidentiality of individual health information.

General Security Requirements

After April 21, 2005, the Security Rule applies to most covered entities,[58] but only to their receipt, creation, use, storage, and transmission of ePHI.[59] It is therefore more limited in scope than the Privacy Rule,

---

[54] J. R. Christiansen, *An Integrated Standard of Care for Healthcare Information Security: Risk Management, HIPAA, and Beyond* (American Health Lawyers Association, 2005), 14–15; see also National Institute of Standards and Technology (NIST), *Risk Management Guide for Information Technology Systems*, NIST Special Publication 800-30 (Oct. 2001).

[55] Institute of Medicine, Health Data in the Information Age (Washington, D.C.: National Academy Press, 1994).

[56] See OTA, Protecting Privacy 91; AHIMA, *Practice Brief: Portable Computer Security (Updated)* (June 2003), available at http://library.ahima.org/expdio/groups/public/documents/ahima/pub_bok1_019872.html.

[57] 45 C.F.R. §§ 164.302 et seq.

[58] The compliance date for small health plans is April 21, 2006.

[59] 45 C.F.R. § 164.302.

which applies to PHI in any form.[60] (For a discussion of HIPAA generally and of covered entities, see Chapter 6.) However, the Security Rule applies to ePHI in whatever form it may be transmitted or stored, and whether or not it is transmitted in a standard transaction prescribed by the HIPAA regulations governing electronic transactions and code sets (TCS Rule).[61] Transmissions using any electronic media, the physical movement of data from one location to another in any removable or transportable electronic storage media, transmissions using the Internet (wide open), extranet, leased lines, dial-up lines, or private networks, and "fax-back"[62] and telephone voice response systems are all subject to the Security Rule.[63] Paper and voice transmissions, paper-to-paper facsimiles, video teleconferencing, and messages left on voice mail systems are not subject to the rule, because the information they contain was not in electronic form before the transmission.[64]

The Security Rule also makes no distinction between transmissions of ePHI within a corporate entity and those made to external parties.[65] Thus, members of a covered entity's workforce who work at home or who are mobile will be subject to the rule and must be included in a covered entity's security compliance program. The challenges facing covered entities will increase as their workforces become more mobile and dispersed. The entities must establish the safeguards required by the rule in order to protect the ePHI they transmit across remote access networks or carry in portable computers and handheld devices. Covered entities with wireless data environments must also implement technologies that will prevent signals from escaping secure work environments.

The Security Rule requires all covered entities to:

- Ensure the confidentiality, integrity, and availability of all ePHI that they create, receive, maintain, or transmit

---

[60] For a discussion of the distinctions between the Privacy Rule and the Security Rule, see 68 Fed. Reg. 8335 (Feb. 20, 2003).

[61] 68 Fed. Reg. 8342 (Feb. 20, 2003).

[62] "Fax-back" is "a request for information from a computer made via voice or telephone keypad input with the requested information returned as a fax." 68 Fed. Reg. 8342 (Feb. 20, 2003).

[63] 68 Fed. Reg. 8337, 8342 (Feb. 20, 2003).

[64] 68 Fed. Reg. 8342 (Feb. 20, 2003).

[65] 68 Fed. Reg. 8337 (Feb. 20, 2003).

- Protect against any reasonably anticipated threats or hazards to the security or integrity of such ePHI
- Protect against any reasonably anticipated uses or disclosures of such ePHI that are not otherwise permitted or required by the Privacy Rule
- Ensure compliance with the Security Rule by their workforces[66]

To achieve these requirements, the Security Rule sets forth standards for security and integrity, which covered entities are expected to meet. These standards have a unique feature, however. They state fairly general objectives, but provide no detailed instructions concerning how to meet them. The standards are essentially technology neutral. The rule permits covered entities to design the specific safeguards that will achieve those objectives in their own organizations and operational environments. Covered entities may use any security methods that enable them "to reasonably and appropriately implement" the security standards of the rule.[67] Their choice of security protections will depend upon the complexity of their organizations, the security capabilities of their hardware and software, the likelihood and severity of risk to ePHI in their systems, and the cost of implementing security safeguards.[68] The rule establishes the general specifications for ePHI security measures, and leaves to covered entities the discretion to determine how best to build them.

The security safeguards are presented as standards and supporting implementation specifications. The specifications are divided into "required" specifications and "addressable" specifications. Required specifications are mandatory, and covered entities must implement them in order to comply with the rule. An addressable specification is more discretionary, and permits a covered entity to determine whether the specification is appropriate for the entity's particular organization, operations, and environment.[69] In making this determination, the covered entity has three options:

- If it determines that the specification is reasonable and appropriate, the entity must implement the safeguard

---

[66] 45 C.F.R. § 164.306(a).
[67] 45 C.F.R. § 164.306(b).
[68] 45 C.F.R. § 164.306(b)(2).
[69] 45 C.F.R. § 164.306(d).

- If it determines that the specification is not reasonable and appropriate for its operations, the entity must document why, and implement an equivalent alternative security measure
- If the covered entity determines that it can achieve the standard by using another, completely different security measure (that is, one that is neither an addressable specification nor an equivalent alternative safeguard), the entity may elect to implement the different measure and not to implement either the measure called for in the Rule or the equivalent alternative, in which case the covered entity must document the rationale for its decision[70]

Where the rule establishes a standard without implementation specifications, the standard is also the implementation standard.[71] Although the government recognizes that no information system can be totally secure,[72] the security standards and implementation specifications together set a high standard for ePHI protection.

The Security Rule and the Privacy Rule work together to provide a comprehensive scheme of protection for health information. The Privacy Rule contains its own general security requirement for which covered entities must "have in place appropriate administrative, technical, and physical safeguards to protect the privacy of protected health information."[73] Thus, the Privacy Rule extends the requirement for security protections to include all PHI.

Administrative Safeguards

The Security Rule establishes administrative standards that each covered entity must meet.[74] These safeguards allow covered entities considerable discretion in implementing the specifications in a manner appropriate for the size and nature of their businesses. Even the required implementation specifications provide flexibility for covered entities to design the required safeguards to fit the characteristics of their businesses and the likelihood of security incidents in their operations.

---

[70] 45 C.F.R. § 164.306(d)(ii); 68 Fed. Reg. 8336 (Feb. 20, 2003).
[71] 68 Fed. Reg. 8336 (Feb. 20, 2003).
[72] 68 Fed. Reg. 8346 (Feb. 20, 2003).
[73] 45 C.F.R. § 164.530(c)(1).
[74] 45 C.F.R. § 164.308.

Security Management Process

The Security Rule requires covered entities to establish a security management process that will prevent, detect, contain, and correct security violations.[75] This standard requires covered entities to conduct risk analysis and risk management and to establish a sanctions policy. Before covered entities can take effective steps to eliminate or minimize the risks to, and vulnerabilities of, their ePHI, they must identify and assess those risks. The government views the security management process as the foundation upon which all the other HIPAA security standards are based.[76] The risk analysis specification requires covered entities to keep their security measures "current," but allows the entity to determine how best to do so. The standard does not mandate formal internal security audits, but a covered entity is expected to conduct reviews as frequently and in as much detail as its security environment requires.[77] Security policies should identify the kinds of problems, events, and developments that will trigger a determination of whether a security assessment is needed. To effect a thorough and accurate risk analysis, covered entities must consider "all relevant losses" expected if security measures were not in place. "Relevant losses" include those caused by unauthorized uses and disclosures and loss of data integrity expected to occur in the absence of adequate security measures.[78]

A covered entity must impose "appropriate sanctions" against any member of its workforce who fails to comply with its security policies and procedures.[79] The Security Rule reflects the government's view that punishment is a customary component of effective security programs and is necessary for effective compliance. However, covered entities may determine the type and severity of sanctions imposed based on their security policies and the relative severity of the violation. A covered entity must meet the standards set forth in the rule, but the entity is free to create additional protections for information it believes requires additional security.[80]

---

[75] 45 C.F.R. § 164.308(a)(1).
[76] 68 Fed. Reg. 8344 (Feb. 20, 2003).
[77] 45 C.F.R. § 164.308(a)(1)(ii)(D).
[78] 68 Fed. Reg. 8347 (Feb. 20, 2003).
[79] 45 C.F.R. § 164.308(a)(1)(ii)(C).
[80] 68 Fed. Reg. 8347 (Feb. 20, 2003).

Security Official

The administrative safeguards require each covered entity or covered component of a hybrid entity to appoint one official to be responsible for compliance with the Security Rule.[81] The security official's responsibilities include management and supervision of the use of security measures and the conduct of personnel in relation to the protection of ePHI. The Security and Privacy Rules assign to the security official and the privacy official the same responsibilities with respect to the rules, and the same person may fill both positions.[82]

Workforce Security

A covered entity must ensure that members of its workforce have appropriate access to ePHI, and must establish policies that will prevent access to ePHI by unauthorized members of its workforce.[83] The policies should establish procedures for determining which employees may have access to ePHI; the methods of granting, reviewing, and modifying access to a workstation or program; and the methods for supervising those employees in their use of ePHI. For example, a health clinic that is a covered component of a larger organization must establish policies and procedures to prevent unauthorized access to its ePHI by personnel in other components of the organization.

The Security Rule does not require employee background checks as part of a covered entity's workforce clearance procedure, but a covered entity must determine that the access of a workforce member is appropriate.[84] How that is accomplished is left to the entity's discretion. An entity's risk assessment should identify the need for, and extent of, an appropriate screening procedure and its feasibility. These specifications permit large covered entities to establish formal procedures for screening employees, and permit sole practitioners, who have limited staff, to establish minimal, if any, workforce clearance procedures. Whatever procedures a covered entity ultimately develops will have to be justified by the circumstances of that entity's structure, operations, and environment.

---

[81] 45 C.F.R. § 164.308(a)(2).
[82] 68 Fed. Reg. 8347 (Feb. 20, 2003).
[83] 45 C.F.R. § 164.308(a)(3)(i).
[84] 45 C.F.R. § 164.308(a)(2)(ii)(B).

The standards include a related addressable implementation specification that requires covered entities to create procedures for terminating access to ePHI when a workforce member's employment ends.[85] Although the standards provide no detailed termination procedures, they require covered entities to document the policies and procedures they will use to implement the termination specification. The purpose of this documentation is not to specify all the circumstances under which employment will be terminated, but to ensure that termination procedures include actions (for example, revoking passwords) that will protect the security of ePHI.

Information Access Management

A key standard in the Security Rule is the requirement policies and procedures for authorizing access to ePHI that enable covered entities to comply with the Privacy Rule. Where a clearinghouse function is part of a larger organization, these policies and procedures must isolate and protect ePHI that is used in a clearinghouse function from access by the larger organization.[86] Covered entities must also address methods of authorizing access to ePHI and for reviewing and modifying authorizations.[87]

Security Awareness and Training

Like the Privacy Rule, the Security Rule requires each covered entity to provide ongoing, reasonable, and appropriate security awareness training for its workforce.[88] The elements of a security training program are addressable implementation specifications, so although security training should be part of the entity's overall training program, covered entities may design their programs and methods to fit their size, risks, and operations. The rule suggests that training include periodic security reminders, user education on virus protection, and training on the importance of monitoring log-ins and password management.[89] Business associates and other nonworkforce members with potential access

---

[85] 45 C.F.R. § 164.308(a)(2)(ii)(C).
[86] 45 C.F.R. § 164.308(a)(4)(ii)(A).
[87] 45 C.F.R. §§ 164.308(a)(4)(ii)(B) and (C).
[88] 45 C.F.R. § 164.308(a)(5)(i); 68 Fed. Reg. 8350 (Feb. 20, 2003).
[89] 45 C.F.R. § 164.308(a)(5)(ii).

to ePHI must be made aware of a covered entity's security policies, but a covered entity is not required to provide training to business associates or anyone else who is not a member of its workforce. Covered entities therefore may, but are not required to, train vendors, independent contractors, temporary personnel, and consultants. Given this requirement, a covered entity should consider what information it will give these individuals and what documentation of receipt, if any, it will require.

Security Incidents

A "security incident" is "the attempted or successful unauthorized access, use, disclosure, modification, or destruction of information, or interference with system operations in an information system."[90] The rule requires a covered entity to establish policies and procedures for responding to and reducing the harmful effects, if any, of a security incident.[91] A covered entity's risk assessment and security management programs should identify security incidents, document their occurrence and their outcomes, and provide direction for managing them.[92] The Security Rule permits, but does not require, covered entities to report security incidents to outside parties. Such reporting will depend upon a covered entity's business operations and other legal requirements to which it is subject (for example, local or state reporting requirements).[93]

Contingency Planning

Covered entities are required to develop a security contingency plan—which includes a data backup plan, a disaster recovery plan, and an emergency mode operation plan—and to address the need for an applications and data criticality analysis and testing and revision procedures.[94] DHHS views this requirement as the "only way" to protect the "availability, integrity, and security of data" during unexpected events or crises. The agency suggests that each covered entity determine its own potential risks in the event of an emergency that results in a loss of operations.[95] Each covered entity is permitted to design its contingency

---

[90] 45 C.F.R. § 164.304.
[91] 45 C.F.R. § 164.308(a)(6)(i).
[92] 45 C.F.R. § 164.308(a)(6)(ii).
[93] 68 Fed. Reg. 8350 (Feb. 20, 2003).
[94] 45 C.F.R. § 164.308(a)(7).
[95] 68 Fed. Reg. 8351 (Feb. 20, 2003).

plan to accommodate its individual structure, size, and operations, so long as it includes appropriate procedures for maintaining critical health information in a crisis.

Security Safeguards Evaluation

The Security Rule requires covered entities periodically to evaluate the technical and nontechnical components of their security measures to demonstrate and document the extent to which they comply with the rule and their own security policies and procedures.[96] Although covered entities are free to establish policies that define the frequency with which they must evaluate their security measures, any events or developments that affect ePHI security—such as a security incident, implementation of new technology, or a material change in the structure or operations of the organization—should trigger consideration of whether an evaluation is warranted. Covered entities are free to consult with external compliance certification organizations, but no formal external certification of compliance with the Security Rule is required.[97]

Physical Security Standards

The Security Rule requires covered entities to establish policies and procedures that will provide physical safeguards for ePHI.[98] The rule defines physical safeguards as "the physical measures, policies, and procedures to protect a covered entity's electronic information systems and related buildings and equipment, from natural and environmental hazards, and unauthorized intrusion."[99] This broad standard extends to a covered entity's facilities, computer devices, and workstations.

Facility Access Controls

This standard requires covered entities to implement policies and procedures that control physical access to electronic information systems and to all facilities that contain such systems. "Facility" is defined as

---

[96]   45 C.F.R. § 164.308(a)(8).
[97]   68 Fed. Reg. 8351 (Feb. 20, 2003).
[98]   45 C.F.R. § 164.308.
[99]   45 C.F.R. § 164.304.

physical premises and the interior and exterior of buildings.[100] The standard focuses upon protecting ePHI from unauthorized access and ensuring that authorized personnel have appropriate access. It contains the following addressable implementation specifications that should be evaluated and implemented as needed by the covered entity:[101]

- *Contingency operations.* Implement procedures for facility access in support of data restoration as part of the covered entity's disaster recovery efforts and for emergency mode operations in the event of an emergency. A covered entity's contingency plan should include a data backup plan that defines what information should be retrieved to allow the entity to continue operating in an emergency.[102]
- *Facility security plan.* Implement policies and procedures for protecting equipment and facilities housing ePHI from unauthorized physical access, tampering, and theft. A covered entity remains responsible for facility security, even when it shares space in a building with another organization. Facility security may include electronic and physical security systems.[103]
- *Access control.* Implement procedures for controlling and validating individuals' access to facilities based on their role or function in the organization or their status as visitors and their access to software programs for testing and revision. Access-control procedures should identify, address, and resolve any conflicts of authority between individuals with access to ePHI and those responsible for checking and maintaining access controls.[104]
- *Maintenance records.* Implement policies and procedures for documenting repairs and modifications to a facility's physical security measures (for example, doors, locks, surveillance).

Workstation Use and Security

The Security Rule requires covered entities to implement policies and procedures to protect the confidentiality of ePHI contained in or used

---

[100] Ibid.
[101] 45 C.F.R. § 164.310(a)(2).
[102] 68 Fed. Reg. 8351 (Feb. 20, 2003).
[103] 68 Fed. Reg. 8353 (Feb. 20, 2003).
[104] Ibid.

at its workstations.[105] A "workstation" is both the computer and any electronic media stored in the immediate vicinity.[106] An appropriate solution to a workstation security problem will depend upon a covered entity's risk assessment. Its policies and procedures should specify which functions should be performed and how they can be performed at workstations that contain ePHI. Security policies and procedures must also address the physical location and surroundings of workstations to maximize the security of ePHI, determine the activities an employee may conduct at such workstations without jeopardizing the confidentiality of ePHI, and govern the design of workstations and the work areas in which they are used so that unauthorized persons cannot see or use the workstations. These safeguards include locking portable workstations to desks to prevent their theft and limiting access to work areas that include computers that contain or have access to ePHI.

Device and Media Controls

The rule also establishes a standard requiring covered entities to implement policies and procedures that control the acquisition, receipt, and movement within the facility of hardware and electronic media that may contain ePHI.[107] The standard includes two required implementation standards. The policies and procedures must provide for the final disposition of hardware and electronic media and the removal of ePHI from media before the media are reused or recycled. Covered entities must be certain they have stripped ePHI from all electronic media that will used for a new purpose or that remain in hardware being discarded. Thus, a covered entity should develop procedures for disposing of hardware and software containing ePHI and for maintaining a record that will show proper implementation of procedures.

The standard also includes two addressable implementation standards. Covered entities must determine whether they need a record of the movements of hardware and electronic media that contain ePHI, as well as a record of the persons responsible for such movements. Movement records are useful for demonstrating compliance with the standard and in defending against negligence actions alleging the

---

[105] 45 C.F.R. §§ 164.310(b) and (c).
[106] 45 C.F.R. § 164.304.
[107] 45 C.F.R. § 164.310(d).

improper disclosure of ePHI. Covered entities should also consider creating a retrievable, exact copy of the ePHI before moving equipment. A covered entity that knew that the ePHI would be needed for healthcare purposes and failed to retrieve it could have exposure to liability for improper disposal of ePHI.

Technical Security Standards

The technical security standards of the Security Rule follow the administrative and physical security standards in their general nature and their focus on requiring covered entities to implement methods and technologies appropriate to their business operations.[108] DHHS recognized that the speed with which technology changes would make highly specific regulations obsolete almost immediately.[109] Although these broad standards are disquieting to some covered entities who prefer clearly delineated guidance from DHHS, many have taken advantage of the flexibility the rule provides, and have developed policies and procedures tailored to their own organizations.

Access Control

The standards require covered entities to implement policies and procedures to grant access to ePHI only to individuals and software programs that have been granted access rights as outlined in the administrative security safeguards of the rule.[110] These procedures must assign unique user identifications to each individual granted access to ePHI, so that users can be identified and tracked. What types of access controls and other implementation features should be used is up to each covered entity to determine in light of its operations.[111] Covered entities must also develop procedures for providing access to ePHI in an emergency so that access to essential ePHI will not be lost. Although the rule suggests that covered entities consider installing an automatic log-off feature in their information and communications systems, entities are not required to use the feature if they determine and document that other security features will adequately protect their

---

[108] 45 C.F.R. § 164.310.
[109] 68 Fed. Reg. 8343 (Feb. 20, 2003).
[110] 45 C.F.R. § 164.312(a)(1).
[111] 68 Fed. Reg. 8355 (Feb. 20, 2003).

ePHI.[112] Covered entities may also use encryption/decryption as another safeguard if they have determined that the risks to their information systems require it.[113]

Audit Controls

Information systems that contain or use ePHI must incorporate audit control mechanisms to record and examine system activity.[114] This safeguard may use any combination of hardware, software, and procedural mechanisms to enable covered entities to track system activity, and may need to comply with state laws not preempted by HIPAA.[115] This audit control and tracking requirement should not be confused with the accounting requirement of the Privacy Rule, which mandates creating a record of a covered entity's disclosures of PHI.[116]

Integrity and Authentication

Safeguards for the integrity and authenticity are essential protections for ePHI. Covered entities are required to implement policies and procedures to protect ePHI from improper alteration or destruction,[117] and may use whatever mechanisms and technology are appropriate for their operations.[118] Error-correcting memory and magnetic disk storage are examples of protection mechanisms often used. The standard also requires covered entities to implement procedures that will verify the identity of a person or entity seeking access to ePHI.[119]

Transmission Security

In addition to the safeguards required for stored data, the rule requires that each covered entity consider security measures to protect ePHI being transmitted over its communications systems.[120] The implemen-

---

[112] 45 C.F.R. § 164.312(a)(2)(iii); 68 Fed. Reg. 8355 (Feb. 20, 2003).
[113] 45 C.F.R. § 164.312(a)(2)(iv).
[114] 45 C.F.R. § 164.312(b).
[115] 68 Fed. Reg. 8355 (Feb. 20, 2003).
[116] For the Privacy Rule accounting provisions, see 45 C.F.R. § 164.528.
[117] 45 C.F.R. § 164.312(c)(1).
[118] 68 Fed. Reg. 8356 (Feb. 20, 2003).
[119] 45 C.F.R. § 164.312(d).
[120] 45 C.F.R. § 164.312(e).

tation standards address the use of encryption software and preventing unauthorized modifications during data transmission.[121] These addressable standards do not require data encryption, unless a vulnerability exists in the transmission network or unless transmissions are made over the Internet or other open networks that are susceptible to interception.[122]

Organizational Security Safeguards

The Security Rule establishes standards for transmissions of ePHI between covered entities and their business associates and between different groups within an organization. The rule also establishes special security standards for group health plans and healthcare clearinghouses and the documentation requirements for all covered entities.

Business Associates

The Security Rule expands the Privacy Rule provisions governing the relationship between a covered entity and its business associates.[123] (See the detailed discussion of business associates in Chapter 6.) The administrative security standards require the business associate agreement to include additional provisions that create an obligation in business associates to comply with both the security and privacy protections of the rules. In addition to the requirements established by the Privacy Rule, the business associate agreement must provide that the business associate will

- implement administrative, physical, and technical safeguards that reasonably and appropriately protect the confidentiality, integrity, and availability of the ePHI that it creates, receives, maintains, or transmits on behalf of the covered entity;
- ensure that any agent, including a subcontractor, to whom the business associate provides such information agrees to implement reasonable and appropriate safeguards to protect it;

---

[121] 45 C.F.R. § 164.312(e)(1).
[122] 68 Fed. Reg. 8357 (Feb. 20, 2003).
[123] For the Privacy Rule provisions concerning business associates, see 45 C.F.R. §§ 164.502 (e) and 504(e).

- report to the covered entity any breach of security of which it becomes aware; and
- authorize termination of the contract by the covered entity if it determines that the business associate violated a material term of the contract.[124]

The use of a business associate agreement is not required for transmissions of ePHI to a healthcare provider for treatment purposes, by a group health plan to a plan sponsor, or from or to certain government health plan programs.[125] Consistent with the Privacy Rule, different requirements apply if the covered entity and the business associate are both governmental entities.[126]

Hybrid and Affiliated Entities and Group Health Plans

Hybrid entities are organizations that are composed of several components, at least one of which is a covered entity and one is not.[127] Affiliated covered entities are legally separate, but functionally or structurally related, covered entities that choose to operate as one covered entity for purposes of complying with the Privacy and Security Rules.[128] (For a detailed discussion of hybrid and affiliated entities, see Chapter 6.) The covered components of a hybrid entity are subject to both the Privacy Rule and the Security Rule. The security safeguards they establish must protect ePHI from unauthorized use or access by the other components of the organization that are not subject to HIPAA. Affiliated entities may operate under joint privacy and security policies and procedures.

The Security Rule also imposes on group health plans organizational standards that are similar to those of the Privacy Rule. The standards mandate that agreements between group health plans and plan sponsors generally require a plan sponsor to implement safeguards to protect the confidentiality of ePHI that the sponsor uses or transmits to a health plan, and to report to the plan any breach of security of which the spon-

---

[124] 45 C.F.R. § 164.314(a)(2)(i).
[125] 45 C.F.R. § 164.308(b)(2).
[126] 45 C.F.R. § 164.314(a)(2)(ii)(A).
[127] See 45 C.F.R. §§ 164.103 and 105(a)(1).
[128] See 45 C.F.R. § 164.105(b)(1).

sor becomes aware.[129] These mandates ensure that group health plan documents will require the sponsor to protect the ePHI it creates or receives on behalf of the plan, except for ePHI disclosed to a plan sponsor that is summary health information or enrollment/disenrollment information discussed in the privacy regulations.

Policies, Procedures, and Documentation

The Security Rule requires that covered entities develop and implement policies and procedures designed to enable them to meet the standards of the rule.[130] These policies must be in written (including electronic) form, and must be maintained for six years from the later of the date they were created and the date they were last in effect.[131] The covered entity's documentation should also include a record of actions it has taken in compliance with the Security Rule.[132] Thus, security risk assessments, interventions in response to security incidents, implementation of security safeguards, and other actions specified in the rule should all be in the covered entity's record of security compliance. If a covered entity amends its policies and procedures for any reason, the entity must also document those revisions. Finally, a covered entity must periodically review its policies and procedures and make any revisions required by environmental or operational changes.[133] The frequency with which a covered entity conducts its reviews will depend upon the entity's size, configuration, business environment, operational changes, and the particular security measures already implemented.[134]

Security Requirements in Health Data Networks

In any health data network, the HDN or the participating covered entities will be required to implement for the HDN operations all the security measures that meet the standards set forth in the Security Rule—including assessing controls and tracking methodologies and ensuring that the EHRs it maintains or uses will be free from improper

---

[129] 45 C.F.R. § 164.314(b).
[130] 45 C.F.R. § 164.316(a).
[131] 45 C.F.R. § 164.316(b)(2)(1).
[132] 45 C.F.R. § 164.316(b)(1)(ii).
[133] 45 C.F.R. § 164.316(B)(2)(iii).
[134] 68 Fed. Reg. 8361 (Feb. 20, 2003).

alteration or destruction. In addition, authentication procedures must be in place to ensure that the person or entity seeking access to the ePHI used or maintained by the HDN is authorized and authentic. The Security Rule gives HDNs the flexibility to design and implement security safeguards that are appropriate for their particular structures and operations, so long as the security standards of the Security Rule are met.

The additional challenges facing HDNs include determining what security safeguards to establish, whether all participants in the HDN must use the same safeguards regardless of their size and function, how those safeguards relate to each other in the HDN's operations, and how to manage the security requirements in an arrangement involving many participants. In addition, if the HDN includes a clearinghouse function as part of a larger organization, additional structural challenges will be presented by the Security Rule requirement that ePHI used in that clearinghouse function be isolated and protected from access by the larger organization.

State Data Security Laws

Some states have enacted laws dealing specifically with information security, as opposed to privacy, issues. For example, at this writing, 8 states have enacted security breach notice laws, and 34 states have such legislation pending.[135] These statutes are quite similar, and require persons covered by the law to disclose any breach of the security of an information system following discovery of the breach. The disclosure must be made without delay to any resident of the state whose unencrypted information was, or was reasonably believed to have been, acquired by an unauthorized person.[136] These statutes differ in two areas. The first is the description of the persons required to make disclosures of a breach. Some statutes refer to "any person or business." Others limit required action to state and local governmental agencies. The second is the definition of "security breach." Some statutes require no disclosure if there is

---

[135] See, e.g., Ill. Pub. Act 94-0036 (June 16, 2005). The 8 states are Arkansas, California, Georgia, Illinois, Indiana, Montana, North Dakota, and Washington.
[136] See Ark. Code § 4-110-105; Cal. Civ. Code § 1798.82; Ga. Code § 10-1-912; Ind. Code § 4-1-11; Mont. Code Ann. § 31-3-115; N.D. Cent. Code § 51-30-02; Wash. Rev. Code § 19.42.17(1)(a).

no reasonably anticipated harm to a resident of the state. Others require disclosure for unauthorized access to personal information.

Following HIPAA, states are also likely to adopt health information security requirement for health industry organizations that create, use, store, or transmit electronic health information. Health information managers must keep current with these developments whether or not they practice in HIPAA covered entities.

Electronic Health Records Contracting Issues

Using EHRs to their fullest extent in support of patient wellness and health care inevitably will require healthcare providers and others to enter into agreements governing the creation, use, storage, disclosure, transmission, ownership, and destruction of health information. If the information is part of a community health record within an HDN, agreements will be needed to govern the formation and operation of the HDN and to control the participation of hospitals, physicians, other clinicians, laboratories, and others in the HDN. Deployment of an EHR inevitably requires agreements with vendors and often with third-party support organizations such as clearinghouses needed to standardize data elements. As more HDNs are formed, they will re-quire agreements for the exchange of data between HDNs for the cre-ation of a true regional health record. All of these agreements will define the rights and obligations of the parties with respect to the data.

Considerations for Contracting

Several considerations will be important in crafting these agreements. The parties must determine what technology infrastructure will be used for data exchange. The infrastructure may foster a true interoper-able EHR, which is maintained in the record systems of various providers, or it may be an HDN providing a centralized data warehouse for community health records. All of the decisions needed to form the relationships between participants in the data exchange must be made as part of infrastructure planning. If an HDN is envisioned, who will serve as the HDN? Will a hospital provide the HDN services, and, if so, for how long? The participants must determine whether the pro-posed infrastructure is technologically feasible and whether sufficient human resources are available to operate it. They must also consider whether they should launch the infrastructure, taking into account the strategic implications of, and potential liability risks arising from, its operation. If the structure is to be an HDN or other data sharing arrangement, the participants must decide whether to create a new legal entity or to use an existing participant; whether that entity will be a tax-exempt, not for profit organization or a taxable business entity; and whether a joint venture would best accommodate their objectives. These questions must be addressed and resolved at the outset so that agreements accurately reflect the parties' intent.

Given the complexity of the information systems needed to implement and support an interoperable EHR, providers must decide whether they will outsource some functions of the network, and, if so, to whom and for how long. Outsourcing agreements are complex and should not be undertaken without the assistance of qualified legal counsel, particularly where one of the parties is a tax-exempt organization that is subject to the restrictions of Section 501(c)(3) of the Internal Revenue Code or where the service provider is domiciled in a foreign country.

Health Data Network Agreements

The specific provisions of an HDN agreement will depend largely upon the nature and structure of the HDN and the participating parties. In most cases, the agreement will include provisions that describe:

- The purpose, goals, and scope of the HDN
- How the data network will function and the HDN's role in it
- The categories of participating members and their rights and obligations
- The allocation of duties among the participants
- The initial and ongoing funding of the HDN
- The governance and how it is determined (for example, by capital contribution, size of participant)
- The decision-making process within the HDN
- Day-to-day management of the HDN
- Items and services to be provided or made available by the HDN
- Role of the HDN with respect to vendors and support organizations
- Communications between and among participants and the HDN
- Removal of participants and addition of participants in the future
- Collaboration with other HDNs

HDN agreements will also describe how the EHR database will be created and managed, how the "help desk" for participants will function, and how the HDN will respond to requests for access to health information from participants, patients, and third parties (for example, government agencies, courts). The agreements should also address the use of ePHI for other than patient care (such as marketing, research, and fund-raising). Most HDN agreements will incorporate business associate provisions required by the Privacy and Security Rules. Allocation of liability will be a key issue in the agreement, as will be provisions governing limitation of liability of the HDN. These liability-related provisions should be calibrated with the liability provisions of agreements with vendors who support the HDN's operations. As with any multiparty agreement, the HDN agreement should address the unwinding of the network and address how remaining participants will function if one or more participants withdraw.

Vendor Agreements

The threshold question in a vendor agreement is who will serve as the contracting party with a vendor. The agreement may be a multiparty contract involving some or all of the participants, or an agreement between the HDN and the vendor. It may be a master agreement that envisions licensees and sublicensees of software and other products. Determining the role of the vendor is a key element. The vendor may perform a support role for the participants or may relate directly with the HDN, which in turn serves as the direct support interface with the participants. Any vendor agreement in the HDN context should provide for growth of the data network and should address pricing of the vendor's products or services as growth occurs. In addition, the agreement should define for all participants the scope their license to use the product.

Vendor agreements for information technology will present all the standard information technology acquisition and support agreement issues addressing the features, functions, and performance of the product. In the context of HDNs and other data sharing arrangements, vendor agreements will present special challenges with respect to system infrastructure, including database design, system interfaces with the contracting vendor and with other vendors, and privacy and security safeguards. Because most vendors will want to use the network's data for purposes other than patient care (for example, marketing), the question of data ownership will be critical. The HDN and/or its participants should consider asserting ownership of the data and restricting the vendor from using data for its own purposes.

Participation Agreements

Participation agreements define the relationship between an HDN and its participants and the nature and scope of the services the HDN provides. The agreements should track vendor agreement provisions to the extent necessary to ensure compliance by participants with those provisions. Thus, participation agreements would likely include provisions concerning license rights, payment terms, support obligations, warranties, liability limitation and disclaimers, indemnifications, term, and termination. They also generally include specifications for the equipment and software configurations required for participation. It is through the participation agreement that the parties are able to enforce standards for data content, accuracy, integrity, and completeness and to establish the HDN's right to audit participants' compliance.

Particular attention should be paid to required business associate terms, so that covered entities participating in the HDN will be in compliance with the Privacy and Security Rules. The participation agreements should define the parties' data access and use rights and restrictions with respect to each participant's own data and those of other participants. How participants respond to requests, including subpoenas, from third parties for access to data is also an important part of the agreement. Given the scope of data network functions, the agreement should distinguish between data that constitute the "medical record" and information that is compiled and used for purely business purposes.

Participation agreements define the financial relationship between the parties, including amounts paid for services, sales taxes, fee adjustments over time, and terms of payment. Because the agreement will determine how a participant may withdraw from the network, the participant's rights with respect to the addition of new participants, and the dissolution of the HDN, care should be taken to draft provisions that ensure a cohesive yet flexible network arrangement. Each participant should be given a clear statement of the consequences of termination or withdrawal—particularly with respect to disposition of the participant's data; the HDN's right to continue to use the data; any applicable penalties, refunds, or credits; and the transition of services.

Regulatory Issues

EHRs exist in a highly regulated environment, and the body of law that affects most healthcare providers will govern how EHRs are used by the various providers who treat a particular individual. Failure to comply with these regulations can have serious legal and financial consequences, so healthcare organizations and practitioners should keep the regulations in mind as they implement EHR systems and HDNs.

Antikickback Laws

Federal and state antikickback statutes prohibit the payment, solicitation, offer, or acceptance of anything of value in exchange for the referral of any items or services paid for by a federal or state healthcare benefit program.[137] The purpose of these laws is to prevent abuse of government reimbursement programs for monetary gain. These antikickback statutes generally are broad, and give regulators and courts considerable discretion in defining when a violation has occurred.[138] Violations may result in both civil and criminal penalties, including fines, imprisonment, and exclusion from reimbursement programs.

These statutes become relevant when institutional providers implement for their employees and medical staffs EHRs that require computers and telecommunication networks in order to operate. If a hospital, for example, makes these devices available to its medical staff physicians, it can be argued that doing so constitutes payment of something of value for the referrals of patients those physicians make to the hospital. The fear that both the hospital and its physicians have of incurring sanctions for violating the federal antikickback law can present a barrier to the acceptance of EHR systems[139]—and with some justification, given the government's hostile position concerning the provision of computer equipment.[140]

---

[137] See 42 U.S.C. §§ 1320a through 7b(b); Ark. Code § 20-77-902(6); La. Rev. Stat. § 46:438.2.

[138] See, e.g., *Hanlester Network v. Shalala*, 51 F. 3d 1390 (9th Cir. 1995); *United States v. Gerber*, 760 F. 2d 68 (3d Cir.), *cert. denied*, 474 U.S. 988 (1985).

[139] See GAO, *HHS's Efforts*, 46.

[140] See K. McAnaney, *General Observations Letter Regarding Free Computers, Facsimile Machines, and Other Goods* (July 3, 1997), available at http://oig.hhs.gov/fraud/docs/safeharborregulations/freecomputers.htm; 56 Fed. Reg. 35978 (July 29, 1991).

The government has provided numerous safe harbors that provide guidance for avoiding antikickback violations.[141] Unfortunately, none of these really adequately covers the relationships that are necessary between providers to establish a viable EHR network. As of this writing, neither Congress nor DHHS has adopted a safe harbor that adequately encompasses the implementation of an EHR network. However, the Office of Inspector General (OIG) of DHHS has published proposed regulations that would create a safe harbor from the antikickback prohibitions for donations to physicians of technology necessary for e-prescribing. In the proposed regulations, the OIG has presented its thinking concerning a possible safe harbor in the future for donations to physicians of technology needed to create interoperable EHRs.[142] The OIG is considering creating two safe harbors—one to take effect before the secretary of DHHS has developed product certification criteria for interoperability, and one to take effect after such criteria are in place. In the first safe harbor, hospitals would be permitted to donate to members of their medical staffs certain software used solely for the transmission, receipt, and maintenance of EHRs, along with certain related training services. In the second safe harbor, the software would have to meet the secretary's product certifications for interoperability in order to fall outside of the antikickback prohibition. The OIG stated that this two-stage approach would be designed to promote interoperable EHRs.[143]

Although the OIG publication suggests that the government is seriously considering some form of relief from the antikickback prohibitions in order to facilitate the adoption of interoperable EHRs, the proposals raise more questions than they answer. Considerable additional analysis and debate will likely be needed to reach a workable EHR safe harbor. The OIG has solicited public comment concerning its ideas for a safe harbor. Until the government implements a practical safe harbor, therefore, institutions seeking to build an EHR system and to have their medical staffs participate, even though the physicians will likely derive no immediate financial benefit from the system, face a challenge in convincing physicians to invest in the infrastructure

---

[141] For an explanation of the safe harbors, see U.S. Department of Health and Human Services (DHHS), *Safe Harbor Regulations*, available at http://www.oig.hhs.gov/fraud/safe-harborregulations.html.
[142] 70 Fed. Reg. 59015, 59182 (Oct. 11, 2005).
[143] 70 Fed. Reg. 59187 (Oct. 11, 2005).

needed to implement EHRs. Given the pressure from the federal government and quality improvement organizations to convert entirely to EHRs, some regulatory agency relief from the burdens of the antikickback regulations is likely in the future. In support of the effort to seek relief, the healthcare industry will likely continue to build a case for the EHR as a fraud-fighting device as well as a benefit to patient care.[144]

Stark Law

Closely related to the antikickback statutes are prohibitions against physician self-referrals. These are known as the Starks laws at the federal level,[145] and little Stark laws or baby Stark laws when enacted by the states.[146] These statutes prohibit a physician from referring patients to an entity for services paid for by federal or state health benefit programs if the physician has a financial relationship with the entity. They also prohibit the entity from billing for services provided to patients referred in violation of these laws. (A financial relationship is defined in most of these statutes as including an ownership interest in, or receipt of compensation from, the entity). Thus, when a hospital believes that it must provide equipment, software, and services to its medical staff members in order to encourage them to participate in an EHR network, the physicians fear that their acceptance of the donated goods and services will be construed under the Stark law as remuneration that will disqualify their subsequent referrals of patients to the hospital, thus subjecting the physicians to possible penalties.

Like the antikickback laws, the Stark law provides some exceptions that permit physicians to make referrals, but most of these exceptions provide little protection for EHR systems other than systems that qualify as community-wide health information systems—that is, available to all provider, practitioners, and residents of the community who desire to participate.[147] This exception is not practical, particularly for newly established EHR systems that are limited primarily to hospitals and their medical staffs. Another Stark law exception that may be more useful is one that permits any payments by a physician for goods or

---

[144] See, e.g., "Detective Work: AHIMA to Study How Information Technology Can Help Fight Healthcare Fraud," *Modern Healthcare* 30 (May 16, 2005).

[145] 42 U.S.C. § 1395 nn.

[146] See, e.g., Fla. Stat. § 456.053; 225 Ill. Comp. Stat. §§ 47/1 et seq.

[147] 42 C.F.R. § 411.357(u)(1).

services at fair market value.[148] Under this exception, a hospital may charge physicians the fair market value of the goods or services it provides in support of the EHR system. The disadvantage of this exception is that the parties must demonstrate and document that their pricing is at fair market value, and that the physicians will incur material costs to participate in the EHR network.

However, the pressure from the federal government and quality improvement organizations to convert entirely to EHRs will likely result in additional Stark law exceptions in the future that will more effectively accommodate the formation of EHR systems and HDNs. Toward that end, DHHS has proposed regulations that would create exceptions from the Stark law prohibitions for donations to physicians of technology needed for e-prescribing and for interoperable EHRs.[149] Under the proposed regulations, hospitals would be permitted to donate qualifying technology to members of their medical staffs, and physician group practices would be permitted to donate such technology to their physician members. Two exceptions would be created— one for the period until the secretary of DHHS adopts product certification criteria for interoperability, and one to take effect thereafter. For the first exception, qualifying technology for EHRs would include software used solely for the transmission, receipt, or maintenance of EHRs and directly related training services. After certification criteria are in place, the software would have to meet these criteria in order to fall within the exception. In addition, the regulations would set a maximum value on the technology that could be donated, and would establish additional conditions designed to prevent abuse. The proposals provide only a broad outline of the exceptions that DHHS is contemplating, and the agency is soliciting public comment on virtually every element of the proposed regulations. Although some form of relief from the Stark self-referral prohibitions is inevitable, the question remains at this writing whether the eventual relief will be sufficiently practical to be of use to the healthcare industry.

Tax Laws Affecting Tax-Exempt Organizations

In any multiparty arrangement that involves one or more charitable, tax-exempt organizations, complex legal issues arise, the resolution of

---

[148] 42 C.F.R. § 411.357(c)(2)(i).
[149] 70 Fed. Reg. 59015, 59182 (Oct. 11, 2005).

which can have a material effect on the ability of those organizations to retain their tax exemptions. The principal laws that define an organization as exempt from federal taxation are found in Sections 501(c)(3) and 509(a) of the Internal Revenue Code and the corresponding Treasury regulations.[150] The issues concern the status and operation of an HDN that includes tax-exempt organizations.

Tax Status of the Health Data Network

Section 501(c)(3) creates tax exemptions for organizations formed for charitable purposes, such as education, religion, social services, and the promotion of health. Although little authority exists for granting tax-exempt status to an HDN, the government's clear mandate for a national health information infrastructure and the substantial emphasis placed on the development of EHRs and HDNs by both private and government agencies provide a strong rationale supporting charitable status for HDNs that consist primarily of charitable, tax-exempt organizations. In addition, earlier precedents suggest that the Internal Revenue Service (IRS) is favorably disposed to such networks, which have as their purpose the improvement of health for the community.[151]

Section 501(c)(3) organizations must also qualify as nonprivate foundations under Section 509(a), unless they want to be subject to the burdensome requirements imposed on private foundations. A "public" charity has the advantage of less regulation and fewer restrictions. Although the requirements for nonprivate foundation status are quite complex, they offer HDNs several options, and HDNs should be able to qualify, particularly as the number of participants increases and community involvement in the organization grows.

Tax Pitfalls for Tax-Exempt Health Data Networks

The most serious risk a tax-exempt organization faces with respect to its status is the loss of its exemption. This can occur if the organization per-

---

[150] I.R.C. §§ 501(c)(3) and 509(a).

[151] See, e.g., Rev. Rul. 81-276 (finding that a professional standards review organization promoted health of the community); Rev. Rul. 76-455 (finding that the creation of a nonprofit regional HDN for the purpose of, among other things, providing aid for the development of uniform health record data-keeping and reporting procedures and providing related educational programs qualified for a tax exemption); Rev. Rul. 74-553 (finding that a physician peer review board of a state medical association qualified for tax exemption under § 501(c)(6)).

mits its assets to inure to the benefit of an individual or a taxable entity or if the organization's activities result in more than incidental benefit to an individual or taxable entity. However, if the financial relationships between the participants of an HDN are established and implemented strictly on a fair market basis, it will be unlikely that the HDN will violate the prohibitions in the Internal Revenue Code against private inurement and private benefit. Determining what is fair market value in an HDN that participants join at different times with different information technology infrastructure needs can be a daunting task. The participation agreement among HDN participating entities should address how the parties will allocate fairly the capital and operating costs of the HDN, and should provide a basis for demonstrating that the tax-exempt HDN and its tax-exempt participants adhere to the Internal Revenue Code requirements.

Antitrust

The federal antitrust laws prohibit contracts, combinations, and conspiracies that unreasonably restrain trade,[152] and prohibit monopolization, attempts to monopolize, and conspiracies to monopolize.[153] Thus, any arrangement among competitors in a market creates the need for a consideration of these laws. Collaborative enterprises undertaken for legitimate reasons should not run afoul of antitrust prohibitions. Competitors may combine their talents and resources to create new or better services that will actually enhance competition in a market rather than suppress it. Therefore, the antitrust laws should not prevent competing healthcare providers from forming an HDN to improve the quality and efficiency of health care in a community.

However, the competing providers should be careful to avoid conduct that might suggest an antitrust violation. For example, they should avoid exchanging information that may be competitively sensitive, unless they provide the information in a manner consistent with guidelines provided by the Federal Trade Commission (FTC) and the Justice Department. Likewise, if the HDN's standard-setting activities are used by participants as a device to exclude competitors from the market, antitrust exposure will arise. Implementing objective criteria and standards for participation and vendor selection will substantially

---

[152] 15 U.S.C. § 1.
[153] 15 U.S.C. § 2.

reduce this exposure. Finally, agreement to share costs of creating an HDN will raise antitrust concerns unless the allocation of costs benefit all participants.

Creating an HDN is a complex and challenging undertaking that should not be attempted without the advice of qualified legal counsel, including experienced antitrust counsel.[154]

Electronic Health Records as Evidence

In addition to enabling providers to respond properly to the healthcare needs of patients, medical records serve as a diary of a healthcare provider's actions. It is therefore important that the information contained in a record be admissible as evidence in court when the care received by the patient or the patient's medical condition is an issue. As commercial organizations have moved to electronic business records, Congress and state legislatures have enacted statutes that make electronic records equivalent to written or paper records, and courts have developed standards for determining the trustworthiness of computerized records.[155]

The Rule Against Hearsay

One barrier to the introduction of any medical record as evidence in court is the rule against hearsay. Hearsay is generally defined as a statement made by a person who is not present in the court, the statement being proffered by one of the parties as evidence to prove the truth of the matter asserted. Hearsay statements are viewed as inherently unreliable because they generally cannot be challenged effectively by an opposing party. Therefore, courts exclude hearsay from evidence, unless one of the exceptions to the hearsay rule applies. Because all medical records, regardless of form, are written statements made outside the courtroom, they are classified as hearsay if offered as evidence to prove the truth of any matter asserted in them.

---

[154] For a more detailed discussion of the antitrust risks of HDN development, see Christine L. White, "Information Exchange with Electronic Medical Records," N.Y.L.J. (May 9, 2005).

[155] See E-SIGN; UETA; UCITA; Fed. R. Evid.1001(1) and (3).

One important exception to the hearsay rule is the business records exception. Although the wording of this exception may vary from jurisdiction to jurisdiction, the general rule is that to come within the business records exception, records must be kept regularly in the ordinary course of business and must not have been prepared specifically for trial. The business records exception applies only to record entries made at or near the time of the event recorded. In addition, the identity of the person making or recording the entry must be captured in the record, and the record must have been prepared by a person with firsthand knowledge of the event recorded or from information transmitted by such a person. The person making the record or transmitting the information for the record must be acting in an ordinary business capacity at the time the record is made.[156]

An EHR made in the ordinary course of a provider's business should meet the requirement that the record be kept regularly and in the ordinary course of business. An EHR system typically records the date and time of each entry and each update to a patient record, so the time of the entry or update and its timeliness can be shown in court. The identity of the person who makes each entry or update is also typically captured by the system. If employees or health professionals share passwords or make entries under an identifier that is not their own, it will be impossible to ensure that the system's record of the identity of the person making the entry is accurate. The Security Rule standards for access and authentication are designed to prevent this problem.

It is important that errors in EHRs be corrected appropriately. The system should preserve both the original entry and the correction, and should record the identities of the persons making each original entry or correction so as not to create an appearance that the record has been altered or that records on the system are not reliable and trustworthy as evidence. If a system uses reliable software and preserves erroneous entries, tracking the history of each entry and correction, the provider should be able to demonstrate the reliability of the record in court.

It is advisable for the provider to have an employee or technical consultant who can testify concerning the reliability of the system's identification and entry-dating features and the trustworthiness of the system as a whole, including system security features and procedures.

Records created and stored on a properly designed and maintained EHR system should come within the business records exception to

---

[156] See, e.g., Ala. R. Evid. 803(6); Cal. Evid. Code § 1271.

the hearsay rule (or a similar exception applicable to medical records) if the Security Rule standards, which encompass the procedures described above, are met. Under the business records exception to the hearsay rule, statements contained in such EHRs may also be admissible if made by providers or staff acting in the ordinary course of business. Statements contained in such records may also be admissible if made by the declarant for "purposes of medical diagnosis or treatment and describing medical history, or past or present symptoms, pain, or sensations, or the inception or general character of the cause or external source thereof insofar as reasonably pertinent to diagnosis or treatment."[157]

Best Evidence Rule

Another evidentiary rule relevant to the admissibility of EHRs is the best evidence rule, which expresses a judicial preference for the original of a writing if the contents of a writing are in dispute. In the EHR context, a question arises as to whether a hard copy of the contents of the record is an "original" for purposes of the best evidence rule. The Federal Rules of Evidence state the requirements for data stored on a computer or similar device. Rule 1001(3) states that "[i]f data are stored in a computer or similar device, any printout or other output readable by sight, shown to reflect the data accurately, is an 'original.'"[158] The Federal Rules of Evidence also provide that duplicates are admissible to the same extent as originals, unless a genuine issue of authenticity or unfairness arises.[159] Some states' evidentiary rules also provide that computerized documents shall be accepted as originals.[160] Other states permit admission of reproductions into evidence when the reproductions are made in the regular course of business and satisfy other criteria for trustworthiness.[161] The trustworthiness of a record created on a computerized system refers to the reliability of system hardware and software, the use of proper procedures for creating and storing records, the assurance that entries are made by adequately trained personnel, and the prevention of unauthorized access to the records and of tampering with

---

[157] Fed. R. Evid. 803(4). This exception to the rule against hearsay is known as the medical records exception.
[158] Fed. R. Evid. 1001(3).
[159] Fed. R. Evid. 1003.
[160] See, e.g., Fla. Stat. Ann. § 90.951.
[161] See, e.g., Cal. Evid. Code § 1270-1272.

the system. Again, the Security Rule standards are designed in part to protect the integrity of EHRs, and, if these standards are met, output from EHRs should meet evidentiary requirements.

The Difficulties of E-Discovery

The enormous growth of electronic business records has created severe problems in lawsuits when parties attempt through discovery to view information that is relevant to the issues in dispute. The cost of e-discovery preservation, collection, and production in commercial litigation in the United States was approximately $700 million in 2004, and was predicted to reach almost $2 billion in 2006.[162] Discovery is a formal process described in the rules of, and supervised by, a court. Through this process, the parties to a dispute gain access to information that they need in order to prosecute or defend the case. For example, in a dispute between a hospital and a diagnostic imaging instrument manufacturer in which the hospital alleges negligent manufacturing that caused injury to patients examined with the defendant's machine, the defendant may want to review the hospital's records of treatment so as to determine the scope of damages. If those records are stored in an EHR system, the hospital will have to determine whether it has the records and whether they can be retrieved without jeopardizing the hospital's ongoing operations. Gaining appropriate access to these records can present serious difficulties.

The amount of data contained in electronic records can be enormous, so in some cases the sheer volume of information can be overwhelming.[163] Much information is stored in dynamic databases that do not correspond to paper materials, and the routine operation of these databases makes retrieving relevant information difficult. For example, some computer programs routinely overwrite and delete information as new information is developed. Some of the "deleted" information may still exist. The files may also contain metadata that is hidden and not

---

[162] Leigh Jones, "The Surging Evolution of E-Discovery," *National Law Journal* (Aug. 12, 2004), available at http://www.law.com/jsp/article.jsp?id=1090180322383.

[163] 17.5 trillion electronic documents were expected to be generated in 2005. Ronald Raether, "Email Maelstrom" *Business Law Today* 13(1) (Sept./Oct. 2003), available at http://www.abanet.org/buslaw/blt/2003-09-10/raether.html.

reproduced in full form when the records are printed.[164] In addition, some of the information may be incomprehensible when separated from the information system that created it. All of these problems make it extremely difficult to obtain information relevant to a dispute that occurred at a specific time, especially when the rules of discovery were designed for obtaining access to paper records, not electronic records. Failure to comply with e-discovery can lead to monetary penalties,[165] loss of the ability to call witnesses,[166] adverse instructions to the jury,[167] or a default judgment.[168]

In response to these problems, some federal courts and a few states have revised their discovery rules to address the unique characteristics of electronic records. In addition, it is likely that the federal rules of practice will be revised to set a national standard for cases coming before the federal courts.[169] For example, one of the problems that electronic records create is the risk of destroying privileges that may otherwise protect information from discovery. This may occur by inadvertently releasing data in a large electronic record. Practice rules permit parties to release a large volume of data and later "take back" information that would have been privileged if not released. Such rules help reduce the enormous cost in time and money of having attorneys review every single bit of information in a discovery request before the data are released, the purpose of the review being to make certain that no privileged information is being released. Federal and state practice rules will continue to evolve to accommodate the use of electronic records, and healthcare organizations should keep abreast of these rules as they apply to EHRs.

---

[164] "Metadata is information about a particular data set which describes how, when and by whom it was collected, created, accessed or modified and how it is formatted (including data demographics such as size, location, storage requirements and media information." *Sedona Guidelines* (September 2004 Public Comment Draft), 81–82.

[165] See, e.g., *Procter & Gamble v. Haugen*, 179 F.R.D. 622 (D. Utah 1998); *In re Prudential Insurance Company of America Sales Practice Litigation*, 169 F.R.D. 598 (D.N.J. 1997).

[166] See, e.g., *United States v. Philip Morris USA, Inc.*, 327 F. Supp. 2d 21 (D.D.C., July 21, 2004).

[167] See, e.g., *Zubulake v. UBS Warburg LLC*, No. 02 Civ. 1243, 2004 U.S. Dist. LEXIS 13574 (S.D.N.Y., July 20, 2004).

[168] See, e.g., *Essex Group v. Express Wire Services*, 578 S.E. 2d 705 (N.C. Ct. App. 2003).

[169] See Committee on Rules of Practice and Procedure of the Judicial Conference of the United States, *Report of the Civil Rules Advisory Committee* (May 17, 2004; revised August 3, 2004).

The key to dealing with e-discovery is to manage EHRs and other electronic records effectively, especially with possible litigation in mind. Healthcare organizations and practitioners should take the following action in managing their electronic records in connection with possible litigation:

- *Preserve electronic records by suspending ordinary destruction practices and identify the individuals with authority to impose this suspension.* A party's failure to halt document retention and destruction policy can constitute bad faith and potentially justifies sanctions.[170] Notify the necessary records management personnel both orally and in writing of document preservation obligations. Have a defensible preservation plan that will demonstrate a reliable preservation process.
- *Identify and gather relevant sources of data.* Determine where the electronic information is stored (for example, on hard drives and backup media), and consider the time periods relevant to the case. Ensure that the chain of custody for the data can be maintained and demonstrated.
- *Process the collected data.* Once collected, the records must be processed so that they are accessible for attorney review. This involves restoring backup tapes or evidentiary images, recovering deleted files, removing password protections, and extracting data from proprietary formats to more usable forms. Cull potentially responsive files from irrelevant data through use of search criteria.
- *Review the data.* Categorize the documents as responsive to the discovery request, privileged, confidential, and so on.
- *Produce the data.* Increasingly, production will be in electronic form. Determine in what file form (such as .tif, .pdf, or native file format) and in what physical form (for example, hard drives, backup tapes, DVDs, or CD-ROMs).

Professional Liability

A concern for healthcare providers is whether EHRs will increase their exposure to negligence liability. The same rules of negligence that have

---

[170] See, e.g., *Wiginton v. CB Richard Ellis, Inc.*, No. 02 C 6832, 2003 U.S. LEXIS 19128 (N.D. Ill., Oct. 27, 2003).

governed the outcome of professional liability lawsuits in the past will apply to healthcare providers in the age of the EHR, but the standard of care to which providers are held will certainly change. A substantial body of law does not yet exist to determine whether EHRs present new risks to practitioners and healthcare facilities. Several issues have begun to emerge, however. The principal question is whether new EHR technology will change the standard of care to which healthcare providers are held. For example, the rapid access to EHRs—and particularly interoperable EHRs that form community health records held in HDNs—suggests that a duty to consult prior health records may arise where no duty exists today. In addition, a practitioner's reliance on electronic data in an EHR or in practice guidelines may lead to exposure if the data are unreliable.

In one medical malpractice case in which the patient died following surgery, the plaintiff asserted that the defendants breached the applicable standard of care by failing to consult the patient's past medical records. The defense experts testified, however, that the standard of care did not require such consultation, and the appellate court upheld the trial court's summary judgment for the defendant.[171] Also, in *Susnis v. Radfar et al.*, the parents of a child born with an undiagnosed congenital heart condition sought recovery for injuries sustained to the growth plate in their child's left leg while undergoing treatment for cardiac arrest.[172] Had the defendant properly diagnosed the infant's chest X-ray, the defendants claimed, treatment of the condition could have minimized or avoided the damage to the child's growth plate. The trial court granted a directed verdict for the defendant radiologist. The verdict was affirmed by the appellate court, holding that the plaintiffs failed to demonstrate that the failure to diagnose was the proximate cause of the injuries to the growth plate.[173] But in another case, the physician failed to diagnose the plaintiff's breast cancer despite numerous examinations, and the plaintiff alleged negligence for failure to consult her prior health records. The parties presented conflicting expert testimony on the applicable standard of care, and the jury's verdict for the plaintiff was upheld on appeal.[174]

---

[171] *Suniga v. Eyre*, 2004 Tex. App. LEXIS 486 (unpublished).
[172] 739 N.E. 2d 960 (Ill. Ct. App. 2000).
[173] *Susnis v. Radfar et al.*, 739 N.E. 2d 960, 965–966 (Ill. App. Ct. 1990).
[174] *Primus v. Galgano*, 329 F. 3d 236 (1st Cir. 2003).

As it has over the past decades, the standard of care to which health-care providers are held will likely continue to evolve as the use of technology and the body of medical knowledge continue to increase. It is inevitable that the ways in which practitioners use electronic health information will evolve. Just as, in the past, providers have had to keep abreast of new treatment protocols, medical devices, and pharmaceuticals, it will be essential for them in the future to keep current with accepted practices concerning the use of health information in treating patients. A major challenge for healthcare providers will be keeping pace with the dramatic speed at which the technology supporting EHRs changes.

Specific Electronic Health Records Security Issues

Facsimile Transmission of Health Information

The widespread use of facsimile (fax) machines to transmit information, including medical records, from one location to another creates a potential threat to confidentiality, and may, in some circumstances, call into question the integrity or authenticity of orders and other medical records entries transmitted by fax. Both paper and computerized records can be sent via fax machines, and the use of a computer fax modem makes possible transmission of EHRs from one computer to another without generating a hard copy of the record as a necessary by-product of the transmission. In either case, fax transmissions to external parties generally travel over telephone networks or other public channels of communication. Because there is a significant risk that fax transmissions will be misdirected, use of facsimile machines to transmit confidential medical records information is risky, and is extremely risky if highly sensitive patient information (such as the diagnosis of HIV) is involved.

The transmission by a covered entity of a facsimile copy of PHI stored electronically in a computer is subject to the Security Rule and must enjoy all the security safeguards prescribed by the rule. (See the detailed discussion of the Security Rule requirements earlier in this chapter.) The transmission by fax of health information from a paper copy to a paper copy is not subject to the rule, however. The paper copy created by the fax machine generally will be subject to the Privacy Rule if it is received by a covered entity, and thus must be accorded all the protections required by the Privacy Rule, including its general requirement for security protections for PHI.

The confidentiality and security risks to health information transmitted by fax can be reduced, however, if proper maintenance and security techniques are used and if proper procedures are followed in transmitting medical records. Nevertheless, it is unwise to send highly sensitive health information by fax, except in encrypted form or over nonpublic channels of communication that are highly secure (such as a local area network within a facility). AHIMA notes that the use of fax machines to transmit health information has become commonplace in healthcare organizations, and that a provider sending confidential information by fax off-site should take the following precautions:

- Establish fax policies and procedures based on federal and state law and consultation with legal counsel
- Describe in the covered entity's Notice of Privacy Practices required by the Privacy Rule the uses and disclosures of PHI by fax machine
- Obtain patient authorization for transmission of health information when the transmission is not otherwise permitted by law
- Take reasonable steps to ensure that the transmission is sent to the appropriate destination (for example, preprogram and test destination numbers, remind frequent recipients to update their fax numbers, train staff to double-check the recipient's fax number before transmitting, and verify that the recipient is authorized to receive the transmission)
- Include a confidentiality statement on the cover page of the fax
- Request the recipient to return or destroy the fax if it becomes known that the fax was misdirected
- Place fax machines in secure locations[175]

In addition, some—but by no means total—protection against unauthorized access to a fax transmission can be obtained by calling the recipient before sending the transmission, alerting the recipient to stand by for the transmission, and verifying with the recipient that the fax number to which the transmission will be directed is the correct number.

---

[175] AHIMA, *Practice Brief: Facsimile Transmission of Health Information (Updated)*, available at http://library.ahima.org/xpedio/groups/public/documents/ahima/pub_bok2_000116 .html (2001).

Encrypting faxed information is another method of protecting its confidentiality. However, this process generally requires that the receiving fax machine or computer be equipped to decode the encrypted information, and this will often not be the case. When sending faxes off-site, a provider should retain a record of each fax transmission (including the phone number of the receiving fax machine) and the contents of the fax.

When receiving orders or other medical records information from outside the facility, a provider should also take special precautions. If caller identification is available, the receiving fax machine should be equipped with a mechanism for recording the number of the telephone from which the fax transmission originated. The personnel operating the fax machine should have a list of telephone numbers from which medical staff members transmit orders, and should verify that the telephone number identified on the fax machine appears on that list.[176] A hospital may also treat faxed orders like verbal orders, and require authentication of the order by the appropriate medical staff member within the time period permitted for authentication of verbal orders.

Technologies for protecting data sent by facsimile will evolve, and healthcare organizations, whether or not they are HIPAA covered entities, must keep current with the latest technologies. Using what are considered best practices in the industry to protect health information is a sound approach to reducing liability for negligent disclosure of health information.

Providers should also refer to state rules of evidence to determine if, and under what circumstances, facsimile transmissions that become part of a patient record are admissible in court.[177] Fax machines that are used to transmit orders internally should also be equipped to print the date, time, and address of the originating fax machine to help support the authenticity of internally faxed documents. The original of each such fax transmission should be retained.[178] A majority of states has adopted the Uniform Photographic Copies of

---

[176] See "Practice Brief: Guidelines for Faxing Patient Health Information," *Journal of AHIMA* 62(46) (1991).

[177] It is important to note that a number generated by the fax machine originating the transmission and printed on the fax may not be a correct number, since some fax machines can be programmed to transmit a number other than that of the originating telephone.

[178] A number of states has adopted legislation that authorizes the admissibility of reproductions made in the regular course of business without need to account for the original.

Business and Public Records as Evidence Act and the Uniform Rule of Evidence, which establish the admissibility of accurately produced records into evidence.[179]

Electronic Claims Processing: The Transactions Code Set Rule

The first element in the rollout of HIPAA was the body of regulations governing electronic transactions and code sets (TCS Rule), which was published August 17, 2000.[180] The TCS Rule established a set of standards for several of the most common electronic transactions by which information is transmitted in the healthcare industry. Unlike some of the other HIPAA rules, the TCS Rule is truly designed to simplify the administration of health care in the United States by reducing the number of electronic data interchange (EDI) formats used in the country from approximately 400 to a few nationally established standard formats. DHHS estimated that the TCS Rule would save healthcare providers and health plans from $1.5 billion to $19 billion over the 10 years following implementation.[181] Using private sector standard-setting organizations, the TCS Rule is designed to create, maintain, and revise national standards that will keep current with technological advances. The TCS Rule is also a basic component in the Privacy Rule, in that "covered entities" are only those healthcare providers, clearinghouses, and health plans that engage in the standard transactions created by the TCS Rule.

The TCS Rule applies only to electronic transmissions between covered entities or their business associates. In addition, a health plan must conduct a transaction using a standard code set if it is requested to do so by any entity, regardless of whether the entity is a covered entity.[182] All covered entities that conduct with another covered entity any electronic transaction for which DHHS has created a standard must use the standard code sets established by the TCS Rule.[183] The following transactions are subject to the rule:

- Healthcare claims or equivalent encounter information
- Healthcare payment and remittance advice

---

[179] http://www.law.upenn.edu/bll/ulc/ulc_frame.htm.
[180] 65 Fed. Reg. 50312 (Aug. 17, 2000).
[181] 65 Fed. Reg. 50345 and 50358 (Aug. 17, 2000).
[182] 45 C.F.R. § 162.925(a).
[183] 45 C.F.R. § 162.923(a).

- Coordination of benefits
- Healthcare claim status
- Enrollment and disenrollment in a health plan
- Eligibility for a health plan
- Health plan premium payments
- Referral certification and authorization
- First report of injury
- Health claims attachments
- Other transactions prescribed by DHHS[184]

Although covered entities may use code sets prescribed for these transactions in connection with other transactions, they are required to use the national standard code sets only with the transactions set forth in the TCS Rule from time to time by DHHS. The TCS Rule applies to electronic transmissions using most forms of media, including (a) electronic storage media, such as computer hard drives, and movable digital memory media, such as magnetic tapes or disks and digital memory devices; and (b) transmission media used to exchange information already in electronic form, such as the wide-open Internet, extranet, leased lines, dial-up lines, and private networks.[185]

A code set is any set of computer codes used to encode data elements, such as diagnosis, demographic information, and medical procedures. The code set standards adopted by the TCS Rule establish the computer codes that covered entities must use to conduct the covered transactions. Each transaction described in the rule has a prescribed set of codes and data elements that must be used. For example, transmissions of medical information concerning diseases require the use of the *International Classification of Diseases, 9th Edition, Clinical Modification (ICD-9-CM), Volumes 1 and 2*, as published by DHHS. Other standard code sets are required for the transmission of other types of information (for example, pharmaceuticals, physician services, clinical laboratory tests, and so forth).[186]

The HIPAA regulations establishing the National Provider Identifier as the standard unique health identifier for healthcare providers

---

[184] 45 C.F.R. § 160.103.
[185] Ibid.
[186] 45 C.F.R. § 162.1002.

(NPI Rule) were published on January 23, 2004.[187] After the compliance date for the NPI Rule,[188] healthcare providers that are covered entities must use only one unique identifier in all standard transactions, as defined by the TCS Rule.[189] Covered providers that have subparts may also obtain NPIs for their subparts if they would qualify as covered healthcare providers if they were separate legal entities.[190] Covered providers may discard the variety of other numbers they now must use to communicate with health plans and others. Providers who are not covered entities may take advantage of the unique numbering system by applying for and receiving an NPI.[191]

The NPI is a 10-digit numeric identifier with a check digit in the 10th position and no information about the provider in the number.[192] The check digit is recognized by the International Organization for Standardization (ISO), and is used to assist in identifying erroneous or invalid NPIs. The National Provider System (NPS), which is part of CMS, is responsible for assigning and regulating NPIs and for collecting and maintaining information about each healthcare provider that receives an NPI.[193] CMS has published an NPI Application/Update Form for use by healthcare providers.[194]

Because NPIs will be required to engage in standard transactions, including those to obtain payment for healthcare services, healthcare organizations should have a keen interest not only in their own compliance with the NPI Rule, but also in the compliance of others who may be part of the payment process. For example, hospitals that are billing for services that include physician services may have to use the physicians' NPIs. If the physicians have not obtained their NPIs, payments to the hospital could be delayed. Close coordination among such related providers and among subparts of single covered healthcare organizations will be required in order to take advantage of the efficiencies offered by the NPI Rule.

---

[187] 69 Fed. Reg. 3434 (Jan. 23, 2004).
[188] The compliance date for the NPI Rule is May 23, 2007, for all covered entities—except small health plans, which must comply by May 23, 2008. 45 C.F.R. § 162.404.
[189] 45 C.F.R. § 162.406(b).
[190] 45 C.F.R. § 162.410.
[191] 69 Fed. Reg. 3438 (Jan. 23, 2004).
[192] 45 C.F.R. § 162.406(a).
[193] 45 C.F.R. § 162.408.
[194] The form is available at https://nppes.cms.hhs.gov.

Telemedical Records

Telemedicine is the delivery of healthcare services at a distance with the use of interactive telecommunications and computer technology. Telemedicine may or may not use the Internet as a communications device, although the trend toward Internet-based interactions is increasing. Using telecommunications technology, for example, a physician in one location can interview a patient, listen to his or her heart, examine skin lesions, examine X-rays, read EKGs, diagnose conditions, and prescribe treatment. Because the practice of telemedicine relies on electronic signals to communicate medical information from one location to another, it raises significant legal issues with respect to the accuracy, confidentiality, and security of healthcare data that are transmitted this way.

The clinical applications of telemedicine are varied and differ technologically. Currently, it is applied in several settings, including in communications between emergency medical technicians providing prehospital care to a patient in an ambulance and a hospital emergency department, and in data-linking systems for remote evaluations of CT scans, radiology tests, and similar examinations. Another application of telemedicine is the development of databases of patient records and the provision of distributed access to these databases in HDNs. Some of the data in HDN databases include multimedia information collected and communicated through sophisticated telemedicine technologies. HDN databases also include patient data from laboratories, pharmacies, medical instrument readings, and other sources. HDN databases allow healthcare providers at different treatment locations within a community to access directly all of a patient's health information.

Telemedicine applications rely on a variety of technologies, many of which require a bandwidth. Although the practice of telemedicine can require different amounts of bandwidth depending on the circumstances, it generally requires the transmission of a large amount of data in a short period of time and the use of a large amount of bandwidth. Through the use of a coder-decoder, the analog signal produced by audio and video equipment can be converted into a digital signal for transmission to another location, and then converted back at the location receiving the broadcast, so as to compress the data, use less bandwidth, and reduce the costs of the communication.

When data are compressed, distortion can occur, raising concerns that the health information that a provider receives via telemedicine is inaccurate and will lead to misdiagnoses. In addition, the potential for breach of confidentiality is significant—for many of the same reasons discussed above with respect to EHRs, and also because telemedicine involves not only collecting and storing patient data electronically, but also broadcasting it off-site. The airwaves are not secure, and the confidentiality of a patient's medical history may not be guaranteed when using telemedicine for video consultation. Individuals may intentionally or unintentionally intercept video broadcasts, leading some telemedicine locations to take precautions to prevent unauthorized access to health information.

In the past, healthcare providers have scrambled their broadcasts to protect confidentiality. They have had technical personnel present at both ends of the transmission during a consultation broadcast, and have required that these individuals be included in institutional policies and training that relate to patient confidentiality. The particular safeguards that healthcare providers use when engaged in telemedicine will depend upon the state of technology at the time, and providers must keep current with best practices in the industry. The Security Rule permits covered entities to implement safeguards that accomplish the goals set forth in the rule's security standards and that are appropriate for a given covered entity. The periodic security assessments that covered entities perform should alert them to the need for revising their security policies and procedures to protect health information used in telemedicine.

There are very few legislative or accreditation requirements that govern the creation or maintenance of telemedical records. AHIMA has addressed these topics in a practice brief, recommending minimum content standards for telemedical records and suggesting specific actions to protect confidentiality and security.[195] Accreditation standards do not specifically address telemedical records, but the Joint Commission on Accreditation of Healthcare Organizations has specified that a facility using telemedical information in patient treatment decisions must comply with all relevant standards.[196]

Electronic Mail

Increasingly, consumers of healthcare services seek to communicate with their care providers via electronic mail, or "e-mail," and text messaging. Communications via e-mail may be transmitted through direct

---

[195] AHIMA, *Practice Brief: Telemedical Records*, available at http://library.ahima.org/xpedio/groups/public/documents/ahima/pub_bok1_000074.html (1997).
[196] Ibid.

modem-to-modem links; in-house routers, servers, and bulletin boards; commercial third-party host services; and the Internet. (For a more detailed description of security risks related to Internet e-mail, see the discussion of the Internet later in this chapter.) As people become more accustomed to the benefits of e-mail, they use this medium to transmit a wide variety of sensitive information, including patient data, large documents for research projects, budgets, and other confidential time-critical information. At many healthcare organizations, e-mail is used as a communication vehicle between patients and their caregivers.

The development of e-mail technologies (that is, modes of e-mail communication) has been occurring at such a rapid pace, however, that at times the related implementation of technological safeguards has lagged behind. This raises confidentiality and security challenges for healthcare facilities in relation to the transmission of patient healthcare information via e-mail. Organizations that are HIPAA covered entities must comply with all the requirements of the Privacy and Security Rules with respect to the transmission of PHI by e-mail. Others involved in the healthcare industry will likely be subject to state laws governing health information privacy and security.

Among other things, this will require healthcare facilities to provide their staffs with training to ensure organization-wide recognition of the security risks associated with e-mail and compliance with applicable privacy and security policies and procedures. All healthcare professionals using e-mail to transmit patient healthcare information should understand that e-mail affords individuals no more confidentiality than written memoranda or letters—and, in the absence of adequate technological safeguards, may in fact offer less privacy and security. Healthcare professionals who use e-mail must recognize the necessity of exercising caution when transmitting patient information, and should be trained concerning the importance and means of sending e-mail messages that do not compromise the integrity of data, create the potential for a privacy or security breach, or contain inappropriate statements that could be misconstrued.

Before outlining recommended safeguards that healthcare facilities may want to consider in addressing e-mail security risks, it is worth briefly noting relevant federal law (and corresponding state laws) enacted with the legislative intent to provide enhanced protection for the privacy of electronic communications. Title III of the Omnibus Crime Control and Safe Streets Act of 1968, also known as the federal wiretapping law, was amended by the Electronic Communications Privacy Act of 1986 (ECPA) to provide protection against improper interception of new forms of electronic communications such as e-mail, and thereby to increase acceptance of e-mail and other electronic data transmissions as a secure means of communication.[197] In addition, some states have adopted wiretapping statutes modeled after the ECPA.[198] The ECPA imposes civil and criminal liability on individuals who intentionally intercept any wire, oral, or electronic communication; disclose or use the contents of such communication with knowledge or reason to know that it was unlawfully intercepted;[199] or access without authorization an electronic communications facility and thereby obtain, alter, or prevent authorized access to stored communications.[200] The ECPA provides several exceptions to these prohibitions for certain access to messages by the communications service provider and the government (for example, law enforcement agencies).

Although these federal and state wiretapping laws generally indicate what types of e-mail communications activity may lead to liability, they provide little guidance on how to protect the privacy of such communications. With respect to the transmission of health records, this practical information regarding steps to be taken for the protection of e-mail communications is of utmost importance. The healthcare organization must ensure that adequate security technology is being used, and that confidentiality standards (set forth in its policies and procedures) are being met on an organization-wide basis. Staff training is also a crucial element for effective e-mail information security programs in the workplace.

Implementing security technology that adequately protects the confidentiality of e-mail communications involves setting up a well-managed system of access controls. All e-mail users should be required to have user IDs and passwords to access their electronic mailboxes, and should be informed as to the importance of adherence to user personal identification procedures. Users should also periodically be reminded not to leave e-mail messages on their screens when they are away from their computers. Without such controls and training, e-mail

---

[197] 18 U.S.C. §§ 2510 through 2711.
[198] See, e.g., Minn. Stat. § 626A.02; Va. Code Ann. § 19.2-61; Utah Code Ann. § 77-23a-1.
[199] 18 U.S.C. § 2511(1).
[200] 18 U.S.C. §§ 2701(c)(1) and (2).

messages may be forged and may be retrieved by unauthorized persons. Moreover, to minimize the risk of misdirected messages, users should be trained to verify the address of an e-mail account and confirm that the message has been received by the intended recipient. The healthcare organization's policies and procedures also should address ways to ensure the confidential handling of messages within both the sender's and the receiver's organizations. A policy may require that, prior to sending a confidential e-mail communication, a sender take certain steps to verify that the recipient has sole access to his or her electronic mailbox.

In addition, systems controls (such as encryption methods) should be considered as a way to prevent unauthorized review of e-mail messages by systems and network support personnel. A very significant security risk in relation to patient healthcare information may well be posed by a healthcare organization's network administrator who, in monitoring traffic on certain parts of the network to ensure proper functionality, is tempted to read e-mail that contains information about an individual with whom he or she is acquainted, or about a public figure. Moreover, if e-mail messages are stored off-line, access to such storage facilities should be restricted.

With respect to developing policies and procedures on the use and retention of e-mail communications, the healthcare organization should first take into consideration any existing policies regarding the security of patient healthcare information. Many healthcare organizations have successful information security policies in place, but need to develop additional policies specifically directed at strengthening the security of e-mail communications. Because the content of an e-mail communication can range from a request for a consultation to a detailed report on the patient's current medical status, healthcare organizations should adopt specific standards with respect to the use and retention of e-mail for patient care related purposes.

These standards should prohibit the use of e-mail for transmitting sensitive patient information (such as HIV infection status and AIDS records, alcohol and drug abuse diagnosis and treatment records, mental health and developmental disability records, and genetic screening and test results) unless such e-mail messages are encrypted or otherwise protected by highly secure technology. In healthcare settings, unencrypted e-mail messages can be an unnecessary temptation to breach patient confidentiality. For example, one individual may send an unencrypted e-mail message containing patient information to another individual external to the organization, and later find that the message has been widely disseminated to other individuals through a forwarding mechanism or some other means. Even an inadvertent disclosure can result in a breach of patient confidentiality and consequent liability, statutory penalties, and licensure sanctions for the healthcare organization. Accordingly, policies regarding sensitive e-mail communications should include a prohibition against the forwarding of such messages to others without the prior permission of the sender. As an additional safeguard, healthcare organizations may want to consider displaying a warning notice on its e-mail system reminding users that electronic mail should not contain information that could identify any patient, directly or indirectly, unless the message is secured via encryption.

As technology of e-mail advances, any one of these security safeguards may be rendered ineffective. Healthcare organizations and practitioners, particularly those who are HIPAA covered entities, must stay current with developing security safeguards and best security and privacy practices, and periodically update their policies and procedures. Keeping ahead of potential security and privacy breaches resulting from the transmission of electronic health information is an enormous challenge, but one that must be met in order to avoid liability.

A healthcare organization's information security policies should also address e-mail retention issues; these policies should address whether all or certain e-mail communications should be archived, and, if so, for what period of time. The organization's document retention and destruction policy should cover treatment of e-mail communications, including messages saved on the central computer system, backup media, and individual computer hard drives. Many healthcare organizations require that e-mail communications be included in the patient's medical record, in which case retention of these communications will be subject to medical records retention requirements. The healthcare organization may want to consider a policy encouraging individual healthcare providers to read sensitive e-mail messages immediately upon receipt, and then, to avoid having the messages being retained in the system's nightly backup medium, to delete such messages promptly.

In addition to access controls and specific policies covering the use and handling of e-mail communications, healthcare organizations must provide adequate staff training and education in this area. Individual healthcare providers should understand how e-mail communications regarding patient care are to be recorded, and the risks of conveying information in an e-mail message. It is particularly important that healthcare professionals who use e-mail to transmit patient healthcare information are informed that any e-mail communication containing information relevant to the patient's diagnosis and treatment should be included in the patient's medical record in hard copy or linked to or inserted in an existing EHR. This procedure follows the same rule that applies under circumstances in which the healthcare provider transmits patient information over the telephone; these telephone calls typically are recorded in a patient's medical record, and e-mail communications should also appear in the patient's medical record. The healthcare organization's policies should identify the individuals responsible for including the communication in the patient's medical record (for example, sender, receiver, or both).

With respect to the content of e-mail messages, healthcare professionals should be trained to understand that e-mail communications pertaining to patient care must be checked for accuracy and appropriate language. A training program should emphasize the importance of drafting e-mail messages with the same caution that users would exercise in writing a formal memorandum, because e-mail messages may ultimately be forwarded to numerous individuals other than the original recipient. In addition, given the breadth of e-discovery in lawsuits, healthcare professionals should recognize that statements made in e-mail are easily discoverable,[201] and that informal, often hastily written but widely disseminated e-mail can adversely affect the outcome of the defense in a professional liability action, external investigation by law enforcement personnel, or internal security investigations.

Moreover, many healthcare organizations have decided to officially support e-mail communications with patients. In these settings, physicians and other healthcare professionals must be trained as to the risks of electronically relaying health information to the patient. For example, a physician may create a physician-patient relationship without realizing it simply by engaging in e-mail communications with an unknown individual. Perhaps a more common occurrence is that patients may perceive a physician's e-mail messages to be impersonal, and thus become dissatisfied with the care they are receiving, when no such

---

[201] See, e.g., *United Air Lines, Inc. v. Hewins Travel Consultants, Inc.*, 622 A. 2d 1163 (Me. 1993) (computer printouts of system data were admissible as evidence in breach of contract action); *Boone v. Federal Express Corporation*, 59 F. 3d 84 (8th Cir. 1995) (e-mail messages offered as evidence of a conspiracy); *Strauss v. Microsoft Corporation*, 856 F. Supp. 821 (S.D.N.Y. 1994) (defendant's motion in limine to exclude e-mail messages into evidence denied).

complaints would have arisen in a person-to-person exchange where emotions are more effectively communicated. As a risk management strategy, the healthcare organization may want to consider providing patients with written material describing the risks of breaches of confidentiality, and adopting a policy that requires patients requesting e-mail communications from their physicians to submit signed forms that acknowledge such risks. Certainly, providers who are HIPAA covered entities should consider including a description of their e-mail policies and procedures in their notices of privacy practices.

Healthcare professionals should be trained to handle a number of other content-related problems that may arise in using e-mail for patient care purposes. For example, e-mail messages may be ambiguous to the receiving healthcare professionals. In such instances, they must recognize the need for follow-up with a telephone call to the sender. Also, if e-mail is used by healthcare professionals to update a patient's status, an unanswered e-mail can trigger liability concerns. Where the recipient of an e-mail fails to respond to a message requesting an urgent consultation, for example, the sender who fails to take appropriate steps to treat the patient in the absence of such response may incur liability in negligence. In addition, e-mail communications containing patient information are increasingly common between the healthcare organization and third-party payers with authorized access to such information; if an e-mail contains incorrect information in these circumstances, the result may be denial or delay of reimbursement, and potential liability or other sanctions. Healthcare organizations should also have protocols in place regarding approved uses of e-mail, and procedures to follow under all of these circumstances.

AHIMA's recommendations provide a good summary of issues that healthcare organizations should consider as they develop and implement their information privacy and security policies and procedures:

- Create a policy that establishes criteria for the provider-patient e-mail communication and consent process before initiating electronic communication with the patient
- Develop procedures for the patient's authorization to use e-mail as a communications medium
- Develop policies addressing issues that require incorporating e-mail into the patient record
- Establish and enforce policies for retaining e-mail in the patient record

- To guide the use of group e-mail messages, develop policies and procedures that describe the necessity of protecting identities of addressees
- Develop criteria to determine a patient's health literacy level and ability to use an e-mail application
- For requests that do not meet content guidelines, establish procedures to instruct the patient to follow up in person or by telephone
- Establish a policy for e-mail turnaround time
- Develop a policy and educate patients about appropriate types of e-mail
- Research state law governing e-mail communications
- Develop a policy that addresses security issues when using remote access
- Develop a policy that addresses special issues presented in patient e-mail and the response to that e-mail (for example, mental health, substance abuse, HIV status, urgent health conditions)
- Develop policies defining and prohibiting emergency e-mail messages
- Develop procedures addressing a workable documentation mechanism for responding to e-mail by telephone and responding to telephone calls by e-mail
- Develop a policy and procedure to guide termination of a patient from e-mail communications
- Establish a method to audit all e-mail correspondence
- Establish organizational procedures for cleaning computer hard drives
- Update current confidentiality policies to incorporate references to e-mail[202]

Transmission of Health Information Through the Internet

Whether known as e-medicine, telemedicine, e-health, telehealth, or cyber-medicine, electronic transmission of health information over the Internet is used in various ways related to healthcare delivery. Some offer health and medical content to consumers, some provide healthcare services, some host support groups for particular medical condi-

---

[202] AHIMA, *Practice Brief: E-mail as a Provider-Patient Electronic Communication Medium and Its Impact on the Electronic Health Record*, available at http://library.ahima.org/xpedio/groups/public/documents/ahima/pub_bok1_021588.html (2003).

tions, and some sell medical products and supplies and provide business support services. They are operated by various types of organizations, including not for profit organizations, the government, and commercial enterprises. For example, the University of Virginia Medical Center, the Virginia Neurological Institute, and Hewlett-Packard have collaborated on a project to enable the viewing of patient records by using an application called the Virtual Electronic Medical Record.[203] Another electronic medical records system developed by the University of Kansas Medical Center links the medical center's e-mail and radiology systems so that an attending physician can automatically receive a radiologist's dictation, and the physician can then log on to the Internet to view a patient's X-ray and download it to a local computer.[204]

The July 2002 *Journal of the American Medical Association* reported that the use of telemedicine in the United States has been "relatively slow and uneven," due in part to insurers' reluctance to provide reimbursement for telemedicine services, and physicians' reluctance to use "new and often inconvenient" telemedicine technologies. According to the report, U.S. telemedicine referring sites averaged fewer than 40 consultations per site in 1998. Nonetheless, the report predicts that "telemedicine will continue to evolve slowly but steadily."[205]

The myriad legal and regulatory requirements applicable to the face-to-face delivery of health care also apply to the virtual delivery of health care and related services through the Internet. The rapidly evolving electronic revolution has generated significant legal and regulatory initiatives directed to the use of the Internet in the health industry. Such legal and regulatory initiatives include the Electronic Signatures in Global and National Commerce Act (E-SIGN),[206] the Children's Internet Protection Act (CIPA),[207] the Children's Online Protection Act (COPA),[208] the Children's Online Privacy Protection

---

[203] J. Kazmer, A. Crosby, and K. Oliver, "The Creation of a Virtual Electronic Medical Record" (paper presented in Proceedings of the 1996 Annual HIMSS Conference, Atlanta, March 1996).

[204] See W. Hardin, D. Masys, C. McDonald, and D. Voran, "Medicine Across the Internet" (paper presented in Proceedings of the 1997 Annual HIMSS Conference, San Diego, March 1997).

[205] *American Health Line* (July 29, 2002).

[206] 15 U.S.C. §§ 7001 through 7031.

[207] 47 U.S.C. § 254.

[208] 47 U.S.C. § 231.

Act (COPPA),[209] the Uniform Computer Information Transactions Act (UCITA),[210] the Health Insurance Portability and Accountability Act (HIPAA), and enforcement initiatives by the Food and Drug Administration (FDA), the Federal Trade Commission (FTC), and various state attorneys general. Among other things, these requirements relate to the privacy and security of health information.

Failing to take the full spectrum of legal and regulatory issues into account early in the design phase of the Web site development process, as well as throughout the ongoing operation and maintenance of the site, may give rise to the need for significant Web site design changes and may expose the organization to the risk of adverse regulatory action. These issues and the corresponding liability risks must be carefully managed through Web site disclaimers, terms and conditions of use, consents, privacy, security, and other policies, and agreements with third-party Web site development, hosting, and maintenance.

Two significant security risks related to Internet access are unauthorized access to the healthcare organization's computer systems and networks, and unauthorized disclosure of confidential patient information. To address these concerns, healthcare information managers should consider the following necessary elements of a secure electronic medical records system involving the Internet:

- Authentication of users to ensure that patient information is accessed only by those authorized to do so
- Access control mechanisms so that each user's access to patient information in the system is limited to data that the individual has a legitimate need to know
- Data integrity to ensure that patient information is not altered during transmission
- Reliability of the network to ensure the continued availability of clinical information

Identifying the true identity of the individual with whom a provider is communicating over the Internet is essential to protecting the privacy and confidentiality of healthcare information. Family and house-

---

[209] 15 U.S.C. §§ 6501 through 6506.
[210] Uniform Law Commissioners, "Summary: Uniform Computer Information Transactions Act," available at http://www.nccusl.org/Update/uniformact_summaries/uniformacts-s-ucita.asp.

hold e-mail accounts make it difficult to rely on an e-mail address in order to validate identity. The identity authentication requirements imposed on covered entities by the Security Rule require continuously secure authenticating methods.

Moreover, if the healthcare organization makes use of the Internet to exchange patient-identifiable information, healthcare information managers should devote special attention to security weaknesses associated with the Internet. Finally, one other concern related to Internet use is the potential for introducing computer viruses and other computer contaminants into the organization's computer systems and networks.

The need for network security does not apply to the healthcare industry alone, however; many industries now rely on the Internet for commercial purposes. Therefore, a growing demand exists for techniques to secure information relayed in transactions over the Internet. Accordingly, health information managers should become knowledgeable about such techniques, including the establishment of standards for encryption of documents as well as choices of software and hardware for user authentication.

The HIPAA Privacy and Security Rules will likely apply to PHI maintained on, and transmitted through, the Internet by a covered entity. In addition, as states update their health information privacy laws, individually identifiable health information on the Internet will become subject to state law. Thus, sending sensitive health information such as that concerning HIV testing, genetic counseling, mental health, and substance abuse over the Internet may be inadvisable. Such information is given special protection under some federal laws and many state laws that contain provisions likely to preempt even those of the Privacy Rule. Therefore, healthcare organizations must implement measures to ensure network security and the confidentiality of patient medical records. Most healthcare organizations already have implemented comprehensive information security programs, in which case many of the policies, training procedures, and controls will be in place to address Internet information security risks. Because the Internet is changing so rapidly, however, health information managers should continually review information security measures to ensure sufficient protection of healthcare information; an organization-wide information security program should facilitate ongoing attention to this objective.

Liability risk relating to privacy and confidentiality can be managed in part through appropriate patient authorizations, together with appropriate disclaimers. Before beginning an Internet communication with an individual, providers should obtain his or her authorization. The authorization should describe the intended communications, describe the risks of using the Internet for those communications, acknowledge those risks, consent to the uses, and agree to follow the instructions provided on the site. This authorization form should not be a substitute for other consents required by law, including state laws governing informed consent for treatment and authorizations required by the Privacy Rule. If the individual is a patient with whom the provider has physical contact, the provider should have the individual sign the form during a face-to-face consultation, perhaps when administering the execution of the general consent for treatment. Copies of Internet consents and authorizations and all other Internet communications should be included in the patient record as either a physical copy in a paper record or as an easily accessible electronic copy in an EHR.

AHIMA has outlined steps for developing and/or enhancing policies and procedures related to Internet security.[211] A starting point, according to AHIMA, is to determine how the Internet is being used within the healthcare organization. For healthcare professionals, use of the Internet usually falls within one or more of the following categories:

- Accessing the vast amount of available information through online libraries or other sites
- Extending an organization's network by connecting with other healthcare providers (for example, linking an employee's computer to another organization's computer system to participate in a joint research project, providing remote access for staff members, or transferring files to other organizations)
- Using electronic communications, such as sending and receiving e-mail and participating in mailing lists and discussion groups

After evaluating how the Internet is used by the healthcare organizations, health information managers should determine how the Internet connection is actually made. Some means of connection present far greater security risk than others. According to AHIMA, high-speed

---

[211] D. Miller, "Internet Security: What Health Information Managers Should Know," *Journal of AHIMA* 67(8), (1996).

connections to the healthcare organization's networked computer systems create far greater risk than a dial-up connection from a personal computer solely for browsing the Internet. In either case, however, AHIMA recommends that healthcare organizations have an organization-wide information security program and an information systems department specifically responsible for establishing and maintaining the organization's links to the Internet and for developing related policies and procedures.

One important security-related responsibility of the information systems department is ensuring that the organization's connections to the Internet are protected by one or more "firewalls"—the computer hardware, software, and network equipment used to control the link to the Internet. The department also should be responsible for ongoing monitoring of the firewall and, as necessary, updating its functions to protect against new security threats. The department may also want to recommend that an organization-wide information security program include policies specifically prohibiting (a) the establishment of other connections to the Internet from the organization's computer, and (b) connecting to the Internet from personally owned computers while those computers are on the organization's premises (if those computers are also connected to the organization's network at the same time).

Access to the organization's systems and network from the Internet also should be totally prevented or stringently controlled. The information systems department should be responsible for implementing and maintaining strong system access controls and firewalls to prevent unauthorized access from outside the organization. Remote log-ins, telnet, remote procedure calls, and other functions that permit accessing the organization's computers from the Internet should be blocked by the firewall. Moreover, any staff education undertaken by the information systems department should include a recommendation that file transmissions using file transfer protocol (FTP) be done with caution.[212] As AHIMA has explained, using FTP to transfer files into the organization may result in downloading software in violation of copyright laws or infecting the organization's computers with viruses, and FTP used for file transfers outside the organization may result in disclosing confidential patient information.[213]

---

[212] FTP allows files to be transferred from one computer to another via the Internet, often without verifying the identity of the requester.
[213] Miller, "Internet Security."

In developing policies regarding the use of the Internet to send e-mail to other Internet users, the healthcare organization, in conjunction with the information systems department, should emphasize that the Internet is not secure as a communications mode. E-mail messages sent over the Internet have the potential for being read by many persons and stored on many different systems prior to delivery, and for easily being copied and forwarded by the recipient to many other people. As a safeguard in this area, healthcare organizations that intend to use e-mail for communication with patients should require the patient to request in writing that e-mail be used and to acknowledge the potential for breaches of confidentiality. Other policies governing the use of Internet e-mail should be implemented and made known to all Internet users in the organization. (For a more detailed description of policies in this area, see "Electronic Mail" earlier in this chapter.)

An information systems department may also want to develop policies regarding the use of Internet e-mail in relation to mailing lists, discussion groups, or bulletin boards. Internet users who subscribe to mailing lists and who send e-mail messages to the list should know that the e-mails usually are available to all subscribers. Although these groups can be a valuable source of information, they may also be the cause of inadvertent disclosure of confidential or proprietary information. Aside from areas involving confidential patient information, staff members should be educated as to other restrictions on e-mail sent to mailing lists.

For example, a typical message to a mailing list might involve one healthcare organization interested in developing specific policies requesting from another organization a copy of that organization's established policies. Some healthcare organizations do not permit such distribution of proprietary materials; thus, staff members should be informed about the organization's policy for participating in mailing lists, the type of information subscribers can post, and whether or not they are permitted to provide comments on behalf of the organization. Staff members also should be informed that patient-identifiable information must never be posted to these lists in order to illustrate procedures or methods.

Although use of the Internet gives rise to significant information security risks, the benefits of the Internet when used properly as a research and information source and a communications tool are probably more significant. Use of the Internet will likely continue to increase at a rapid pace, and health information managers therefore must keep abreast of the latest developments in this area. It is likely that the future will bring increased Internet-related responsibility for health information managers as they face the challenges of ensuring that their organizations have established formal information security programs that include policies, training, and controls specific to Internet use, while also ensuring that all systems and networks storing and processing patient information with links to the Internet are protected with firewalls.

CHAPTER 14

Health Information in Medical Research

Chapter Objectives

- Introduce the stakeholders in medical research
- Describe federal law governing the use of health information in medical research
- Describe the HIPAA Privacy Rule requirements with respect to medical research
- Discuss state laws concerning the use of health information in medical research
- Describe international law affecting medical records and clinical trials
- Summarize industry codes, ethical obligations, and guidance on the use of health information in medical research

Introduction

A research trial conducted in the course of providing clinical care to an individual or otherwise using an individual's medical records information involves many stakeholders. The stakeholders include the researchers (often referred to as investigators), the healthcare institutions and other providers who serve as research sites or simply maintain the medical records that other stakeholders are seeking to access, universities whose medical faculty serve as investigators, public and private funding sources such as the federal government and pharmaceutical and device manufacturers, institutional review boards (IRBs) and privacy boards responsible under federal law for approving and overseeing research and the use of health information in research, and vendors and support organizations such as data managers and clinical research organizations.[1] All the stakeholders have a need to access—and an interest in accessing—the medical records and research records information used in the research trial before, during, and after the trial. Potential collection, access, and use include development of research protocols; identification, screening, and recruitment of potential subjects; conducting the trial and ongoing monitoring of the trial; complying with adverse event reporting and other legal reporting requirements; postmarket surveillance; secondary research; and marketing.

Federal, state, and international laws relating to the privacy of medical and other personal information and the protection of human research subjects affect every aspect of the research-related access to, and use of, such information by all these stakeholders. Such laws require creation of a privacy infrastructure around the way patient health information is collected, processed, shared, stored, and accounted for in the course of a clinical trial. Medical privacy laws also affect the use of information in secondary research and the development of blood and tissue banks for use in medical research.

Traditionally, federal laws have protected the privacy rights of human subjects only in federally funded clinical research or in clinical investigations regulated by the Food and Drug Administration (FDA). More recently, however, the Health Insurance Portability and Accountability Act (HIPAA) and the implementing privacy regulations (Privacy Rule) have extended privacy protections to all research—both publicly and privately funded—thus establishing a federal floor of privacy protections for most individually identifiable health information.[2] The Privacy Rule establishes conditions for the use and disclosure of such information—referred to in HIPAA as "protected health information," or "PHI"—by certain healthcare providers, health plans, and healthcare clearinghouses. Because the Privacy Rule does not preempt all state laws, compliance with state privacy and health law confidentiality laws remains an important consideration. (For a detailed discussion of the

---

[1] Institutional review boards (IRBs) were created by the federal law governing human subject research, known as the "Common Rule." See 45 C.F.R. §§ 46.101 et seq. The Common Rule requires that all federally funded research be reviewed and monitored by an IRB so as to identify and weigh the relative benefits and human subject risks of the proposed research.

[2] 42 U.S.C. §§ 1320d et seq. The federal regulations implementing the HIPAA statute can be found at 45 C.F.R. pts. 160, 162, and 164.

Privacy Rule, see Chapter 6.) So, too, is compliance with international privacy laws that govern the sharing of data in research across international borders, such as the European Union's (EU's) Data Protection and Clinical Trials Directives and national EU member states' laws implementing these directives, and other relevant foreign nations' laws. Finally, those conducting clinical trials and medical research must abide by applicable industry and professional codes, professional ethical obligations, publication requirements, clinical trial agreement terms, and other commonly recognized and followed guidelines, such as the Guideline for Good Clinical Practice (GCP), issued by the International Conference on Harmonisation of Technical Requirements for Registration of Pharmaceuticals for Human Use (ICH).

In many respects, healthcare providers, as the ones who maintain medical records, are an initial and ongoing source of the medical and personal information that is so critical to a research trial. Therefore, the primary responsibility of compliance with this complex body of statutes, regulations, and standards rests with such providers and with the health information professionals responsible for managing, overseeing, and administering their health information operations. Meeting this compliance burden requires a thorough working knowledge of these legal and regulatory requirements and corresponding professional standards.

This chapter will briefly discuss the various federal, state, and international laws and other guidelines and standards relating to the privacy of medical information in clinical research. However, because of the complexity of this area, healthcare organizations should seek the advice of qualified legal counsel.

U.S. Federal Laws Relating to Acquisition and Use of Health Information in Connection with Medical Research

The Common Rule

Generally

All federally funded research involving human subjects must comply with the "Federal Policy for the Protection of Human Subjects," which is generally referred to as the "Common Rule."[3] The Common Rule

---

[3] 45 C.F.R. §§ 46.101 et seq.

delineates broad requirements relating to research involving human subjects.

Even the mere use of individuals' private information, without interaction with the individuals in a clinical setting or otherwise, can be considered human subject research that is subject to the Common Rule. However, the "[P]rivate information must be individually identifiable (*i.e.*, the identity of the subject is or may readily be ascertained by the investigator or associated with the information) in order for obtaining the information to constitute research involving human subjects" that is subject to the Common Rule.[4] In addition, although the Common Rule is not specifically a privacy regulation, IRBs must make sure that adequate processes exist to ensure the privacy and confidentiality of data obtained in research involving human subjects.[5]

The Informed Consent Requirement

Among other things, the Common Rule requires that an IRB ensure that researchers obtain and document adequate informed consent of all human subjects, except where the IRB finds that waiver of such requirement is appropriate.[6] An adequate informed consent must contain the following elements:[7]

- A statement that the study involves research, an explanation of the purposes of the research and the expected duration of the subject's participation, a description of the procedures to be followed, and identification of any procedures that are experimental
- A description of any reasonably foreseeable risks or discomforts to the subject
- A description of any benefits—to the subject or to others—that may reasonably be expected from the research
- A disclosure of appropriate alternative procedures or courses of treatment, if any, that might be advantageous to the subject
- *A statement describing the extent, if any, to which confidentiality of records identifying the subject will be maintained*

---

[4]   45 C.F.R. § 46.102(f).
[5]   See 45 C.F.R. § 46.111(a)(7).
[6]   See 45 C.F.R. §§ 46.101 et seq.
[7]   45 C.F.R. §§ 46.116 and 45.117 (the Common Rule's general requirements for adequate informed consent and the documentation of such consent).

- For research involving more than minimal risk, an explanation as to whether any compensation is available, and an explanation as to whether any medical treatments are available if injury occurs—and, if so, what the treatments consist of, or where further information may be obtained
- An explanation of whom to contact for answers to pertinent questions about the research and research subjects' rights, and whom to contact in the event of a research-related injury to the subject
- A statement that participation is voluntary, that refusal to participate will involve no penalty or loss of benefits to which the subject would otherwise be entitled, and that the subject may discontinue participation at any time without penalty or loss of benefits to which he or she would otherwise be entitled[8]

Under the Common Rule, an IRB may modify or partially or completely waive the requirement of obtaining informed consent where an IRB finds and documents that all of the following apply:

- The research involves no more than minimal risk to the subjects
- The waiver or alteration will not adversely affect the rights and welfare of the subjects
- The research could not practicably be carried out without the waiver or alteration
- Whenever appropriate, the subjects will be provided with additional pertinent information after participation[9]

In addition, there are two cases in which an IRB may waive the requirement of obtaining documentation of written informed consent.[10]

---

[8] 45 C.F.R. § 46.116(a). Generally, a human subject's informed consent must be documented in a written informed consent form that has been approved by the applicable IRB and signed by the human subject or his or her legally authorized representative. An informed consent form can either specify all of the Common Rule requirements in writing, or it may consist of a shorter form stating that the subject was informed of the necessary elements. In the latter case, the IRB must have approved the written form of the verbal summary used to communicate the requisite information, and a copy of the written verbal summary must be given to the subject. In addition, the written verbal summary must be signed by a witness to the verbal informed consent process, who also has signed the short informed consent document.

[9] 45 C.F.R. § 46.116(d).

[10] 45 C.F.R. § 46.117(c).

First, an IRB may waive the requirement where the informed consent document would be the only record linking the subject with the research, and the principal risk from the research would be the possible harm resulting from a confidentiality breach.[11] In this case, however, each subject must be asked whether or not he or she wants documentation connecting the subject with the research, and the subject's wishes must be honored.[12] Second, an IRB may waive the requirement where the research presents only minimal risk of harm to the subject, and involves no procedures for which written consent would be required outside of the research arena.[13]

Certain federally funded research is exempt from the Common Rule requirements. In particular, research involving the collection or study of existing data that either are publicly available or are recorded in a manner such that the subjects of the data cannot be identified directly or indirectly is not subject to the Common Rule.[14]

FDA Protection of Human Subject Regulations

The FDA Protection of Human Subject Regulations (FDA Regulations),[15] govern all clinical investigations regulated by the FDA.[16] The FDA Regulations apply to "any experiment that involves a test article and one or more human subjects" where the data are submitted, or are intended to be submitted, to the FDA. The FDA Regulations do not regulate secondary research.[17] Unlike the Common Rule, the FDA Regulations apply regardless of whether the study is funded by the federal government.

The FDA Regulations require that clinical researchers obtain legally effective informed consent from a research subject or the subject's legally authorized representative in circumstances that give the consenting individual understandable information in a noncoercive atmosphere.[18] The FDA Regulations permit a limited exception to the

---

[11] 45 C.F.R. § 46.117(c)(1).
[12] Ibid.
[13] 45 C.F.R. § 46.117(c)(2).
[14] 45 C.F.R. § 46.101(b)(4).
[15] 21 C.F.R. pts. 50 and 56.
[16] Additional requirements relating to investigational new drug applications and investigational device exemptions are found in 21 C.F.R. pts. 312 and 812.
[17] See 21 C.F.R. pts. 312 and 812.
[18] See 21 C.F.R. § 50.20.

general informed consent requirement in emergency situations where the subject's life is at risk and it is not possible to obtain the consent of the subject or the subject's legally authorized representative's in the time needed to engage in a lifesaving intervention.[19] The FDA Regulations' requirements for the content and documentation of informed consent are identical to those set forth in the Common Rule, except that the subject must be informed of the possibility that the FDA might inspect medical records relating to the clinical investigation.[20] The consent would include, therefore, a statement describing the extent to which confidentiality of records identifying the subject will be maintained.

HIPAA Privacy Rule

HIPAA Generally

The HIPAA Privacy Rule establishes a federal floor of privacy protections for most individually identifiable health information. In particular, the Privacy Rule sets forth the conditions under which protected health information (PHI) may be used or disclosed by certain healthcare providers, health plans, and healthcare clearinghouses, and the means by which individuals will be informed of such uses and disclosures.[21]

Unlike the Common Rule and the FDA Regulations, the Privacy Rule applies *directly only to* HIPAA-defined "covered entities" that use or collect "protected health information," or "PHI." Covered entities include providers who electronically bill and collect for their services, health plans (including self-insured plans), and clearinghouses.[22] The Privacy Rule defines PHI as individually identifiable health information that is held, maintained, or transmitted in any form or medium (orally, or in paper or electronic form) by a covered entity or by a business associate acting for the covered entity.[23] The Privacy Rule defines a business associate as a person, other than an

---

[19] 21 C.F.R. § 50.23.

[20] See 21 C.F.R. §§ 50.25 and 50.27.

[21] Healthcare providers that transmit health information electronically in connection with certain transactions, such as claims or eligibility inquiries, are considered covered entities under HIPAA. See 45 C.F.R. § 60.103.

[22] 45 C.F.R. § 160.103.

[23] Ibid.

employee, who performs a function involving the use of PHI—such as billing, claims processing, quality assurance, utilization review, or practice management—or who provides legal, actuarial, accounting, consulting, data aggregation, management, administrative, accreditation, or financial services to or for the covered entity where the provision of services involves PHI.[24]

As a general rule, HIPAA prohibits use and disclosure of PHI by a covered entity without a specific, written authorization from the individuals involved, unless an exception applies. HIPAA provides many exceptions to this general rule. For example, healthcare providers may freely exchange an individual's identifiable health information in the course of treating the individual or as necessary to bill and collect for such treatment.

Applicability to Medical Research

Pursuant to the Privacy Rule, a covered entity may access, use, and disclose PHI in connection with research only if it (a) has obtained a valid authorization from the subject of the PHI, (b) has a valid waiver to the authorization requirement from an IRB or a privacy board,[25] or (c) if the use or disclosure falls within one of several specified exceptions that are described further in the section "Research Exceptions to Authorization or Waiver Requirements."[26]

Because HIPAA does not apply directly to other than "covered entities," the act does not directly apply to medical researchers or to other stakeholders in clinical trials, such as industry sponsors. The act has indirect application, however, in various respects. First, before a

---

[24] Ibid.
[25] A privacy board is a special review body that the Privacy Rule allows to be established to review requests for a waiver or alteration of the Privacy Rule's written authorization requirement in connection with a particular research study. Privacy boards do not exercise any other powers or authority granted to IRBs under other federal laws, such as the Common Rule or the aforementioned FDA regulations. In addition, the Privacy Rule does not grant privacy boards the authority to approve authorization forms or to monitor uses and disclosures of PHI made pursuant to an authorization. See National Institutes of Health (NIH), "Privacy Boards and the HIPAA Privacy Rule" (posted Sept. 25, 2003), available at http://privacyruleandresearch.nih.gov/privacy_boards_hipaa_privacy_rul .asp (accessed Sept. 14, 2004).
[26] See NIH, "Privacy Boards"; 45 C.F.R. § 164.508.

covered entity will release medical records information to a researcher requesting it, the covered entity will require written documentation of the fact that the researcher has obtained a valid HIPAA authorization or IRB or privacy board waiver, or that the researcher's access to, and use of, the information qualifies for an exception to the authorization or waiver requirement. In practice, many, if not all, covered entities insist that such documentation be produced as part of the IRB or privacy board review process using forms that have been approved by the IRB or privacy board. This indirectly places on IRBs and privacy boards part of the responsibility of implementing the authorization, waiver, and exception provisions of HIPAA, even though HIPAA itself does not impose that responsibility on the IRB.[27] As the common point of contact for researchers seeking access to the medical records maintained by providers, the health information managers of providers also bear part of the HIPAA compliance responsibility. A significant aspect of their role is to collect for the covered providers' compliance records the various forms of HIPAA-related documentation they obtained through the IRB process.

Second, HIPAA also indirectly extends to other stakeholders, such as industry sponsors, who seek, and in many cases contractually mandate, that they be given access by a researcher to PHI. These stakeholders will likely be contractually bound, under the terms of the applicable written research agreements, to comply with the requirement of the particular authorization, waiver, or exception.

Third, many researchers also function as HIPAA covered providers, both apart from and in connection with certain clinical trials. In all cases, it is important for researchers who from time to time function as covered providers to remember that they may not freely use for research the PHI that they obtain from the medical records of their patients. HIPAA sets forth specific requirements with which covered providers must comply when using the information for what

---

[27] For example, HIPAA requires no IRB involvement in the determination that an exception to the authorization or waiver requirement applies in a particular case. Nor does HIPAA require an IRB review and approval of the authorization used in connection with a study when the authorization is not included as part of the same form as the Common Rule informed consent.

is considered research within the meaning of HIPAA.[28] Finally, a researcher who is also an employee or other workforce member of a covered entity also may generally be obligated as such to comply with that entity's new HIPAA privacy policies and procedures.[29]

Valid Authorization

HIPAA sets forth the requirements for a valid authorization.[30] A valid authorization must be signed and dated by the person giving authorization, must be written in plain language, must be specific as to the information to be collected and permissible uses and disclosures, must list the expiration date or event (which, in the case of research, may be "none" or "end of research"), must discuss the effect on treatment or healthcare payment, must warn of any redisclosure risks, must discuss the subject's right to revoke the authorization, and must contain a waiver of access to information where appropriate.[31] If an authorization is signed by a subject's personal representative, the authorization must provide a description of the representative's authority to act for the individual.[32] Any authorizations obtained for use or disclosure of PHI must be retained for six years from the later of the date the authorization was created or the date the authorization was last in ef-

---

[28] It is important to distinguish between "research" and quality improvement activities in this context. HIPAA covered entities are permitted to use PHI without an authorization in connection with their "health care operations." Healthcare operations are defined as including: (1) conducting quality assessment and improvement activities, including outcomes evaluation and development of clinical guidelines, provided that the obtaining of generalizable knowledge is not the primary purpose of any studies resulting from such activities; and population-based activities relating to improving health or reducing healthcare costs, protocol development, case management and care coordination, contacting of healthcare providers and patients with information about treatment alternatives, and related functions that do not include treatment—and (2) reviewing the competence or qualifications of healthcare professionals; evaluating practitioner and provider performance; health plan performance; conducting training programs in which students, trainees, or practitioners in areas of health care learn under supervision to practice or improve their skills as healthcare providers; training of nonhealthcare professionals; accreditation, certification, licensing, or credentialing activities. 45 C.F.R. § 164.501.

[29] See NIH, "Clinical Research and the HIPAA Privacy Rule" (last edited June 22, 2004), available at http://privacyruleandresearch.nih.gov/clin_research.asp (accessed Sept. 14, 2004).

[30] 45 C.F.R. § 164.508.

[31] 45 C.F.R. § 164.508(c).

[32] 45 C.F.R. § 164.508(c)(1)(vi).

fect.[33] As further discussed later in this chapter, in order to comply with special federal and state health information privacy laws, a special authorization form may be required for research involving the use or disclosure of psychotherapy notes or information relating to HIV, mental health, genetic testing, or drug or alcohol abuse.

A Research Authorization

An authorization to use or disclose an individual's PHI in connection with human research is different from the informed consent to participate in the clinical research that is required by the Common Rule and the FDA requirements.[34] A HIPAA authorization focuses on privacy risks, and states how, why, and to whom the researching person or entity will use and/or disclose the individual's PHI in connection with research. In contrast, informed consent provides research subjects with a description of the study and of its anticipated risks and/or benefits in addition to a description of the extent to which the confidentiality of records will be protected. Further, the provisions of the informed consent relating to confidentiality historically have been less specific than the HIPAA required provisions of an authorization.

Valid Waiver

The Privacy Rule allows an IRB or privacy board to grant a waiver of the authorization requirement when the board determines that the following three criteria have been met.[35] First, use or disclosure must involve no more than minimal risk to the data subjects' privacy because the IRB or privacy board finds present at least the following three elements: (1) the research project contains an adequate plan to protect health information identifiers from improper use or disclosure, (2) the research project has an adequate plan to destroy identifiers at the earliest opportunity absent a health or research justification or legal requirement to retain them, and (3) the research sponsor provides adequate written assurances that the PHI will not be used or disclosed

---

[33] 45 C.F.R. §§ 164.508(b)(6) and 164.530(j)(2).
[34] Whether to combine the Common Rule informed consent and the HIPAA authorization remains the subject of debate among stakeholders and practitioners. A discussion of that issue is outside the scope of this chapter.
[35] 45 C.F.R. § 164.512(i)(1)(i).

to a third party except as required by law, for authorized oversight of the research study, or for other research uses and disclosures permitted by the Privacy Rule.

Second, the IRB or privacy board must determine that the research could not practicably be conducted without the waiver or alteration. Finally, the board must decide and document that the research could not practicably be conducted without access to, and use of, PHI. The grant of waiver or alteration of the authorization requirement must be adequately documented, and documentation of such waiver must be maintained for at least six years from the later of the date of creation or the date when the authorization was last in effect.[36] The waiver provision has been used from time to time to grant a limited waiver solely for the purpose of recruiting subjects. Following recruitment, an authorization would be needed to actually conduct the research.

Research Exceptions to Authorization or Waiver Requirements

The Privacy Rule contains three explicit exemptions that permit covered entities to use or disclose PHI in connection with medical research without obtaining a valid authorization or valid authorization waiver: (a) review preparatory to research,[37] (b) research involving use of PHI regarding decedents,[38] and (c) disclosures in connection with certain obligations to report information in connection with certain public health activities and FDA reporting requirements. [39]

This exception permits a researcher to use or disclose PHI in connection with activities preparatory to research, such as preparation of a research protocol (including, without limitation, designing a study, assessing the feasibility of conducting a study, and assessment of whether a sufficient and appropriate subject pool exists to support the study), if both of the following criteria are met: (a) the principal investigator does not record or remove the PHI from the provider entities, and (b) the information sought is necessary for the purposes of the research.[40]

---

[36] 45 C.F.R. § 164.530(j)(2).

[37] 45 C.F.R. § 164.512(i)(1)(ii).

[38] 45 C.F.R. § 164.512(i)(1)(iii).

[39] 45 C.F.R. § 164.512(b)(1). In addition to these research-related exceptions to the Privacy Rule, covered entities do not need to obtain individuals' authorization to use PHI in treatment, payment, or healthcare operations. 45 C.F.R. §§ 164.506(c) and 164.502(a)(1)(ii).

[40] 45 C.F.R. §§ 164.506(c) and 164.502(a)(1)(ii).

When using or disclosing PHI under this exception, however, reasonable efforts must be made to limit the PHI to the minimum necessary to accomplish the intended purpose of the use, disclosure, or request. In addition, this exception may not be available for the use or disclosure of PHI that contains psychotherapy notes or data relating to HIV, mental health, genetic testing, or drug or alcohol abuse.

A researcher may use and disclose a decedent's PHI for research without an authorization or an IRB waiver if all the following criteria are satisfied: (a) the use will be *solely* for research on the PHI of a decedent, (b) the principal investigator has documentation of the death of the individual about whom information is being sought, and (c) the data sought are necessary for the purposes of the research. Note, however, that when using or disclosing decedents' PHI, reasonable efforts must be made to limit the PHI to the minimum amount necessary to accomplish the intended purpose. In addition, this HIPAA exception may not be available for decedent PHI that contains psychotherapy notes or information relating to HIV, mental health, genetic testing, or drug or alcohol abuse.

Information Protected Under the Family Educational Rights and Privacy Act

HIPAA does not apply to information that is considered "educational records" covered by the Family Educational Rights and Privacy Act of 1974 (FERPA) or to "student health records" that are exempted from the coverage of FERPA.[41] Therefore, education records and student health records may be used or disclosed for research purposes without obtaining either an authorization or an IRB waiver. However, the principal investigator must secure a valid consent from the student.[42]

Transitional Rule

The Privacy Rule created a transitional provision that allows a covered entity to use or disclose PHI that was created or received for research before or after the initial HIPAA compliance date (April 14, 2003), so long as the researcher received: (a) the subject's express legal permission to use or disclose PHI for the research, (a) the subject's valid informed

---

[41] 20 U.S.C. § 1232g(a)(4)(A) (2002); 20 U.S.C. § 1232g(a)(4)(B)(iv) (2002).
[42] 34 C.F.R. § 99.30 (2002).

consent to participate in research, or (c) a valid IRB waiver of informed consent pursuant to the Common Rule or FDA's human subject protection regulations.[43]

Use of De-Identified Information and Limited Data Sets

Researchers must not only comply with the Privacy Rule in connection with primary research, but also before using already collected PHI in secondary research. One form of secondary research is the use of data from a primary research study to conduct a separate and unrelated study. HIPAA considers use of PHI in a secondary research study to be use in a new study for which a new authorization or IRB waiver is required, unless the secondary research was disclosed with adequate specificity in the authorization that the subjects signed for the primary study. Two important possibilities exist for secondary use of the PHI from the primary study. First is to strip the PHI of identifiers and create "de-identified data." The second is to strip the information of certain of the identifiers so as to create a "limited data set." As with authorizations, waivers of authorizations, and exceptions to the HIPAA authorization requirement, a covered entity will need to document its compliance with the detailed HIPAA requirements relating to use of de-identified data and limited data sets. Further, the covered entities are likely to rely on IRBs and privacy boards, as well as their internal health information administrators, for assistance in creating and collecting such compliance documentation. (For a detailed discussion of de-identified information and limited data sets, see Chapter 6.)

It is important to note that research protocols involving certain types of information are subject to stricter regulation under HIPAA or state law. In addition, use of limited data sets containing psychotherapy notes or PHI relating to HIV, mental health, genetic testing, or drug or alcohol abuse may be limited or prohibited under applicable special federal and state laws protecting the privacy and confidentiality of such categories of information. The ability to use a limited data set is an important substitute for the use of de-identified data because, in many cases, de-identified data does not contain sufficient information for effective use in research studies.

---

[43] 34 C.F.R. § 164.532.

Other Accommodations for Research in the HIPAA Privacy Rule

In addition to the previously discussed exceptions to the authorization requirement, the Privacy Rule also makes certain other accommodations to limit the burdens of HIPAA on medical research.

The Privacy Rule gives individuals the right to receive an accounting of a covered entity's disclosures of their PHI. However, covered entities need not account for disclosures made pursuant to an individual's valid authorization for a research study.[44] In addition, covered entities need not include in PHI disclosure accountings any disclosures of limited data sets to researchers.[45] Finally, the Privacy Rule allows simplified accounting of PHI disclosures involving at least 50 records that are made for research purposes pursuant to a valid waiver or pursuant to the specific HIPAA research exceptions (that is, review preparatory to research, and research involving decedents' information).[46]

In connection with clinical trials, the Privacy Rule also grants an exception to patients' general right of access to information in their medical records. Specifically, HIPAA authorizes covered entities to suspend research subjects' access to the research medical records results during a clinical trial if the research subjects agree to this as part of the informed consent process.[47] (For a more detailed discussion of an individual's HIPAA rights, see Chapter 6.)

Certificates of Confidentiality

The Privacy Rule generally does not require an authorization for disclosure of PHI when required by law, such as in response to a judicial subpoena.[48] However, Section 301(d) of the Public Health Service Act (PHSA) allows the secretary of the Department of Health and Human Services (DHHS) to authorize persons engaged in biomedical, behavioral, clinical, or other research to provide special privacy protection for individuals who are research subjects by granting "Certificates of Confidentiality."[49] DHHS, in

---

[44] 45 C.F.R. § 164.528(a)(ii).
[45] 45 C.F.R. § 164.528(a)(viii).
[46] 45 C.F.R. § 164.528(b)(4)(i).
[47] 45 C.F.R. § 164.524(a)(2)(iii).
[48] 45C.F.R. §§ 164.512(a) and 164.512(e).
[49] 42 U.S.C. § 241(d).

turn, has delegated to the National Institutes of Health (NIH) its authority to grant Certificates of Confidentiality.[50]

Certificates of Confidentiality may be granted for studies collecting PHI that, if disclosed, could have adverse consequences for subjects— such as damage to their financial standing, employability, insurability, or reputation.[51] Certificates of Confidentiality allow investigators and others who have access to research records to refuse to disclose identifying information in any civil, criminal, administrative, legislative, or other proceeding.[52] Researchers may still voluntarily disclose information about research subjects, such as evidence of child abuse, so long as the researcher discloses his or her intent to make such voluntary disclosures in the informed consent process.[53] The regulations regarding Certificates of Confidentiality authorize DHHS to compel disclosure, for audit purposes, of records protected by a Certificate of Confidentiality if the research is federally funded or if the information is required to be disclosed by the Food, Drug, and Cosmetic Act (FDCA).[54] However, the regulations governing Certificates of Confidentiality do not appear to authorize DHHS to compel disclosure of records related to research that is not federally funded.

When researchers have been granted a Certificate of Confidentiality in connection with research, investigators should disclose in the informed consent form that a Certificate of Confidentiality is in effect.[55] As noted, the informed consent form should also disclose whether a researcher intends, notwithstanding a Certificate of Confidentiality, to make voluntary disclosures in certain circumstances, such as to report child abuse.[56]

---

[50] See 42 C.F.R. § 2a.3(a); NIH Office of Extramural Research (OER), "Certificates of Confidentiality: Background Information," available at http://grants2nih.gov/grants/policy/coc/background.htm; Department of Health and Human Services (DHHS) Office of Human Research Protections (OHRP), "Guidance on Certificates of Confidentiality" (Feb. 25, 2003).

[51] OER, "Certificates."

[52] 42 C.F.R. § 2a.7.

[53] See OER, "Certificates."

[54] 42 C.F.R. § 2a.7(b)(2).

[55] 42 C.F.R. § 2a.4(j).

[56] See 42 C.F.R. § 2a.4(j)(4); OER, "Certificates," 2; OHRP, "Guidance," 2.

State Laws Relating to Acquisition and Use of Health Information in Connection with Medical Research

The Privacy Rule preempts all contrary state laws relating to the privacy of health information unless the state laws are more stringent.[57] However, the Privacy Rule specifically exempts from preemption state laws that (a) the secretary of DHHS finds are necessary to prevent fraud and abuse, to ensure appropriate regulations of insurance and health plans, to engage in state reporting on healthcare delivery or costs or for other compelling public health needs; (b) address controlled substances; (c) provide for reporting of disease or injury, child abuse, birth or death, or for conducting public health surveillance, investigation, and intervention; or (d) relate to management and financial audits, program monitoring or evaluation, or licensure or certification of facilities or individuals.[58]

State HIPAA Statutes

Some states have adopted health information privacy laws that generally have a broader scope than the Privacy Rule. Ambiguity in such state privacy laws often broadens their scope, perhaps unintentionally.[59]

Many such state privacy laws extend the notice, access, amendment, and safeguard requirements to a broader range of entities, including pharmaceutical companies. For example, the California Confidentiality of Medical Information Act (CMIA) covers pharmaceutical companies and requires that they generally preserve the confidentiality of medical records, and that they obtain special authorization to disclose medical information.[60] The CMIA also contains a provision requiring employers that receive medical information to take steps to maintain the confidentiality of the information and prevent its unauthorized disclosure.[61] Texas's health privacy statute also contains an expansive definition of what is deemed a "covered entity"; in Texas, a covered entity

---

[57] 45 C.F.R. § 160.203.
[58] Ibid.
[59] See, e.g., 45 C.F.R. § 181.001(b)(2).
[60] Cal. Civ. Code § 56.05(c).
[61] Cal. Civ. Code § 56.20.

includes any person who "comes into the possession of protected health information," or "obtains or stores protected health information. . . ."[62] Pharmaceutical companies and medical device companies are covered by the Texas medical records privacy statute.[63] In addition, unlike the Privacy Rule, many state privacy laws also regulate data recipients. For example the CMIA requires authorization for secondary disclosures of any identifying health information. In addition, as noted, Texas law includes data recipients as covered entities, and that state's law also specifically prohibits any efforts to reidentify the subject of PHI without obtaining the data subject's consent or authorization.[64] Finally, many state privacy laws, unlike the Privacy Rule, create private rights of action to enforce their provisions.[65]

State Common Law

State common law and other statutes provide additional protections for the medical records of research subjects. In particular, informed consent forms must be guided by cases such as *Moore v. Regents of University of California*,[66] which held that patients have a right to discover any financial interests that their healthcare providers may have in a given course of treatment before the patient gives true "informed consent" to the course of treatment. In addition, those involved in medical research should be cognizant of state common law causes of action for invasion of privacy as they relate to medical records. State employee privacy laws may provide additional protections.[67] Finally, as previously mentioned, many state privacy laws provide additional protection for particularly sensitive health information, such as mental health records and information relating to HIV/AIDS or genetic diseases.[68]

---

[62] Tex. Health & Safety Code ch. 181, § 181.001(b)(2).
[63] See Tex. Health & Safety Code ch. 181, §§ 181.001(b)(4) and (b)(5).
[64] See Cal. Civ. Code §§ 56.05(g), 56.13, and 56.245. The Texas Insurance Code requires that health insurers obtain authorization to disclose nonpublic personal health information except to the extent that disclosure is necessary to perform certain specified insurance functions. See Tex. Ins. Code. arts. 28B.02 and 28B.04.
[65] See, e.g., Tex. Health & Safety Code § 241.156.
[66] 793 P. 2d 479 (Cal. 1990).
[67] See Cal. Civ. Code § 56.20.
[68] See Chapters 5 and 8.

International Laws Relating to Medical Records and Clinical Trials

Various international laws govern the use of personal information in connection with research. The application of these laws includes the exchange of information in cross-border studies and the use of information obtained from foreign sources solely in connection with domestic studies. The breadth of these laws can result in an inadvertent violation of them in the context of research, particularly research that involves the use of the Internet to recruit and otherwise gather and exchange information from foreign subjects.

European Union (EU)

The European Union (EU) has engaged in an extensive effort to protect the privacy of personal information, including health information. In 1995, the EU published the EU Data Protection Directive (EU DPD).[69] The EU DPD is broader than the HIPAA Privacy Rule, both in terms of the data covered and the parties regulated, and significantly impacts the conduct of clinical trials. The principal difficulty the EU privacy protections seem to present for domestic research activities is the transfer of personal data from the EU to the United States.

Applicability

The EU DPD protects individuals' right to privacy with respect to the processing of *any* personal information—not just health data.[70] Health data are considered "sensitive," and thus are subject to even more stringent regulation than other personal data are.[71] The information collected in clinical trials is likely to be personal data. The EU DPD provisions apply to every person or body that processes personal data, not merely providers or health plans—including the investigator; the private industry sponsors of clinical trials involving human subjects,

---

[69] Directive 95/46/EC (EU Data Protection Directive, or EU DPD), *Official Journal of the European Communities* (O.J.) L 281 (Nov. 23, 1995): 31–50.
[70] EU DPD art. 1, no. 2.
[71] EU DPD art. 8.

such as pharmaceutical companies and device manufacturers; and contract research organizations (CROs).

In general, the EU DPD prohibits individuals and organizations from using or exporting from the EU sensitive personal information, such as health data, unless an exception applies.[72] Under the EU DPD, the data controller—a natural or legal person who alone or jointly determines the purposes and means of processing personal data—is ultimately responsible for compliance with the EU DPD principles.[73] A data controller must obtain a subject's unambiguous consent to the processing of personal data, or must ensure that information is processed only by health professionals or others subject to stringent secrecy obligations.[74]

The EU DPD and other EU directives do not legally bind national citizens, but instead are addressed to EU member states, who are required to pass national legislation implementing the EU directives.[75] Because of the varied implementation of laws in member countries, analysis of relevant national law with the help of local counsel is necessary.

Exporting of Medical Data

The EU DPD and national implementing legislation limit the ability of individuals and organizations to export medical data to the United States to four circumstances.[76] First, the EC has specifically authorized information to be exported where the data recipient has signed up for a

---

[72] EU DPD arts. 8 and 25.

[73] See United Kingdom, Data Protection Act of 1998, ch. 29, pt. I ("data controller" means, subject to subsection (4), "a person who (either alone or jointly or in common with other persons) determines the purposes for which and the manner in which any personal data are, or are to be, processed....")

[74] EU DPD art. 8.

[75] Ibid.

[76] Under the EU DPD, a data controller may transfer data to a third, non-EU (and non-European Economic Area) country only if the third country ensures an "adequate level of protection." EU DPD art. 25, p. 6. The commission has recognized Canada, Argentina, Guernsey, Hungary, and Switzerland as providing adequate protection, but not the United States. See Stephen Bernstein et al., "Transfer of Clinical Research Data from the European Union to the United States," *Medical Research Law & Policy Report*, Issn. 1539-1035, at 4, reprinted from 3(7): 271–276 (Apr. 7, 2004).

"Safe Harbor" sponsored by the U.S. Department of Commerce.[77] The Department of Commerce created the Safe Harbor framework in consultation with the EC, and the EU approved the framework in July 2000.[78] To qualify for the Safe Harbor, a U.S. organization must self-certify to the Department of Commerce its compliance with either the Safe Harbor Principles or the principles set forth in a similar self-regulatory privacy program.[79] Under the Safe Harbor Principles, organizations collecting and using personal information must inform data subjects about the purposes for which information about the data subject is being used and collected; the types of third parties who will be receiving the data; and mechanisms to communicate complaints and inquires regarding the information, including requests to limit its use and disclosure.[80] Organizations must also promise to take reasonable precautions to protect data security.[81] Finally, to qualify for the Safe Harbor, organizations' failure to comply with the principles or self-regulatory program must be actionable under Section 5 of the Federal Trade Commission Act (FTCA).[82]

A second way to legally transfer health information from the EU to the United States is for the data exporter and the data recipient to enter into a special contract with "appropriate contractual clauses."[83] The appropriate contractual clauses include a requirement that the data subject be a third-party beneficiary of the agreement between the data exporter and data importer.[84] In addition, in the data use contract, the data importer (for example, a clinical trials sponsor based in the United States) must commit to process personal information in accordance with certain data protection principles, including agreeing to either

---

[77] "Safe Harbor Privacy Principles" were issued by U.S. Department of Commerce and were approved by the EC. Decision of the Commission 2000/520/EC of July 26, 2000, art. 1, p. 1 (*O.J.* L 215/7, Aug. 25, 2000).

[78] Department of Commerce, "Introduction to the Safe Harbor" (updated June 29, 2004), available at http://www.export.gov/safeharbor.

[79] Department of Commerce, "Safe Harbor Privacy Principles" (issued July 21, 2000), available at http://www.export.gov/safeharbor/SHPRINCIPLESFINAL.htm.

[80] Ibid.

[81] Ibid.

[82] Ibid.

[83] EU DPD, art. 26, p. 2.

[84] Ibid.

strong encryption for health data transmission or retention of a record of access to such health information.[85]

A third approved mechanism to export PHI to the United States is for the data recipient and the data exporter to obtain a regulatory waiver by appropriate national supervisory authorities for a specific code of conduct to govern the transfer.[86]

The fourth, and final, approved means for legally transferring health information from the EU to the United States is for the data exporter and the data recipient to obtain the data subject's unambiguous consent to such transfer.[87] The latter is the most practical manner for entities conducting international clinical trials to comply with the EU DPD, because it is the least burdensome; the subject's consent to information transfer can be incorporated into his or her informed consent to participate in a clinical trial.[88]

More recently, the EU adopted the EU Clinical Trials Directive.[89] The EU Clinical Trials Directive contains an overarching scheme of principles and rules regarding good clinical practice in the conduct of clinical trials, which are to be implemented by domestic legislation of EU member states. In particular, the EU Clinical Trials Directive emphasizes that informed consent must be obtained from legally competent individuals.[90] Accordingly, those conducting clinical trials in Europe should ensure that informed consent documentation adequately reflects the consent of a legally competent individual.

United Kingdom

The United Kingdom has enacted legislation implementing the EU Directives. The Data Protection Act of 1998 implements the EU

---

85 See Decision of the Commission 2001/497/EC of June 15, 2001 (*O.J.* L. 181/19, July 4, 2001), which sets forth a standard set of contractual clauses stipulating the transfer from a European-based data controller to a data controller in a third country that the EC has approved.
86 Decision of the Commission 2001/497/EC.
87 Decision of the Commission 2001/497/EC, art. 26, art. 2(h).
88 International Conference on Harmonization of Technical Requirements for Registration of Pharmaceuticals for Human Use (ICH), Guideline for Good Clinical Practice (GCP) No. 4.8.10(n).
89 Directive 2001/20/EC of April 4, 2001 (*O.J.* L. 121/34, May 1, 2001).
90 Ibid. The EU Clinical Trials Directive also requires that every EU clinical trial now have a sponsor that is established or has a legal representative in the EU and that has registered with the appropriate national body where the data are being collected or processed. See Directive 2001/20/EC, art. 9.

DPD,[91] and covers all data controllers that are incorporated or otherwise conduct data processing activities in the United Kingdom.[92] Meanwhile, the Medicines for Human Use (Clinical Trials) Regulations 2004, which came into force on May 1, 2004, implement the Clinical Trials Directive. The Medicines for Human Use (Clinical Trials) Regulations 2004 establish the Medicines and Healthcare Products Regulatory Agency as the body responsible for authorizing clinical trials and enforcing regulations.[93]

Generally, the Medicines for Human Use Regulations 2004 require that all clinical trials be conducted in accordance with Guideline for Good Clinical Practice (GCP) principles, which were developed by the International Conference on Harmonisation of Technical Requirements for Registration of Pharmaceuticals for Human Use (ICH) and are discussed later in this chapter. In addition, the Medicines for Human Use Regulations create certain additional protections for minors and physically or mentally incapacitated adults who are candidates for clinical trials.

Canada

Canada has established its own council governing the protection of human subjects in clinical research. The *Tri-Council Policy Statement: Ethical Conduct for Research Involving Humans* (1998, with 2000 and 2002 updates) generally requires notice, including of any proposed secondary use, and consent before researchers may use and disclose personal information about clinical subjects.[94] The Canadian rule is subject to a reasonableness standard regarding notice and consent.[95] The EU allows data exports to Canada, because Canada is seen to be an "approved country" that adequately protects the privacy of health information.[96]

---

[91] A copy of the Data Protection Act of 1998 can be found at http://www.hmso.gov.uk/acts /acts1998/19980029.htm.

[92] Data Protection Act of 1998, ch. 29, pt. 5.

[93] The Medicines for Human Use (Clinical Trials) Regulations 2004 came into effect in May 2004 and can be found at http://www.legislation.hmso.gov.uk/si/si2004/20041031 .htm.

[94] Clinical Trials, § 3.

[95] See Clinical Trials.

[96] Decision of the Commission 2002/2/EC of Dec. 20, 2001 (*O.J.* L. 2/13, Jan. 4, 2002).

Japan

In 2003, Japan enacted a new Personal Information Protection Act (PIPA).[97] PIPA is similar to the EU DPD in that it creates broad protections for all personal data and regulates all entities handling personal information. The act requires that individual businesses must specify the purpose for collecting and using personal information and promptly notify data subjects of such purpose. PIPA, which became effective in April 2005, is in many ways more restrictive—but in other ways weaker—than the EU DPD.

Generally, PIPA strongly protects personal information; a business may not supply personal data to an unaffiliated third party, whether inside or outside Japan, without the data subject's prior consent, except in four narrow circumstances. The four circumstances in which a business entity may transfer an individual's personal information to a third party without the individual's consent are: (a) the transfer is made pursuant to a law or ordinance; (b) the transfer is necessary in an emergency to protect life, safety, or property; (c) the transfer is made for the improvement of public hygiene or to promote children's health; or 4) the transfer is required by a public authority, where informing the data subject might impede execution of government business. However, PIPA leaves enforcement to "competent Ministers," and does not allow a private right of action to enforce the act.

Currently, PIPA does not distinguish between general personal information—such as names, addresses, and birth dates—and data that the EU considers more sensitive, such as health information. However, on June 1, 2004, the Japanese national government announced that it planned to offer personal data protection guidelines for every industry sector.[98] The Japanese government also stated that it might introduce sector-specific privacy and data protection laws for industry sectors that handle particularly sensitive types of personal information, such as the medical, financial and credit, and telecommunications sectors.[99]

---

[97] 2003 Law No. 57.
[98] *Mainichi Newspaper Tokyo* morning edition (June 2, 2004), cited at http://www.privacyexchange.org/japan/nf0406.html#1e.
[99] Ibid.

Other Guidance

In addition to federal, state, and international laws, those involved in clinical research should also consider other sources of applicable guidance relating to medical records—such as industry and professional codes, ethical obligations, publication requirements, and clinical trial agreement terms. The most prominent of such other applicable guidelines is the Guideline for Good Clinical Practice (GCP).

International Conference on Harmonisation

In 1990, six regulatory bodies and research-based industry groups in Europe, Japan, and the United States established the International Conference on Harmonisation of Technical Requirements for Registration of Pharmaceuticals for Human Use (ICH). The six founding members are: in Japan, the Ministry of Health, Labour and Welfare (MHLW) and the Japan Pharmaceutical Manufacturers Association (JPMA); in Europe, the European Commission (EC) and the European Federation of Pharmaceutical Industries and Associations (EFPIA); and in the United States, the Food and Drug Administration (FDA) and the Pharmaceutical Research and Manufacturers of America (PhRMA).[100]

In its first meeting, the ICH unanimously agreed to expand its Steering Committee membership to include representatives from the World Health Organization (WHO), the European Free Trade Association (EFTA), and Canada as "observers."[101] The ICH seeks to make developing and registering new medicinal products in Europe, Japan, and the United States more efficient by harmonizing the regulatory processes within these three regions.[102]

---

[100] See http://www.ich.org/MediaServer.jser?@_ID=406&@_MODE=GLB.
[101] Ibid.
[102] Ibid. ("The objective of ICH is to increase international harmonization of technical requirements to ensure that safe, effective, and high quality medicines are developed and registered in the most efficient and cost-effective manner."); 62 Fed. Reg. 25691, 25692 (May 9, 1997) ("one of the goals of the harmonization is to identify and then reduce the differences in technical requirements for drug development among regulatory agencies").

In July 1996, the ICH adopted the GCP.[103] In addition to establishing proper procedures for clinical trials, the GCP lays out general rules for the protection of clinical research subjects. Although protecting the privacy of medical records is not the principal goal of the GCP, the guideline does explicitly endorse the idea of medical information privacy. In particular, the GCP states that "[t]he confidentiality of records that could identify subjects should be protected, respecting the privacy and confidentiality rules in accordance with the applicable regulatory requirement(s)."[104]

The GCP also contains standards relating to obtaining proper informed consent. The standards state that the informed consent form should tell subjects that records identifying them will be kept confidential, subject to relevant laws and regulations.[105] Like the Privacy Rule, the GCP calls for an IRB to review and approve the methods and materials to be used in obtaining and documenting trial subjects' informed consent and all other written information provided to subjects.[106]

The FDA has specifically stated that the GCP should be followed in any clinical trials involving data that are intended to be submitted to regulatory authorities.[107] However, the FDA also notes that the GCP "does not operate to bind the FDA or the public," and that entities may follow an alternate approach that satisfies all applicable laws and regulations.[108]

The PhRMA[109] Principles on Conduct of Clinical Trials and Communication of Clinical Trial Results ("PhRMA Principles") explicitly endorse the GCP standards. The PhRMA Principles specifically state: "All participation in a clinical trial is based on informed consent, freely given without coercion. Any proposed payments to research participants should be reviewed by an independent IRB/EC. The privacy

---

[103] Issued as CPMP/ICH/135/95/Step 5, and Explanatory Note and Comments, issued as CPMP/768/97.
[104] CPMP/ICH/135/95/Step 5, § 2.11.
[105] CPMP/ICH/135/95/Step 5, § 4.8.10.
[106] See ICH GCP at §§ 1.31, 3.1.2.
[107] 62 Fed. Reg. 25691, 25692 (May 9, 1997).
[108] Ibid.
[109] Pharmaceutical Research and Manufacturers of America (PhRMA). See http://www.phrma.org.

rights of research participants and the confidentiality of medical information are safeguarded."[110]

Other professional associations likewise endorse the principle of protecting the privacy of medical records. For example, the American Medical Association (AMA) Code of Medical Ethics states that "[t]he physician should not reveal confidential communications or information without the express consent of the patient, unless required to do so by law."[111] The code also specifically provides that "data collection from computerized or other patient records for marketing purposes raises serious ethical concerns."[112] The code notes that collection of information on physicians' prescribing practices on behalf of pharmaceutical companies may violate principles of informed consent and patient confidentiality if patients have not given their permission after being fully informed about the purposes of such disclosures.[113]

Finally, as noted, many publication requirements and clinical trial agreements contain specific provisions relating to the confidentiality of medical records information. Accordingly, those involved in clinical research should always consult publication requirements and clinical trial agreements for additional requirements relating to medical records information.

Conclusion

Those involved in medical research should be careful to ensure that their collection and dissemination of health information complies with all applicable U.S. federal and state laws, international laws, and other appropriate professional or contractual requirements. Given the complexity of this area, those involved in large, multistate, or international clinical trials should consult counsel in order to ensure compliance with all relevant laws.

---

[110] PhRMA, *Principles on Conduct of Clinical Trials and Communication of Clinical Trial Results,* available at http://www.phrma.org/publications/quickfacts/20.06.2002.428.cfm.
[111] AMA, Code of Medical Ethics, E-5.05—Confidentiality.
[112] AMA, Code of Medical Ethics, E-5.075—Confidentiality: Disclosure of Records to Data Collection Companies.
[113] Ibid.

Glossary: Acronyms and Definitions

Note: Terms followed by an asterisk were taken from the Centers for Medicare & Medicaid Services (CMS) Web site at http://www.cms.hhs.gov/.

ADA
Americans with Disabilities Act

Administrative code sets
Code sets that characterize a general business situation, rather than a medical condition or service. Under HIPAA, these are sometimes referred to as nonclinical or nonmedical code sets. Compare to medical code sets.*

Administrative simplification
Title II, Subtitle F of HIPAA, which authorizes DHHS to: (1) adopt standards for transactions and code sets that are used to exchange health data; (2) adopt standard identifiers for health plans, healthcare providers, employers, and individuals for use on standard transactions; and (3) adopt standards to protect the security and privacy of personally identifiable health information.*

Administrative tribunal
The place in which a governmental agency conducts a legal proceeding, usually a hearing before an officer of the agency.

Advanced directive
A written instruction, such as a living will or durable power of attorney for health care, that is recognized under state law and that expresses an individual's wishes regarding

	future medical treatment should he or she become incompetent.
AHIMA	American Health Information Management Association
AHRQ	Agency for Healthcare Research and Quality
Authentication	The process that requires the physician or other medical practitioner to sign the medical record(s) or a portion thereof. A handwritten signature, a rubber stamp, or a computer key are acceptable authentication methods.
Auto-authentication	The process by which a physician authenticates a report by computer code before the report is transcribed.
Bill of Rights	The first 10 amendments to the U.S. Constitution.
Breach of confidentiality	A legal theory under which a patient may sue a healthcare provider for the improper disclosure of medical records information. Also known as breach of physician-patient privilege.
Business associate	A person or organization that performs a function or activity on behalf of a covered entity, but is not part of the covered entity's workforce. A business associate can also be a covered entity in its own right. Also see Part II, 45 C.F.R. § 160.103.*
Business records	Documents that are made in the regular course of business at the time that, or within a reasonable time after, the recorded event occurred and under circumstances that reasonably might be assured to accurately reflect the actual event.
CDC	Centers for Disease Control and Prevention
Centers for Medicare & Medicaid Services (CMS)	The DHHS agency responsible for Medicare and parts of Medicaid. CMS has

historically maintained the UB-92 institutional EMC format specifications, the professional EMC NSF specifications, and specifications for various certifications and authorizations used by the Medicare and Medicaid programs. CMS is responsible for oversight of HIPAA administrative simplification transaction and code sets, health identifiers, and security standards. CMS also maintains the HCPCS medical code set and the Medicare Remittance Advice Remark Codes administrative code set.*

Code of Federal Regulations (CFR)

The official compilation of federal rules and requirements.

Code set

Under HIPAA, this is any set of codes used to encode data elements, such as tables of terms, medical concepts, medical diagnostic codes, or medical procedure codes. This includes both the codes and their descriptions. Also see Part II, 45 C.F.R. § 162.103.*

Common law

The principles of law that evolve from court decisions resolving controversies.

Compliance date

Under HIPAA, this is the date by which a covered entity must comply with a standard, an implementation specification, or a modification. This is usually 24 months after the effective date of the associated final rule for most entities, but 36 months after the effective data for small health plans. For future changes in the standards, the compliance date would be at least 180 days after the effective date, but can be longer for small health plans and for complex changes.*

Compliance program

A healthcare organization's or facility's program that enforces internal controls and monitors conduct in order to prevent and correct improper activities.

Confidential intermediary   A person authorized to contact one or both of the biological parents of an adopted person and to request information sought by the adoptee.

Constitution of the United States   The supreme law of the land, establishing the general organization of the federal government, granting certain powers to the federal government, and placing certain limits on what the federal and state governments may do.

Coordination of benefits   Process for determining the respective responsibilities of two or more health plans that have some financial responsibility for a medical claim. Also called crossover.*

Corporate compliance programs   A document that outlines standards and procedures to be followed by an organization's employees and agents for the purpose of preventing and detecting criminal or illegal conduct involving the organization.

Covered entity   Under HIPAA, this is a health plan, a healthcare clearinghouse, or a healthcare provider who transmits any health information in electronic form in connection with a HIPAA transaction.*

Data content   Under HIPAA, this is all the data elements and code sets inherent to a transaction, and not related to the format of the transaction.*

Data element   Under HIPAA, this is the smallest named unit of information in a transaction.*

Data security   A process or mechanism that protects data from improper disclosure or alteration.

Defamation   A legal theory under which patients may file civil lawsuits for unauthorized disclosure of medical information. Libel is the written form of defamation; slander is the oral form.

Designated code set   A medical code set or an administrative code set that is required to be used by the adopted implementation specification for a standard transaction.*

Designated standard

A standard that DHHS has designated for use under the authority provided by HIPAA.*

Designated standard maintenance organization (DSMO)

An organization designated by the secretary of DHHS to maintain standards adopted under Subpart I of 45 C.F.R. Part 162. A DSMO may receive and process requests for adopting a new standard or modifying an adopted standard.*

DHHS

U.S. Department of Health and Human Services

Direct data entry

Under HIPAA, this is the direct entry of data that are immediately transmitted into a health plan's computer.*

DNR

Do Not Resuscitate

DRG

Diagnosis related group

Due process of law

A legal concept that requires that the rules being applied are reasonable—not vague or arbitrary—and that fair procedures are followed in enforcing the rules.

ECPA

Electronic Communications Privacy Act of 1986

Effective date

Under HIPAA, this is the date that a final rule is effective, which is usually 60 days after it is published in the *Federal Register*.*

Electronic data interchange (EDI)

Refers to the exchange of routine business transactions from one computer to another in a standard format, using standard communications protocols.*

Electronic health record (EHR)

A system that captures, stores, retrieves, and transmits patient health data, including clinical, administrative, and payment data. A fully automated, computer-based patient

	record is one in which all the data images collected over the course of a patient's health care are created, authenticated, modified, stored, and retrieved by the computer.
Emancipated minors	A term describing the legal status of minors when they are married or otherwise are no longer subject to parental control or regulation and are not supported by their parents. The specific factors necessary to establish emancipation usually are established by statute and vary from state to state.
Employer identifier	A standard adopted by the secretary of DHHS to identify employers in standard transactions. The Internal Revenue Service's Employer Identification Number (EIN) is the adopted standard.*
EMTALA	Emergency Medical Treatment and Active Labor Act
Encryption	A method of encoding data to protect the information from unauthorized access or tampering when the data are transmitted or stored in a computer.
Enforcement Rule	The HIPAA regulations governing the procedures for enforcement of other HIPAA regulations, found at 45 C.F.R. §§ 160.500 et seq.
Entry errors	Minor errors in transcription (such as spelling) or more significant mistakes involving test results, physician orders, inadvertently omitted information, and similar substantive errors.
ePHI	Protected health information in any electronic medium.
EPO	Exclusive provider organization
Equal protection	A legal concept utilized to ensure that like persons are treated in like fashion, and applied by analyzing the legitimacy of the classification used to distinguish persons for various legal purposes.

ERISA	Employee Retirement Income Security Act of 1974
Express consent	The consent given by direct words, whether orally or in writing.
FDA	Food and Drug Administration
FOIA	Freedom of Information Act
Fraud and abuse	A term referring to a complex and expanding array of legislative restrictions on the way healthcare providers conduct business and structure relationships among themselves. Provisions governing this conduct are found primarily in the Medicare/Medicaid statute, Stark legislation, and the civil False Claims Act. Violations of these provisions generally consist of executing a scheme or artifice to defraud a healthcare benefit program, or obtaining through false representations money from a healthcare benefit program. Other federal offenses relating to healthcare fraud include theft or embezzlement, false statements, and obstructions of criminal investigations.
Freedom of information laws	The laws that enable the public to get access to records maintained by state agencies. In some states, the statute is called the "public records" or "open records" law.
GPWW	Group practice without walls
Group health plan	A health plan that provides health coverage to employees, former employees, and their families, and is supported by an employer or employee organization.*
Healthcare clearinghouse	A public or private entity (entities including, but not limited to, billing services, repricing companies, community health management information systems or community health information systems, and "value-added" networks and switches are healthcare clearinghouses if they perform these functions) that does either of the following:

(1) processes, or facilitates the processing of, information received from another entity in a nonstandard format or containing nonstandard data content into standard data elements or a standard transaction, or (2) receives a standard transaction from another entity and processes, or facilitates the processing of, information into nonstandard format or nonstandard data content for a receiving entity.*

Healthcare Provider Taxonomy Code (HPTC)

An administrative code set that classifies healthcare providers by type and area of specialization. The code set will be used in certain adopted transactions. (Note: A given provider may have more than one Healthcare Provider Taxonomy Code.)*

Health plan

An entity that assumes the risk of paying for medical treatments—that is, uninsured patient, self-insured employer, payer, or HMO.*

Hearsay

An out-of-court statement introduced into a legal proceeding for the purpose of proving the truth of the facts asserted in that statement.

HIPAA (Health Insurance Portability and Accountability Act of 1996)

A federal law that allows persons to qualify immediately for comparable health insurance coverage when they change their employment relationships. Title II, Subtitle F of HIPAA gives DHHS the authority to mandate the use of standards for the electronic exchange of healthcare data; to specify what medical and administrative code sets should be used within those standards; to require the use of national identification systems for healthcare patients, providers, payers (or plans), and employers (or sponsors); and to specify the types of measures required to protect the security and privacy of personally identifiable healthcare information. Also known as the Kennedy-Kassebaum Bill, the Kassebaum-Kennedy Bill, K2, or Public Law 104-191.*

HMO Health maintenance organization

Hybrid entity A covered entity whose covered functions are not its primary functions.*

IDS Integrated delivery system

Implied consent The consent inferred from the patient's conduct and consent presumed in certain emergencies.

Incident report An administrative record of an adverse event affecting a healthcare facility. The report allows the facility to identify potential problems by evaluating occurrences and monitoring trends.

Informed consent The process by which a patient is apprised of a procedure's risks and benefits, and freely agrees to undergo the proposed treatment.

Interoperable The ability of different information systems, software applications, and networks to communicate and exchange information in an accurate, secure, effective, useful, and consistent manner.

IPA Independent practice association

IRB Institutional review board

IRS Internal Revenue Service

JCAHO Joint Commission on Accreditation of Healthcare Organizations

Legal process Refers to all writs issued by a court during a legal action, or by an attorney in the name of the court but without court review. There are two types of legal process—the subpoena and the court order.

Living will A document providing direction as to medical care, if the adult becomes incapacitated

	or otherwise unable to make decisions personally.
Local codes	A generic term for code values that are defined for a state or other local division or for a specific payer. Commonly used to describe HCPCS Level III Codes.*
Long consent form	A form with a detailed description of a patient's medical condition, proposed procedure, consequences, risks, and alternatives to treatment. Also called a detail or special consent form.
Managed care	Any method of healthcare delivery designed to reduce unnecessary utilization of services and provide for cost containment while ensuring that high quality of care or performance is maintained; a system to minimize cost of care and "churning" while still delivering good access to high-quality health care; arrangements made by payers to promote cost-effective health care through establishing selective relationships with healthcare providers, developing coordinated or integrated delivery systems, and conducting medical management activities.
Maximum defined data set	Under HIPAA, this is all of the required data elements for a particular standard based on a specific implementation specification. An entity creating a transaction is free to include whatever data any receiver might want or need. The recipient is free to ignore any portion of the data that is not needed in order to conduct their part of the associated business transaction, unless the nonessential data are needed for coordination of benefits.*
MCO	Managed care organization
Medical code sets	Codes that characterize a medical condition or treatment. These code sets are usually maintained by professional societies and public health organizations. Compare to administrative code sets.*

Medical group practice	A traditional practice structure in which physicians combine their resources. Also known as a consolidated medical group.
Medical record	A collection of data relating to the medical and healthcare services that a patient receives from a healthcare professional or other licensed healthcare provider. Also known as patient records.
Medicare contractor	A Medicare Part A Fiscal Intermediary (institutional), a Medicare Part B Carrier (professional), or a Medicare Durable Medical Equipment Regional Carrier (DMERC).*
MSO	Management services organization
NAIC	National Association of Insurance Commissioners
National drug code	A medical code set maintained by the FDA. The code set contains codes for drugs that are FDA approved. The secretary of DHHS adopted this code set as the standard for reporting drugs and biologics on standard transactions.*
NCQA	National Committee for Quality Assurance
NLRB	National Labor Relations Board
Notice of Proposed Rulemaking	A document that describes and explains regulations that the federal government proposes to adopt at some future date, and invites interested parties to submit comments related to them. These comments can then be used in developing a final regulation.*
NPI (National Provider Identifier)	A system for uniquely identifying all providers of healthcare services, supplies, and equipment. A term proposed by the secretary of DHHS as the standard identifier for healthcare providers.*
NPI Rule	The HIPAA regulations establishing and governing National Provider Identifiers, found at 69 Fed. Reg. 3434 (Jan. 23, 2004).

OCR (Office for Civil Rights) — Part of DHHS. OCR's HIPPA responsibilities include oversight of the privacy requirements.*

OIG (Office of Inspector General) — The OIG was established by law as "an independent and objective oversight unit of the [DHHS] to carry out the mission of promoting economy, efficiency, and effectiveness through the elimination of waste, abuse and fraud." It is empowered to conduct audits and investigations, identify systemic weaknesses that permit fraud, coordinate efforts to detect fraud and wrongdoers, and keep the Secretary of DHHS informed concerning problems and deficiencies in the administration of DHHS programs. 69 Fed. Reg. 40386 (July 2, 2004).

Peer review — A process by which a hospital's medical staff members review the qualifications, medical outcomes, and professional conduct of other staff physician members and applicants to determine whether such physicians may practice in the hospital, and, if so, the parameters of their practice.

PHI — Protected health information. Defined as individually identifiable health information transmitted by electronic media, maintained in electronic media, or transmitted or maintained in any other form or medium. Some exceptions apply.

PHO — Physician/hospital organization

Physician-patient privilege — A legal privilege, often created by statute, that protects the communications between a patient and a physician from disclosure in judicial or quasi-judicial proceedings under specified circumstances. The purpose of this privilege is to encourage the patient to tell the physician all the information necessary for treatment, no matter how embarrassing.

Plan sponsor	An entity that sponsors a health plan. This can be an employer, a union, or some other entity.*
Power of attorney	A written document that authorizes an individual, as an agent, to perform certain acts on behalf of, and according to the written directives of, another—the person executing the document—from whom the agent obtains authority. The agent is called the attorney-in-fact, and the person executing the document is called the principal.
PPO	Preferred provider organization
Privacy Rule	The HIPAA regulations governing the privacy of protected health information, found at 45 C.F.R. §§ 164.500 et seq.
PRO	Peer review organization
PSDA	Patient Self-Determination Act
QIO	Quality improvement organization
Qualified legal counsel	In the context of addressing legal questions concerning health information, qualified legal counsel are attorneys who have meaningful experience and expertise related to the specific health information legal issues presented. For example, if the issue presented is one of HIPAA preemption of state law, qualified legal counsel would be attorneys who have dealt with numerous HIPAA preemption issues. Although any licensed attorney should be capable of advising on any legal issue that may arise, attorneys who have experience with the specific issue usually are able to provide advice most efficiently.
Quality improvement	A management engineering theory for obtaining continuous and incremental improvements. Quality improvement identifies problems in healthcare delivery, tests solutions to those problems, and tracks implemented solutions.

Reasonable patient standard One of the two standards used to determine the adequacy of the information that the physician has given to the patient during the informed consent process. Most states have adopted this standard whereby the physician's duty to provide information is determined by the information needs of the patient, rather than by customary professional practice.

Reasonable physician standard One of the two standards used to determine the adequacy of the information that the physician has given to the patient during the informed consent process. This standard requires the physician to provide the information that a reasonable medical practitioner would offer under same or similar circumstances.

Risk management A four-step process designed to identify, evaluate, and resolve the actual and possible sources of loss. The four steps are risk identification, risk evaluation, risk handling, and risk monitoring.

Security Rule The HIPPA regulations governing the security of protected health information, found at 45 C.F.R. §§ 164.302 et seq.

Self-insured An individual or organization that assumes the financial risk of paying for health care.*

Short consent form A form that provides space for patient name and description of the specific procedure, and that states the following: (1) the person signed has been told about the medical condition, consequences, risks, and alternative treatments; and (2) all the person's questions have been answered to the individual's satisfaction. The short form does not list the particular risks and benefits that were described to the patient. Also called a general or battery consent form.

Small health plan Under HIPAA, this is a health plan with annual receipts of $5 million or less.*

Stare decisis

A legal doctrine imposing on the presiding court the requirement to follow the precedents of higher courts in the same court system that has jurisdiction over the geographic area where the presiding court is located. For example, each appellate court, including the highest court, generally is bound to follow the precedents of its own decisions, unless it decides to overrule the precedent due to changing conditions.

Statute

Law enacted by a legislature.

Statute of limitations

A period of time established by statute, usually measured in years, during which a party may bring a lawsuit.

Strategic National Implementation Process (SNIP)

A national Workgroup for Electronic Data Interchange (WEDI) effort for helping the healthcare industry identify and resolve HIPAA implementation issues.*

Subpoena ad testificandum

A written order commanding a person to appear and to testify at a trial or other judicial or investigative proceeding. These orders are used to obtain documents during pretrial discovery and to obtain testimony during trial.

Subpoena duces tecum

A written order commanding a person to appear; give testimony; and bring all documents, papers, books, and records described in the subpoena. These orders are used to obtain documents during pretrial discovery and to obtain testimony during trial.

System Security

A process in which a specified system functions in a defined operational environment, serves a defined set of users, contains prescribed data and operational reports, defines network connections and interactions with other systems, and incorporates safeguards to protect the system against defined threats to the system and its resources and data.

TCS Rule	The HIPAA regulations governing standard electronic transactions and code sets, found at 45 C.F.R. §§ 162.100 et seq.
Telemedicine	The delivery of healthcare services at a distance with the use of the Internet, interactive telecommunications, and computer technology.
Therapeutic privilege	An exception to the informed consent doctrine that permits a physician to withhold information when disclosure of the information poses a significant threat of detriment to the patient.
Third-party administrator	An entity required to make, or responsible for making, payment on behalf of a group health plan.*
Trading partner	External entity (for example, customer) with whom business is conducted. This relationship can be formalized via a trading partner agreement. (Note: an entity's trading partner for some purposes may be a business associate of that same entity for other purposes.)*
Transaction	Under HIPAA, this is the exchange of information between two parties to carry out financial or administrative activities related to health care.*
UHCIA	Uniform Health Care Information Act
URO	Utilization review organization
Utilization review	The function of evaluating the medical necessity of nonemergency care.
Virtual private network	A technical strategy for creating secure connections, or tunnels, over the Internet.*
Workforce	Under HIPAA, this means employees, volunteers, trainees, and other persons under the direct control of a covered entity, whether or not they are paid by the covered entity. See, for example, 45 C.F.R. § 160.103.*

**Workgroup for Electronic Data
Interchange (WEDI)**   A healthcare industry group that has a formal consultative role under the HIPAA legislation (also sponsors SNIP).*

Index

A

abortion
  disclosure requirements, 256–257
  Planned Parenthood v. Casey, 6
  Robin v. Incorporated Village of Hempstead, 7
absolute privilege, 402
abstention, defined, 16
abuse. *see also* fraud and abuse investigations
  of controlled drug prescriptions, 255
  disclosing child, 249–252, 264–265, 278, 305–308
  disclosing disabled persons, 253–255
  disclosing elder, 278, 305–308
  disclosure to law enforcement agencies, 310
Abused and Neglected Child Reporting Act, 380
access control
  e-mail security, 501–502
  ePHI safeguards, 467, 469–470
accreditation standards
  authentication systems, 63
  copies of medical records, 45
  medical record entries, 53, 57, 140–141
  quality assurance and utilization review, 206
  retention of medical records, 46–47
  special disclosure concerns, 329–331
  statutes for, 40
ACEs (affiliated covered entities)
  documentation of designations for, 153
  ePHI safeguards, 472–473
  HDNs qualifying as, 451
  Privacy and Security rules for, 151–153
acquired immunodeficiency syndrome. *see* AIDS (acquired immunodeficiency syndrome)
ADA (Americans with Disabilities Act), 434
addressable specifications, ePHI, 460–461
administrative requirements, HIPAA, 242–245
administrative search records, 314–315
Administrative Simplification provisions, HIPAA, 115–117
admissibility of electronic medical records, 485–490
  best evidence rule, 487–488
  difficulties of e-discovery, 488–490
  fax transmissions, 494–495
  overview of, 485
  rule against hearsay, 485–487
admissibility of medical records, 383–393
  defined, 374
  of fax transmissions, 494
  of hearsay, 383–386
  of incident reports, 390–393
  in negligence actions, 53
  other healthcare documentation, 386–387